Vladimir Biti
Tracing Global Democracy

Culture & Conflict

Edited by
Isabel Capeloa Gil and Catherine Nesci

Editorial Board
Arjun Appadurai · Claudia Benthien · Elisabeth Bronfen · Joyce Goggin
Lawrence Grossberg · Andreas Huyssen · Ansgar Nünning · Naomi Segal
Márcio Seligmann-Silva · António Sousa Ribeiro · Roberto Vecchi
Samuel Weber · Liliane Weissberg · Christoph Wulf

Volume 7

Vladimir Biti

Tracing Global Democracy

Literature, Theory, and the Politics of Trauma

DE GRUYTER

ISBN 978-3-11-057782-2
e-ISBN (PDF) 978-3-11-045764-3
e-ISBN (EPUB) 978-3-11-045706-3
ISSN 2194-7104

Library of Congress Cataloging-in-Publication Data
A CIP catalog record for this book has been applied for at the Library of Congress.

Bibliographic information published by the Deutsche Nationalbibliothek
The Deutsche Nationalbibliothek lists this publication in the Deutsche Nationalbibliografie;
detailed bibliographic data are available on the Internet at http://dnb.dnb.de.

© 2016 Walter de Gruyter GmbH, Berlin/Boston
This volume is text- and page-identical with the hardback published in 2016.
Cover image: Old map of Suriname, 1853. By Lithograaf: Spanier, Elias (Het geheuden van Nederland) [public domain], via Wikimedia Commons.
Typesetting: PTP Protago-T$_E$X-Production GmbH, Berlin
Printing and binding: CPI books GmbH, Leck

♾ Printed on acid-free paper
Printed in Germany

www.degruyter.com

Acknowledgments

While working on this book I have published portions of it in different forms. To adapt them to the final shape of argument, I have revised all of them with one exception.

Chapter 1 is a modified version of the essay "The Divided Legacy of the Republic of Letters: Emancipation and Trauma," *Journal of Literature and Trauma Studies* (University of Nebraska Press) 2: 1 (2012), 1–30.

Chapter 2 is a modified version of the essay "The Fissured Identity of Literature. The Birth of National Literary History out of International Cultural Transfers," *Journal of Literary Theory* (De Gruyter) 1–2: 7 (2013), 1–30.

Chapter 3 is an extended and revised version of the essay "Two Concepts of Literary *Bildung*: Education and/or Self-Formation?" in Vladimir Biti, ed., *Reexamining the National Philological Legacy: Quest for a New Paradigm?* Amsterdam and New York: Rodopi, 2013, 23–42.

Chapter 4 draws on portions from "The Divided Legacy of the Enlightenment: Herder's Cosmopolitanism as Suppressed Eurocentrism," in Marc Maufort & Caroline de Wagter, eds., *Old Margins and New Centers: The European Literary Heritage in the Age of Globalization*, Bruxelles et al.: Peter Lang, 2011, 73–83.

Chapter 5 is an original contribution.

The argument taken in Part Two is sketched in the German-language essay "Theorie und Weltbürgerlichkeit," in Mario Grizelj and Oliver Jahraus, eds., *Theorietheorie: Gegen die neuerliche Theoriemüdigkeit in den Geistes- und Kulturwissenschaften*, Paderborn and Munich: Wilhelm Fink, 2011, 291–303.

Chapter 6 is an extended and revised version of the essay "The Adulterous Theory," *Neohelicon* (Springer) 1: 40 (2013), 11–21. This essay was published in slightly modified version, in German, under the title "Die verinnerlichte Außerhalbbefindlichkeit: Über die weltbürgerliche Legitimierung der theoretischen Wahrheit," in Mario Grizelj, Oliver Jahraus and Tanja Prokić, eds., *Vor der Theorie: Immersion – Materialität – Intensität*, Würzburg: Königshausen & Neumann, 2014, 163–183.

Chapter 7 is an extended and revised English version of the German-language essay "Anschlussfähigkeit und postkoloniale Welt: Zum Stellenwert des Romans in Luhmanns Systemtheorie," in Grizelj, Mario and Daniela Kirschstein, eds., *Riskante Kontakte: Postkoloniale Theorien und Systemtheorie?* Berlin: Kadmos, 2014, 251–278.

Chapter 8 is an original contribution.

Chapter 9 substantially extends and reworks portions taken from the essay "The Self, the Novel and History: On the Limits of Bakhtin's Historical Poetics," *Orbis Litterarum* (Blackwell&Viley) 4: 66 (2011), 255–279.

Chapter 10 substantially extends and reworks portions taken from the essay "Distance and Proximity," *Neohelicon* (Springer) 2: 37 (2010), 469–475.

Chapter 11 substantially extends and reworks portions taken from three essays: "From Literature to Culture – and Back?," *Primerjalna književnost* 1: 31 (2008), 15–25, "Narrative Identification," *Arcadia* (De Gruyter) 1: 43 (2008) and "Toward a Literary Community?" in Theo D'haen und Iannis Goerlandt, eds., *Literature for Europe*, Amsterdam, New York et al.: Rodopi, 2009, 27–42.

Chapter 12 draws on the short draft of "Literature as Deterritorialization: Gilles Deleuze and Jacques Rancière," in Sonja Stojmenska-Elzeser and Vladimir Martinovski, eds., *Literary Dislocations*, Skopje: Institute of Macedonian Literature, 2013, 19–27. It was published in the given form under the title "Disaggregating Territories: Literature, Emancipation, and Resistance," in *Umjetnost riječi/The Art of Words: Journal for Literature, Theatre and Film Studies* 3–4: 58 (2014).

The epilogue was written especially for this book.

I offer my thanks to the publishers for their permission to use revised versions of these essays here.

Contents

Acknowledgments —— V

Introduction
The Cosmopolitan Axis: Agencies and/or Enablers —— 1

Part I: Toward a Global Community: The Emergence of the Modern Idea of Literature

1   The Divided Legacy of the Republic of Letters: Emancipation and Trauma —— 33

2   The Fissured Identity of Literature: National Universalism and/or Cosmopolitan Nationalism —— 57
2.1   Intertwined opposites —— 57
2.2   The emergence of the national literary historiography —— 60
2.3   Cosmopolitan patriot and democratic tyrant: Jean-Jacques Rousseau —— 68
2.4   Who is authorized to represent "natural communities"? —— 74
2.5   Identification by alienation —— 79

3   The Janus Face of Literary *Bildung*: Education and/or Self-Formation? —— 83
3.1   "Having the other" and "being the other" —— 83
3.2   Differences between the *Bildung* concepts —— 84
3.3   Mirroring and interweaving —— 89
3.4   Resolving ambiguity, instituting difference —— 94

4   Who Voices Universal History? Kant's "Mankind" and/or Herder's "Nature" —— 99
4.1   Introduction —— 99
4.2   Kant's advocacy of mankind —— 105
4.3   Herder's advocacy of nature —— 118

5   Who Worlds the Literature? Goethe's *Weltliteratur* and Globalization —— 133
5.1   Comparative literature as the promoter of globalization —— 133
5.2   Goethe's detachment from globalization —— 137

5.3	Getting out of the crowd: Goethe's elitist cosmopolitanism —— 139	
5.4	The acting out of the traumatic experience —— 141	
5.5	A retroactive reinvestment of Goethe's cosmopolitanism —— 146	
5.6	Goethe's trauma narrative: Repositioning German literature —— 148	
5.7	From exemption to expansion: Toward the Roman imperial cosmopolitanism —— 153	
5.8	Translating the "iron law of kinship" into the "free competition of values": The U.S.-American trauma narrative —— 157	

Part II: An Observer under Observation: The Cosmopolitan Legacy of Modern Theory

6	Interiorizing the Exteriority: The Cosmopolitan Authorization of the Theoretical Truth —— 179	
7	The Narrative of Permanent Displacement: Early German Romanticism and Its Theoretical Afterlife —— 195	
7.1	Reappropriating the early Romanticist legacy —— 195	
7.2	The pattern of irritated overcoming: the entangled opponents —— 198	
7.3	Literature against philosophy: Niklas Luhmann's autopoietic turn —— 202	
7.4	Passionately commited to the memory of the whole —— 203	
7.5	The European entangled legacy —— 206	
7.6	The novel as the epitome of evolutionary necessity —— 209	
8	The Oppositional Literary Transcendental: The Russian Formalist Rewriting of Early Romanticist Cosmopolitanism —— 213	
8.1	The post-imperial hyphenation and early Romanticist legacy —— 213	
8.2	Literature's persistent self-exemption – modern literary theory's cosmopolitan operation —— 220	
8.3	The resurgence of the disempowered law —— 224	
8.4	Unleashing the force of self-exemption —— 227	
9	The All-Devouring Modern Mind: Bakhtin's Cosmopolitan Self —— 235	
9.1	Confronting mind with self-displacing life —— 235	
9.2	A utopian cosmopolitan community —— 239	
9.3	The authorial operation: expanding the self by consummating the others —— 242	

| 9.4 | A counterfactual compensatory project —— 245 |
| 9.5 | The divine and the devalued other – a constitutive interdependency —— 250 |

10	Countering the Empirical Evidence: From Immigrant Cosmopolitanism to a Cosmopolitanism of the Disregarded —— 257
10.1	Abstracting from natural transcendentals —— 257
10.2	Dis/empowering the cosmopolitan police —— 264
10.3	At the empowering service of a powerless victim: Emmanuel Levinas —— 266
10.4	The disabling enablement of the theorist: Maurice Blanchot and Michel Foucault —— 272
10.5	Empowering the literary transcendental: Jacques Derrida —— 281

11	Political and/or Literary Community: From Class to Messianic Cosmopolitanism —— 285
11.1	Singularity – a European mission? —— 285
11.2	The class cosmopolitanism of Cultural Studies —— 291
11.3	Cruelly attached to unfathomable singularity —— 299
11.4	The counter-narrative of singularity —— 306
11.5	Vanishing mediation —— 315

12	Literature as Deterritorialization: New Vistas for Democracy? —— 319
12.1	Gilles Deleuze: emancipation through dehumanization —— 319
12.2	Jacques Rancière: emancipation through deregulation —— 329
12.3	Reintroducing the agent of universality: politics turned into police —— 340

Epilogue
The Practice of Recommencing: Toward a Cosmopolitanism of the Dispossessed Belonging —— 345

References —— 357

Index —— 385

Introduction
The Cosmopolitan Axis: Agencies and/or Enablers

This book investigates the emergence of the cosmopolitan idea of literature and its impact on the democratic reconfiguration of the European and non-European cultural and political spaces. The birthplace of this idea, as I interpret it, is its designers' traumatic experience as induced by the disconcerting social and political configuration of their abode. Since the early modern colonial era, Europeans have perceived themselves as historical latecomers in a world dominated by the "exotic" customs of foreign civilizations. Shocked by the compartmentalized and authoritarian political space that they have encountered, they undertook its recalibration and democratic restructuring. Inasmuch as democratic rule is distinguished by the inclusion of the majority of the ruled populace within political decision making, as Aristotle states in his *Politics* (III, 1279a 25–30), Europeans have typically associated themselves with dialogic openness and inclusiveness, as opposed to the despotic exclusiveness and violence of the others' manner of rule (*Politics*, III, 1285a 6–7; VII, 1327b 24–33). The tradition of European peaceful and cosmopolitan self-perception being singled out against the background of others' bellicose provincialism is well documented. However, what has often remained suppressed, probably owing to this rich tradition, is that the progress of humankind's unification, triggered by Renaissance colonialism – and the Renaissance is generally taken to be the cradle of European modernity – was accompanied by exclusions and atrocities. Because plantation, factory, and colony were the principle laboratories of today's global humanity, its infrastructure translates into power asymmetry. Colonialism rather than generous hospitality paved the way for what is usually reclaimed as common human history (Mbembe 2010: 57, 80). The much trumpeted liberation of all humans was therefore overshadowed by their silent division into the *agencies*, those politically entitled to conduct the dialogue of equals, and the non-political *enablers*, excluded from this dialogue in order to procure its prerequisites. The democratic freedom of the European political space was thus purchased at the price of the normative pressure intensified toward its frontiers as well as violence applied outside its walls.[1] In accordance with Jacques Rancière's interpretation of Aristotle's concept of good democracy, "[t]he centre is assured not by presence but by absence, by virtue of a gap which serves to

---

[1] For a similar recent conceptualization of Europe, from a sociological perspective, see Brunkhorst 2014. She depicts the history of Europe as a continuous suppression of its colonial past, arguing that the suppressed returns and refuses the offered appeasement.

keep interests apart" (1995: 17). According to Rancière, "imparity" is democracy's "essential part" (102). It grows out of an original division that undermines all attempts to superimpose a consensus upon it. This irremovable and permanently resurfacing gap between the agencies and enablers points to the "anarchic traumatism" of European global democracy.[2] Despite the latter's increasing denial of the imparity underlying it, or rather *because* this asymmetry was so consistently obliterated, democracy reinvigorated the division between the entitled and the disqualified humans. As the imposed consensual platform of human commonality systematically gained in volume from the Renaissance onwards, the traumatic gap within this commonality grew deeper. I argue that the contribution of the modern idea of literature to the European cosmopolitan restructuration of time, space, and meaning took place in this exclusionist frame, which fissured modern literature's identity.

My thesis is that the usually celebrated cosmopolitan extension and homogenization of the political space that constitutes the gist of European modernity announces the process that is usually termed globalization today. The eighteenth and nineteenth century's cosmopolitan projects trace the twentieth century's global democracy, confirming the thesis that "[g]lobalization is not an alternative reality that makes previous knowledge and social reality irrelevant. It is a long emerging if only recently visible and represented reality" (Alexander 2012: 155). However, since the cosmopolitan "compression of time, space, and meaning" (157) grows out of what its promoters either *denied* as their individual or *reclaimed* as their collective trauma, the usual representation of modernization as a progress from the particular to the universal is misleading. Such simplifications belong to the European myopic self-perception and self-aggrandizing rhetorics that have to be dismantled rather than uncritically resumed. What makes them questionable is precisely the traumatic origin of cosmopolitan projects. It prevents cosmopolitanism from being a sovereign *action* of responsible subjects, disclosing it as an enforced *reaction* of the instances dispossessed by injury.

As I will try to demonstrate in what follows the pattern of trauma *denial* underlies, for example, Voltaire's project of the Republic of Letters as well as Herder's utopian vision of humanity and Goethe's idea of world literature for that matter; German Romanticists, on the contrary, *reclaimed* the experience of a long-term national victimhood in their trauma narrative. In the former cases, we have to deal with the *covert and individual* trauma narratives developed from the "poisonous knowledge" acquired by their narrators in shattered social relationships (Das

---

2 For the term "anarchic traumatism," see Levinas 1974: 194. He employs "anarchic" in the etymological sense of being without an identifiable cause.

2007: 54), while in the latter with an *overt and collective* trauma narrative aimed at the public retribution of the collectively experienced pain. Individual narratives indirectly *indicate* the experience of pain, and the collective ones directly *present* it. Given that the technique of camouflaged indication is implemented by the suppressed, whereas the technique of public presentation is by acknowledged voices, this constitutes an important difference. Nevertheless, the voices that create covert and overt trauma narratives are always tightly related to one another.[3] It is not only that the acknowledgment of one kind of voice implies the refusal of the other, but also that this refusal tears apart the acknowledged community. This is why, under certain exceptional conditions, the agents of both the acknowledged and suppressed voices experience the parameters of action and the intelligibility of their political space as restrictive and in need of restructuring and recalibration.

In this book, I will primarily focus on clandestine trauma narratives that try to heal their authors' suffering through its subtle indication. The problem from suppressed sufferers' perspective is entering into action without being seen, i.e. unnoticably navigating internal and external perimeters in order to change the existing communal order (Povinelli 2011: 97). But since they experience their pain as poisonous, they frequently deny it to themselves, which turns their action into a kind of "gesturing toward" rather than a strategic public performance. Given that their traumatic experience hides itself, it has to be identified as such in the first place. This is the "diagnostic" task of the following analyses. My argument is that such covert narratives, once invented by Voltaire, Herder and Goethe, resurfaced more or less spontaneously with the conceptions of the Russian Formalists, Mikhail Bakhtin and Gilles Deleuze, amongst others, albeit with a different distribution of accents due to the completely altered traumatic constellation.

In addressing the concept of trauma in this book that deals with prominent writers and outstanding intellectuals, I do not refer to the psychic devastation of persons as an effect of catastrophic impacts as is the case in the common, and re-

---

3 For an elaboration on this point, see Das 2007: 18–39. She argues that the narrators of national trauma narratives, while using the suffering of particular social groups as the main instrument of the nation's establishment, sentence the victims of the same suffering to anonymity and silence. For example, the figure of the violated woman was an important mobilizing point for the discourse of the Indian nation as a "pure" and masculine space in which the "right" kinds of men keep the "right" kinds of women under control. However, in creating such hegemonic discourse, the hegemons not only usurped the right of the woman to decide her future course of action, but also deprived her of her own language of pain. Under the pressure of such discourse, she experienced her body as a container of poisonous knowledge, which was unutterable in the public space and thus forced into the form of "gesturing" or fiction. This is how the technique of indicating one's pain was set in motion.

cently seriously challenged, psychoanalytically inspired concept of trauma (Das 2007: 101–104; Berlant 2011: 9–10; Alexander 2012: 10–13). Without undermining the devastating experience of individual and collective human suffering, I merely question its *unmediated character* by maintaining that this everyday premise of victims as helpless "inscription surfaces" is unwittingly drawn from today's lay commonsense. Some thirty years ago, the victim was tarred as illegitimate and suspect; meanwhile, the reconfiguration of the contemporary society's moral space transformed it into a widely recognized identification target. This is why, as Didier Fassin and Richard Rechtman stress in their *Empire of Trauma* (2009: 7, 12), today's concept of trauma has to be denaturalized whilst its concept of the victim repoliticized. As they are by no means self-evident, the process of their universalization, in the form of an uncritical shift from "historical" to "structural" trauma, (LaCapra 1998: 47) needs to be counteracted and defamiliarized. To avoid such an indiscriminate leveling of trauma, my argument rehabilitates its concrete historical form, which in turn requires further differentiation. Since there exists no unitary subject of trauma, the task is to reconstruct the social and political conditions under which it becomes possible to speak of traumatic experience. We need to establish exactly *who* speaks of traumatic experience in the complex knotting of the various social actors differently involved in it. This reconstruction is, for example, undertaken in chapter five "Who Worlds the Literature?" Generally, I argue that victims are social agents in their own right, conducting their own politics via "carrier groups." As indicated above, they are never homogeneous but rather are divided into representative agencies (the speaking "survivors") and represented enablers (silenced victims). This approach does not aim to deny victims' *suffering*, but rather seeks the critical examination of their *representation*. Under closer inspection, the latter often uncovers the needs and desires of "narrators" projected onto the representation of victims as their "figures." "We are not asking whether […] trauma is a relevant concept from the medical or social viewpoint: we are aware that it is considered as such in medical and social circles. […] These viewpoints have their logic, but they are not ours. […] [A] critical reading of trauma rejects the naturalization of the concept." (Fassin and Rechtman 2009: 7)[4]

Taking into account that even victims are "figuring out how to stay attached to life from within it" (Berlant 2011: 10), Jeffrey Alexander even goes so far to speak of a "naturalist fallacy" about absolute victimhood which analysis must carefully distance itself from. Interpreted from a more elaborate analytical view-

---

[4] For the most recent reiteration of this perspective, see Brunner 2014. According to him, the ultimate target of such denaturalization of trauma is the violence and injustice inherent in any representation of it. I will be arguing in the same direction.

point, trauma is a socially and culturally mediated attribution (Alexander 2012: 13).⁵ As cultural imagination is intrinsic to the very process of its representation, I argue that it originates not in an enforced *Erlebnis* linked to an exceptional *event* but rather in an uncertain and complex *Erfahrung* of something that I will call a traumatic *constellation*.⁶ I interpret a traumatic constellation as a historically induced political arena or dramatic tableau characterized by asymmetries along its many intersecting and overlapping axes, each of them for its part a potential generator of trauma. The process of their mediation, responding to the discomfort and challenge that enters into the core of one's sense of collective identity, therefore "seizes upon an inchoate experience [...] and forms it, through association, condensation, and aesthetic creation, into some specific shape" (Alexander 2012: 14). The "inchoate experience" that Alexander is speaking of here means, in Berlant's terms, nothing "more concrete than a sense of the uncanny" or "free-floating anxiety" that has to be confronted – and processed – in "the situation of being without genre" (Berlant 2011: 80). In Elisabeth Povinelli's corresponding terms, a series of quasi-events that usually saturate potential worlds begin to aggregate and become apprehended, evaluated and grasped as ethical and political demands in the actual world (2011: 3–4, 13). In this way, they set in motion a social project, dependent on a host of interlocking concepts, materials, and forces that attempts to capacitate an alternative set of worlds. The task of this complex operation is to manage many co-present disquieting axes, or their frustrating configuration, in a manner capable of attracting performances of adjustment and energizing affective attachments. The objective is a new, refashioned and recalibrated kind of commonality.

---

5 According to Brunner (2014: 12–13) the agents of this complex and multiple mediation comprised in the concept of the *politics of trauma* are, for example, cultural values, conventions and habits, mental dispositions, political convictions, the state, government, parliament, political parties, scientific and media discourses, etc. In the final analysis, such an extensive political mediation also underlies the idea of the Holocaust, raised some time ago to be the standard for judging all traumas. For its critical reexamination from this perspective see, for example, Rothberg 2000: 179–186, or Alexander 2012: 31–96.

6 For a further elaboration on this concept, see Biti 2014b. For the engagement of Benjamin's (and Freud's) opposition between *Erlebnis* and *Erfahrung* in the context of trauma, see LaCapra 2004: 54–55. Berlant's re-description of trauma goes in the same direction when she speaks of the "convergence of many histories," "an ongoing activity of precariousness in the present" or "systemic crisis" built into ordinary situations which can, but need not, coagulate into a traumatic event and induce trauma (10). The outcome of such situations depends on the reaction of the involved. She defines *situation* as a state of things in which "something in the present that may become an event" is emerging, "an intersecting space where many forces and histories circulate," (5) which is a definition that disaggregates and dynamizes the concept of trauma in a similar way to that which I am trying to do with "constellation."

The series of situated cosmopolitan operations[7] that I will be discussing was set in motion by a gradual realization by outstanding individuals or "carrier groups" that the community no longer exists as an effective source of their support. Its well-established form of life underlies gradual disaggregation. An unexpected doubt casts shadow on its familiarity, systematically making its habitual world hollow, numb and uncertain. The most usual words are suddenly untethered from their well-known meanings, circulating around as if emptied out. In such traumatic constellations generated by the public political space, the complex mediation of their discontinued axes, as undertaken by outstanding intellectuals, is probably expressed more transparently than in personal traumas disconnected from the ongoing problems of social identity. As I will be dealing primarily with the politically induced kind of trauma, which works slowly, insidiously and unevenly into the awareness of those afflicted by it and mobilizes them to counteraction, I will distance myself from the concept of trauma as a unique and homogeneous experiential substance that directly acts out an original traumatic event. In Veena Das' pregnant rendering, "encounter with pain is not a one-shot, arm's length transaction" (Das 2007: 90). Contrary to reacting in a passive and uniform manner, suffering collectivities distributed across divided constellations are imagined into being in complex and controversial, i.e. political, ways.

As one's *Erfahrung* of such constellations remains exposed to the suspicion of others who, due to their different position in the same constellation, do not experience it in the same way, it meets serious obstacles on its way to social and political affirmation. The latter requires a considerable reconfiguration of the starting distribution of agencies, values and forces by attracting, galvanizing and convincing the presumed affiliates, interlocking with them and establishing an efficient collective agency. Even if it is regularly presented as an enforced *break* with the constellation of forces that engenders it, collective trauma is affirmed as a combined *outcome* of the retroactive operations by many agents. It is an induced re-

---

[7] Recent theory insists that cosmopolitanism is of a similarly plural and protean character as nationalism. "Like nations," states Bruce Robbins (1998: 2) for example, "cosmopolitanisms are now plural and particular." Kwame Anthony Appiah was the first to attentively elaborate the thesis of the social, historical and geopolitical rootedness of cosmopolitanism against the habitual thesis of its universal character (2005: 213–272, 2006). However, he connects cosmopolitan projects with *belonging* to particular communities and not with *traumatic constellations*; he does not introduce an irresolvable gap into them as I am trying to do. The same holds for other prominent U.S.-American theorists of cosmopolitanism such as Martha Nussbaum, Will Kimlicka, or Seyla Benhabib. An exception is Bonnie Honig whose concept of cosmopolitanism draws on Jacques Derrida's "hostipitality" (as developed in Derrida 2000b, 2001b, 2005) and is closer to mine. See, for example, Honnig 2006.

configuration rather than a violent rupture. Although it systematically denies and obliterates that, it is an equivocal construct established through a battle of the interpretations by victims, participants and observers, who share this constellation in different ways, sometimes overlapping and sometimes conflicting.[8] This is why the recognition of trauma does not definitely overcome but merely reconfigures the divisions that gave way to it. As soon as it becomes the ground for amelioration and reconciliation, one's trauma risks suppressing other's trauma. The very spread of a trauma community necessitates such a discriminating effect. In Rancière's terms (1999: 21–42, 61–65), the establishment of a consensus on trauma turns its "politics" into a "police."

To take an illustration from the postcolonial world, the proudly proclaimed social contract of the Indian nation-state, founded on the figure of the woman abducted by the enemy during the Partition, ultimately became a discriminating sexual contract. It allocated women, as sexual and reproductive beings, to the domestic sphere, placing them at the service of their entitled "masters" (Das 2007: 19). Furthermore, the emancipating project of the postcolonial Indian nation suppressed the suffering of innumerous concrete human beings in pursuing the nation's magnified image (Guha 2002: 75–94; Das 2007: 41–44). Finally, the homogenized national public space established a series of enemies, gradually turning the community of victims into the perilous community of revenge. To be sure, such a transformation of trauma communities from victims into killers (Mamdani 2002) does not only take place in postcolonial or post-imperial societies but also in "imperial" ones. Consider, for example, the United States' official politics after the event of 9/11.

Multidirectionally engaged in the political space of its emergence as well as beyond it, collective trauma is not an objective but rather a political given.[9] With a disputable redistribution of values and forces built into its infrastructure, rather than directly to an original *Erlebnis* of inflicted injury as in the common

---

8 Advocating a social theory of trauma along the same performative lines, Alexander states: "Which narrative wins out is a matter of performative power. The emotional experience of suffering, while critical, is not primordial." (2012: 2) Trauma is thus relegated from the private psychic into the public political space. Brunner (2014: 24) has recently endorsed this view, stating that trauma discourse cannot speak "by itself" but only via social carriers and mediators who are in possession of necessary resources to put it into circulation. For him, trauma equally emerges from the knotting of heterogeneous discourses that underpin, question and defy each other (2014: 41–45).

9 Not long ago, in a significant move to the theory of trauma continued by Lauren Berlant, Michael Rothberg subjected trauma to an ongoing negotiation, cross-referencing, and borrowing by placing it in the intercultural dynamic of interaction, entanglement and intersection (2009: 3–4).

understanding, it points to the equivocal *Erfahrung* of a political space. The latter is, per definition, divided by a gap between the entitled agencies and the denied enablers. I am going to call their relationship, characterized by a perpetual renegotiation of the traumatizing terms of their reciprocity, *the cosmopolitan axis*. My argument will be that the cosmopolitan fusion of enablers with agencies along this axis – passionate investment in their commonality obtained by the prospect of continuity – cannot but produce new enablers. Far from being unquestioningly redeeming as they often present themselves, all of the destabilized agencies' attachments to an expanded mode of commonality amount to controversial achievements. Their "politics" invisibly slips into a "police." As soon as it is established, "We" bifurcates into the enablers assigned to the brackets of the disagreeable on the one hand and agencies that decide what is agreeable on the other; two fundamental constituents of the cosmopolitan axis that "never have to meet" (Povinelli 2011: 183). The carriers of cosmopolitan projects usually expect such an affective grasping toward a stabilizing form of commonality to guarantee endurance amid the frustration of constitutive inequality, but their projects ultimately turn out to be endangering this prospect (Berlant 2011: 48). Irrespective of their plans and objectives, all goods emerge in a system of distributed misery. Sovereignty is a fantasy of an agency intentionally opposed to fraying and attrition but in fact permanently exposed to them. The engineers of cosmopolitanism may be an aggregation vis-à-vis their intentions to build a project of commonality, but they are constantly disaggregated by the world outside them. It is this which makes the bipolarity of the cosmopolitan axis with its asymmetry between the agencies and enablers endure.

As any rendering of a common traumatic experience is situated, divergent, and even contradictory, its "truth value" eschews ultimate verification. In Kantian terms, it underlies reflective rather than determining judgment. What achieves the status of "trauma" emerges from the crossing, overlapping and sometimes conflicting back-projections with which, provisionally and temporarily, one wins the battle in given circumstances. This one interpretation that succeeds in becoming the truth-producer for the whole constellation, in providing authenticity to the suffering it bespeaks, and in creating a new language for this suffering, will be what Richard Rechtman calls the *trauma narrative* (Fassin and Rechtman 2009: 7–8). As Jeffrey Alexander (2012: 16–30) has spelled out, carrier groups, variously located within the social structure, transfer their feelings of being traumatized to a broader audience, assimilating the latter into the trauma community by means of such covert or overt self-medicating narratives. These groups put themselves in abeyance by attaching themselves to the space of others so as to get out of the disconcerting experience that they have been confronted with. I interpret their attachment as a cluster of vague prospects expected to elongate the narrators' time horizon and to assure them, by way of their genuine commitment to these prospects, a large-scale historical existence. Thus understood in the performative terms of its concrete enabling conditions rather than in the extraterritorial and extrahistorical terms of its truth-value, trauma becomes an important resource of the politics of reconfiguration for the constellation giving rise to it. However fantasized it may be, the force of affective attachment turns out to have more righteousness than anything considered "objectively true."

Created through a non-sovereign reaction by an interrupted and injured individual or group agency, trauma community remains profoundly controversial. While gaining public recognition for the pain of its newly established agencies, it simultaneously sentences the suffering of its new enablers to invisibility and silence. As I will try to show in more detail in chapter two, in revolting against the assimilating pressure of French culture throughout the eighteenth century, German Romanticists affirmed the right to self-determination of all nations that had up until then been exposed to French hegemonic aspirations. Yet while they established a new ethnolinguistic platform for assimilating co-nationals diffused over foreign countries in order to affirm that right, this platform turned out to dissimilate non-national fellow-citizens at home. Concomitantly, it was gradually dismantled as an instrument of powerful exclusion. To provide another illustration from the same chapter, the same holds for Rousseau's vision of community "from below" established via the social contract of its participants. By obliging the woman to teach the man how to renounce his attachment to her in order to give life to "his" political community, Rousseau reduces her to an instrument for the inauguration of men's sovereignty. His all-uniting social contract amounts to a discriminating sexual contract.

Following a delineated performative thread, Fassin and Rechtman parenthesized the question of whether trauma is real in favor of a more Foucauldian question of "what the choice to read violence in these terms produces in the social world and in the moral sphere. Thus our approach necessarily proceeded from a critique of common understandings, not in order to refute them but rather that we might better analyze the assumptions behind them and their consequences" (2009: 278). Along the same lines, in this book I am going to critically analyze, alongside the concept of trauma, common understanding of several key concepts of European modernity such as democracy, cosmopolitanism, literature, and theory. The objective is certainly not to discard them but rather to disaggregate their apparent essences until they become variable and contingent bundles of relations, or controversial constellations. Keeping in mind that all these important European concepts contain *zones of suppressed possibilities*, the strategy consists in the liberation of this hidden potentiality, with the social and cultural otherwise inhibited by their structure. The European imperial and colonial conquest across the globe relegated this into the pockets of a "past perfect being," cut off from the vibrant potentiality of the future world (Povinelli 2011: 27). In order to dismantle such European usurpation of potentiality, we need to translate the enrooted generous and universal understanding of cosmopolitanism into the performative value of a particular "carrier group." This group produces and contours its trauma narratives at the expense of the denial of other traumas. No community can achieve common harmony without sentencing "the part that has no part" within it to invisible suffering. However democratic and cosmopolitan they declare themselves to be, all communities are containers of the "poisonous knowledge" expelled from their public space. To prevent this infective anxiety contagiously spreading into its everyday relationships, the community that contains it has to be re-inhabited, its anonymous space renamed and its signs of subjection recrafted (Das 2007: 62). This is the argumentative strategy for the following chapters.

Some examples can be drawn upon for the sake of illustration. Behind the proudly proclaimed universal human objectives of French cosmopolitanism, there lurks the struggle of the French Catholic high bourgeois elite to defend its endangered privileges by forging a transnational class alliance. Or, behind Herder's generous idea of common *humanitas*, there lies a carefully elaborated social and cultural hierarchy by which the natives are recruited to lower positions whilst the Germans are assigned the highest ones. Finally, Goethe's concept of *Weltliteratur* aims at the consolidation of German national literature against the homogenizing pressure of a rapidly uniting world. He establishes this idea so as to force his compatriots into a progressive national self-formation through an attentive self-differentiation, which he trusts is the only method to assure their supremacy. In a word, both Herder's and Goethe's "hospitable" cosmopolitanism were put at the service of the German national self's consolidation, which at that time was deeply wounded and frustrated. Their covert trauma narratives projected a circuit of repair for their broken relation to their community. In stating this, I do not intend to underplay the huge emancipating impact which they have been part of within the constellations as well as far beyond them. I only want to draw attention to the parallel oppressive dimension that came to expression in historically, politically, socially and culturally remote constellations, for example of the so-called Third World. After such "welcoming" cosmopolitanism was instituted in the latter's postcolonial and post-imperial societies, their "subaltern subjects" were confronted with the impossible task of transporting their "ancient indigenous identity," over many centuries of complete colonial or imperial suppression, back into the "liberated" present of their twentieth century. As this (self-)imposed "mission impossible" was clearly destined to failure,[10] instead of the envisioned relief, it generated persistent lament, grief and self-reproach in these subjects (Povinelli 2002: 39, 49). This paved the way for their ill reputation of being irreparably infantile, irresponsible, and driven by instincts and compulsions.

Through such an analysis, the ambition of a common understanding of cosmopolitanism to abstract from its concrete political stakes for the benefit of its universality will be systematically counteracted. As cosmopolitanism cannot solve the problems that it generates, it will be confronted with questions such as: what produces the conviction that we so badly need it, who calls and who is called to it, what ramifications does it have beyond the superficial aim of conflict resolution (Brown 2006: 86–87)? What groups does it serve, protect and maintain, who is spared of conflict by its establishment and who in the last instance owns global democracy as its crucial historical achievement (Povinelli 2002: 29)? Why does cosmopolitanism systematically cause inequality under the cover of equality, crimes under the cover of justice? When thinking of it in customary generous terms, we should probably remind ourselves that "nothing was more cosmopolitan than the Nazis' concentration and extermination camps" (Levy and Sznaider 2007: 31, trans. mine). Parallel to its undeniable liberating dimension, cosmopolitanism also demonstrates restricting, suffocating effects. Perpetuating losses that in turn induce the need to emotionally invest into it, cosmopolitanism is an instance of "cruel optimism." It firmly attaches people to vague prospects that actively impede the aim of their attachment (Berlant 2011). It depends on the historical constellation of a given political space as to whether the emancipation or the enforcement, that in such projects continually go hand in hand, will provisionally take the upper hand. But, inasmuch as it recreates this inequality instead of bridging it, the cosmopolitan staging of equality amidst the structural inequality of global democracy seems to be less a reliable scenario of repair to which we ought to attach our hopes than a problem in its own right which we ought to reflect upon.

---

10 By "(self-)imposed," I mean that "hospitable" cosmopolitanism was not only imposed by colonial and imperial nations but also enthusiastically embraced by the native "carrier groups" that governed the process of respective national liberations. By adopting the Western teleological pattern of history, these groups rejected on their part the alternative (literary) representations of the past within their own cultures (Guha 2002: 49). By producing "historical accounts in which the nationalism of the colonized competes with metropolitan imperialism in its bid to uphold the primacy of the state (74)," they emulated the statism of their European mentors, i.e. silenced the creativity of domestic subjects involved in the complex and volatile "prose of the world." The colonized peoples thus fell apart into the representative agencies and represented enablers, offering another example of the non-homogeneous corpus of victims.

In view of that insight, this book's strategy is a consistent repoliticization of its central concepts in order to counteract their relentless depoliticization, or naturalization, on the part of their agencies. The envisaged repoliticization amounts to the following questions: What makes these concepts possible in their given form? Who is by this condition of their possibility forced into the state of "off-the-world" (*hors-monde*, Mbembe 2010: 79) and sentenced to "bare life?" In a word, who surreptitiously becomes an enabler in the process of an agency's establishment? Such contestation of common understanding is interpreted as the enactment of democracy. Oriented toward a persistently reopening *practice* rather than an accomplished legitimate *state*, democracy constitutively resists realization, merely materializing itself through the work of stubborn recommencing. It re-inhabits a given political space by liberating it from the "poisonous knowledge" that is destined to silence and invisibility by this space's distribution and configuration. By redistributing and reconfiguring it, critical theory engages the disaggregating potentiality of its various "heterotopias" and "zones of indeterminacy." Instead of norming this space in the manner of "police," it introduces new possibilities into its normative horizon in the form of "politics" (Rancière 1995: 11–20, 1999: 21–42, 61–5, 2001). "Policing" means imposing a consensus on a political space by suppressing the gap amid it. By pointing out, ever anew, the gap between what is *claimed* and what *is* within the given space, politics "makes a difference even if it does not immediately produce a propositional otherwise" (Povinelli 2011: 192). It avoids the production of a proposition precisely in order not to turn into a consensual platform. The goal of recommencing from ever-new "diasporic" perspectives is to uncover the dissensual politics behind the consensual platform of established democratic principles. If these principles regularly turn out to be equivocal, they lack the universality that they proudly claim to possess.

If cosmopolitan projects arise from frustration – and what prevents the universality of law is that it always comes into being in response to an injury (Benjamin 1996: 250) – they are enmeshed in the specific traumatic constellations for which they seek a remedy by magnetizing the like-minded against their otherwise-minded opponents. This partisan and antagonizing operation, on the one hand, desirably mobilizes people for the restructuring of the unsatisfactory forms of human commonality, yet on the other hand, it regrettably undermines the proclaimed universality of the projects of reform. "One man's imagined community is another man's political prison." (Appadurai 1996: 32) The envisioned "modernity at large" turned out to be profoundly ambiguous, announcing the Janus face of today's globalization. Contrary to its habitual self-presentation in the rhetoric of liberal democracy, globalization does not simply translate into justice and the good life. Rather than displacing enslaving religious dogmas with liberating reason, globalizing ideologies merely provided secular versions of equally heinous constraint (Alexander 2012: 159). This point about the secular transmission of religious dogmas has been made by a number of political theorists such as Charles Taylor, Talal Asad and William Connolly. The triumphant break of secularization from religious doggedness regularly relapsed into the resurgence of discrimination.

Yet despite this equivocation inherent to the cosmopolitan tracing of global democracy, I argue that it has creatively recalibrated and developed human commonality. Departing from the inflicted humiliating experiences, it worked out their scenarios and shaped new social and political configurations. Certainly, by no means does every deadening human experience manage to gain public attention, but solely the one that became, in the hands of its carrier group, an instrument of social and political reordering. As I will spell out in the final chapter, Deleuze's and Rancière's "literary" operation of a consistent self-exemption from any given identity amounts to a method of reasserting sovereignty through a continuously changing "alocation of differences." While this operation rescues the "literary" subject from restrictions imposed upon his or her freedom, at the same time it also frees him or her from any responsibility toward the others pinned down by the same operation to their restricting identity. The "literary" subject only escapes the trauma of identification by transferring it to its "non-literary" counterparts. They become riveted to their indigenous roots, whereas the "literary" subject freely fashions his or her prospective individuality.

Unexpectedly coming up "from below" and switching established perspectives, trauma marks a new beginning. Any process that inflicts social and political pain can simultaneously stimulate the birth of new social and political agendas. If his or her work of survival is transformed and not broken, the subject of the traumatizing event is opened to a new habitation of history (Berlant 2011: 81). By moving "the glacial force of the habitus into the quickened beat of improvisation," forced migrations immensely increased the mobility of the imagination (Appadurai 1996: 6). Included in a controversial political space, trauma is as ambivalent and bidirectional a process as Foucault described power to be at the other end of the scale. Yet if it, like power, escapes attribution to an ultimate agency, because its address is dispersive and multidirectional, then a moralizing approach to it seems to be equally misplaced. Such re-conceptualization of trauma, liberating it from the sublime passivity of those exposed to its strike, underpins a recent thesis that "trauma narratives can trigger significant repairs in the civil fabric," along with instigating "new rounds of social suffering" (Alexander 2012: 2). To reiterate, I am primarily interested here in the denigrating experiences that wounded the social and political identity of distinguished writers who, by having invented (frequently covert) trauma narratives such as those of the Enlightenment or Romanticism, raised these experiences to the status of a *common* social and political agenda. Having crossed the boundaries of their communities, their precarity became a broader intercommunal concern, an agency on its own. This transformation into a transnational and transcultural consensual platform is the way in which the repressive side of trauma narratives comes to the fore.

When thinking of Enlightenment trauma narrative, Kant might be taken as a case in point. As a long-term university teacher of anthropology, he was confronted with the overwhelming abundance of human races discovered by colonizers all over the globe.[11] The disaggregating potentiality of world's "heterotopias" entered his universe in the form of a disconcerting "inchoate experience" with these races. Given that in his eyes it threatened to destroy the providential design of man created by the divine *ratio*, Kant apprehended this "free-floating anxiety" as a philosophical and political demand. He responded to it by introducing the concept of *Menschenrasse* that associated man with the divine *ratio*.[12] However one-sided and problematic, this association was fully natural at the time and enabled him to distinguish man from irrational animals and animal-like human beings (such as women, children, and barbarians). Using this "self-evident" criterion, he instituted the regulative idea of mankind to put the immature self-willingness of humans, which unconcernedly serve their benighted inclinations and habits, under pressure. In such a way, he forced these humans to obey the allegedly universal will of mankind as a historical necessity. Whichever individual or collective subject proved itself to be unable to meet this hard requirement was taken to have fully deserved the sufferings connected with this failure, which is why s/he or it was then mercilessly abandoned to his, her or its grim destiny.

The Romanticist trauma narrative is a kind of response to the harsh effects of the delineated Enlightenment one. More an anti-Enlightener than a Romanticist proper,[13] Herder was the first to take strong exception to Kant's statement that humans are animals in need of a master by insisting that the reverse is actually true: humans who need a master are animals. To summarize his opinion, any force

---

[11] Safranski (2009: 26) points out in his book on German Romanticism that Herder was surrounded in Riga by a colourful mix of peoples consisting of Russians, Livonians and Poles. This holds even more for Kant as the inhabitant of multiethnic and multicultural Königsberg, who, in addition, regularly visited its port to collect stories about "exotic" human races from sailors, overseas entrepreneurs and adventurers.

[12] For the naturalness of this association at that time, see Apter 2006: 32.

[13] Safranski (2009: 17) aptly compares him with Rousseau, meaning that his ideas announced Romanticism rather than really representing it. Considering the variety of German Romanticism, one in any case ought to be cautious with the "Romanticist label." However, as Lucy (1997: 28) rightly puts it, "'romanticism' is a signifier. As with any signifier, there is no natural or predetermined signified attached to it. Whatever 'romanticism' signifies, then, is always going to have to be textual…"

despotically imposed from above is unable to hold the people together; a political order must express the will of the people itself, its common affects, beliefs and traditions, its natural roots; it has to be built from the bottom up. As genuine *Bildungswesen*, men are able to breed and govern themselves without external custodians. They are summoned to *Bildung*, moreover, by the linguistic and cultural *Umwelt* as their nurturing sole, saturated with the aspirations, habits and customs of predecessors; any descendant is obliged to cultivate it in order not to stagnate and perish. Thus, turning nature into a shelter of familiar tradition, Herder generously opens its doors to everybody, yet only on the condition that the invitee consents to the cultivating imperative. Unfortunately, this does not seem to be a much easier task than the requirement which was imposed by Kant's historical necessity; by no means is everybody qualified to meet it. In sum, Enlightenment and Romantic trauma narratives, the latter of which was further developed, refined and finally established by Friedrich Schlegel's and Novalis's invention of a "literary subject," roughly correspond to the successive types of European colonial attitude toward "barbarians": the "hard" assimilating and the "soft" regenerating one (Amselle 2003; Mamdani 2012).

It is through such a performative *politics of trauma* (Fassin and Rechtman 2009: 8) that the modern idea of literature was established and thereupon translated into its postmodern shape. "It is people who make traumatic meanings, in circumstances they have not themselves created and which they do not fully comprehend." (Alexander 2012: 4) Carried out under such dispossessing restrictions, in my interpretation the liberating reconfiguration of the inherited horizon of meaning is the essential feature of trauma narratives in both their overt and covert forms (with the latter being predominantly the case in my examples). Their truth-value is an effect of the "regime" established by their performance rather than being their natural property. Their inventors rescue themselves from the anonymity of enablers by appealing to the unknown "elective affiliates" beyond the restrictive boundaries of their inherited horizon. Yet it should not be forgotten that, in becoming a "multidirectional" platform for the recovery and reconciliation of various traumatized collectivities,[14] these symbolic constructions display the potential to trigger horrific group conflicts. All of a sudden, victims can turn into killers (Mamdani 2002). However mutually underpinning and cross-fertilizing they come to be, while solidifying and expanding the circle of the "we" via these literary constructions, cosmopolitan narratives obstinately refuse to rec-

---

[14] As Michael Rothberg (2009: 1–22) has argued, trauma narratives offer unpredictable encouragement, support and enforcement to each other across social, cultural, and historical boundaries.

ognize the pain of others, most probably because the latter was created by their remedial expansion. While the cosmopolitan healing of social and political trauma paves the way for the forthcoming global democracy, it also foreshadows new traumas by multiplying new destitute enablers.

My study of these equivocal cosmopolitan narratives consists of two parts. Part One, *Toward a Global Community: The Emergence of the Modern Idea of Literature,* deals with the rise of the modern cosmopolitan idea of literature from the French Republic of Letters to Goethe's *Weltliteratur*. In the first place, it focuses on the French-German cultural and symbolic transfers and the concomitant political and intellectual battles between the Enlightenment and the early Romantic idea of literature. I argue that these European contests over the sharing of the common – which I take, like Rancière, to be the very gist of democracy (Rancière 1995: 102) – proliferated out of the continuously frustrating co-articulation of political agencies and non-political enablers, i.e. various perturbations along the *cosmopolitan axis*. Although fiercely embattled with one another, the Enlightenment and early Romanticism nonetheless represent a "joint venture." Although from different angles, both are committed to the suppression of the irresolvable gap inherent to the European project of democracy. It was the insight into their simultaneous *heteronomy* and *proximity* that made the relationship between the agencies and enablers increasingly frustrating. The constitution of agencies turned out to be doggedly followed by the deconstitution of enablers, which is why enablers ghostly resurfaced. The presence of agencies was already increasingly haunted by their spectral absence in the second half of the European eighteenth century. Kant, the founder of the modern idea of cosmopolitanism, had already realized that exotic aliens inhabit the same Earth as his fellow beings. This *explosive entanglement*, which in the imperial and colonial regimes of the time corroborated serious turbulences, required political appeasement without much hesitation and, if possible, without the loss of sovereignty. Although extermination remained a continuously tempting solution, it was not a feasible political alternative. The integration into "common humankind" was therefore preferred. However, driven by ambitions to possess and exploit the "barbarians," it resulted in "necropolitics" (Mbembe 2010: 82), i.e. the systematic allocation of precarity, malnutrition, abandonment, and social death to vast anonymous masses. "Common" history thus turned out to have been internally divided from the very beginning of European modernity. In order for agencies to maintain sovereignty, enablers were exposed to slow deaths. Albeit from different angles, both the Enlightenment and the Romantic agencies publicly proclaimed the complete opposite, i.e. entirely "human" objectives. Their declared plan was to translate the "or" of ruling out of enablers into the "and" of building a community with them, to transfer an uneasy cohabitation into a peaceful coexistence, and to transform a blatant discontinuity into an apparent continuity of the cosmopolitan axis. Due to their successive and combined efforts, novel multiple and indirect technologies of domination have been invented. Agencies responded in a new way to the question of who has the right to exist and who does not, redefined the prerogatives and limits of public power, recodified rights, privileges and inequalities and refashioned financing (Mbembe 2001: 67). The rise of cosmopolitanism softened and dispersed, but precisely in such a way reconfirmed and reinstated sovereignty. *Pace* Foucault, sovereignty did not disappear as an antiquated fantasy after its translation into governmentality but persevered as a cruelly intensified attachment to that fantasy.

Laying bare, unintentionally, the *déjà vu* of its undertaking, the cosmopolitanism of the French Enlightenment drew on the tradition of Roman imperial cosmopolitanism opened toward the inferior foreign enablers. Its political agency endorses the inclusion of enablers (i.e. foreign constituencies) into the community frame, but under the condition of their compliance to the established legal rules. Enablers are only welcomed by agencies as long as they accept subordination to their law. Roman imperial cosmopolitanism, despite its seemingly generous attitude toward the inclusion of enablers, obviously displayed the same internal constraints as its French descendant would do much later on. Whoever does not comply with the restructuration of his or her identity as envisioned by cosmopolitan law is mercilessly excluded. In the process of the requested adjusting, the inassimilable otherness is eliminated. This is how the inclusionary logic of the imperial cosmopolitan operation surreptitiously turns into the exclusionary one, how the "and" between the agencies and enablers is gradually translated into the "or," and their interaction transfigured into the interruption. Ultimately, this is why the envisioned global democracy then fails. The foreigner in the Roman empire was included among the contractual allies not "out of mercy but for the sake of the expansion of the polis which, from now on, was expected to affiliate even the most foreign members to the new alliance of comrades" (Arendt 2010: 114–115). Concomitantly, the French cosmopolitan expansion, by inviting foreign "comrades" into the French community on the basis of the same model, implied a silent occupation of the international space by French national norms. Despite its revolutionary ambition to lay the foundations for a completely new and truly global community, it would reintroduce an uncanny *déjà vu* experience.

In opposing this Roman imperial cosmopolitanism, German early Romanticist cosmopolitanism drew on the tradition of the Greek elitist cosmopolitanism directed against the inferior local enablers. It declared itself ready to open the broadest possible dialogue between international agencies, but only on condition that its distinguished participants first exempted themselves from the selfish interests of their "domestic" enablers. The Greek cosmopolitan dialogue commences at the point where existential necessity ends, which means that, forced to perform hard labor outside the walls of the polis or, for that matter, outside its political agora, the population in permanent need (slaves, women and barbarians from abroad) constitutes the tacit condition of its possibility. Coerced into subordination, such a population is disqualified a priori from the democratic behavior of respecting and seriously considering the other's (and this also means the enemy's) opinion (Arendt 2010: 44–45). Indulged in compulsive reactivity, these enablers are too belligerent for a well-balanced impartial reflection of autonomous individuals. In the Greek exclusionist understanding, therefore, democracy is everything but omnipresent and a matter of course (41–42). As one has to qualify for it in the first place, freedom is reserved for the enlightened agencies capable of permanent self-extension through the assimilation of many of the others' points of view, whereas their benighted enablers are sentenced to a restrictive condition of their selves. The latter's excommunication is therefore the necessary prerequisite for the former to include the broadest possible range of opinions and thus ensure the democratic character of the judgment passed. As a result the Greek elitist cosmopolitan creates his broad intellectual horizon through the patient and open exchange of attitudes recruited from the most heterogeneous political, social and cultural regions – and this is precisely how the *interaction* reenters the initial *interruption* between the agencies and enablers, or the intellectual *as-well-as*-logic rearticulates the political *either-or*-logic established between them. In such a way, Greek cosmopolitanism traces an alternative path to democracy, based on self-formation rather than the educational shaping of others. Yet, as if repeating the unplanned entanglement of Roman imperial cosmopolitanism's inclusion and exclusion, the unparalleled judgmental mobility and independence of Greek elitist cosmopolitanism proved to be limited to the political elite. It was precisely the walling off of the foreigners', slaves', women's and children's perspectives which paved the way for the exhaustive consideration of the greatest variety of the others' opinions. In order for the thinking subject to achieve freedom, those unable of the activity of thought must first be ruled out of the polis. The thinking subject is expected to transgress every single imaginary boundary, with the exception of the established political boundary between the agencies and enablers.

To summarize, the cosmopolitan axis based on the disquieting *and/or*-relationship between the agencies and enablers gives way to two operations which are ferociously opposed to one another, but equally determined to erase this discontinuity. These operations engender alternative mappings of today's global democracy. In the first, the political agency is oriented toward the assimilating reconfiguration of its enablers whilst, in the second, it is devoted to its own rigorous self-reconfiguration, which is destined to surpass its enablers through the identification of their differences. However, after being historically redoubled by the Enlightenment and early Romanticist response to it, these seemingly mutually inimical strategies, turned out to have been intermingled from the outset. As we will see in the last chapter, the same holds for the imperial (sovereign) and the elitist (governmental) type of colonialism. As Hannah Arendt (2010: 108) has noticed, Roman politics, engendered on foreign soil, "came into being precisely at the point where for the Greeks it reached its limit and end, in the in-between; that is to say, not between citizens, but between peoples, foreign and unequally opposed to each other and brought together only by conflict as they are." Yet such substantial recalibration of human community did not entail its liberation. As the recent specialist in the field Greg Wolf (1998: 105) has put it, we may conceptualize this process as the expansion of Roman society through the recruitment of a colonized population to various underprivileged roles and positions in the social order. This is why two cosmopolitan mappings of global democracy, while fiercely attempting to defeat and replace each other, proved interdependent.

In lieu of being overcome in a sovereign cosmopolitan fashion, the traumatic co-articulation of the agencies and enablers underlying European democracy ultimately resurfaced in the form of the division of imperial and elitist cosmopolitanism. Joined by a common striving to undo the conjunctive disjuncture of agencies and enablers, neither of the opposed operations could get rid of the embarrassing company of the other. Destined to disappear, the uneasy cohabitation persevered. This frustrating reiteration induced ever new, more ambitious and more sophisticated projects designed to consolidate the threatened sovereignty of the democratic agency by virtue of the expansion of its jurisdiction. In the Part One's five chapters, the victorious *break* with the traumatic constellation and its consecutive uncanny *reintroduction* are tackled from various angles, focusing on different concepts and their interrelations. Not only was the borderline between two types of cosmopolitanism permanently on the move from the very establishment of European modernity, but the rift *between* them reappeared *within* each of them respectively, blurring the boundaries of their reclaimed autonomy. Such a development follows from democratic agencies' persistent denial, their endeavor to obliterate their constitutive dependency on enablers against all contrary evidence. As Arendt has stated:

> Wherever the few separated themselves from the many, they obviously became dependent on them, that is to say, in all those matters of coexistence which have to be really negotiated. [...] This is why the realm of the freedom of the few is [...] dependent on the many for its very existence. [...] [I]t becomes a necessity that on the one hand opposes the freedom, and is its precondition on the other. (2010: 58–59)

Part Two, *An Observer under Observation: The Cosmopolitan Legacy of Modern Theory*, traces the destiny of modern literary theory, which emerged in response to the age of national philologies. In taking up the suppressed cosmopolitan idea of literature in new historical and political circumstances, this theory questioned the consequences of the establishment of the new nation-states after the breakdown of East Central European multinational empires. My aim is to examine which redistribution of emphasis and roles this historical and geopolitical re-contextualization of the divided cosmopolitan project entailed in the argument between Roman imperial and Greek elitist cosmopolitanism, the polemics between the Enlighteners and the Romanticists respectively. To keep in sight the long trajectory of the cosmopolitan axis' perturbations, reconfigurations and recalibrations, the permanent efforts of its constituents to adjudicate and adapt to the transformed drama of their present situation, I reverse the systematically applied translational methodology of Part One: *new* debates on the nature of literature are consistently refracted through the lens of the *old* ones. As long as imperial and elitist cosmopolitanisms oppose each other's enabling structure while neglecting the enablers at their own basis, the uneasy cohabitation of these two types of cosmopolitanism seeks resolution in vain. This is why the failure of the present cosmopolitan agencies to break with the benighted past enablers, as detected in the unfolding of modern literature in Part One, resurfaces in the unfolding of modern literary theory as presented in Part Two. In lieu of the triumphant surmounting of the one of the cosmopolitan axis' poles by the other, their "missed encounter" re-arises. The debate between imperial and elitist cosmopolitanism continues in ever-new forms, inducing their new entangled manifestations such as intranational, immigrant, class, messianic or "cosmopolitanism of the disregarded." In focusing in subsequent chapters on each of them in turn, my principal interest is to represent their covert trauma narratives as compensatory responses to the pressing historical, social and political circumstances of their emergence; I focus on the infrastructural stress they have been exposed to. While these various forms of cosmopolitanism are destined to work through the circumstances that destabilize their carriers, they cannot but simultaneously act out these circumstances. Cosmopolitanism is not merely an opening but a defense as well. Nonetheless, I do not aim at their utter disqualification through the disclosure of hidden prejudices at the heart of these narratives' cosmopolitan orientation. Rather, in carefully analyzing their structure and argument, I intend to obviate the recent uncritical resumption of cosmopolitanism's sovereignty ambitions. As I try to argue in the Epilogue, theory today is better advised to examine the possibility of a non-sovereign and non-narrative kind of cosmopolitanism whose premises are not given in advance but are perpetually sought outside of the established political space. To put this in Rancière's terms, cosmopolitanism must not turn into a consensually imposed police but rather take care to maintain the form of dissensual politics. Such politics takes recourse to the uneasy cohabitation with distant and dissimilar others with whom I apparently have nothing in common but must nonetheless responsibly share one and the same earth (Mbembe 2010: 85). This is why the departure from the relational and dispossessed, rather than the sovereign cosmopolitan subject stubbornly regenerated by the European myopic self-perception, is recommendable.

In the first chapter of Part One, "The Divided Legacy of the Republic of Letters: Emancipation and Trauma," I discuss Voltaire's retroactive canonization of the Republic of Letters as a cosmopolitan project induced by the deep social inequalities of the French monarchy of the time that undercut Voltaire's social ambitions and damaged his private life. In taking up for remedial purposes a half-century-old idea of Bayle's, Voltaire established an extraordinarily fertile elective affinity between the victims of religious and political discrimination, enabling the translation of two different traumatic constellations of French and European modernity into one another. His "World Republic of Letters," related to Bayle's compensatory invention, created a basis for an open and free international exchange of opinions against the nationally isolated and despotic model of the eighteenth century's absolutist monarchies. It envisioned the dissolution of self-confined traditional communities into which the human being was pressed by his or her very birth, and the replacement of these with the politico-economic community whose rules were expected to be freely accepted and strategically created by him or her. This is why the modern idea of literature was actually deeply involved in its shaping, contrary to the entrenched opinions that oppose it to the world of economy and politics by highlighting literature's autonomy. Its democratic circuit of ideas was inextricably intertwined with the free circulation of money, commodities, and people, i.e. with the processes of unbounded market exchange. Accordingly, modern literary intercourse took an active part in the huge reconfiguration of Western European political, economic, and intellectual space and the concomitant modes of individual and collective identification that were set in motion in the second part of the eighteenth century. Yet for the vast majority of the world's population, entrapped in a variety of political, economic, and social bonds and strictures, the requested freedom of behavior and thinking was completely unattainable. This is why ultimately only select individuals could become the beneficiaries of "republican" rights. Voltaire's republican project gradually underwent a similar "perversion," as did that of the French Revolution for which it paved the way, substituting an intolerant exclusiveness for the envisaged inclusiveness.

The second chapter, "The Fissured Identity of Literature: National Universalism and/or Cosmopolitan Nationalism," focuses in the first place on the German national response to the French expansionist "republican universalism." Like all "dominated nationalisms," this national awakening demonstrated interlocking cosmopolitan inclinations in order to defend itself from the French "dominating nationalism." Struggling for their own emancipation, German intellectuals affirmed the right to self-determination of all nations put under similar assimilatory pressure. While bearing in mind this peculiar international constellation of forces around 1800, I claim that rather than having taken place between cosmopolitanism and nationalism as is usually assumed, the French-German confrontation in question stood between *national universalism* and *cosmopolitan nationalism*. Once the habitual opposition between cosmopolitanism and nationalism is reintroduced into each of the opposites, they unexpectedly enter a mirror relationship with one another. Such an "inverted reflection" of one another indicates that they are not only excluding but also enabling each other, i.e. acting as the irritating internal condition of the possibility of the opponent. In order to rid itself of the haunting frustration induced by this internal enabler, the self undertakes the enabler's disabling externalization by making him or her into the object of distancing, enmity, and aggression. That is to say, the external confrontation of cosmopolitanism and nationalism is an outcome of their enduring and disconcerting mutual implication. Following these reconfigured terms, I investigate the tacit entanglement of French "literary cosmopolitanism" with political-national aims, as well as the secret political agenda of German "literary nationalism," most appropriately expressed in Friedrich Schlegel's establishment of national literary historiography. All such unifications via "trauma narratives" entail new divisions, as I seek to demonstrate through the internal French resistances of Jean-Jacques Rousseau and Mme de Staël to the universalism of the Parisian intellectual elite. Trauma inflicted by the pressure of Parisian universalism, by crossing historical, national, and cultural boundaries, spawned a series of transnational and transhistorical transferences and elective affinities.

The confrontation between the French Enlightenment and the German Romanticist idea of literature introduces a significant rift into the concept of literary *Bildung*, which now signifies *public education* directed toward the other, as well as *private formation* directed toward the self. In the third chapter, "The Janus Face of Literary *Bildung:* Education and/or Self-Formation," I argue that these seemingly opposite *Bildung* functions of literature simultaneously oppose and imply one other. As for their divergences, whereas Voltaire illustrated the historical progress of humankind by a spatial journey from Eastern to Western Europe, Herder as the forerunner of Romanticism perceived the development of the *Volksgeist* exclusively in historical terms. In order to create the not-yet-established German national self, he privileged historical interaction with the spirit of deceased ancestors over cultural interaction with distant living neighbors, which extended the already established French self. Friedrich Schlegel accordingly reversed the paternal attitude of the present toward the past, transforming the relationship between them into genetic lineage. The past now belonged to the same national geographic and cultural space as the present; it thereby lost its alien traits, acquiring familiar ones instead. Consequently genetic dependence was substituted for cognitive sovereignty, initiating the *re-evolutionary* paradigm in distinction to its French *revolutionary* counterpart. Since ancestors with all their intentions and attitudes are inscribed in their descendants' memory, without sensitively researching this rich genetic archive descendants cannot properly identify themselves. The retroactive self-finding operation acquires the pattern of an ongoing specification of the self through the subtle differentiation from its otherness-to-itself. The nation is expected to work normatively on its disentanglement since it has to be suitably created. Yet dissent re-emerges among the constituents of the one and the same national self, i.e. among individual selves with regard to the question as to which *particular* other is in the final analysis most suitable to contrastively determine the national self. This quarrel turns a purportedly consensual normative work into a conflict-ridden task. Normative work tacitly translates into oppression, which makes it reiterate the basic gesture of its Enlightenment opponent by forcing nationalism into an uneasy interweaving with cosmopolitanism. Simultaneously contradictory and co-implicated correlates of literary identities, literature is their ambiguous co-creation.

In the fourth chapter, "Who Voices Universal History? Kant's 'Mankind' and/or Herder's 'Nature'," I analyze the debate between Kant and Herder on the authorizing principle of human history as testimony to a traumatic rift in modernity's project of humanity's secular reconstitution. This rift points to the equivocal and/or-relationship inherent to European democracy, whose re-emergence will on the one hand hinder the latter's progress and on the other hand instantiate various operations expected to eliminate this hindrance. Yet what was designed to suspend the stubbornly resurfacing bifurcation in the envisaged democratic community simultaneously contributed to its reenactment. Kant introduces the historical agency of mankind in order to emancipate man from his basically "animal" natural disposition, epitomized by the obedience to lower, bodily drives. Yet the difficulty that his argument must face is that man's self-willingness characterizes the very agency expected to carry out his emancipation. The agency called upon to supervise man's long journey to final freedom displays significantly coercive traits. As it cannot be present or available in any way, mankind appears to be an imagined godlike instance demanding unconditional obedience, which lends it an almost terrorist character. Accordingly, emancipation characterizes the emergence of modern man only in a firm pairing with despotism. The same holds for Herder's advocacy of nature in response to the despotic attributes of the "absolutist" instance of mankind. In clear opposition to Vico's inimical representation of nature as a wild beast whimsically inclined to sudden disasters and devastations, Herder's organic nature assumes an almost idyllic shape of a familiar and caretaking human *Umwelt*. Nevertheless, it remains questionable whether this environment really suspends coercion as Herder claims. Inasmuch as it provides paternal protection from wild external forces through the measure of loyalty demonstrated by its dependants in return, it may be merely transposing brute fatherly force into more sublime terms. Instead of liberating dependants from coercion, as is envisioned, it only replaces the visible violence of an external despot with the invisible pressure of an internal master. This is how discrimination is subtly reintroduced into the desired common harmony.

The idea of *Weltliteratur* is a hotly debated topic in today's global world. The latter seems to have antiquated national literatures in the same way, it is claimed, as did Goethe and Marx with their idea more than a century and a half ago. In the fifth chapter titled "Who Worlds the Literature? Goethe's *Weltliteratur* and Globalization" I contest this claim, showing, first, that Marx, even though critical of nationalism, was ambivalent with regard to the formation of the world market, anticipating its compartmentalizing consequences. Second, I argue that Goethe's concept of *Weltliteratur*, far from being opposed to national literature, which in the Germany of the time was still in the process of self-finding, has to be regarded as an attempt to consolidate national literature against the homogenizing pressure of a world rapidly and superficially uniting. Parallel to that, however, Goethe's enlightened and considerate (inter)nationalism countered the aggressive German ethnonationalism launched by the brothers Schlegel in an embittered reaction to the French revolutionary expansion and the splintering of the German empire. Goethe was resolutely against such compensatory national exclusionism, but he was equally firmly against the gaudy flux, overall dilettantism, and bad taste of the culture emerging from the commercial and communicational uniting of the world. Like his immediate predecessor Kant in *Toward Perpetual Peace* (1795), he was an advocate of a dialogic internationalism which implied that a necessary departure toward other literatures and cultures with the aim to achieve an in-depth knowledge of them could not be permitted to amount to self-abandonment, but should rather lead to improved self-acquisition of German literature on a higher level. The final goal of Goethe's world literature was therefore never-ending national self-formation through an attentive self-differentiation in the turbulent worldwide flux. His *Weltliteratur* was conceived as an ever-changing outcome of literary exchanges between distinguished national literatures as its participants, an ongoing dialogue from which German literature, which at the time was the weakest among them, was expected to benefit the most. In the same way as Goethe's "trauma narrative," aimed at a consolidation of his disturbed personal and the shaky German self at the time, was a sovereignty-warranting method, I argue this to be the case, in an altered world configuration, with its recent re-instantiations, such as those of Casanova, Moretti and Damrosch.

The second part of the book opens with a genealogy of the exilic consciousness of modern theory, which enables it to transcend literature's embeddedness into "native" habits by contemplating its abstract laws from abroad. In the sixth chapter, "Interiorizing the Exteriority: The Cosmopolitan Authorization of the Theoretical Truth," I argue that such contemplation proves to be a well-established legacy of European theory since the time of Greek *theōría*. The Greek word *theōrós* designated a special envoy sent to inter-communal religious ceremonies to request divine wisdom and relay it back to community members. His or her authorized gaze tranquilized community fears caused by inexplicable occurrences by disclosing the truth underlying them. Yet the same "adultery with the foreigners" that enables the detection of truth prevents its easy acknowledgment, exposing it to the suspicion of the fellow citizens. To counter the mistrust of these "simple minds" and to foster consensus for its contemplation, theory was forced to make its sublime vision of the truth available to a broad spectatorship. Because of this exposure to the same mob prejudice that was to be dismantled, theory gradually became a public performance, dependent on the confirmation of the earthly gaze. Without ever being able to completely assimilate this gaze in the divine truth provided by "adultery," despite its strenuous efforts to deactivate the community's ignorant self-evidence, theory was at constant risk to reaffirm it. This permanent exposure to pollution explains why in early German Romanticism, as the most important relay between Greek *theōría* and modern theory, no observer was authorized in advance, but was rather compelled to reflect critically on its earthly dependencies in the detection of literature's truth. Concomitantly, the truth in continuous historical displacement substituted the Greek truth received from abroad, but in early German Romanticism this history was taken at its word equally piously, as was the truth from abroad in Greek times. Truth was now deduced from its most diverse historical effects. Early Romanticist theory thus set itself the "infinite task" of interiorizing all exterior critical observers of literature's truth in order to establish a completely sovereign observation, which means that it was ultimately dedicated to the consolidation of the given theorist's self rather than its cosmopolitan interrogation.

The seventh chapter, "The Narrative of Permanent Displacement: Early German Romanticism and Its Theoretical Afterlife," investigates this early German Romanticist "narrative of permanent displacement" lurking behind the differential paradigm of poststructuralist theory. It starts by taking issue with the recent German mainstream interpretation of this legacy, which neglects the striving of the Romanticist self towards a sovereign observing post, insisting on the putative reciprocity between the self-affirmation and self-negation in the formation of this self. This reciprocity, the argument goes, is better represented in the work of German poststructuralist thinkers, such as Niklas Luhmann, than in the one-sided interminable subversion of identity in the work of Derrida or de Man. My exploration therefore starts with Luhmann's basic assumption that no single observer is capable of identifying by itself the blind spot of its observation. Constitutively dispossessed by another observation, it cannot escape delusion. Displacement is therefore promoted into the structural condition of theoretical knowledge, meaning that each and every site of knowledge implies delusion. As the blind spot of an observation can be detected only retroactively by subsequent observation and the blind spot of the latter again only retroactively by the next one, narrative concatenation of observations into a progressive temporal sequence charts the trajectory of theoretical knowledge. Thanks to such enlightening continuity, the Enlightenment doctrine unexpectedly catches up with its Romanticist polemic partner. By surreptitiously reintroducing the former's educational terms, early Romanticist theory resumes the ambition to capitalize, once the divinely absolute insight has been achieved, on having patiently pushed through the prior state of delusion. To fulfill this imperial self-educational ambition, truth abandons its initial self-enclosed and self-satisfied "site in life," entering the enriching temporal medium of displacement and postponement. In such a way, the horizon of the theoretical observation hugely benefits from its strategic "exile." Its course is delineated not just as a blind and hollow trajectory, but as a goal-directed plot. Each new phase demonstrates a more developed synthetic capacity. Luhmann's systemic observer therefore seems to be guided by the know-all attitude whose truth can come into being only against the background of the deluded first-order observers. He needs the latter less to question his truth than to affirm its superiority.

In the eighth chapter, "The Oppositional Literary Transcendental: The Russian Formalist Rewriting of Early Romanticist Cosmopolitanism," I turn to the Russian Formalist rewriting of Romanticist Cosmopolitanism taking place in substantially altered circumstances of the nationally reconfigured post-imperial Eastern European space. Being deficient in the national-historical continuity established by the Western European national philologies, these literatures were shaped by principles deeply inimical to linear national evolution. Their internal cultural hybridity was still evident and irreducible. Therefore the East Central European literary theorists, instead of soliciting their national identity like their compatriot literary historians, aimed to break out of its inappropriateness. In order to subvert national terms, they searched for an intrinsic *literary quality*. Their "defamiliarizing" operation followed the exclusionary logic of "neither this familiar national nor that familiar national literary identity" diametrically opposed to the assimilating as-well-as logic of Western European national literary historiography. "Literariness" was accordingly expressed in negative, oppositional terms. However, by authorizing the theoretical truth of literature's contesting character against the historical delusion of literature's affirmation of the *Volksgeist*, Russian Formalists surreptitiously reintroduced the hierarchy between the two observations of literature inherent to early Romanticist theory, i.e. the cosmopolitan disengaging and the nationally engaged perspective. Along with the enlightening attitude to "benighted opponents" they reaffirmed the commitment to the world of unimplemented possibilities beyond the nationally familiar reality. By catapulting its readers out of comfortable consuming habits, literature enters "foreign alliances" in the way early German Romanticists claimed it does. Yet whereas German Romanticists deployed cosmopolitanism for the therapeutic enhancement of their politically frustrated national soul, Russian Formalists redistributed its emphases to defy the identity pressure of their new state authorities. While Romanticist international cosmopolitanism mobilized the process of a nation's self-finding in foreign literatures, East Central European intranational cosmopolitanism implemented the affirmation of literature's innate strangeness.

In the ninth chapter, "The All-Devouring Modern Mind: Bakhtin's Cosmopolitan Self," I explore Bakhtin's rewriting of Kant's cosmopolitanism, taking issue with the neo-Kantian reading of his ideas and drawing them closer to the German Romanticist tradition and its central concept of life. Bakhtin aestheticizes life in the spirit of §46 of the *Critique of Judgment*, which defines aesthetic quality as the ability of the work of art to mobilize human mind through the disengagement of its automatic application. Bakhtin attributes to life the same quality that Kant had attributed to the work of fine art. Such aestheticization raises life to a supreme authority that, in Bakhtin's philosophy, "authors" all human achievements, including art. Life becomes an unfathomable performer of self-exemption from all forms of its appropriation, including the artistic forms. They are for Bakhtin merely derivative, instead of being absolute as in the Formalist rendering. Confronted with this evasiveness of life, can the authoring subject find any reliable retreat in its a priori schemata? To answer this question, Bakhtin developed a conception of the mind's authoring activity, conceived as the never-ending dialogic consumption of life's inaccessibly heterogeneous forms. He understands modernity as the age in which the self begins to experience its existence as an open life event without transcendental guarantees. Its mind becomes aware of the challenge addressed to it by different dispositions of other minds. This makes the self's responsibility unique. Rather than just representing an example of a pre-given universal rule, it now looks for the new form of commonality departing from its uniqueness. This utopian community, aesthetic in nature by virtue of its loyalty to life-in-becoming, comes into being – following Kant's equivocal *sensus communis* (*Vernunft/Verstand*) – through reflective judgment. Life rises as the new universal horizon because the modern self loses its previously ensured social and political site. Being faced with the plural grammar of disjointed norms, each of them deficient in itself, it is reoriented toward their dialogic completion and reconciliation. However, while looking for the compensation for its loss of a secure "site in life" in the new public sense (*Vernunft*), Bakhtin's self, by involuntarily slipping into common sense (*Verstand*), inadvertently produces new losses.

The tenth chapter, "Countering the Empirical Evidence: From Immigrant Cosmopolitanism to a Cosmopolitanism of the Disregarded," traces the transition from immigrant cosmopolitanism, characteristic of the structuralist generation of French theory, to what I term "cosmopolitanism of the disregarded" genuine to its poststructuralist generation. I argue that French Eastern European immigrants such as Greimas, Todorov, and Kristeva, in order to undermine the author as the literary representative of the free human individual placed in the foundation of French universalism, systematically interrogate the empirical evidence on which a given author unquestionably relies when disclosing the illusions of his or her figures. Precisely by being empirically rooted, these "dismantling" authorial insights fall victim, in their turn, to the author's restricted horizon mistakenly taken to be universal. To become truly universal, this horizon must evaporate into non-empirical qualities, which is why structuralists trace back the authored works to an anonymous structure postulated to be their transcendental condition. Yet the uninvolved theoretical disclosure of the latter proves to be impossible since, unavailable to direct observation as it is, its terms must be invented, which means that as it stands it meets the inventors' compensatory needs. Therefore, by imposing its transcendental quality upon all literary works, the structure turns out to be a harsher dogma than the author previously had been. The resistance to this ruthless structuralist colonization developed by Althusser, Bourdieu, Derrida, Lyotard, or Cixous – all of them, in one way or another, associated with decolonized Algeria – corresponded with the resistance to French colonialism that, in the footsteps of the famously inconsiderate "national universalism," left the otherness of the included others unaccounted for. Albeit poststructuralist cosmopolitanism was of the same subordinated kind as the structuralist one, the global extension of the delineated colonization implied diverse forms of resistance to it, unlike the homogeneous resistance of immigrants to universalism. The "uncounted" others subverted the truths established by the colonial theoretical discourse at their scattered locations in an incomparably larger "radiation field." I meticulously investigate three interconnected forms of this heterogeneous subversion, epitomized in the thought of Levinas, Derrida as well as in the intellectual exchange between Blanchot and Foucault.

In the eleventh chapter, "Political and/or Literary Community: From Class to Messianic Cosmopolitanism," I track the concept of singularity, whose popularity rises at the outset of the twenty-first century, in the context of the European intellectual legacy. Unlike particularity, it is claimed, singularity offers hospitality to unforeseeable alterity in the way the European culture did from its very nascence in contradistinction to all the others. From Aristotle onwards, Europeans have liked to perceive themselves as being dialogically open, unlike the others who therefore had to be either enlightened or, if necessary, excommunicated from humanity. In invisibly mediating the becoming of humankind, the Europeans accordingly combined the overcoming of certain admitted others with the extermination of those they deemed inadmissible. But the rising shadow of the sacrificed, contrary to their expectations, gradually polluted their vision of an all-inclusive human community. To examine the globalizing role allocated to literature in this profoundly equivocal mission, I first reject the established thesis that British Cultural Studies aimed to abandon the study of literature in favor of the study of cultures. My claim is that it, on the contrary, surreptitiously reaffirmed and extended the idea of literature inherent to the contested Literary Studies' programs, associating its typically European self-exempting mediation of others with the culture of the working class. This culture, according to Cultural Studies, engages with literature in the performing rather than representing manner, as does the culture of the ruling class. In following that thesis I state that if the concept of literature in Literary Studies was determined by the cultural practice of those in power, then the concept of culture in Cultural Studies was shaped by the literary practice of the subordinated class. The culture of the dispossessed was thus silently placed at the service of Cultural Studies' cosmopolitan empowerment; the former's subversive mimicking of the high culture legitimized the latter's "permanent displacement" characteristic of the European "vanishing mediation" of humankind (Balibar). As a result, the gap between the powerful and the disempowered that Cultural Studies intended to bridge was deepened. The desperate tactical maneuvering of the disempowered was strategically capitalized on by the powerful. Yet the messianic "poetics of singularity" which, with the "anti-culturalist turn" at the outset of the twenty-first century claimed to be disengaging this imperial pattern of assimilation in the name of the redemption of singularities suffocated by it – this is the second step of my argument – involuntarily reapplied the same European literary model of "vanishing mediation." The messianism of the literary community cannot cure the exclusions of the political community, since it reintroduces them. These two communities are not only opposed to but also involved with each other, i.e. captured by the relationship *and/or*. I demonstrate this shortcoming of the "poetics of singularity" through a close reading of, among others, Agamben's, Cavarero's, and Nancy's messianic arguments.

In the final chapter, titled "Literature as Deterritorialization: New Vistas for Democracy?," I focus on the implementation of literature for the democratic opening of the human being-in-common in the philosophy of Gilles Deleuze and Jacques Rancière. Deleuze and Guattari advocate a quasi-traumatized, "animally" disfigured kind of discourse that testifies to the impossibility of bearing witness to the unpredictable whirl of becoming, not only in philosophical but also in literary writing. Kafka exemplarily blurred the boundaries between his representing and represented subjects, drawing them into an unrestrained field of immanence. It is through such persistent revivifying of polyphony that his minor literature unleashed the suppressed creativity of major literature and language. It subverted literary language from within its identity, deterritorializing its monolingual molecules and pushing its subjects beyond the politically acknowledged threshold of representation. Invading the subject's speech, action, and behavior, minor literature revolutionizes its agency. Rancière also makes the political regulation of the subject from above the main target of the oppositional literary deregulation from below. For both of them, literary politics consists of the disarticulation of the politically authorized selection of sensations by an unpredictable revolutionary assemblage that escapes it. Now oriented inwardly toward the subject's perception apparatus, instead of outwardly toward other political subjects as before, revolutionary politics in their rendering deactivate the agency, departing from an inarticulate molecular area excluded from the scope of its activity. Despite undeniable divergences between their thoughts, this paradoxical "action through non-action" connects their conceptualizations of literature. Both of them place literature at the service of a transcendental force of negation deprived of all marks of identity and destined to dissolve all established agencies with such marks. However, as the genealogy of the messianic tradition has shown, the deactivation of "majoritarian" agencies does not merely achieve emancipating affects; it simultaneously empowers the "minoritarian" assemblage introduced in the place of agencies. As a result, the initially democratic (because minoritarian) assemblage suddenly resurfaces as the major agency of revolutionary terror. I argue that placing literature at the service of the allegedly egalitarian force of negation entertains this risk in both Deleuze's and Rancière's philosophies.

Finally, in the Epilogue, as an alternative to the delineated forms of cosmopolitanism that consistently strive for sovereignty, I design a cosmopolitanism that meets the challenge of an uncanny but unavoidable cohabitation with the anonymous "exilic" enablers located outside the dominating political space. This cohabitation cannot come into being in terms of narrative progression that follows the principle established by that space but, on the contrary, by way of an obstinate liberating leaping outside its "global" determination. Keeping oneself receptive for "diasporic injunctions," and thereby for the permanent rebirth of one's freedom out of imposed "natural necessity," is the conditio sine qua non of democracy.

Part I: **Toward a Global Community:
The Emergence of the Modern Idea
of Literature**

1 The Divided Legacy of the Republic of Letters: Emancipation and Trauma

Literature's gradual emancipation from the restrictive horizon of traditional communities into the purportedly unlimited horizon of "world" community is today most often traced back to Voltaire's canonization of the Republic of Letters undertaken in his *The Century of Louis XIV* (1751). Such a genealogy however, runs the risk of undertaking a surreptitious canonization on its own. In *The World Republic of Letters* (2004) for instance Pascale Casanova presents it in such a way as to legitimate her own managerial projection of a "world literary space" (2005: 72). She argues that today's World Literary Republic, as "a market where non-market values are traded" (72), greatly benefits from Voltaire's project of liberating literature from political, national and economic constraints. As self-enclosed national literary spaces are today suspended, Casanova argues, literary texts "must be thought and described in the relational terms" of a coherent "global structure" that determines them (73). In this argument, 'literature' make sense only "by taking the route" "through the vast, invisible territory" that Casanova calls the 'World Republic of Letters' (73). Casanova pitches this project *"against* the vast mass of conventional thought about literature" (82) as a decidedly "abstract, hypothetical model" (73). This global and all-determining literary territory is consecrated by the Nobel Prize for literature delivered by the Swedish Academy, which, in Casanova's terms, is estimated to be "totally independent in making its choices" (74–75). However, if we recall Casanova's argument about the mode of operation of the Swedish Academy presented in her book several years before, the academy's consecration of the World Republic of Letters, far from having endorsed the Republic's autonomy has been all the time clearly favoring one and the same "monopolist of universality" (2004: 154), that is, the French literary taste:

> This new degree of autonomy came about as a result of the structural complementarity obtaining between the Nobel Prize and the power of consecration enjoyed by Paris. In effect, the Academy affirmed (or reaffirmed) the verdicts of the capital of literature and, as it were, grounded them in law: by making these decisions official, the Swedish Academy – with few exceptions at least through the 1960ies – endorsed, ratified, and made public the judgments of Paris (153).

We are brought to the conclusion, then, that the "world structure" that provides "intellectual categories, and recreates its hierarchies and constraints" in the mind of "writers, readers, researchers, teachers, critics, publishers, translators and the rest" (2005: 81–82) has actually from Voltaire's time till today, been dominated and orientated by French literary authority. This seems to be considered as something to be welcomed because the typical representatives of this French literary power enjoyed and still enjoy the "greatest autonomy" (83) unlike "the newcomers" who, to get rid of non-literary pressures at home, must struggle to be recognized by the French "central authorities" (87). Casanova infers that "literature itself, as the common value of the entire space, is also an instrument which, if re-appropriated, can enable writers – and especially those with the fewest resources – to attain a type of freedom, recognition and existence within it" (90).

She therefore advises marginal writers to follow "the common value of the entire space," i.e. literature as it has been defined by Paris. This stance is very much in line with the instruction recently given by the Princeton Enlightenment specialist Jonathan Israel (2010: 11). He states that "the Western World most basic social and cultural values in the post-Christian age" such as democracy, equality, individual liberty and so on, representing the quintessence of "Radical Enlightenment" thought,

> especially in many Asian and African countries, as well as in contemporary Russia – has also become the chief hope and inspiration of numerous besieged and harassed humanists, egalitarians and defenders of human rights, who, often against the great odds, heroically champion basic human freedom and dignity […] in the face of the resurgent forms of bigotry, oppression, and prejudice…

In short, the enlightenment of the "Western World," with France as its main trademark, holds the transnational Enlightenment torch that helps those newcomers from "borderlands" and "subordinated regions" to come to grips with the nationalist "forces of darkness" in their own countries.

As a matter of fact, for many reasons that we will come to see shortly, it is much more difficult than it first appears to frame Voltaire and his work into "a hegemonic Archimedean point from which to leverage a dominant discourse of global supremacy" (Kadir 2012: 64). True, with his *Republic of Letters*, Voltaire not only translated the two centuries old Latin *Respublica litteraria*, the first international institutional network for the collection, classification, and distribution of knowledge, into vernacular national terms. He also substantially modernized its pre-given transnational Greek-Roman foundation by connecting it to the principle of a free commerce of ideas between various European nations. In such ways, he really contributed to the transition of European modernity from a *religious* (i.e., Christian) global design typical of the Renaissance to the *civilizing* one typical of the Enlightenment. Nevertheless, this secularizing transition involved – and this is usually all too easily overlooked – the tacit reintroduction of the *colonial difference* inherent to the Renaissance global design. However secular Enlightenment rationalism was, it shares structural similarities with the "dogmatic" religion it sought to displace (Connolly 2000). The international or universal Christian mission of early European modernity was underpinned by the exploitation of the Americas in much the same way as its secular civilizing follow-up rested on the ongoing British, Dutch, and French plunder of Asia and Africa (Mignolo 2000: 722, 725–726). This may be why modern cosmopolitanism, contrary to its predominant humanist self-representation, rehearses the colonial difference between European and non-European peoples. Far from eliminating the imparity, as we will come to see in the fourth chapter, its founder, Immanuel Kant, gradually complemented and refined it with the *imperial difference* between the North, South, and East European nations. Hegel's dialectics, a kind of synthesis of the sketched development from the Renaissance onwards, treated both the colonial (intercontinental) and imperial (intracontinental) differences as unquestionable matters of fact.

Yet as exemplified by Casanova and Israel who are here, to be sure, speaking for the broad international community of scholars, European modernity demarcated its beginning with the eighteenth century by resolutely repudiating colonial and religious discrimination, that is, *the asymmetric division of humankind as its very condition of possibility*. Within this "scientific community," in the competition for symbolic power, each group of scholars favors its own national Enlightenment as the putative agenda for humanity, as we will come to see shortly. The question who was tacitly providing the *prerequisites* for this symbolic competition to take place remains bypassed. Due to the systematic cancellation of this question, the key Western achievements of democracy and equality tend to present themselves as being untainted by colonial atrocities and exploitation. "The post-Christian age" is, against all evidence to the contrary, postulated as the "natural" secular origin of these values. In order to stylize themselves as the founding fathers of modernity, the prominent Enlighteners themselves, followed by a series of contemporary adherents who symbolically benefit from this progeny, in a typically *traumatic* abnegation, tend to obliterate their disconcerting colonial background by shifting it to the supposedly premodern past. This may be why we are today, while attentively working through the constitutive trauma of modernity instead of unconcernedly acting it out, obliged to read the masterworks of the prominent Enlighteners against the grain and apply them, with all due respect, with the necessary reservations and theoretical attentiveness. There is an underlying awareness, that those who non-reflectively invest their concepts as analytical tools tacitly mask or even endorse their contaminated and disturbing legacy. With the Enlightenment, neither religious nor colonial discrimination was really overcome and in many respects, as we see from the observations concerning "world literature" above, this discriminating difference was reaffirmed or re-articulated. This is why "literature," as the most genuine representative of "Enlightenment achievements," was by no means freed from institutional, economic, and political strictures, constraints, and pressures. It was not merely exposed to them but exerted their pressures in a different form. So as to prevent this, literature's still predominating Enlightenment interpretation has to be revisited through the uncovering of a *trauma denial* at its core.

To obviate the uncritical forwarding of Voltaire's revolutionary project of the Republic of Letters in the current literary research, the traumatic constellation with which he attempted to get to grips must be reconstructed against Voltaire's own consistent denial. What started as an emancipating project toward transnational conviviality, having a suppressed traumatic wound as its motor, has turned in the hands of Voltaire's recent interpreters into a universal project to manage the literary "world." By denying rather than examining its divided legacy, this world literary "design" retains the initial traumatic experience in the form of a rising frustration that looks after an ever-stronger remedy. While resisting the unjust communal constraints imposed upon their carriers, because all cosmopolitan projects nevertheless arise from *within* them, they tend to reintroduce the managerial frames that they are criticizing. In order to avoid slipping into this "complicity with regimes of terror" genuine to the neocolonial and neoimperial discourse (Kadir 2006: 74–75), as well as in order to escape "producing a facile globalism in which distinct literary worlds are flattened to fit homogeneous paradigms" (Apter 2009: 56–57), in what follows we are going to ask not merely *why* such cosmopolitan projects are launched in the first place but also from *where*, by which *agency*, within which specific geopolitical and ideological *frame* and with which direct or collateral *effects and victims*. In such a pattern of argument the introduction of the new "abstract model" for the "mapping" of world literature, inasmuch as it would support instead of question global designs, can only be viewed as at best misplaced or at worst complicit. The intention here is to liberate literature's suppressed potentials by re-describing its up-to-date proposed cosmopolitan forms and by raising the question of their unintended consequences.

The accepted point of departure is that *every* attempted cosmopolitanism is historically, geopolitically and socially rooted rather than universal and all-uniting (Appiah 2005: 213–272). This is why, in trying to come to terms with the particular traumatic constellation introduced by the gradual spreading of the suppressed "poisonous knowledge" along the axes of the commonly accepted truth, cosmopolitanism does not transcend but merely restructures the asymmetry between the truth and this knowledge. To illustrate, the French Enlightenment idea of the citizen attempted to transcend the Renaissance division of the Christian and the *infidel*, but instead of transcending it, it replaced this division by the new division of the citizen and the *foreigner*. To transcend the latter, the idea of man was invoked, but instead of transcending the division of the citizen and the foreigner, it merely exchanged it with the new division of "man" and "*inhuman*" beings. Therefore, with their narratives, cosmopolitanisms – or at least those that are well positioned to enact and devise global designs – repeatedly reproduced the exclusion that they were trying to overcome. Despite intentions and declarations, they never became truly all-encompassing. Because of that, according to Kadir (2004: 2), "[t]o *world* and *to globalize* [...] would have to be parsed in light of their subject agencies and their object predicates. World and globalization, thus, would be imputable actions, rather than anonymous phenomena." Accordingly, the local historical borders of such powerful universals have to be attentively drawn from the combined perspectives of various enablers classified, positioned and/or excluded by their global agency. At whose cost were the naming, defining, and canonization of "proper literature" all the time taking place (Coopan 2009: 41)? Who was tacitly denigrated to the status of a temporally anterior and spatially exterior object in the very act of literary recognition by "global authorities" (Shih 2004: 17)? For example, what would some nine-tenths of humankind (according to Voltaire's own calculation), the so-called common people whom he, contrary to a tiny intellectual elite (*un petit nombre de sages*), in a letter to Damilaville of April 28, 1766, scornfully estimated to be so benighted that they did not deserve to be enlightened (*ne meritent pas que l'on les éclaire*) (Voltaire 1968–1977: XXX, 194), what would *they* have to say about his egalitarian and all-embracing Republic? Next to the colonized and imperially dominated peoples who worship another God than he did, these "illiterates" were subjected to the whole grandeur of Voltaire's "epochal progress of literature," exposed to the suppression that accompanied its enactment and thereby transformed into its "ghostly repetition" and "uncanny haunting" (Coopan 2009: 41). Whoever renders the so called cosmopolitan universals abstract and anonymous by systematically attributing them to God-like, supraindividual, irrefutable "authorities" (like nature, humankind, reason, history, economy, capitalism, world-systems etc.), is, viewed from these persistently obliterated and silenced perspectives, trying to repress his or her particular responsibility not just for their establishment but also for their effects and consequences.

***

The crucial notion of a free commerce of ideas was put forth already in Voltaire's 1733 *Essay sur la poésie épique* (printed as an addendum to the third edition of *La henriade*). It might have been inspired by his stay in England from 1726–1728 where, at that time, the religious unity of society was already transformed by the market ideology of circulation and mutual exchange and contract. By adapting this ideology in his vision of the secular literary republic, he suspended the Renaissance preordained transnational pattern of literature, introducing in its "oppressive" place a version of permanent negotiation and commerce among diverse national-literary models. This is how the broad, internationally recognized French Classicism, and its version of monopolizing universality, became a substitute for the "eternal" claims of Greco-Roman antiquity. Under this pattern of analysis, we can see that Voltaire's enlightenment intention was to replace the older, imposed religious and hereditary bonds and fixed relations by a free international exchange of ideas associated with the rising circulation of commodities and money in a putatively "open" cultural marketplace. Yet because of its predominantly economic base, what he saw as human freedom ultimately functioned less as a moral force in the service of those at the mercy of the rising system of exchange, as was envisioned, than as an instrument of the mercantile "cost and benefit" logic. The free market exchange of ideas was, despite Voltaire's intention, as regards its discriminating effects quite similar to the former political and religious pressures and constraints exerted upon the population by the older elites. It was everything but liberating for each and everybody in the world. Due to uneven political and economic developments caused by the social, imperial, and colonial exploitation of one group of national, social, or political constituencies by another, the intended free exchange between them was in reality determined and filtered by existing hierarchies of power and by already firmly established divisions of labor. "The ideal of the autonomy of each person," curiously enough, "became established among men who were dependent on one another for material things to a much greater extent than all their predecessors" (Dumont 1980: 11). Yet not just persons as such but, at the more general level, the European reconfigured states as well were affected by the reinforcement of the new privileges that replaced those of the aristocratic elites. These states and peoples had entered a "liberal" global economy, but instead of uniting them under general Enlightenment principles, this form of economy ultimately divided them up. This process continued in the transnational cultural exchanges set in motion by literary modernity, which was always permeated with inequality, asymmetries, and dependencies to a much greater extent than Western self-congratulating interpretations of democracy, equality, and individual liberties allow (Huyssen 2005: 10).

As a matter of fact, Voltaire's literary republic itself, with humanity's free individual disposition built into its very fundament, grew out of clear social and economic inequalities that poisoned Voltaire's personal life. It established such a profoundly utopian vision of human communal belonging – an *imagined* cosmopolitan community (Robbins 1998: 2) as it were – that it often strikes us today as compensatory action derived from bitter personal experience. One is probably stating the blatantly obvious by saying that a "society as conceived by individualism has never existed anywhere for the reason […] that the individual lives on social ideas (Dumont 1980: 10)." Far from being the self-evident measure of

1 The Divided Legacy of the Republic of Letters: Emancipation and Trauma — 39

all things, individual freedom was therefore, from the outset, shaped as a projection of the frustrated minds of the new political and cultural "engineers." Voltaire rebelled against the unjust and exclusionist hereditary principle that, being the basis of the French political and social order of his time, ruined his intellectual and social ambitions and restricted and damaged his private life, among those of innumerable others, of course. Celebrating the historical initiator of this Republic, the French Protestant scholar Pierre Bayle, Voltaire might have recognized in Bayle's traumatic situation his own troubles and sufferings under the despotic French monarch and the arrogant nobility. After having fallen victim to the religious intolerance in France toward the end of the seventeenth century, Bayle advocated during his Dutch exile a cosmopolitan collaboration of international scholars on an equal basis (Dainotto 2007: 87). Both Bayle and Voltaire acted as versions of a cosmopolitanism deeply rooted in French religious, political and social divisions, Bayle deriving his cosmopolitanism out of the traumatic experience in terms of religious belief and Voltaire out of the traumatic experience in terms of citizenship. But as Mignolo (2000: 724) has pointed out, "[...] the ideological configuration of one moment does not vanish when the second moment arrives but is reconfigured. The Renaissance did not disappear with the Enlightenment!" Such a persistent *translation* of one asymmetric configuration of European modernity into another, instead of being the decisive *rupture* between them, explains not just the stubborn reemergence of the question of rights as a constitutive hindrance to modernity's project but also the elective affinities between the victims of its various traumatic constellations, as demonstrated by Bayle and Voltaire.

Elaborating on the rebellious idea of man's free disposition in the voluminous *Essai sur les moeurs et l'esprit des nations* (1756), Voltaire marked the beginning of his history with man's emancipation from Oriental bondage, letting the human being thereafter slowly progress toward its complete sovereignty in the Occident. Charting a "sun-like" trajectory (1904: 184), his history moves from the East to the West until it reaches the "golden century of Louis XIV." For, according to Casanova (2004: 69–70), where else in the world could have had emerged such a peerless free summit of writers like Corneille, Racine, Molière, Pascal or La Rochefoucauld? Yet Voltaire sees that the whole process of emancipation that entailed this unique achievement of human history could hardly have been set in motion if man's basic disposition had not been disobedient from the very outset. "Man" is accordingly promoted into a genuinely revolutionary being destined to a steady individual overcoming of his natural and communal dependencies.[1] As

---

[1] Here and in the following I am deliberately skipping "his or her" for "man" taking the habitual point of view of Enlighteners.

the chief architect of the glory of the Republic of Letters, which epitomizes this eminently bourgeois idea of man, Voltaire sharply opposes Bossuet's *Discours sur l'histoire universelle* (1681) and Montesquieu's *De l'esprit des lois* (1748). In a typically aristocratic manner, both make man's natural disposition heavily dependent on the landed "necessities" of topography and climate. Voltaire rejects Bossuet's degrading rendering of the Arab, Chinese and Indian civilizations in these terms (1904: 158–189) reminding that they were shining in their entire splendor at the time the Europeans were living in huts. It should not be forgotten that Europe is a historical newborn (215), that is, impossible to be imagined in its contemporary brilliance without the merits of its non-European predecessors.

As for the other, more contemporary and prominent opponent Montesquieu, an insistent polemic against him was taken up already in *Le siècle de Louis XIV* (1751), culminated in the eighteenth chapter of the *Essai sur les moeurs* (1756), and continued in some shorter pieces like *Suppléments* (1763) (1906: 111), *Dialogue entre A, B, C* (1768) (1891: 323), *Commentaire sur l'Esprit de Lois* (1778) (1895: 409), and *Pensées sur le Gouvernement* (1802) (1892: 530). Voltaire accuses Montesquieu of surreptitiously defending the old aristocratic privileges which Montesquieu "disguised" by blaming Louis XIV, who had actually suspended them. Montesquieu had launched his critique of Louis's, though in a covert fictional form, already in the *Persian Letters* (1725). The correspondence beteween the figures meticulously delineates how the legitimate and lawful monarchic order descends into a lawless order of a whimsical "family father," the process continued in France of the eighteenth century. The same argument continues more overtly in *On the Spirit of Laws*. According to Montesquieu's thesis, concludes Voltaire (1906: 112–113), a new governmental form was introduced next to the republican and monarchic one with Louis's regime, namely one that knew no other law but the caprice of its sovereign. Through recourse to Aristotle's *Politics*, Montesquieu compares this capricious form with the Asian pre-political tyrannical regimes in which sovereigns completely disregarded the opinion and rights of their subjects. He shares Aristotle's conviction that the hot and humid Asian climate makes Asian peoples simply incapable of having a reversible political relationship with their sovereigns and so they, as opposed to the naturally democratic European peoples, eventually *deserve* their tyrants.[2]

Voltaire warns that such a pre-political form of despotism is Montesquieu's pure invention, introduced with the aim to legitimate his constructed thesis on Louis's unlimited despotism. In addition, his equating of despotism with tyranny, so goes the argument, falsifies the original meaning of this concept as it was pre-

---

[2] See for this argument Aristotle's *Politics*, Book III, 1285a 6–7 and Book VII, 1327b 24–33.

sented in the first book of Aristotle's *Politics* (1255a: 15–20). Aristotle designates with the concept of the "despot," next to the unilateral and asymmetric relationship between the sovereign and subjects, also the reversible dialogic relationship based on the common political interest of both parties. So he allows for two kinds of despotism, the Asian and the European. Voltaire accuses Montesquieu of having deliberately skipped this "European," caretaking kind of despotism because it was precisely the model exemplified by Louis XIV. Louis's despotism was "enlightened" and political unlike the purely "Asian" prepolitical one "invented" by Montesquieu. Such an idea of "Asian" despotism, constructed by a rising French anxiety concerning the threatening Ottoman invasion during the sixteenth and seventeenth century, is pure nonsense, as no people would ever allow one man to sacrifice a multitude of other men out of mere caprice.

Voltaire therefore insists on the free character of Asian despotic regimes placed as they are at the outset of human history. They are not different from European regimes in essence, but only in the gradation of fatherly care – it is a difference of degree, not of kind. A clear aim of such a linear gradation of human history, rid of substantial breaks and mechanical repetitions,[3] is to lay bare all the glory of the "European" despotic regime of Louis XIV that marks its culmination point. In order to prove this triumphant historical pattern, Voltaire reveals that behind Montesquieu's contention that all Ottoman people were slaves, with the single exception of their sovereign,[4] lies his personal frustration with the French Ottoman's (that is to say Louis's) abolition of hereditary privileges in favor of citizens' equality. But by consistently drawing attention to Montesquieu's distortions of history in the service of his selfish interests, Voltaire diverts attention from his own comparable maneuver. In a homogenizing move typical of his new philosophy of human history based on the principle of humankind's consistent self-overcoming, he readily grants the ancestors historical priority in order to reserve for the descendants their intellectual and cultural domination. In accordance with this, he states that Asians to be sure, started the process of humankind's emancipation,

---

[3] Voltaire officially introduced this linear conception of *human* history based on the bourgeois principle of man's self-overcoming – in contradistinction to a futile circuit of *natural* history – in the booklet *Philosophie de l'Histoire*, published in Amsterdam 1765 under the pseudonym of Abbé Bazin, actually a kind of "retroactive" introduction to his *Essai sur les moeurs* (1756). In the article on history written at the same time for Diderot's and D'Alembert's *Encyclopédie* (Voltaire 1765: 220–221) he resolutely relegates natural history to physics, disconnecting it from human history. The historical pattern of self-overcoming was obviously already established.

[4] In the fourth chapter, we will see Hegel repeating this derogatory thesis on the Asian political regimes.

but it was brought to its incomparable contemporary height only by the European spirit epitomized by Louis XIV. If the golden age of Asian civilizations today happens to be over, opines Voltaire, this is because they remained in the state "like we were two hundred years ago" (Voltaire 1904: 217).

With this somewhat enigmatic hint made around 1756, that is, after the Republic of Letters was already established, Voltaire may have had in mind that around the middle of the sixteenth century universal Latin was being replaced by the vernacular French language that, according to Casanova, paved the way for his own Republic of Letters. This linguistic "development" introduced a broad dialogue of equals in which, at the declarative level at least, everybody was invited to join irrespectively of his religion, nation or hereditary qualities and status.[5] As such "literature," in principle, addresses all human beings rather than the Frenchman or German, the nobleman or peasant, the Catholic or Protestant, it, rather than consolidating the traditional self-enclosed communities, constitutes an open-ended and future-oriented community of humankind. Envisioning a world community of humans regardless of their inherited identities, literature therefore putatively abandons its previous identity-*confirming* services and appropriates an identity-*building* function. Like the historically forthcoming "political republic" for which Voltaire's "literary republic," if only unknowingly, paves the way, it affirms and mobilizes the free individual will of its citizens, suspending their hereditary privileges.

In this way, with Voltaire's Republic of Letters, obviously in polemics against the restrictive political order of the French absolutist monarchy, European literature began its cosmopolitan career (Goodman 1994: 15). In the wake of the groundbreaking research carried out by Reinhart Koselleck in *Kritik und Krise* (1957) and Jürgen Habermas in *Strukturwandel der Öffentlichkeit* (1962), it is clear that Europe owes its bourgeois culture of public opinion and even civil society in general, which it often advertises as its distinctive achievement, precisely to such the project of cosmopolitan Enlightenment literature. What this meant was that it created a basis for an open and free international exchange of opinions against the nationally isolated and despotic model of the eighteenth century's absolutist monarchies. If the French Revolution, as stated by Koselleck (1973: 135, 156), logically resulted from the transformation of public opinion initiated in such a way, then the political ambition of the modern concept of literature – keeping in mind the idea of an open community of equal citizens that it entailed – becomes obvious. For the first time in human history, in an unprecedented utopian project of re-

---

[5] Roberto Dainotto (2007: 93) interprets the same phrase in a more neutral way, as if having had referred to the English scientific revolution.

sistance, no limits have been set to this coming community; it aimed to encompass the entire world. For the first time no transcendent idea, no general rule, no pregiven hierarchical order was declared to determine relations among its members beforehand; it was left to a free dialogic exchange between autonomous individual wills to find out the principle of communal cohesion. What was rising on the European horizon for the first time, thanks to modern literature, was a republican community of equals involved in steady extension and progression, predestined as still-to-come.

In all these interconnected respects, that is, global ambitions as regards its geopolitical range, equality pertaining to the rights of its members, constitutive freedom of their decision-making as well as steady transformation and extension, the *World Republic of Letters paved the way for the politico-economic model of Western liberal democracy*. It envisioned the dissolution of self-confined traditional communities into which the human being was pressed by his or her very birth and the replacement of these by the politico-economic one whose rules were expected to be freely accepted and strategically created by its participants. This is why the modern idea of literature was deeply involved in the shaping of the neoliberal world of economy and politics, the entrenched opinions highlighting literature's autonomy notwithstanding. Its democratic circuit of ideas was inextricably intertwined with the free circulation of money, commodities, and people, that is, with the processes of unbounded market exchange (Koch 2002: 55–56). Being a constitutive part of the "monetary mania of relations" (*monetärer Beziehungswahn*, Hörisch 1996: 111–112), the modern idea of literature, which was turned into the "universal currency" for various "national wares," operated as an ally of expanding capitalist economies, which is why it systematically abolished political, national and religious constraints.

Communicational, mercantile, monetary, and spiritual mobility are the joint agenda of a European modernity that ultimately establishes an uneven flow of lucrative transmission and translation, appropriation and expropriation. This flow systematically deepened the inherited asymmetry, or the constitutive imparity of Western democracy, because the mobility of those who possessed money was purchased at the price of the immobility of those who possessed just the merchandize and the labor. As without spiritual innovation no trade extension is imaginable and, vice versa, without new commercial routes no propulsion of ideas, so the stream of ideas and commodities foster and accelerate each other (Koch 2002: 62). *Esprit de commerce* and *commerce des esprits* belong together. Accordingly, modern literary intercourse took an active part in the huge reconfiguration of Western political, economic and intellectual space and the concomitant modes of individual and collective identification that were set in motion in the second part of the eighteenth century. Defying the static, inert, and repressive aristocratic political order that prevented the great majority of citizens from governing their identification routes, it laid the foundation for the democratic order based on the willing and permanent revolutionizing of selves (Koselleck 1973: 135). Opening toward a progressive future, the new political community of humankind resolutely attached itself to the mobile horizon of expectation (*Erwartungshorizont*) as opposed to the inert space of experience (*Erfahrungsraum*) of traditional telluric communities (Koselleck 1989: 359). As the world of unforeseeable potentials gained the upper hand over the constrained familiar reality prevalent until then, the very meaning of the word subject was turned upside down substituting "the lord" for "the bondsman."

Unfortunately, not everybody was ready to meet the propulsions of human history by a relentless separation of the past from the present in the name of the future (Certeau 1975: 9–10). On the contrary, the introduction of a unitary version of political order serving a "liberal" economy into a multitude of traditional communities, established deeply unsettling effects among the non-European and marginal European populations and peoples. All the while claiming a new and very ambitious role of mastering entire human history as well as freeing individuals from inherited social and religious bonds, the liberal economic model deprived the majority of its constituencies of the necessary prerequisites to instrumentalize the advantages of such a profound change. Not all the starting positions for the forthcoming competition enjoyed equal chances because the cultural richness, communicational velocity, and economic propulsion of the great Western countries rested on the enslavement, exploitation, and plundering of others. European modernity was enabled by colonialism, conquest, and the hard labor of various subordinated regions and peoples. "With the European overseas expansion begins the history of its art collections, cabinets of curiosities and museums." (Koch 2002: 51, trans. mine) Oriental literature was implemented, not unlike Oriental spices, to enrich the available sources of pleasure, expand the space of choice as well as heighten the joy of combination of elite Western individuals. Such an accumulation of wealth was the basic precondition of individual freedom, which is why only the elect, like French, British, Dutch, or eventually North American societies, were able to make the individual into the self-evident point of reference.

Voltaire, after all, did not countenance great swathes of populations and actually envisioned his Republic as composed of a very limited social elite. Koselleck therefore appropriately translates *République des Lettres* as *Gelehrtenrepublik*, that is, a republic of scholars among whom, in addition, Voltaire would hardly have welcomed such radical and "impious" thinkers like Spinoza, Diderot, Hélvetius, or d'Holbach. For the vast majority of the world population, entrapped into a variety of political, economic and social bonds and strictures, the requested freedom of behavior and thinking was completely unattainable. And yet such

1 The Divided Legacy of the Republic of Letters: Emancipation and Trauma — 45

people(s) are blamed and scorned not only by Voltaire because of their "benightedness" but also by Kant because of their regrettable immaturity (*Unmündigkeit*) that prevents them from achieving a necessary "personality." It is from the perspective of such a completely overlooked colonial history that the Argentinian philosopher living in Mexico Enrique Dussel (1993: 68) comments:

> For Kant, immaturity, or adolescence, is a culpable state, laziness and cowardice is existential ethos: the *unmündig*. Today, we would ask him: an African in Africa or a slave in the United States in the eighteenth century: an Indian in Mexico or a Latin American mestizo: Should all of these subjects be considered to reside in a state of guilty immaturity?

Far from being *free by nature* and *autonomous in their decisions*, all individual identities emerge from the familiar sets of solidarities, affiliations, and allegiances that, in their turn, are located within the broader social networks of relations and therefore, depending on such location, differently developed, mobile, and flexible. The pattern and content of these micro- and macrosocial relations are in their turn powerfully conditioned by a national and international constellation of forces. In sum, by its continuous and parallel operations of inclusion and exclusion, this web of practices of situating, positioning, ascribing and attributing *continuously dispossesses the sovereignty of identities*. It also determines their uneven power distribution or the various degree of strictures to which they are exposed. Far from being autonomous in their self-shaping, individual identities are mere outcomes of maneuvering between political, economic and social rules, pressures, and closures imposed upon them in the historically, politically and socially given constellations of forces. Their freedom is dependent on the available room for maneuver. Despite the usual privileging of the "French" "civic" or cosmopolitan over the "German" "ethnic" or national type of individual identity bounding – because the first allegedly fosters individual liberties and the second suppresses them – citizenship proved to be no less powerful an instrument of social closure than ethnicity (Brubaker 1992: 21–35). The civic mode of exclusion that characterizes the French tradition is still "probably far more important, in shaping life chances and sustaining massive and morally arbitrary inequalities, than is any kind of exclusion based on putative ethnicity" (Brubaker 2004: 141). Yet paradoxically it was created precisely with the intention to unconditionally extending the range of its inclusiveness.

***

How did the web of political practices look like in which Voltaire launched his Republic of Letters? In the Ancien-régime that provoked his republican oppositional project, state citizenship was based on a legal inequality between the orders of the nobility and clergy on the one hand and the so-called third estate on the other, as well as numerous political, social, religious, regional, guild, and gender privileges (Brubaker 1992: 35–39). What Voltaire was therefore understandably fighting for, even if only on the restricted symbolic level, was the principle that was thereupon established by the French Revolution on the political level, namely the substitution of a common law (or citizenship) for privilege (or private law). What Emmanuel Joseph Sieyès presented in his famous 1789 broadside *What Is the Third Estate?* is on the political level more or less equivalent to Voltaire's conception of unmediated, undifferentiated and individual membership in the Republic. He certainly extended it to a larger population:

> I picture the law as being in the centre of a huge globe; all citizens, without exception, stand equidistant from it on the surface and occupy equal positions there; all are equally dependent on the law, all present it with their liberty and their property to be protected; and this is what I call the *common rights* of citizens, the rights in respect of which are all alike. (Sieyès 1963: 162)

Already French absolutist monarchs undertook the first steps toward the more abstract meaning of law in their attempts, in the second half of the eighteenth century, to establish a central fiscal, monetary, and administrative control over the territories of their monarchies against the liberties, immunities, and privileges of feudal lords and municipalities. But even though absolutist monarchs generalized law and power and extended their coverage in such a way, the emergence of the general status of the citizen was impeded. Not only the nobility who defended their hereditary privileges but also the citizens of autonomous city-states accustomed to actively participating in the business of rule resisted it, Jean-Jacques Rousseau being the most prominent among the latter. The citizens of these city-states could not make common cause with either the distant and anonymous power of state sovereigns or with their own abstract and faceless state-citizen status (Brubaker 1992: 42–43). Many German intellectuals of that time as well, Herder being the most prominent among them, felt extremely denigrated because their absolutist monarchy turned them into what they saw as the generalized, empty, and uniform signs or anonymous items of the centralized power (Koch 2002: 93–95).

Voltaire projected his Republic, therefore, on the endangered model of *city-states*, that is, on the mode of active participation of its elected members; and French revolutionaries followed him. This might be the reason why, although the French Revolution attempted to transform active participation in the business of rule from a privilege enjoyed by a tiny elite into an all-inclusive form that pertains to every nation-state citizen, it did not suspend the discrimination genuine to the practice of the city-states (and concomitantly of Voltaire's Republic). On the contrary, it reintroduced it on a more general level. As the citizenship of the nation-state now became more important than the membership of orders, guilds, provinces, and other subnational groupings (the so called hereditary privileges), the French Revolution abolished internal legal, moral, and personal barriers, *but instead established national boundaries in their place* (Febvre 1973: 213–214). Such a redrawing of the lines of identity politics resulted in marking foreigners as paradigmatic outsiders. As Hannah Arendt has shown in her famous argument on the origins of totalitarianism, in the key declarations of the French Revolution human rights were identified with national citizen rights which left stateless populations and individuals without "the right of bearing rights" (1979: 299–300). The poor, women, the workers, and the old were now all included, but at the cost of excluded foreigners:

> By inventing the national citizen and the legally homogeneous national citizenry, the Revolution simultaneously invented the foreigner. Henceforth citizen and foreigner would be correlative, mutually exclusive, exhaustive categories. One would be either a citizen or a foreigner, there would be no third way. [...] The Revolutionary invention of the nation-state and national citizenship thus engendered the modern figure of the foreigner – not only as a legal category but as a political epithet, invested with a psychopolitical charge it formerly lacked, and condensing around itself pure outsiderhood. (Brubaker 1992: 46–47)

Inasmuch as this "sacred" obligation toward the nation made modern man, as Marx was one of the first to notice, into an "egotistic man, man separated from other men and community" (1971: 102), the war against foreigners was set in motion by the very act of emancipation from the constraints of the previous era.

This can go some way in explaining the well-known and abrupt shift away from cosmopolitanism and international outlooks to nationalism and xenophobia in France after 1793. All were not ready or willing to simply acknowledge the Jacobin principles and so the universal brotherhood rapidly turned into a universal war against the 'foreigner' up until the *Proclamation des Consuls* at the end of 1799, when the dream of universal monarchy was finally substituted for the dream of the universal republic (Fink 1993: 32, 41). Carl Schmitt (1996: 54) may have had such a kind of development in mind with his characteristically apposite comment: "When a state fights its political enemy in the name of humanity, it is not a war for the sake of humanity, but a war wherein a particular state seeks to usurp a universal concept against its military opponents." Costas Douzinas (2007: 159) infers that "[...] cosmopolitanism starts as a moral universalism but often degenerates into imperial globalism. [...] The continuous slide of cosmopolitan ideas towards empire is one of the dominant motifs of modernity." Such a typical development makes the French Revolution, from today's point of view, into the promoter of the discriminatory age of nation-states rather than the harbinger of the tolerant age of a "universal" humanity (Kristeva 1991: 165). The French Declaration of the Rights of Man and Citizen States in Article 1 states that men are born free and equal in their rights, but in Article 3 it is stipulated that the source of this equality and freedom is the Nation. This is how the national citizen became the principal beneficiary of human rights. Universal human rights and national sovereignty were born together, making the latter into the condition of the possibility of the former. Yet this leaves open the question

> whether the law thereby declared is French or human, whether the war conducted in the name of rights is one of conquest or one of liberation [...] whether those nations which are not French ought to become French or become human by endowing themselves with Constitutions that conform to the Declaration? (Lyotard 1988: 147)

If the national is the only persistent universal, does this ultimately mean that "Chechnya, Scotland, Kyrgistan, the Basque country, Quebec, Corsica should all become independent in order to confirm" this principle (Douzinas 2007: 98)? Or should they be considered as being beforehand disqualified from such a comparison with "proper nations"?

Significantly, Voltaire's project of the literary republic, which helped pave the way for the forthcoming French Republic, underwent a comparable "perversion" of its envisaged inclusiveness into an intolerant exclusiveness. As Hans Blumenberg meticulously demonstrated in *The Legitimacy of the New Age* (1988: 471), the Enlightenment lust for knowledge (*Wißbegierde*), which mobilized an up to then unknown theoretical curiosity for what in our familiar life-world remains out of sight (*innerweltlich Unsichtbare*),[6] was gradually coming to a halt at the peak of

---

[6] Luhmann (1990a: 46, trans. mine) traces the genealogy of this "observation of latency" in the following way: "The technique is some two centuries old. It was probably first practiced in the novel, then in the counter-Enlightenment, then in the critique of ideology, that is, in the first place always with the better-knowing attitude. The first-order observer was in such a way removed into the zone of the harmless, the naïve, or he was treated as someone who, without knowing it, has something to hide. The better-knowing nurtured itself by a suspicion and the generalization of the suspicion principle enabled whole disciplines – from psychoanalysis to sociology – to establish themselves with additional competences in a world in which everyone knows or believes to know for what purpose and in which situation he acts." Luhmann's thesis that the investigation of latency beyond the familiar reality was started by literature and thereupon continued by various scientific disciplines was recently endorsed, within another theoretical frame, by Jacques Rancière (2007). Rancière interprets modern literature as the promoter of democracy, because it introduced equality into the hierarchy of the everyday distribution of the sensible. The realist novel, being the paradigmatic agent of such democratic revolution, transfers its original hermeneutic impulse thereupon onto the sociological, psychoanalytic, or Marxist theories that are, on their part, trying to explain the novel. Both Luhmann and Rancière therefore, important differences

Enlightenment. In his famous *Dictionnaire Philosophique* (1764) (1961: 472–473), a kind of summa of his entire oeuvre, Voltaire accordingly opts for a reintegration of a consistent scientific search for truth back into the pragmatic context of the familiar life-world. The radical theoretical truth claim rests on a sacrifice of ordinary human happiness and needs, because of which it must be adapted to the servicing of the latter. "Man! God has given you reason in order to behave yourself and not in order to penetrate into the essence of things created by him (14, trans. mine)." A relentless transgression of God-given boundaries spawns scholastic dogmatism and intolerance (60) and must be replaced by "apt behavior." This "apt behavior" amounts to a reassimilation of the disclosed background of acknowledged reality into the social horizon of shared meanings. In the name of this pragmatic strategy Voltaire now criticizes Diderot's *Encyclopédie*. A broad team of collaborators on Diderot's encyclopedia, once celebrated by Voltaire as a crucial achievement of Bayle's Republic of Letters, was in his dictionary replaced by a fake collective enterprise that in reality was *one man, one orchestra* (Hempel 1989: 257–259). Once Voltaire found in the familiar national milieu the *bonne compagnie* that he had previously searched for amongst widely dispersed humankind, the free spirit of man that was previously supposed to break out of all pre-imposed divine principles was mercilessly suspended and replaced by a decidedly *consensual* collective horizon. Whoever could or would not conform to such a consensus was condemned by the great enlightener (1961: 60) as an *orgueilleux imbécile* (imbecile nose-in-the-air) who jeopardizes the happiness and health of the collective body. The previous revolutionary dogmatism established in the name of a (supposedly) free individual, instead of being attentively worked through, was thus in a typically compulsive re-enactment, replaced by a conservative dogmatism as a (putative) representative of traditional community.

In Voltaire's late writings, especially after the publication of his *Dictionary*, animosity toward radical Enlightenment ideas, epitomized in Spinoza's, Diderot's, and d'Holbach's materialism and atheism, increases (Israel 2010: 199–220). Against their rejection of final causes and teleology in nature Voltaire reveals, contrary to his previous opinions, the divine power behind its workings. The aged philosopher now subjects man's freedom to nature's "grand" and "supreme intelligence" (1879: 442–443; 462–464). He accuses some of the leading French Enlighteners of "philosophical atheism" derived from Spinoza (437–442, 457–458); even Bayle is criticized for not having read Spinoza carefully enough (1770–1772:

---

between their arguments notwithstanding, insist on the democratic effect of the "hermeneutics of suspicion" mobilized by the modern "joint venture" of literature and science; but neither of them considers the consequences of such democratization. See chapters seven and twelve.

III, 59–63; IV, 281; V, 330–332). *Le grand tout* has a will to which every individual will must submit, following it by its experience rather than by reasoning. Unexpectedly, nothing is left of the former active participation of every individual in the common interest of knowledge. The frustrated and embittered Voltaire allied himself with the court and the nobility against his former intellectual comrades whom he then, as it were, expelled from his Republic. Who does not believe in the Christian God does not belong to it, including Bayle (1770–1772: V, 330–332; II, 287)! If the Christian God ultimately takes hold of the Republic of Letters, what then remains of the proudly proclaimed literary autonomy?

We see, then, that the curious contortions and perversions of the generous "republican idea" exemplified by "modern literature" are far from accidental. In attempting to resolve one traumatic experience, the modern idea of literature paved the way for the emergence of another, inflicted upon those who were deprived of an appropriate identity position capable of meeting the tests set by the Republic of Letters itself. From the very beginning, mutual respect and the rational and dialogic exchange of opinions set as the basic premises of Voltaire's Republic of Letters could not have been within the abilities of the general body of humanity at that time. In addition to extraordinary linguistic and educational competences, they demanded finely tuned manners, and the refined skills of communication and polite conversation that were the polygons of the subject-formation of world citizens in the eighteenth century. If the literary republic denied religious, national, linguistic, and cultural barriers, it expected the reunion of people to take place on a much more refined and sophisticated basis. The political, economic, educational, technological, and institutional support necessary for the success of such a project had been, at the time, very unevenly distributed among individuals and peoples of the world. How can one exchange opinions with foreign scholars without knowing their language, literature, and culture, without commanding the skills of an elegant and cultivated conversation (Goodman 1994: 90–135)? Besides, as foreign scholars are often far removed from one's home, one must rely on correspondence, which implies a developed postal service. Further, the reading of their publications can hardly be imagined without a well-established press technology and the so-called literary life that makes possible the distribution of written goods. Finally, in order for the requested exchange to properly take place, institutions like salons, clubs, associations, and academies or literary journals are indispensable (136–183, 233–280). All the above prerequisites for the emergence of the Republic of Letters were provided precisely by the critically targeted French monarchy, which discloses the surreptitious entanglement of the cosmopolitan idea with the interests of national politics from the outset. This might be the reason why mainstream of French culture still proudly promotes cosmopolitanism as one of its leading achievements.

Along with those outlined so far, a number of further important points underpin this argument. The refined, civilized manners of this elected *bonne compagnie* that laid the grounds of the Republic of Letters are hardly imaginable without the impact of women in the French salons of that time (99–111). It was this environment and the behaviors that adhered to it that taught French men to acquire a friendly and tolerant attitude toward others much before other European men were able to do so. It was only on condition of overcoming their aggressive selfishness, that is, putting their instincts and affects under control, that they would become able, among other things, to ironically secure their dominance over women. This is partly how the famous French generosity that would come to characterize the forthcoming paternal inclusion of the other European and non-European nations and cultures into its own cosmopolitan narrative initially came to into being. Its basic trait is a readiness for self-cultivation through a respectful, patient, and polite dialogue with others.

In the chapter on commerce at the beginning of the second book of *The Spirit of the Laws*, Montesquieu points to the civilizing function of commerce that rests on mutual understanding. Trade introduces tolerant habits in the place of rude ones and peace in the place of war. Its spirit unites peoples and cultures by making them mutually dependent and forbearing. As one could meet such tolerance and generosity nowhere else in Europe of that time, the cosmopolitan idea of literature was created by a stratum of French society with all the social, technological, and institutional privileges that such a national élite had established for itself. But the agonistic spirit of French men was not to be entirely suspended with their acquisition of politeness; it was just relegated from the former bellicose and contested relationship between French men onto the relationship between them and outsiders. By opposing narrow-mindedness, self-cultivation was from the outset structurally prevented from becoming the property of each and every social stratum, religion, culture, language, nation, or individual for that matter; in order to progress, it desperately *needed its negative foil*. As it was constitutively directed against the self-enclosed minds inaccessible to self-overcoming and refinement, discrimination then became its necessary corollary.

This is why the republican cosmopolitan idea in both its preparatory literary and triumphant political form unleashed, parallel to the potentials of human freedom, the up to then unknown potentials of generalized human cruelty against those who failed to conform to the envisaged trajectory. "Man 'born free and everywhere in chains has become man born human and everywhere inhuman." (Rancière 1999: 125) As Carl Schmitt (2003: 104) once put it, "only when man appeared to be the embodiment of absolute humanity did the other side of this concept appear in the form of a new enemy: the *inhuman*." A merciless victimization of vulgar non-humans who blindly remained loyal to their inherited clannish bonds therefore followed on from the imperative of overcoming of all such bonds in favor of true "humanity" that was proudly displayed on the flag of the Republic of Letters. This republic was apparently patterned for all humans, but in practice it ultimately acknowledged only "proper" cultivated citizens. Its smooth narrative of a progressive humankind was "consciously or unconsciously designed to expunge the traces of the trauma or loss that called that narrative into being in the first place" (Santner 1992: 144). Its biased compensatory basis was, that is to say, resolutely repudiated and this is why its putatively universal project was consistently buttressed by blame, stigma, condescension, and sanctions toward individuals and communities who simply could not qualify for it. As the envisioned advancement persistently failed to attract the whole of humankind, the disinterested, indifferent, incapable, and resilient individuals and communities were blamed and sanctioned for having impeded its triumph. However, paradoxically enough, it was precisely in relation to this non- or premodern alterity as a necessary correlate that modernity was from the very beginning able to establish its dominant identity.

The delineated problems that the modern republican idea was continuously confronting from its first "literary" manifestation onwards can be traced back to its basic postulate that the equality of human beings results from a free exchange of opinions between "free" liberal individuals oriented toward persistent self-overcoming. What was expected to be established through such an exchange, which step by step was to transcend all set boundaries, was the general community of humankind. That is to say, Western modernity deprives not just the past of the right to restrict the present but also non-modern collectives of the right to constrain their constituencies. The *present* and the *individual*, in a clearly polemical gesture against the past monarchic political and social order, became the sovereign masters of a "modern" destiny. Foucault regarded such "eventialization" (1996: 393, *événementialisation* (1990: 47–48)),[7] that is, the persistent disengagement of constituencies from the whole as well as the separation of the present from the past, as the decisive feature of modernity that Kant was the first to notice and single out. Instead of being determined by history, each present event assumes a potentially determining, that is to say critical, position with regard to the past. According to Foucault, this continuous reassessment of one's limits and

---

[7] As is well known, "event" is an important concept in Foucault's vocabulary but, in this peculiar form, he nonetheless asks his audience to pardon *l'horreur du mot*.

capabilities (*les pouvoirs*) is the only Enlightenment legacy worth taking up after two centuries (2001a: 1587).

Yet one should beware Tocqueville's far-reaching unveiling of the perils of such unconstrained liberal individualism that became the basis for American democracy, that is, when he stated that "the woof of time is any instant broken, and the track of generations effaced [...] [D]emocracy breaks the chain and severs every link of it." As humankind is deemed present in each man's unconstrained freedom, men "are apt to imagine that their whole destiny is in their own hands" (Tocqueville 1945: 18). The progress of humankind and that of the individual therefore run strictly parallel, as they precondition each other. Every single individual, by contracting a social whole with enumerable others of its kind irrespective of their geographic, ethnic, or cultural affiliation, enters the free market of competing individuals whose basic principle has to be determined exactly through this competition, that is, as its result. It is generated out of the relationship between units rather than imposed beforehand as a transcendental principle (Dumont 1977: 84). All transcendental principles are systematically suspended in order for the liberal individual to take their place.

However, due to the vacancy left behind by the "discarded transcendence" that was expected to be reestablished sometime in the remote future, all markers of this global identification market turned out to be permeated by a radical indeterminacy (Lefort 1988: 17). Every liberal unit of the whole was entitled to raise the claim of representing its traumatically absent centre but not one of them was able, precisely due to the constitutive absence, to prove the appropriateness of its own representation. This is why the imagined cosmopolitan community that was expected to come was continually exposed to a fierce battle of representations. Each constituency struggled to compensate for the castrated cohesion of the whole by instituting a new political bond in its place (217–219). Who, in the final analysis, is called upon to define the universal currency for everybody's wares? Yet the only result was a continuous litigation between representatives over the basic principle of the whole. Though the latter is the condition *sine qua non* of the proclaimed equality between constituencies, its fundamental uncertainty and indeterminacy could not be overcome (19). Lefort's portrait of liberal democracy confronts us, however, with the following question: While uncertainty and indeterminacy may stimulate and encourage those competitors who are entitled to access and engage a broad range of various resources, what about those for whom such an access is denied, let alone those who were beforehand excluded from the competition in general?

The real problem is therefore that the competition for equality between the representatives of humankind, as stated clearly in Voltaire's literary republican idea, does not rest solely on a basic inequality but also on *excommunication* and *expulsion*. As Rancière (1999: 11–12) spells out, the people who are called to authorize democracy are not simply the poor, but primarily those who lack any recognizable position in the established putative democratic order. The constitutive violence of the democratic community escapes the logic of reparation because it necessarily results in a part of those who have no part. It is not just that the vast majority of constituencies of the "World Republic of Letters" were bereft of the means, abilities, or "room for maneuver" necessary for the exchange among equals as envisaged by it, because this is not the main aspect. It is, more fundamentally, that, as an alleged "universal currency" of Voltaire's Republic, literature outlawed an undifferentiated mass of people(s) with its declared distribution of values. Rather than being identified and properly positioned, this currency sentenced them to a state of inarticulation and accordingly locked them in a "zone of indeterminacy." The "wrong" by which politics occurs is not a flaw underlying reparation. It is rather the introduction of an incommensurable element into the heart of the distribution of identities (Rancière 1999: 19). This element, which in turn disseminates an infective anxiety into the reigning distribution, induces the latter's erruptions and implosions. "Zones of indeterminacy" are reservoirs of suppressed possibilities which distribute their potentiality into the social aggregate that they are (an unacknowledged) part of, setting in motion this aggregate's spectralization and disarticulation. They errupt as soon as their potentiality, which spreads in the form of quasi-events and diffuses traumatic experience into ordinary relations, reaches its agencies (Povinelli 2011: 3–4, 11–13), i.e. the carriers of the projects of reordering. For whoever has no part in the shaping of human community cannot in fact have any part other than *all or nothing* (Rancière 1999: 9). The outlawed and miscounted people(s), exposed to the violence perpetrated upon them by *all* partakers in the "universal currency" of literature, stay for a literature that disqualifies *all declared denominators* (and is therefore a *nonidentifiable no-thing*) rather than for any particular literary *currency* promoted by one of the competing parties. They are the incommensurable element that, disaggregating the grammar of the ordinary that it belongs to (without belonging), recruits the projects of its reconfiguration.

Not competition is germane to the literary republic, but rather an *anarchic traumatism* (Levinas 1974: 194). Although those who have inherited material and symbolic means, resources, and abilities from a putatively "relinquished past" are much better equipped for the future global community on the proclaimed way of its becoming, this is not the main aspect. Instead, it is more substantially that those who created the very terms of equality excluded a considerable share of people(s) from the possibility of implementing them from the outset. Resting on that basis, the French democratic parole of universal equality fed upon an enduring universal inequality and gradually became a symbol of oppression and humiliation (Douzinas 2007: 94–95). The proudly declared free competition was secretly reconnected with violence, coercion, and discrimination and the only remaining choice for the dispossessed human agencies was to react to this *traumatic constellation* either out of the individual "poisonous knowledge" or the collectively "experienced pain." Translated into the terms of the "literary republic," this amounted to an uneasy choice between literary cosmopolitanism with its covert trauma narratives and literary nationalism with its overt ones. Overcoming this binary from the perspective of a *nonidentifiable no-thing* or "diasporic injunctions" is a non-consensual project that is still awaiting its enactment.

2 The Fissured Identity of Literature: National Universalism and/or Cosmopolitan Nationalism

> Those for whom nation simply does not exist make this matter too easy. [...] But those for whom the idea of the supranational does not exist also proceed too comfortably. [...] The most irritating obstacle to the natural organization of human society is the imposition of the two ideals, nation and state, upon the human. There is nothing else left but to strengthen that which was developed independently of these ideals, awakening and keeping alive the idea of their obsolescence. (Musil 1978: 1035, trans. mine)
>
> (Die, für welche die Nation einfach nicht existiert, machen es sich zu leicht. [...] Aber auch die, für welche die Idee der Übernationalität nicht existiert, machen es sich zu bequem. [...] Einer natürlichen Gliederung der menschlichen Gesellschaft steht [...] nichts ärger im Weg als die Überhebung der beiden Ideale Nation und Staat über den Menschen. Es bleibt nichts übrig, als an der Verstärkung des an ihnen sich vorbei Entwickelten zu arbeiten und den Gedanken an ihre Überholtheit zu wecken und wach zu halten.)

2.1 Intertwined opposites

Aimed at a redistribution of benefits and merits in the international order of Europe, the rise of the German national idea toward the close of the eighteenth century was a response to the Europe-wide cultural expansion of France as demonstrated throughout that century. Having resisted French cultural hegemony, German national awakening set the standards for the "dominated nationalisms" (Balibar 2002: 62) that were to come. Looking for allies to strengthen their own resistance and forming thus a new basis for international solidarity, these "petty nationalisms" display a strong interlocking inclination. Struggling for their own emancipation, therefore, German intellectuals affirmed the right to self-determination of all nations put under similar assimilatory pressure, in the first place the forthcoming East-Central European post-imperial ones. As opposed to the French self-sufficient and invisible "dominating nationalism" in the guise of a generous *universalism* orientated toward humankind, German other-related and all-too-visible "dominated nationalism" reclaimed *cosmopolitanism* in the form of a peaceful coexistence of autonomous nations. Returning to Arendt's distinction between Roman imperial and Greek elitist cosmopolitanism that I have sketched out in the Introduction, I claim that French "national universalism" spontaneously resumed the tradition of the first and German "cosmopolitan nationalism," the tradition of the second model.[1]

---

[1] As regards French self-sufficient and German other-related cosmopolitanism, which is a distinction that neatly corresponds to Balibar's distinction between dominating and dominated

The relationship between French and German cosmopolitanism, however, has been recently interpreted by the French literary historian Pascale Casanova in more conventional, strictly oppositional terms. She claims that German cultural emancipation "was the ultimate consequence of the enterprise inaugurated by du Bellay and the humanists against the supremacy of Latin" (2004: 69). It follows that, although both French and German cosmopolitanism at the moment of their rise open the door to liberty, French cosmopolitanism precedes German, paving the way for truly world-oriented nations, and therefore does not result in a self-centered national literature. On the contrary, thanks to "the enormity of accumulated literary capital [...] engaged in by French men and women of letters," it spawns a complete freeing of writers "from subjection to the national cause" (69). Hence French cosmopolitanism is in her discreetly self-complimentary view tantamount to a *purely symbolic republic of letters* devoid of any economic (as in England) and political (as in Germany) connotations and stakes. "French came to be generally established, without the assistance or cooperation of any political authority, as a common language – the language of cultivated and refined conversation, exercising a sort of jurisdiction that extended to all of Europe." Having been "never recognized as national, but accepted instead as international," it is represented by Casanova as having an indisputable advantage over German and English cosmopolitanism (68). An unreserved equating of one's own national identity merely with letters is, however, far from being a widespread inclination of all nations but a typically French habit. "Only in France does the entire nation consider literature to be the best representative expression of its fate," remarked Curtius in 1930 (Kristeva 1993: 44). Casanova's attitude therefore cannot but recall what Julia Kristeva dubbed the "abstract cosmopolitanism" of the French "left-wing intellectuals" who "sell French national values" at the same time as they deny "national determinations" (Kristeva 1991: 37, 15).[2] In this man-

---

nationalism, self-sufficiency would be the cosmopolitan perspective of dominant agencies completely unsuitable for the dominated ones: "One can grasp French cosmopolitanism of this time without entering into the German one, but not vice versa ..." (Fink 1993: 24, trans. mine). Accordingly, Wieland was once called the German Voltaire but "nobody, alas, ever called [Voltaire] the French Wieland" (Appiah 2006: 15). In opposing such self-sufficiency, the dominated "have especially great need to band together in order to be effective" (Calhoun 2007: 295).

[2] However justified this critique undoubtedly is it does not spare Kristeva herself from reproducing another sort of Francophone cosmopolitanism. She asserts that "[t]he French national idea ... can make up the *optimal rendition* of the nation in the contemporary world" because it is "achieved in the *legal and political pact* between free and equal individuals" (Kristeva 1993: 39–40). Deriving her cosmopolitanism from the liberal individualism that was notoriously available only to elite classes and elected nations, she exposes herself, however, to the same criticism she makes regarding stoic cosmopolitanism when she states that it was "separated from the remain-

ner, they continue the powerful tradition of republican universalism, which from the outset flattered national pride while freeing the French nation from obligations toward other peoples. As regards the promotion of liberal individualism, that is to say, French republican universalism was convinced it was beating even the United States as the inventor of this powerful ideology with its strong prejudices against ethnic attachments and in-group solidarity (Fink 1993: 25; Calhoun 2007: 288).

In the course of the international expansion and institutionalization of French cosmopolitanism, however, the hegemonic class universalism of its carrier group gradually entered center stage. In such a way, a transnational class formation that struggled to defend its elite privileges was dismantled behind the proudly proclaimed liberal individualism (Calhoun 2007: 291–292). It provoked in return the ethnonational solidarity of those who, lacking the elementary cosmopolitan prerequisites to practice such a luxurious attitude (such as wealth, network of communication, administrative or educational services, established set of social rules and customs, or technological equipment), found themselves oppressed or denied by it. This is why the politically "dominating nationalism" inhered to French "literary cosmopolitanism" from its very beginning, the noblest intention and proclamation of its architects and chief proponents notwithstanding. As soon as the relationship to its enablers was altered, this previously invisible nationalism became all too visible. Contrary to Casanova's strong opposition between nationalism and cosmopolitanism, or politics and literature for that matter, these apparent opposites turned out to be closely interrelated. It is not merely that narrow-minded nationalism always underlies bright-minded cosmopolitanism and vice versa, it is also that "selfish" politics always underlies "altruistic" literature and vice versa. The literary and the political are as inextricably intertwined as nationalism and cosmopolitanism. Both pairs of putative opposites are captured in a mutually conditioned relationship.

---

der of humanity that was incapable of the same effort of reason and wisdom [...] this produced a new strangeness – the strangeness of those who do not share in our reason" (1993: 20–21). She also heartily endorses Kant's cosmopolitan vision of humankind as a progressing unity in diversity (Kristeva 1991: 171–173) forgetting that it relies on the concept of *person*, which seriously restricts its inclusiveness. "The fact that the 'person' is Kant's beginning and reference point is already indicative of the presuppositions implied in the universal neutral imaginary that for him constitutes the person. Kant obviously was not thinking about the Amerindians, the Africans, or the Hindus as paradigmatic examples of his characterization." (Mignolo 2000: 734)

2.2 The emergence of the national literary historiography

Such an intricate interplay of national and cosmopolitan, literary and political, attributes that subversively condition each other, casts new light on the German national project preventing its direct association with perilous self-enclosure and requiring a more attentive political, social and historical contextualization. However unpopular the so-called ethnic nationalisms understandably appear to be, in all their incontestable cruelty they are but bitter reactions to the much less acknowledged and considered cosmopolitan cruelty. "Ethnic solidarity is not always a matter of the powerful exclusion of others; it is often a resource for effective collective action and mutual support among the less powerful." (Calhoun 2007: 295) Consequently, disjoining and conjoining the foreigners often run parallel which hinders their clear-cut separation from one another. That is to say, while it *assimilates* co-nationals diffused over foreign countries, ethnic nationalism *dissimilates* non-national fellow-citizens at home (Verdery 1996: 84). In ethnonational exclusionism, the problem of the citizen or people locked in the traumatic constellation of being deprived of "the right to bear rights" looks for its remedy. Whoever treats ethnicity just as a deliberate and hence blamable choice neglects the omnipresence of discrimination as the determination of social identities (Calhoun 2007: 301). Many ethnocultural claims are intended to rectify injustices caused by the group classifications (Valadez 2007: 314) imposed by the imperial cosmopolitan policies.

Ethnic nationalisms therefore usually choose the pattern of *public trauma narratives* that affirms their collective agency in an embittered response to the experience of long-term victimhood. Friedrich Schlegel's invention of national literary historiography is a case in point. Yet this remedy turns out to be double-edged. Even if, on the one hand, it triggers "significant repairs in the civil fabric," on the other hand such public trauma narrative simultaneously instigates "new rounds of social suffering" (Alexander 2012: 2). That is to say, in becoming a multidirectionally connectable platform for collectivities established by traumatic experience that begin to support and enforce each other across social, cultural, and historical boundaries (Rothberg 2009: 1–22), these creative symbolic constructions gradually develop huge symbolic power on their own. Invented by the "engineers" of social and cultural memory for the primary sake of reconciliation and consolidation, they gradually set in motion horrific group conflicts. In order to win the battle against the multitude of social and political rivals, they must display not only a persuasive distribution of roles but also high competitive abilities. This complex mediation of the underlying traumatic experience that engages various discourses and media might be described as the politics of trauma. Such politics cannot be caried out without violence and injustice (Brunner 2014:

12–13) or, in the case of German Romanticist ethnonational trauma narrative, the brute implementation of discriminating ethnocratic strategies. In order to oppose the assimilation strategy of French imperial cosmopolitanism efficiently, its carrier group demanded ethnic homogenization. Therefore, national literary historiography has to be interpreted not as a sovereign action of its "designers" but as their reaction to what they perceived as a *traumatic constellation*. Other-related as it was, national literary historiography undertook a reconfiguration of that constellation.

Such *relational and translational methodology* does not lead to a solution in favor of either cosmopolitanism or nationalism. In fact, it systematically avoids such an easy solution, regarding it as the practice of policing. In reinstating inner tensions and perplexities within both cosmopolitanism and nationalism, it adheres to recommencing rather than teleological terms. It underpins, among others, the opinion of Michael Rothberg (2000: 10) who stated that "[t]hinking in terms of relationality and overlap may seem to risk producing an ahistorical account of culture, but in fact it is precisely in the specific modes of interaction [...] that historical particularity can be grasped." The use of clear oppositions in the writing of history makes historical temporality progressing from one to the other pole function as a strategy of exclusion and a figure for the assertion of a historian's cognitive, axiological and social privilege. Instead, the systematic translation of apparent "opponents" into one another, continuously introducing other possibilities into their respective normative horizons, prevents their turning into universal values.

The reconfiguration along these lines of the relationship between cosmopolitanism and nationalism will be employed to examine the emergence of the organicist pattern of national literary historiography. It attributed to literature for the first time a particular *ethnolinguistic identity* as well as a historically *singular character*. Aimed at the consolidation of the shaken German national self, the organicist pattern was an invention of German Romanticism, more specifically of Friedrich Schlegel, who in his *History of the Old and the New Literature*, a series of lectures delivered in 1812 at the University of Vienna, presented the peculiarity of German literature in the historical frame of other and older national literatures. Vienna was at that time not just a refuge for Napoleon's German Catholic opponents (Echternkamp 1998: 196), but also the birthplace of the politically frustrated idea of the revival of the Great German Empire, which was supposed to counter Napoleon's expansion. Born like the majority of the forthcoming national literary histories out of a bitter political frustration – in this case ensuing from the immediately preceding collapse of the Empire in 1806 – these lectures are usually taken to represent a regression compared with August and Friedrich Schlegel's previous European and world literary histories. The ideological orientation of these earlier histories, composed at the very beginning of the nineteenth century, allegedly takes its bearing from Schiller's *Universalgeschichte* whereas that of the somewhat later German literary history owes much to Herder's *Nationalgeschichte* (Neubauer 2007). Yet this is a further normative opposition between cosmopolitanism and nationalism that ignores their interrelatedness and intertwinement.

A short quotation from Friedrich Schlegel's *History of European Literature* (1804–1805) might suffice to illustrate my point:

> The newer literature begins with the Christian-Latin; thereupon follows the old French, the source of Italian and Spanish-Portuguese, the Nordic as the middle source of all these literatures, the English and finally the German which has comprehended, moreover swallowed up all these literatures; and it is the only one that blossoms forth with the most free life force, the only one from which an important fertile epoch is to be expected. (Schlegel 1958: 140)³

Bearing in mind the nationally impregnated cosmopolitanism in Germany around 1800 (Albrecht 2005: 308–309), I would instead opt for more continuity in the transition from August and Friedrich Schlegel's European to Friedrich Schlegel's national literary history (Fohrmann 1989: 69–130; 1994). The Schlegel brothers, by gradually shifting emphasis from antiquity to modernity, almost imperceptibly transferred the agency of universal history from a petrified ancient model to the modern German nation in emergence. The latter was expected to revitalize the ancient Greek republican (against the aggressive Roman imperial, i.e. French universalist) "world republic" model in the rising plural and divided Europe (Schlegel 1979b: 639, 1979a).

Deeply concerned with the disintegration and atomization of modern society, Friedrich Schlegel complained that the political culture of modern republics remains decidedly inferior to that of the ancients in respect of the common public spirit. Modern egoist communities lack the genuine affection and love between fellow citizens exemplified by the ancient Greek "community of morals" (1966: 18). As he gradually lost faith in the power of modern Germans to develop a true community through their own spontaneous efforts and in the power of art to promote such an unselfish attitude in the same way as it did in ancient Greece, he shifted emphasis from (Greek) art to (German) religion as a more popular and comprehensible means for achieving the desired unity (Beiser 1992: 241). This drove him to the conclusion that the former Christian unity of Europe, which was, in his opinion, still lurking behind national differences between cultures needed to be restored through an "endless progression" in the faith oriented toward the remote but desirable future (Schlegel 1979a: 225–226, 231). And, this point being decisive for his "patriotic cosmopolitan" vision, the German Romanticist *Welt-*

---

3 All translations from German in the following are mine unless otherwise indicated.

geist fitted much better than the Greek cosmopolitan model with such a revival of the former Christian unity of European nations (Schlegel 1971a: 280).

He privileges the German instrument of unification because the *Weltgeist*, unlike the Greek *fixed canon* of *artistic rules*, affirms itself in the *mobile medium of a language*. The latter was instituted with Luther's secularization of the Holy Script and from then on, through a series of translations from Classic and modern languages, continuously expanded its resources, options and possibilities. "The adoption of the foreign through poetic transposition [...] is a domestic habit in Germany from ancient times," as August Schlegel avers, in common with the prevailing ethos (1965: 36). One of the main preoccupations of German intellectuals from Herder to Goethe was to promote the German language as the key mediator of European languages, as an asylum for those "original spirits" who, because of the "pettiness of their epochs," felt alienated in their own homelands (1965: 26). Thus developed their awareness of the desperate need of the homeless, "humiliated and insulted" individuals and groups at the beginning of the nineteenth century to find an appropriate platform of unification and consolidation. If, as August Schlegel complained, every stranger, being immediately translated into French was turned into a Frenchman, then from Romanticism onwards the German language was envisioned as a welcoming identification mirror for each and every foreigner (1964: 17). To put this in economic terms, the German language was expected to become *universal currency for foreign spiritual wares*. This appropriately reflected the crucial role of the Greek language in the cosmopolitanism of the Hellenist age. The task of German was "to unite all the advantages of most various nationalities" in order "to create a cosmopolitan midpoint for the human spirit" (1965: 36). August Schlegel was therefore convinced "that the moment is not so remote when German will become a general organ of communication for all educated nations" (27).[4] The cosmopolitan ambition of the German national idea could hardly have been expressed in a more transparent fashion. Yet, unlike the French imperial and assimilating cosmopolitanism, theirs was of a Greek, elitist and regenerating kind (Amselle 2003; Mamdani 2012).

---

[4] This was encapsulated in Goethe's famous letter to Carlyle of July 20, 1827: "Whoever understands and studies the German language now finds himself in a market where all the nations of the world are offering their wares for sale ..." (Goethe 1987: 266, trans. mine) One commentator observes: "People have ridiculed this notion of German as the linguistic pivot for *Weltliteratur*, but one should recall that circa 1800 there was indeed a singular plethora of German translations of foreign literature and that in the nineteenth and even into the twentieth century German remained the language for many educated Central and Eastern Europeans, for it was thanks to German that they had access to world literature." (Meyer-Kalkus 2010: 107)

This German *takeover of the command of the world partition of symbolic values* seems, at least in the perception of distinguished intellectuals like Novalis, the Schlegel brothers, Fichte or Jean Paul, to have been a fait accompli by the beginning of the nineteenth century. Even Mme de Staël (1978: 541), in a letter to her compatriot Charles de Villiers who translated Kant into French, stated in 1802: "Je crois avec vous que l'esprit humain, qui semble voyager d'un pays à l'autre, est à présent à l'Allemagne." (Like you I believe that the human spirit, that seems to be traveling from one country to another, is at the moment in Germany.) Such a replacement of the past all-encompassing but frozen Greek mirror by the present mobile German one on the rise – being the key achievement of the Schlegel brothers' cosmopolitan literary histories – prepared the negotiating design of the relationship between the present and the past for the forthcoming genre of national literary historiography. In this organicist design, the national present declared itself generously ready to admit its debt to the cosmopolitan past out of which it emerged, but only at a less generous price of turning this past into its absolved, assimilated legacy. If a nation is like an organism in terms of its permanent growth, then it subscribes to the *imperative of a consistently individualizing development*, i.e., reasoned, differential adaptation to new international relations.

The German national project, and concomitantly literary history as its constitutive part, was therefore far from self-sufficient and self-enclosed. For a nation that pretends to set global terms for the huge diversity of other nations, in the same way in which money sets the terms for the widest variety of wares, limitless adaptability is the most cherished property. According to August Schlegel, nobody can beat Germans in this respect:

> Universality, cosmopolitanism are the true German properties. What made us for a long time inferior in external splendor to the one-sided, limited, but decisive efficiency of other nations was: the lack of one single direction which turns into something positive, i.e. many-sided directions, and this will ultimately bring us supremacy over them. (A. Schlegel 1965: 26)

Turning the long-term inferiority into the present and especially future superiority – no other turn-around can better epitomize the plot of what Jeffrey Alexander has termed "trauma narrative." The German *Volksgeist* was thus transformed step by step from the subservient local enabler into a self-propelling global agency in the relentless search for genuine distinction and comparative advantage. To make Germany into the key agency of human history, select German intellectuals engaged in the huge mission of turning other nations into its enablers. The latter were, in the last analysis, needed only as the continuous backdrop of their agency's emancipating march into the future, or as the clay for its shape and the source of its supremacy. The agency and its enablers parted ways, the first progressing toward the future, the second relegated to the past. In assigning them different tenses, the autonomous and self-determining on the one hand and the constrained and determined on the other, German Romanticists instituted between Europe and non-Europe as well as within Europe itself the opposition of what had been and what was now becoming. Novalis's typically pregnant and paradoxical formulation in a letter to August Schlegel from 1797 might have had exactly this in mind: "Germandom is cosmopolitanism mixed with the most powerful individuality (*Deutschheit ist Kosmopolitismus mit der kräftigsten Individualität gemischt*; Fink 1993: 39)." From this moment onward German obligation toward diversified humankind was manifested only through loyalty to the individual national case (Dumont 1994: 6). The *Weltbürger's* duty was not excluded but filtered by the *Staatsbürger's* commitment.

Having been bitterly directed against the global missionary consciousness of the French Jacobin cosmopolitanism (Fink 1993: 31–32), in such a way, German nationally centered cosmopolitanism imperceptibly acquired the same profile that characterized its fierce opponent. After having accumulated national "symbolic capital" in an enormous acceleration of the opponent's speed as demonstrated throughout the eighteenth century, it raised an analogous claim for domination, as described in August Schlegel's *Lectures on the Art of Drama and Literature* of 1808–1809 (Schulz 1989: 65). The lectures Friedrich Schlegel delivered three years later in Vienna were merely a national extension of this tendency already inherent in the cosmopolitan phase. The discriminating perversion of German patriotic cosmopolitanism was no longer preventable.

This new "recalibration of the German polis" (Tihanov 2011: 134) that progressively *individualized* its own national identity against the background of nationally identified others was a clear reaction to the French Enlightenment type of recalibration that progressively *universalized* its own national identity through the systematic assimilation of national others. Through this defensive national reaction, paradoxically, it invented the regenerating cosmopolitan model. In order to comprehend the German *systematically differential self-propelling* – a continuous "literary deactivation" of German self –, one has to bear in mind that Germany was not only biconfessional (from 1648 onwards) but also, for many centuries, a frontier state between Germans and Slavs in a way that has no parallel in France with its smoothly increasing "stateness" (Brubaker 1992: 5–6). This is why the erected *ethnolinguistic affinity* of the German demos to the imagined future polis, aiming at a disentangling of this frustrating confessional and ethnic entanglement, substituted for its *political affiliation* to the present monarchic state. Simultaneously, this literary un-mixing of the German political space traced the transition from the *self-evident* aristocratic *liberties* specific to the monarchy to the *self-earned* national *rights* specific to the envisaged nation-state. Such a redirection towards an invented or created affinity between its past and present along the temporal axis and its domestic and dislocated co-nationals along the spatial axis, established an imagined "community of fate" (*Schicksalsgemeinschaft*) whose agreeable legacy future Germans will inherit. Yet not merely Germans were urged to gain close acquaintance with this homogenizing construct, but also the representatives of all East-Central European nations who have thereupon heartily embraced this "fateful" model. The ideologies of sustained, collective sacrifice for a common national future find their most fertile soil and evoke a most genuine commitment in the traumatic political constellations generated by the breakdown of empires, in which social uncertainty becomes so pervasive that ordinary actors are unable to stick to any consistent political strategy for long (Hanson 2010). However fantasized it may be, the force of such affective attachment promises a large-scale historical existence, which might explain the recourse of innumerous national liberation movements to it, starting with the German Romanticist, via the East-Central European postimperial and up to the Asian and African postcolonial ones. We will return to them.

The Schlegel brothers established the important link between this ethnolinguistically shaped imagined *national* community and its genuinely *cosmopolitan* past (the latter having been dubiously taken to have preceded the religious schism) in two principal ways: religious and historical. Religion was at the time, and remained up until today, an approbated instrument of human temporal and spatial uniting. Yet not only by Friedrich Schlegel's and Novalis's Catholic and Fichte's Protestant universalism, this link was also powerfully buttressed by August Schlegel's thesis of the medieval German empire as "Europe's motherland." He represented the generous embrace of other national cultures as a traditional German property, and invited his compatriots to adhere to it, to replace their predominantly fanatic and restricted national feeling with a superior and all-encompassing cosmopolitan national pride (1965: 36–39; 26–27). Anticipating Goethe's later disdain for benighted compatriots that I will be dealing with in chapter five, this parenthesizing of the petty nationalism of the narrow-minded co-nationals testifies to the (Greek) elitist character of German cosmopolitan tradition. Its transnational alliances tend to outmaneuver the unenlightened masses of compatriots.

Germany's medieval cosmopolitanism, the Schlegel brothers' argument goes, beats France's modern one: "Never was there more freedom, equality and fraternity than in the Middle Ages," noted Friedrich Schlegel in 1799, "and these were again at their best in Germany." (Schlegel 1963: 293) All Romanticists were convinced that "the destiny of the Germans is to revive the culture of all mankind" (Beiser 1992: 238). August Schlegel's association of the medieval German Empire, depicted as the time when all nations acknowledged German supremacy, with the golden age of the Holy Roman Empire stresses the imperial ambitions of German cultural mission as envisaged by Romanticists (Albrecht 2005: 310). In addition to this, the turn to the corporate medieval state signaled the breakdown of the early republican and essentially counter-statist belief in the true moral community created in spontaneous terms primarily by way of art. Confronted with the violence, compartmentalization and corruption created by the Revolution, German Romanticists now believed that only a paternal state could ensure genuine community. Their nationalism acquired statist treats.

Once it was launched, such statist rendering of the German polis put in long-range historical terms paved the way for Friedrich Schlegel's national literary historiography whose task was to consecrate a new ethnolinguistic and cultural community of shared memories, solidarity and belonging (Benhabib 2006: 65). After the Schlegel brothers' cosmopolitan literary histories introduced the *nationally filtered internalization of external diversities*, Germany's consolidated *Volksgeist* was discretely redirected by Friedrich Schlegel's national literary history toward a *diversification of the established national spirit*. The unity-in-diversity principle of cosmopolitan literary histories was, as it were, turned upside down, from now on displaying diversity-in-unity. In Friedrich Schlegel's national literary history, therefore, literature in its quintessence (*wahrem Wesen*) comprehends a broad variety of arts and sciences, philosophy and religion; in other words, every linguistic activity that takes life and humans for its object (Schlegel 1961: 13). Rather than representing a substantial break, this diversification of the achieved integrity of the "national spirit," like a reflection in a mirror, was substituted for the former integration of diversities. The discriminating pattern of cosmopolitan literary histories was thereby passed on to the national history as well. Accordingly, Friedrich Schlegel not only extends the concept of literature (*Dichtkunst*) but, in his frequent and bold speculations on the obligation of every German intellectual to obey the national imperative, imposes upon literature a firm nation-uniting mission, criticizing all writers who ignored or refused to adhere to it. For example, he openly regrets the German religious schism caused by the Reformation (304), treating it as the personal guilt of given historical actors and deliberately ignoring its ecclesiastic prehistory.

Such obscurities, and there are many more, unavoidably reintroduce new schisms into a story written with a unifying intention; for example, the division between the true and the false national spiritual tradition. The false tradition is significantly represented by literary works unable to qualify for the leading principle of Germanness. According to Fohrmann (1994: 589–590), "they are conceived of as an extrinsic force [...] which remains totally alien to German literature and consequently may be considered only ex negativo for the evolution of German literature." Schlegel's judgment is directed in the first place against esthetically shaped works bereft of moral attitude (*moralischer Gesichtspunkt* (Schlegel 1961:

163)), i.e., devoid of the sacred national memory that is the most excellent business of literature (*das vorzüglichste Geschäft der Dichtkunst*, 15). Such an open display of the historian's ideological conviction is deliberate; the one-sided historian is better than the reserved one without any clear attitude. Friedrich Schlegel's history therefore openly serves his religious and political opinions. The main objective presented in the dedication to Metternich is the formation of national spirit. As testified by the ferocious reactions of his contemporaries, however, the homogenizing national spirit projected by Schlegel was anything but universally accepted in Germany around 1800. In lieu of being united around the allegedly merely *re*constructed genuine national spirit, the Germany forcefully *constructed* through literature was divided into proper and improper Germans.

2.3 Cosmopolitan patriot and democratic tyrant: Jean-Jacques Rousseau

In a peculiar continuation of the Schlegel brothers' cosmopolitan literary histories, Friedrich Schlegel's national literary history set in motion a simultaneously liberating ("upwards") and discriminating ("downwards") transformation of the compartmentalized German polis into an *ethnos* with cosmopolitan cultural consciousness. Yet his fierce resistance to the universalist model of the French Republic of Letters was not an exclusively German enterprise, nor a completely pioneering one, as it was pre-designed by the French dissident Rousseau a good half-century earlier. As Rousseau's rebellion against the shortcomings of French "national cosmopolitanism" takes place within the French culture and not outside it, as does the delineated German "cosmopolitan nationalism," I take it as a welcome reminder that national cultures are never homogeneous and that an all-too-easy opposition between French and German concepts of the age has to be reintroduced into each of these alleged opposites. A continuous clash between the processes of *Vergesellschaftung* (the uniting diversification of society) and *Vergemeinschaftung* (the disuniting homogenization of its particular groups and communities), characteristic of all modern nations, inhered to both of them. As I will try to demonstrate in the following, French cosmopolitanism was torn apart by internal national antagonisms, conflicts and exclusions from its very beginning. Uninterruptedly haunted by such disaggregating social, ideological and cultural tensions between its constitutive parts, modern French culture displayed different values in different directions, and continues to do so today.

In his prized *Discourse on the Arts and Sciences* composed for the Academy of Dijon (1750) Rousseau (1964a: 15) resolutely rejected the polish and grace that, according to him, were expected to make all non-Parisians, within Europe and with-

2.3 Cosmopolitan patriot and democratic tyrant: Jean-Jacques Rousseau

out, as affected, unnatural and artificial as proper Parisians were. In his critique of the self-enslavement of humankind under the principle of equality imposed from above, Rousseau asks why all European nations should strive to become morally corrupted. The Enlightenment rhetoric invoking progress, liberty and equality is designed to conceal tyranny and bondage; so much for Montesquieu's famous geopolitical distinction between European democrats and Asian tyrants (Grosrichard 1979: 50–66). In Rousseau's bitter polemic tyrants have occupied the very heart of Europe, which is why Montesquieu's opposition was no longer to be rendered just in intercontinental terms. Rousseau transferred it to the inner-European axes.

He was therefore the first European intellectual to see behind the declared cosmopolitanism of the French Republic of Letters a suspicious class and religious universalism. If all men are equal, he pointed out in the following *Discours sur l'inégalité* (1755) and *Lettre à M. d'Alembert sur les spectacles* (1758), then they are so only in terms of their unsociability, independence and solitude. Why should they not behave naturally, each in their own way, disregarding the all-equalizing pressure of enlightened French sociability? The backdrop of the independent state of nature is in Rousseau's view the arch-example of the genuinely authentic human substance.[5] The latter, pace Voltaire, is not to be found in the "peaks" but in the "valleys" of history, the broad stretches of anonymous happenings whereby people project themselves into history through spontaneous deeds rather than highbrow parlance (Berlin 1990: 51–52). The French inclination to eloquence disguises the fact that words are the most genuine vehicle of deception and falsification (Barnard 2003: 163–164). They are the instruments of tyranny rather than democracy. The democratic and tyrannical attributes belong to exchangeable rather than permanent properties.

Because Rousseau himself, despite his Geneva origin, allied himself with the French language and culture, his concept of "French tyranny" has to be translated as "the tyranny of the perverted taste of the contemporary French Catholic high bourgeois elite." From Rousseau's point of view this taste was corrupted, artifi-

---

[5] Rousseau's stance is surely controversial as regards the true "human substance" or "nature," which makes the reconstruction of his argument a tricky undertaking. For example, he states in the *Discourse on Inequality* (1965: 175–176) that his idea of the "natural state of man" is a pure hypothesis or invention as it cannot be empirically investigated or checked, but just several pages earlier (170) he calls himself a natural historian who sticks to "nature which never lies" instead of relying on treacherous books. In his *Essay on the Origin of Language* he advocates language as a means of transition from *l'homme naturel* to *l'homme de l'homme* which gives rise to morality, law, and history, but on the other hand despises civilization because it tortures, disfigures and corrupts man's true nature. See more regarding this important ambiguity of Rousseau's thought in Eze 1995.

cial and effeminate (Rousseau 1968b: 100–103). But it by no means characterized the whole French nation in the same way that the resistance to it hasn't characterized the whole German nation but only particular "carrier groups" of the oppositional movement. German aristocracy of the time passionately aped French taste. Inasmuch as such border-crossing elective affinities between the French and German ruling *cosmopolitan agencies* (i.e. the Parisian elite and German aristocracy) on the one hand and their subordinated *national enablers* (i.e. the Southern provincials and German marginalized bourgeoisie) on the other contradict smooth national continuities, they are regularly overlooked in the uncritically homogenizing back-projections of respective national historiographies. What one social, political or religious group within the national corpus experiences as a traumatic constellation, the other such group need not buttress in its turn. In order not to reinvigorate compensatory and simplifying national self-enclosures, the transnational and transhistorical alliances between dominating agencies as well as dominated enablers have to be uncovered. By forging their trauma narratives in an ongoing dialogue, they continuously reinvented the platforms of mutual solidarity. Despite the appearance they are systematically producing, trauma narratives are equivocal, multiconfessional and multicultural composures ridden with internal conflicts.

The first homogenizing retroactive projection that has to be deconstructed along these analytical lines, before we introduce Rousseau's rebellion against the "literary universalism" of the French encyclopedists, is the entrenched identification of the opposition between artificiality and naturalness with the opposition between the French *civilisation* and the German *Kultur*. This misleading identification stems from the German retroactive self-consoling maneuver engendered against the traumatic backdrop of the rise of National Socialism.[6] In the traumatic constellation of the 1930s, the imagined community of the German *Kulturnation* was stressed by some progressive German intellectuals to suppress the statist idea of the *Blut und Boden*-rootedness that was, as we have seen, equally

---

[6] For the pioneering sociological argument in terms of cultural confrontation between two nations see the first chapter of Elias (1978), which was originally published in 1936 and was therefore probably, though not explicitly, linked to the distinction between civilization and culture introduced by Alfred Weber's *Kulturgeschichte und Kultursoziologie* (1935). Roughly speaking, *civilisation* would cover a wide range of social manifestations engendered in the process of human everyday behavior and intercourse, whereas *Kultur* would pertain only to the highest human achievements in the arts, science and philosophy brought about in individual and "splendid isolation." Because German intellectuals in the pre-war atmosphere of the second half of the 1930s obviously side with the latter, they are trying to suppress the incriminating ethnic and political background of their nationalism for the benefit of its apparently pure esthetic character.

2.3 Cosmopolitan patriot and democratic tyrant: Jean-Jacques Rousseau

constitutive of the Romanticist trauma narrative.[7] In such a way, the polarization among the German intellectuals between the "cosmopolitan" and "national" bent, set in motion by Herder and German Romanticists to be taken up by Goethe, was resumed by Elias's elitist cosmopolitanism in the traumatic pre-war circumstances. Yet the suppressed political aspect of the German Romanticist trauma narrative nonetheless contaminated its foregrounded cultural aspect shortly after Elias introduced his influential defense of German tradition. This significantly happened from the non-German perspective. The British historian Robin Collingwood, while writing *The Idea of History* during the Second World War, was struck by the consequences of Herderian theory which his age experienced, qualifying it as "scientifically ungrounded" and "politically disastrous." "Consequently we are not inclined to be grateful to Herder for having started so pernicious a doctrine." (Collingwood 1961: 92) This understandable overreaction notwithstanding, we can risk the thesis that, being deeply traumatized by the Nazi epoch, some post-war mainstream German intellectuals tended to render the Romanticist narrative in purely aesthetic terms by stressing its democratic tenor and disregarding its imperial statist tendency.

On the other hand, Rousseau's internal resistance cautions against the equally strong inclination of certain prominent French intellectuals who for their part, in response to the postcolonial traumatic constellation of the 1960s, retrospectively glorify their Enlightenment cosmopolitanism, as we have seen in Kristeva and Casanova. Both groups of "national representatives," the German and the French, thereby externalize the terror that internally haunts their national project by transforming it into a "foreign enemy." The battle for the adoption of the "soft" and rejection of the "hard" nationalist tradition, that finds expression in these and other transfers, turns the French Enlightenment and German Romanticist trauma narratives into the rich memory sites of the successively stored past and present rivalries and clashes (Schlereth 1977: 13; Albrecht 2005: 17). Whoever deploys the concepts related to them cannot but take sides, advertently or inadvertently, which accounts for the reiteration of antagonisms. What Balibar (2002: 57) stated regarding nationalism – "there is no neutral position or discourse here, no way of being 'above the fray'" – has to be extended to cosmopolitanism as well. Once the camps are homogenized, nobody can escape the traumatizing battle of transfers between them. Stressing their complex mutual implications as

---

[7] It deserves attention in this context that Goethe, who in 1773 edited a collection of Alsatian folk songs together with Herder, was the first to become aware of the disconcerting implications of the national idea this collection has catalyzed. As Meyer-Kalkus (2010: 101) spells out, his late idea of the *Weltliteratur* was a vehement reaction to the German religious-patriotic art his early work gave rise to.

well as various transnational alliances between the antagonized "carrier groups" within the respective national corpuses is an attempt to analytically disaggregate such scientifically inadequate and perilous, albeit in everyday practice probably unavoidable, naturalizing mechanisms.

This then is the reconfigured context in which Rousseau's advocacy of the putatively "typically German" values such as naturalness, frankness and straightforwardness must be placed. Within the one and the same French tradition the Protestant and petty bourgeois Rousseau was rebelling against the Catholic and high bourgeois Voltaire in the same way as Voltaire himself previously rebelled against Montesquieu's concept of the civilized political community, Protestant and aristocratic in its spirit. For Voltaire, who is a tyrant in Rousseau's terms, Montesquieu was a tyrant (Grosrichard 1979: 39–48). Furthermore, just a couple of decades before Rousseau ferociously opposed the artificial imitation of Parisian parlance in the name of the victimized human natural behavior, Voltaire's idea of literature radically opposed the blind repetition of the civilized manners of his aristocratic predecessors. His Republic of Letters broke alliance with the Monarchic "nobility" reproduced through mechanical collective aping by putting forward the Republican imperative of strategic individual self-cultivation. Yet in the process of its international expansion, ironically enough, exactly through the previously rejected automatic imitation, this imperative gradually set the "sacred standard" for all European literatures (Casanova 2004: 87–100). Through its tyrannical institutional pressure it provoked a growing ethnonational resistance within those literatures that were, owing to the unequal distribution of "internal" cosmopolitan resources, unable to keep pace with its acceleration.

Though clearly attached to French literature and culture, Rousseau was a Protestant, dissident and poor petty bourgeois or, in Koselleck's words (1973: 135), "ein Ausländer im französischen Staat" (a foreigner in the French state) and "ein Fremdling in der guten Gesellschaft" (a stranger in noble society). These were the terms of his personal traumatic constellation. Due to this stigmatizing second-class citizenship status which induced his deeply frustrating experience, he was forced to look for influential allies in the Protestant tradition both inside and outside France. Looking for inward support, he had recourse to Montesquieu's praise of the Protestant (i.e., Northern) independent individual disposition as opposed to the socially dependent Catholic (i.e. Southern) one (*The Spirit of the Laws*, XXIV.5 and XXV.2); looking for outward support, he introduced great English literature to the Francophone world. This is how his galvanizing trauma narrative with its richly resonating "multidirectional memory" (Rothberg 2009) came into being.

Let me first briefly tackle this outward alliance, i.e., the "literary cosmopolitanism," that, according to Brunetière's pupil Joseph Texte (1895), was a pioneering endeavor within the French context. A second-class citizen of the French nation establishes *cosmopolitan alliances*, first, to support the outward resistance of other nations to the cultural pressure of his privileged compatriots and, second, to gain their support for his inward resistance. This interlocking inclination unique to dominated individuals and collectivities indicates the traumatic experience underlying Rousseau's envisioned recalibration and transformation of the French polis. The Protestant affiliation drives him as a Southern European writer to forge a cosmopolitan alliance with the Northern English literature, which suspends the bipolarity between the European North and South uniting them in one and the same European literature. On that basis Joseph Texte celebrates him as the first literary cosmopolitan in Europe (1895: 334, 336).

But Texte's judgment is, as usual, one-sided, keeping silent about Rousseau's equally influential recourse to Montesquieu's *individualism* which runs parallel to his literary cosmopolitanism. In order to highlight the French "Northern" individualist spirit, Montesquieu had curiously established the same bipolarity between the European North and South that Rousseau has eliminated. But he nonetheless became Rousseau's invisible *national ally*, contaminating, as it were, his cosmopolitanism. This covert historical continuity with one of the founders of the national tradition who applied French putative geopolitical privilege as a criterion for the discriminative evaluation of other European cultures renders Texte's canonization of Rousseau's cosmopolitanism doubtful. If we interpret Rousseau as a Romanticist cosmopolitan alone, as Texte and many others do, the continuity of his views with the exclusionist legacy of the French Enlightenment passes unnoticed. Yet this hidden link finds clear expression in his conception of the democratic constitution based on the *free and willing decision of individuals* which endorses patriotism. The implication is that patriotism testifies to the legitimacy of the (French individualist) political order which engendered it, whereas (Voltaire's) cosmopolitanism, being imposed as a moral obligation from above instead of earned through democratic consent, testifies to its illegitimacy. In short, cosmopolitanism is antipatriotic. "What the fatherland consists of," writes Rousseau (1964b: 254n) in a letter from 1764, "are the relations of the state to its members," i.e., law, government and constitution. He highlights this constitutional patriotism (tacitly but powerfully endorsed in Kant's famous treatise *On Eternal Peace*) in order to discredit the assimilating cosmopolitanism of the *encyclopédistes*. This influential maneuver forced patriotic loyalty and universal human morality to part company, introducing between them a sharp opposition (Albrecht 2005: 35–36).

In establishing such an opposition in favor of patriotism, Rousseau unfortunately misapprehends that "we, the people," far from being a natural expression of the people's "general will," as he uncritically assumed, was always exercised in the name of a *specific constituency* (or "carrier group") that establishes its sovereignty *against other constituencies* of the same people. Some constituencies, such as women, slaves and servants, devoid of the full membership in the "we," either fall under the protection of the sovereign constituency or remain, strangers and immigrants, completely excluded from it. The USA's restrictive, protectionist and hierarchical immigration policy for example, similar to the French or British for that matter (Kristeva 1993: 10–13), hardly matches the Rousseauan aspiration proudly declared in the golden age of national consolidations for the government to dwell "as a vital principle in the will of every citizen" (James Russell Lowell, 1865). Far from being everybody's concern, democracy surreptitiously reintroduces the tyranny it claims to have dethroned, an outcome that makes patriotism and cosmopolitanism, pace Rousseau, implying rather than opposing each other (Derrida 1986; Benhabib 2006: 33–34).

2.4 Who is authorized to represent "natural communities"?

Keeping this patriotic bond with the national Enlightenment legacy firmly in mind, we should certainly not neglect Rousseau's cosmopolitan dimension. His inclination to England notwithstanding, his underrated citizen status within the French "national body" aroused his sympathies primarily for the "natural" or insignificant nations put under the pressure of acculturation. He resolutely defended their right to choose their own literary and cultural style. This line of argument, motivated by the same inferiority feeling, was taken up and enforced by Friedrich Schlegel's national literary historiography despite the different confessions of these two peculiar "elective affiliates." The right to self-determination of literary and culturally conquered communities mattered more than religion to the small and marginal group of Catholic German intellectuals at the beginning of the nineteenth century. Rousseau's passionate advocacy of the prodigious diversity of European habits, temperaments and characters was launched from the Geneva Republic that, next to its (in the French culture of the age minoritized) Protestant religion, differed from Paris in terms of its "provincial" position and inferior size. Such a marginal and "compressed community," according to Rousseau's explanation in *Discourse on Inequality*, improves the feeling of natural affinity and the sense of co-belonging between the community members. In his opinion, small nations are much better prepared for the future republican constitution that will substitute for the cumbersome and anachronous monarchic one. As another important aspect of Rousseau's intended reconfiguration of the French polis, this sense of co-belonging offering platform of identification for the whole series of inferior provincial communities of the age understandably attracted the attention of German Romanticist intellectuals. In resuming and reconfiguring Rousseau's French trauma narrative, they were engineering the future German "community of fate."

The problem was, alas, that the swift expansion of the French Republic of Letters that paved the way for the political republican set-up consistently ruined and decomposed these organic "social bonds." The modern idea of literature that the Republic of Letters promoted envisioned the dissolution of *natural communities* – into whose holistic horizon of shared meanings an individual was comfortably born but unpleasantly imprisoned – by a huge *political community* that was expected to be strategically, rationally and steadily built up by liberated individuals. Defying the static, inert and repressive political order that prevented the majority of its subjects from shaping their identity routes on an individual basis, the rising political community laid the foundation for the new democratic order based on the willing and permanent revolutionizing of the self (Koselleck 1973: 135). Opening its boundaries toward the progressive future, the newly raised principle of *Selbstbildung* resolutely attached itself to the open horizon of expectation (*Erwartungshorizont*) as opposed to the closed experiential space (*Erfahrungsraum*) of anachronous natural communities (Koselleck 1989: 359).

That is to say, in his advocacy of democratic naturalness Rousseau bitterly reacted to such a triumphant modernization, administration and rationalization of humankind from the traumatized perspective of the "social bonds" victimized by it. Being insufficiently equipped with cosmopolitan resources to get in the engine of grand history, they faced the deeply unsettling effects of this huge global process instead of benefiting from its possibilities. By personally sharing the frustration of "natural communities," Rousseau, followed enthusiastically by Herder, sympathetically endorses their recourse to indigenous myths to protect them from deracination. Mythification is the habitual response of a self-enclosed collective memory stored in oral folklore to the threat of its devastation by the anonymous rationalized memory deposited in written archives (White 2000: 52–55). Endangered communities construct petty moral plots against monumental causal explanations to save what Aleida Assmann described as their active and personal *Funktionsgedächtnis* from being destroyed by a passive and anonymous *Speichergedächtnis*. According to her interpretation, such sentimental and nostalgic attempts to revitalize oral cultural memory proliferate under the pressure of the rising print culture toward the close of the eighteenth century (Assmann 2004: 48–50). By crossing national borders, print culture etiolates and devastates traditions.

Apart from Rousseau's delineated defense of "natural communities," this helps us to understand why a comparably small Switzerland became the refuge for another French Protestant dissident, Mme de Staël. She resisted the aggressive imperial character of Bonaparte's France by affiliating herself instead with the established British literature and with the emergent German one. In the above-mentioned outline of French literary cosmopolitanism, Joseph Texte (1895: 432–448) praises her undertaking as a continuation of Rousseau's cosmopolitan extension of French literature but one should again be wary of replacing this self-congratulatory interpretation with a less generous one. Since Mme de Staël established her Protestant alliance with the European North departing from a deeply dependent and less than sovereign European South like Rousseau, her attachment has to be understood, like Rousseau's recourse to English literature, as the self-empowering reaction of an endangered inferior social bond. One should recall that Montesquieu celebrated the European North for its sovereign independency. Therefore, against the expansive French Enlightenment universalism, Mme de Staël reiterates Rousseau's defense of the right of the Southern "natural communities" to autonomy and self-sufficiency. If the Enlightenment recalibration implied the universal expansion of the French polis, then the Romanticist reconfiguration, as exemplified in Rousseau, Mme de Staël and the ensuing German national project, implied contraction, narrowing down and solidifying isolation. It advocated the defensive *Vergemeinschaftung* above the progressive *Vergesellschaftung*. Traumatized as it was, and forged in reaction, it consolidated the resistance against supremacy.

Both Rousseau and Mme de Staël therefore anticipated the traumatic pattern of Friedrich Schlegel's national literary history, consistently defending the perspective of communities endangered by the self-propelling French universalism and striving to revive their eroded "natural identity." Unlike Rousseau, however, who associated this naturalness with frank masculinity against the embellished femininity of the French bourgeois elite, Mme de Staël, several decades later, associated it with democratic femininity standing in opposition to the despotic masculinity of the Napoleonic regime. It was a feminine rewriting of Rousseau's idea. Rousseau conceptualized loyalty to one's own nature as the purification of all extraneous influences which, as he states in *Émile*, is something that women are simply incapable of:

> She cannot fulfill her purpose in life without his aid, without his goodwill, without his respect: she is dependent on our feelings, on the price we put upon her virtue, and the opinion we have of her charms and her deserts. Nature herself has decreed that woman, both for herself and her children, should be at the mercy of man's judgment. [...] "What will people think" is the grave of a man's virtue and the throne of a woman's. (Rousseau 1977: 328)

Anne Louise Germaine de Staël was not such a woman, however; on the contrary, she was brought up to achieve self-mastery (Richardson 1995: 134). She therefore strongly opposed Rousseau's conviction of the masculine character of naturalness, starting with her *Letters on Rousseau* (1788) onwards. In her opinion, while stimulating manhood, the French republican spirit, proud because of its firm democratic commitment, took up the same despotic attitude toward women that it had previously indignantly criticized as the attitude of Oriental rulers toward their people. Rousseau was therefore accused of reproducing the despotic patterns he for his part attributed to Voltaire. Indeed, he treats Sophie in *Émile* as Emils obligatory passage into sociality expected to renounce his emotional attachment to her in order to give way to his much more important attachment to the political community. The latter is an exclusively masculine enterprise that drowns out women's voices. Yet Mme de Staël's real target was not so much Rousseau but Napoleon. According to Roberto Dainotto (2007: 156):

> The sort of French imperialism that Napoléon had begun with the Italian campaign in 1796 [when the Directorate of the Revolution had planned a strategy of simultaneous wars for the liberation of Europe, V.B.] smacked too much, for Staël, of Oriental despotism. [...] As the despotism of the Orient was based on the enslavement of women in the harem, so was postrevolutionary despotism based on the increasing marginalization of women. [...] After the coup d'état of the eighteenth Brumaire of 1799, Napoléon had been quick to declare that "since women have no political rights, it is not appropriate to define them as citizens"; and the Napoleonic code [...] had marginalized the social role of women to mere "obedience."

Against such harsh gender discrimination, de Staël needed to mobilize some influential *national allies* among whom, surprisingly enough, we find the same powerful figure her antagonist Rousseau had resorted to some decades earlier, though for other reasons and against another enemy. She invokes Montesquieu's thesis on respect for women as the distinctive trait of the European North in comparison with the European South: German culture grants woman the freedom to take responsibility for domestic happiness between husband and wife rather than despotically subjecting her to humiliating sexual services as is the French Southern habit. Such an Oriental harem model forces women to understandable rebellion and (homo)sexual aberrations which are to be avoided at any cost. This petty bourgeois idea of self-enclosed family happiness, cautions Dainotto, authorizes de Staël to subscribe to the North European moderate patriarchal authority, to restrict the proper area of female action to heterosexual marital union and, consequently, to eliminate the Orient, along with Southern Europe, "with its unruly gender confusion and its despotism, from the scene of European literature" (Dainotto 2007: 157). The affiliation to Montesquieu's exclusionist Enlightenment argument, as in the case of Rousseau, erodes the intended democratic character of the "natural community." Its liberation cannot but cast a long discriminating shadow, as was the case with Friedrich Schlegel's aforementioned and contemporaneous "community of fate." Adhering to the "primitive 'common denominator'" of "closest relatives" one usually tends to suppress, as Kristeva (1993: 3) warned, "the petty conflicts those family members so often, alas, had in store for me."⁸ The conflict-ridden profile of "natural bonds" corrupts the proclaimed naturalness of their roots. It associates immediacy and direct historical lineage, suppressing that any such rooting is an invention of the proclaimer(s) engendered to remedy a particular traumatic constellation or more of them.

The project of national literary history for its part, far from being a German "family enterprise," emerged from the elective affinities of various European intellectuals caught into various traumatic constellations consisting of social, cultural, religious and/or gender axes. Their sacrificial narratives, despite democratic intentions, ultimately entailed exclusionist consequences. No liberation pertains to the entire community but merely those instances that set its rules. They alone become the full members of the demos, while the rest of the population stands at the mercy of the exercise of their authority (Benhabib 2006: 35). If Novalis, the German Catholic who wanted to advocate a Europe of peacefully coexisting nations rather than French revolutionary universalism, followed in his *Die Christenheit oder Europa* (1799) the dogmatic lines of the Catholic doctrine (Novalis 1983a), then Mme de Staël, the French Protestant who wanted to reclaim a Europe of democratically reconciled nations, applied the feminine model of domestic happiness that discriminates the Orient and Southern Europe.⁹

---

8 However, Kristeva (1993: 15, 32–33, 37) for her part also wholeheartedly agrees with Montesquieu's "differentiated cosmopolitanism" in order to liberate herself not just from Herder's "mystifying nationalism" but from French abstract cosmopolitanism as well. She celebrates his idea of the nation as a "lay aggregate" of absorbed differences subordinated to permanent transition in favor of a "general interest" (41), praises this "polyvalent community" (35) and "coordinated diversity" on the way to confederation (1991: 133), completely forgetting about the violent exclusionism of such putatively all-embracing inclusion based on the idea of individual free choice. Regarding the questioning of her enthusiastic reading of Kant and Montesquieu from the perspective of Derrida's alternative reading of hospitality limited by hostility, see Leonard (2005: 89–91). That is to say, in the various traumatic constellations of French political and intellectual history Montesquieu re-emerges as a multi-profiled ally always ready to assist but not without, as it were, invoicing his services.

9 For the connection between Rousseau, Mme de Staël and Novalis in this context see Dainotto (2007: 99–150). In an elaborate and convincing argument, Dainotto also adds to these well-known figures the lesser-known Spanish Jesuit Juan Andrés, who was institutionally affiliated to the Italian academy.

2.5 Identification by alienation

Without explicitly referring to his foreign predecessors Rousseau and Mme de Staël, Friedrich Schlegel takes up their fundamental argument on the necessity for all people to dethrone their imposed representatives in order to return to their natural roots. "The moment a people adopts representatives it is no longer free; it no longer exists," states Rousseau (1968a: 143), as if returning to one's roots such as language, folklore or history does not imply the process of their canonization by elected domestic representatives. For their part, these representatives, in a typically interlocking movement, look for outside support to authorize themselves against domestic opponents. To illustrate this customary maneuver, when Rousseau elected Poland, his follower Herder, later on, chose the Jewish people and Herder's follower Friedrich Schlegel finally Hungary to act as their generous protectors, this implied, despite contrary appearance, not so much a generous one-way custody as a reciprocal identification. Let me recall Lacan's thesis that mirrors do not simply reflect but constitute our identity. The latter is therefore necessarily a multilayered and internally antagonistic formation. No self is possible without being alienated via external mirrors; no agencies come into being without enablers.

Hence when Rousseau addressed the Polish nation in his *Considerations on the Government of Poland*, an open letter of sympathy "against a powerful and cunning aggressor," his public collective address was intended as a countermove to Voltaire's personal private letters to the absolutist sovereign Catherina II of Russia. He sided with the victim instead of with the aggressor (Wolff 1994: 238). In the same way as Voltaire identifies with Russian aggressive power, Rousseau as a citizen of the Geneva republic identifies with a defenseless people. It is through the significant bifurcation of outward national sympathies that the class-related, religious and ideological tensions within the body of the French Enlightenment came to the fore. Via such transfers, Voltaire and Rousseau conducted the battle for the status of the national representative. "If you make it so that a Pole can never become a Russian, I answer you that Russia will never subjugate Poland." (Rousseau 1990: 170–171, trans. mine) Nobody can destroy a nation so naturally rooted in its tastes, manners, prejudices and vices (163), i.e., so clearly distinguished from its neighbors. With this distinctive perception of Poles Rousseau was countering Voltaire's indiscriminate and careless lumping together of Russians, Poles, Tartars, and Hungarians. Whereas the whole of Western Europe becomes uniform under the pressure of French taste, the Poles must defend their peculiar national feeling by nurturing it with careful national education (Wolff 1994: 240–241). Only by learning their historical cultural roots can they shift from being subjects to becoming members of the world community of nations.

The same transition from the monarchic political culture of subjection to the republican political culture of participation that the French Republic of Letters had used to emancipate the imprisoned *individual* lives of French citizens was redirected in Rousseau's counter-Enlightenment project to liberate the suppressed *national* feeling of other European peoples. With his multidirectionally connectable trauma narrative he struggled to open up public space for people whose identities were put under strong pressure by the imperially imposed technique of individual emancipation which they were unable to apply. Anticipating the German national project, Rousseau's idea of a nation emerged as a remedial vision of the democracy of European peoples who were prevented from enjoying the individual rights established by the ruling European nation-state of the age. Yet was not this homogenization of national identities – denying the internal non-national fellow citizens, treating other nations as enemies and excluding women from the "social contract" – predestined to repeat the same discrimination that was violently applied against them?

Some ten years later, Johann Gottfried Herder's similarly homogeneous political convictions, this time concerning the future of the German people, were given tacit expression in the treatise *The Spirit of Hebraic Poetry* (1783). The question of Jewish nationality in contemporary Europe was significantly discussed in a retrospective historical perspective. "Just as Germany in his days was a nation of many states and Austria a state of many nations, so ancient Israel portrayed 'a most excellent example' of a nation [of twelve independent republics or tribes] long before its emergence as a *state*." (Barnard 2003: 20) As if giving an example to his own people, he highlighted the ability of Jewish people, thanks to their loyalty to common law, their shared historical language and folklore memory, their fostered and perpetuated family ties as well as love and reverence for their forefathers, to preserve their sense of identity in a predominantly hostile environment for over two thousand years. A sustained combination of all these determinants gradually paved the way for a communitarian order free from power as a central source of coercion. "That law should rule and not the legislator, that a free nation should freely accept and honor it, that invisible, reasonable, and benevolent powers should guide us and no chains enslave us" (23) was not only the achievement of Moses but Herder's democratic vision of how modern Germany should come into being. We know the outcome. Though he strongly opposed Voltaire, like Rousseau before him, Herder was no less egalitarian in his visions and no less republican in his heart than the French Enlightener. It is simply that the republic he envisioned was of a different kind and of a different discriminatory pattern.

To conclude this list of significant identifications by transference, the reason for Schlegel's enthusiasm for Hungary, some thirty years later, becomes transparent in his tenth Vienna lecture where he celebrates the Hungarian national resistance to King Matthias Corvinus in the sixteenth and seventeenth century (Schlegel 1961: 237). The similarity of Corvinus's Italian and Latin preferences with the French predilections of the late Prussian king, Frederick the Great, is striking.[10] In the same way as the Hungarian national movement, by resisting contemporary Austrian hegemony, had recourse to Hungarian legends from Corvinus's time, Schlegel expects his compatriots to resist the European offensive of French culture, reflected in the prevalent taste of the ruling German aristocracy, by recourse to German literary and cultural memory.[11] His first intention was to promote German literature in the making, as opposed to the acknowledged French literature, as the epitome (*Inbegriff*) of the spiritual formation of the German people. The aim of his literary history was therefore to establish the German national spirit in order to rescue his compatriots from French cultural appropriation. But this meant that Schlegel subscribed to a much broader idea of literature as an identification vehicle for people who, because they were politically, culturally or linguistically appropriated by the imperial nation-states, were deprived of access to their own identity and bereft of the possibility to use the first person pronoun. In inventing his unexpectedly influential trauma narrative he met with Rousseau and Herder, all of them convinced "that an enhanced consciousness of one's identity, in and through one's grasp of historical roots, could produce a shift in one's understanding":

> First, it would further people's reflective self-identification and self-location within time, space, and the context of others; and, second, it would make them realize that they were not meant to be merely passive observers, but that they could also think of themselves as active participants. (Barnard 2003: 161–162)

To become active participants in history was the only way for these people to rid themselves of the traumatic experience of their downgrading, denigration and exclusion. Consequently, thanks to a number of outstanding interconnected European intellectuals who opposed the central identification power as an inadmissible tutelage replacing it by a broad democratic participation of nations in the

---

10 "This happened to Hungarians in the fifteenth century and would surely happen to us Germans in the eighteenth if the great king of the age, who like Matthias respected and knew only the foreign spiritual formation, had reigned equally unconstrained over all of Germany as did Corvin in Hungary" (*So ging es den Ungarn im fünfzehnten Jahrhundert, wie es auch wohl uns Deutschen im achtzehnten ergangen sein würde, wenn ein großer König dieser Zeit, der wie Matthias auch nur ausländische Geistesbildung ehrte und kannte, eben so unumschränkt über das gesamte Deutschland geherrscht hätte, wie Corvin in Ungarn* (Schlegel 1961: 237)).
11 An attentive and inspiring investigation of this subject, on which I am drawing here, was performed by Neubauer (2004).

world community, the liberating cosmopolitan potential of national literary history came to the fore. If humankind was to be established according to their vision, a self-regulating ensemble of many cooperating self-regulating smaller wholes was the only viable option. Humankind was expected to unfold from within and come from below instead of being imposed from above as in the universal model of the Republic of Letters. This affirmation of autonomous literatures and cultures was clearly meant as an alternative, an international vision of the cosmopolitan recalibration of the polis. Yet as soon as Europe was nationally reconfigured, i.e., dismembered into sovereign nation-states, the intended bright democratic vistas of this recalibration reintroduced harsh discrimination and, moreover, reinvigorated its traumatic consequences, as some constituents of this reorganized humanity came to experience.

3 The Janus Face of Literary *Bildung*: Education and/or Self-Formation?

3.1 "Having the other" and "being the other"

Friedrich Schlegel's transfer of literature's theatre of operation from the external social and political scene to the interior of the national self is usually considered to have established the principal difference between the Romanticist and Enlightenment idea of literary *Bildung*. Following Herder's redefinition of language as no longer an instrument of external communication but a repository of an overall way of thinking (*Denkart*) passed on and treasured by previous generations, the Romanticists relegate literature from the collective public sphere of *education* to the private individual domain of *self-formation*. Although they still employ the concept of *Bildung* to designate the main function of literature, in Romanticist use this concept gradually shifts its meaning from "cultivating or educating others" to "constituting or building the self (as the other)." The "difference between" the self and the others apparently becomes the "difference within" the self which ceaselessly separates this self from its falsifications (Currie 2004: 93).

It deserves attention that these seemingly opposite *Bildung* functions of literature, "having or possessing the other" and "being or becoming the other,"[1] roughly correspond to two of Foucault's modes of conceptualizing state power, sovereignty and governmentality. Whereas sovereignty attempts to integrate the diverse population into the law of the state, governmentality suspends law by disarticulating it into a heterogeneous set of administrative tactics, the so-called technologies of the self, which does not draw its meaning from any unitary source. Yet contrary to Foucault's celebration of governmentality as the liberation of pop-

---

[1] For two excellent discussions of the Freudian distinction between *desire* (libidinal bond to the other-as-object whom the self wishes to possess) and *identification* (emotional tie to the other-as-model on whom the self bases him- or herself) see Borch-Jakobsen (1988: 164–72) and Fuss (1995: 11–16). Both of them claim that "to have" the other (which is a relation) and "to be" the other (which is a non-relation since it is preconscious) cannot be clearly distinguished from one another because they constantly reappear within each other. As I will try to demonstrate, the same holds for the distinction between the Enlightenment "difference between" and Romanticist "difference within." Despite all the efforts made to keep its items separate, this distinction is equally untenable in the final analysis. Literature has resisted all the appropriation, inclusion or "narrative accommodation" (by literary history) to which it has been exposed. Because "literary experience negates determinate space and time" (Saussy 2011: 292), it cannot be located or "mapped." This literary negation of any coverage is, however, a permanent source of frustration that continuously invites attempts to come to grips with it.

ulation, a series of political theorists have meanwhile argued that it is an invention of the sovereign state exposed to crisis, or the failure of its universalistic principle for that matter (Amselle 2003; Butler 2004b; Brown 2006). If governmentality's implementation is really better interpreted as a response to the sovereign state's legitimacy deficit, i.e. its historically diminished capacity to embody universal representation, then the state power is, rather than being replaced, reproduced, revitalized and enlarged by governmentality.

Returning to my analogy and following this thread, I will argue that the "hard" Enlightenment concept of literary *Bildung*, that eradicates differences between the humans and focusses on intellectual elites, and the "soft" Romanticist concept of literary *Bildung*, that affirms differences between the humans by orienting itself toward the broad readership, do not merely exclude but also imply each other. The affirmative regeneration of the reader's distinctive identity is a creation of the endangered educational project of his/her assimilation into the predetermined identity matrix. Therefore, in what follows I am going to describe the paradoxical relationship between the two projects of literary *Bildung* as a disabling enablement of one by the other.

3.2 Differences between the *Bildung* concepts

This does not mean that the differences between them that define the entire intellectual horizon of European modernity ought to be downplayed or neglected. Let us begin with the *first* difference. In the French Republic of Letters, authoring literature was identified with consistent self-affirmation through the dialogic overcoming of others. It was interpreted as a practical, rational and goal-oriented enterprise in which the superior self profitably assimilates either its barbaric predecessors (in historical terms) or exotic foreigners (in geographical terms) into its own civilized present or cultivated domestic condition. Within the horizon of such an undertaking historical and geographical terms appear to be inextricably entangled. For most of the eighteenth century, a spatial journey from "alien" Eastern parts of Europe to the familiar Western ones, such as that undertaken by Voltaire in *Essai sur le moeurs* (1756), also entailed a temporal progression through history (Wolff 1994: 284–331).

Now, taking the opposing German point of view, Herder introduced a deliberate asymmetry into this spontaneous association of geography with history. He perceives the national spirit (*Volksgeist*) exclusively as a historically emergent entity. Concentrating on the affirmation of dominated national identities (in the first place the exemplary German one) he privileged historical interaction with the undying spirit of deceased ancestors over cultural interaction with geographically distant living neighbors (Barnard 2003: 139). This "regenerative attitude" explains why Schlegel envisioned the memory archive of national literature, taken to be the epitome of the *Volksgeist*, as the most appropriate medium for German self-finding (*Selbstfindung*). As opposed to the proud French self of the time, the German self was non-existent, and therefore bereft of the possibility to be simply asserted (*Selbstbehauptung*). It had to be *invented*, an operation which ambiguously oscillates between the investigative *detection* and imaginative *creation* (as it is always possible that the past facts that have now "just" been detected in their original condition are in the given form created or back-projected by the same "now"). This irresolvable ambiguity at the heart of the project of national self-formation initiated by its stubborn reappearance the forthcoming unprecedented self-propelling (*Selbststeigerung*) of the German spirit. As all detections of the past turned out to be the retroactive creations of the present, the German *Volksgeist* tirelessly strove to disengage these undesired "forgeries" in order to reach its proper "indigenous form."

In order to carry out this ambitious project, which makes the *second* important difference between the two concepts of literary *Bildung*, Schlegel reversed the sovereign educational attitude of the present toward the past as established by the French Enlightenment rationalism, transforming the relationship between them into genetic lineage. The past now belonged to the same national geographic and cultural space as the present; it thereby lost its alien traits, acquiring the familiar ones instead. Being forerunners rather than foreigners, ancestors are considered by Schlegel to be grandparents of sorts, and descendants become their grandchildren. Consequently, *genetic dependence is substituted for cognitive sovereignty*. That is to say, family descendants can now take possession of themselves only through family ancestors. Successive perspectives of past generations treasured in the national literary memory archive chart the trajectory of the present national self. But the latter is at the same time the vertex of the ancestors' centuries-long differential, individualizing, and self-disentangling self-identification directed toward national peculiarity. If the ancestors represent the body, then the descendants are the mind of the national self; without them the slumbering national community *in* itself could not be transformed into the awakened national community *for* itself and the self-finding could not be successfully accomplished. Herder invented this highly influential interactive historical pattern in his early *Fragments on the New German Literature* (1766/7) in order to define the profile of European literature. At the outset of the third collection (Herder 1985: 374), he describes this "colossus" as consisting of an Oriental head, a Greek breast, a Roman belly, Nordic-Gallic legs, and German feet. Paying tribute to all European nations, he reserves the earthly fundament and the only dynamic part of the European colossal body for the Germans who are now expected to move the magnificent European whole forward. "The present carries the past, traditions are founded not in the hidden origin, whence they emerged, but in the reflective acknowledgment and interpretation attributed to them by the present." (Koch 2002: 98)[2]

According to the *re-evolutionary paradigm* he in such a way prepared for the forthcoming Schlegel's application to the history of national literature, material history evolves out of the past toward the present, whereas its intellectual invention (detection and/or creation) takes the reverse direction. The evolutionary *material* and the re-evolutionary *intellectual* unfolding of history are however inseparable, since only the rose as the highest point of maturation can appropriately explain the bud; only the fruit its seed; and only humans their basic natural origins. However, as Hobsbawm (1983: 2) pointed out against this organicist metaphorics, nobody invents his or her tradition without being challenged by the present break with it. Let us translate his insight in the following way: If the retroactive invention rescues the descendants' endangered identity formation, then this invention is generated by a *traumatic constellation*. There is the risk of fabrication inherent in such a traumatized operation which ultimately determines what will enter the present self-formation and what will be suppressed by its profile: the past has to be "suitable" (1). In bypassing this *normative work of self-formation*, Herder designates it as the *Einfühlungsvermögen* or ability of the present self to enter into the mindset of the past others. In this manner he clearly substitutes detection for creation. Since ancestors with all their feelings, intentions, attitudes and ends are inscribed in their descendants' memory, without sensitively and meticulously researching into this rich genetic archive, descendants cannot realize who they really are or where they fit in; they cannot properly identify themselves. Identifying deceased grandparents, the argument goes, is the most appropriate way to identify ourselves. The retroactive self-finding operation accordingly acquires the pattern of an ongoing specification of the self through the subtle differentiation from its otherness-to-itself. Whereas, according to this pattern, the truth of the self is to be judged in terms of its future potentiality (or *Erwartungshorizont*, to speak with Koselleck) the truth of the others is to be judged in terms of a past perfect being (or *Erfahrungsraum*). An internal incommensurability or inability for the further development is projected onto their recognition.[3] Herder obliterates that he *creates* their disability in order to confirm

---

[2] This and the following translations from German are mine unless otherwise indicated.
[3] According to Amselle (2003: 8–31), Herder is the founder of the Western ethnologic tradition that celebrates the diversity of the world's population. However, this praise amounts to a significant polarization, as Herder assigns the representatives of this diversity to a "class" of either privilege or disability. As regards the latter "class," the outcome "is a very close network that [...]

the self's ability.⁴ Race and tribe are European inventions; these concepts did not exist before the colonization of Africa (Mamdani 2012: 73–74). They were engaged as the backdrop of European superiority.

After Herder's *Fragments* (1985: 375–378), German literary spirit was for a very long time, ever since Frederick II introduced European education, a mixture of various cultural strata, yet the confrontation with these foreign elements raised the awareness of its distinctive quality. This is what Herder invented to equip the future national literary historians. Starting with the existing genres, styles and techniques of German literature, he retrospectively identifies its early modern genuine national quality (*Eigenart*), which helps him to pin down and gradually outmaneuver the Oriental, Greek, Roman, French and British cultural strata in the subsequent course of history (Koch 2002: 102). The German self thus revolutionizes him- or herself through the retroactive disentangling of his or her evolution. S/he moves toward the self-conscious future unity through selective and reflexive delving into the past diversity of his or her preparatory stages. This is how Herder envisages the self-finding operation (or canonization) of the German spirit: a continuous affirmation of national singularity and cultural distinction against the background of Greek antiquity and the contemporary European context. As far as he is concerned, all people certainly belong to humanity but do not occupy its same tense. To engage Elisabeth Povinelli's vocabulary (Povinelli 2011: 41–42), *autological subject* and *genealogical communities*, i.e. individual freedom and collective destiny, gradually part their ways on the global, European, and national level simultaneously from Herder onwards.

Let us finally address the *third* difference between the Enlightenment and Romanticist concepts of literary *Bildung*: contrary to the Enlightenment public self directed toward the assimilating cultivation of the political, social and cultural others, Schlegel's interiorized self-formation (*Selbstbildung*) aims at shaping the in-dividual, i.e. unsharable or differential self. Beware, however, that, owing to Herder's cultural transfer of the French principle of individuality to the people (Dumont 1994: 10), Friedrich Schlegel's individual self is identified with the *Volk*.

---

endows each person with a specific weight depending on his or her place in a real or virtual group (deaf mutes, paraplegics, etc.). The result of this proliferation of identities is that individuals can no longer be compared to one another on an equal basis and that they lose personal responsibility for themselves (12–13)." Taken to be in need of assistance, and stigmatized as such, they underlie protection and custody. Yet this protection is, for its part, only a technology of governance or a strategy to contain social and political change (Mamdani 2012: 28).

4 As we will come to see, Hegel will follow him in depriving, for instance, Africa of history. As Mamdani (2012: 53) puts it, the basic premise of colonial historiography is that history only came to Africa with the advent of its colonizers.

Collective phylogeny is equated with individual ontogeny, which means that it has to be invented in the same way. This is what Schlegel aims at when he subscribes to Novalis's association of literature with the domain of self-formation postulated in the famous passage quoted by Benjamin (1974: 64): "The beginning [of the self] emerges later than the self; this is why the self cannot have begun. We see therefrom that we are in the realm of *art* here ..." (Der Anfang entsteht später, als das Ich, darum kann das Ich nicht angefangen haben. Wir sehn daraus, dass wir hier im Gebiet der *Kunst* sind ...) Because the beginning of the self is necessarily retroactively, i.e. artistically, constructed, the self consists of artificial (*künstlich*) rather than natural data, it is a 'work of art,' "*the self must be constructed*" (Novalis 1983b: 253 [emphasis mine]). Instead of being unquestionably natural and original, its shape is an arbitrary after-effect. Stating its artistic nature, Novalis clearly reacts against the thesis of Fichte and Schelling that the self is a natural given. When Schlegel treats biography as the work of life-art (*Werk der Lebenskunstlehre*, Schlegel 1988: 125), he actually refers to Novalis's view: "Das Leben soll kein uns gegebener, sondern ein von uns gemachter Roman sein" (Novalis 1981: 563; We should not take life to be a novel given to us, but one made by us.)

In the Romanticist interpretation, literature is a narrative invention of the self that carefully examines others, rather than the self's inconsiderate conquering of others. In Friedrich Schlegel's vision, this self-invention applies to the *Volksgeist*. The *Volksgeist* does not eradicate the difference of the others but shapes, defines and manages them in order to derive from this management a distinctive national self. The nation is expected to work normatively on its disentanglement if it is to reach, once in the future, its peculiarity (*Eigenart*). This is why the *Selbstbildung* (self-formation) amounts to the *Selbststeigerung* (self-propelling). Yet the re-emerging dissent among the constituents of the one and the same national self, i.e. among individual selves, with regard to *which particular other* this peculiarity is to be accomplished, turns this purportedly consensual normative work into a conflict-ridden task. First disentanglement of the national self pertains of course to the non-European natural, i.e. indigeneous selves of "natives," irrevocably riveted to the *Umwelt* they are born into, but this is obviously not the point at which the self-differentiation of the *Volksgeist* can stop. It has to be continued within Europe, differentiating its West from the East, or North from the South. Within the West, further on, the Germans are to be distinguished from the French, Brits or Spaniards. The problem is, however, that these "negative foils" cannot be outmaneuvered in such a way to rescue the *Volksgeist* from their contamination, as they turn out to be resurging within the national corpus of one's own in the form of "foreign bodies," "misfits" or "internal enemies."

3.3 Mirroring and interweaving

This undesired reintroduction of the putatively excluded external others in the form of permanent internal dissents within the national self complicates the establishment of a firm opposition between the two concepts of literary *Bildung*. They are forced, almost imperceptibly, to become mirror reflections of each other. Let us now examine this unexpected mirroring. *First* of all, as regards the opposition between individual and collective identity-building, every self-formation necessarily takes place in the medium of national literary memory. As in the Enlightenment idea of literary *Bildung*, the individual and community formation run parallel; the one is the condition of the possibility of the other. If in the Enlightenment argument humankind emerges through the emancipation of individuals from their national community domains, then in the Romanticist argument, conversely, the individual comes into being by inventing his or her national memory archive.

The individual and the collective interfere, and this is the *second* aspect of the mirror reflection of the two models, because the Romanticists abandon the Enlightenment idea of common human nature that neglects the linguistic variety of humankind. Human nature is in their view always linguistically constituted, and, owing to the multitude of national languages, structurally diverse. National language is not an external instrument of intercourse between its users, but the internal structure of collective thinking, perception and imagination into which one is born. Romanticists therefore insist on seeing humankind in its diversity instead of in its unity. Yet just as the unity of humankind in the Enlightenment interpretation comes into being by overcoming the diversity of national languages, so its diversity in the Romanticist interpretation requires the unification of national languages. Unity and diversity cannot emerge without each other, they are closely interdependent. A given national language can take its distinctive place in the diversity of national languages only after it has been *internally unified*. Inasmuch as the unity of a given national language could not be accomplished without overcoming a variety of dialects, local usages, anachronisms, loan phrases, idioms and words, intersections and overlaps with other national languages, the coercive unification carried out by the Enlighteners at the level of humankind is relegated by the Romanticists to the level of national languages. Hence coercion is by no means abandoned in favor of an unlimited diversity. Of this diversity only unified national languages can partake.

Without this internally undertaken homogenization, the German language could not have acquired the self-confidence it needed in order to compete with other great European languages, such as Italian or French (Fohrmann 1994: 585). This is why Schlegel focused his intellectual energy on the national unity instead of global diversity, as Goethe did subsequently in an obvious polemical reaction. Following Herder's dictum (Herder 1985: 638), Schlegel undertook the principal philosophical task of researching the inexhaustible sources of the German mother tongue, i.e. its supposedly genuine life-world sphere disentangled from the hybridizing international cultural exchange. He wanted to rescue the genuinely German way of thinking and feeling (*Deutschheit*) from being corrupted by the ever-growing intercultural communication. From Goethe's point of view, expressed in the polemical articles he published in his journal *Über Kunst und Altertum* from 1805 onwards, this neo-Catholic euphoria of violent national purification was doomed to fail from the moment it was launched in Schlegel's Parisian journal *Europe* (1802). Having banished from German culture everything that was secular and non-German, it not only effectuated this culture's regrettable impoverishment, but disqualified Germany outright from serious international competition. In order to become truly competitive, German literature had to accept the hybridity of its origins and historical destiny, rather than retreat into a utopian and compensatory self-isolation (Koch 2002: 241–247). Only an identity that generously acknowledges the others within itself, Goethe argued, can confront the others outside itself with the necessary dignity. For example, in his essay *Shakespeare without End* in 1816, (1987: 135) he pointed out that only an author equipped with self-consciousness can properly understand foreign tempers and mentalities (*Gemütsarten*). He obviously had in mind the French counterpart. Heterogeneity of other literatures can be profitable only if a literature confronting them has already established its own esthetic credentials (1987: 243, 280). Without the necessary self-confidence and established criteria of selection, one is annihilated by the marvelous mirror, which was engaged to reflect oneself to advantage. Even in the second edition of *Wilhelm Meister's Journeyman Years* (1829), in the chapter "Makariens Archiv" Goethe notably warns that such impressive foreign talents as Shakespeare or Calderón might damage the shaky German self-formation (1987: 282).

Yet if the German self around 1800 was fragile and frustrated because of humiliating historical experiences, how justified was Goethe's demand for its self-confidence, openness and generosity? Mme de Staël (1985: 167) celebrated his power to court the forces of destruction in his works like a true conqueror in the real world, but she was an external (French!) admirer, and his compatriots have not been adequately equipped to embark on the same dangerous adventure of commanding the powers of historical furor. His imperial readiness to drag identities into the process of an endless mutual reflection, dissolving them until they become almost unrecognizable, for example in the *West-Eastern Divan* (1819, 1827), induced a threatening vertigo in the consciousness of his compatriots. They have not been able to match Goethe's calm and superior world-view whose fluidity perilously bordered on indifference. "Contemporary literary critics were equally overwhelmed as was the forthcoming literary scholarship. An author who dissolves genres expects natural scientists to produce world literature, fills *Wilhelm Meister's Journeyman Years* with scientific literature and riddles the Second *Faust* with allegories; such an author cannot reckon with the recognition of estheticians" (Günther 1990: 116). This is why, in order to cure Germany's wounded national self in the traumatic constellation induced by the breakdown of the Empire, Schlegel undertook an almost militantly self-defensive historical unification of German national spirit. He emphasized the deep national unity of German literature in order to contrast it to the broad international unity of world literature espoused by the French Republic of Letters.

But, and here we come to the *third* point of the mirroring of the two models, by reducing the internal diversity of German national literature, he reiterated the basic gesture of its Enlightenment opponent, which for its part subsumed the *ethnolinguistically* diverse world literature into the *spiritual* unity of humankind. To undo this enforced unity of world literature and broadcast its ethnolinguistic diversity, Schlegel, as Goethe noted, presses for the internal diversity of German literature to be subsumed into the historical pattern of national unity. Relinquishing the coercive unification of the World Republic of Letters for the benefit of a democratic consensus of national literatures, he reiterates coercion on the national level. Fascination with the unity-in-diversity inherent in the Enlightenment idea of world literature does not disappear in the Romanticist idea of national literature, but is, through a peculiar reversal, reaffirmed instead; diversity now pertains to world literature and unity to national literature. But despite this permutation of the two key agencies of literary *Bildung*, humankind and nation, in the dominating position, two conceptions of literature remain firmly entwined. Even the reversed operation of re-extending the narrow national perspective, that was carried out in the rise of so-called comparative literature about a century later, does not alter the underlying pattern. What unites humankind and nation as the ordering principles of literary history is a common normative character that assigns derogatory attributes to all deviations, implements corrective measures, applies disciplinary sanctions, and finally orders the expulsion of that which is considered to be irrecoverably deviant from the canon.

As if to offer further proof of this complex and uneasy interweaving of the two *Bildung* attitudes, in the development of his Romanticist idea of national literary history Schlegel drew largely upon his Enlightenment predecessor Herder, who himself characteristically oscillated between the two opposing and mutually implicated orientations. He was the first of the German Enlighteners to downplay the obligation of writers to the future of humankind, typical of the French enlightenment, in favor of their commitment to the national past, stored in their national language. One is born into one's linguistic, literary and cultural community which is why one is not expected to acquire individual identity by overcoming all one's predecessors, but rather communal identity by learning from the most familiar of them. Humans are obligated to their particular community roots rather than to the whole of humankind. The latter all-equalizing obligation is imposed upon the small, poor nations by the large, rich ones; it is an accommodation imperative imposed by European masters on extra-European and intra-European bondsmen.

> It would be the most stupid vanity to imagine that all the inhabitants of the World must be Europeans to live happily. Should we ourselves have become what we are out of Europe? He who placed us here, and others there, undoubtedly gave them an equal right to the enjoyment of life. [...] [A]n other has as little right to constrain me to adopt his feelings, as he has power to impart to me his mode of perception, and convert his identity to mine. (Herder 1968: 71)

Sharply opposing Kant's vision of humankind as a politically ordered society, Herder imagines national communities as extended families bound to particular natural environments as well as a continuous transference of linguistic and habitual patterns from one generation to another (73–78). This holistic thesis derived from the relegation of responsibility for communal human harmony from a divine agency to human activity clearly aligns him with the looming German Romanticism and against the French Enlighteners. Following Rousseau, Herder resisted general deracination, dematerialization and defacing of human existence in large absolutist monarchies trying to return humans to their site in life (*Sitz im Leben*) genuine to the telluric (*bodenständig*) communities (epitomized by the numerous small city-republics of that time). Through this resistance, he anticipates the governmental type of state power that would introduce free association of national differences in lieu of their assimilation into a homogeneous humanity. He suggested replacing the enlightening and civilizing treatment of the Other by the protecting and preserving approach to the most diverse world population, which anticipated the switch from the "direct" to the "indirect" rule that will take place in the British, French and Dutch colonies in the second half of the nineteenth century (Mamdani 2012). Yet this by no means exhausts his complex argument that also contains an important Enlightenment aspect.

While turning the *Volksgeist* into the principal moving force of national self-formation, being a loyal pupil of Leibniz, Herder always envisages the possibility of its extension into the *Welt* via the mediation of a particular *Umwelt*. Nationalism and cosmopolitanism are for him two facets of the same process: in *Ideas* he insisted that the idea of humanity is necessarily nationally colored, in *Letters on the Advancement of Humanity* (1793) he repeatedly laid emphasis on the unity of humankind. That is to say, he never neglected the manifold interconnections between national languages, as Schlegel would do, but left the door open for Goethe's forthcoming heterogenization of the national spirit. One must not forget, after all, that the processes of circulation, bifurcation and exchange of money, commodities and ideas constitute the fundamental anthropological paradigm of the second half of the eighteenth century. "The free circuit of ideas becomes the social ideal: the more self-induced the to-and-fro commerce of intellectual stimuli, the more illuminating a group." (Koch 2002: 55–56)

As an inexhaustible archive of collective memory, national language for Herder is an expandable nurturing source with flexible identity borders. This makes national identity formation an interminable task in which every individual is invited to enroll. Since every language is but a branch of the common tree of humankind, however, it connects any individual not just with its own *Volk*, but extends the links well beyond it into the endless labyrinths of humankind and – this is the point where Herder parts company with the French Enlightenment and Kant – *nature*. Herder conceives nature as an incessant process of growth and becoming that is reflected in each of its particles, confronting it with the task of steady development; its obligation is an active understanding of the given *Umwelt*, which is linked to the *Welt* by a sort of umbilical cord. Such understanding invents the *Welt* beyond the *Umwelt* paving the way for Hegel's *Weltgeist* as the ultimate horizon of the development of the *Volksgeist*. Herder, however, still uses the concept of nature in its place. All constitutive parts of nature are called upon to participate in its relentless re-invention, even though not all of them are capable to properly respond to that call. Yet nature is not so much hospitable as inimical to all its passive, inert and non-creative constituents, i.e. environments unwilling or unable to take control of themselves. This "filtering" dimension of Herder's cosmopolitan argument, taken up and further developed by Goethe, implies that every individual is rooted in his/her particular linguistic community; this community is for its part just a branch on the linguistic tree of humankind; whereas humankind itself draws its sustenance from the all-embracing and all-pervading power of nature (Barnard 1965: 25–53). The power of nature, thereupon transformed by Hegel into the *Weltgeist*, continuously differentiates its future-oriented *autological* subjects from its past-addicted *genealogical* subjects. This makes the "telluric communities" regrettable side effects rather than revivifying generators of this activity. If site in life implies sentencing to the past perfect tense or the waiting room of history, then Herder's regenerative approach rests on discrimination.

3.4 Resolving ambiguity, instituting difference

Schlegel restricts this abysmal cosmopolitan horizon, in a typically Romanticist way, to the horizon of a single national spirit. Cutting off limitless bifurcations and ramifications engendered by the unfathomable unifying power of nature (*Naturkraft*), he purposely narrows the scope of his literary history to facilitate the selection of materials, strengthen its structure, and enhance its inner connections (Dainat and Kruckis 1995: 125, 136). That is to say, he uses Herder's diversification of humankind into the multitude of self-regulating units to turn it, via Herder's equation of these units with particular national languages, literatures, and cultures, into the national pattern centered on the power of the "national spirit." Yet, as regards the process of *Bildung* that inheres in this pattern, Schlegel reiterates Herder's model of self-regulating unity-in-diversity (*Einheit in Vielfältigkeit*), representing the history of national literature as an analogously spontaneous overcoming of religious, cultural, and dialectal diversity by means of a single unifying principle. Owing to this eminently Herderian legacy, he cannot get rid of the ambiguity with regard to the final agency of unification: *is it original or back-projected?* On the one hand, Herder conceives of it as an internal force (*Kraft*), which is why it must be evaluated bottom-up, in each of its particular manifestations respectively, and not as a top-down regulating principle. On the other hand, unification becomes explicable only in terms of destinations, not origins; the discovery of purpose provides clues that disclose antecedents; the ends decide the relevance of the originating antecedents. For Herder, to put it in a nutshell, the purposive direction of nature consists in the unfolding actualization of something that is already there (Barnard 2003: 113). Yet what is "already there" in the past seems to have been put there (i.e. created, not only detected) by the present. Being thus constitutively dependent on its retrospective understanding, the profile of nature's unifying force turns out from the outset to be in compliance with the restrictive horizon of this hypothetic understanding – and therefore coercive, instead of egalitarian as proclaimed. The same goes for the unifying force of Schlegel's nation, shaped in the same fashion. Any constitutive part that does not comply with the retroactively declared national unity principle is subjected to correction, emendation, marginalization, and, in the last resort, exclusion.

The first such exclusion that Schlegel proposed in fact preceded his fashioning of national literature, preparing its forthcoming design. In *Concerning the Language and the Wisdom of Indians* (1808), this exclusion privileged the "noble Aryan community" of "organic languages" (Greek, Latin, German and English), taken to be the living seeds of growth and vitality of humankind, over the ignoble languages, thought to derive from Chinese, such as Slavic, American-Indian, or Japanese. The latter, atomized and lacking in depth, form a random community liable to be pulled asunder at any moment (1846: 302). Those languages, "blown together by the wind," do not form part of civilized world history. Therefore,

> the formerly postulated equal value [of languages, literatures and cultures] was transformed into the higher value which led to the thesis on the right of the German nation to take over the scepter of the *translatio studii*. In order to stake such claims, one needed the philosophical-historical reinterpretations that would make a cultural nursery of Europe out of a nation which appeared to have no character. (Fohrmann 1994: 585)

Such translations of defects into advantages, typical of all trauma narratives, usually bloom in times of bitter political disappointment; the German self-aggrandizement around 1800 is proportional to the feeling of inferiority that underpins it. "If Germans are thus proclaimed as *the* specialists for humanity (*das Menschheitliche*), then the next step is within reach, to see the others as superficial in the construction of the building of humanity. The rest of Europe is relegated to passive bystanders." (Koch 2002: 241) What therefore affiliates the German Romanticists' with the German and French Enlightenment's idea of literature is the common discriminating pattern of overcoming, rooted in the traumatic experience of wounded or humiliated identity. Even though the meaning of literary *Bildung* shifts from the education or cultivation of others in the Enlightenment to the formation or constitution of the self in Romanticism, the therapeutic imperative of overcoming, whether of the self or others, remains. By attempting to overcome my inferior self with my superior community, I am trying to heighten its competitiveness with respect to other communities that are meant to be overcome.

As Aleida Assmann (1993: 23) pointed out in her genealogy of the *Bildung* concept, the "reflected formation and taking hold of one's own life" (*bewusste Gestaltung und Ergreifung des eigenen Lebens*) remain germane to this project of European modernity throughout its history no matter whether it refers to the individual or the community. As mentioned above, Herder's *Volksgeist* is nothing but an adaptation of the French (and North American) triumphant individualist ideology to Germany's less than individualist society of the time. In lieu of rejecting individualism of its most fierce opponent, Herder surprisingly raises it to a higher level, i.e. transfers it "from the level of human individuals to the level of individual cultures or 'peoples'." Because of this maneuver, they are now considered as being equal to each other (Dumont 1994: 10). The principle of equality in Herder's teaching is applied to the relationship between nations and not between individuals. This is why *both* literary imperatives strive toward replacing the subordination of the self to the other with the relationship of their equality. In both its basic forms, the Enlightenment and the Romantic, modern literature is an essentially liberal, democratic, and egalitarian project.

Yet in order to liberate oneself – either in the collective form of *revolution* that gets rid of the despotic external other, or the individual form of *re-evolution* that disentangles the self from its internal otherness – one cannot but launch the imperative of overcoming the other. "Just as there is progressive radicalization in a revolution, [in the opposite German *Bildungsprojekt* of re-evolution, V.B.] we can detect a progressive reassertion of the collective identity." (Dumont 1994: 30) This explains the increasing propensity of the German Romanticist intellectuals to adopt an unprecedented intensifying of themselves. An educated man, proclaims Schlegel (1988: 154), must be able to transform him- or herself at any time to get rid of the provisional position he holds. Following the postulated ideal of the persistent shaping of oneself, the leading German intellectuals passionately strove to surpass and outdo each other, which ultimately entailed a kind of collective self-aggrandizement in the form of "a German equivalent of the French Revolution." Many of them, affected with the traumatically induced mania of *Selbststeigerung*, believed in the final instance that "Germany was called by a sort of birthright to dominate other peoples" (Dumont 1994: 23).

Though certainly not a direct continuation of his ideas, such a "perversion" of Herder's democratic *Bildungsprojekt* was by no means accidental; it followed from its highlighted equivocation as regards the power that dictates the *Bildung*. On the one hand, Herder insists on the primary genetic force of *Volksgeist*, but on the other interprets it as the resulting sum of the individual *Bildung* efforts undertaken in the long history of national spirit.

> To insist on the unchanging nature of genetic sources would have involved the denial of the (much-emphasized) dynamic of historical causation. To allow, on the other hand, for the complete changeability of genetic sources would have seriously threatened, if not invalidated, the notion of a persistent identity implied by the term "national character." (Barnard 2003: 123)

This internal equivocation has driven Herder's inheritors to split up his project. As a result, the "underdeveloped" nations have been expected to militate, doggedly sticking to their genuine tradition, against the peril of change; and the "developed" ones like Germany to choose relentless redirection, recreation, and innovation of tradition, injecting a continuous element of unpredictability and enhancing thereby their competitiveness. "Great literatures" were thus not only liberated from the "sacred duty" to respect continuity between ancestral intentions and descendants' implementations but in point of fact obliged to break anew this loyalty to enable the permanent rebirth and renewal of their nations. Their development was thus made possible at the price of stagnation of "small literatures" doomed to occupy the position of Fichte's *Nicht-Ich* against which the forward-pushing energy of *das Ich* had to be mobilized. It is "extraordinarily important" for a poet, states Hölderlin (1961: 264), "to take nothing as given [...] or positive." The task of great literatures was formulated as *ein immerwährendes Durchbrechen von festen Gehäusen* (Behler 1997: 112), i.e. a consistent tearing apart of the strongholds in which the small literatures have been sentenced to dwell. This rendering of the Western mission as an active negation of the otherness had an enormous impact on the further development of the Western self-representation:

> On key matters, the Hegelian, post-Hegelian, and Weberian traditions, philosophies of action and philosophies of deconstruction derived from Nietzsche and Heidegger, share the *representation of the distinction between the West and other historical human forms* as, largely, the way the individual in the West has gradually freed him/herself from the sway of traditions and attained an autonomous capacity to conceive [...] norms [...] by individual, rational wills. (Mbembe 2001: 10)

The rest of humanity was treated as the necessary material for this self-liberating negation of the otherness. This is why the modernizing of literature could not be a democratic undertaking without simultaneously being a coercive project, an insight hitherto mostly downplayed, neglected or repudiated. Literature's emancipating and coercive effects, owing to the compulsive reemergence of the one kind of effects in the other ran parallel since the establishment of its modern concept. Thus if we want to ameliorate the iterative acting out of the traumatic experience of prevented, suppressed, or frustrated identity, a consistent reintroduction of the division *between* the "opponents" *within* each of them respectively might be a better strategy than the simple blaming of the "opponent" for our frustration. We might not heal our traumatic experience but rather reinvigorate it if we just relegate it to the other by imposing upon him or her a consensus derived from the denial of such experience on our part. The uncompromising nature of the Western self had the counter-effect of reducing the discourse of non-Western selves to a simple polemical reaffirmation of Western sovereignty. The nativist passionate preoccupation with the native's originality and authenticity gave rise to a historiography that ultimately implemented the same statist agenda as its proclaimed opponent (Mamdani 2012: 87). Yet if we reintroduce the traumatic experience into both the agency and enabler, instead of repudiating it as they are prone to do, they turn out to be dispossessed by the other rather than sovereign in their action, which makes the division between them less traumatic and less in need of a violent consensual overcoming. Such diffusion of the dissensual traumatic experience into the agencies and values of the consensual political space is the task of the argumentative strategy taking side with "politics" against the "police."

4 Who Voices Universal History? Kant's "Mankind" and/or Herder's "Nature"

> One man's imagined community is another man's political prison.
> (Appadurai 1996: 32)

4.1 Introduction

The split in the body of the Enlightenment doctrine is usually traced back to the confrontation between its French and German versions. However established this opinion might be, it reduces the complexity of the problem. True, in the early treatise *Another Philosophy of History for the Education of Humankind* (1774) Herder, proposing his alternative conception of human history, elaborates on a *re-evolutionary* pattern in explicit opposition to Voltaire's and Boulanger's *revolutionary* pattern (1891: 15, 18). For Herder, the goal of human history is not a *break* with obedience to a despotic nature, but a gradual *reunion* with nature's generous patronage. Associating the French advocacy of self-governing humanity with the ruthless oppression of absolutist monarchies of the age, Herder raises nature to the agency of human emancipation from such unbearable pressures. But in putting nature in the former supreme position of humankind, Herder was not only countering French Enlighteners, he was also launching an indirect polemical attack on his compatriot and professor Kant. Herder was a life-long adherent of the "pre-critical" Kant represented in the latter's early work *Allgemeine Naturgeschichte und Theorie des Himmels* (1755), in which he argued the history of nature is in a permanent state of flux to which humans are also subjected (Beiser 1992: 193–194). But at the time of their parting company, Kant had already abandoned this "anachronous" natural history in favor of an enlightened critical philosophy based on human supremacy over nature. In an article published in 1765 in Diderot's and D'Alembert's *Encyclopedia*, Voltaire (1765: 220–221) declared the final victory of human over natural history and Kant was renowned for keeping up to date with the work of prominent French contemporaries. In a sense, therefore, Herder was defending the young "pre-critical" from the elder "critical" Kant. From the opposing perspective, while criticizing Herder's sweeping analogies between natural and human law presented in the first book of his *Ideas on the Philosophy of the History of Humankind*, Kant was struggling with his own youthful shadow (Kant 2006a: 201–221; Beiser 1992: 402n.). In the final account of these curiously crisscrossed commitments, while both subscribe to the project of human emancipation from its suppressor, Kant links it to human's responsibility toward *humankind*, whereas Herder connects it to human's constitutive obligation to *nature*.

In the following I propose that this literary-philosophical debate at the turning point of Western modernity reflects a specific traumatic constellation as the birthplace of modernity's project of humanity's secular reconstitution. It points to the fissure in the very origin of European democracy, whose re-emergence will on the one hand hinder the latter's progress and on the other instantiate various operations expected to eliminate this hindrance. To clear the way for the establishment of the sovereign political agency, these operations suppressed the constitutive gap between "speaking individuals" or persons on the one hand and "speechless animals" or misfits on the other, i.e. obliterated the split between the *agencies* and *enablers* inherent to the European project of democracy from its very beginning.

> Ever since its original judicial performance, personhood is valuable exactly to the extent to which it is not applicable to all [...] Only if there are men (and women) who are not completely, or not at all, considered persons, can others be or become such. [...] [T]he process of personalization coincides [...] with the depersonalization or reification of others. (Esposito 2011: 209)

Political agency – the pillar of democracy – is concomitantly inextricably co-articulated with its non-eliminable enabler that puts a demand upon it, making it responsible for dispossession. This uneasy relationship of the *agencies* and *enablers* induces an "anarchic traumatism" (Levinas 1974: 194) laid in the very foundation of democracy. But although agencies ought to take into account this unwilled cohabitation with the "unnamable" beyond their distinctive sphere of belonging (Butler 2012: 23–24), they prefer to turn away from this obligation. Denying their responsibility for the defaced and dispossessed, they claim sovereignty instead.

However contested the sharing of the common has remained from its Greek beginnings to this day, and however appallingly the enablers called their agencies to account for its traumatic effects, both contestation and responsibility were systematically obfuscated by agencies. "Imparity" is democracy's "essential part" (Rancière 1995: 102), but so is its denial. This obstinate disavowal of the exclusion of "the mutes" from the public space characterizes not only political practice but also political philosophy. Both interpret politics as a dialogic search for consensus superimposing in such a way common law upon the original division (Rancière 2001: 15, 1995: 88). Yet consensus cannot cure the disease that it produces (1995: 104, 106). On the contrary, in the very healing of the "disease," consensual "policing" perpetuates, reinforces and rigidifies it. The borderline at which the One meets the Many is the shared brink of the abyss rather than the common agora. It gives way to an *ethical-political encounter* that, by interrupting and displacing identities, persistently induces traumatic experiences instead of harmony. Obstinately refusing to face its true figure, the invisible terror of the consensual One mobilizes the visible terrorism of its inevitable remains. This is why operations that were designed to suspend the stubbornly resurfacing bifurcation in the envisaged democratic community simultaneously contributed to its reenactment. "[T]he community of equals can never achieve substantial form as a social institution. It is tied to the act of its own verification, which is forever in need of reiteration." (84) The passion for unity induces the desire for war. In lieu of tolerance for all involved parties, it meets "the irregulability of the primal horror, the irregulability of the hatred and dread, the pure rejection of the other" (24).

As if summarizing such a paradoxical development – shortly after the repressed European colonialist legacy had experienced its boomerang effect in the Nazi genocide (Césaire 1950 [2000]: 36) – Hannah Arendt (1951 [1979]) dismantled European democracy as a consistent, systemic exemption of the "non-proper people" from what had been declared general human rights. To translate this traumatic outcome of all concensual policies in the terms of the debate between Kant and Herder: Whichever of the two proposed principles was implemented to extend the scope of included historical agencies by instantiating equality among them, Kant's "mankind" or Herder's "nature," it could not but perpetuate the production of the denied non-historical enablers. The traumatic rift *between* humankind and nature was thus reproduced *within* each of them, spawning their internal agencies and enablers. The missed ethical-political encounter thus irritatingly resurfaced.

Hegel's world history, raising Kant's "mankind" to the supreme *Geist*, aimed at the promotion of an even more encompassing democracy but equally ignored the imparity constitutive to it. In sum, as soon as the dissensual concept of *politics* was replaced by the consensual concept of *history* – and precisely this is what happens at the end of the eighteenth century – freedom was banished from the public space of common human affairs to the private space of leisure. History locates freedom "neither in the acting and moving human being nor between humans, but transfers it to the process that takes place behind the backs of acting humans operating conspicuously beyond the visible space of public affairs" (Arendt 2010: 43). The human becomes captured by the current of history, which turns him or her into a mere constituent of its progression and acceleration, pure means to higher ends. This imposition of the consensual horizon eliminates his or her judgmental dignity, thus bereaving the human of its fundamental ability to escape imposed strictures by taking up an external standpoint (Arendt 1992: 9). What makes the idea of world history monstrous, says Arendt, is that it compresses the irreducible multitude of people into *one* human individual (2010: 12) or one imperial principle for that matter. Operating as a strategy of containment, selection and exclusion performed in the name of a higher necessity, it erases the mutuality, dependence, arbitrariness and contingency of human existence or, in the last instance, its freedom (Guha

2002: 46–47). All alternative representations of the past must unquestionably bow to the new master.

Forcing its subjects into guilt for not being able to meet the requirements of progress, history reintroduces violence it claims to have overcome through its equality. Passing its judgments upon these subjects, it transfers on them the entire responsibility as if their sufferings were caused by their own deeds rather than the imposition of its law. Yet how can something that is by itself illegitimate, instituted by an arbitrary act, pretend to legitimize everything else? Arguing that judgment does not occur in history, Levinas (1990a: 23) underpins Arendt's critique of history. Far from being guided by the hand of God, the historical sequence of events is mindless, blind and indifferent in its strikes. Finally, in his "Theses on the Philosophy of History," Benjamin also states that waiting for justice cannot be fulfilled in historical time. On the contrary, by pushing into oblivion its victims it shuts the door for justice. The universality of historical reason, insistently claimed in the Greek philosophical tradition, spawns innumerable atrocities from the Jewish philosophical perspective.

This explains why both humankind and nature as history's uniting principles, designed to democratically expand its responsibility, systematically produced their "subalterns" prevented from becoming legible within the established space of the political.

> [T]he spaces, the liberties, and the rights won by individuals, in their conflict with central powers always simultaneously prepared a tacit but increasing inscription of individuals' lives within the state order, thus offering a new and more dreadful foundation for the very sovereign power from which they wanted to liberate themselves. (Agamben 1998: 121)

If we want to understand the regular violent resurgence of the dreadfully silenced enablers amidst today's liberal democracy, we must expose history's obliteration of the disconcerting ethical encounter. Democracy pertains to the *many*, the contradictory *in-between* created by these many, which is why humankind, contrary to what happens in Kant's and Herder's world history, is not to be reduced to a single Man shaped according to a divine model (Arendt 2010: 119). Against the policy of dissolution of the fundamental disagreement, which, on the consensual basis of these two seemingly opposite cosmopolitan projects, traces forthcoming globalization, the democratic conflict has to be readdressed, reaffirmed and reinstated. "Politics always involves one people superadded to another, one people against another." (Rancière 2010: 85) Because it subsumes political dissensus under consensus as history's alleged common denominator, the apparently generous cosmopolitan pacification of divisions that underlies both path-breaking projects in question will be in the following consistently dismantled as a mission destined to aggravate a given state of affairs.

In order for politics to remain a permanent litigation between two irreconcilable terms, as both Arendt and Rancière, despite the discordances between them, rightly insist it is, the suspension of the agency's uneasy cohabitation with the dispossessed and dispossessing alterity must confront our active disagreement. Its smooth perpetuation perverts into a "democratic despotism" (Rancière 2006: 20). Contrary to the usual understanding of democracy as the best available "political regime," I will conceive it in the following as an untiring exposition of the disquieting frontier between the agencies and enablers. Democracy is a permanent *practice of highlighting the denial* inherent in its political representation rather than a given or desired *state order*. The disagreement between two parties does not *precede* the problem-solving establishment of the democratic state but *follows* it (Rancière 1999: 27). Hence the ethical encounter is inalienably co-articulated with the political and cannot be "efficiently absolved" in favor of an "indivisible democracy." Doomed to share its earthly place with the destitute enabler, political agency is interrupted and dispossessed by its claim. Time and again, it has to wrestle with this "diasporic injection" which traverses the historical sequence of events by escaping all efforts at adoption and assimilation.

With regard to this essentially recommencing character of democracy, i.e., the fact that democratic "succession" implies unpredictable irruptions, Rancière seems to be in fundamental agreement with Arendt despite his repeated critiques aimed at her political philosophy (Abensour 2011: 34, 41). Underlining the frequently neglected Arendtian character of Rancière's thought, Schaap defines democracy as a persistent enacting of the right to have rights (Schaap 2011). Since by its very definition it can never be truly *accomplished*, democracy has to be continuously *implemented*, creating possibilities for the emergence of new forms of participation, new accommodations and, concomitantly, new agencies. Implementing it means untiringly opening the public space up to the new beginning, i.e. to its suppressed otherwise and missed possibilities.

According to the discussion conducted since Arendt's identification of the origins of totalitarianism in Western representative democracy, the perpetuation of exclusion in the project of modernity gradually produced "an effect of apartheid, in flagrant contradiction with the ambition of constituting a democratic model on the continental and world scale. [...] It seems that the constitution of a permanently inferior position in the hierarchical structure of Europe cannot be excluded." (Balibar 2004: 43–44) As the Latin American philosopher Enrique Dussel (1998: 17) put it, "[t]he crisis of modernity [...] refers to internal aspects of Europe. The peripheral world would appear to be a passive spectator of a thematic that does not touch it, because it is 'a barbarian', a 'pre-modern', or, simply, still in need of being 'modernized'." However, the derogating attributes of "barbarity" and "pre-modernity" were repeatedly allocated not just to the non-European *colonial* "periphery" but also, in the form of *imperial difference*, to the inner-European dispossessed enablers. Both "borderlands" were apparently situated beyond the horizon of metropolitan visibility, which is why even the most far-sighted Northwestern Europeans were oblivious to violent exploitation as the premise of their own well-being. Constitutively prevented from grasping "the way the system functions as a whole," they were doomed to a blindness which "no enlargement of personal experience [...] no intensity of self-examination" was able to overcome (Jameson 1990: 51).

Yet once the postcolonial and post-imperial dispossessed enablers entered the very center of the European scene, migrating into the former colonial or imperial metropolises, they prevented the comfortable perseverance of such a blind spot. "What Mexico is to the United States and Maghreb is to France, the South and East of Europe (Turks, Yugoslavians, and now East Germans, *Aussiedler* from Russia and Poles) is to Germany and Austria." (Hassner 1991: 21 as quoted by Balibar 2004: 255n) If read today from these diverse but affiliated subaltern perspectives of the dispersed yet interconnected enablers and victims of the colonial and imperial difference,[1] modernity's intellectual pillars Kant and Herder appear to have met in the exclusionary structure of the envisaged harmony even if they openly disagreed on the latter's profile. Laying new foundations for the forthcoming democratic political order amid the traumatic constellation of their political space toward the end of the eighteenth century, both thinkers spontaneously translated the Renaissance *colonial* technique of *religious universalism* into the Enlightenment *imperial* technique. If the first was directed against the heretic non-Europeans, the second was disdainful of the benighted Europeans. Instead of being overcome as was envisaged, discrimination reemerged. This happened because both Kant and Herder, one or another way, took normative recourse in universal history, assimilating everything into its consensually imposed continuous stream. Yet "[t]he point is not to convert the inassimilable into the assimilable, but to challenge those regimes that require assimilation into their own norms. Only when those norms break apart does universalization have a chance to renew itself within a radically democratic project" (Butler 2012: 23).

Comparing these two modernist techniques of human unification-through-polarization and keeping in mind that the triumph of Christianity was buttressed

---

[1] Mignolo (2000: 765) distinguishes between globalization from above and globalization from below or "diversality": "If you can imagine Western civilization as a large circle with a series of satellite circles intersecting the larger one but disconnected from each other, diversality will be the project that connects the diverse subaltern satellites appropriating and transforming Western global designs. [...] A cosmopolitanism that only connects from the center of the large circle outward, and leaves the outer places disconnected from each other, would be a cosmopolitanism from above ..." I will return to that important suggestion in the Epilogue.

by the expulsion of Moors and Jews from the Iberian Peninsula as well as the enslavement of Africans and Amerindians, we could speak, rather than of a decisive break, of two different faces of the same European imaginary (Mignolo 2000: 730). One should recall that, while religious universalism was suspending the discriminating attitude of telluric communities overcoming their intolerance, it simultaneously required a strict separation of "proper" (i.e., Christian) from "improper" (i.e., non-Christian) loyalties as well as an irrevocable abandonment of "false gods" (Douzinas 2007: 91). In such a way it established the colonial difference as the historical foundation of modernity (Mignolo 2000: 725) that was thereupon translated into imperial terms. This explains why Kant's and Herder's political cosmopolitanism, instead of resolutely breaking with the "telluric mentality" or exclusionist religious universalism for that matter, as it had proclaimed to be doing, tacitly reapplied their discriminating parameters by introducing imperial difference. In the very act of relinquishing the forerunners – the definite rupture with the despotic past having been, as is known, the distinctive emblem of modernity – it surreptitiously realigned itself with them. Modern political cosmopolitanism thus underwent "pollution" by something that for hygienic reasons, it intended to keep at bay. Despite the reemergence of oppositions in the development of modern European democracy, such as those between religious and political terms or between humankind and nature for that matter, in relegating all the harm to their counterparts, none of the oponents managed to liberate themselves from their internal equivocation. The latter doggedly persevered. I interpret this obstinate resurgence of the schism amid the agencies as well as enablers as a direct corollary of its consistent erasure.

4.2 Kant's advocacy of mankind

No wonder then that, despite contrary proclamations, in the German Enlightenment the concept of the human *race* (*Menschenrasse*), still clearly associated with universal *ratio* located in God's mind (Apter 2006: 32), was characterized by divine attributes. Although at the time religion was proudly rejected as a superstition to be overcome if humankind was to achieve maturity, the very idea of the human gradually maturing on his own transfers divine ratio onto the "great chain of being" or, in Kant's rendering, the "series of generations" (*Reihe der Zeugungen*).[2] Kant introduces the historical agency of mankind in order to emancipate man from

---

[2] In the following argument I will be selectively drawing on the theses presented in Biti 2011. I will deliberately use "mankind," "man" and "he" to draw attention to Kant's unconcernedly masculine reasoning (much more understandable at that time of course, considering the political

his basically "animal" natural disposition (*Naturanlage*) epitomized by the obedience to lower, bodily drives. Man, being by his disposition an animal in need of a master (Kant 2006a: 46), as Kant significantly formulates in the treatise *Idea for a Universal History with a Cosmopolitan Purpose* (1784), is only ready to willingly pursue the laborious task of consistent use of his reason in exceptional circumstances (44). Speaking of exceptions, Kant actually means Western European adult males. If history were delivered to man's naturally inborn base and selfish goals, it would amount to a "senseless course" (42) of devastation, upheavals and the complete exhaustion of human powers (47). "For each of them will always misuse his freedom if he does not have anyone above him to apply force to him as the laws should require it." (46) Kant's expectation, however, is that the united world society looming large on the horizon of his age will prevent citizens from living such an inappropriate, animally blind life by subjecting them to the "condition of compulsion" (46, trans. modified, *Zustand des Zwanges*) or the pressure of historical necessity. By his natural disposition constructed from "warped wood," man needs mankind "to break his self-will and force him to obey a universally valid will under which everyone can be free." (46) If he were not compelled to obey this supreme general agency, he would be destroyed by his essentially selfish and hostile nature, instead of developing the ability to reason that distinguishes him from animals. For Kant, the natural disposition is, in a word, a wild compulsive force that has to be domesticated through a patient self-overcoming of man under the custody of mankind.

The difficulty that Kant's argument must face is, however, that man's self-willingness, envisaged by mankind as disciplined, characterizes the very agency expected to carry out his emancipation. The agency called upon to supervise man's long journey to final freedom displays, in Kant's rendering, significantly coercive traits. Kant claims that nothing but the hard pressure of universal history can force man to give up the comfortable condition of concord (*Eintracht*), self-sufficiency (*Selbstgenügsamkeit*), and mutual love (*Wechselliebe*) characteristic of his familiar community (45).³ In order to qualify for the prestigious status of the world citizen

---

and ideological circumstances, although significant for precisely that reason) which explicitly excludes women from the realm of self-governed citizens who enjoy the vote. We should be aware that Schiller's inaugural lecture at the University of Jena (1789) was delivered for an exclusively male audience, as females were strictly forbidden to participate in higher education.

3 In his influential reading of Kant's closely related essay *What is Enlightenment?* composed in the same year (1784), Michel Foucault downplays the moment of pressure in order to promote his own "revolutionary" argument. By highlighting in the freedom to disobey put forth by Kant in this essay, the (French) revolutionary attitude of "voluntary inservitude" (1996: 386), Foucault neglects the key presupposition of this freedom, namely the acceptance of bondage to the master instance of universal history.

(*Weltbürger*) man is now expected to reflect his historical engagement from the cosmopolitan viewpoint, instead of blindly engaging in the given course of events as the state citizen (*Staatsbürger*) would. In Kant's vision, the cosmopolitan imperative that beckons man out of the entirety of mankind relegates the national imperative of his fellow state citizens addressing him from the present political community to second-class status. The hierarchy is clear: Man's *universal moral duty* pertains to the demands of universal history while a citizen's *restricted political duty* pertains to the historical demands of a particular community. The urge of geographically, culturally and historically distant human beings gets the upper hand over the call addressed to man by his immediate fellow citizens. The *cosmopolitan commitment* figures as the crucial proof of human maturity, entreating man – those worthy of the name, which excludes women, children, slaves, and barbarians – to transgress the constraints of his familiar community. Now, was not the same universal claim raised by the Christian community which, subjecting people to God's transcendent law, produced ecumenical uniformity and equality out of national and cultural diversity and differences (Badiou 2003: 109)? If this Kantian cosmopolitan "law is given by higher authority but is willed by us, isn't this the secular version of Christianity" (Douzinas 2007: 94)? Is not Kant in this manner surreptitiously reintroducing into Enlightenment the colonial difference established by the Renaissance *orbis universalis christianus* (Mignolo 2000: 725–726)?

Thus when man avails himself of the freedom to disobey his fellow citizens at the cost of being regarded as unsociable (Kant 2006a: 45–46), this is not just a matter of his free individual choice, but rather an act of subordination to universal law. Kant clearly sets his stakes: "All the culture and art which adorn mankind and the finest social order man creates are fruits of his unsociability (46)." In such a way he raises the universal history of mankind to the master instance expected "to break [man's] self-will and force him to obey a universally valid will under which anyone can be free (46)." Contrary to Foucault's influential reading which recognizes in Kant's cosmopolitan attitude the individual will to revolution, Kant's argument implies that man's cosmopolitan *freedom* follows from the acceptance of *bondage* to the supreme authority of universal history. For Kant, the same obligation of surrendering to the hypothetical "supreme touchstone of truth" also holds for an enlightened scholar. Recurring in his philosophy from *Critique of Practical Reason* to *Anthropology from a Pragmatic Point of View*,[4] this *Probierstein der Wahrheit* refers to the scholar's persistent obligation to test the intrinsic value of his judgments in the pluralism of the public arena. Without such a *criterium veritatis externum*, as Kant calls it in the *Anthropology*, he would not necessarily be-

---

[4] See Kant 1956: 65, where *Probierstein* is translated as "criterion," and Kant 2006b: 17, 113, etc.

come prey to serious delusions, but his judgments would be restricted and biased, rather than general and impartial, this being the aim of such a horizon-widening dialogic self-interrogation. However, as both Arendt (1992: 43) and Lyotard (1991: 224) cautioned in their readings of Kant, this cosmopolitan "public arena" is not something that can be present or available in any way. It is a constitutively absent, imagined world audience (*Weltpublikum*) established to justify the disinterestedness and impartiality of Kant's own philosophical standpoint.[5] It is a godlike instance (i.e. observes individuals in the impartial and all-inclusive way only God, "the omniscient knower of the heart" (*der Herzenskundige*) is apparently able to (Arendt 1992: 49–50)), a hypothesis which is impossible to prove and closely related to the faculty of imagination (*Einbildungskraft*). Kant's reason appears to be concealing an irrational myth that lies at its very heart, which might account for its hideously terrorist character (Dussel 1993: 66). Therefore there is always the danger "that we run of irresponsibly simplifying natural mechanisms by determinedly enforcing an imagined and desired unity. Reason both complies and commands" (Morgan 2000: 122). More accurately, it commands by complying.

In such a way, the allegedly unbound individual freedom of reasoning appears to be from the very beginning disciplined by a hypothetical, improvable authority of humankind as the basic condition of its possibility. In this connection one is tempted to recall Levinas's conclusion from his *Reflections on the Philosophy of Hitlerism* (1990b: 69): "Man's essence no longer lies in freedom, but in a kind of bondage [...] the ineluctable original chain ..." The association of Kant's argument with Hitlerism might be overstated here, as Kant is obviously not to be treated as an avatar of Nazism. I certainly do not want to raise such an absurd claim. Yet the association serves as a welcome reminder that Hitlerism takes to a horrible extreme Kant's covertly *religious demand* that man "obey a universally valid will under which everyone can be free" (2006a: 46). Such a freedom obviously implies bondage. It was the same unquestioned surrendering to such a will that, certainly in a grotesque distortion and an inappropriate reversal of argument, engendered the fascist ideology of kinship solidarity and territorial belonging-together. What distinguishes radical cosmopolitanism from radical nationalism is the kind of hypothetical "chain" each of them surrenders to, and which is clearly far from irrelevant in the final outcome. But the enchainment itself is inherent to both of them.

---

5 In her *Lectures on Kant's Political Philosophy*, Arendt (1992: 43) connects the dialogic extension of one's judgment with the faculty of imagination by pointing to § 40 of the *Critique of Judgment*. In it Kant states the obligation of every enlightened man to compare his judgments not only with the actual, but also merely possible judgments of other people by putting himself in the place of any other man. She also points out the division between the impartial observer and the interested agents of history which results from the insistence on this obligation (44, 52).

Emancipation therefore characterizes the emergence of modern man only in a firm pairing with despotism. In fact, Kant himself discovered the tight entanglement of these two seemingly irreconcilable realms even before he articulated the argument of his late political writings. The disobedience of the individual to the community and the resistance of the present to the past, the two essential features of his later famous injunction *Sapere aude!*, are already inherent in his former and fundamental concept of *critique* rendered as a consistent implementation of reason. If in pre-modern times power tacitly exempted itself from the competence of reason, with the rise of modernity a reversal was taking place. Reason exempted itself from power in order to operate on its own terms. As Agamben (2005a: 24) reminds us, during the Middle Ages self-exemption was the exclusive domain of the despotic sovereign. Only from modernity onwards has it been integrated into the individual competence of each citizen in her or his everyday behavior. Gradually, everybody became authorized to criticize. In 1765, Diderot unreservedly states that everything is submitted to the law of critique, including the sovereign himself (Koselleck 1973: 89, 97). Kant's somewhat later proud intellectual imperative addressed at every responsible individual in the *Critique of Pure Reason* – "Our age is the genuine age of *critique*, to which everything must submit" (1998: 100–101, translation slightly modified: *Unser Zeitalter ist das eigentliche Zeitalter der Kritik, der sich alles unterwerfen muss* (1969: 12n)) – is a continuation of the same tendency.

This is how modern democracy translated pre-political self-willing despotism into its regulated political terms. Eliminated from the central position of power, despotism was accommodated to the circumstances of a democratically multiplied empowerment of citizens. Having been uncoupled from the whimsical sovereign as its bearer, it was turned into the *distinctive feature of reasoning of every individual*. Each single act of reflection was challenged to declare its independence from given circumstances, or to use the register of reason in order to defy the register of power. Hence if in pre-modern time power was authorized to exempt itself from the competence of reason, in modern times reason was authorized to exempt itself from the competence of power by taking a necessarily *arbitrary recourse to the hypothetical authority of humankind*. Yet it is exactly this arbitrary self-empowerment of reason that testifies to its constitutive involvement with the same despotic power it was declared to be firmly defied.

This subtle argument on the entanglement of reason and power, or political emancipation and pre-political despotism for that matter, continues in the paragraphs of *Critique of Judgment* devoted to aesthetic judgment. To understand their co-implication in the very idea of modernity, Kant's analysis of aesthetic judgment is indispensable, as it lays down the law of the modern self in exemplary manner. Even though Foucault, at the time of his investigation into governmentality, recognized that in Kant's interpretation reason is at once despotic and enlightening (2001a: 1587), he skipped this important prehistory of Kant's political writings, which resulted in their one-dimensional interpretation adapted to the purposes of a French internal intellectual debate.[6] Besides, the philosophical persistence of Kant's thought vanishes from the horizon. Foucault interprets the "political" Kant as having implied that reason, instead of just opposing man's immature obedience to an external political instance, acknowledges immaturity as something inherent in itself. Reason consequently does not simply defy external obedience to power, as the Enlightenment from the nineteenth century onwards is usually taken to have claimed, but has always included this obedience in its own operations. In such a way a *stark opposition* between reason and power is replaced by their *mutual implication*. Accordingly, to become critical, reason is supposed to reflect its own internal resistance to critique forever anew; since, if it is continuously oriented just against an external authority, reason itself inadvertently turns into power (Foucault 1996: 387). Reason can reach an emancipating effect only on condition of liberating itself from its own internal constraints (Foucault 2001c: 433), i.e. of introducing the *principle of a consistent self-overcoming* to its operations. What remains to be seen is, however, whether this individual self-overcoming, celebrated by Foucault in his "ethical phase" from 1978 onwards as the only true emancipating operation of the modern self, is not already expounded upon in Kant's *Critique of Judgment* as an unexpected enslavement to go with the envisaged liberation. Significantly, Foucault also skips this perseverance of enslavement at the heart of liberation, in his unliteral rendering of governmentality that represents the latter as the deactivator of sovereignty.[7]

Let us turn to *Critique of Judgment* then to examine Kant's rendering of the problem more attentively. Trying to specify the *reflective* aesthetic judgment in the fourth paragraph of the Introduction (15–16), Kant depicts it as unpredictably searching for an unknown *universal* law of its validity through an interminable series of unsatisfactory individual identifications of a work of art. He opposes this kind of judgment to the *determining* logical judgment that comfortably relies on collectively verified *transcendental* law (see also § 6–7; 21–27). What he namely calls "beautiful (or fine) art" (as opposed both to the "mechanical" and "agree-

---

[6] "La raison à la fois comme despotisme et comme lumière," reads the sentence in *La vie* which is actually Foucault's last authorized paper. But this sentence in the *Introduction*, composed in 1978, is more compressed: "La raison, comme lumière despotique." (2001c: 435) One should bear in mind, of course, that in the French tradition established by Montesquieu, Voltaire and Boulanger, Oriental despotism is considered to be the chief enemy of Western Enlightenment. By coupling them in such an inextricable way, Foucault clearly opposes this powerful tradition too.

[7] For a more elaborate critique of Foucault's rendering of governmentality, see ch. 12.

able" one, § 4) cannot be determined by any transcendental law because it emerges as a product of the genius who makes his own law through it (§ 46; 136–137). Although this latter law initially lacks any validity, it claims it from the forthcoming course of judgment in which it is reflected (§ 44; 134–135) *as if* it were valid for everybody (i.e. as if recipients of beautiful or fine art thereby perform a *logical* judgment even though it is merely an *aesthetic* one, § 4; 15–16). Such a quasi-logical character pending between power and reason, disengaging the one from the other, is absolutely genuine to aesthetic judgment, unlike logical judgment, which unconcernedly implements power.

Kant is aware that such reflection requires a considerable effort, but it is in the very nature of beautiful or fine art to mobilize the *reason* of its addressees instead of merely making their *senses* obey (§ 44). Fine art is essentially connected with reasoning (unlike *agreeable* art, which simply pleases the senses of its recipients), but this is reasoning of a special, disinterested kind (unlike *mechanical* art, which addresses an interested reasoning). If it is, in a word, proper, art mobilizes reason by disengaging its given form, which operates under the spell of power (§ 46). The paradoxical effect of what Kant represents as exemplary fine art could therefore be described as *mobilization of reason through a deactivation of its power-related application*. Through a successive self-exemption from applying any of the available logical laws, exemplary art uncovers its own law as something to be followed exactly in its *unprecedented inapplicability* (§ 46). As its rule cannot serve as a precept, it cannot be (deliberately) *imitated* but only (blindly) *followed* (138–139). By freeing reason of its addressees from unconsciously imposed *ordinary* laws, it powerfully imposes upon them an *extraordinary* law that applies to nothing else but itself. This operation of an absolute but arbitrary self-empowerment by a systematic disempowerment of all pre-given laws is what Kant aims at with his "purposeless purposiveness": a completely self-referential law of art that demands *blind trust* if it is to perform its emancipating function.

In the political writings that followed, Kant extended this systematic operation of self-exemption to the constitution of the supreme authority of mankind. Mankind is empowered through the disempowerment of all "lower" kind of communities, thereby urging an almost *sacrificial loyalty of its subjects*. The same ascetism characterized the "disinterested reasoning" (§ 46) of a highly qualified aesthetic recipient. To recall, in *Critique of Judgment* this kind of reasoning requires a considerable effort, even on the part of the "transcendental philosopher" (§ 8; 45). The uncultivated, narrow-minded and mistrustful "creatures" locked in their pettiness hardly ever care about such distant, abstract and hypothetic unities. They are rather established by the so-called fine souls, and the more obstinately so, the more arbitrary these invented unities appear to be. Moreover, the more obstinate such loyalty to the *superhuman* unity of mankind would seem, the more discrimination of the *subhuman* mass of "savages" by the select "fine souls" it produces. The one invokes the other. "[T]he process of personalization coincides [...] with the depersonalization or reification of others." (Esposito 2011: 209)

Hence Kant's subtle argument operates with two problematic hypotheses. With regard to the first hypothesis, i.e., mankind, Lévi-Strauss's following retrospective observation deserves serious consideration:

> The concept of an all-inclusive humanity, which makes no distinction between races or cultures, appeared very late in the history of mankind and did not spread very widely across the globe. What is more, as proved by recent events, even in one region where it seems most developed, it has not escaped periods of regression and ambiguity. For the majority of the human species, and for ten thousands of years, the idea that humanity includes every human being on the face of the earth does not exist at all. (Lévi-Strauss 1983: 329)

As for the second hypothesis, i.e. "savages," at the end of the eighteenth century knowledge about them was very sparse, conjectural and unreliable. Kant's "idol" Rousseau (1986: 175–176) leveled accusations at the whole genre of travel literature written by sailors, merchants, soldiers, and reverends, who deliver dilettante and distorted reports of European "others." These are mostly pure inventions disconnected from the empirical truth. As Williams Dickson thereupon complained in his *Letters on Negro Slavery* (1790), such invented tales were dangerously close to ambitious scientific treatises. "The travel literature, often a by-product of other activities such as trade, war or missions, offered curious and extraordinary, as well as exemplary and instructive, tales for the pleasure and entertainment of the reading public." (Sebastiani 2000: 200) Collecting his knowledge on "savages" from travelogues, light fiction, the exotic stories of explorers, missionaries, and fortune seekers as well as conversations with merchants, sailors, and adventurers in the Königsberg seaport (Eze 1995: 230),[8] Kant admits that his shrewd speculations on the beginnings of human history, based on scarce evidence, are of a vaguely conjectural character. "[T]he journey on which I am about to venture is no more than a pleasure trip..." (2006a: 221)

So it is possible that the persistent evasiveness of both of these hypotheses, of rational mankind in the supposed future and the irrational "savage" in the supposed past, accounts for their tight interrelatedness in Kant's thought. The one, superhuman, continuously invokes the other, subhuman, as its secret prerequi-

---

[8] In a significant footnote to the Preface of his *Anthropology* (2006b: 4) Kant states that Königsberg, "a city which by way of rivers, has the advantages of commerce both with the interior of the country and with neighboring and distant lands of different languages and customs, can well be taken as an appropriate place for broadening one's knowledge of human beings as well as of the world, where this knowledge can be acquired without even travelling."

site condition until Kant, seemingly irritated by their deep mutual dependence, finally decides to oppose these two "phantoms" to one another. To render the resulting polarization of human species in Rousseau's terms, which are of course close to Kant's argument, the "phantom" of *human nature* opposes the "phantom" of the *natural human*. The latter "creatures," essentially being disqualified to take up the laborious task (2006a: 44; *mühseliges Geschäfte* (1985: 25)) of the commitment to human nature, behave like "animals in need of a master" (2006a: 46; *ein Tier, das einen Herr nötig hat* (1985: 28)) which is why they cannot be regarded as proper humans. The degree of this animal submissiveness depends of course on the race in question but the animalization of a considerable part of humanity is an indispensable consequence of Kant's entire philosophy and not just his "less-than-philosophical" anthropology. As Foucault (2008a) has convincingly demonstrated and as I have tried to argue, Kant's anthropology forms an organic part of his entire philosophy and especially of his cosmopolitan project. Whoever bypasses it by departing from his critiques or "post-critical" writings misses colonial, imperial and gender difference as its constitutive feature.

Kant in fact systematically opts for a differentiation within the body of mankind that, first of all, derogates the so-called ordinary man: "Nothing straight can be constructed from such warped wood as that which man is made of" (2006a: 46; *[A]us so krummem Holze, als woraus der Mensh gemacht ist, kann nichts ganz Gerades gezimmert werden* (1985: 29)). In addition to ordinary men, he also treats women and children as animal-like dependents in both senses of the word: they need a master to *support* as well as *guide* them.[9] Animal-like beings, devoid of the ability to reason, cannot stand or speak for themselves; they have to be taken care of, to be represented. Accordingly, in the treatise *On the Use of Teleological Principles in Philosophy* (1788) Kant classifies human races according to their dependence on the long-term bodily lineage. As European races are considered to be free moral agents primarily determined by reason, he makes the physiological body the repository solely of the non-European racial identity. Possessing all forces and talents as well as the capability of unlimited progress, Europeans set the ideal model of universal humanity (Eze 1995: 203–204, 216). As he stated in his *Physical Geography*: "Humanity is at its greatest perfection in the race of the whites. The yellow Indians do have a meagre talent, the Negroes are far below them and at the lowest point are a part of the American peoples." (Kant 1997b: 63) Unlike Europeans,

---

[9] The American translation of his treatise *On the Common Saying* considerably softens his contention that the "natural qualification" of the citizen consists in "not being a child, a woman", *dass es kein Kind, kein Weib sei* (1985: 143), rendering it as "apart, of course, from being an adult male" (2006a: 78). As an admirer of Rousseau, Kant was rather close to his predominantly masculine worldview (Eze 1995).

none of these three "lowest human races" can continue to grow in intelligence (63–4). This explains why Blacks or Indians remain "loiterers" (*Umtreiber*) even after moving to Europe, where people are "naturally diligent" (*emsig*, i.e. behaving like ants, *Emsen*) or enduringly driven to activity (2006a: 104). Kant remarks in a typical association of the non-European with the European animal-like human beings (Sebastiani 2000: 223–225)[10] that, like "Gypsies" among us, Blacks abandon any proper work as soon as they are set free from slavery. As he stunningly formulates, they give up even the easy handicraft they were previously forced to perform as slaves (2006a: 104; *ein leichtes Handwerk, welches sie vormals als Sklaven zu treiben gezwungen waren*). If the American Indians are completely bereft of all talents and cannot be educated, the "Negroes" underlie education, yet only through physical coercion and corporal punishment (Eze 1995: 215). They are namely "so talkative that they must be driven apart from each other with thrashings" (Kant 1960: 111).[11] No wonder, as if a "fellow" is "quite black from head to foot," this is "a clear proof that what he said was stupid" (Kant 1997a: 57).

In sum, it is precisely through the unifying movement of mankind that a clear hierarchy is established among human races related to the degree of their independence from their bodily heritage. Having been consistently resilient to racially engendered restrictions, says Kant, only European nations have unremittingly exempted themselves from them. They are therefore associated with the *mobile mind* as opposed to the *inert body* associated with non-European races. Kant ultimately divides humankind into the European *selves in permanent making* whose mind defeats reification through a remorseless entanglement with other subjects' representations and the non-European reified *body-bound selves*, the boundaries of whose minds end on the threshold of their skin. In such a way his unification amounts to polarization. It goes without saying that in the aftermath of Kant the same essential distinction between "proper agencies" and their "regrettable enablers" was drawn and perpetually redrawn between races and nations within Europe as well. If Kant stated that "in hot countries the human being [...] does not [...] reach the perfection of those in the temperate zones" (1997b: 63), then Hegel inferred therefrom

---

10 In *The Crisis of European Humanity and Philosophy*, Husserl (1954: 318–319) says for example about the Roma that they "incessantly rove around Europe [...] while we, if we understand each other correctly, will for example never become Indians (*die dauernd in Europa herumvagabundieren [...] während wir, wenn wir uns recht verstehen, uns zum Beispiel nie indianisieren werden*)."

11 The third edition of the Encyclopedia Britannica (1788–97), which is roughly contemporary with Kant's treatises in question, values American Indians higher than the Negroes. As Sebastiani (2000: 220) puts it: "The 'black race' [...] remained branded with superstition and immorality, while the American Indians were re-evaluated as free, generous and wise."

that the hot Southern Europe is no longer the theatre of world history because the temperate Northwestern Europe has now become its heart (Hegel 1997: 149). Once set in motion, the normative work of the dualist anthropological machine could not be stopped, according to Reinhart Koselleck (1985: 186),

> the dualistic criteria of distribution between Greek and Barbarian, and between Greek and Heathen, were always related, whether implicitly or explicitly, to humanity as totality [...] the *genus humanum*, was a presupposition of all dualities that organized humanity physically, spiritually, theologically or temporally.

So what was initially intended to become cosmopolitan emancipation eventually turned out to be coupled with racial and national discrimination. In order for one race to appear predestined for the infinite spiritual adventure, other races within the one and the same humankind were rendered desperately riveted to their finite corporeal destiny. "The notion of a universalist definition of the self [...] is inapplicable without a criterion of exclusion..." (Lang 1990: 190) It includes varieties, but they can be tolerated only within the margins fixed by a stipulated conception of reason. Outside those margins, i.e., in the domain of the excluded enablers, question of degree hardly matter. According to Kant:

> The Negroes of Africa have by nature no feeling that rises above the trifling. Mr. Hume challenges anyone to cite a single example in which a Negro has shown talents, and asserts that among the hundreds of thousands of blacks who are transported elsewhere from their countries, although many have been set free, still not one was ever found who presented anything great in art or science or any other praiseworthy quality, even though among the whites some continually rise aloft from the lowest rabble, and through superior gifts earn respect in the world. So fundamental is the difference between these two races of man and it appears to be as great in regard to mental capacities as in color. (1960: 110)

Finally, Kant reinforces the inference that universal history, which was supposed to unite mankind, effectuates a division of it with the significant remark that state constitutions are regularly improved only in one part of the world, which he calls "ours," stating that this part will eventually probably legislate for all the other parts (2006a: 52). As we know, once this Western European legislation took place, "[i]nferior and no longer merely different, other races were completely excluded from its compass and became prehistoric as well as extracultural" (Gilroy 2000: 64). Taking their own culture to be representative of a universally valid human history, Western Europeans systematically produced antagonists as objects of a biological and cultural judgment of inferiority. In a first step they associated Negroes with orang-utans (e.g. Edward Long in his *History of Jamaica* (1774) (Sebastiani 2000: 215)). In a second step they associated remote savages with domestic workers on the basis of their inclination to rebel against legitimate sovereigns but also on the basis of what was considered their "improvability," provided they were treated with enough "educational care" like domestic servants (Sebastiani 2000: 223, 225). And in a third step they also established finely tuned inner-European differentiations. In the section of Kant's *Anthropology* entitled "The Character of Nations" we read that England and France "are the two most civilized nations on the earth" (2006b: 226). However, the German "has a fortunate combination of feeling, both in that of the sublime and in that of the beautiful; and in the first he does not equal an Englishman, nor in the second a Frenchman, yet he surpasses both in so far as he unites them" (1997a: 53–54). Whereas England, France and especially Germany are empires on the rise, Spain is an empire in decay. What disqualifies Spaniards is that they "evolved from the mixture of European blood with Arabian (Moorish) blood" (2006b: 231). "The Spaniard's bad side is that he does not learn from foreigners; that he does not travel in order to get acquainted with other nations; that he is centuries behind in the sciences. He resists any reform; he is proud of not having to work; he is of a romantic quality of spirit, as the bullfight shows; he is cruel, as the former auto-da-fe shows, and he displays in his taste an origin that is partly non-European." (231–232) So Spaniards belong together with Italians and Portuguese on the second, Southern European rank whereas the Eastern European nations (Russians, Turks, Greeks and Armenians), located at the outmost European margin, belong to a third division.

In a more advanced phase of the same normative tradition, the phase of world history in which the *Geist* takes up the guidance, Hegel did not hesitate in legitimating this constitutive division of universal history elaborated by Kant in very explicit terms, insisting on the tripartite division of Europe into the core, the South, and the Northeast (Hegel 1956: 102). He is even more explicit with regard to Africans. "The peculiarly African character is difficult to comprehend, for the very reason that in reference to it we must give up the principle which naturally accompanies all *our* ideas – the category of universality." (93) The universals like God, justice, and the state are namely completely unknown to Africans. The Negro is an "animal man" and "nothing consonant with humanity is to be found in his character" (Hegel 1997: 127–128). Africa "has no historical interest of its own, for we find its inhabitants living in barbarism and savagery" (124). "Life there consists of a succession of contingent happenings and surprises [...] There is no subjectivity, but merely a series of subjects who destroy one another." (126) Africans are by nature so submissive that they see "nothing improper about their slavery and they have even opposed English attempts to abolish it" (134). "In all the African kingdoms known to the Europeans, this slavery is endemic and accepted as natural." (135) "Anyone who wishes to study the most terrible manifestations of human nature will find them in Africa." (142) Bereft of a fully developed statehood that qualifies nations for their place in world history – each of them a particular stage of development – Africa belongs to preconscious and prepolitical Prehistory (1991:

§ 352–364). If Hegel entitles West Europeans to treat as barbarians other nations that belong to the former epochs of world history, such as Orientals or Romans, "in the consciousness that the rights of these other nations are not equal to theirs and that their independence is merely formal" (1991: § 351), then what about Africans who are excluded from world history outright? Treating them without any respect is, in Hegel's perspective, a "higher undertaking [...] grounded in a higher necessity," "the world-historically justified victory of the higher principle over the lower" (1975: 1061–1062).

To translate these significant series of Hegel's inferences into the more contemporary Agamben's biopolitical vocabulary: Never having constructed a human world, "Africans are the included exclusion, they are bare life. Or, to put it another way, their inclusion within the realm of the human is precisely the source of their exclusion" (Rothberg 2009: 57–58). "They were," according to Hannah Arendt (1979: 192), "'natural' human beings who lacked the specifically human character, the specifically human reality, so that when European men massacred them they somehow were not aware that they had committed murder." Kant regrettably anticipated this stance, stating that to beat "the Negro" efficiently, because he is by nature stupid, idle and lazy, one requires "a cane but it has to be a split one, so that the cane will cause wounds large enough that prevent suppuration underneath the Negro's thick skin (Neugebauer 1990: 253)" (*Die Mohren* [...] *haben eine dicke Haut, wie man sie den auch nicht mit Ruthen, sondern gespalteten Röhren peitscht, wenn man sie züchtigt, damit das Blut einen Ausgang findet, und nicht unter der Haut eitere*) (Kant 1831 [1977]: 353).

In order for universality to be rescued, therefore, "it is quite conceivable that one fine day, a highly organized and mechanized humanity will conclude democratically – namely by majority decision – that for humanity as a whole it would be better to liquidate certain parts thereof" (Arendt 1979: 299). Indeed, Africans were, with respect to their supposed inhumanity, just a pre-figuration of the European twentieth century's stateless refugees and concentration camp inmates slated for death. If Western Europeans in their colonialist phase were shocked by their encounter with African "natural" human beings, in their totalitarian phase they attempted to effectuate within the European space, conversely, a regression of human beings to that natural state. The Nazi genocide as a boomerang effect of colonialism namely kills human dignity in both victims and perpetrators, reverses man's fragile victory over nature and thus sets the stage for totalitarianism (Rothberg 2009: 58). "Men insofar as they are more than animal reaction and fulfillment of functions are entirely superfluous to totalitarian regimes. Totalitarianism strives not toward despotic rule over men, but toward a system in which men are superfluous." (Arendt 1979: 457) Reduced to "bare life," as Agamben has argued with reference to Arendt, they become disposable (Agamben 1998: 126–134). This utter disposability of declassified humans was the final consequence of the long, consistent and sophisticated normative work of the dualist anthropological machine mobilized by the Enlightenment idea of humankind. It followed on from the consensual conception of democracy.

4.3 Herder's advocacy of nature

In a bitter reaction to Kant's review (1785) of the first book of his *Ideas* (1784), in the second book (eighth chapter), Herder addresses precisely these harshly discriminating consequences of Kant's coercive agency of mankind. He returns to the topic several times, culminating in his *Metakritik* (1797). To summarize his opinion, any force despotically imposed from above is unable to hold the people together; a political order must express the will of the people itself, its common affects, beliefs and traditions, its natural roots; it has to be built from the bottom up. If people are properly educated, they do not need the master and can govern themselves. "Hence Herder took strong exception to Kant's statement that humans are animals in need of a master. He insisted that the reverse of this *Bildungswesen* statement is true: humans who need a master are animals." (Beiser 1992: 212) As genuine, they are able to breed and govern themselves without external custodians. While transferring the harsh despotic attributes to the "absolutist" instance of mankind,[12] Herder reserves for his natural law only generous and friendly attributes, which results in a much less ambiguous attitude to nature than is to be found for example in the enduring source of his inspiration, Rousseau's *Discourse on Inequality*. In clear opposition to Vico's inimical representation of nature as a wild beast whimsically inclined to sudden disasters and devastations, Herder's organic nature assumes an almost idyllic shape of a familiar and caretaking human *Umwelt* (Barnard 1979). He misinterpreted the ambiguous transformation of the *animale rationable* into the *animale rationale* through the development of the faculty of speech, as delineated by Rousseau in his *Essay on the Origin of Language*, as a clearly unilateral progress. On that basis, he reduced Rousseau's equivocal concept of nature to a linguistically cultivated, humanized environment isolated from the self-willing and violent behavior of external natural forces.

Therefore, it remains questionable whether the *Umwelt* really suspends coercion as Herder claims. Inasmuch as it provides – like all self-enclosed communi-

---

[12] Herder actually opposes the absolute lawgiving character of mankind, insisting on a freedom of choice of human agents who must not be coercively centrally determined instances but rather act as freely and autonomously determining agencies (Barnard 2003: 93–94).

ties – paternal protection from wild external forces through the measure of loyalty, devotion and care demonstrated by its dependants in return, it may be merely transposing brute fatherly force into more sublime terms. Far from being offered freely and in equal measure, such family shelter seems to bind and oblige its inhabitants to a strictly committed belonging. Instead of liberating them from coercion, as is envisioned, it merely replaces the visible violence of an external despot (wild nature, mankind or a sovereign) with the invisible pressure of an internal master (the educationally acquired consciousness or disposition). In the Preface to the *Ideas on the Philosophy of the History of Mankind* (1784–91) Herder accordingly cautions mankind to extend and deepen its domestication of (wild) nature in order not to perish from the two greatest tyrants on earth, chance and time, which mercilessly harass it beyond the cultivated domestic sphere. The same imperative responsibility for historically, linguistically and culturally infinitely resonating *Umwelt* certainly holds for races, peoples, nations and individuals respectively (1989: 15–16). This implies that in order to come to expression the potentially inexhaustible memory archive of the past generations, whose acts, thoughts and feelings are treasured in the *Umwelt*'s resources, requires of communities and individuals a proper education, committed reflection and continuity of cultivation. Herder's *Umwelt* is by no means an immediately available and universally accessible given. To become rich nurturing soil, it has to be persistently relived, reinterpreted and recreated from the perspective of each single phase of its historical unfolding. Therefore only very diligent and qualified communities and individuals can properly channel, filter, and articulate the *Umwelt*'s open-ended natural energy; all the others are destined, as Rousseau (1968a: 31) puts it, to "no more social structure than family, no laws but that of nature, no language but that of gesture and some inarticulate sounds."

It is under such consistent paternal care retroactively engraved by its elected representatives into its very structure that Herder's *Umwelt* acquires its friendly sheltering shape. If it cannot welcome every inhabitant in the same way but restlessly classifies, discriminates and devaluates its affiliates, this is because this *Umwelt* amounts, on closer inspection, to Herder's feverish wishful projection launched from his desperately factionalized, conflict-ridden and "yoked fatherland." Confirming the initial thesis of a powerful impact of religious terms on the political universalism of the Enlightenment, the rising pietism and evangelism throughout the disunited petty city-states in the Germany of Herder's time was clearly enmeshed into his remedial projection. "Through the concept of community and longing for unity, pietism became concerned with the fatherland. […] Thus, the inner fatherland of Christ was projected outward onto the national community." (Mosse 1985: 8) And as Protestants never question God himself but only the believers' relationship to Him (Dumont 1994: 30–31), Herder blindly trusted his all-embracing Nature as Kant did his Mankind. Both perpetually challenged man alone, and especially their German compatriots, to become worthy of their Supreme Caretaker.

The same invisible but reliable paternal care that Protestants humbly expect from their god pertains to the way in which history, according to Herder, hosts its inhabitants. As early as in *Another Philosophy of History for the Education of Mankind*, Herder raises not just the very beginning of history, but each of its stages to a necessary condition for the possibility of the next one, which ultimately makes the present the peak of historical development. In the course of such organic growth depicted as the noble implementation of human history, subsequent stages refer to one another, grow out of one another, thus making one the means to the ends of another. As Herder sees the present end as the sustaining source of the entire past's unfolding, each of the series of events preceding it is determined solely by its relevance to this end, as without the latter's paternal selection and protection these "dependants" would never have come into being as such. Yet the self-congratulating character of this retrospection shaped from the present point of culmination remains completely unquestioned. Such a perspective "does not allow the investigating subject to recognize himself or herself as also the figure he or she is investigating. It stops the subject from seeing his or her own present as discontinuous with itself" (Chakrabarty 2000: 239), i.e. as arbitrary, contingent and coercively involved in his or her apparently generous historical presentation. In other words, Herder's conception of human history, similar in this regard to Kant's conception of universal history, rests on the denial of the traumatic constellation that engenders it. This self-exemption from the law imposed upon all the others explains why discrimination inheres to it.

As early as 1815, an all encompassing intellectual and moral program by Friedrich Carl von Savigny neatly comprised Herder's discriminating proto-historicist pattern that would determine the development of German historiography over the course of the nineteenth century:

> It is necessary that we understand each particular man simultaneously as a member of a family, a people, a state, each epoch of a people as the continuation and development of all bygone epochs; [...] if this is so, then none of the epochs produces its world for itself and arbitrarily but in an inseparable communion with its entire past. [...] History is, then, not a mere collection of samples but the only route to a true cognition of our own condition. (Savigny 1850: 110–111, trans. mine)

In sum, Herder interprets human history as an organic process of ripening in which each generation prepares the soil for the emergence of the next, in an unbroken advancement of cultivation from one stage to another up to the final present one, which like a denouement comprehends and resolves them all. This ultimate all-embracing and superior perspective is reserved for the philosopher of history, that is to say for Herder himself, who generously enlightens all his predecessors. He describes it as the "vantage point" (*Standpunkt*) that permits the "command of the totality of mankind" (*das Ganze [...] unsres Geschlechts zu übersehen*) (1891: 107)[13]. Confirming the thesis that his foremost interest was not so much the past for its own sake but "the pastness in the presentness" (Barnard 2003: 4), Herder summarized his proto-historicist epitome as follows:

> Ich
> bins, in dem die Schöpfung sich
> punktet, der in alles quillt
> und der alles in sich füllt!
>
> (I
> Am the one in whom creation
> Peaks, who pours into all beings
> And whose self is full of them all!) (Quoted in Kittler 2000: 65)

What deserves special attention in these lines is the colonial principle of asymmetrical reciprocity. As the (colonized) enabler, the past passes onto the present its raw genetic energy; as the (colonizing) agency, the present replies with its well-balanced and reasonable *Einfühlungsvermögen* or "the capacity to feel oneself into the minds, motives, moods, purposes, aspirations, habits and customs" of predecessors (Barnard 2003: 5–6). Thus when Herder concludes: "The barbarian subjects, the educated overcomer cultivates" (*Der Barbar beherrscht, der gebildete Überwinder bildet*) (1989: 706), what he means by the preferable *Überwindung* is obviously this systematic cultivation of the past as opposed to Kant's subordination of it to the pattern of the present. Turning his nature into a domestic place, Herder generously opens its doors to everybody, yet only on condition that the *invitee consents to the hard self-cultivating rule of the host*. To be included, one has to be disciplined. "To be truly human, one needs to be corrected." (Rasch 2005: 145)

The Voltairean pattern of the successive overcoming of each prior historical constituency by the subsequent one persists despite the substantial reversal of Kant's argument.[14] Not unlike that of his antagonist, Herder's historical time appears to be posited as a measure of cultural distance that allocates to "unreasonable" peoples either a pre-modern place "elsewhere" or an outdated time "not yet," with the only difference that they are now kindly and generously relegated to a "waiting room of history" (Chakrabarty 2000: 7). Herder's cosmopolis leaves no

---

13 All translations from the German editions of Herder's works are mine.
14 In his article "Histoire" prepared for the 8. Volume of *Encyclopédie*, Voltaire explicated the pattern on the very structure of the encyclopedia: "Une article doit corriger l'autre; et s'il se trouve ici quelque erreur, elle doit être relevée par un homme plus éclairé." (1765: 224)

barbarians outside its gates but, as they are now allowed to enter among the citizens of the world, the pressure of the *Bildungsimperativ* placed upon them considerably grows. This certainly pertains only to those who are able to educate themselves; those whom nature "was obliged to deny nobler gifts" she has taken care to compensate for this denial by "an ampler measure of sensual enjoyment" (Herder 1997b: 77):

> That finer intellect, which the creature whose breast swells with boiling passion beneath this burning sun, must necessarily be refused, was countervailed by a structure altogether incompatible with it. Since then a nobler boon could not be conferred on the negro in such a climate, let us pity but not despise him; and honor that parent who knows how to compensate, which she deprives. (77–78)

As it is usually suppressed in the dominant contemporary interpretations of Herder's legacy, this blatantly discriminating aspect of his philosophy of history deserves scrutiny. Herder's idyllic projection of mankind's history liberated of all antagonisms develops out of the traumatic constellation of a man deprived of paternal political protection in a desperately compartmentalized country deeply divided along religious, political, and social axes and ruled by a large number of despotic and whimsical princes and dukes. Recollecting the basic life-experience of his desperate youth in Germany, in his *Journal of My Travel in the Year 1769* Herder (1997a: 15) states in a significant self-apostrophe: "The familiar, firm [...] center disappeared, you are fluttering in the airs or swimming in a sea – the world vanishes from your horizon." Would Herder have ever empathized with foreign countries if he hadn't been expelled from his country of origin (*Herkunftsland*, 14) himself? His "yoked fatherland" consisting of about 300 princely states existed only nominally and was described by Herder as *terra obedientiae* (Barnard 2003: 3).[15] Its subjects have been cut off from all political activity, which was a source of Herder's permanent bitterness as well as enduring sympathy for the small city-states, like the Republic of Riga, whose hospitality he enjoyed for five wonderful years of his life (1764–1769), in which people managed their own affairs independent of absolute control. His deep political frustration with the mechanical contrivances of a German monarchy lacking the consensual support of its sub-

---

15 Herder developed his vision during so-called Weimar Aesthetic Humanism (1775–1795) after accepting the invitation of the young Thuringian duke Carl August to join Wieland and Goethe in the capital of his duchy Weimar, less "une petite ville" than "un grand château" (Mme de Staël) numbering at that time some 6,000 inhabitants. The duchy, consisting of around 106,000 inhabitants, was an accurate reflection of the German *Kleinstaaterei* of the age. It made "an unremarkable patchwork of territories ruled vaguely from a capital city", each of whose four portions "maintained separate administrations and tax systems" (Chytry 1989: 40).

jects joined his inborn hostility towards the nobility because of its undeserved hereditary privileges that authorized it to rule and denigrate other human beings (Barnard 2003: 29). The accumulated bitterness ultimately effected a perversion of his conciliatory projection, which was meant to suspend such contrivances and privileges. His megalomaniac projects stand in direct proportion to the depth of his trauma denial. At the beginning of the *Journal of My Travel in the Year 1769*, which describes his remembrances during his return to the West upon completing his five-year stay in Riga, he recollects his youthful condition as being catapulted out of his motherland (1997a: 15); "everything was against me" (7). Considering this "feeling of emptiness, lack of reality" that haunted him throughout his life (113), Blumenberg characterizes him as an "incessant balloon blower" (*Blasenwerfer*; 1984: 428). Herder's utopian political vision directly acted out his personal and generational traumatic experience rather than carefully working through it.

To overthrow the despotic and whimsical monarchs of the age, he established the authority of nature expected to offer all its inhabitants an equal opportunity to rule themselves autonomously. Yet grasping this opportunity was, as demonstrated, far from a matter for all, as it required the hard work of permanent self-cultivation. While deriving such a *Bildungsimperativ* from man's environment, Herder obviously implied a linguistically cultivated nature as opposed to the animal's "bare" one. If not appropriately humanized, nature remains inimical to human beings. What distinguishes human beings from animals is the faculty of language. This thesis closely corresponds to Rousseau's *Essay on the Origin of Language*, as he also sees language as a means of transition from the *natural human* to *human nature*. While sharing with animals the inherited natural disposition, the human establishes a distinctive community of human beings precisely via his linguistic activity. This explains why Herder states that apes may be similar to humans, but can never be their "brothers" like the "Negro," who speaks human language (1989: 255). Human linguistic ability allows for creativity in order to compensate for the weakened natural disposition of the human in comparison with the animal. Because man is "the crown of earthly creation" (665) who arrives only at the very end of evolution, his natural disposition is already substantially etiolated.

> Man has no such uniform and narrow sphere where just *one* job is to be carried out; he is surrounded by a whole world of businesses and intentions. His senses and organization are not focused on *one* thing: he has senses for *everything*, and hence naturally these senses for everything that is particular are weaker and duller. (Herder 1966: 107)

Both animals and man express their affects through language but, unlike animals, who in their exclamations express just themselves, man is also capable of naming the distinctive feature of other beings (117–118). His language is not strictly self-referential, because climate does not influence his behavior in the same compulsory way as it determines the behavior of animals (121). The newborn human is characterized by "so dispersed, so weakened a sensuousness," "dormant abilities," "divided and tired drives," but "destined to belong to a great circle," "born mute, but –" (107). In lieu of natural instincts which automatically drive animal behavior, the human can afford the freedom of cultural creation; in lieu of natural sound genuine to animal voicing, he possesses the ability to choose whatever sound he wants (107). In the human world, as opposed to the animal one, potentiality takes the place of actuality. Whereas actual (natural) beings flourish and perish, the potential (cultural) ones persist, passing the torch of Enlightenment from one generation to another. Firmly riveted to their natural environment, animals and animal-like beings produce no historical continuity.

To summarize, the human is a *Bildungswesen*, obliged to go beyond his inherited limits in order to compensate for the lost union with nature. If nature is the roots of mankind's tree, and various languages nothing but its branches, then each of them cannot but be deficient in comparison with the comprehensiveness and richness of their descent and their nurturing source. It is this initial lack that has to be compensated for through a systematic and incessant work of further human differentiation. Mankind's potential for language is thus transformed into innumerable actual languages, each of them suitable for the part of nature that it linguistically creates. This proliferation of languages makes up for the lack of each particular linguistic disposition which is, its "naturalness" to respective "native speakers" notwithstanding, substantially deficient. Only this cosmopolitan imperative inherent to each natural language can explain why for Herder races and peoples are just various branches sprouted by the same "linguistic tree," each of them enjoying its proper place and time in the historical extension of mankind. Unlike Kant, who in *The Different Races of Mankind* (1775) advocated a genetically inborn concept of race turned into an unchanging substance, Herder develops an environmental theory which explains race in terms of its geographical and climatic surroundings, turned into a particular linguistic and cultural disposition that can be changed and does change through the history of a race. Unlike Kant (2006b: 223), who divides mankind into separate races, Herder advocates "one and the same species (*Geschlecht*)" in an "ongoing metamorphosis." "Passages are as transformable (*wandelbar*) as they are unnoticeable (*unmerklich*) [...] The colors become lost in each other [...] so that finally everything amounts to a shadowing of one and the same large canvas (*Gemälde*) that extends through all the spaces and times on earth." (1989: 256) Keeping in mind this broad human brotherhood, Herder cautions the European slaveholder not to mistreat the "Negro";

"you should not oppress, kill or rob him because he is human like you yourself" (255).

But even though he democratically declares the transformability of races, as one language and culture is continually translated into the "brotherly" other, this claim nevertheless does not seem to hold equally for all races and in all parts of the world. Some of them conceive their "nurturing roots" in a strikingly restrictive fashion, firmly adhering to what *comes naturally* rather than to an inexhaustible and all-encompassing linguistically humanized nature. Their languages are consequently less translatable than others, first and foremost of course their European counterparts. This is because the "general spirit" of Europe amalgamates the "tribe formation (*Stammesbildung*) of many European nations" (705). Due to numerous modifications and ameliorations of ethnic narrow-mindedness that took place in the course of many centuries in this climatically privileged part of the world, "everything in Europe tends toward a gradual suspension of national characters" (706).[16] Therefore Herder's tolerant and democratic vision of a broad human brotherhood could originate nowhere else but in Europe; its birthplace is Europe's paternal care for the rest of the world. Contrary to his professor Kant, who established a monogenetic theory of races, Herder certainly advocates polygenetic theory, but distributes races along a progressive historical axis of mankind's development that peaks with Europe. All races deserve their place, but Negroes are allocated to the beginning of history, Europeans to its end. Herder's racial theory becomes a philosophy of history that supplies the grounds for the shift from the assimilating to the emancipating colonial attitude and practice. In the place of the negation of "Negroes," he advocates their reaffirmation. Yet even so, as measured against proper "human nature," Africa is represented as elementary, primitive, and irrational, enabling the Europeans to accede to their infancy and subconscious desires and realize the supremacy of their adult rational state (Mbembe 2001: 1–3). In such a way, the emancipating attitude toward the non-Europeans, precisely in protecting the traditions of the "poor," surreptitiously reaffirms their constitutive inequality. Much thereafter, in following this interiorization of inequality, "[b]iological science would move [...] from the visible to the invisible factors of inequality, from the beauty of the race to the purity of the blood and genes" (Sebastiani 2000: 227).

---

16 Hegel (1997: 112) will thereupon provide a further specification and refinement stating that "the northern part of the temperate regions is particularly suited to that purpose [i.e. to become the theatre of world history], because at this point the earth has a broad breast and in the South it separates into many distinct points." Such compartmentalization is an enduring feature of barbarity.

The fundamental problem with Herder's conception is that it constitutively allows for ambiguity in the basic idea of human nature. On the one hand, inasmuch as humans are *natural* beings like animals, they physically *inherit* their natural disposition. On the other hand, inasmuch as they are *linguistic* beings unlike animals, they spiritually *create* their natural disposition. Which human nature is then, so to speak, more natural – the physical or the spiritual? Though Herder repeatedly insists on the spiritual being of the human, he realizes that not all humans are of a spiritual kind. His explanation is that the *bodily disposition* prevents some races and nations from taking up their *spiritual disposition*. But if this is so, does this not diminish the proclaimed universal validity of the thesis of the human as a *Bildungswesen*? How is one supposed to change his or her inherited disposition creatively if one is naturally prevented from doing so by that same disposition? If races restricted by their bodily disposition exist, then the human cannot be a creative spiritual being by definition.

In order to escape this vicious cycle, in a second step comparable to the one undertaken by his opponent Kant, Herder introduces discrimination to mankind. He states that the European races emerged through a long process of formation characterized by mixtures and migrations.

> In no other part of the world did peoples mix one with one another like in Europe: in no other part of the world have they changed their dwelling places and with them their art of living and customs so intensely and frequently as in Europe. (1989: 705)

This must have lead to a substantial weakening of the European's inborn instincts, but, as Herder (1966: 107) put it, "in lieu of instincts, other hidden forces must be dormant in it." Due to such mobility, European races developed and enriched their "inborn genetic life force" (1989: 272), i.e. cultivated themselves. The Mongols, on the contrary, "belong to no other world landscape (*Weltstrich*) but grass plains (*Steppen*) and mountains" (256), whereas the Arabs, for example, unfold their "original character" "all for one" (*alle für Einen*) in a neat communion with their horses and camels (257). No wonder they can understand the language of their horses so well, with whom they are "of one piece" (1966: 89). In sum, in Herder's finely tuned outline of races, which is close in its shape to his contemporaries Blumenbach, Lavater and Camper,

> nature has placed the Negro close to the ape and entrusted the solution of its great problem of humanity to all the peoples of all epochs leading from his (the Negro's) reason up to the brain of the finest human development (*Menschenbildung*). That which is most necessary, produced by drives and needs, is to be found in almost each and every people on earth; but only finer peoples of milder climates were capable of producing a finer development of the state of mankind (*zur feinern Ausbildung des Zustandes der Menschheit*) (1989: 633–634).

Like all plants, the environmentally bound, i.e. non-European, races and peoples flourish and wither (571), but in the more mobile and advanced, i.e. European, races culture goes forth (*rückt fort*, 628), taking on the seeds of withered peoples in order to continue with nature's vital creation (*lebendige Schöpfung*, 573). This is the outcome of the initially proclaimed equality of all races and nations around the globe. According to William Rasch's Derridean remark, once

> the term used to describe the horizon of a distinction becomes also that distinction's positive pole, it needs its negative opposite [...] something that lies beyond the horizon [...] completely antithetical to horizon and positive pole alike [...] the inhuman (Rasch 2005: 143).

In other words, the colonial difference between animally "physical" and genuinely "spiritual" human beings is, far from being a natural given, a product of the uncritical implementation of the then prevailing norms of European culture.

As regards the proclaimed equality of all *inner*-European nations, Pascale Casanova (2004: 77–82) spoke for many other scholars when she attributed a huge liberating potential to Herder's doctrine of the linguistic autonomy of nations, as it democratically assigned every nation in possession of its own language a place on the literary chart of Europe. Nonetheless, apart from many nations who do not possess their own distinctive literary languages (like the Irish, Swiss, Belgians or Austrians for example, not to mention the European Jews or Serbs, Croats, Bosnians, Montenegrins and Kosovars for that matter), a lot of places on the literary chart of Europe generously allocated by Herder have turned out to be remote, modest and restricted, certainly when compared to the centrally located German site. Indeed, only rare European peoples were capable of realizing and developing their allegedly inherent *Bildungswesen*. "There is nothing less certain than this word [culture, V.B.]," Herder observes, "and nothing deceives us more than the implementation of culture on all peoples and epochs. How many members of a cultivated people are indeed cultivated (1989: 12)?" So even if one and the same "acting principle" drives all peoples, i.e. "*one* human reason that strives to produce the one out of the many, order out of the disorder, an even whole of enduring beauty out of the diversity of forces and intentions" (649–650), this "inner genius" (273) does not amount to the same in all cases.

After all, not only was their own *language* completely withheld from particular races and peoples – consider only the North and South American, Australian and New Zealand nations, who do not speak their own languages – some of them were deprived of *nature* too, if nature is the instance that provides races and peoples with a proper piece of land, climate and environment. How can one expect anything distinctive from such peoples? Taking such a withholding of natural shelter to be their own fault, Herder does not hesitate to declare: "We regard here the Jews as a parasitic plant hanging onto almost all European nations and drawing more or less profit from their juice." (702) However, this does not exhaust his list of parasites among the peoples that hardly deserve to be called peoples at all. The Gypsies are for instance called "strange, pagan, underground people" equally spread all over Europe, a people that is "by its birth far removed from everything that is called divine, decent and civilized," stubbornly "keeps loyalty to this humiliating destiny" and is therefore "good for nothing but harsh military discipline" (703). No wonder that in the post-Herderian world, in which his nexus between language, people and state predominated for a very long time and is still far from antiquated, the Gypsy argot failed to qualify as a language (Agamben 2000: 64). In the forthcoming jockeying for power and respect in the field of language this argot, like for example Catalan, Basque or Gaelic, has been bereft of chances because its speakers were denied any acknowledged territory. That is to say, they lacked the necessary telluric quality (*Bodenständigkeit*). In a word, not having one's own language is bad enough, but being deprived of a country is even worse.

Although Herder generously included these destitute stateless peoples in the human species based on the model of the (great) family, they nonetheless could not enjoy common human rights; rather they remained subject to abuse, torture and annihilation. As Arendt has noticed, structuring human species according to the model of family kinship brutally erases its political plurality and irreducible diversity (2010: 10–11). The family principle forbids calling into question its consensual truths, which jeopardizes politics as the genuinely dissensual space. Political judgment acquires its validity by engaging multiple foreign perspectives, which is opposite to subsuming particulars under pre-given family rules. It deserves attention that Plato, in elaborating his influential antidemocratic argument taken up by his contemporary followers (Milner 2003; Lévy 2002), passionately adhered to and repeatedly insisted on the *iron law of kinship* (Rancière 2006: 30). Woe to those a priori disqualified from respecting and following the rules of the "family father": they were exposed to the revenge of his self-appointed representatives! No wonder, then, that along with the "parasitic" Jews, Gypsies were ultimately slated for death in the Nazi extermination camps. They were afforded a responsibility as low as they themselves were able, according to Kant, to demonstrate toward others: "A man [...] who is brought up by gypsies until the habit of evil conduct has become a necessity, is responsible to a lesser degree." (Kant 1997c: 164)

Significantly, contrary to "natural" peoples deprived of their own distinctive language or moreover the "unnatural" ones bereft of their own cultivated *Umwelt*, Germans in Herder's rendering can be proud of their *Volksgeist*, developed enough to be, like the exemplary Greeks, free from any "intermixtures with foreign nations" (1989: 566–567). This is how Herder introduces them into universal history:

> We now approach the tree of peoples (*Völkerstamm*), which has contributed to the wealth and evil of this part of the world more than other peoples through its undertaking, its bold and enduring combativeness [...] along with its wide conquering and constitution established completely in the German fashion ... (690)

According to Herder, Germans occupied, protected and fertilized the most valuable part of Europe, laying down the foundations for its freedom, culture, and security.

> The common constitution of German peoples was in the history of the world, as it were, a firm envelope, which protected the culture that remained after the storm of the epochs, developed the common spirit of Europe and slowly and conspicuously ripened to effectuate all the world regions on earth. (805)

It appears as if, unlike other environmentally determined peoples, Germans are, as the most proper European representatives, the single nation liberated from such determination. As often the case, it is Hegel (1997: 149) who provides the most cogent explanation: "European man also appears naturally freer than the inhabitants of other continents, because no one natural principle is dominant in Europe." Europe can consider itself happy not to have Huns or Bulgarians as inheritors of the lands of the ancient Roman Empire, but precisely Germans with their "stark, beautiful and noble stature (*Bildung*), decent customs, reliable reason, and honest disposition" (*Gemütsart*) (Herder 1989: 706). Interestingly enough, this point seems to be in full accordance with the opinion of his fierce polemical opponent Kant: "The tallest and most beautiful people on the dry land are on the parallel and the degrees which run through Germany (Kant 1997b: 59)."

Though Herder was broadly acclaimed as the father of the Slav national revival (Barnard 1965: 170–177, 2003: 13–14, 85–104), on closer inspection he described the Slavs as "taking up a much larger space on earth than in history" (1989: 696).[17] Whereas the Germans are celebrated for possessing their own genuine substance, "we encounter [the Slavs] [...] there among the Goths, here

---

[17] Slavic nations' intellectual elites embraced Herder's humiliating "protective attitude" that raised them to an object of domestication and grooming with the same enthusiasm, and at approximately the same time, as the elites in African colonies embraced the shift in colonial rule toward the enforcing of "native" traditions. They perceived this reorientation as the affirmation of their genuine substance by misapprehending what it had really been. "Enforcing tradition became a way of entrenching colonial power. The fact is that colonial powers were the first political fundamentalists of the modern period. They were the first to advance and put into practice

among the Huns and Bulgarians, along with whom they had heavily disturbed the Roman Empire, mostly as itinerant (*mitgezogene*), auxiliary or serving peoples. Despite their incidental deeds, they never were as undertaking, belligerent and adventurous a people as the Germans; they rather tacitly followed behind them, occupying the emptied places and lands." (696) "Is it astonishing that, after centuries of subjugation and the deepest embitterment of this nation through its masters and robbers, their soft character has been degraded to the most cunning, terrible slavish inertia" (*Knechtsträgheit*) (698)? They simply refuse any prosperity, as Engels (1970: 172) would bitterly observe after the failure of the national revolutions of 1848: "[T]hese scrapings of people (*Völkerabfälle*) are always the fanatic carriers of the counter-revolution, and will remain so until their complete annihilation or de-nationalization." In fact their de-nationalization had already been undertaken by Herder, who in the wake of the Italian abbot Alberto Fortis treated all the Slavs as one sole nation. Like many other similar amorphous "agglomerations," they were thereupon much better suited for "area studies" than the "national-philological" treatment (Spivak 2003: 8). Herder's characterization of Slavs, in a sense, anticipates Hegel's characterization of South American natives as victims of great violence, employed in grueling labor and subjected to every kind of degradation, which in the final account made them submissive and incapable of independence (Hegel 1997: 113). Once Slavs have gotten such a slavish profile, who is to expect a proper literature and culture from them? They have to be content with language and folktales instead of Shakespeare, quite contrary to the Germans, who are on their way to acquiring the latter, much more desirable "symbolic property."

That is to say, Shakespeare was permanently on the agenda in Herder's and Goethe's time not just because, as Casanova (2004: 76) puts it, the leading German intellectuals relied on English literature to oppose the dominant French influence, but primarily because he was regarded as the "naïve," "natural" and "authentic" poet in the *sense of originality* that the German writers themselves pretended to be. This artistic sense of naturalness has to be clearly distinguished from the primitive sense in which the writers of the "small nations" have been considered to be "natural." "Small nations" identify the whole of nature with their geographically and culturally restricted plot of land; in fact, as pointed out above, they must remain loyal to their traditional *Volksgeist* in order not to perish. Accord-

---

two propositions: one, that every colonized group has an original and pure tradition, whether religious or ethnic; and two, that every colonized group must be made to return to that original condition, and that the return must be enforced by law. Put together, these two propositions constitute the basic platform of every political fundamentalism in the colonial and the postcolonial world." (Mamdani 2012: 50)

ing to the "naïve" portrait of Goethe offered in Schiller's treatise *On Naïve and Sentimental Poetry* (1799), the leading German writers of that time imagined their naturalness in Shakespearean rather than these primitive terms. The latter were reserved for "backward" nations whose folksongs and sagas were taken by German writers only as a neat source of artistic inspiration or as a raw material to be carefully worked on. There is a clear gradation of naturalness that inheres to Herder's democratic doctrine: the first-rate naturalness of ingenius literary works reserved for literatures of great European nations, which must be approached in hermeneutic fashion, and the second-rank naturalness of folktales and folksongs reserved for Slavs, which can be approached in philological fashion alone. Approving this tacit hierarchy, Casanova (2004: 80) also adds the third-rank naturalness of rituals and customs of decolonized African and Asian countries, which can be evaluated only by "the model provided by ethnology."

Besides, as the *Bürger* are interpreted by Herder to be the propelling force of national *Bildung* and as they merely constitute, in small nations, a very thin social layer, who was expected to consistently nurture the national spirit in such a precarious social milieu? In the social profile of these modest peoples the selfish, blind, and inarticulate mob prevailed, which is why Herder envisaged for them another kind of self-determination directly opposed to the restless individual improvement of the German tradition. Continuously exposed to external threats, they were supposed to strengthen their integrative determinants and internal bonds by indiscriminately using non-rational molding agents such as myths, legends, rituals, customs, prejudices, "parochialism," mob-judgment and narrow nationalism. All this may be good in its time and place, for "self-esteem and happiness may spring from it. It urges peoples to converge upon their centre and attaches them firmly to their roots" (Herder 1891: 510). After all, as Herder unambiguously formulated in his *Essay on the Origin of Language* (1966: 107), the abilities of animals grow in power and intensity in reverse proportion to the extent and diversity of their sphere of action; only humans can adequately use the breadth and variety of the latter. Like "Negroes," with regard to these abilities, Slavs seem to be much closer to animals. These are some of the harshly discriminating consequences of the "natural" pattern of overcoming introduced by Herder's philosophy of history in favor of the "great family" of all nations. Nature did not prove to be a more just principle than mankind, and nor did family.

As for the equality of estates (*Stände*) ultimately, Herder quickly realized, like his opponent Kant upon the introduction of the agency of mankind, that of all the social strata called upon to partake in nature's creation, only citizens (*Bürger*) were able and willing to take advantage of this opportunity. The nobility (*Adel*) relied on the old hereditary rights, whereas the rabble (*Pöbel*), acting out of bitterness and frustration, used its creative gifts for destructive ends, wrecking the fragile and gentle fabric of social mutuality (Barnard 2003: 32). Two of the three social strata therefore had to be carefully kept at bay during the creation of the common public space of the nation. The envisaged equal participation in the business of rule, on the model of Rousseau's *Social Contract*, ended with the same outcome as in Rousseau's exemplary Geneva, where out of four distinct orders of inhabitants "only two compose[d] the Republic" (Rousseau 1978: 54). In addition to that, as we have seen, Rousseau asigned women to the function of pure enablers of male agencies, which were taken to be constitutive of the social contract. In such a way, far from being just an agency of democratic harmony, the proclaimed republican force of the *Volksgeist* proved to be an agency of racial, ethnic, gender, and social discrimination. Instead of emancipating itself from all antagonisms that drive humanity apart, it simultaneously not only generated but also reinforced them.

5 Who Worlds the Literature?
Goethe's *Weltliteratur* and Globalization

> Ich fordere Sie ernstlich auf: Lust und Luft für alle!
> (I am urging you seriously: lust and air for everybody!)
> Elfriede Jelinek, *Lust* (1987)

5.1 Comparative literature as the promoter of globalization

If at the time of its establishment Goethe's *Weltliteratur* was indeed a "literary-political concept" (Günther 1990: 104), the same holds even more for its contemporary interpretations and appropriations.[1] We usually see them adapting the idea, in a more or less inconsiderate manner, to new political investments and compensatory reconfigurations. In an essay which caused a considerable stir in the academic enclave of comparative literature, Franco Moretti (2000: 54) took as a point of departure Goethe's famous remark to his secretary Eckermann of January 31, 1827 that national literature no longer meant a great deal (*will jetzt nicht viel sagen*) and that the epoch of world literature had arrived (*die Epoche der Welt-Literatur ist an der Zeit*). Goethe's views (1987: 250)[2] were endorsed, as it were, some twenty years later by Marx's and Engels's adoption of the concept in terms of the emerging world market: "National one-sidedness and narrow-mindedness (*Beschränktheit*) become more and more impossible, and from many national and local literatures, there arises a world literature (*bildet sich eine Welt-literatur*)." (Marx and Engels 1952: 421, Marx and Engels 1974: 466) Taking these two sentences to be proclaiming more or less the same thing, namely the final revelation of literature in the shape of a "planetary system," Moretti puts forth the thesis that the discipline of comparative literature, having long been restricted to a very narrow international scope, "has not lived up to these beginnings" (2000: 54). It is not just that its focus has remained limited mostly to Western Europe and that it has failed to give equal consideration to everything published as literature

---

[1] I would like to express my gratitude to Galin Tihanov for suggestions that helped me improve and strengthen my argument in this chapter. He is of course in no way responsible for the deficits that remain.
[2] My translation of this passage from *Conversations with Eckermann* slightly differs from both the American translation by John Oxenford (San Francisco, 1984: 132) used by Damrosch 2003 and Moretti's own translation. All following translations from German will be mine if not otherwise indicated.

throughout world, rather the principal shortcoming is that it has not addressed the *problem* or approached its object through an appropriate methodology. Citing Max Weber's maxim that "A new 'science' emerges where a new problem is pursued by a new method," Moretti proposes a return to Goethe's and Marx's vision of *Weltliteratur* as a systemic whole with closely interdependent constituents.

As is often the case when past thinkers are brought into play so as to legitimize present methodological revolutions, and Moretti is determined to introduce a completely new critical method to the field (55), they tend to be read one-sidedly and narrow-mindedly. Long ago, it was precisely Marx and Engels who rendered the narrow-minded treatment literature antiquated. Nevertheless, given that Moretti's new method openly dismisses so-called close reading as a technique that pertains only to canonical literary texts, the unilateral interpretation of Goethe's views might come as no surprise. According to Moretti, "if you want to look beyond the canon (and of course, world literature will do so: it would be absurd if it didn't!) close reading will not do it" (57). As there is however always a point at which an examination of the texts of world literature must employ a close reading requiring linguistic competence, Moretti leaves this task to "the specialist of the national literature" (66). Although he considers all texts to belong to national and world literature simultaneously, there is an asymmetrical division of labor between them: "[Y]ou become a comparatist for a very simple reason: *because you are convinced that that viewpoint is better*. It has greater explanatory power; it's conceptually more elegant; it avoids that ugly 'one-sidedness and narrow-mindedness'." (68) He therefore supports and propagates distant reading in his more recent book *Graphs, Maps, Trees* (1) as well. But what is a comparative literature that, in order to create "authoritative totalizing patterns" (Spivak 2003: 108), leaves informed close reading to national literary scholars on the periphery (i.e. beyond the great Western languages that comparatist is expected to understand) and therefore depends on "untested statements by small groups of people treated as native informants" (108)? What is comparative literature whose fundamental division of labor amounts to the slogan "the others provide information while we know the whole world" (108)? What else can such comparative literature be but precisely a *one-sided and narrow-minded* discipline practiced by the scholars who are convinced they are in possession of the "better viewpoint"? If, in the envisioned division of labor, it creates the global methodological design as a technique of distant reading in order to "dominate the literary world system" (Apter 2009: 49) and relegates the dominated modest and restricted jobs to others, then ultimately it can be nothing other than "nationalism, U.S. nationalism masquerading as globalism" (Spivak 2003: 108).[3]

---

[3] If I am here siding with Spivak's critique of Moretti, this does not mean that I endorse her own revision of comparative literature. With its opposite privileging of native informants and

Goethe's and Marx's ideas of world literature, if we take a *closer* look at them, are deeply resilient to their deployment for such purpose. First of all, the very merging of these two figures into a homogeneous thesis of a substantially new world order is misguided. For Marx, world literature was an unavoidable corollary of the formation of the world market and as such an *instrument of the expanding bourgeois capital* which destroys national industries, economies and cultural self-sufficiency. Unlike Goethe's *Weltliteratur*, Marx's concept was directed against the nation-states by opposing a statist nationalism that was unknown to Goethe. But even though Marx was certainly critical of nationalism, associating it with the manipulative politics of nation-states, his stance on cosmopolitan world literature, as an instrument of the bourgeois suspension of all differences, was far from being clearly affirmative (Cheng 1998: 28). The homogenizing pressure of this cosmopolitanism spawned the proliferation of nationalisms (as well as national philologies) in the second half of the nineteenth century and it is pretty obvious that today's globalization produces exactly the same effect. As a number of scholars who resisted the flattening of distinct literary traditions into a single "systemic rhythm" of world literature have noted, this legacy of the expanding cosmopolitanism, as disconcertingly manifested in today's global world, might be a more appropriate point of departure for the establishment of analogies between Marx's time and ours. One of the lessons that might be drawn from Marx's characteristic ambivalence regarding "globalization" is that the annihilating fragmentation follows the triumphant integration of the world like a shadow. Not long ago Derrida was warning that the "spectre haunting Europe" is a "dispersal into a myriad of provinces, into a multiplicity of self-enclosed idioms or petty little nationalisms, each one jealous and untranslatable" (Derrida 1992a: 39). Such an unfortunate self-enclosure in untranslatability is, however, a direct response to the celebrated imperative of universal translatability.

As John Pizer (2006: 20) for example noticed, economic globalization disrespects popular ethnic sentiments, blindly trusting that rational politics can balance the interests of all parties. Yet, on the contrary, tribal solidarities fiercely react to the threat of such a globalized economy and the concomitant loss of distinct national identities by clinging to them with ever-greater tenacity. "Globalization puts us in a position to reflect on inequality all the time. [...] Inequality is not on the way out," remarks Haun Saussy (2006: 28). "The many states [...] fold [...] onto the one global economy; but the single economy divides up what it unites." This systemic misbalance might be the reason that the harsh critique of "nation-

---

comparatists (2003: 14, 22), it overemphasizes the particularity of languages and cultures in a typically liberalist, multiculturalist spirit.

alist ideologies and their imperial projections" in recent academic practice "has turned out to coexist quite comfortably with a continuing nationalism" (Damrosch 2003: 285). Nationalism is not an outdated or retrograde phenomenon to be downplayed, neglected and hushed up. Cosmopolitanism that argues in these terms is "all the more national for being European, all the more European for being trans-European and international; no one is more cosmopolitan and authentically universal than the one, than this 'we' (Derrida 1992a: 48)," no one is more particular than a 'we' that "specialize[s] in the sense of the universal" (74). Therefore, "it is the task of our transnational, diasporic, global times to rethink the national paradigm. On the other hand, it is imperative to understand the continued relevance of the nation-state form to the still unfinished project of decolonization." (Coopan 2009: 37) According to Stephen Greenblatt (2010: 1), the bodies of the deceased national identities refused to stay buried and violently returned onto the scene of the contemporary world. Thus "mobility studies," which were set in motion by the persistent colonization, exile, emigration, wandering, contamination and métissage caused by globalization, "need to account as well for the fact that cultures are experienced again and again [...] as fixed, inevitable, and strangely enduring" (16).

However, contrary to Marx's ambivalent stance on such a monolithic shaping of the world, Moretti, in a kind of better-knowing Marxism rather remote from the "father's" reflectively undecided and cautious attitude (not to mention Derrida's reading of Marx, with which both he and Pascale Casanova are quite unfamiliar), does not give the slightest account of these disturbing effects of globalization. Rather it places comparative literature, resolutely and unconcernedly, *at the service of its affirmation*. Like Casanova, who "wholly subscribes" to his clear-cut power opposition (ignorant of Foucault's revision because it is shaped à la Bourdieu), he pretends to be in full possession of the analytical tool of the "literary system." As opposed to him (her), all other literary agents, including the "specialist in national literature," are doomed to blindness for this system's surreptitious operations. The non-reflected legacy of the American and French Revolution seem to be marching hand in hand here. It is only an informed Marxist comparatist who, being properly instructed in world-system theory, is in a position to dismantle this all-pervading human astigmatism (Casanova 2005: 80, 82; Moretti 2000: 66). For Moretti and Casanova, the putatively discarded discipline of comparative literature, now refashioned into a revolutionary world literature, celebrates its heyday.

5.2 Goethe's detachment from globalization

If we now turn to Goethe, who is Moretti's second chosen foothold for the justification of his "literary world systems theory," he is completely unambiguous with regard to the accelerated economic, traffic and communicational uniting of the world of his time. Far from offering praise, he is *deeply concerned* by it and thus develops a consistent *defensive strategy* against this abundance of superficial impressions. The result of "all possible facilities of communication," he writes for instance to Zelter on June 6, 1825, is a generalization of a terribly mediocre culture (WA IV 39: 216).[4] Already a quarter of a century before, in the Introduction to the first issue of the journal *Propyläen* (1798), he cautioned the young writer not to get lost in the gaudy flux of a world trivialized in such a manner. Far from being merely liberating (from the constraints of local cultures), the enormous variety of world literature is simultaneously overwhelming and dangerous. One cannot feel at home in every part of the world and every century and hence one often falls prey to what seems natural in its respective context (letter to Friedrich von Müller on January 27, 1830; 1987: 287–288). Yet one should beware of such easy familiarizing projections, which are the usual business of the mob bereft of proper insight. Goethe interprets such a swift adoption of the foreign that unconcernedly accommodates its foreignness to one's petty domestic universe as vulgar cosmopolitanism, from which he clearly distances himself. His approach is similar to Plato's treatment of Athenian democracy in Chapter VIII of the *Republic* (562d–563d), in which he speaks of a chaotic reign of selfish individuals who do anything they please. Only through a heightened attentiveness for other cultures can a writer resist the overall dilettantism of the contemporary literary market that, because of the superficial and dispersive everyday habits of literary consumers, requires from literature nothing more than swift and powerful effects (1987: 173–175). Indifferent as listeners and readers usually are, writes Goethe (302–303) again in one of his late notes characterized by resignation and animosity to the "crowd," they prefer to hear and read always the same thing, expecting the writer to treat them as one would a maid (*Frauenzimmer*), telling them only what they would like to hear.

Contrary to Moretti's and Casanova's claim, the restrictive rules of the emerging literary market tame and impede the emancipating nature of world literature. Whereas in ancient times such mechanical repetition was regarded as a rare

---

4 I will be quoting, in the following, various critical editions of Goethe's works (*Weimarer, Berliner, Frankfurter Ausgabe*) according to the following principle: division (here IV), volume (here 39), page number (here 216).

illness, in modern times it instead became endemic and epidemic (304). But contrary to mere imitators who unquestioningly consent to the low taste of the ignorant crowd, the true artist is required to uncompromisingly adhere to the strategic task of a proper representation of nature beyond what just comes as natural, i.e., he must undertake meticulous comparative study of world-wide cultures and discover a deep unity beneath their confusing diversity. In short, a necessary departure from oneself toward the other must not amount to an all too easy self-abandonment but on the contrary, *improved self-acquisition on a higher level*. If one is too devoted to the admirable other, one loses one's own characteristic national nature (282), which is the only basis for the international recognition of a particular literature. Each product has first to display (*aufstecken*) its national symbol (*Nationalkokarde*) clearly, whereupon it will be accepted benevolently into the privileged circle of world literature (letter to Reinhard, June 18, 1829; 1987: 278). The final goal of Goethe's world literature is therefore a tireless *Selbststeigerung* or self-propelling. "You have to incessantly change, renew, rejuvenate yourself," he confesses to Müller on April 24, 1830, aged no less than 80, "in order not to ossify" (291). Continuously at risk of falling victim either to the aggressive pressure of worldwide uniformity or to the static provincial taste of his compatriots, a world writer, as Goethe understands him, bears responsibility to withstand and reject both. Always counteracting both inconsiderate all-equalizing cosmopolitanism and petty local nationalism, he is to be unremitting in his never-ending self-formation.

Faced with the worldwide vulgarization of literary taste, Goethe reacts to it by defending the exclusive right of the creative writer to speak in the name of the whole of humankind/humanity (*die ganze Menschheit*) against the grotesque distortion of its universal human substance (*das allgemein Menschliche*) carried out in the name of non-reflected elementary habits. Such a writer must engage humanity in its entirety, must go beyond his immediate neighbor who provides him the ready security of "house piety" if he wants to embrace the true amplitude of "world piety" (FA I 10: 514). In a letter to Carlyle from July 20, 1827 Goethe states that the endeavor of the best poets of all nations has for some time been concerned with that which is universally human while trying to transcend the selfishness and appease the bellicosity of earthly human creatures. It is exactly this uncompromising universality that in world literature shines and shimmers through the particular (1987: 265). Yet under the pressure of the mob that expects everything to fit its false concepts and prejudices and thus does untold harm (*großes Unheil*) to humanity, true works of art remain unrecognized and unacknowledged (303). Threatened by the "flood" of market-influenced literature as if it were about to swallow up his delineated elitist claim, towards the end of his life Goethe bitterly complained to Eckermann that barbarous times had come (March 22, 1831; 1987:

297). He was literally overwhelmed by that insight, helplessly acting out of the "poisonous knowledge" induced by it. New barbarians misapprehend true art as that which is exemplary (*Vortreffliche*) for humankind, i.e., precisely that to which he was at pains to remain loyal throughout his literary career (letter to Zelter on the same day; 297). If we take the tripartite process of a writer's development outlined in his earlier essay *Simple Imitation of Nature, Manner, Style* from 1789 (BA 19: 77–82) as a criterion, Goethe obviously placed himself, in opposition to his German contemporaries, at the highest level of "style." This level renders the writer capable of capturing the unique essence of the object represented unlike pure imitators, who simply reproduce its externally visible surface.

5.3 Getting out of the crowd: Goethe's elitist cosmopolitanism

As a great admirer of ancient Greek culture, Goethe in the presented deeply frustrated considerations, deliberately or not, draws on the tradition of Greek elitist cosmopolitanism directed against the narrow-minded plebs of compatriots. Such cosmopolitanism declared readiness to open the broadest possible dialogue among equals only on the condition that its distinguished participants are completely freed beforehand from the selfish interests of their inferior fellow citizens. The latter have to be kept at bay, as they care solely about enjoying rights and pleasures at the cost of others. Used to subordination, they are disqualified in advance from the intellectually free behavior of truly considering the otherness of the other and caring equally about his or her rights and pleasures (Arendt 2010: 41–45). Since one must achieve such freedom of thought through engaging bright-mindedness and courage, the Greeks reserve it for enlightened individuals, i.e., *agencies*, whereas the benighted crowd, i.e., *enablers* expected to provide through their persistent work all the necessary prerequisites for this remarkable achievement, is sentenced to compliance and delivered to its restricted habits. *Agencies are those who think and act, enablers those who work and produce.* The free democratic world, the Greek cosmopolitan argument goes, can be created solely through the well-balanced exchange of thoughts between agencies, who therefore expect their truth to be universally valid.

However, being established on the disagreement between two parties who, although seemingly speaking the same language, do not understand the same thing in what the other is saying (Rancière 1999: 10), the truth of the political elite can never gain universal validity. Its terms systematically prevent the subaltern from becoming legible by allocating these "dissimilar items" to the "pockets of disability," "zones of indeterminacy" and "regimes of confinement" and by depriving them of all symbolic profits of the citizen status. In Greek democracy as well as in its neoliberal descendants, caesura separates agencies from enablers, the entitled "subject of" from the outlawed "subject to." Enablers are sentenced to a subliminal, silent, and animal existence. The boomerang effect of such a hideous incarceration is a "systemic crisis" of democracy, "an ongoing activity of precariousness" within its established institutions, modes, and relationships (Berlant 2011: 10), the spreading of the fear into its grammar, the spectralization of its events, and the disaggregation of its political aggregate. This is why, the efforts of the agencies to impose their rule upon the enablers notwithstanding, the stubbornly reemerging split between them hinders the establishment of a harmonious democracy.

Therefore, when he founded his Academy as an isolated space of intellectual freedom in opposition to the false freedom of the polis that inflicts the opinion of the agora upon all citizens, Plato obviously realized the delineated restricted nature of the public truth. This insight into the limits of democracy induced his resolute refusal of its universal claim that entitles everybody to partake in the business of rule. In his view, such an unnatural attitude was derived from the traumatic absence of the "divine shepherd," the only authority naturally entitled to take care of the human flock. All the evils of democracy commence with the separation of the *human* principle of government from the *natural* law of kinship as well as the establishment of this principle on the elimination of the "family father." Illegitimately usurping the natural rule of the "murdered shepherd" (Lévy 2002), democratic rulers falsify, invert and perturb his order. Instead of being based on the principle of *arkhé*, which lets the firstborn and the highborn rule, the democratic entitlement is based on the *anarchic* principle of the drawing of lots. Democracy is ruled by chance or chaos, an unbearable condition that it owes to the patricide. This crime lets the human orphans wander in the "empire of the void" whose "empty center" (Lefort 2000) persistently lures them into taking pleasure in its seizure, representation and dissemination, and they do not hesitate to disrespectfully enjoy this pleasure (Rancière 2006: 30–41).

However, through the founding of Academy, Plato opposed Athenian democracy by redeploying its own *maneuver of self-exemption from the deluded dominant opinion in the name of the forgotten divine truth*. He reintroduced this self-redeeming cosmopolitan maneuver because the shepherd's archaic truth was in his opinion subjected to democratic perversion into the human anarchic truth. While the democratic government claimed to be the only authentic representative of God, beneath this appearance he discerned the egotistical individual with its quick and petty pleasures. Yet considering that Plato took recourse to the same maneuver of invoking the divine truth against the truth of blinded fellow citizens, must not the same critique, to which he exposed the Athenian democracy, necessarily undermine his own argument too? To counteract the selfishness of democratic individuals, Plato likewise holds on to the eliminated pastor, taking him as "the reference point by which an opposition between good government and democratic government is established" (Rancière 2006: 35). For Plato, we can rescue ourselves from the perils and crimes of democracy only by distancing ourselves from its anarchic multitude, turning back toward the lost family father, his golden law of kinship and the sheep's (i.e. our) bond to him. Looking after both the whole flock and each its member, He alone neatly harmonizes the One with the multiple – and precisely this uniting is required of a good government. Confronted with Plato's thesis based on such redoubling of the opponent's argument, one can hardly resist the impression that it relies on the same human misappropriation of the divine truth that it fiercely condemns on its behalf.

I propose to take this as a welcome warning against Goethe's elitist cosmopolitanism. Yet an outright rejection of it, skipping the much-needed explanation for why Plato's argument stubbornly resurfaces in humankind's history, ultimately in Goethe's idea of world literature itself, would be of very little help. Whence this obstinate holding on to the (imagined) shepherd against his self-appointed false representatives, i.e., betrayers (Rancière 2006: 34–5) which in its turn runs the risk of repeating and being blamed for the same betrayal? We will not eliminate very influential ideological formations emerging from such "misplaced prejudices" by setting up a truth putatively superior to their blinded assertions. As no cosmopolitanism hitherto could pass judgments without recourse to a legitimating "higher truth," it could not but redouble nationalism's argument. Instead of raising absolute claims to the universal truth, it seems therefore advisable to uncover dissensual judgments underneath consensual prejudices (in Arendt's terms), or politics underneath the police (in Rancière's terms). "In the course of this replacement it is necessary to trace back these prejudices to the judgments inherent to them and to affiliate these judgments for their part to the underlying experiences which once gave rise to them" (Arendt 2010: 79).

5.4 The acting out of the traumatic experience

Taking up such an attitude to Goethe's elitist cosmopolitanism, in what follows I will affiliate it with the traumatic constellation of forces he had to cope with. Uncovering such a constellation as the mobilizer of Goethe's cosmopolitanism, I will not deny the legitimacy of the judgment generated by it, yet simultaneously, from the perspective it tried to obliterate, expose its claim to the universal truth as a prejudice. Hence the analytical objective is not to dispose with prejudices altogether because of their failure to realize the universal truth. The aim is instead to lay bare the claim of these prejudices to the status of universal truths as a pretension *unsuitable for the dissensus constitutive of democracy*. Democracy is not an accomplishable *state order* – which is precisely the main cosmopolitan *prejudice* to be dismantled – but rather an interminable *practice* of the incalculable human many carried out in the form of *judgments*. Provoked by the dissemination of various "zones of indeterminacy" into the established social aggregate, these judgments interrogate the political line separating "one life from the other" (Rancière 2004b: 303), life from inanimate matter (Hägglund 2011: 272–276) and persons from things (Esposito 2011: 209). Rather than an ultimate unification of this incalculable human many, the task of democracy is raising awareness of the violence inherent to such therapeutic cosmopolitan undertakings. In an attempt to remedy human traumas finally, they give rise to more devastating traumatic experiences.

Before we return to Goethe by following this line of argument, let us recall that another important predecessor of his "Greek" cosmopolitanism alongside Plato, i. e. Voltaire, engaged the same nostalgic recourse to the forgotten divine truth so as to direct it against the dominant opinion of blinded compatriots. Each of these prominent intellectual figures operated as the author of a trauma narrative in their own right. In establishing his international Republic of Letters, Voltaire equally attempted to outmaneuver his ignorant aristocratic compatriots. Blindly attached to their inert and selfish habits as they were, they were suddenly exposed to critical observation by an international circle of intellectually mobile agencies. The latter conducted an emancipating dialogue with each other by distilling from it their growingly encompassing, convincing, and eventually binding truth. Once publicly recognized, however, Voltaire's remedial narrative transformed the elitist *exemption* from its monarchic surroundings into the international *expansion* of the "republican" truth. Goethe's trauma narrative undertakes the same cosmopolitan recalibration and sophistication of the local public truth, yet now distances itself from the "idyllic," i.e., the parochial and self-enclosed type of petty bourgeois readership (1987: 298) which, to Goethe's deepest disgust, increasingly took command of the literary market of the time. To defend himself from this flood, in *The Epochs of Social Formation* (1831) he takes recourse to the unity of all educated circles across the globe. His intention is to write for this kind of readership.

Regarding a somewhat frustrated late remark, it makes a huge difference whether one reads instinctively for pleasure and reanimation (*Genuß und Belebung*) or reflexively for insight and instruction (*Erkenntnis und Belehrung*) (308), even if readers preferring the latter, profound benefit of literature are extremely rare. But only those who are able to enjoy this benefit can claim to be reading with regard to what is universally human (as one is obliged to read world literature) rather than reading in the leisurely manner of the most deluded part of humanity (as one normally reads trivial literature). Such capable (*tüchtige*) people who really care about "the true progress of humanity" by striving to shed their narrow intellectual skin are certainly few and far between, but in their rarity they are nevertheless scattered all over the world. Step by step, the initial distinction between the true (or world) and the false (national or trivial international) works, writers and readers turns into a harsh opposition. Along with its international position, Goethe's literary oeuvre consolidates its pretensions to universality.

Ultimately, Goethe does not hesitate to introduce a *clear-cut division to literature*, placing the benighted majority of its agents on one side, and the select minority on the other: "Yet the route they take, the pace they keep is not everyone's concern." Their sublime task is to rescue the world from descending into narrow-mindedness or barbarity. They belong to the "quiet, almost chastened church" (*eine stille, fast gedrückte Kirche*) of the serious-minded (*die Ernsten*) who, because it would be futile (*vergebens*) to oppose the wide current of the day (*die breite Tagesfluth*), must nonetheless "steadfastly (*standhaft*) try to maintain their position till the flow (*die Strömung*) has passed" (FA I 22: 866–867). Their solitary position, removed from the silly worldwide crowd orientated toward immediate consumption, is tantamount to "aesthetic autonomy." However, one might ask whether the aesthetically autonomous world literature, if it must be restricted to a "quiet church of the serious-minded," the initiated circle of agencies walled in against the masses of their enablers, really deserves the name of *world* literature. How encompassing can a literature that rests on the exclusion of those without whose persistent work it cannot possibly come into being be? In order to answer this question, one is well advised to recall the paradoxical character of the relation between agencies and enablers or freedom and coercion for that matter:

> Wherever the few separated themselves from the many, they obviously became dependent on them, that is to say, in all those matters of coexistence which have to be really negotiated (*in allen Fragen des Miteinander-Lebens, in denen wirklich gehandelt werden muss*). [...] This is why the realm of the freedom of the few is not only at pains to maintain itself against the realm of the political determined by the many, but is dependent on the many for its very existence; the simultaneous existence of the polis is existentially necessary for the existence of the academy. [...] [I]t becomes a necessity that opposes freedom on the one hand, and is its precondition on the other. (Arendt 2010: 58–59)

As Dana Goodman convincingly demonstrated, all the prerequisites for the emergence of Voltaire's Republic of Letters, i.e., all the political, economic, educational, technological and institutional support necessary for its establishment and functioning, were provided by the same French monarchy which was ferociously criticized by him (Goodman 1994: 90–183, 233–280). Yet if his literary republic denied religious, national, linguistic and cultural barriers, it expected the reunion of people to take place on a culturally elevated basis, which relied on extraordinary linguistic and educational competences, finely tuned manners, and the refined skills of polite conversation, and from which the inert crowd of compatriot-enablers was necessarily excluded. Exemplified in the line from Plato through Voltaire to Goethe, the self-redeeming reintroduction of freedom on an elevated level thus unavoidably implies a reintroduction of the others' bondage on the lower levels. It seems as if compliant enablers doggedly accompany free agencies, inducing ever-new attempts on the part of the latter to purify their freedom from pollution.

Goethe's personal investment in the Platonic antidemocratic and discriminatory reasoning can hardly be overlooked. Besides his narrow-minded provincial audience and the worldwide rise of bad taste, he had to fight fierce battles against the misunderstanding of his nationally inflamed Romantic German contemporaries (Mandelkow 1980: 57–65). Against all these bitter disappointments, he found a welcome consolation in the reception of his work by some distinguished French and English Romanticists once Mme de Staël's influential book *De l'Allemagne* was published in England (1813) and France (1814).[5] Using categories like double force, double light, play and floating, the French exile writer portrayed him as a protean, mobile, contradictory and ironic poet who in the presentation of his self and others tends to maneuver incessantly back and forth, establishing and destroying identities in the same move. A couple of years later, structuring his *West-Eastern Divan* (1819; expanded second edition 1827) in a deeply polyphonic way, Goethe readily recognized himself in her categories in order to distance himself from and defend himself against his inimical and provincial German milieu (Koch 2002: 187).

Far from holding the representatives of this milieu in high esteem, he constantly expressed the opinion they might be crushed in their intellectual mis-

---

[5] This might be one possible answer to the "rarely asked" but fundamental question from Thomas Beebee's illuminating discussion of Nietzsche's skeptical stance to world literature: "[W]hat kind of consolation can the teaching and propagation of world literature provide?" or, even more specifically, "[W]hom is world literature consoling, and in what way?" (Beebee 2011: 367, 376) Goethe himself found in *Weltliteratur* a consolation for his traumatic situation at home in the same way as, to take up Beebee's examples, the students in Kathleen Komar's class in Los Angeles or Roberto Bolaño's character Urrutia did. Yet if Goethe's specific traumatic experience effectuates world literature's ability to console, then Michael Rothberg's concept of "multidirectional memory" (Rothberg 2009) might be an apt instrument for specifying this ability. *Weltliteratur* is always responding to a nationally situated traumatic experience but possesses the ability to work through the remote affiliate traumatic experiences as well. Such elective affinities among the injured are however always established at someone's cost and it is precisely this "side effect" of world literature's "therapy" that must not be forgotten. Its politics must not degenerate into policing.

ery by such impressive foreign talents like Shakespeare or Calderón. Each of the latter "is too rich and too powerful" to be taken even as the mirror of their self-identification. Shakespeare for example forces the rising German talents to reproduce him mechanically while they falsely believe to be producing themselves (1987: 289, 282). "How many excellent Germans have been ruined by him and Calderón!" In the same conversation with Eckerman conducted on December 25, 1825, Goethe highlights the grotesque effect of Shakespeare's plays on his compatriots, who put their potatoes into his silver dishes (228). The magnificent Calderón drives the young Schiller into madness, threatening to erode his humble virtues while the unprecedented Molière becomes desperately weak in German treatment, he remarks to his secretary on May 12, 1825 (226). No matter how much German novels and tragedies imitate Goldsmith, Fielding and Shakespeare, they nonetheless pollute and pervert their models (December 3, 1824; 223). No wonder Goethe warns Eckermann himself, in a conversation conducted at the beginning of their acquaintance (September 18, 1823), to beware of great undertakings and inventions of his own: they are almost destined to fail! One cannot expect a real sense for what is true and capable (*echter Sinn für das Wahre und Tüchtige*) in German petty circumstances, he tells his secretary on October 15, 1825. The masses who dominate them abhor whatever is truly great, tending to banish it from the world (227) (including Goethe himself, we might add, to elucidate his obvious bitterness). "For, we ordinary people (*kleine Menschen*) are not capable of retaining (*bewahren*, also in the sense of "making true") in us the greatness of such things ..." (226)

This is a simulated modesty of course: Goethe surely (and of course rightly) did not perceive himself to be an ordinary man, at least not of the sort to which he thought the majority of his compatriots belonged. He recognized himself much more in another "we" applied in a diary note from January 27, 1827, which enthusiastically comments on the rich French reception of his play *Torquato Tasso*. He famously writes, "a universal *world literature* is emerging in which an honorable role is reserved for us Germans" (243). However, as in the letter to the editor Cotta the day before and the translator Streckfuß on the same day (WA IV, 42, 26–28), with this "us" he obviously means just himself, since no other German writer enjoyed comparable international attention at that time. Probably the most exemplary proof of this is the huge success of his *Young Werther* far across national borders.[6] Lord Byron dedicated one of his works to Goethe, Manzoni adored him, Gérard de Nerval translated *Faust* and Delacroix illustrated it, Walter Scott translated *Götz von Berlichingen*, and there were much more fruitful refractions of

---

[6] I thank Galin Tihanov for this reminder.

and reflections on his work, for instance those of the French literary critic Jean-Jacques Ampère and the translator Albert Stapfer, not to mention Thomas Carlyle. Whereas contemporary British, French and Italian intellectuals accordingly *recognized themselves in Goethe*, other German writers recognized themselves in foreign writers and translated them passionately. With regard to these modest but diligent compatriots, Goethe found himself, along with for example Hegel in his impressively erudite contemporaneous *Lectures on Aesthetics*, in the comfortable position of being able to benefit, in the medium of the German language, from the extraordinarily rich and fruitful translation work of two previous generations (Günther 1990: 113; Wiedemann 1993: 545ff.). So despite the rhetorically or prudently deployed "we," Goethe was clearly aware of the real division of labor and prominence among German writers and intellectuals of his time. The majority of them only provided the background and sources enabling the expression of the whole splendor of the select few. Being regarded as too provincial, they were prevented from entering the latter's "hall of fame."

5.5 A retroactive reinvestment of Goethe's cosmopolitanism

Surprisingly, this traumatically resonating antidemocratic stance of Goethe's escapes David Damrosch in the first chapter of his admirably knowledgeable book on world literature, in which he treats German identity in Goethe's age as a homogeneous body rather than, as I have tried to demonstrate, something internally divided and antagonistic. He certainly portrays Goethe in a historically more careful and adequate way than Moretti, but with the same restrictive aim of deriving his own recent design of world literature from this not exactly informed, if not biased, interpretation. Unlike Moretti, who complains that nobody can really master all that was ever written in the world – as if this is what Goethe meant with his concept of *Weltliteratur* and not the contrary – Damrosch clearly states that "world literature is not an infinite, ungraspable canon of works, but rather a mode of circulation and of reading" (Damrosch 2003: 5). This he presents, as it were, as the Goethean approach *from below*, a perspective that is, it would seem, engaged to circumvent the delineated perils of global designs *from above*. As I have tried to emphasize, Goethe does associate *Weltliteratur* with mutually enriching interaction, but he means an interaction among a number of initiated agents who exempt themselves from the mob at home and abroad. If one takes into consideration that this elitism induced by the aggressive pressure of common understanding and bad taste, more or less habitual in the select social circles of the day, is inherent in the idea of *Weltliteratur,* such a literature was anything but projected from below. Quite the opposite of being truly all embracing, in order to overcome the traumatizing effects of the surrounding ignorance, Goethe based it on the *retaliating exclusion* of this "ignorant crowd."

Goethe's argument is complex and sometimes contradictory, yet unambiguously directed against the domestic as well as the worldwide mob because of the latter's inability or unwillingness to engage in the spiritually capitalizing exchange. However, although Damrosch's reading emphasizes Goethe's "constantly shifting personality" of "a diamond [...] that casts different color in every direction" (1, actually quoting Eckermann's preface), he rejects the interpretation according to which Goethe's idea of world literature would amount to an "imperial self-projection" or a "self-confirming narcissism" of German literature. At that time, he remarks, German culture was lacking a great history, political unity and a strong literary tradition, having been unable to stand comparison with its French or English counterparts, which were in sovereign possession of all these dimensions (2003: 8). Whereas the leading French critic of that time, Philarète Euphémon Chasles, in stressing the infinite receptiveness and sensitivity of French culture clearly displays triumphalist cosmopolitanism with imperial aspirations, Goethe's cosmopolitanism emerges from the "provincial anxiety" of a nation with "relatively weak culture" that strove for international recognition and political unity (9–13).

Curiously identifying Goethe with a nation from whose dominant public representatives he consistently remained aloof, Damrosch accordingly proposes that a "provincial writer," being "free from the bonds of an inherited tradition," "can engage all the more fully, and by mature choice, with a broader literary world." His intention would be "to seek out a variety of networks of transmission and reception" (13) for his or her literature. Yet of what use is this paradoxical *provincially anxious freedom* if, as Goethe demonstrated with the examples of his compatriots, including Schiller, it ultimately entails madness, weak imitation, grotesque distortions, vulgarizations and failures, in short the desolate bankruptcy of the great majority of German writers who searched for the secure abode of their selves in great foreign models? As Goethe untiringly pointed out, German writers resided in the small and self-enclosed world of "home piety" (*Hausfrömmigkeit*), taking care exclusively of their own individual security (*Sicherheit des Einzelnen*; FA I 10, 514): "German poetry offers, just look at the daily production, as a matter of fact only expressions, sighs and interjections of benevolent individuals. Every individual presents himself (*tritt auf*) by his natural disposition (*Naturell*) and formation (*Bildung*); hardly anything tends toward what is universal, higher …" (Letter to Hitzig, November 11, 1829; Goethe 1987: 285) In such depressing circumstances, where is the free ability and mature readiness for engaging with the broader literary world about which Damrosch boldly speculates?

It is not the freedom from national tradition, then, but the lack of recognition and overall misapprehension or the traumatic experience of undeserved isolation and the neglect of his work at home that motivates Goethe's enthusiastic engagement with world literature (Bohnenkamp 2000; Koch 2002). When read against its public presentation, his elitist choice uncovers a self-exempting, self-rescuing maneuver aimed at international self-expansion. He significantly hopes that "the differences which prevail within a given nation will be corrected by the perspective and judgment of others" (Letter to Sulpiz Boisserée from October 12, 1827; WA IV 43: 106). In the previous letter to Reinhard from June 10, 1822 we find the following remark: "I have a general impression that nations learn to understand each other more than ever; misunderstandings seem to be residing within each of their own bodies." (WA IV 36: 61) This biting comment is clearly addressed at his compatriots after the publication of the four-volume French translation of his dramas (Bohnenkamp 2000: 197). Far from being a "provincial writer" (Damrosch 2003: 13), in the 1820s Goethe was, to his great personal satisfaction, a widely internationally acknowledged author. As a complete foreigner in the nationally inflamed petty German circumstances, he attentively and efficiently established numerous international coalitions and foreign alliances to outmaneuver homeland pressures and suppress domestic enemies.

5.6 Goethe's trauma narrative: Repositioning German literature

However, he simultaneously undertook the maneuver of the self-exemption of *German literature* from its dominant international surroundings, which instructively redoubles his cosmopolitan project. This consoling self-glorifying maneuver of turning the lack of an autochthonous literary tradition into an advantage in comparisons with France or England – characteristic of all trauma narratives – was almost a commonplace in the culturally inferior Germany around 1800 (Herder 1991: 551; A. Schlegel 1965: 26; Wiedemann 1993, 545ff.; Koch 2002: 234; Albrecht 2005: 308).[7] Following this domestic habit, Goethe wittily employed a slightly derogatory image of Germans as, from the French perspective, "a not complete, acknowledged, but vital neighboring people, striving and involved in

---

7 An American philosopher, having researched the German intellectual corpus around 1800, had this impression: "There is, so to speak, quite a promiscuous theoretical as well as stylistic dependence of one writer on another. [...] In this climate of in- and cross-breeding of citations and cross-references, one writer being quite dependent upon others in the trading of ideas and authorities..." (Eze 1997: 6–7)

controversies" (a typically multi-voiced commentary from the *Kunst und Altertum* (1826); FA I 22: 259) to counteract the French national-universal tendency to instantiate global cultural uniformity. Defending his Greek "cosmopolitanism against the inferior local others," he resisted the French national universalism based on the model of Roman imperial "cosmopolitanism toward the inferior foreign others." Yet as is often the case with such compensatory revolts, this initial opposition gradually turned into substitution. Invisibly, the German "bondsman" adopted the imperial behavior of the French "lord." One inadmissible appropriation of the global truth substituted for another.

Let us examine this transformation of self-exemption into self-expansion, briefly exemplified above in Plato's and Voltaire's cosmopolitan arguments, in more detail. Already in a much earlier polemical reaction to the literary legacy of the French Revolution, significantly entitled *Literary Sanculottism* (1795), Goethe stated unequivocally: "We do not wish for the upheavals which could prepare classical works in Germany." (1987: 66) In other words, state revolutions established classical national literatures in France and England, which from his perspective is unacceptable, as no single national literature deserves the status of the classic. This status seems to be reserved for the *pre- and transnational* literature of Greek Antiquity. For Goethe, any modern European nation making such universal claims is an improper usurper (Günther 1990: 109) in the same way as Plato blamed democrats for their inappropriate occupation of the divine shepherd's throne. Such *political* national sovereignty vainly pretends to erase the rich sediments of universal *cultural* memory inherited from Greek Antiquity because the latter's archive ultimately proves victorious (Koch 2002: 151–158). Considering the fragmentation and dispersion of this social and cultural legacy induced by modernity, it is no longer possible for any modern agency to be sovereign on its own terms. Literary sovereignty is therefore imaginable merely in terms of a "joint venture" of many agencies, which have to patiently learn to know each other in order to somehow put together these scattered fragments. Appropriating solely for themselves the universal Greek cultural legacy and occupying for their petty purpose its constitutively "empty throne," modern national agencies falsify its universality.

Even from the perspective of individual writers, Goethe admits to Eckermann on May 15, 1825 that it makes no sense speaking of someone's originality if one considers that the world leaves its imprints on the human being from his beginning to his end. "If I were able to mention everything that I owe to great predecessors and contemporaries, very few things would remain," i.e. beyond energy, power, and the will [to go through others in order to find out for oneself] (1987: 226–227). Indeed, as Goethe learns by reading his *Faust* in French translation, one cannot affirm the self without encountering the other, and the same goes for the reflections of German literature in the mirror of French or English criticism. "Like individual man, each nation also relies on what is ancient and foreign much more than what is its own, inherited or self-made," he writes in a letter to Carl Ernst Schubarth on November 3, 1820 (188). No modern national literature can erase the old Greek transnational fundament, which is why Goethe prefers a corporate aesthetic redemption of its cultural legacy. "In the evaluation of the foreign (literatures) we must not stick to anything specific in wishing to regard this as exemplary," he tells his secretary Eckermann on January 31, 1827; "if we need something exemplary, we must always return to the Ancient Greeks... (250)."

But the Ancient Greeks are gone forever. After their definite departure, their legacy lost its binding power, henceforth figuring merely as a regulating idea. As the Lord was now irrevocably absent, His throne became empty and up for grabs. In order to expose its improper usurpers after the historical dissolution of the Antique pattern, Goethe invented *Weltliteratur* as a permanent *supervising negotiation* between them. Every modern writer must accordingly courageously confront the turbulent worldwide flux, expose his own body to its erasure, and stubbornly drive his spirit through its mess if he wants to gain the real overview and achieve representative status in the ongoing European competition. (As far as Goethe is concerned, the non-Europeans are involved not so much as distinguished competitors but rather as the not quite distinguishable sources for exploitation). Xenophobic self-isolation (which dominated the German Romantic scene) would not do. Contrary to recent quantitative interpretations of Goethe's concept (as if it comprises all literatures in their entirety) or the qualitative ones for that matter (as if it means "a symphony of masterpieces from different nations" like for example in Thomsen 2008: 13), one cannot overemphasize the importance of prominent international literary exchanges for Goethe's vision of world literature. It pushes all national literatures in the process of *making*, as testified by his constant concern for the participation of Frenchmen, Englishmen, Scots and Italians in the shaping of German literature (Birus 1995: 8; Günther 1990: 124).

The basic principle of self-propelling toward the common future ideal holds therefore not just for writers but national literatures as well:

> Left to itself, every literature will exhaust its vitality, if it is not refreshed by the empathy (*Teilnahme*) of a foreign one. What nature researcher (*Naturforscher*) does not take pleasure in the wonderful things that he sees produced by reflection in a mirror? Now what mirroring (*Spiegelung*) in the field of morals (*Sittliche*) means, everyone has experienced in himself if only unconsciously, and once his attention is aroused, he will understand how much in the formation of his life he owes to this mirroring. (Goethe 1987: 245)

Not everybody, though, was in a position to capitalize on the proposed process of mutual mirroring, as in order to participate in it one first had to be legitimized

5.6 Goethe's trauma narrative: Repositioning German literature

as an agency. In his essay *Shakespeare without End* of 1816, Goethe (1987: 135) pointed out that only an author equipped with self-consciousness (i.e. in the final analysis Goethe alone!) can properly understand foreign tempers and mentalities (*Gemütsarten*); others are too frightened by them to explore them carefully. In the same manner, heterogeneity of other literatures can be profitable only if a national literature confronting them has already established its own aesthetic credentials and identity (243, 280). In Goethe's understanding, world literature implies an ongoing dialogue of equals. Far from being a universal concern, equality requires merits. Unlike the French or the English, the Germans of Goethe's time had not yet succeeded in accomplishing this equality; they were the only nation-in-the-making among the prominent Europeans.

In proposing a world literature based on the German future-oriented pattern of becoming, Goethe allocated to the Germans a completely different role from being just one of its national participants. To avoid misappropriations, his *Weltliteratur* refuses to adopt the national model as the basis of its identity but searches instead for its identity in an open process of permanent mediation, exchange and negotiation. As among the select few only the shaky German identity was at that time engaged in such a self-finding process, Goethe ultimately *expands the ongoing German search for identity to the dialogic becoming of world literature*. Other nations were thus expected to participate (or, in the case of non-European or less-than-European literatures: to serve) with their particular national currencies in an open exchange set up on the German identity pattern permanently on the move. In such subtle fashion, *elitist self-exemption* turned into *democratic expansion* not only on the individual (i.e., Goethe's personal) but also on the collective level: the Germans were surreptitiously appointed as the only legitimate guardians of the Greek transnational legacy. Developing his idea of *Weltliteratur*, Goethe invented a reconfigured cultural space, which allocated to his compatriots the prestigious role of the custodians of the Holy Archive. Additionally, they were presented as self-denying agencies acting in the name of the forgotten Shepherd who, beyond any selfish interest typical of the French and English pretenders, merely foster a reunion of fractured literatures and cultures. The media of this mutually (yet substantially unequally) enriching and empowering intellectual trade between accredited European literatures that were expected to spawn the consolidation, improvement and final triumph of German self-understanding were "journals and books, correspondence, and translations, the journeys and encounters of writers as well as an expanding book market" (Meyer-Kalkus 2010: 106).

As John Pizer (2006: 22–24) has rightly pointed out, "impersonal" German literature could not produce a typical classical author infused by a national spirit. It was bereft of recognizable national agency, decentered through its enduring exposure to foreign influences, marked by sub-national disunity and a lack of cohesion and, still in the dialogic process of national self-finding, internally heterogeneous and contradictory. Yet precisely this set of features made it suitable as the *open dialogic model* for the establishment of world literature and world classical authors. This German pattern of subtle mediation and negotiation was directed against the bellicose competition between the strong, nationally infused French and British literatures. Not that Goethe was hoping the world will by means of literature achieve "a universal peace" – he was no less skeptical than Kant in this regard – but he was confident that "the unavoidable quarrel will gradually subside and the war will become less cruel, the victory less imperious (*übermüthig*)" (FA I 22: 433–334). Of course, nobody can expect that nations will suddenly reconceive themselves, "but they must become aware of one another, grasp each other, and if they are unwilling to love one another (*wenn sie sich wechselseitig nicht lieben mögen*), learn to tolerate each other" (FA I 22: 491). For "if we have to communicate in our everyday life with resolutely other-thinking persons, we will find ourselves moved to be on the one hand more cautious, but on the other more tolerant and lenient" (FA I 22: 868). Nevertheless, a core motivation behind these scattered remarks is not so much "the desire for productive and peaceful coexistence among the nations of Europe," as Pizer (2006: 21) surmises, incautiously taking Goethe at his word. Rather, beneath Goethe's cosmopolitan proclamations there lurks a compensatory raising of the German national pattern of becoming into the sovereign moderator of international intellectual traffic. Germany is envisaged to become the *divine shepherd of world literature.*

In this regard, Goethe was, after all, just a loyal inheritor of a number of his reputed domestic predecessors. In 1793, Herder had stated that Germans should "appropriate the best of all the peoples and in such a way become among them what man became among his fellow creatures (*Neben- und Mitgeschöpfe*) from which he learned his skills (*Künste*). He came at the end, took from every one of them his art and now *he surpasses and rules all of them*" (Herder 1991: 551 [emphasis mine]). Several years later, Novalis, in the equally cosmopolitan project *Christendom or Europe* (1799), put forth the thesis that, while other European countries are "occupied by war, speculation and partisanship (*Parthey-Geist*), the German makes himself with all diligence into an associate (*Genosse*) of a higher epoch of culture. This preliminary step *must give him, over the course of time, a large predominance* (ein großes Uebergewicht) *over the others*" (Novalis 1983b: 519 [emphasis mine]). In the same vein, Goethe entrusted the German language with the role of the medium of permanent translation or commerce of one with another literature. German is called upon to set the course for everybody's national currency (*Münzsorten*) "not by repelling the foreign but devouring it" (1987: 243). What Goethe ultimately envisaged was "the take up and complete appropriation (*das völlige Aneignen*) of the foreign" (238), which is tantamount to the complete denial of the foreignness inherent to Roman imperial "cosmopolitanism toward the inferior foreign others."

5.7 From exemption to expansion: Toward the Roman imperial cosmopolitanism

Unlike the Greeks, the Romans refused to acknowledge the other in his or her otherness, regarding him or her as a mere extension of their own noble breed. They simply could not imagine that there existed anybody who could be equal to them in terms of greatness and still be different from them (Arendt 2010: 121). By tacitly shifting from the Greek elitist attitude to this Roman imperial one, Goethe ultimately disqualified, or at least disregarded, any individual or collective identity reluctant or unable to persistently enrich itself, i.e., to adopt his and the German self-propelling behavior and standards. In the famous letter to Thomas Carlyle from July 20, 1827, he states:

> The Germans have long contributed to the mediation *[Vermittlung]* between individual and national particularities *[das Besondere der einzelnen Menschen und Völkerschaften]* and their mutual recognition. Whoever understands the German language finds himself in a market where every nation displays its merchandize, plays the translator while enriching himself. (1987: 265)

Being himself an internally dialogic author whose consciousness was able of devouring an incredible polyglossia,[8] Goethe wanted to transfer the vivid spiritual cohesiveness of individuals characterizing the French *esprit général* and the English *public spirit* from the national to the world literary level. However, in so doing he also wished to open the *historical stream of the entire human community* engendered in such a way, by applying to it the German "dialogic principle" of self-finding.[9] In an address to the society of nature researchers and physicians

---

[8] As regards Goethe's overarching creative consciousness, it strikes his attentive readers as "'what we Germans call spirit [*Geist*], which is predominant in an upper leader (*das Vorwaltende des oberen Leitenden*)' (FA III 1: 181), a weightless, on-hand intelligence that 'especially belongs to a man of age or an aging epoch' and qualifies itself through a 'worldwide overview, irony' and 'free use of talents'" (Koch 2002: 201).

[9] I deliberately deploy this famous concept of Mikhail Bakhtin's literary and linguistic theory to indicate the importance of his in-depth reading of Goethe for its shaping. However, unlike Pizer, who enthusiastically endorses Bakhtin's empathic understanding of Goethe, I interpret the dialogic principle – in both cases – as an operation of imperial self-empowerment that aims at the establishment of a supreme authority or what we, using Bakhtin's own terms, could dub the "authorial self." See ch. 9.

from 1828 he stated that what is of real concern in world literature is that "vivid and striving men of letters become acquainted with one another and find themselves stimulated for social action through their mutual inclination and common sense" (*Neigung und Gemeinsinn*, FA I 25: 79). The works of world literature concern us only inasmuch as they concern each other (Günther 1990: 124). It is only if they create such select common sense, caught in the unlimited process of perfection, that they substitute, to deploy Thomas Mann's apt opposition, what is capable of or valid for the world (*Weltfähige* or *Weltgültige*) and characterized by a true world horizon (*Weltbezug*) for what is at present simply the way of the world (*Weltläufige*; Birus 1995: 16).

> Given Germany's own lack of a strong, immanent, infrangible national identity in his time, it is not surprising that Goethe was particularly aware of and open to the possibility of a super- or transnational literary modality. Perhaps Goethe's insights into the contemporary impossibility of creating a "classical" (national) German literature made the formulation of a *Weltliteratur* desirable as the only possible alternative to cultural fragmentation. (Pizer 2006: 24)

Goethe's *Weltliteratur* was undoubtedly a *trauma narrative* in the meaning Jeffrey Alexander attributed to this concept: coming up "from below" (i.e., both from an unrecognized Goethe in the German literary space and from an underrated Germany in the European political and cultural space), it therapeutically reconfigures the existing political, literary and cultural space. The *Weltliteratur* narrative, in a word, works through and acts out both a personal and a collective traumatic experience. Yet no trauma narrative can achieve necessary public recognition without instigating "new rounds of social suffering" (Alexander 2012: 2). At the very moment at which it predicates the equal dignity of all its imagined worldwide community's invited participants, it proves unable to remove the gap, which produces "the part that has no part" in it.

This essential simultaneity of the narrative's *construction* and *destruction* of community accounts for its slide from emancipation to supremacy. Undertaken under the pressure of deprivation and humiliation, it gradually rises to the status of an international intellectual agenda and thus, if only with delays and hesitations, becomes a powerful "multidirectional" platform for the recovery of various traumatized collectivities. This is what had happened meanwhile to Goethe's *Weltliteratur*, whose global impact increased in an almost daily rhythm. Yet without denying its politically intended integration of political and cultural fragmentation at home and abroad, his trauma narrative of world reconciliation (*Weltversöhnung*) was basically structured on the German *Einheit-in-Vielfalt* model of steady self-expansion: *The greater your diversity, affiliates of* Weltliteratur, *the more magnificent grows my dialogic unity in becoming!*

5.7 From exemption to expansion: Toward the Roman imperial cosmopolitanism

Having been initiated in the form of Greek elitist "cosmopolitanism against the deluded fellow citizens," that is to say, Goethe's idea of world literature tacitly perverted into Roman imperial "cosmopolitanism toward the inferior foreigners" open to the inclusion of any agency able and ready to comply with the set rules of exchange. According to Costas Douzinas (2007: 159), "[…] cosmopolitanism starts as a moral universalism but often degenerates into imperial globalism. […] The continuous slide of cosmopolitan ideas towards empire is one of the dominant motifs of modernity." It is significant that, following this same path, Voltaire's project of the world literary republic underwent a comparable "perversion" of its envisaged inclusiveness into an intolerant exclusiveness. It finally asked "those nations which are not French […] to become French" (Lyotard 1988: 147) and thus turned its initial war of liberation into the war of conquest. No wonder then, the same imperial model already defined the true, albeit hardly deliberate agenda of the famous manifesto of Weimar Classicism, composed by Schiller but subscribed to by Goethe. It set its sails, in the interest of "pure humanity" (*rein menschlich*), to "unite again the politically divided world under the banner of truth and beauty (*die politisch geteilte Welt unter der Fahne der Wahrheit und Schönheit wieder zu vereinigen*)" (Schiller 1991: 109). After all, aesthetics in the service of Germany's own political recalibration and reconfiguration was, as Joseph Chytry (1989) has convincingly demonstrated, the main agenda around 1800.

In harmony with this broadly politically motivated aesthetic program, Goethe's idea of the aesthetic autonomy of world literature, expected to represent the Greek transnational legacy in modern national conditions, takes recourse to § 49 of Kant's *Critique of Judgment*, which makes the appropriate reception of a work of art a constitutively open but authoritatively guided undertaking. "The recipient's interpretational designs are endless precisely because it 'gives us so much to think about'; exactly because the aesthetic idea keeps the observer in a continuum of the search for meaning, it turns out that art's domain is not entirely incommensurable with our normal experiential reality. The understanding of works of art is certainly 'endless', but they give us something to understand" (Koch 2002: 202–203). That is to say, the reader's imagination is, although free, not completely directionless and unleashed but hideously orientated and guided by the integrative movement of an ultimate authority. In Goethe's literary area of interest, this remote governing Godlike authority of the Ancient Greek legacy is called *Weltliteratur* and in Kant's philosophical domain the *Probierstein der Wahrheit* (touchstone of truth; in Kant 1956: 64, translated as "criterion," 2006a: 249, 2006b: 17, 113). In both cases, it is associated with a worldwide community as the last-resort corrective of individual or national judgmental aberrations. According to § 40 of the *Critique of Judgment*, the task of the reader's imagination is to compare his or her judgments not only with the real, but also with the *merely possible* judgments of other readers. The reader is expected to put himself or herself in the place of everybody else (*dass man sein Urteil an anderer, nicht sowohl wirkliche, als vielmehr bloß mögliche Urteile hält, und sich in die Stelle jedes andern versetzt*).

This act of self-authorizing transposition into the others (*Hineinversetzen*) is how Kant's and Goethe's "sensus communis" (*Gemeinsinn*) that is expected to unite the community's diversity ultimately comes into being. Far from being present or available in any way – the Ancient Greek artistic model is gone, as is the Ancient Greek philosophical truth – the community that authorizes this sensus communis is *constitutively absent and has to be imagined* (Lyotard 1991: 224; Arendt 1992: 43). As is the case with every "imagined community" based on elective affinities (*Wahlverwandtschaften*) among its *membra disjecta*, it can arise only through an *act of institution or collecting mobilization* performed by the "carrier group" that establishes its common concern, takes responsibility for it and draws most benefits from its endurance and expansion. Figuring as "multidirectional" platforms for the transnational reconciliation, trauma narratives proved to be attractive instruments of such cross-cultural mobilization of adherents. While having enthusiastically joined the imagined community established by them, its most diverse participants authorized its inventors, the engineers of the new cultural and political space, to pass judgments and correct their aberrations on their behalf.[10] This normative procedure applied by the engineers of world literature to those who for their part had authorized them by joining the venture is how Goethe expected the global polis to be gradually reshaped and recalibrated. Put in the "obvious" terms of the untiringly self-propelling German spirit, world literature community was hoped to eventually become an "expanded fatherland," according to Goethe's own formulation in the essay on Carlyle's translation of Schiller (FA I 22: 431–434). Accordingly, the entrance to this expanded fatherland was surreptitiously supplied with an invisible "garbage disposal." Not everybody was equally welcome within the family.

---

10 My point is that the world literature's community is not a *precondition* but *effect* of its institution, in the sense in which Derrida for example, in his critique of Rousseau's theory of the social contract in *Of Grammatology* or in his reading of Freud's *Totem and Taboo* in *Préjugés*, derives social consensus from the *political authority of its inaugurators*. Because of this, the process of the institution of the common sense necessarily rests on the repression and exclusion of those who subscribe to it. Being based on such constitutive violence, common sense established by world literature turns out to be not that common as it usually claims to be.

5.8 Translating the "iron law of kinship" into the "free competition of values": The U.S.-American trauma narrative

This *spontaneous authorization* of world literature by the most heterogeneous participants who self-sacrificially consent to join it undermines the enthusiastic reading of Goethe's *Weltliteratur* proposed by the Moroccan *Germanist* Fawzi Boubia (1985, 1988). Unreservedly endorsed by Pizer (2006: 27–28), he refutes the charges against its Eurocentric character. Goethe respects the particularity of non-European "others," the argument goes, advocating the movement toward the non-European Other and not a dominion over it or its leveling to European dimensions. This thesis finds a supporter in David Damrosch (2003: 13). Damrosch, quoting a passage from Eckermann in which Goethe dismisses medieval Germanic and Serbian poetry by treating both as "barbaric popular poetry" of only provisional interest for the serious writer, regards this to be "not, or not primarily, Eurocentrism," since elitism and Eurocentrism strike him as partly "competing values." The problem is, unfortunately, that in Goethe's argument they go strictly hand in hand, making a quite inseparable couple. The incessant normative activity of passing judgments and correcting aberrations – disciplining the most diverse participants to comply with the set rules of participation by abandoning their "inherited identity garbage" – transforms *Weltliteratur* tacitly from an emancipating agency into one which is oppressive. Being constitutively dependent on *verification* by its manifold adherents, the cosmopolitan operation of trauma narratives cannot avoid perversion into an instrument of their *colonization*. The same "democratic malformation" happened, after all, to Herder's *Weltpoesie* based on *Naturdichtung* as well as to August Schlegel's *universal poetry* (canon of masterpieces, A. Schlegel 1965: 14) and Goethe's *Weltliteratur* proves, albeit long after his death, unable to escape it, – all the advertent or inadvertent "makeup" applied by his domestic and international interpreters notwithstanding. Yet Goethe himself, being a well-trained pupil of Plato, was terrified by this sinister prospect of an idea, which was forged to circumvent it. This is why he tirelessly, albeit ultimately vainly, reaffirms its elitism.

In the famous conversation of January 31, 1827 (1987: 249–250), for example, he firstly shares with Eckermann the democratic thought that poetry is a common good of humankind in which some are a little bit better, swim a little bit longer at the top than the others, and that's all. As poetry is a universal human matter, nobody should delude himself he is a great poet just because he has written a good poem. Yet he was at that time already frightened by the consequences of this initially Herderian literary doctrine to which he subscribed in 1773, when he edited a collection of Alsatian folk songs together with Herder. In the meantime, this early democratic initiative of hugely expanding the idea of literature gave rise to the neo-German religio-patriotic art (*neu-deutsche religiös-patriotische Kunst*) which he now abhorred (Meyer-Kalkus 2010: 101). What was once intended to be broadly democratic was thus turned into the self-enclosed national-conservative opposite. With his *Weltliteratur*, Goethe pretended to obviate this destiny of *Naturdichtung*, which is why he could not permit everybody to usurp it. It had to be saved from such vulgarization by its uncultivated consumers in the same way as the restriction of the Greek nomos to a small circle of domestic agencies tended to prevent the (forthcoming Roman) evaporation of the political in an incalculable system of imperial expansion (Arendt 2010: 119).

He therefore immediately, in the continuation of the same conversation, returns to the Greek elitist cosmopolitan position: Such universal poetry certainly concerns Chinese, Serbian poetry or the *Nibelungenlied*, which are exclusively of a transitory historical interest, but not Greek Antiquity, which is of an immortal aesthetic interest. In the slightly later notes from the *Makariens Archiv* (1829, 1987: 284) he is even more unambiguous: "Chinese, Indian, Egyptian antiquities are always just curiosities; it is recommendable to make oneself and the world acquainted with them; but they would be not especially fruitful for our moral and aesthetic education/formation (*Bildung*)." This is the reason why "Orientals" can never stand comparison with the Greeks and Romans or the *Nibelungen* with the Iliad for that matter (174); they simply belong to different categories, since the first represent false or transient values and the second those that are true or deep. Because of the "Oriental predilection" to lump together what is most remote, contradictory and incommensurable (169), Goethe also rejects the literary work of his younger contemporary Jean Paul (175–177). Instead of trying to distill from the world's diversity its underlying true equivalent (*wahres Äquivalent*) patterned according to the Ancient Greek model, Jean Paul uses this diversity as a coin for momentary rhetorical effects. Such "Oriental" literary rhetoric only degrades poetry, bereaving it of its true substance (178). Poetry is therefore no longer a universal human matter: all Oriental literatures, the Serbian and the old Germanic epic as well as Romantic mannerists like Jean Paul are expelled from its blessing.

They are not completely inapplicable, admittedly, but of restricted use in the envisioned world literary community of elective affiliates. Oriental culture can be used just as a "refreshing source" to "strengthen the peculiarity of our spirit," but certainly not as its law-giving pattern (FA II 6: 642). "Goethe has never abandoned Shakespeare in favor of Nizâmî." (Birus 1995: 19) The same holds for *Naturdichtung*: original but primitive, it can be reasonably exploited only as a raw material. Even if Goethe urges his compatriots to apply the Herderian *Einfühlungsvermögen* (empathic ability) in their approach to Serbian folk poetry, when he accordingly advises them to pay the Serbs a "personal visit" he describes the Serbian "rough land" as if it lay somewhere far behind, "several centuries ago" (FA I 22: 686). And when he was indeed once invited, during his journey through Italy, by the Prince of Waldeck to cross the Adriatic Sea and pay the "Morlacks" a "personal visit," he declined with uneasiness, "distinctly not interested in travelling across the Adriatic" (Wolff 2001: 192). The imagined geography, pleasing by its self-complimenting operations, refuses to be embarrassed by the real one. Even if he recommended "to read every poet in his own language and the peculiar district of his time and habits" (FA I 3: 270) and "to strive to approach the foreign as closely as possible" (FA I 3: 293), he himself read the Chinese novel of manners *Yü-chao-li* – a "marginal Chinese literary work of minor importance" (Wang 2011, 296) – in a free French translation and adaptation (*Les deux cousines*, 1826). In the same way, he retranslated the Serbian epic from the poor Italian translation. Recalling this episode fifty years later, he even claims he translated it from the accompanying French in Countess Rosenberg's *Morlackische Notizen*, which were not published until 1788, i.e. too late to be used for his translation (Wolff 2001: 192) – a neat example of how unconcerned he was about translations of "barbaric" literary products. It seems he did not exactly expect the translation of such marginal literary works to be of the highest sort – according to his typology (1987: 181–185) – that gives up its own language in order to closely stick to the original; an informative, plainly prosaic translation, which is the lowest sort in his hierarchy, completely suffices. The "heightened attentiveness" that protects one from "easy familiarizing projections" practiced by the ignorant mob is not exactly necessary here. Oriental non-European or indeed European literatures all serve merely for rude orientation. From the Western perspective, they make up "the rest" which "we must look at only historically; appropriating for ourselves what is good, so far as we can" (250). The non-European or less-than-European literatures and cultures, in a way, remain up for arbitrary grabs for their prominent European counterparts; what counts are their motives, certainly not language, discourse or style.

The great West European literatures, on the contrary, serve Goethe as highly important refracting mirrors that, unlike the Oriental ones, fully deserve the attentiveness of Kantian *Hineinversetzen* or Herderian *Einfühlungsvermögen*. If one wants to truly understand them, meticulous and patient translation of their genuine otherness has to penetrate what is untranslatable in them (*Beim Übersetzen muß man bis ans Unübersetzliche herangehen*, 308). Goethe does not fear to be crushed by them like his modest compatriots, since the French, British and Italians were the first to acknowledge and invite him into their international company and not vice versa. His almost imperially self-confident *Weltliteratur* therefore does not emerge from German literary and cultural inferiority as Damrosch claims. At stake is an initiative not merely richly prepared by numerous domestic translations, as indicated above, but also powerfully corroborated from abroad. Nobody comes upon the idea of forging global designs without such accreditations. Because of outlined interferences between these cultures, Damrosch's clear-cut opposition between French cosmopolitanism "from above" and German cosmopolitanism "from below" has to be substantially revised, i.e., reintroduced within each of these respective corpuses. They are far from being as robust as Damrosch (along with many others) portrays them for the polemical purpose of defending his own argument. As cosmopolitanism splits into agencies and enablers, those who speak for it and those in the name of whom it speaks – and this not only along national but also economic, social and gender lines, – it necessarily contains an *internal redoubling*. Underneath its "elitist" face, the "democratic" element is submerged, underneath its "mind" its "body." No external opposition or "blaming of the ignorant" can cancel out this constitutive gap. No "subject of" exists without a "subject to" that persistently undermines its sovereignty. Rather than being consistent and continuous, cosmopolitanism is a split and discontinuous undertaking.

As the Goethe specialist Anne Bohnenkamp was the first to notice, his idea of world literature was "directly connected with *his perception of the international reception* of his own works" (2000: 187 [emphasis mine]). It was not that he initially and anxiously *looked after* the foreign mirrors but instead, in a creatively sovereign reaction, *reflected* on their mirroring, mirrored their refractions back, retransferred their transfers, received their reception, retranslated their translations. In sum, he creatively enhanced and propelled the process of literary exchange, and precisely this is how his equivocal narrative of world literature came into being. In the final analysis, all this consolatory acceptance, praising, translating, staging, reviewing and censoring of his work (Goethe 1987: 243, who here again "modestly" speaks of "us") enormously contributed to Goethe's imperial self-understanding (Meyer-Kalkus 2010: 105–106). As the refractions "from one mirror to another do not fade but ignite each other" (FA I, 17: 371) the wide world suddenly became an "expanded fatherland," i.e. a substantially improved version of what he was desperately missing at home. After all, a number of his distinguished contemporaries such as Novalis, the brothers Schlegel, Fichte, Jean Paul, and Mme de Staël were also firmly convinced that the moment had come for Germans to take command of the world partition of symbolic values. They were expected "to unite all the advantages of the most varied nationalities" in order "to create a cosmopolitan midpoint for the human spirit" (A. Schlegel 1965: 36). To reiterate "[...] cosmopolitanism starts as a moral universalism but often degenerates into imperial globalism. [...] The continuous slide of cosmopolitan ideas towards empire is one of the dominant motifs of modernity." (Douzinas 2007: 159)

Thus the conclusion would be that, opposite to Damrosch's consistently one-dimensional reading in favor of the "free competition" of cultural values, Goethe's *Weltliteratur* nonetheless amounts to an imperial "system of self-securing" of his and the German shaken self in the sense defined by Barbara Herrnstein Smith (quoted by Damrosch, 8). This *imperial self-securing system of world literature*, "in enlarging its view 'from China to Peru,' may become all the more imperialistic, seeing in every horizon of difference new peripheries of its own centrality, new pathologies through which its own normativity may be defined and must be asserted" (Smith 1988: 54). Smith's characterization neatly harmonizes with Arendt's description of Roman "cosmopolitanism toward the inferior others," which regards the other as a mere extension of the noble Roman breed (Arendt 2010: 120). In Roman imperial terms, the other was saved from annihilation not "out of mercy, but for the sake of the expansion of the polis, which from now on was expected to include even the most foreign members in a new alliance of comrades" (116). Far from being a firm and enclosed canon (as was the contemporary Romantic *Universalpoesie*), Goethe's adaptable and steadily contextually fed movement of world literature that swallows up ever-new participants thus gradually, despite his reluctance, acquired the Roman profile. Goethe as the engineer of world literature and the Germans as its collective beneficiaries systematically capitalized the "reiterated mirroring" and "mutual illuminations" (Bohnenkamp 2000: 202–203) provided by its numerous adherents. According to a lucid early remark by Ernst Robert Curtius, world literature was from the very beginning meant as a "meeting point of many references, a center of diverging perspectives: formulated as a mission" (*ein Aufgegebenes*; Curtius 1954: 46; Bohnenkamp 2000: 202), it accumulated profit as capital does by its very definition. Being shaped as steadily agglomerating symbolic capital – and note that without exception recent German interpreters also avoid this point – it was meant exclusively for *agencies* in the globalizing operations of circulation. The remaining unfit candidates (like the non-European, less-than-European, pre-modern or indeed Romanticist mannerist literatures for that matter) were expelled in advance from the international circulation, transformation and translation that enables the symbolic enrichment of its participants – as Damrosch (2003: 4–5) significantly circumscribes the essence of world literature. Being rejected by a fine-tuned "garbage disposal" that hideously supervised its normative procedure, they were relegated to the category of *enablers*, the "working and producing" residue of all compensatory trauma narratives. This amorphous surplus follows the triumphant rise of world literature like an uncanny shadow.

Systematically stamped, marginalized, and excommunicated by the relentless normative work of this global *autopoetic system*,[11] these enablers were captured in the immobile, restricted and benighted realm of national literatures (Damrosch

---

[11] According to Niklas Luhmann (1984), who coined the term and extensively elaborated upon it, autopoietic systems are systems that maintain, differentiate and propel themselves by relentlessly reintroducing the fundamental difference between them and their environment into the

2003: 6). Locked in such a way, they were prevented from gaining and benefitting from cultural exchanges and concomitantly bereft of any chance to function as the prestigious exchange value for all the others. Destined to be deployed at best selectively, partially and occasionally as raw material, rather than permanently exchanged, differentiated and refined in the ongoing globalizing operations, they were condemned to the status of local and anonymous use values devoid of global identity, relevance and acknowledgement. To put their condition in the famous terms of Arendt, they were bereft of the right to bear rights. "Certainly some works are so culture-bound that they can be meaningful to a home-grown audience and specialists in the area," Damrosch points out in his recent book on *How to Read World Literature* in a sentence that strongly reminds us of Moretti. "[T]hose texts remain within the realm of their original national or regional culture." (Damrosch 2003: 2)

Yet *who* is authorized, and *by whom*, to ultimately determine which texts have deserved confinement within their village fence? And is such "systemic judgment" not necessarily biased and culture-bound itself, i.e., induced by the ignorance or fear of the disqualified "exotic" language, literature and culture? Besides, if the production and proliferation of such telluric, indistinctive, non-exchangeable and untranslatable "pockets of disability" is an unavoidable corollary of the self-propelling autopoietic system of world literature, then the habitual attitude of the inhabitants of these pockets to world literature has to be reexamined. The enthusiastic endorsement of its operations, feverishly trying to scratch and crawl the enabler's way into their "blessed realm" at the cost of thereby being denigrated to the status of a temporally anterior and spatially exterior object with

---

systemic operations themselves. Unlike the structuralist system concept applied by Wallerstein, Moretti or Casanova, these poststructuralist systems are caught in the process of incessant becoming, i.e. the devouring, reworking and rearranging of their environment. By back-projecting this contemporary concept onto Goethe's understanding of *Weltliteratur* I intend not just to uncover the historical sources of Luhmann's "super-theory," which attempts to embrace all particular disciplines in the same way as *Weltliteratur* attempts to embrace all particular literatures. My intention is also to point out that the fundamental difference between system and environment (*Umwelt*) that sets in motion the systemic differentiation and propulsion is rooted in *constitutive asymmetry* and *exclusion*. This is why the ceaselessly improving system's connectability (*Anschlussfähigkeit*) on the one hand – like the tireless expansion of Goethe's *Weltliteratur* – is like a shadow followed by an extension of the disabled, because disconnected environment on the other. The same point holds of course for Damrosch's system of world literature even though it presents itself, deliberately or not, in an underreferenced and under-theorized form. Applying to this conception of world literature Luhmann's over-referenced and overtheorized conception of autopoietic systems I wanted, in a sense, to fully articulate what Damrosch prefers to leave in the state of a "dotted line," or to dismantle a theory behind this conception's less than theoretical appearance. For more on Luhmann see chapter seven.

5.8 From the "iron law of kinship" to the "free competition of values" — 163

regard to the systemic mainstream (Shih 2004: 17), risks the elimination of these "systemic outputs" from the field of political attention. Are we therefore not better advised to raise the question as to who in the last analysis is authorizing, promoting, and canonizing this imperial system, and with what motivation, purpose and benefit? "*To world* and *to globalize*, then, would have to be parsed in light of their subject agencies and their object predicates. World and globalization, thus, would be imputable actions, rather than anonymous phenomena." (Kadir 2004: 2)

If we are about if not to stop, then at least ameliorate the devastating national compartmentalization of literature which, as a number of scholars indicated, turns out to be the direct consequence of the much-trumpeted and triumphant integration under the banner of world literature, are we not obliged to reopen and explore this question again and again? If the conflict between proper citizens or persons and the ignorant and amorphous mob is inherent in the cosmopolitan project of democracy since the Greeks, then, in order to proceed democratically we should not permit its obliteration, but reiterate it. Democracy pertains to the *many*, the contradictory *in-between* created by these many; no single model of Proper Man conceived as imago Dei can erase this contradiction (Arendt 2010: 119). Therefore, in order for democracy to remain a permanent litigation between the many, the relation of global domination based on the imposition of common law, as represented in the existing projects of world literature, must confront continuous disagreement rather than be smoothly perpetuated. If world literature does indeed want to be democratic, then it has the task of highlighting the irresolvable conflict that underlies its cosmopolitanism rather than the task of persistent suppression of this conflict for the benefit of a supposed "unity-to-come." In lieu of being an "unfinished project" that has to be brought to its harmonic completion, world literature is a project *never to be finished* because of the split inherent to it. Maintenance of its democratic character, not its celebrated "dialogue of equals" but its neglected *constitutive disagreement* between agencies and enablers has to be *consistently practiced*. What this unflagging practice is intended to foreground is that world literature is not so much a generous project of reconciling the divided parties, as it is regularly presented to be, but rather a compensatory project designed to come to terms with the underlying trauma of division. While systematically healing one traumatic experience, however, it cannot but inflict others.

World literature can treat these daily multiplying and "heterotopic"[12] *systemic outputs* in two principal ways. The one well-established approach devoted to the

---

[12] Foucault (1986: 24) uses the concept of heterotopias to indicate a steady proliferation of "counter-sites" that "simultaneously represent, contest and invert" the system that for its part tries to isolate or exclude them. His important point is that a system affirms its norm precisely through a reiterative delimitation of the unruly energy of deflections. Initially destined to lock

maintenance and expansion of the system at all costs is to hideously clean them up and channel them away, using, to put it metaphorically, the technique of toilet paper, water closet and septic holes. In the consensual circles of agencies, this is dubbed "decent behavior" and is understood. This approach amounts to the *state* conception of democracy. The other approach is to explore how it comes that, due to such habitual self-maintaining operations of the autopoietic system of world literature, numerous literatures are doomed to suffocate in "the pockets of poverty" relegated to marginal zones envisioned for the "garbage disposal." This approach does not acknowledge the taken-for-granted assumption that such a proliferation of "outcasts" is necessary if *we* are to have world literature but focuses instead both on the restricted character of the *worldness* of such literature as well as the limited nature of this *we*. This is an attitude that amounts to the conception of democracy as *practice*. However, as we have seen, the two delineated conceptions of democracy do not only oppose, but also imply each other.

David Damrosch enlists the following core attributes of world literature: (1) the profitable *overlapping* of different groupings of works, (2) the establishment of highly intriguing *family resemblances* between them (2003: 281–288), (3) the concomitant work's *abstraction from its origins* (300), as well as (4) the *detached engagement* that this requires on the part of the researcher (297). In a stunning passage, which clearly anticipates this list, Manfred Koch, in his informed, attentive and well-documented study on *Weimar's Inhabitants of the World*, states:

> In the interplay with other stories, the use value of a particular story recedes in favor of the equivalence value. In this toing and froing between stories and their groups, the imagination liberates itself from the fixation to particular times and topics and, almost levitating, dissects the fundamental motives of human coexistence. If this deepening succeeds, one can discern in what is newest that which is oldest. (Koch 2002: 176)

For Koch, Goethe undertakes a systematic dissolution of the historical boundary drawn by the moderns with the aim of securing the global transnational character of their literary achievements. To such a feverish novelty addiction, he opposes the deep quietude and steadiness of collective memory (154). This is how Roman imperial cosmopolitanism oriented toward the assimilation of others reemerges in "Greek clothing." That is to say, in the same move in which Goethe denies the

---

these unaccountable systemic forces into a sort of "inner colony" or "inside pocket of outsideness," these "foreign bodies," however, incessantly grow until they finally "undermine language because they make it impossible to name this *and* that, because they shatter and tangle common names." They "desiccate speech, stop words in their tracks, contest the very possibility of grammar at its source; they dissolve our myths and sterilize the lyricism of our sentences" (Foucault 1971: 18).

imperial global sovereignty of the new he establishes the elitist global sovereignty of the old, vastly extending its area of responsibility. With this global restaging of the ancient, the departed legacy renews its claim to sovereignty. Goethe thus subjects the form of the *systemic interpretation of the world* to harsh critique whenever the moderns as its carriers are concerned, but it powerfully resurfaces in relation to the ancients (156). This means that Goethe, surreptitiously as it were, takes up the idea of sovereignty from the French revolutionaries with whom he otherwise waged a war on all levels. It is not the systemic ambition itself that changes, but merely its terms. Instead of being *immediately given*, the systemic whole of the world shaped by the lost Greeks has to be earned through *mediation*. If modern artistic revolutionaries namely claim they have forever broken with self-enclosed domestic tradition in the name of universality, he, as if quieting the disquietude provoked by their "revolution," discovers in this supposedly discarded tradition a continuity of analogous breaks. "The sovereignty of Goethe the observer stems from his ad hoc exhibition of the structure of the new and modern experience of time which enables him, through a retreat from it, to escape into the ancient and perpetual." (157) Perpetuation guarantees continuity, which for its part levels all conflicts and controversies.

Yet this disclosure of the deep-seated ancient structure of the new, if it wants to make itself convincing, is by no means an easy operation, as the latter is an immensely mobile, diverse and multifaceted phenomenon. "In *Notes and Essays on the West-Eastern Divan* the poet is clearly presented as a bazaar trader who picks up the goods of the most diverse cultural provenances and composes from them new collections, which makes him a governor and mixer of traditional stocks rather than an autochthonous creator." (Koch 2002: 161) Goethe is aware that the consciousness of the modern reader is overloaded with stories of various origins and imageries, differing narrative techniques and levels. Therefore he, to attract this reader's attention, includes in *Conversations of German Expatriates* (1795), like a good tradesman in the warehouse, a colorful mass of catchy stories, anecdotes and news next to the high literature. That is to say, the unity of scattered expatriates must be achieved not through a declaratory imposition from above but rather through an integrating examination of their discordances from below, which makes Goethe prefer the polyphonic stream of an open-ended conversation (168). His entire hope is that thereby "the whirl of modern dispersed memory could be transferred, by means of the reiterated mirroring evoked by his text, into a slow rhythm of foundational memory" (175). The compromise with the bazaar and the warehouse, conceived as the epitomes of despised vulgar cosmopolitanism, is evidently transitory. There is a carefully organized system behind them.

A systemic integration of a huge stockpile of the mutually historically, linguistically and culturally very remote literary works, introduced by Goethe two centuries ago as a *sovereignty-warranting method* and reestablished by Damrosch today, is therefore a *foundational work* that distills from their very specific *use values* their basic and profitable *exchange value*. It performs this (symbolic) capitalization, to reiterate Damrosch's list of world literature's core attributes, through (1) the careful detachment of the project's "carier group," (2) abstraction of literary works from their origins, (3) their concomitant intersection, translation and overlapping which ultimately force them into (4) new family resemblances. Literary works give up their old families not in favor of a different type of their common-being but in favor of a *new family* grouped around the absent, i.e. obliterated father. Reintroducing via His self-appointed representatives the passion for unity, the systemic project of world literature opens the door for the renewed terror of the One over the Many. As Arendt noticed, structuring human species on the model of family kinship brutally erases its political plurality and irreducible diversity (2010: 10–11), paving the way for the terrorism of all those who do not fit it.

This is exactly what Goethe's *Weltliteratur* does. Published for the first time almost a quarter of century after the *Conversations*, the *West-Eastern Divan*, an exemplary work of world literature *avant la lettre*, intensifies unification of the most disparate elements via the mutual mirroring and splitting of opposites. In order to force an overarching family unity into the potentially broad diversity, Goethe pushes such dissolution and volatilization of identities to a hitherto unimaginable limit which eventually effectuates a melting of national individualities into what appeared to him to be universally human (Koch 2002: 195). God is, after all, presented in the *Divan* as a liberal old man whose indifferent command of the world does not allow for beginnings and ends, boundaries and restrictions. To his "neutrality" comparable to the one of Bakhtin's "Third in the dialogue" (Bakhtin 1979: 305–306, 371) everything appears to be provisional and contingent, caught in the dissolving movement of becoming.[13] Yet how truly indifferent and detached can an instance be that eventually capitalizes the whole process, forcing its participants to comply with its terms? In a significant self-apostrophe in the poem "Unlimited" (*Unbegrenzt*), written just four years before the *Divan*, and omitted

---

[13] Koch refers neither to Bakhtin nor Luhmann but analogies can be drawn with Bakhtin's contention that from the point of view of the constitutively external "third consciousness" every identity appears to be depersonalized and exchangeable and every meaning interminable, groundless and limitless (Bakhtin 1979: 305–307, 371). As for Luhmann's superior observer, the social world strikes him as an interminable bifurcation and its dissent is resumed with every observation. The identification of the fundamental difference is thus replaced by a relentless differentiation (Luhmann 1995b: VI) which is, significantly, hard to follow as it "requires considerable intellectual effort" (1986a: 181). It is therefore not to be expected from inert and asleep observers but only from those equipped with a better-knowing ambition, readiness and ability to enter into vertiginous self-reflection. As in Goethe's vision of *Weltliteratur*, differentiation implies discrimination.

by Koch, Goethe, as the forthcoming engineer of world literature, seems to have come as close as possible to the highest commanding position bereft of all other interests except the steady accumulation of (symbolic) profit:

> Daß du nicht enden kannst das macht dich groß,
> Und daß du nie beginnst das ist dein Los.
>
> (That you can never end is what makes you great,
> And that you never begin is your destiny.) (1987: 133)

Tirelessly switching between the registers of perception, imagination and remembrance as well as the multiple roles in which he alternately presents his "I" (emigrant, traveler, merchant and poet), in the *Divan* Goethe is at constant pains to integrate the dispersed and heterogeneous readership aesthetically. He thereby creates "an alliance of those who understand what is at stake in these texts – and who are united without the statute, without knowing each other, but through the bond of common aesthetic experience" (Koch 2002: 218). Building an abstract network of mutual understanding and social intercourse, the *Divan* is a standing invitation to those readers willing to participate to firstly drop their inherited cultural baggage, intellectual affiliations and alliances, to disregard the goal-oriented performances of their everyday lives in order to join the "grand family of the initiated" "scattered all over Germany and the world" (218). Through such an extension of the bonds of human affection toward a cosmopolitan family of like-minded individuals securely severed from the ignorant masses of their anonymous fellow creatures, Goethe trusted, as Bakhtin (1986: 23) once enthusiastically observed, that he could enable the becoming of his self to be realized parallel to that of the world. After all, Kant, especially in his political philosophy, tended to observe the world from the same imperial and apparently impartial cosmopolitan perspective and with the same supposedly selfless participation (*uneigennütziger Teilnehmung*) that in the *Critique of Judgment* he required for the judging of a work of art (Arendt 1992: 73).[14] But how many people could afford the same dissolution of a local identity refuge, the need for which was keenly felt, in the systematically postponing, relaxed creative and divinely sovereign manner of these "world family" engineers? As Ken Hirschkop (1999: 238) caustically noticed, "what Goethe

---

[14] The same "impartiality" and "unselfishness" holds for the observer position in Luhmann's super-theory, which strives to add nothing to the existing state of facts other than to bring itself into complete accordance with the structure of this state, providing nothing but a report on the process of its self-production. All observers that appropriately decipher the calculus inherent to it will, the astounding thesis goes, ultimately derive from it the same sense (*Gleichsinn*; Luhmann 1996).

saw [around himself] was not the evidence of a generalized human creativity." "Only some of the subjects of Goethe's time laboured 'creatively'; most of them worked technically, to satisfy immediate needs and the commands of their superiors." This is why very few of these "local enablers" could recognize his invitation to join the prosperous "world literature community," let alone accept and follow it systematically. It was after all, in its elitist self-exemption, from the very start structured to maintain itself *against those who could not recognize the same invitation*. Behind the Roman cosmopolitan assimilation of others lurks the Greek cosmopolitan separation from them. The two thus continually intersect.

As Goethe takes care to permeate the *Divan*'s consistent "rustle of intertextuality" and "arabesque combinatory" with a clear authorial will organically linked to the exemplary antique legacy, an arrogant aristocratic gesture is directed against the deluded "Oriental crowd" because of its inability to establish a clear connection with it. In fact, the vertiginous presumptuousness of this work is engaged with the aim of fencing off such "Orientals" (identified with the "moderns") lacking insight into the magnificent past that shimmers through the work of art (Koch 2002: 225). For what is truly universal in literature, its final truth, cannot possibly be expressed in a direct way, but only through the most diverse effects, refractions and mirroring (Bohnenkamp 2000: 203). Nonetheless, an attentive reader (*Aufmerkende*) will know how to penetrate to it beyond the distracting appearance (Goethe WA IV 43: 83). "That which is truthful is godlike, it does not appear immediately; we must divine it from its manifestations." (FA I 10: 746) This holds for the true writer's approach to nature, in whose confusing abundance s/he must capture the all-uniting essence, as well as the true reader's approach to a literary work, in whose dense particularity s/he must discover the shine of universality. Yet befallen by the myriad of diverse manifestations, how many readers can carry out such complex derivation in an appropriate way? And who is in the final instance authorized to determine which one of the manifold ways is appropriate? Who can claim to be in possession of the truth? Complaining that in Goethe's magnificent whirl "everything invokes everything, which makes one's mind quite dizzy," none other than Hugo von Hofmannsthal was to be one of its innumerable perplexed victims among German contemporaries (Hofmannsthal 1979: 442; Koch 2002: 188). "The society of readers with aesthetic feeling is in principle endlessly extendable; the only entrance ticket is the sense of 'excellence' and the will to affirm it in the face of the changing fashion of the zeitgeist." (Koch 2002: 225) Whoever lacks this sense and the will to accomplish 'excellence,' from the systemic perspective that sells the entrance tickets for it of course, inevitably finds that the door to the world community is locked. "The *West-Eastern Divan* is an invocation of memory and the eternal legacy of the past and its founding books." (227)

5.8 From the "iron law of kinship" to the "free competition of values" — 169

In establishing an instructive genealogy of Goethe's idea of world literature, Manfred Koch emphasizes, contrary to the usual "generously democratic" interpretations, the concept's covert elitist, classicist and discriminating structure. Surreptitiously suppressing its initially *emancipating historical character* of a literary-political alliance with the affiliate foreign writers against the domestic strictures and pressures, world literature gradually acquires an *oppressive aesthetic profile* of a detached community of the like-minded. They systematically disconnect themselves, freely and playfully exchanging their symbolic values, from all obligations toward their cultural origin and associated fellow creatures. Their exchange values ultimately come to be inapplicable and strange for these creatures. Yet the established "world literature community" with its strong inclination toward the *exemption from, parenthesizing* and *abstraction of* the inherited identity constraints does not just disqualify and discriminate innumerous writers, works and readers that existentially depend on them and are therefore doomed to the existence of this community's systemic outputs. Beyond this expulsion, it substantially impoverishes the systemic constituents themselves. In order to participate in the established equivalence value and to profit from the intellectual trade set in motion by it, they must be relegated to the suitable series, mode and category, which forces them to abandon everything unfitting to these identity marks and in so doing to give up their resilience to the imposed terms of trade.

David Damrosch in *How to Read World Literature* (2009: 5) stresses that "discussions here are by no means intended as full-scale readings, but are given as examples of general issues and as portals into extended readings." Yet the whole argument developed above guides us to the inference that the very methodology of the system theory of world literature[15] – whether this system is autopoietic or, as in the case of Moretti and Casanova, self-enclosed – necessarily transforms literary works into "examples" and "portals" of systemic operations. Close reading of literary works is equally remote to Damrosch as it is to Moretti or Casanova for that matter: they are systemic thinkers dealing with arbitrary, abstract items compelled to dispose with their immobilizing social and cultural inheritance in order to prepare themselves for the mobile process of their capitalization. Without respect for the foreignness of the foreign, Damrosch accordingly bereaves literary works of their specific memory. Freeing them in such a way from their cultural resilience to or historical ignorance of the new "world family," he transfers them into its abstract terms with regard to which they, despite their deeply unequal and hardly reconcilable starting positions, must prove equally responsible. Contrary

---

[15] Damrosch (2006: 45) postulates that world literature is *by nature* a systemic construct continually remaking itself diachronically and dialectically.

to Goethe's Greek elitism, such a powerful assimilation of the foreign obviously draws on the tradition of Roman cosmopolitanism, limitlessly ready to integrate others upon the condition that they comply with the terms set by the heir. In the process of the Romanization of the provinces, Roman components, although interactive and adaptable rather than given and static, dominated at the expense of the indigenous ones. Their dissemination assured historical progress. Roman rule was presented as providing the conditions for human beings to fully realize their potential by becoming civilized and so truly human. This is why Roman civilizing "might be compared to the demolition of street upon street of old houses, materials from which were used to create a towerblock to house the former inhabitants in a new style" (Wolf 1998: 47). The same kind of restructuring holds for the Americanization of world literature.

Damrosch eliminates Goethe's German-centered elitism from his interpretation of the idea of *Weltliteratur* exactly in order to obliterate his world literature's culturally impregnated profile. As we have seen, he states that a "provincial writer," being "free from the bonds of an inherited tradition," "can engage all the more fully, and by mature choice, with a broader literary world," "to seek out a variety of networks of transmission and reception" (2003: 13) for his or her literature.[16] Goethe's pre-national approach *from below* becomes a mobile systemic perspective that is, it would seem, taken up by Damrosch in order to circumvent the delineated perils of the static systemic designs *from above* rooted in given national identities. Like Goethe, Damrosch interprets the latter as being inappropriate usurpers of that which has to remain universal. He launches an alternative project of world literature in comparison with the national, i.e. French and American appropriations of Casanova and Moretti. What is germane to it is not a fundamental difference between the proper (national) and the improper (non-national), but merely a relentless differentiation.

---

16 This rendering of world literature's generously liberating mission strongly recalls Pascale Casanova's statement that world literature "as the common value of the entire space, is also an instrument which, if re-appropriated, can enable writers – and especially those with the fewest resources – to attain a type of freedom, recognition and existence within it" (2004: 90). It is also in line with Jonathan Israel's conviction, quoted in the first chapter, that French Enlightenment, "especially in many Asian and African countries, as well as in contemporary Russia" has become "the chief hope and inspiration of numerous besieged and harassed humanists, egalitarians and defenders of human rights, who, often against the great odds, heroically champion basic human freedom and dignity" (Israel 2010: 11). In short, despite the differences between Damrosch's and Casanova's pattern of world literature, they seem to agree that the Western "global" intellectual achievements help newcomers from "subordinated regions" to come to grips with the nationalist "forces of darkness" in their own countries.

Nevertheless, obliterating the huge asymmetry between the German *pre*national and his U.S.-American *post*national point of departure, Damrosch misuses Goethe's elitist idea for the sake of imperial globalization. Like Greek elitist cosmopolitanism, Goethe's structuring of world literature, being directed against the provincial national self-enclosure, eventually aims at an international affirmation and consolidation of the national self. As opposed to it, being established in exile, on foreign soil, the U.S.-American democratic cosmopolitanism belongs to the Roman type:

> What happened when Trojan descendants arrived on the Italic territory amounted to the following: Their politics came into being precisely at the point where for the Greeks it reached its limit and end, in the in-between, that is to say, not between citizens, but between peoples, foreign and unequally opposed to each other and brought together only by conflict. (Arendt 2010: 108)

Developed from an irrevocably hyphenated or grafted identity, this cosmopolitanism is oriented toward establishing the in-between areas between the opponents; it dissolves oppositions in favor of the mutual implication of the parties. Because Aeneas is a newcomer among the Latin settlers, he must rely on his contract with them. Inasmuch as the Romans owe their historical existence to this contract, they are oriented towards protecting the inferior foreigners by means of ever-new contracts, until the entire globe is finally clamped down in a system of contracts (114–115). Their imperial slogan reads: Do not destroy, expand! As Greg Wolf, the specialist in ancient Rome, puts it, Romans understood their expansion as "the means by which the potential of the world and the entire human race might be fulfilled" (Wolf 1998: 57). Being of the same hyphenated, postnational character, U.S.-American cosmopolitanism displays the same patronizing attitude. Yet we should recall that this tireless creation of bonds and alliances on the pre-given contractual basis ultimately pushed the Romans "very much against their will and without any lordliness on their part, into domination of the entire globe" (Arendt 2010: 119). Their generous democratic cosmopolitanism relied on the utter ignorance of the otherness of the other. The Romans simply could not imagine that there existed something equal to them in terms of greatness and yet different from them (121). Precisely this appropriation of the space between peoples, Arendt claims, "created the Western world as a world in the first place" (121), pushing it, we could add today, into its recent globalized form.

Deriving this imperial Roman type of U.S.-American *post*national cosmopolitanism from Goethe's *pre*national cosmopolitanism putatively developed *from below*, Damrosch not only purifies it from all national claims but also tacitly and subtly uncouples ill-reputed globalization from selfish and profitable U.S.-American "engineering." Considering the huge collateral damages inflicted upon globalization's innumerous "enablers," and especially the devastating terrorism leveled to globalization's leading "agency" as a kind of retribution of these damages, one can detect the traumatic experience of the shaken U.S.-American identity as the birthplace of Damrosch's idea of world literature. His leading question, rescued from its hiddenness, reads: Why does the U.S.-American identity suddenly act in *national* fashion if it is genuinely *postnational*? Unlike the official U.S.-American politics that, blindly denying national trauma, all the more fiercely acts it out, Damrosch's elaboration of the idea of world literature invests considerable effort in working through it. His somewhat apocryphal thesis, when seen in the light of day, is that the engineers of *violent* globalization are, by necessity, of the provincial *national* kind. He therefore clearly rejects the U.S.-American narrow-minded nationalism just as Goethe was opposed to its German forebear. The fundament of his *reconciling* idea of world literature instead becomes the *postnational* U.S.-American identity, which cannot but be a product of the relentless differentiation, crisscrossing and overlapping the most diverse national literatures.

Yet what if the U.S.-American *post*nationalism is equally *nationally* oriented as Goethe's German *pre*nationalism? What if postnational mobility, as Haun Saussy (2006: 20–21) pertinently cautions, is not so much a "common substrate" distilled from compared literary works, i.e., from below, but, on the contrary, projected onto them by the "act of comparing itself," i.e., from above? What if this act, departing from what comes naturally to an U.S.-American researcher, reifies their identity? "[T]he internationalism of our academic life is a direct consequence of our economic, cultural, and political hegemony, our position at the center of a de facto empire," warns Katie Trumpener (2006: 191). She points to the counter-example of Central and Eastern European countries where the nation-state was to develop incomparably later than in the West and therefore *against* the Western postnationalism. There are many more such countries in the world of course. It is precisely because Damrosch's conception of world literature is decisively postnational that it forgets that one important part of the world is still *pre*national (like Goethe's Germany was some two centuries ago) and that world literature should not advance at the expense of this part of the world.

In accordance with this basic suppression, Damrosch's theory of "profitable translatability" seems to also cancel out the geopolitical power differential between the great and minor languages and literatures that does not allow for equal mobility and concomitantly equal profit of world literature's participants. More than being just provisionally unequal, the immobility of the minor literatures is the condition of im/possibility for the mobility of the great ones (Biti 2002). "[T]he intercultural relations in which translation figures are, in any historical moment, not just asymmetrical but hierarchical." (Venuti 2012: 180) If the "translational gain" is, according to Damrosch, the royal road to the much-desired status of world literature, and if translation is, for the reasons delineated above, not exactly the coequal mutual traffic, then it is clear whose symbolic status mostly benefits from it. Is the status of world literature reserved just for great literatures and those "minor writers" who readily consent to their preferences and predilections? In the same way that Goethe concealed the fact that the German prenational search for identity forms the basis of his idea of world literature, Damrosch conceals how the American postnational search for identity forms the basis of his idea of world literature. However, despite this obliteration, or precisely because of it, neither of these ideas can eliminate discrimination from its operations.

However, even beyond this structural discrimination inherent in Damrosch's interpretation of world literature, the postulated *ideal of translatability* bereaves literary works of everything that, from the systemic perspective, impedes their exchangeability. The result is

> a sort of restrictive literariness – based on an author's or a work's potential for international or European influence – but also an unspoken hierarchy for the different European literatures based on the extent of their respective transnational-philological potential. From this came the principle of translatability – that is, the special capability of certain cultural languages to take in a wide diversity of literary productions, thus guaranteeing their admittance to the international scene. (Aseguinolaza 2006: 420)

In the outcome, this autopoietic system of world literature, while largely outmaneuvering the otherness of the other in order to carry out its sweeping comparisons as well as to establish its new family resemblances, transforms literary works into the exemplars of the *supremacy of the signified over the signifier*. To provide an illustration, in the chapter "What is 'Literature'" in his book *How to Read World Literature*, Damrosch juxtaposes three examples of love poetry. He analyzes an Indian short lyric from around the year 800, a lyric of an anonymous sixteenth-century English poet, and a poem by the Chilean poet Alejandra Pizarnik from 1965, instantiating a kind of *experiential exchange* between their "speakers" across languages, cultures and centuries. Hence even though the focus of the chapter is the question "what is 'literature'," instead of concentrating on the establishment of the literary quality of these examples Damrosch introduces their common denominator on the level of the experiences presented. He speaks of the strong focus on the speaker's or lover's "interior state of mind" (or the "interior drama" "inside the speaker's head") induced by an almost strategic concealment of the setting of the speech act (9–10). What connects three otherwise very remote literary examples would be roughly the following: The reader is driven into the position of "overhearing a single speaker" (10), which channels his hermeneutic effort toward the reconstruction of the missing parameters of the speaker's communicational and overall situation. This is especially demanding in the case of the old Indian poem with a different set of social and cultural assumptions. Damrosch (13) therefore advises the reader to linger upon moments that seem puzzling or absurd on first reading and, by "learning enough about the tradition" and clearing up these moments "with some detailed specialized knowledge that we lack," to use them in the second reading as "windows into the writer's distinctive methods and assumptions." Yet how can the reconstruction of the *represented* (i.e. the *speaker's*) communicational situation tell us something about the specific literary quality of the poem? Would not the reconstruction of the *representing* (i.e. the *writer's*) communicational situation be more appropriate?[17] And the latter situation can hardly be invoked by the reader's stumbling over "illogical, overdone, or oddly flat" moments of the poem, as it requires prior knowledge of the historically, socially and culturally specific literary conventions that *precede and frame* the very act of writing. Love is after all not just a socially coded relationship but one coded in literature too (Luhmann 1982). Such knowledge would, for instance, advise us against talking about the "individual thinking aloud" and the "interior state of mind" in a sixteenth-century poem since the silent thinking linked to the interior state of mind, as the distinctive feature of individuality, does not enter Western literature until the late nineteenth century. In view of such knowledge, we would probably also hesitate to apply the same category of the "speaker" (which implies a clear distance from the author) to all three examples indiscriminately. And finally, the very division of the question "What is 'literature'" into "The World of the Text" (8), "The Author's Role" (13) and "Modes of Reading" (16) would, as a historically much later tripartition of literary studies, probably also have to be questioned.

Such unreflected supremacy of the signified over the signifier follows, it would seem, from the *tacit relinquishment of differential theory* that marks the transition from comparative to world literature as well as the accelerated canonization and institutionalization of the latter. Denuded of their otherness and consequently devoid of any chance to resist the "sacred imperative" of systemic circulation, these works, their huge historical, social, cultural and linguistic diversity notwithstanding, function as a sort of merchandize in the systemic operations of transfers, combinations, translations, orderings and mappings or, in the final analysis, gains and losses. We thus testify to the glorious revival of the basic principle of Goethe's *Weltliteratur* – *The greater your diversity, participants of*

---

[17] Considering the manual character of his book, Damrosch is sparing with references but his reading of lyrics as a staged or quoted speech event strongly reminds us of Barbara Herrnstein Smith (1978) and Félix Martínez-Bonati (1981), whereas his two-level-interpretation of the reading of lyrics recalls Riffaterre (1978). These conceptualizations of lyrics characterized by the methodology of their time have been meanwhile, however, exposed to critique and revision.

world literature, the more magnificent grows my unity – with the important caveat, however, that new world literature, reintroduced in all its splendor after centuries of apocryphal existence, *turns the very spirit of this principle upside down.* As the unity of world literature now progresses through the *suspension* instead of *affirmation* of its national diversity, everything is put down to the common denominator of mobility, exchangeability and translatability. This is why new world literature – exactly opposite to what Goethe envisaged for the old one – celebrates the triumph of what is globally habitual (*Weltläufige*) and therefore *indifferently valuable* over what is capable for the world (*Weltfähige*), and therefore *irreducibly individual*. Nietzsche's sinister diagnosis that world literature is tantamount to an assemblage and compilation of items uncoupled from any creative potential, an indiscriminate mixture of the most diverse arts and senses produced by the metropolitan, deracinated and adaptable man "without qualities" (Beebee 2011: 373–374) – this diagnosis was surely unjustified with regard to Goethe's *Weltliteratur*. However, it wonderfully fits the new worlding of literature. We are advised therefore, instead of taking its putatively democratic character at face value, to insist like Nietzsche on the necessity of pinning down such transnational visions of literature to their historical, geographical, national, social and cultural, almost "physiological" location. Despite its detached global appearance, this "world literature" is firmly located within a recognizable, i.e., U.S.-American *part* of the world. It is precisely the indifferent detachment from the irreducible otherness of its participants and its works that announces this part's global imperial ambitions.

Part II: **An Observer under Observation:
The Cosmopolitan Legacy of Modern Theory**

6 Interiorizing the Exteriority: The Cosmopolitan Authorization of the Theoretical Truth

The shortest possible definition of theory might read "an eye-opening affair with someone beyond our familiar world." As proper insight without the risk of self-estrangement seems to be impossible, theorizing would be a brave act. Yet it is not necessarily a deliberate undertaking. Displacement into the amazing area "beyond the boundary," initially resonating with pulse-quickening and adrenalin-increasing associations, can sometimes mean the most desperate emigration or exile uncoupled from any eye-opening intention. Despite the much-trumpeted cognitive benefits of border-crossing, émigrés and exiles, if they had the choice, would probably prefer, however short-sightedly, to stay in their familiar world. Is it therefore advisable, as Hans Mayer (1975) and Edward Said (1993: 403) suggested, to distinguish between the two kinds of "outsiders," the "heroic" and "enlightened" intentional ones and the "sacrificial" and "benighted" existential ones? Alternatively, are we better advised to treat enlightenment and benightedness or heroism and victimhood as co-extensive attributes of "theoretical outsideness?"

Charting a genealogy of American comparative literature as the institutional domicile of literary theory after the Second World War, Emily Apter, for example, derived its endemic feeling of placelessness out of exilic consciousness continuously passed and refined from one comparatist generation to another. According to Apter, this deeply ingrained constant of the field lent it its "consistency of character as a relentlessly distantiating mode of criticality" (1995: 87), i.e. a profile which is today usually attributed to literary theory. Early American comparatists, many of them European emigrants like Leo Spitzer, Erich Auerbach, René Wellek, and Wolfgang Kayser, had a distaste for nationalism which paved the way for "the nation-neutral textuality of American New Criticism" and developed theoretically based pedagogies for which "no visa was necessary" (88). Because the lingua franca of the burgeoning discipline was German, similarly to the theories of alienation and subjective estrangement expounded by the likes of Marx, Freud, Simmel, Benjamin and Lukács, comparative literature was characterized by an ethics of linguistic estrangement and secessionism from mainstream American culture (89). Through their exilic experience first comparatists were banished from the world of purely esthetic forms but the trauma of exodus resonated even louder for the next melancholic generation of deconstructionists who, beginning with Jewish epistemological placelessness, speak of the "anxiety of influence," "agonism," and "criticism in wilderness" (90). The current postcolonial generation of exilic critics, finally, is anti-Eurocentric, non-German-speaking, non-white, antipatriarchal, and hostile to elite literariness and yet, like its antecedents, imbued with "melancholia, Heimlosigkeit, cultural ambivalence, consciousness of linguistic loss, amnesia of origins, border trauma" (90). Like Leo Spitzer, Homi Bhabha for instance activates cultural difference and disinheritance as engines of literary analysis, which is why theorization of *Heimlosigkeit*, with its unbroken decades-long persistence, turns comparative literature as the traditional domicile of literary theory into "a placeless place that is homely in its un-homeliness," "the institutional and pedagogical space of not-being-there" (93). "This unhomely voice, together with the restless, migratory thought patterns of the discipline's theory and methods, highlights the extent to which comparative literature's very disciplinarity has been and continues to be grounded in exilic consciousness." (94)

In her more recent book *The Translation Zone* (2006), which explores the genealogy of exilic consciousness of comparative literature, Apter turns to what she terms "philological humanism" of Jewish prewar and war émigrés to Turkey, such as Spitzer and Auerbach in their pre-American emigrant episode that produced the conditions conducive to the establishment of American comparative literature.

> A fascinating two-way collision occurred in Istanbul between a new-nations ideology dedicated to constructing a modern Turkish identity with the latest European pedagogies, and an ideology of European culture dedicated to preserving ideals of Western humanism against the ravages of nationalism. (Apter 2006: 50)

Leo Spitzer claimed in his essay *Learning Turkish* (1934), that "any language is human prior to being national," i.e. associating philology with linguistically interrelated and intertwined etymological roots as well as human *ratio* rather than *race*, defended a kind of transnational humanism or global *translatio* of national languages. His "resistance philology" was used as a prophylactic against the nationalist leveling differences to rescue them from reductive politicization (57–58). Being a foreigner in the Turkish national corpus, he developed an interest for bottomless, dehumanized aspects of language which, according to de Man's interpretation of Benjamin, (De Man 1986: 85–86) cause suffering in the authenticity of every mother tongue (*die Wehen des Eigenen*) in the manner, the most valuable translations do.

> Spitzer forged a worldly paradigm of *translatio studii* with strong links to the history, both past and present, of *translatio imperii*. [...] The practice of global *translatio*, as Spitzer defined it, is patterned after untranslatable affective gaps, the nub of intractable semantic difference, episodes of violent cultural transference and countertransference, and unexpected love affairs. (Apter 2006: 64)

What else but such amazing affairs could better suit "the pulse-quickening thrill of dangerous liaisons" (63) inherent to today's comparative literature and its representative product theory?

Yet in the aftermath of the First World War, many of the East-Central European literary theorists developed their ideas out of the political dislocation and consequent linguistic and cultural displacement. The lives, for example, of Trubetskoy, Jakobson, Lukács, Bogatyrëv, Šklovskij and Wellek were deeply marked by the experience of exile and emigration, coercive evacuation from their familiar universe. As Galin Tihanov (2004: 419) pointed out, their

> [e]xile and emigration were the extreme embodiment of heterotopia and polyglossia, triggered by drastic historical changes that brought about the traumas of dislocation, but also, as part of this, the productive insecurity of having to face and make use of more than one language and culture.

Living as dislocated remnants of the broken multinational East-Central European empires within the environments of the new nation-states, these intellectuals embodied "transcendental homelessness," an existential feeling detected by Lukács, in a typical transference maneuver, in the behavior of the novelistic hero. As the elected representatives of this post-imperial generation were unable to identify either with German or Russian culture as their own meaning horizon, they consistently challenged both of them, raising the evacuation of empirical evidence to the basic operation of modern literary theory. "Appropriating literature theoretically meant, after all, being able to transcend its (and one's) national embeddedness by electing to position oneself as an outsider contemplating its abstract laws." (420)

Interestingly enough, far from being an exclusive feature of modern theory, such contemplation of abstract laws after an enforced detour is, after Hans Blumenberg (1987), a well-established legacy of European theory since the time of Greek *theōría*. The Greek word *theōrós*, according to Hannelore Rausch, designated a special envoy sent to inter-communal religious ceremonies to request the divine wisdom and relay it, with consecrating effects, back to community members (Rausch 1982: 9–10). The purpose of *theōría* and the objective of *theōrós* were therefore to tranquilize community fears caused by inexplicable occurrences (Blumenberg 1987: 12). Jean-Michel Rabaté observed: "in his authorized gaze everyday deeds will be integrated into a sacred 'theater'; there, things will be seen under their most essential aspect, so that they can be recorded officially" (2002: 114). Aristotle dubbed this essence of community life, discerned from an authorized remote position by means of theoretical insight, the truth (Rausch 1982: 11). The truth introduces the divine perspective into the shattered community horizon, re-centering it through its extension. As European culture, because of its persistently enforced detours, was challenged to continuously extend its communal horizon in this manner, Blumenberg (1987: 158–159) interprets theory as its consistently unifying telos. Theory's persistent search after the truth, as long as it has the ambition to restore the community's jeopardized consensus through a cosmopolitan reordering of the disquieted habitual perspective, seems to be warranted for the unbroken continuity of European history. The tacit corollary to Blumenberg's argument is that this distinguishes Europe from the self-enclosed history of other cultural circles ignorant of or inimical to the others.

In the conclusion of his book, Blumenberg adheres to Husserl's consensual conception of theory that persistently assimilates earthly resistances to its truth in a broadening horizon as against Heidegger's revolutionary conception of theory that, as exemplified in *The Question after the Thing* (1935 and 1936), ignores and rejects these resistances. Following Nietzsche, Heidegger refuses any communal verification of theory's judgment, making the truth the privilege of an elected and insightful minority (1987: 148). This philosophical minority finds the confirmation of its superiority in the community's rejection of its truth, an elitist stance that, after Blumenberg, betrays the democratic function of theory in the history of European culture and ends its development. According to Jacques Taminiaux, Blumenberg's tacit disagreement with Heidegger's dismissal of public judgment broadly corresponds with the attitude of Hannah Arendt, who openly criticizes Heidegger's alienation of professional philosopher from human beings in terms of practical concerns (Taminiaux 1998: 132–133). Both Blumenberg and Arendt, who otherwise hold different philosophical positions in a distinctively European tradition, the argument goes, advocate a democratic reintegration of theory into communal horizon through the cosmopolitan extension of the latter. Never calling into question the possibility of such reasonable dialogue between community and its *theōrós*, neither of them considers the irrevocable and inassimilable character of theorist's outsideness.

Theory was nonetheless from the Greek time constantly subject to misunderstandings that questioned its pretension to truth. Apparently, the theorist's "adultery with the foreigners" that in the first place *enabled* such pretension simultaneously *prevented* its acknowledgment. It suddenly jeopardized the entrenched prejudices of the community; and whenever such a threat arises, people who find existential shelter in these prejudices tend to consolidate them further thereby burying themselves ever deeper into their self-defending phantasms. This is the gist of the famous anecdote on Tales and the Thracian maid recounted by Socrates in Plato's *Theaetetus*, whose numerous transformations Blumenberg attentively investigates to demonstrate theory's persistent vulnerability to laughter and mockery. The theorist's privilege with regard to peasant or philistine community members cannot be accomplished without his/her simultaneous exposure to their down-to-earth judgment. To counter the mistrust of "simple minds" and foster the necessary consensus for its supposedly divine contemplation, theory was forced to make its sublime vision of the truth available to a broad spectatorship

(Gasché 2007: 198). Because of this brutal exposure to the same mob prejudice that was envisaged to be dismantled, theory, instead of providing a privileged private insight into the divine truth, became a public performance dependent on the confirmation of the earthly gaze. Without ever being able completely to assimilate this benighted philistine gaze in the illuminating divine truth provided by "adultery," but remaining dependent on the crowd's uncertain approval, theory, despite its strenuous efforts to deactivate the community's ignorant self-evidence, was at constant risk to reaffirm it.

In an entirely characteristic contradiction to her consenting to Blumenberg's hermeneutic argument, presented above,[1] Hannah Arendt has tackled this paradox in her instructive exegesis of the political in the ancient Greek-Roman context. In the Greek polis, the political rests on the non-coercive action between human subjects, from which the slaves and barbarians are, however, excluded (Arendt 2010: 37). By repeating this emphasis, Hannah Arendt obviously presents herself a theorist of social exclusion rather than of reasonable human communication. The price of the latter is the former, which puts into question the reasonable character of political activity. The liberation of people for the broad-minded exchange of opinions is inconceivable without slave labor; freedom and non-coerciveness are preconditioned by violence and coercion (38–39). The political commences where necessity ends, and is therefore by no means omnipresent and a matter of course (41–42). It requires the courage to put at risk one's private being and allegiance to the family, both apparently not to be expected from the slavish souls that passionately stick to them (44–45). Used to compliance, they are unable to live the life of equals, i.e. to be free. The free world is created through a permanent exchange of opinions between equals, i.e. as something common to the many. Yet because such freedom demands coercion and violence toward the outcasts, it cannot be regarded as true freedom. Plato obviously realized this when he founded his Academy as the space of true freedom, as opposed to the feigned freedom of the polis. Once again, liberation from the coercion of the public marketplace is made the prerequisite of the true freedom of academia; Academia reinstated, if it

---

[1] The early Habermas of *The Structural Transformation of the Public Sphere* (1966) subjected Arendt's philosophy, to an influential hermeneutic appropriation, translating it eventually into the consensual frame of his later theory of communicative action. Comparing Arendt's and Heidegger's philosophy, Jacques Taminiaux takes up his thesis of the neo-Aristotelian revival of the category of praxis in Arendt. Though not completely unfounded, this thesis suppresses the dissent-oriented moment of the new beginning, and with it, the discontinuity of the public sphere in Arendt's political thought. For the critique of the consensual appropriation of her thought, the reduction of its complexity and the suppression of its antagonistic character, see Disch 1997: 149 and Villa 1995: 204–205.

did not reinforce, freeing of the few through enslavement of the many (55–56). It thus reaffirmed the work of self-exemption from the deluded crowd characteristic of Greek cosmopolitanism (and resumed, as we have seen, by Voltaire, Kant and Goethe, or by Heidegger's philosophical elitism addressed above).

Now, the Arendt's sketched elaboration of the relation between freedom and coercion elucidates Blumenberg's paradox of theory outlined above:

> Wherever the few separated themselves from the many, they obviously became dependent on them, that is to say, in all those matters of coexistence which have to be really negotiated. [...] This is why the realm of the freedom of the few is not only at pains to maintain itself against the realm of the political determined by the many, but is, dependent on the many for its very existence; the simultaneous existence of the polis is existentially necessary for the existence of the academy. [...] [I]t becomes a necessity that on the one hand opposes the freedom, and is its precondition on the other. (58–59)

The gist of this paradox, according to Arendt, is that philosophy is determined to rescue the value which disappeared from the public space of the self-sufficient polis, i.e. the greatest possible survey of the greatest variety of opinions. When a community conducts a war against another community, like the Greeks against the Trojans, it tends to obliterate the point of view of the other. But the political judgment demands at least two parties, which is why it has to liberate itself from the destructive belligerent attitude towards the other in order to pay respect to both sides; to equally consider both points of view in conflict. Yet such mobility of thought, even if it enables an unparalleled independence of Greek judgment (96), remains constrained to the space within city walls and pertains neither to the abroad (i.e. foreigners) nor to the family space (i.e. women and children) (99–100), both determined as they are by the relation of domination.

> The free space of the political appears like an island; solely there is the principle of violence and coercion excluded from human relations. What remains outside that tiny space, the family and the relation of the given polis to other political units, remains subject to the principle of coercion and the power. (100)

To apply to foreign policy the patient consideration of many points of view is therefore unthinkable for the Greeks. Because legislation is by definition limited to the space within city walls there is no common legislation that regulates relations between political communities. Precisely this walling off of the outside world paves the way for the internal political world characterized by free communication between humans. Whoever ventures beyond the pale transgresses the law and exposes himself or herself to its force. Insofar as the legislating bridge building between peoples did not belong to the Greek world, the founding of an empire of the Roman kind was under such conditions simply impossible (114). We can therefore conclude that the unparalleled mobility of thinking in the Greek polis was purchased at the price of violence against the insiders and outsiders excluded by its law. In order for the thinking subjects to be free, those who are disqualified from the activity of thought had to be ruled out. To occupy as many points of view as possible – yes, but not those of slaves, women, children and foreigners! Those who think are expected to transgress every single boundary, excepting that between the free and the bound. As the hard won ability of judgment keeps aloof from any relation of domination, it is reserved for the elect few or philosophers, such as Nietzsche and Heidegger in Blumenberg's argument about theory. The many or the philistines are on the contrary delivered to domination, which makes them incapable of free theoretical thinking. Operating as it does with the continuous engagement of the otherwise minded, theory is for the Greeks tantamount to a domestic policy that relies on an elect elite.

Since the Romans established their city in exile, on foreign soil, their relation to foreign affairs was completely different.

> What happened when Trojan descendants arrived on the Italic territory, amounted to the following: Their politics came into being precisely at the point where for the Greeks it reached its limit and end, in the in-between; that is to say, not between citizens, but between peoples, foreign and unequally opposed to each other and brought together only by conflict as they are. (108)

Turning their former enemies into future allies by means of peace treaties, the Romans transferred politics to the relation between peoples, owing to which from their perspective law amounts to the establishment of an in-between area between former opponents. Because Aeneas is a newcomer among the Latin settlers, he must rely on his contract with them. Inasmuch as the Romans owe their historical existence to this contract, they are oriented to protect the inferior foreigners by means of the always-new contracts, until the entire globe is finally clamped down in a system of contracts (114–115). Their imperial slogan reads: Do not destroy, expand! The life of the other had to be saved not "out of mercy, but for the sake of the expansion of the polis, which was from now on expected to affiliate even the most foreign members to the new alliance of comrades" (116). Yet the cosmopolitan Societas Romana envisioned as an endlessly expandable alliance system turns out to be a boundless and insatiable enterprise. The Greek restrictive nomos wanted, according to Arendt, to prevent exactly this evaporation of the political in an incalculable system of relations. However, neither Greek elitism (as exemplified in Heidegger's stance towards the benighted mob), nor the Roman cosmopolitan attitude (as exemplified in Husserl's opening up of theory to include the most diverse affairs from the everyday), saved their ideas of free judgment from ultimate breakdown. Arendt therefore states:

> There is no doubt that at the end the whole Hellas collapsed because of the nomos of their political units, city-states which could multiply by way of colonization but were not able to unite into an enduring bond. But we could with equal justice state that the Romans became prey to their "lex," which, although it made possible for them to create bonds and alliances wherever they arrived, was for its part uncontainable because it pushed them, very much against their will and without any lordliness on their part, into the domination over the entire globe which, as soon as it was established, fell apart again by itself. (119)

The final price for the boundless expansion of the empire was the loss of Greek impartiality. Unlike the Greeks, the Romans refused to acknowledge the other in its otherness, regarding him or her as a mere extension of their own kind. The Romans could simply not imagine that there existed something equal to them in terms of greatness and different from them (121). Precisely this paternalist appropriation of foreign cultures, Arendt claims, "created the Western world as a world in the first place" (121). Even though Roman imperial rule followed the ideal of inclusiveness, it crushed out the local customs of the included in favor of imperial institutions. The more it became universal, the less the Roman citizenship respected the rights of the lower classes, women, or ex-slaves (Mamdani 2012: 76). Arendt seems to be claiming that the same kind of discriminating absorbtion of foreign cultures underlies the much-trumpeted Western openness toward the others.

Arendt's interpretation of the Roman cosmopolitan extension of their own political truth to the others advises caution with respect to Gasché's thesis on the early German Romanticist, typically European *democratic* cosmopolitanism. In *The Honor of Thinking* (2007), he interprets early Romanticists as rescuing the honor of the mobile Greek theoretical thought, because at the time, accelerated confrontation with foreign cultures stimulated them to question all empirical truths of literature. As communal judgment at the micro and macro level was, almost overnight, immensely diversified, empirical truths turned into non-reflected self-evidence in need of enlightenment. Under such world-opening conditions, theory was obliged to dismantle the self-enclosure of these local truths raising the universal truth of literature to the dialogic horizon of their eventual reconciliation. Early Romanticists thus introduced the self-reflective age of modern theory, compelled to observe the intracommunal and intercommunal differences and measure them against each other. However, they undertook a comparative detour through the reigning *dissent* in order to accomplish a truly universal *reconciliation*, which is a moment heavily downplayed in Gasché's reading. They focused first on the difference between literature and every acknowledged truth of it, instead of directly upon literature, systematically evacuating the self-evidence of the latter. No theoretical location was authorized in advance but all were compelled to reflect critically on their down-to-earth indebtedness. Unlike a substantially less mobile Greek theory whose divine truth enjoyed an only domestically questioned authority, such a mutually questioning relating of numerous earthly truths to each other followed from their growing social and international dispersal. No particular literary work, genre or corpus, however broadly acclaimed by a given social group or national community, could represent the final truth of literature anymore. However, what early Romanticists were eventually aiming at, pace Gasché's portraying of their cosmopolitanism in predominantly oppositional terms, was literature's truth as an indifferent, impartial and unselfish metteur-en-scene of this dialogue. The truth they envisaged was therefore of a similar status to Kant's observer addressed above, Goethe's engineer of world literature or Bakhtin's "Third in the dialogue." Far from being disinterested, the integration of the mutually historically and culturally very remote views on literature into the final truth of literature was an operation serving the consolidation of this instance's sovereignty.

The early German Romanticists' self-reflective concept of literature, Gasché states, is "rooted in a comparative approach to literature that transcends linguistic and national boundaries" by making literature into the medium of permanent reflection of one national literature or literary genre in the other (2007: 178). He prioritizes the logic of permanent opposition following Benjamin's insight that the early Romanticist concept of criticism comprises not just the direct knowledge of its object but also an indirect knowledge that this knowledge will not suffice and that, as nobody's knowledge is all-inclusive, this insufficiency is inevitable. The self-reflective critic must therefore be able (Gasché refers here to August Schlegel) "to block out his personal predilections and blind habits in order to transpose himself into the singularities of other peoples and ages, and to experience them from their center as it were" (Schlegel 1966: 18). According to August Schlegel (1964: 21),

> ... there is no fundamental force in the whole nature that would be so simple as to prevent self-division, and not separate into opposite directions. The whole play of living movement is based on agreement and opposition. Why would this phenomenon not repeat itself on a grander scale in the history of mankind?

Consequently, if dissent is the driving force of the whole history of humankind, why should be theory spared the endless differentiation of its judgment? On the contrary, it ought to be its highest representative.

After its elaboration by Kant in a number of treatises from 1785 to 1798 (Kant 2006a), cosmopolitanism loomed large on the intellectual horizon, entailing the proliferation and juxtaposition of the firsthand evidences which the truth was expected to assimilate in order to authorize itself. Yet, pace Gasché, this infinite detour, because it surpassed the "visited" self-evidences, obviously did not mean that the truth lost control of the alluring labyrinth of theirs. On the contrary, it aspired to the complete surveillance. Discussing the establishment of proper esthetic judgment in §40 of the *Critique of Judgment*, Kant obliges the reader to compare his or her judgments not only with the real but also merely possible judgments of other readers by transposing himself or herself into the place of everybody else (*dass man sein Urteil an anderer, nicht sowohl wirkliche, als vielmehr bloß mögliche Urteile hält, und sich in die Stelle jedes andern versetzt*). He imagined the appropriate reception of an artwork as a constitutively open yet nonetheless authoritatively guided undertaking. The reader's imagination is, though free in terms of its adulterous "foreign affairs," not completely directionless and unleashed but hideously orientated and governed by the integrative movement of an ultimate authority. Kant associates the latter with worldwide community (*Weltpublikum*) as the last-instance corrective of judgmental aberrations. This *Weltpublikum* functions as what, especially in his late philosophy, he repeatedly calls the "touchstone of truth" (*Probierstein der Wahrheit*; in 1956: 64, translated as "criterion," 2006a: 249, 2006b: 17, 113).

Kant's secularization of the authorization procedure of the truth, compared with the divine character of the truth in Aristotle's philosophy, paves the way for the early Romanticists' democratic repositioning of literary theory as the official purveyor of literature's truth. Nonetheless, neither Kant nor Romanticists, despite the undertaken secularization and democratization, suspend but reaffirm the truth's divine character. The innumerous questioning detours notwithstanding, the theorist remains unquestioningly loyal to this "deity." This is exactly the point at which Gasché's interpretation of early German Romanticist legacy, which follows the exegesis introduced by Walter Benjamin and continued for example by Ernst Behler, Winfried Menninghaus and Samuel Weber, falls short in its generous attempt to save the "honor of thinking." Kant's *Weltpublikum* is obviously aligned with his key political-philosophical concept of the human race (*Menschenrasse*), introduced as a long-term historical agency necessary to emancipate a short-term human being from its basically "animal" natural disposition (*Naturanlage*). Still clearly associated with the universal *ratio* in God's mind (Apter 2006: 32) Kant's human race is saturated with divine attributes. Although religion was proudly rejected as a superstition to be overcome if humankind was to achieve maturity, the very idea of the human being gradually maturing on its own transfers divine ratio onto the "great chain of being" or, in Kant's rendering, "series of generations" (*Reihe der Zeugungen*). Universal history is a quintessentially divine enterprise. The divine substance is from the outset constitutively involved in its course keeping a watch on it. In early German Romanticism the truth in continuous historical displacement is a substitute for the Greek truth sent from abroad, but history is *equally piously taken at its word* as was this "abroad." Now, how honorable can thinking be if it requests authorization from an instance, which it in advance exempts from questioning?

Goethe as usual hit the nail on the head in *Makariens Archiv*: "The truth is god-like; it does not appear to us immediately; we have to derive it from its manifestations" (*Das Wahre ist gottähnlich; es erscheint nicht unmittelbar, wir müssen es aus seinen Manifestationen errathen* (FA I 10: 746)). Far from being accidental and isolated, this claim is in full accordance with a motto from *Kunst und Altertum* (VI 1) in that one can learn the truth only from its effects (*Die Wahrheit lässt sich erst an ihren Folgen erkennen*). It is also in line with the letter to Iken of September 27, 1827 in which the God-like author Goethe confides in his addressee that he long ago decided to drive his attentive reader to derive the secret meaning of his work from its counter-positioned and mutually mirroring constituents (*so habe ich seit langem das Mittel gewählt, durch einander gegenüber gestellte und sich gleichsam in einander abspiegelnde Gebilde den geheimeren Sinn dem Aufmerkenden zu offenbaren*) (BA IV 43: 83). This explains why Romanticist artists and philosophers must authorize their truth – the community's homogenizing common sense (*Gemeinsinn*) – through the accumulation and mutual comparison of its most manifold international effects. The truth emerges through a series of self-transpositions into the most diverse perspectives, i.e. a complex management of frustrating differences carried out by a disquieted self that searches for accreditation.

What therefore distinguishes the early Romanticist from the old Greek theorist is that this authorizing "adultery with the foreigners" does not take place in the *real world* but in the *imagination* of the theorist's disconcerted self. As Lauren Berlant (2011: 26) has put it, the object of desire must be *absent* in order for the desiring subject to stabilize his or her proximity to it and to invest its hopes into it. This is to say, the inter-community that is expected to accomplish the reconciliation of the theorist's shattered and divided community by introducing the ultimate truth into it is projected out of the theorist's *traumatic experience*. Working into the awareness of those afflicted by it insidiously, differently and unevenly, the community's traumatic constellation mobilizes some of its destabilized members to counteraction, primarily those most sensitive to its traumatizing impact. The carriers of this counteraction put themselves in abeyance by attaching themselves to the vague prospect of the truth expected to warrant them a large-scale historical existence, or at least assure them continuity amid the process of its brutal discontinuation. In the traumatic constellations characterized by heightened uncertainty, such passionate attachments to potential long-term collective benefits usually flourish at the expense of an orientation to short-term individual interests (Hanson 2010: 29).

Yet why should other members of the same community, who occupy different political, social, ethnic or gender positions in the same constellation, experience this constellation in the same traumatic way as the theorist unreservedly committed to the redemptive prospect of the truth does? The traumatic constellation, as I interpret it, is a controversial knotting of heterogeneous perspectives and discourses that underpin, question and defy each other (Brunner 2014: 41–45). This is why the community's suspicion of the theorist's "foreign affairs," as analyzed by Blumenberg in the case of the old Greek *theōría*, must hold sway over early German Romanticism as well. The early Romanticist assimilation of antagonistic self-evidences in the international horizon of literature's truth is as equally problematic as was their domestic assimilation in the Greek polis. The sovereignty of the early Romanticist truth is, like the sovereignty of the Greek theoretical truth, a therapeutic phantasy exposed to communal attrition. However grandiose the aggregate envisaged by its cosmopolitan detour comes to be, this truth cannot but experience disaggregation by the forces excluded from it. It produces a compensatory heterotopia of sovereignty, elongating the time horizon of its carriers and their adherents. Because of that, we should treat this scenario of repair as a problem in its own right rather than attaching our hopes to it (Berlant 2011: 49) in the way that Gasché does. This is the task of what follows.

Let me begin with the thesis that the insight into the arbitrary character of the early German Romanticist authorization of the theoretical truth already lurks behind Hannah Arendt's and Jean-François Lyotard's illuminating readings of Kant's political philosophy (Lyotard 1991: 224; Arendt 1992: 43). Kant's cosmopolitan transpositions were led by his intention to establish an impartial and superior philosophical self. Yet far from being all-inclusive in this attempt, Kant was at permanent pains to exclude his philosophical gaze from the ordinary perspectives of uncultivated fellow-creatures and lower human species. Unlike fine souls, they were not the destinations of his self-transpositions. Both "savages" and "natural humans" whom Kant (2006a: 46) describes as "animals in need of a master" are already excluded from this elite company. As for the "savages," he is disarmingly frank in his *Physical Geography*: "Humanity is at its greatest perfection in the race of the whites. The yellow Indians do have a meagre talent, the Negroes are far below them and at the lowest point are a part of the American peoples." (1997b: 63) Unlike Europeans, none of these three lowest human races can continue to grow in intelligence (63–64). In the treatise *On the Use of Teleological Principles in Philosophy* (1788) Kant classifies human races after their dependence on long-term bodily lineage. As European races are considered to be free moral agents primarily determined by reason, he makes the physiological body into the repository solely of the non-European racial identity. Possessing all forces and talents as well as capability for unlimited progress, Europeans are the ideal model of universal humanity (Eze 1995: 203–204, 216). This is why the authorizing series of transpositions, instead of entailing an othering of the self, amounts to the exploitation of others for the sake of its own aggrandizement.

Kant was not isolated in the self-centered and Eurocentric authorization of his truth. Proposing the prismatic refraction of the truth and its multifaceted effects, Goethe was aiming at the similarly sovereign German-centered European self as we have seen. The latter is a clear distance from the ignorant and barbarous mob addicted to the security of "house piety" (FA I 10: 514). To feed its superficial and dispersive consumer habits the crowd only requires from literature swift and powerful effects (1987: 173–175). Next to these benighted creatures that dwell in parochial self-sufficiency, Goethe is equally critical of the self-enclosed non-European cultures as well. To recall: "Chinese, Indian, Egyptian antiquities are always just curiosities; it is recommended to make oneself and the world acquainted with them; but they would be not especially fruitful for our moral and esthetic education/formation (*Bildung*)" (284). This is the reason why "Orientals" can never stand comparison with the Greeks and Romans or the *Naturdichtung* like Serbian epic or *Nibelungen* with the Iliad (174). Oriental culture can be used just as a "refreshing source" to "strengthen the peculiarity of our spirit" but certainly not as its law-giving pattern (FA II 6: 642). The same goes for *Naturdichtung*: being original but primitive, it can be reasonably exploited only as a raw material. From the Western perspective, together they constitute "the rest" which "we must look at only historically; appropriating to ourselves what is good, so far as it goes" (1987: 250). Yet even prominent European literature like the French, English or Italian that acknowledged, praised, translated, staged and reviewed Goethe's work (243) in the final analysis contributed merely to his imperial self-understanding (Meyer-Kalkus 2010: 105–106). Through their activity, the world became for Goethe an "expanded fatherland," i.e. a substantially improved version of what he was desperately missing at home.

Neither was Goethe alone in his elitist predilections. In 1793, Herder stated that Germans should "appropriate the best of all the peoples and in such a way become among them what man became among the fellow and co-creatures (*Neben- und Mitgeschöpfe*) from which he learned his skills (*Künste*). He came at the end, took from everybody his art and now *he surpasses and rules all of them*" (Herder 1991: 551 [emphasis mine]). Several years later Novalis in an equally cosmopolitan project *Christendom or Europe* (1799) suggested that whereas other European countries were "occupied by war, speculation and partisanship (*Parthey-Geist*), the German builds himself with all diligence into an associate (*Genosse*) of a higher epoch of culture. This preliminary step *must give him in the course of time great predominance* (ein großes Uebergewicht) *over the others*" (Novalis 1983a: 519 [emphasis mine]). In the same self-fostering vein, Goethe entrusted German language with the role of the medium of permanent translation of one into another literature. It is called upon to set the course for everybody's national currency (*Münzsorten*) through "the take up and complete appropriation (*das völlige*

Aneignen) of the foreign" (1987: 238). If such "complete appropriation" is the true background of the early Romanticists' generous world reconciliation (*Weltversöhnung*), then there is something other than "pure humanity" (*reine Menschlichkeit*) behind Weimar's esthetic program which tried to "unite again the politically divided world under the banner of truth and beauty" (*die politisch geteilte Welt unter der Fahne der Wahrheit und Schönheit wieder zu vereinigen*) (Schiller 1991: 109). When August Schlegel, the key figure of Gasché's cosmopolitan argument, stated "that the moment is not so remote when German will become a general organ of communication for all educated nations" (1965: 27), allocating to the Germans the mission "to unite all the advantages of most various nationalities" in order "to create a cosmopolitan midpoint for the human spirit" (36), he was merely expressing the common view of the time. Novalis's typically pregnant formulation in a letter to him from 1797 reflects the same cosmopolitan patriotism: "Germanness is cosmopolitanism mixed with the most powerful individuality" (*Deutschheit ist Kosmopolitismus mit der kräftigsten Individualität gemischt*) (Fink 1993: 39). As this was obviously a compensatory response to the deep-seated inferiority feeling of Germans at that time, we must agree with Manfred Koch (2002: 235) that such megalomaniac statements "strike us today as extravagant, if not explicitly funny." Contrary to Gasché's claim, therefore, the early German Romanticist cosmopolitan literary theory was dedicated to the self-consoling glorification of the German self. If early Romanticists took the latter to be the very epitome of universal human spirit, what obliges us today, equipped as we unfortunately are with the privilege of retrospection, to endorse their opinion?

This point is important not just because it revises the entrenched stereotypic distinction between the allegedly cosmopolitan early and the allegedly nationalist late German Romanticism. Usually the first is praised at the cost of the second that, especially if looked at retroactively, "pollutes" the German putatively genuine cosmopolitanism. By dismantling their unstoppable intertwining, we question the putatively open cosmopolitan spirit of "proper literary theory." If early Romanticist theory set itself the "infinite task" of interiorizing all its exterior critical observers in order to establish a completely sovereign observation of the world, then it was German-centered and Eurocentric rather than truly cosmopolitan and open. It represented a specific "carrier group" rather than all those in whose names it pretended to speak. This group drew the most substantial profit from it on the model of Roman cosmopolitanism by means of which Romans capitalized their idea of *humanitas*. Developing the notion of *humanitas* in response to anxieties generated by the encounter with Greek culture over the last centuries BC, the Romans shaped it in such a way that only those foreigners who adopted Roman values received acknowledgment of properly exhibiting *humanitas* (Wolf 1998: 58, 63). Remedially expanding the Roman self against the frustrating impact of the superior Greek culture, *humanitas* aggrandized this self in the same way that early German Romanticist cosmopolitan theory therapeutically extended the German and Western self.

In his genealogy of modern literary theory, Gasché uncritically resumes this gesture. Also in the title of his most recent book, inspired by the idea of Europe developed in the late work of Edmund Husserl, he uses the term "infinite task" and thus endorses the philosophical tradition embraced by Blumenberg in *Das Lachen der Thrakerin*. Husserl attempted to solve "the crisis of European humanity" in the same way as Blumenberg and Gasché do, by reattaching Europe to its genuine "task" of rescuing "universal humankind" by gradually suspending limitations caused by others. According to these thinkers, theory is an eminently European mission. Being open "toward transcendence, toward the other, and what is other than Europe" (Gasché 2009: 27), an inborn "interiorizer of exteriorities" so to speak, Europe is interpreted by Gasché to be the most reponsible representative of universal humankind (31). It is an epitome of theoretical behavior that never stops questioning itself. One of Gasché's spokespersons, Jan Patočka had this to say: "In contrast to ordinary life which confines itself to never questioned self-evidence and security, never aiming at anything beyond, spiritual man lives expressly from the negative" (221; Patočka 1990: 247). Associating this consistently self-interrogating life with the spiritual rather than historical or geographical Europeans, Gasché confronts every human being irrespective of location (2009: 27) with this "common task." In the same way Kant confronted every man with the obligation to become a responsible person, forgetting that the great majority of humans, put under the long-term rule of Europeans, were made incapable of assuming such responsibility. As Walter Mignolo once put it: "Kant obviously was not thinking about the Amerindians, the Africans, or the Hindus as paradigmatic examples of his characterization" (2000: 734). If we subscribe uncritically to the idea of theory as the infinite task of suspending all material differences for the benefit of one spiritual truth, we are, advertently or otherwise, fostering the early Romanticists' remedial heroization of the self. It may be that Europe today desperately needs such consolation but, if theory is to maintain its democratic character, it must not strive toward a compensatory suspension but consistent reaffirmation of its non-theorizable "output." Since it is never so universal as it claims to be, the authority drawn from its "murky foreign affairs" ought to be unremittingly exposed to observation if it is to remain politics and not pervert into policing.

7 The Narrative of Permanent Displacement: Early German Romanticism and Its Theoretical Afterlife

7.1 Reappropriating the early Romanticist legacy

Through the early work of Walter Benjamin, the legacy of early German Romanticist thought has been disclosed behind the differential paradigm of poststructuralist theory by interpreters such as Ernst Behler, Winfried Menninghaus and Sigrid Weigel in the German tradition, Philippe Lacoue-Labarthe and Jean-Luc Nancy in the French tradition and Rodolphe Gasché, Beatrice Hanssen, and Samuel Weber in the U.S.-American tradition. Moreover, having meticulously compared Benjamin's somewhat enforced and not completely informed reading of this legacy with Friedrich Schlegel's, Novalis's and Hölderlin's original theses on "infinite redoubling or reflection"[1], Menninghaus did not hesitate to state:

> It is even difficult to see what Derrida has to offer that is substantially new in comparison with the early Romanticists, but it is much easier to see where he lags behind them. The more comprehensive and multifaceted character of early Romanticist thought entails that the critical objections to the metaphysics of the self-present identity do not amount to the negation of the philosophy of identity, but are conceived as their redemption through extreme straining. The figures of différance do not merely possess supplementary quality, but *are* a version of identity themselves, for the Romantics ultimately the only tenable one: identity as the effect of the game played by difference itself. (1987: 131)

This Romanticist redemption of identity would namely go against Derrida's claim that his deconstruction of the metaphysics of presence sounded the death knell for identity philosophy *per se* (131). However, contrary to Menninghaus's contention, Derrida *never* made such a claim. Carefully avoiding the key Romanticist concept of *reflection*, he spoke of the constitutive postponement of identity that is, because of its inbuilt temporal differential, vainly struggling to gain ownership of itself. This makes the final historical reconciliation of identity with itself,

---

[1] The respective part of Menninghaus's book *Unendliche Verdopplung* (1987) is available in American translation and concludes with the following sentence: "Within this line of argument, the general exposition of the Romantic theory of reflection – which is the essential innovation of Benjamin's study – relates to its 'application' in a seemingly paradoxical fashion, in that the general philosophical grounding of his arguments does not hinder him from undertaking a largely valid 'derivation' of the cardinal concepts of Romantic poetology from the theory of reflection as their centre." (2002: 50)

which Menninghaus correctly puts forth as the very gist of the early Romanticist doctrine, impossible from the perspective of deconstruction. Yet if early Derrida, doggedly adhering to undecidability, takes a clear distance from the early Romanticist "literary absolute" (Lacoue-Labarthe and Nancy 1988) or from the replacement of philosophical truth by literary fiction characteristic of Friedrich Schlegel's conception of literature (Bowie 1997: 53–65), how justified is then Menninghaus's remark that he "lags behind" his "forebears?"

Like Menninghaus, the second important German interpreter of the early Romantic intellectual legacy, Ernst Behler (1997: 111), points to the transfer of the Kantian transcendental subject, by way of "transcendental poetry," from philosophical into literary terms. For the brothers Schlegel, in contradistinction to Kant, the imagination is "the primary faculty and reason the secondary, which is why the world manifests itself as an artwork, i.e. in all its original poetry; reason tends toward unity, imagination toward the abundance and manifoldness, beautiful confusion, 'original chaos of human nature'" (Behler 1993: 78). Such an infinitely self-reflective "poetry of the world" that breaks through all the firm cognitive abodes by re-describing ones by means of the others enables the self to go beyond itself on the empirical level and return to itself on the transcendental one. Unlike philosophy or other arts, poetry permits the integration of the most comprehensive variety with the highest possible unity (90). With its infinite perfectibility, it reflects the desire of modern man to realize the Kingdom of God on earth. "Whatever has no relation to the kingdom of God is of a strictly secondary importance." (Schlegel 1971b: 193) As Friedrich Schlegel clarifies in his *Philosophical Apprenticeship* (1796–1806), God is the guarantor of the freedom of man's formation (*Bildung*) inasmuch as He demands the incompleteness of earthly beings to be completed by their counterpart. The peaceful residing in one's own identity is, for this reason, inadmissible. "For a man who has achieved a certain level and universality of formation, his inner being is an ongoing chain of the most enormous revolutions." (1963: 82–83)

From 1800 onwards, Schlegel describes this antithetical or antinomy principle of self-formation as cosmic irony. Both this immense cosmic detour of irony and Nietzsche's famous imperative to the self to permanently switch perspectives, being its evident follow-up, are therefore in the final analysis placed at the service of the God-like formation of the self:

> Far beyond the dialectics of the process of artistic creation, Schlegel's irony designates the propelling energy of man's formation (*Bildung*). It becomes the force that protects from the one-sided, all too fast solidifications and, by pushing incessantly forward, holds the spirit on track. (Behler 1997: 112)[2]

---

[2] All translations from German here and in the following are mine, if not otherwise indicated.

7.1 Reappropriating the early Romanticist legacy

Although Behler (74) strongly insists on the *reciprocity* between the affirmation and negation, the creation and annihilation of the self as the core of Friedrich Schlegel's concept of irony, his analysis nonetheless privileges the *steady progression* of the self towards a divine observing post. Departing from the double-sidedness of irony, Behler objects to the American reception of Schlegel's concept of irony on account of its one-sidedness, just as Menninghaus did to the French reception. He points out the "typically German" predilection for life's entirety instead of just its active part, which is allegedly the French and English tendency (286–287). De Man for example overlooks the affirmative side of irony, insisting on its annihilating power, which betrays the complexity and richness of the original German concept. "Little remains from Schlegel's and Nietzsche's notion of irony, which consisted exactly therein that with the aid of irony we willfully, by means of a skillful tactic, transgress and outplay the linguistic borders set upon us." (309) Instead of starting out from the *power of personal will*, de Man delivers the self to the *inaccessible impersonal language* that repeatedly subverts all its intended meanings (308–309). But is the delivery of man's self to the absolute Kingdom of God that forces it into a *relentless self-propelling* not just as one-sided as its delivery to the absolute Kingdom of Language that forces it to display *sacrificial grief*? Are not sovereignty and victimhood merely the opposite sides of the same coin?

Yet the celebration of Nietzsche's creative concept of *life* that is, according to Thomas Mann, "elevated" in typically German spirit "to the highest rank and spiritual mastery" (288–289) appears to be much closer to the heart of German interpreters of the early Romanticist legacy, for one reason or another, than the celebration of the related demolishing concept of *death*. Having demonstrated their dissatisfaction with the foreign misinterpretations of the German legacy of *Lebensphilosophie*, both Menninghaus and Behler therefore approvingly return to the domestic revival of the authentic Romanticist spirit in Niklas Luhmann's autopoietic system theory (Menninghaus 1987: 208–224; Behler 1997: 324–327). The fundamental insight of Luhmann's theory is that one can never directly observe *objects* as such, rather only their various *observations* (Luhmann 1995b: 50), which concomitantly leads to an infinitely concatenated *observation of observations*. This thesis would indeed be unimaginable without the delineated early Romanticist heritage. Nonetheless, the German usurpation of the exclusive authorial rights to this legacy is questionable, since the same perpetuation of observations holds for example equally well for Gilles Deleuze's translation of the firm difference of structuralism into the poststructuralist terms of continuous differentiation – and Deleuze undertook this far-reaching substitution of differentiation for difference almost twenty years earlier than Luhmann:

> Each point of view must itself be the object, or the object must belong to the point of view. [...] Difference must become the element, the ultimate unity; it must therefore refer to other differences which never identify it but rather differentiate it. [...] Every object, every thing must see its own identity swallowed up in difference, each being no more than a difference between differences. Difference must be shown differing. (Deleuze 1994a: 56)

From the primacy of difference over identity highlighted by both Deleuze and Luhmann in the wake of the early Romanticist legacy, it follows that no single observer is capable of identifying by itself the blind spot of its observation. Constitutively dispossessed by another observation, it cannot escape delusion. Displacement is therefore promoted into the structural condition of theoretical knowledge, meaning that every site of knowledge implies delusion. "The impossibility of differentiating the difference that makes possible our differentiation is the fundamental condition of all knowledge *(Erkenntnis)*." (Luhmann 1990a: 47) As the blind spot of an observation can be detected only retroactively by the following observation and the blind spot of the latter again only retroactively by the next one, narrative concatenation of observations into an *enlightening temporal sequence of redescriptions* charts the trajectory of theoretical knowledge. Luhmann's continuous "observation of observations" transposes us in the mid of the Voltairean pattern of successive overcoming of each prior historical constituency by the subsequent one: "Une article doit corriger l'autre; et s'il se trouve ici quelque erreur, elle doit être relevée par un homme plus éclairé." (Voltaire 1765: 224)

7.2 The pattern of irritated overcoming: the entangled opponents

In such a surreptitious way, the Enlightenment doctrine unexpectedly catches up with its Romanticist counterpart. By unconsciously reintroducing the Enlightenment educational terms, Romanticist theory resumes the ambition to capitalize, once the divinely absolute insight has been achieved, on having patiently pushed through the delusion. If this imperial self-educational ambition is to be realized, the truth abandons its initial self-enclosed and self-satisfied "site in life," entering the enriching temporal medium of displacement and postponement. Yet as each new phase amounts to the enlightenment not just of the immediately preceding phase but all the previous ones in the given sequence, the sequence underlying enlightenment through such narrative progression grows in scope and complexity with each new step. In the long run, therefore, the horizon of the displaced theoretical observation gradually expands. Its course is delineated not just as a blind and hollow trajectory but as a goal-directed plot. Each new phase demonstrates a more developed synthetic capacity, gaining obvious profit from the previous ones.

Tracing this enlightening progression of his systemic observer back to its Romantic origins, Luhmann most accurately identifies the ambition that sets it in motion as "the know-all attitude" (*die besserwisserische Einstellung*). This pertinent term foregrounds not just the agency-enabler-relationship, but also the *power asymmetry* germane to it. The Romanticist truth can come into being only against the background of delusions or, more accurately, through the rejecting of previous truths as delusions. The truth of the second-order observer who "knows better" can be affirmed only through the derogation of the truth of the first-order observer who knows less:

> In such a way, the basic observer was relegated to the zone of the harmless and naive, or treated as someone who, without knowing it, has something to hide. He who knows better nurtured himself through suspicion, and the generalization of the principle of suspicion enabled whole disciplines – from psychoanalysis to sociology – to establish themselves with additional abilities in a world in which everyone knows or believes to know for what purpose and in which situation he acts. (Luhmann 1990a: 46)

Yet this cosmopolitan project of the gradual enlightening of the narrow-minded observers ran into serious difficulties from the very start. Although the Enlighteners persistently strove to assimilate the benighted individuals and groups through their correction and improvement into the growing unity of humankind, the instances they treated so generously nonetheless doggedly resurfaced as obstacles on the envisaged path of progress. To single out two prominent examples for the sake of illustration, in Kant's late treatise *The Conflict of Faculties*, he puts forward the free and autonomous use of human reason as the necessary principle of commensurability of dismembered academic domains. This treatise was a reaction to the Prussian state's censorship threat induced by his previous essay, in which Kant had tried to place religion within the limits of pure reason. Precisely because the Prussian state prefers obedience over free reason, in its academic division of faculties, theology, law and medicine enjoy the status of major faculties, whereas philosophy, the only representative of reason, is devalued as a minor faculty. Kant now proposes an exact reversal of this, which would instantiate philosophy, considered useless in the reigning disposition of knowledge, as the critical judge over the major disciplines, since philosophy is "independent of the government's command" (1979: 27) and these disciplines are obedient to the state. Kant (25) condemns their representatives as "the tools of the government" (*Werkzeuge der Regierung*) or mere "businessmen or technicians of learning" (*Geschäftsleute oder Werkkundige der Gelehrsamkeit*) as opposed to the representatives of philosophy, which in its search for the truth is "by its nature free and admits to no command" (29). Because philosophy, as indicated by its dislocation in the academic distribution of knowledge, serves the truth as opposed to located disciplines that serve the government, philosophy is authorized by Kant to dispossess the latter of their petty "private property" for the benefit of a future "common freedom" of humankind (59–61). The narrow-mindedness of scholarly disciplines comes to the fore in their readiness to place their discourse in the direct service of the extramural "populace consisting of idiots" (25; translation modified, *das Volk* [...] *welches aus Idioten besteht*, Kant 1991: 280) instead of serving the all-unifying human truth.

Kant's significant irritation with the resurgence of the non-academic "idiotic populace" in the form of academic *Fachidioten* finds a modified continuation in Friedrich Schiller's contemporaneous argument from the *Aesthetic Education of Man*. Countering Kant's privileging of philosophy, Schiller, along with Friedrich Schlegel, raises *literature* to the only true representative of mankind as a whole. Literature is, after all, much more reader-friendly than philosophy, and considerably easier for a broad readership to become acquainted with. But he was astonished to discover that readership did not appear to be very enthusiastic about following his call to join the future-oriented community. As if redoubling the gesture of Kant's *Fachidioten*, many readers preferred narrow-minded self-approving and self-asserting literature over its bright-minded self-finding and self-reflexive counterpart. The expected worldwide readiness for self-enlightenment turned out to be a rather rare phenomenon. This irritatingly massive inadequate reception of literature ultimately induced Schiller's resignation. He bitterly concluded that one can meet "the state of beautiful appearance" only in "very few elite circles" and cannot prevent naïve readers from following their ridiculous habits of identification (Schiller 2000: 123). Aesthetic consciousness strikes him as an unevenly distributed natural gift genuine only to the moderate European climate. Peoples who lack this natural gift because of their inadequate climatic environment must simply renounce the aesthetic blessing (106). Completely leaving aside the growing social divisions of the modern world along with a blatantly uneven distribution of wealth, power and education, Schiller ultimately took recourse in Herder's anthropological argument backed by Montesquieu. Because non-Europeans as well as misplaced Europeans do not count among the peoples capable of partaking in humankind's evolution, they must be dropped from it.

Due to such a persistently restrictive application of the cosmopolitan idea – not everybody is up to the challenge – the history of humankind finally acquired the same discriminating pattern as did the course of its later opponent, *national history*, in Ernest Renan's famous lecture from 1892, *What Is a Nation?* According to the French political philosopher, every national history is bound to exclude from its goal-oriented course parts of the population (such as women, workers or minorities) which by their regressive and reactionary profile hinder free national self-determination. Although the ideal of free self-determination is associated with the French Republican tradition – the structure of Renan's argument leaves no doubt about this origin – the demonstrated resurgence of the Enlightenment progressive pattern in the Romanticist argument also sees this ideal reappear in the German Romanticist conception. The only difference is that the self-overcoming self is now transferred from the individual to the collective level. But the distance between the carriers of the historical progress and those in whose name it is tirelessly carried on perseveres. In spite of the repeated attempts at overcoming, polarization between the agencies and enablers stubbornly reemerges in the line from Voltaire via Kant, Herder, Schiller, early German Romanticists and Renan up to Luhmann.

This leads to the conclusion that French national universalism centered on the individual and German cosmopolitan nationalism centered on the collective self go hand in hand. The pattern of triumphant overcoming cannot tolerate self-satisfied instances neither in the first nor in the second. In both seemingly opposite variants of cosmopolitanism, identity-building entails marginalization, gradual assimilation and/or complete elimination of self-enclosed identities. In both, the *agency* is expected to continuously widen its horizon at the expense of *enablers*. Instead of transcending the discriminating profile of nationalism, as it proclaims to be doing, cosmopolitanism reiterates it on a more comprehensive level. It perpetually faces hindrances to its realization because it cannot stop producing an *inferior other as a necessary negative foil for the affirmation of its "know-all" self*. This enabler is not just the condition of impossibility of the agency's maintenance, but also the condition of its possibility.

As an "officially approved" theoretical descendant of early Romanticist ancestors, Niklas Luhmann also inherits their deepest frustration with this inferior other that Kant translated straitforwardly as "idiot." For a long time he polemisized relentlessly against the so-called national sociology because of its ridiculous benightedness in the face of today's global society. What disqualifies national society in the contemporary world society is that the latter discloses the latent zone of possibilities hidden from the self-enclosed perspective of the former (Luhmann 1975). As the world's becoming expands the zone of human possibilities, modern theory must endorse and accelerate it. Following his Romanticist predecessors, who for their part celebrated the exuberant abundance of life (*überschäumende Lebensfülle*), Luhmann demands that theory obey the imperative of the world's becoming that progressively uncovers the utter contingency of human affairs. Even if theory can never take full cognizance of this original chaos, with every further evolutionary step it comes to grasp more of the world's infinite complexity, drawing closer to its unfathomable truth.³

7.3 Literature against philosophy: Niklas Luhmann's autopoietic turn

Following the development of such a progressive "observation of latency" (*Latenzbeobachten*) from the anti-Enlightenment age onwards, Luhmann (1990a: 46–47) interprets its emergence in early Romanticism as a *literary* opposition to Kant's *philosophical* transcendentalism. This obviously reflects the way his own autopoietic system theory opposes Habermas's transcendental philosophy (Luhmann 1995b). Siding with literature against philosophy, Luhmann continues the early Romanticist struggle for unrestrained human freedom. As suggested by the introduction of the re-describing concept of autopoiesis into what had been, until the mid 1980s, a theory of self-enclosed systems, he associates literature with the self-finding second-order and philosophy with the self-asserting first-order observation. The latter's blindness must be denounced, corrected and supplemented whenever it hinders the advancement of human history in the direction of contingency. In such a way Luhmann, in the wake of Friedrich Schlegel's and Schiller's Romanticist argument, inverts the Enlightenment distribution of roles in which the philosopher figures as the paradigmatic second-order observer. Exactly because he *inverts* rather than *reworks* it, the Enlightenment pattern of "policing" the other resurges in his literary version of system theory.

Following Friedrich Schlegel's gesture of the "novelizing of theory" in *Letter on the Novel* (from *Dialogue on Poetry*), Luhmann (1990a: 46) engages literature so as to liberate humans from their narrow-mindedness and benightedness and places the novel, as its representative, at the historical origin of the know-all theoretical ambition. In his interpretation, this ambition separated the novelistic author from his or her figures: whereas the latter directly conflate their fictions with reality, the former does not just systematically disclose their respective delusion but also exposes his or her own constitutive entrapment into fiction in the course of this "enlightening operation" (Roberts 1992: 88–91). That is to say, the second-order observer does not hide that it does not see something. On the contrary, in exemplary democratic fashion, it "observes the world in such a way as to make itself observable" (*die Welt beim Beobachtetwerden beobachtet*) (Luhmann 1990b:

---

3 For the second-order observation as the gradual discloser of the world's complexity, see Luhmann 1990b: 25.

26, 1991: 149–150). As we have seen in the previous chapter, Gasché allocated this persistently self-questioning manner of behavior to an eminently European tradition. Would the corollary be that the first-order observations are to be associated with the non-European manner of behavior?

Such a self-reflective character is, Luhmann's argument goes, the distinctive feature of *modern art* conceived of as an autonomous social system, since other systems such as politics, the economy, the law or science blindly stick to their restricted perspective. Through self-reflection, modern art, which is best represented in the novel, "reclaims its right to objectivity" (Luhmann 1990b: 40). At stake is an objectivity of the second order, as it persistently refers to the *abundant world* of latency and contingency beyond the *restricted reality* established through the systemic activity of the first-order observers (Luhmann 1995a: 142ff.). Only since modernity, that is, can we speak of "world art" (1990b), taking into account modern art's loyalty to the world of unimplemented possibilities excluded by systemic reality. Now, in the same way as the novel reminds other literary genres of the restrictions of their "systemic reality," modern literary theorists remind their predecessors of their narrow-minded rendering of literature. By redrawing the boundaries of any established *reality* in the name of the *world-in-the-making*, modern art and theory thus ceaselessly remind other social systems of the contingency of what they take to be real. Through their unreserved commitment to the world's unimplemented potentials, they press other systems into consistent expansion. Each systemic observation becomes immediately deactivated through its unremitting re-description from a superior know-all perspective.

7.4 Passionately commited to the memory of the whole

Luhmann inherits the Romanticist worldview not just through the consistent literarization (or novelizing) of his second-order observation but also through the cosmopolitan commitment of his know-all attitude. Just as modern art is authorized by the *world's whole* lost through the functional differentiation of society, so the individual, whom Luhmann interprets as a remainder of the same social differentiation, is authorized by the lost *whole of humanity* (*Menschheit*, both in the sense of humanness and humankind) (Luhmann 1989: 212). Since this humanity became equally lost in the course of its social differentiation, all an individual can do is adhere to its memory by a consistent negation of any particular social identity put in its place. This entails the paradoxical principle "I am what I am not" (244), meaning that "an individual can see him- or herself only as an unfinished and interminable process, an inherent infinity of striving and becoming" (*kann das Individuum sich nur als unabgeschlossenen und unabschliessbaren Prozeß be-*

greifen, als innere Unendlichkeit des Strebens und Werdens) (215). With such a radical project of the consistent abandonment of all short-term identity interests for the elusive long-term benefits, Luhmann seems to be exemplifying what Lauren Berlant has called "cruel optimism": a passionate attachment to an object that actively impedes the aim of that attachment (Berlant 2011: 1).

The ideal of a stubborn re-description that was established in such a way connects the becoming of the individual with that of the novel. The novel displays it on various levels: the narrator re-describes the restricted realities of figures, the implied author re-describes the narrator's restricted reality, the novelistic genre itself re-describes the restricted realities of other genres; or, finally, each subsequent novel re-describes its predecessors. Both the individual and the novel are accordingly devoted to the compensatory ideal of uncompromising self-propelling (*Selbststeigerung*) which was the key concept of German Romanticism. According to Dumont (1994: 30–31), German Romanticists relegated, in the form of the *Bildungsideal*, the revolutionary ideal that in the French case applied to society, to the self. Every self (individual or collective) was expected to overcome its predecessor by dismantling the latter's inadmissible self-contentment (*Selbstgenügsamkeit*).

If the individual is for Luhmann accordingly "an identity that is not one," then the novel is analogously a "genre that is not one," always in the process of becoming, as is the world itself. This cancellation of the specific generic boundaries of the novel until it completely merges with the world-in-the-making and becomes universal fully accords with Friedrich Schlegel's contention in the *Athenäum*-Fragment no. 116 that the endless number of modern genres in the final analysis amount to one all-embracing genre. Luhmann's know-all attitude therefore, far from liberating from all transcendental frames, merely replaces the located philosophical transcendentalism with an unfettered literary version that is no less coercive and violent. How powerful a weapon this literary know-all attitude authorized by the world as a "horizon postponed with every operation without ever becoming available" (Luhmann 1995a: 151) can become, is exemplified by Luhmann's unremitting unveiling of all transcendental truths as empirical delusions. Taking inspiration in modern art's shocking unmasking of all transcendental frames by their "empirical grounding," he blames contemporary philosophy for its inability to take cognizance of art's epochal achievement despite a century and a half of *Ideologiekritik* and a full century of psychoanalysis (Luhmann 1995b: 52, 1995a: 137–138). His significant point is that the modern artistic observation of latency, which entailed the final "explosion of the world's unity" would have been betrayed by its later translation into religious and scientific observation, had his own radical constructivism not rescued scientific observation from such a betrayal of the radical challenge of art.

For Luhmann, whereas contemporary religion, science and philosophy still hesitate to completely dissolve the world's unity (Luhmann 1995a: 139), stubbornly adhering to their self-sufficient transcendental frames, only radical constructivism, while giving up every kind of transcendentalism, properly responds to the message of modern art. If theory nevertheless eventually replaced modern art thanks to this heroic achievement of radical constructivism, this only happened because radical constructivism is strict in keeping pace with the *evolution of society*. Society namely first engaged art to play with this explosive latency, to test its applicability to the dissolution of the "great life unity, the visible universe and the structured cosmos." Once "sufficient evidence has been gained," latency was translated into the "more serious, since more consequential, areas of religion and knowledge" (138–139). In Luhmann's rendering, this society's progression strongly reminds us not just of Hegel's famous tripartite scheme of the development of the Absolute Spirit – art, religion, philosophy – but first and foremost of the Hegelian "iron necessity" of evolution from which nobody is allowed to escape. This is how he, surreptitiously, re-claims transcendentalism he allegedly gave up.

However, as Luhmann was, of course, a sociologist, the unfolding of the Hegelian Spirit remains in his project subordinated to the differentiation of society which, in a mirror reversal of the course of the Spirit's development, results in unbound contingency instead of firm certainty (as it does in Hegel's philosophy). This reverse direction of the differentiation of society explains why radical constructivism, in Luhmann's opinion, suits the actual condition of the multifocal world much better than transcendental philosophy does. It is liberated from the philosophical prejudice that it is possible to show "how the world really is" (Luhmann 1990a: 47). "It is only with radical constructivism that all the remnants of the world's certainty are dissolved." (Luhmann 1995a: 139) If Hegel speaks in the name of the Absolute Spirit, Luhmann's inverted Hegelianism just smoothly observes the unfolding of the world society toward an unlimited contingency of human affairs. His super-observer is strictly at pains to add nothing for its part to the existing state of facts. Instead, it seeks to bring itself into complete accordance with the structure of this state, providing a sheer report on the process of its self-production (Luhmann 1996). It is from this ongoing evolutionary perspective, and in the name of its "iron necessity," that Luhmann passes his verdicts, determines what is timely and what is anachronous, what is progressive and what is regressive, unmasks eternal truths as transient illusions. In such a way, he inadvertently lends expression to all the latent consequences of the cosmopolitan imperative introduced by the relentless re-descriptions of early Romanticism. Building on this tradition, Luhmann's cosmopolitan restructuring of the world society amounts to discrimination.

7.5 The European entangled legacy

The perpetual displacement of Luhmann's observer, forming a smooth and continuous narrative, finds its birthplace at the very heart of European modernity. Via its mainstream intellectual tradition from Kant onwards, modern Europe defined itself, in sharp contrast to other continents defined in terms of location and belonging, in terms of the *infinite adventure of self-creation*, i.e. unbound intellectual mobility (Bauman 2004: 6). The persistent detachment of European agency from its non-European or not-quite-European enablers was, however, not always associated with literature. As I have argued, the Enlightenment cosmopolitan imperative associates the relentless self-creation of its agency with philosophy, which was then, in the early Romanticist pattern, reversed in favor of literature. Yet the seeming opposites appear to be mirroring each other's policing operation. The replacement of philosophy with literature does not abolish but reinstate the control of agencies over enablers. Considering this, one could put forth the thesis of the entangled legacies of philosophy and literature with regard to their shaping of cosmopolitanism. In order to substantiate it, in the following I will briefly discuss two recent influential revivifications of the tradition of Enlightenment cosmopolitanism.

The *philosophical* form of the asymmetry between the open European and the self-enclosed non-European mentalities resurges for example in the recent reflections on Europe of Luhmann's yearlong antagonist Jürgen Habermas. He interprets Europe as a post-traditional, i.e. post-national society "oriented towards social, political and cultural inclusion" (Habermas 2001: 9) as well as "shared values," opposing it to traditional national societies – or *völkisch* communities, to be more accurate – oriented around their own values as well as the exclusion of the other. Taking recourse in Kant's enlightened cosmopolitan ideas (Habermas 1996: 192–236, 2004: 113–193, 2005: 324–365) as the blueprint for German post-war constitutional patriotism in opposition to wartime irrational ethnic nationalism, Habermas transfers this putatively typically German[4] legalizing of politics in the form of an imperative to the transnational European level (Habermas 2011: 44–47). In the same way as Germany learned from its irrational Nazi aberrations, Europe should learn from the dark side of its history. It should abandon prescribed rules and unquestioned authorities and choose instead the rational way of continuous negotiation with others on the common terms of international coexistence. Yet as Robert Fine put it,

---

4 Habermas (2011: 39, n. 47) celebrates the discussion of international law in constitutional terms as a prominent accomplishment of German jurisprudence.

> [t]he paradoxical sense of German pride Habermas gives to the theory of constitutional patriotism, a pride in having learnt from history, carries with it an equivalent sense of guilt for those who still think in nationalist terms. [...] The theory of constitutional patriotism declares that a key political struggle of our age is between those who believe that their nation should be based on universal constitutional patriotism and those who still base their nation on ethnic or at least culturally specific membership. If all nationalism is Janus-faced, containing within itself both the values and the barbarities of the idea of national self-determination, Habermas puts all that is positive on the side of constitutional patriotism and all that is negative on the side of nationalism. This conceptual dichotomy, however, splits the good from the bad without confronting the equivocations of nationalism as such. (Fine 2007: 47)

Such an idealizing of the cosmopolitan self backed by the stigmatizing of the nationalist other forgets that constitutional patriotism might be "closer to nationalism than its advocates would like to think and its compatibility with cosmopolitanism less secure" (48). The rational cosmopolitan vision of Europe might turn out to be "a kind of nationalism writ large that may not be appealing to all its constituent parts, let alone to those outside its borders" (51). As far as Habermas's discarding of irrational nationalism is concerned, the insistence on the nation-state could prove to be a plausible self-defensive response to the transnational character of totalitarianisms, especially if one considers the specificity of the East European historical experience (51). Such blind spots compromise Habermas's Enlightenment type of cosmopolitanism epitomized, according to him, in post-war Germany as well as the European Union in the form he has envisaged (Habermas 2011: 39–96).

Another recent and renowned representative of the idea of Europe as a consistent cosmopolitan self-creation is Ulrich Beck. However, he explicitly counters the Enlightenment universalism sketched in above, calling it "deformed cosmopolitanism" since it strongly opposes nationalism and thus generates conflicts (Beck 2007: 5). The either-universalism-or-nationalism logic belongs to the antiquated "first modernity" that reigned in Europe over 300 years from the Peace of Westphalia (1648) until the terrorist attack of 9/11, whereas the proper European cosmopolitanism belongs to the "second modernity" that introduced the "global community of fate" (Beck 2002a; 2002b). As for the first either-or logic, despite mutual exclusion "[t]here is an inner affinity between the national and universal perspectives." "One's own society serves as the model for society in general, from which it follows that the basic characteristics of universal society can be derived from an analysis of *this* society." (Beck 2006: 28) This is why the other must not be subordinated to the self and why national differences, instead of being abolished, should be recognized and integrated. "As a result, under conditions of radical global insecurity, all are equal and everyone is different." (Beck 2007: 14) The only cosmopolitanism that is appropriate to the second modernity is, in opposition to postmodern absolute particularism, a consistent integration of differences according to the both-and principle.

How is this integration of a *Europe of difference and national diversity* expected to proceed? If it is not to degenerate into postmodern particularism and/or into open violence, it requires a certain fund of universal norms as stabilizers of difference which are necessarily nationally rooted and therefore in need of permanent reflection. Such a typically European reflexive cosmopolitanism "changes and preserves, it *opens* the past, the present and the future of particular national societies and the relations among national societies" (2007: 16). After all, Europe is "not a fixed condition" but "geared to movement, to a process that transcends and interconnects the internal and the external" (6). As a single genuine nation-transcending, i.e. cosmopolitan region from its beginning (19), "Europe cannot be discovered (*gefunden*), it must be invented (*erfunden*)" (7). It exists only as Europeanization, i.e. future-oriented self-creation. "The 'We' who legitimize the cosmopolitan legal regime are the *prospective* Europeans who in this way become the subject of their own history" (8), and an extremely self-critical subject at that, with regard to the European traditions of colonialism, nationalism, expulsion and genocide (9). In a word, Europeanization is envisaged by Beck as an unremitting expansion of the European self-reflective cosmopolitan spirit in two directions: "*inwards*, through constant extensions of the powers of the EU and the resulting structural adaptations in the member states; and *outwards*, through the constant enlargements of the community and the export of its norms and rules" (10). This blatantly colonial and imperial "political project" of the Europeanization of the world is so "highly complex and highly differentiated" that Europe "cannot be defined clearly and precisely [...] in a binding way" (11); it must remain a dynamic, open process, an "infinite task" and "infinite adventure." Being permanently on the move, cosmopolitan Europe becomes in such a way not just the subject of its own history but of world history too.

Yet far from having been the messenger of the forthcoming final freedom for humanity, this modern European cosmopolitanism, despite Beck's unreserved championing, announced the new bondage of non-Europeans and less-than-Europeans subjected to its imperatives. Having Odysseus as its prototype, a "compulsive and indefatigable wanderer [...] among those who would rather live their lives in a world ending at the outermost village fence" (Bauman 2004: 3), the European project presents itself as a transgressive, expansive civilization allergic to borders (7). But in the name of this adventurous compulsion, it "made more history than it could consume locally" (8), forcing "the rest of the planet to partake in its consumption" (14). In the end, the non-European and less-than-European cultures were turned into "a handmaiden, a fuel station and a repair workshop servicing" European culture (12), provided "the war of attrition" was not declared on them or they had not initiated the production of "human waste" if they "failed to rise to the standards" set by European culture (13).

In sum, the entangled legacies of the literary and philosophical shaping of modern European cosmopolitanism jointly established an imperative and permanently self-re-describing evolutionary paradigm. This paradigm set the standards of everybody's visibility, but remained for its part invisible. Evolution was presented as having unfolded naturally, logically necessarily and inevitably. Once its legislation was in power, "[i]nferior and no longer merely different, other races were completely excluded from its compass and became prehistoric as well as extracultural" (Gilroy 2000: 64). Other, more related or less abhorrent entities permitted to remain within its overarching perspective, were allocated a firmly restricted place in the past. The future-oriented process of permanent displacement, as the ultimate beneficiary of the whole development, was neither locatable nor identifiable in its parameters. It was precisely this divinely unfathomable character that raised it to the status of "historical necessity."

7.6 The novel as the epitome of evolutionary necessity

Let us concludingly return to Luhmann's inverted Enlightenment established on the early German Romanticist model that renders the evolutionary "iron necessity" in novelistic terms. It turns out that the proclaimed rise of this evolution's inclusive potential (*Anschlussfähigkeit*) amounts to a parallel increase of its potential to exclude. Concerning his pattern of the evolution of society, Luhmann (1997: 609–615) eventually must admit that its progression reproduces, even reinforces the previous underdeveloped phases instead of resolving them. The same undercutting of the universal claim holds for the evolution of art that continuously "heightens the requirements for participation in it" because "deciphering the artistic moment in a work of art requires specialist training." "The final outcome of the heightening of the inclusion requirements is exclusion." (Luhmann 1986c: 649–650) Very few readers appear to be ready to keep under observation all the complex re-describing operations of the novelistic text, but instead become stuck at the lower levels of identification. Erich Schön (1987: 223–226) pointed out that the quality as well as the scope of reading novels increased only through the self-isolation of its readers toward the end of the eighteenth century. In such a fashion, the reader was liberated from the obligation to identify on the one hand with the novelistic figures and on the other with fellow readers. S/he could detach him- or herself from the norms of reception typical of the collective reading performances that had previously been common practice. Postponing the immediate and passionate responses to the actions and behaviour of novelistic heroes, this gave the reader the opportunity to develop a more patient, in-depth and complex reading, shifting from one perspective to another and building in such a way a sort of "balancing identity" (177–182). Yet the substitution of patient and self-controlled reading for the fast and passionate projections into the figures was a rather slow, troublesome and uneven process of the suppression of affective reactions that faced the resistance of the lower readership's strata (219). Only a select few readers could afford the luxury of self-isolation, hence the reading aloud of novels in the family circle continued deep into the nineteenth century. But even in the rare cases of readers with well-developed empathy, the accumulated emotional energy was engaged much more arbitrarily than the former projections had been (220). This especially holds for female readers passionately devoted to a kind of narcotic reading as opposed to male readers, who performed reading of a rationally disciplined kind (Assmann 1985).

As the authors produced their works for the market, this effectuated a differentiation of novelistic production. Many authors decided, as in the case of the so-called Gothic or sensational novels, to meet the abundant fantasy of female readers rather than to support the male self-control as in the case of educational novels.

> The specificity of the sensational novel in nineteenth-century fiction is that it renders the liberal subject the subject of a *body*, whose fear and desire of violation displaces, reworks, and exceeds his constitutive fantasy of intact privacy. The themes that the liberal subject ordinarily defines himself against – by reading *about* them – are here inscribed into his reading body. (Miller 1988: 163)

The Gothic novels also address sensations rather than the reason of their readers, which is why they are treated as inadequate instances of this representative genre and excluded from the canonic histories of English novels such as Ian Watt's *The Rise of the Novel* (Azim 1993: 26–27, 184–185). Instead of uniting various empirical readers by calling them to occupy the uniform observing post of the so-called implied reader, the history of the novel diversified and polarized them along social, gender and/or age axes. Thus the novelistic production of the reader's unbound individuality already confronted serious hindrances in the European space, not to mention the "backward" and "delayed" non-European zones that either postponed or completely skipped the introduction of the novel into their genre system. Toni Morrison explains:

> My sense of the novel is that it has always functioned for the class or group that wrote it. The history of the novel as a form began when there was a new class, a middle class, to read it, it was an art form that they needed. The lower classes didn't need novels at that time because they had an art form already: they had songs and dances, and ceremony and gossip and celebration. (Evans 1983: 340)

As the rise of the novel in Europe is parallel to the rise of the European colonial project, the resilience to it in the postcolonial world is hardly astonishing. "The appropriation of history, the historicization of the past, the narrativization of society, all of which gave the novel its force, include the accumulation and differentiation of social space, space to be used for social purposes." (Said 1993: 93) In the earliest novels, the figures of the savages and aborigines are introduced as a background against which the sovereignty of the European figures can come to expression. This is how Firdous Azim presents the identity of the implied author of the European novel:

> [T]his subject was held together by the annihilation of other subject-positions. The novel is an imperial genre, not in theme merely, not only by virtue of the historical moment of its birth, but in its formal structure – in the construction of that narrative voice which holds the narrative structure together. (Azim 1993: 30)

The envisioned all-inclusive authorization of the novelistic and, concomitantly, Luhmann's autopoietic observer will hardly ever be achieved, as they constitutively need and relentlessly foster exclusion.

8 The Oppositional Literary Transcendental: The Russian Formalist Rewriting of Early Romanticist Cosmopolitanism

8.1 The post-imperial hyphenation and early Romanticist legacy

Although the East Central European nation-states acquired their political autonomy in the aftermath of World War I, their literatures remained historically, linguistically and culturally entangled with the literatures of their neighbors due to their long coexistence within their respective imperial frames. Such *intra*national hyphenation of East Central European literatures explains the resistance of some of their representatives to the *inter*national dialogue between sovereign national literatures. The latter was promoted and fostered by prominent Western European national philologies but also enthusiastically embraced by East Central European national elites. According to Galin Tihanov (2004: 419–420), it is precisely this internal resistance to the Western European model of national literary history that marks the cosmopolitan beginning of modern European literary theory. As the prescribed national terms of the envisaged international cooperation between established literary nations were hardly applicable to entangled post-imperial legacies, the resistance to their application by a select group of literary critics steeped in more languages, literatures and cultures generated an *intra*national kind of literary cosmopolitanism amidst the newly established nation-states.

In the terms introduced and developed in several previous chapters, we can describe this as the old conflict between the Roman international and Greek intranational cosmopolitanism, however now taking place for the first time on the new, i.e. East Central European, ground. Herder who, as I have spelled out at length in chapter four, had (re)invented the hospitable, affirmative type of cosmopolitanism against the exclusive, assimilating type of his professor Kant, had already left an indelible impression on the regional national "engineers" through his acknowledgment of cultural distinctions. However, in accordance with the original Roman concept, there lurked a carefully elaborated social and cultural hierarchy which recruited the Slavs to lower positions and assigned the Germans to the highest ones behind Herder's generous idea of common *humanitas*. This did not prevent the Slav intellectual elites from embracing his paternal protection of their cultural distinction enthusiastically, as they trusted that this would help them acquire their much-desired national sovereignty. Their enthusiasm only increased in the aftermath of World War I, after Western nation-state powers, in the Versailles Treaty, translated the principle of self-determination from Herder's cultural terms into nation-state, opening the geopolitical dismemberment of the region. Carried by triumphant national elites, national revolutions were ushered in, without uprisings, through the terms of peace treatise (Berend 1998: 154).

Contrary to the opinion of such nationally inflamed compatriots, the literary historians who wanted their literatures to be acknowledged based on national sovereignty, the East Central European literary theorists were convinced such international cosmopolitanism betrays the genuinely hybrid identity profile of their new nation-states. Their hyphenated, intersected and intermingled histories as well as their hybrid and perplexed present, lacking a continuous and stable national identity, could hardly have been pressed into the sovereign national terms of the Western European nation-states, which had meanwhile become completely oblivious to the erstwhile brutal establishment of their national identities.[1] On that basis, following the model of Greek elite cosmopolitanism, these regional states' literary theorists took a clear distance from a compatriot literary history longing for national recognition. However, behind these domestic "benighted souls" they actually targeted the dominant Western European national-philological paradigm by challenging it to reexamine its premise of sovereign national literatures. Deficient in the national-historical continuity established by the Western European national philologies, the East Central European literatures were shaped by principles deeply inimical to smooth national evolution. If West-

---

[1] The first Western European nation-states, such as France, England and Holland, were knowingly established by means of the gradual expulsion, dislocation and various forms of cleansing of their minority populations. However, as these operations were undertaken during the Middle Ages and early modernity, they were pushed into oblivion. Forgetting the terror and massacres committed in the name of nation is, according to Renan (2006: 45), constitutive of the French (and every other) sovereign national consciousness. According to Todorova (1997: 175): "Ever since the fifteenth century (and in the case of England much earlier), Western Europe has embarked on a huge homogenization drive with various degrees of success (the Spanish reconquista, England's expulsion of the Jews in the twelfth century, the religious wars in France and Germany), which, in conjunction with the strong dynastic states, had laid the foundations of the future nation-states. [...] In fact, democracy as a political form became an attribute of the West European nation-states only in the twentieth century (and for Germany only after World War II), after they had achieved in the previous centuries a remarkable, although not absolute, degree of ethnic and religious homogeneity and disciplined society, at an often questionable human and moral price." So the establishment of the East Central European nation-states, which was a sort of ultimate Europeanization of this area, was for the Western European nation-states a traumatic "return of the repressed," a painful reminder of the deeply problematic identification of nations with states. The harsh critique of East Central European ethnonationalisms was intended to suppress this disquieting reminder.

ern nations had already forgotten or suppressed their nationally entangled past, the new nations still vividly remembered it. To pick up just two illustrations of this from the region, at that time Czechoslovakia consisted of 6.5 million Czechs, 2.2 million Slovaks and 0.5 million Ruthenians, with large German, Hungarian and Polish minorities. Yugoslavia for its part consisted of 43% Serbs and Montenegrins, 23% Croats, 9% Slovenes, 6% Bosnians, 5% Macedonians and also embraced a further 0.5 million Germans, Hungarians, Albanians and "others"; its Orthodox population amounted to 5.6 million, Catholic to 4.7, Muslim to 1.3, and Protestant to 0.3 million (Berend 1998: 170–174). What is most important, though, is that these extremely heterogeneous consituents were, due to the long imperial past, inextricably entangled with one another. Feeling obliged to this specific post-imperial situation, the East Central European literary theorists acted in the name of hyphenated identities which were marginalized, derogated and excluded by the imposition of national homogeneity. They generated their intranational cosmopolitanism from the traumatic experience of these identities put under the imperative of disentangling. From their perspective, in order for a national literary history to establish the difference of its own literature from other national literatures, it tends to suppress the internal national difference of its own literature from itself, from its stubborn intrinsic alterity. Literary theorists wanted to break out of such violently constructed national-spiritual continuity by introducing a cosmopolitan quality that disengages its allegedly decisive national substance into literature.

This is why, while the Western European literary-historical perspective, based on national philology, envisaged the gradual *unification* of all national literatures into a higher international unity, the East Central European literary-theoretical perspective aimed at a gradual *deactivation* of national literatures. It searched for a genuinely literary quality in order to subvert the "familiar" national terms. Such a consistently "defamiliarizing" operation, as resolutely mobilized by early Russian Formalists, followed the *self-exempting* logic of "*neither* this national *nor* that national but instead a specifically literary identity," diametrically opposed to the *assimilating* logic that "this *as well as* that national literature constitute the international literary community" as advocated by Western European national philologies.[2]

---

[2] As the Soviet Union was constituted as a multinational state, Russian Formalists cannot be smoothly subsumed under Tihanov's category of East Central European literary theorists put under the pressure of their new nation-states. Yet Soviet socialist internationalism was nonetheless structured along national lines both internally and externally (Brubaker 1996: 23–54). This internationalism, following the "welcoming" cosmopolitan pattern, did not erase but preserve the boundaries between nations. Strategically responding to numerous national movements across

However, having been directed against literature's "familiar" perception acquired in the environment one was born into, Formalist "literariness" was conceived in purely *negative, oppositional terms*. Following the Greek elitist "cosmopolitanism against," it looked for the "sublime" literary truth by distancing itself from the deluded "ordinary" truth of compatriots. Shklovsky's imperative of seeing reality afresh from a "strange" perspective, proposed in his path-breaking essay *The Resurrection of the Word* (1914) (Shklovsky 1973), strove to exempt literature from such "natural," self-evident terms. As this "empty objective" was genuinely revolutionary in its spirit – "cosmopolitanism without a polis" in Tihanov's apt phrasing (Tihanov 2011) – it is no wonder it came under heavy attack at a time when Soviet state bureaucracy had suppressed such spirit. The Russification of the Soviet Union started by the mid-1920s. As the Hungarian exile Ervin Sinkó bitterly noticed in Moscow by the mid-1930s, "[i]t is not easy to be a revolutionary in the country where the revolution had triumphed" (Sinkó 1962, 116; quoted after

---

the former Russian empire, Lenin advocated a federation of equal nations from the very establishment of the Soviet Union (Martin 2001: 1–3). This is why the Declaration of Rights of the Peoples of Russia (November 1917) proclaims the right of self-determination for all Soviet peoples. Yet by the mid-1920s, after socialism failed to affect the Western nation-states, which was considered by Lenin to be the prerogative of its survival, Stalin mobilized the process of Soviet nation-building under Russian control and leadership. This turn toward national homogenization was expected to accelerate the so-called socialist modernization determined to beat the capitalist West (Berend 1998: 213–214). Yet, with the consolidation of the nation-building by the mid-1930s, people bereft of national belonging were stigmatized and endangered. For example, being deprived of their own language and land, Jews could in no way qualify as a nation (and the most prominent Formalists, like Shklovsky, Eikhenbaum, Brik and Jakobson, were of Jewish origin). Stalin, in his ill-reputed anti-Semitic campaign after World War II, reinforced by the reawakened mythology of Russian uniqueness and other Soviet nations' accelerated process of *korenizatsiia* (rooting or indigenization), associated the Jews with a "rootless cosmopolitanism." Being non-indigenous, they were deprived of electoral rights at their dispersed locations (*lishentsy*) and forced into separate agricultural communities in order to create national territorial units. "This policy deepened the feeling among national minorities that they did not belong and so should move to a territory where they formed the national minority. Most importantly, it reinforced the belief of national majorities that minorities did not belong and should be expelled." (Martin 2001: 44) As Arendt (1979: 269) summarizes, after Word War I "denationalization became a powerful weapon of totalitarian politics" followed by the expulsion and extermination. In addition to that, in the Soviet Union it was backed by tradition: unlike the assimilated West European Jews, Russian Jews lived in ghettoes exposed to regular pogroms throughout the nineteenth century. Before the 1890s they did not even begin to enter Russian literature and the doors of Russian universities were only thrown open to them after 1917 (Deutscher 1968: 55, 64–69). By adhering to the Revolution's early "cosmopolitanism without a polis" (Tihanov 2011) – after all, Revolution was their "entrance ticket" to the culture that for centuries had kept them at distance – Russian Formalists attempted to prevent the consequences of Soviet nationalization.

Tihanov 2011: 131), i.e. established a fixed political abode. The rise of the nation-state logic explains the Soviet suspicion toward, pressure upon and policing of Formalist literary theory. With the rise of Stalin's state bureaucracy, the feverish ideology of "true believers" – still genuine to Formalist revolutionary literary theory – was replaced by the cynical *Realpolitik* of cold pragmatic calculations.[3]

Paradoxically enough, it was precisely this relegation of Formalist ideas from the official to the apocryphal political space that opened the door for the emergence of a transnational community of their adherents. This calls to remembrance the constitution of Voltaire's Republic of Letters on the same Greek elitist model. Thrown out from the embattled political scene, both were freed from the obligation to pragmatically sacrifice their long-term ideological convictions for their short-term positional interests. If the uncompromising revolutionary ideology (including that of Russian Formalism) celebrated its heyday in the turbulent environment of the Soviet post-October society, then with the development of the bureaucratic Soviet state it was forced into an oppositional ideological enclave. The permanently resurging conditions of the political, social and economic instability of the Soviet as well as other East Central European regimes induced the reemergence and proliferation of such enclaves, enabling the wide resonance, numerous intellectual attachments and ultimate success of Formalist learning. Their counterfactual literary truth, promising long-term potential benefits in the manner which all cosmopolitan projects do, turned into a prospect worthy of the sustained sacrifice of more pragmatic (i.e. national) individual choices.

All that said, Russian Formalists were far from being as revolutionary as they believed they were. By claiming for literature a character that constitutively contested the national-philological thesis of literature's affirmation of the *Volksgeist*, they resumed the hierarchy between the two ideas of literature established by early German Romanticist theory, i.e., the primacy of the *cosmopolitan disengaging* over the *nationally engaged* idea of literature.[4] Along with this enlightening attitude to their nationally "benighted opponents," they reaffirmed the early Romanticist commitment to the contingent *world* of free possibilities beyond the narrow-minded national *reality*. If literature catapults its readers out of their comfortable consuming attitude, as Formalists insisted it does, this is because it deviates from the familiar norm, crosses the boundary of the habitual, and enters free "foreign alliances" in the way early German Romanticists claimed it does. Yet Formalists pushed this project even further. In their rushed evolution through

---

[3] For the important role of ideology in unstable post-imperial democracies, see Hanson 2010.
[4] Tihanov (2004: 424) rightly associates the Formalist with the Romanticist conception of literature but does not develop this thesis further.

several developmental phases (Hansen-Löve 1978: 175–464), they repeatedly re-described literary quality, from (1) the exemption of the "strange" form from the "familiar" material, over (2) the disengagement of the one form from the vantage point of the other, up to (3) the parenthesizing of past literary constellations by means of the present one. In this manner literature's truth, bereft of any stable identity, was ultimately drawn into a vertiginous process of self-negations. Each consecutive Formalist truth of literature, by accumulating all the former detachments from its forerunners, turned out to be more contingent than the previous one. Having extended its identity into a network of mobile relations broader than the previous one, it was interpretable in a greater variety of ways. This growing dependence on the interpretive context, once again, remained perfectly loyal to the early German Romanticist advocacy of the fundamental arbitrariness of life.

Antoine Compagnon (13) therefore hits the nail on the head when he describes modern literary theory as "a lesson in relativism, not pluralism." Its reactions, "instead of adding up to a total and more complete vision [...] are mutually exclusive [...]" A modern literary theorist "is the eternal devil's advocate, or the devil himself" (11). Nevertheless, this ruthless exclusionary logic of neither–nor, if we are to distinguish it from the early German Romanticist nation-*consolidating* cosmopolitan terms, must be put into the perspective of a nation-*opposing* cosmopolitanism. Early German Romanticists and Russian Formalists acted out of two diametrically opposed frustrations, which is a specification that fails to materialize in Compagnon's – as well as Gasché's and Rabaté's – rather linear genealogies of modern literary theory (Compagnon 2004; Rabaté 2002; Gasché 2007). Resuming the early Romanticist legacy engendered in the *pre-statist* Germany in the Russian *post-imperial* circumstances of Soviet statist pressure, the Formalists redistributed its emphases, adapting them to their continually self-exempting task. Considering that, this was not a simple transmission but rather a profoundly transformative, rewriting encounter. The estrangement of the benighted observer, as a cosmopolitan transgression genuine to theory from its ancient Greek beginnings (Rausch 1982; Blumenberg 1987), contains both a liberating and an appropriating potential, which is why it easily slips from politics into police and vice versa. By directing their "politics of estrangement" (Tihanov 2005) against the predominating national orientation of their compatriots, the Russian Formalists turned the early Romanticist model of supervising other nations upside down. They transformed the imperial into the elitist cosmopolitan model.

With this important move, the re-articulation of theory's cosmopolitanism was by no means exhausted. Being constitutively equivocal, cosmopolitanism caries the seed of its re-signification. In the same way that the early German Romanticist cosmopolitanism's ambitions of supremacy were translated by Russian Formalists into an emancipating mission, their theory's later geopolitical and cultural relocations spawned an exact reversal. Through the gradual international expansion of modern literary theory, the intranational oppositional truth of literature was converted into international self-asserting terms. The early Formalist revolutionary spirit underwent an institutionalization comparable to that of the October Revolution, albeit, fortunately, without the same consequences. Because of this intrinsic convertibility, cosmopolitanism ought to be be uncoupled from the intentions of its particular carriers. Its patterns are transferable, modifyable and variously implementable. If its attribution to its carriers' specific objectives is almost unavoidable in terms of everyday practice, theoretical analysis must consider unforeseen *co-articulations* of cosmopolitan patterns along various social and political axes, which outmaneuver the original investments of their particular carriers. As Rogers Brubaker (2004: 7–27) recently warned with regard to the closely affiliated concept of nationalism, its carriers are just naturalized variables rather than "moral" or "immoral" constants. Detaching our analytical perspective from such moralizing attributions, however, amounts to the detaching of modern literary theory from the generous plot of emancipation, which is a wishful projection inherent to Compagnon's, Rabaté's and Gasché's genealogy.[5] As a genuinely cosmopolitan operation, theory cannot but couple the effects of liberation with those of supremacy.

To reiterate, as enforced intranational remnants of the linguistically and culturally entangled imperial past, the East Central European theorists were subjected to the accelerated identity pressure of their new state authorities. As opposed to them, the German Romanticist theorists, supported by a rising atmosphere of domestic "cosmopolitan patriotism," deployed cosmopolitanism for the therapeutic consolidation of their politically frustrated national soul. For them, cosmopolitanism was a matter not of castrated remembrances to be rescued from their present renunciation by the deluded compatriots, but of a prosperous future to be taken up and implemented for the benefit of one's own nation. The German Romanticists acted in the name of their political nation-to-come and not against the violence of its present political establishment, as did their Formalist inheritors. While early German Romanticist international cosmopolitanism mobilized the process of a nation's *self-finding* in foreign literatures, against its narrow-minded *affirmation* merely in national literature, East Central European intranational cosmopolitanism in the early twentieth century implemented the affirmation of literature's *innate strangeness* against its national *domestication*. With modern literary theory, as established at the beginning of the twentieth cen-

---

5 For the conservative deployment of the oppositional Formalist concept of estrangement, as well as its constitutive ambiguity, see Tihanov (2005: 686).

tury, literature entered a process of relentless self-exemption from given terms. It returned to Greek cosmopolitan tradition behind the early German Romanticist Roman cosmopolitanism. Instead of assimilating particular national literatures one after another into an international "dialogic transcendental," it unworked national literatures one after another in favor of literature's aesthetic autonomy.

8.2 Literature's persistent self-exemption – modern literary theory's cosmopolitan operation

This literature's accelerated self-exemption from all external identifications, national or otherwise, explains why literary theory in the twentieth century led a "savage and rejuvenating struggle against received ideas in literary studies" (Compagnon 2004: 5). Ultimately, it was drawn into "the process of hystericization" of knowledge, a desire that can never be satisfied because it refuses satisfaction in advance (Rabaté 2002: 100). Yet before this feverish self-re-description took place, and even before the operation of self-exemption from inherited terms was engaged by the early German Romanticist idea of literature, Kant already associated it with modern art in his *Critique of Judgment*. In the final analysis, the Russian Formalists creatively transferred modern art's self-exemption from pre-given rules, as conceptualized by Kant and thereafter developed by the early German Romanticists, into modern literary theory. But there is an even longer tradition behind this "cosmopolitan operation" because Kant did not invent it out of nothing. He also reconfigured it, in the ecstatic atmosphere of the French Revolution, by applying it to modern art. Such operations are by definition established through a series of displacements, (mis)translations and transmutations. Being dependent on dissemination rather than original creation in order to become what they are, they unfold through consecutive "re-signifying transfers." If their eventual use and meaning is often worlds apart from their origins, this is because their extension rests on such "conjunctive disjunctions" (Butler 2012: 8–9). The convertibility of cosmopolitanism that I have reiteratedly called attention to follows from this constitutive co-articulation of its self-exempting operation with a spatial, temporal, social, cultural and/or political "elsewhere."

Therefore, the establishment of literary theory at the beginning of the twentieth century was not a historically unique occurrence and/or a direct response to World War I (Tihanov 2005: 685), as it is usually interpreted. It resulted from the series of transformations of the operation of relating oneself to the others, genuine to European culture from its beginnings. Hannah Arendt was the first to call attention to the opposition between Greek self-emancipating and Roman other-assimilating cosmopolitanism (Arendt 2010: 37–121). They are obviously dependent on different departing positions, the subordinated and the superordinated one. However, relating oneself to the others *à la Grecque* and *à la Romain* are not only opposing, but also coextensive cosmopolitan operations. Giorgio Agamben (2005b: 95–112) derived this operation of re-signifying oneself by dis/joining the others from the Greek verb *katargeín* (meaning to deactivate, to disengage, or to unwork). Employed for the first time in St. Paul's *Letters*, it was thereafter transferred from the religious into the philosophical realm and set in motion by Hegel's dialectical engagement of Luther's translation of the Greek verb as *aufheben* (to cancel on the lower level in order to maintain on the higher level). Nietzsche's untiringly reevaluating philosophy crowns this philosophical redeployment. At stake is therefore an operation with a vibrant history of migrations and reinvestments.

Kant associated it with modern art by thus lending the latter a clearly cosmopolitan character. He defines aesthetic quality as the *ability of the proper work of art to deactivate its familiar reception* by exempting itself from communal rules that supervise its creation (Kant 2007: 134–137). In his account, the self-exemption from communal rules by both the artistic producer and the philosophical recipient closely correspond. Both aim for a superior attitude of disinterested benevolence and, in order to achieve it, are obliged to first subject their spontaneous observation to a meticulous dialogic interrogation. In following the philosophical recipient's self-exemption, any enlightened scholar is expected to test the value of his judgments within the pluralism of the world arena as an indispensible *criterium veritatis externum* (Kant 1956: 65, 2006a: 249, 2006b: 17, 113).[6] There is no other way of achieving sovereignty over the benighted judgments that blindly adhere to the locally inhabited criteria.

The *producer's* aesthetic quality, on the other hand, is defined as the ability to achieve absolute self-exemption, which implies coming to terms with all inadequate judgments encountered along the way. Kant's statement in the *Critique of Judgment* (§ 40, 123) that the duty of every enlightened man is to weigh his judgment not so much against actual, but rather the *merely possible,* judgments of others by putting himself in the position of everyone else (*dass man sein Urteil an anderer, nicht sowohl wirkliche, als vielmehr* bloß mögliche *Urteile hält, und sich in die Stelle jedes andern versetzt*) occurs with reference to the faculty of imagination. Kant thus, via the intuitions provided by cosmopolitan imagination rather than familiar surrounding, clearly associates production with the reception of works of art. As Arendt (1992: 43) and Lyotard (1991: 224) cautioned in their readings, both the artist and the enlightened man, in order to accomplish the impartial observation of life or work of art, systematically exempt their judgment from all

---

[6] In Kant (2007: 65), *Probierstein* is translated as "criterion."

pre-ordained communal rules, deactivating them dialogically in the space of an *imagined* world arena. "Critical thinking is possible only where the standpoints of all others are open to inspection." (Arendt 1992: 43) This is the only way to pull oneself out of "common sense" understood as common (vulgar) understanding (*Verstand*) and reach "common sense" understood as a public sense or the collective reason (*Vernunft*) of humankind (Kant 2007: § 40, 123, 125). Favoring a never passive, unprejudiced and broadened thought, Kant clearly privileges the *sensus communis aestheticus* over the *sensus communis logicus* (124–125).

In line with the self-evacuation from restricted sensations, Kant states in the *Critique of Judgment* (§ 46, 136–137) that a work of beautiful or fine art (as opposed to both "mechanical" and "agreeable" art (§ 44, 134)) cannot be determined by given communal law (i.e., habitual practices of judging works of art) because it emerges as a product of genius that sets its own law through this work. Such exemplary art mobilizes the reason of those who enjoy it through the disengagement of their form of perceiving art, operating under the spell of habit. The paradoxical effect of an exemplary work of art could be described accordingly as the *mobilization of a recipient's reason through the deactivation of its automatic application.* The Russian Formalists, to my knowledge, never directly refer to this paragraph celebrating the victory of reflective judgment (guided by an unrestrained world community) over determining judgment (guided by restricted communal rules) in the sense these two concepts are given in the Introduction (§ 4, 15–16). Nevertheless, the associations with the de-automatizing operation placed by them within the very foundation of modern literature are blatant and irresistible. Through its consistent self-exemption from the application of any of the established rules of reception, the work of fine art, according to this paragraph in the *Critique of Judgment*, reveals its own law as something that exists exclusively in its inapplicability. Inasmuch as this unprecedented law cannot serve as a precept, because no artist who engages it is capable of formulating it, it cannot be identified and imitated by recipients. It can be only indirectly gathered from its execution, through its series of deactivating effects (§ 47, 138–139). It systematically escapes both the producer and recipient of an exemplary work of art – both the artist and theorist – since it disengages all rules of identification applied by them. Through such avoidance of all attempts to locate it cognitively, fine art develops its distinctive *world-disclosing* capacity (unlike "mechanical" or "agreeable" art that just affirms the established *reality*). Only by implementing this interminable self-finding operation can a literary work of fine art, conceived of as a purely negative force, obtain its unbeatable law-giving status.

Although the delineated operation initially lacks the recipient's immediate recognition, it claims validity from the forthcoming course of judgment in which it is reflected (§ 4, 15–16; § 49, 144–145). It proceeds *as if* it is valid for everybody, i.e. as if recipients of fine art thereby perform a collectively verified *logical (i.e. determining)* judgment even though, as a matter of fact, *aesthetic (i.e. reflective)* judgment is at stake, dialogically searching for its verification (§ 4, 6, 7). This quasi-logical character pending between the bounded communal and the free individual reason, and disengaging the one through the other, is absolutely genuine to reflective aesthetic judgment. Kant points out that such reflection requires a considerable effort, as it involves a higher kind of reasoning that consistently disengages ordinary reason (§ 46, 136–137). Yet as human beings earn their generic distinction exactly through such *reasoning on reasoning*, any human is, as far as Kant is concerned, urged to reflect immediate experiential engagements of his or her reason critically from the cosmopolitan viewpoint.

Thus, from the outburst of modernity, according to Agamben (2005a: 24), everybody – and not only sovereigns, as in pre-modern times – was expected to exempt him- or herself from the communal experiential rules. Since such rules untiringly resurface, self-exemption turns out to be an interminable task for human individuals. In his later political treatises, Kant regarded the operation of this consistent evacuation of one's own prejudgments as the sign of human maturity. Instead of being rare and exceptional as before, this unremittingly self-finding life trajectory slowly instituted itself as the universal human obligation, which everybody was pressed to follow irrespective of his or her existential premises. Whoever adhered to the communally restricted determining judgments was stigmatized as immature. Kant states in the *Critique of Pure Reason:* "Our age is the genuine age of critique to which everything must submit" (1998: 100–101).[7] This universal imperative, evenly imposed upon very unevenly prepared, positioned and/or entitled individuals and collectives, has induced with its consistent daily pressure immeasurable "collateral damage."

To return to the Russian Formalists, without directly referring to this risky superimposition of reflective upon determining judgment (Ferrara 1999: 6–7), let alone pondering its dangerous consequences, they reintroduced it in a curiously *reversed form*. By adopting it, they translated Kant's assimilating into their emancipating cosmopolitanism. Their perilously explosive idea of "literariness," revoked in the atmosphere of the October Revolution in the same way that its covert inspiration – Kant's aesthetic quality – was engendered in the atmosphere of the French Revolution,[8] transformed literature from an instrument of national affirmation into its mirror opposite. Literature became an inducer of individual self-

---

[7] Translation slightly modified: *Unser Zeitalter ist das eigentliche Zeitalter der Kritik, der sich alles unterwerfen muss* (Kant 1969: 12n).
[8] As Arendt (1992: 44–45) reminds us, not only Heine and Marx called Kant the philosopher of the French Revolution, but also the prominent representatives of French revolutionaries them-

exemption from national constraints. In the same way that revolutions, each in their own way, introduce the "state of exception" (Agamben) in the realm of law, Kant and the Formalists introduced it in the realm of art. However, if the early German Romanticist theory employed reflective judgment as an instrument of the national spirit's expansion then the Formalist theory employed literariness to disempower national (familiar) reception habits. The Formalist theorist does not *deliberately* transpose himself in the place of others in order to assimilate them into his expanded world but compulsively subjects his socially inhabited literary disposition to literature's *deactivating* aesthetic operation. He thus renounces sovereignty in favor of the freedom from any attributed identity. The literary work of art inscribes its revolutionary quality into his reception habits acquired in the familiar community, inducing their unworking. In that process, the empirical patterns that effectuated his immediate recognition of represented literary subjects gradually dematerialize into abstract techniques (*priëm*) devoid of the "flesh" that was keeping them together.

8.3 The resurgence of the disempowered law

Yet, as was the case already in Kant's argument, determining logical judgment stubbornly resurfaces amidst the consecutive disengagements of its law-giving character. One should recall that, according to Kant (2007: 15–16), even if determining judgment inadmissibly departs from the pre-given rule by subsuming the particular under it, neither is reflective judgment (which departs vice versa from the particular) capable of operating without the overarching principle of the purposeness of nature. Kant therefore does not reserve transcendentalism for determining judgment alone, as is often mistakenly assumed, by completely detaching reflective judgment from it. He merely privileges the *mobile* "transcendental principle" (or what he calls the regulative idea (15)) of reflective judgment over the *fixed* transcendental principle of determining judgment, because such mobility putatively outmaneuvers the empirically restricted reception of art genuine to the latter. Nonetheless, reflective judgment repeatedly turns out to be laying down the law, i.e. performing the same determining activity Kant wanted to dispose with.

---

selves. Yet what truly affiliates him to the French Revolution are less his scattered remarks on the topic in *The Conflict of the Faculties, Perpetual Peace* or *The Metaphysics of Morals*, but rather the genuinely self-revolutionizing obligation assigned to every individual to systematically evacuate, by way of reflective judgment, his or her experientially generated communal prejudgments. For the connection between Kant's unprecedented aesthetic judgment and the inapplicable legal norm of the French Revolution, see Agamben (2005a: 37).

8.3 The resurgence of the disempowered law

To illustrate to what extent this surreptitious entanglement of two Kantian types of judgment influenced the development of modern literary theory let us recall that early Formalists, in the first phase, raised the technique of estrangement (*ostranenie*) to be a distinctive feature of the literary work. Such estrangement, it was said, hampers, slows down, distorts – in a word, contests – the work's determining reception based on transcendental artistic rules. Yet once this contestation has been recognized by recipients, it was established as the new transcendental rule that, unfortunately, prevents any further estrangement. This is why Formalists in the second phase refused to reduce estrangement to a poet's intentional device, drawing it instead from the dynamic and competitive field of functions. The latter, superseding the poet's control, effectuates its negating shift (*sdvig*). Unlike technique (*priëm*), which is conceived as the sovereign action of an artistic form on the passive life material, the shift results from a provisional constellation of conflicting forces that is unstable and permutable. As soon as the development of the conflict entails the transformation of the constellation, the now subordinate functions can become the dominant ones. This makes the aesthetic deactivation performed by literary work a reflex of antagonisms induced first between the functions within a given work, second between the series within a given literary system and third between the literary and non-literary series within the broader system of a given culture. Whatever the case, the historical condition of the system becomes the new focus of Formalist attention – which is, despite all the invested theoretical reflection, again a transcendental rendering of literature. Such consecutive retroactive disengagements of introduced definitions of literature, each of which proved to be inadmissibly saturated with the empirical content, triggered the incredible rhythm of modern literary theory's development.

In an early but the "most extended and scholarly critique of OPOIAZ ever undertaken by a Marxist" (Erlich 1965: 114), whose essentials, despite its publication in 1928, "retain the most vital significance" (Kozhinov 1972: 100; Bakhtin and Medvedev 1978: 25), Bakhtin and Medvedev (61) unmistakably address exactly this "subtraction and elimination" of "essential aspects." The Formalists, in other words, eliminate the all-uniting ideological meaning from "the elements of the artistic work." In Bakhtin and Medvedev's opinion, the systematic emptying of these elements from their "whole intrinsic meaning" results in "the naked device." Following this thread, they point to "polemical emphasis" as "the main and only concern" of Formalism. It "penetrates every Formalist term," tying it "tightly and inseparably" "to that which it negates and rejects." On that basis, they ultimately interpret Formalism as an abstract, "nihilistic" negation of semantic significance, a "simple opposite" of the rejected ideological fullness and, as a consequence, "a *purely reactive formation*" (62 [emphasis mine]). The Formalist insistence on the deautomatization, defamiliarization and denudation inherent in the artistic word stems from their tendency "not so much [to] find something new in the word as [to] expose and do away with the old" (60). "The novelty and strangeness of the word and the object it designates originates here, in the loss of its previous meaning." (60)

This abstraction of the ideological meaning of the elements of literary works, which for Bakhtin and Medvedev (65) is *pushed too far* to be acceptable for a serious literary scholar, appears to be from the Formalist perspective *never radical enough*. The Formalists cannot reach their envisioned *transcendental literary quality* because the empirical remnants of the ideological meaning stemming from the prejudices of the theorist's "ordinary reason" stubbornly adhere to it. Such irritating remnants point to the previously addressed resurgence of the determining in the reflective judgment, which must be immediately deactivated if literariness is to become a true "regulative idea." An idea can become law-giving only if it is elusive, undeterminable. How unreservedly the Russian Formalists' "permanent revolution" surrenders to the compulsive logics of *judgment-in-the-making*, comes to the fore in a quotation from Boris Eikhenbaum's outline, "The Theory of the Formal Method" (1926). It epitomizes the same resilience of modern literary theory to any kind of dogmatic "isms," i.e. the application of determining logical judgments, which a good half-century later culminated in Derrida's famous defense of deconstruction from American "deconstructionism" (Derrida 1989):

> The principle of evolution is extremely important to the history of formalism. Our opponents, and many of our followers, lose sight of this. We are surrounded by eclectics and epigones who would turn the formal method into some fixed system of "formalism" that would work out terms, schemes and classifications for them. This system is quite convenient for criticism, but not at all characteristic of the formal method. We do not have, nor did we ever have, such a finished system or doctrine. In our scholarship we only value theory as a working hypothesis which might help to reveal and comprehend facts, i.e., help comprehend their laws and make them material for research. Therefore, we do not occupy ourselves with the definitions epigones so desire, nor do we construct the general theories eclectics find so pleasing. We establish concrete principles and retain them, to the extent that they are verified in the material. If the material demands that they be elaborated or changed, we elaborate or change them. In this sense we are sufficiently free from our own theories, as scholarship should be, inasmuch as there is a difference between theory and conviction. There is no finished scholarship – scholarship does not live by establishing truths, but by overcoming mistakes. (Eikhenbaum 1927: 116–117; Bakhtin and Medvedev 1978: 71)

That is to say, because the literary transcendental is from the very beginning established by opposition, its identity remains dependent on that empirical particularity which it negates. Such a constitutive relation to an "elsewhere" spoils its transcendental quality by a particular empirical character, its open reflection by determining activity, its abstractness by materiality, its absoluteness by relativity, and its inclusiveness by exclusivity. The theorist's supposedly limitless individual freedom ultimately amounts to an empirically limited community. Such a *recurrent empirical collapse of the literary transcendental* does not diminish but on the contrary stokes its opposition to the empirical. As the delineated reintroduction of the empirical into the heart of the transcendental becomes increasingly irritating, the temptation to expel this internal otherness from the self becomes increasingly fierce and aggressive. This couples Formalist cosmopolitanism, originally envisaged as emancipation, with discrimination.

The Formalist theorist, by way of literariness, strives to exempt his individuality from the ideological constraints of his community in order to meet individuals from other communities in the space of freedom attained through such exemption. Yet he at the same time, in the name of the envisioned "imagined community," wages a war against the readers who, instead of following him, adhere to their constraints. In Eikhenbaum's quotation above, these frustratingly "benighted" readers are labeled as "eclectics," "epigones," or literary "critics" reliant on "convictions." They are disparaged as dogmatists whose restricted reception of literature must be theoretically disengaged. Eikhenbaum blames them for sticking to the polis in the same way Stalin will thereafter blame the Formalists for lacking it (which was, to be sure, an accusation with the incomparably harsher corollaries). This Formalist exclusionist attitude is strongly reminiscent of Greek "detached," i.e. elitist cosmopolitanism. In the subsequent structuralist revision of Formalist theory, epitomized in Chatman's hierarchical model of narrative communication in which the higher levels supervise the lower ones (Chatman 1978: 151), this enlightening subjection of lower to higher agencies acquires a more systematic form. The theorist is expectedly positioned at the top of this "panoptical" of mutual observations, to ensure the ultimate disengagement of all inappropriate empirical identifications taking place on lower levels (Gibson 1996: 214–215). In one of the manifests of French narratology, Gérard Genette (1969: 68–69) declared that the reading of literary works within the representational modality is "a thing of the past," and whoever applies it – and here Genette seems to be implying not just the worldwide dilettante readership but so-called literary hermeneutics as well – belongs to the antiquated past. Such readers must be exposed and derogated, subjected to continuous enlightenment. As they nonetheless proliferate unceasingly, theory multiplies its enemies and accelerates its tempo of exclusions.

8.4 Unleashing the force of self-exemption

In the form it takes with Russian Formalism, such systematic opposition to any positive identification of a work of art represents an extension of the technique of oppositional thinking as we find it in the work of Friedrich Nietzsche.[9] This is an "elective affinity" hitherto barely noticed,[10] although, considering the underlying operation of self-exemption delineated above, not really unexpected. The German philosopher worked out the idea of permanent revaluation (*Umwertung*) or reversion (*Umkehrung*) of perspectives primarily in his late writings, *The Joyful Wisdom* (1882/1887) and especially *On the Genealogy of Morals* (1887), which is significantly subtitled "A Polemic" (*Eine Streitschrift*). As such a switch of perspectives is a logical follow-up of Friedrich Schlegel's antinomy principle of self-formation (Behler 1997: 112), Nietzsche can be interpreted as a relay in the reconfiguration of the "cosmopolitan operation" that took place between the early German Romanticists and the Russian Formalists.

To open the discussion of the link between Nietzsche's technique of oppositional thinking and the Formalist oppositional theorizing of art, let us begin with *The Joyful Wisdom*. In paragraphs 354 and 355 Nietzsche, typically paradoxically, interprets consciousness as the site of the herd's most efficient appropriation of the individual. If we want to exempt ourselves as individuals from such a deceptive communal mentality, we are advised to dismantle our familiar perceptions of reality as something problematic, foreign and remote. However, directly opposed to Bakhtin and Medvedev's blaming of the Formalist de-familiarization for the lack of creativity, Nietzsche resolutely states in § 58: We can destroy only by creating! (*Nur als Schaffende können wir vernichten!*)

This is a provocative thesis, considering that Nietzsche links his philosophical technique with the histrionic operations of the "plebeian spirit" prevalent in the age of a declining culture in which whimsical masses determine the course of human history. Even if the Formalists never established such an explicit association of their oppositional theorizing with the unpredictable "plebeian spirit," their theory was developed in the atmosphere of the October Revolution, which

---

9 Nietzsche is, to recall, the last "link" in Agamben's genealogy of what I have interpreted as the cosmopolitan operation (Agamben 2005b: 95–112).

10 To mention just two "classical works," Aage Hansen-Löve in his voluminous *Der russische Formalismus* refers to Nietzsche only three times and Peter Steiner in *Russian Formalism* for his part not at all. In his genealogy of Shklovsky's concept of estrangement, Ginzburg (1996) also completely omits Nietzsche, as does Tihanov (2005). A modest exception to this rule is James M. Curtis, who briefly touches on the question in the conclusion of his *Mikhail Bakhtin*. A more notable exception, however, is Dragan Kujundžić's book-length investigation of Russian Nietzscheans after modernity. He refers to one of Groy's unpublished manuscripts in which the "Formalist interpretation of the history of culture as a battle of various artistic wills" (Kujundžić 1997: 12) is firstly derived from the Nietzschean understanding of the world as a power struggle and secondly from Nietzsche's philosophy of vitalism. But Kujundžić focuses in the first place on the concept of history, whereas my *tertium comparationis* is the "cosmopolitan" creativity of the "plebeian spirit."

exemplified Nietzsche's diagnosis of the human masses' takeover of the scene of history. This is why Nietzsche's attempt to authorize his own thought by the creativity of the "plebeian spirit" deserves closer inspection. Deepening this association of his explosive philosophy with the revolutionary spirit of human masses, in *The Joyful Wisdom* (2010: § 377) he rejects the idea of any "reality" by stating that "we, the people without homeland" are "an agency" that breaks with all "realities." "The people without homeland (*Heimatlose*)" is to be understood here in the broader sense of numerous humans and collectivities devoid of possession and therefore, in their identity formation, constitutively dependent on their "owners." Bereft of their own form of identification, they borrow it from their "owners" by adapting themselves to the idea their "owners" have of them, yet not without simultaneously disfiguring and distorting it.

Following Nietzsche's example of a woman who spontaneously impersonates herself (*gibt sich aus*) – i.e., acts by assuming but never really appropriating various roles attributed to her by men – Derrida (1979: 46–50) has meticulously analyzed this creative deformation inherent in the everyday revaluation operation of the "people without homeland." With regard to the latter, Nietzsche, along with women, Jews or publicists addresses the mob as the case in point. As far as the mob is concerned, due to the contempt and humiliation with which it is confronted and forced to live on a daily basis, it pollutes, poisons and draws into failure whatever values it adopts (Nietzsche addresses values such as intellect, culture, possession and/or even solitude (§ 359)). However individual and subtle such a value, due to the strenuous efforts of the "owner" over many years, may have become, the mob disparages and bereaves it of its distinctiveness through inappropriate exchanges and mixtures with lower values. Accordingly, contrary to the incessant differentiating activity of the owners, the disowned conceive happiness as "narcotic, anesthetic, calm, peace, 'sabbath'," a pure *passivity* (Nietzsche 1996: 23–24).

> While all noble morality grows from a triumphant affirmation of itself, slave morality from the outset says no to an "outside," to an "other," to a "non-self"; and *this* no is its creative act. The reversal of the evaluating gaze – this necessary orientation outwards rather than inwards to the self – belongs characteristically to *ressentiment*. In order to exist at all, slave morality from the outset always needs an opposing, outer world; in physiological terms, it needs external stimuli in order to act – its action is fundamentally reaction. (22)

In short, in lieu of *responsibility* that characterizes the sovereign masters, "slave morality" is characterized by the *responsiveness* of the dependants. Let us recall that Bakhtin and Medvedev describe Formalism as a polemical and "purely reactive formation" most closely related to the values that it negates and rejects. In a kind of secret revenge of the passive "slaves" on their active "masters," the latter's dominant values are pulled into a peculiar economy of repudiation that empties out, decomposes, and redeploys everything it adopts.

In *On the Genealogy of Morals* Nietzsche represents *ressentiment* as an inventive literary author that searches for new figures to enact the imaginary scenarios of his meanness (Bernstein 1989: 206). In such a way, s/he turns his or her mortal destructiveness into a regenerative creation. According to Foucault's interpretation of Nietzsche's genealogical method, this profound re-description of master values follows from their inscription into the deformed slave bodies involved in the accelerated process of aging, disease, malformation and mutilation (Foucault 1984d: 82–83). In an interview conducted in 1977 by Jacques Rancière, Foucault (2001b) speaks not so much of an identifiable plebs as of something "plebeian" that, as a kind of reverse or reverberation, sets the boundaries of the power relations among the entitled agencies in a given society. By thereafter developing his political theory, Rancière (1999: 8) transformed this destitute plebeian element into the undifferentiated mass of those who, being the necessary surplus of society, have no positive qualification whatsoever. They figure as the "part of those who have no part" (11) in the partition of what is common in the democratic community.

What links the *ressentiment* generated in this "part of those who have no part" with Nietzsche's subversive philosophical thought and, via it, essentially unhomely, persistently disquieting Formalist literary theory? In order to provide an answer, let us depart from Nietzsche's opposition of consciousness (*Bewusstsein*) and knowledge (*Erkenntnis*), as developed in *The Joyful Wisdom* (§ 354, 355). Techniques like understanding and comprehension, rooted in the collectively trained consciousness, are therein discarded as ruthless falsifiers of reality and replaced by the analytical techniques of knowledge. But even knowledge, to prevent its inadmissible domestication of unfamiliar appearances, is transferred by Nietzsche from conscious into bodily terms. Because of the body's ceaseless physiological and chemical processes, its mechanisms of fragmentation, dissolution, binding, mixing and blending, its openness for life's incessant becoming, Nietzsche represents it as the only proper medium of knowledge. The same exposed, vulnerable and infective body is, significantly, the birthplace of *ressentiment*. Yet in the case of *ressentiment* bodily operations are supervised by the body's external "owner" and in the case of knowledge they are mobilized by the body's bearer him- or herself.

Consequently, Nietzsche claims that, in attentively implementing the chemically disfiguring bodily techniques, knowledge transforms *ressentiment* from a defensive adaptation technique of the disowned masses into the *free subversive technique of disowned individuals*. This is obviously how Nietzsche's genealogical method itself comes into being. It operates with a disconcerting surplus of adaptabilities, refusing to be satisfied with immediate benefits (§ 361). Unlike the masses physically deprived of the homeland, the unhomely individuals successfully disengage their immediate bodily reactions. From the peculiar recapitulation of the history of *ressentiment* offered by Nietzsche in the same paragraph, one can infer that his philosophical technique has to be understood as the culmination of a long development. It began with the "denigrated and humiliated" mob; continued with the actor who has learned to command his instincts with other instincts; then the "artist" (the buffoon, the Pantaloon, the Jack-Pudding, the fool, the clown, the classical type of servant, Gil Blas); thereupon, the proper artist; until the process was finally crowned with the "genius." Nietzsche's genealogical method, it follows, results from the reorientation of negation from an external target (the "owner") to the bearer of this operation himself or herself, or negation's transformation into self-negation. Thus with Nietzsche the opposition becomes interiorized and turned against itself. Consecutively deactivating the deactivation just performed, opposing the opposition – in the same manner that Kant expected the reason of his artistic genius or "transcendental philosopher" to *engage reflective judgment by continuously disengaging the automatic application of reason's habits* – Nietzsche's unhomely thought transforms the popular *ressentiment* directed against the "owner" into an interminable series of self-revolutions. Arriving at the peak of a centuries-long process, and harvesting its fruits, his genealogy triumphantly turns desperate communal passivity into the frenetic individual activity of self-reconfiguration.

According to the first essay in *On the Genealogy of Morals* (§ 8), this process of the profound revaluation of homelessness took no less than two millennia to display its life-affirming side:

> But this is indeed what happened: from the trunk of that tree of revenge and hatred, Jewish hatred – the deepest and most sublime hatred, that is, the kind of hatred which creates ideals and changes the meaning of values, a hatred the like of which has never been on earth – from this tree grew forth something equally incomparable, a *new love*, the deepest and most sublime of all kinds of love. [...] Love grew forth from this hatred, as its crown, as the triumphant crown, spreading itself ever wider in the purest brightness and fullness of the sun, as a crown which pursued in the lofty realm of light the goals of hatred – victory, spoils, seduction – driven there by the same impulse with which the roots of that hatred sank down ever further and more lasciviously into everything deep and evil. (Nietzsche 1996: 20)

Nietzsche liked to present himself as a tree with roots poisoned by material life and branches reaching the heights of the spiritual unknown. Such a magical overturning of the contagious seed of the old into a rejuvenating new substance stimulated Derrida to present him as the *thinker of pregnancy* (Derrida 1979: 64). He takes this metaphor from § 72 of *The Joyful Wisdom,* in which Nietzsche compares the artist's creation with a woman's pregnancy; the single concern of both these solitary undertakings is to produce affirmation out of the negation of life. In the same magical vein, Nietzsche produces his remedial genealogical method from the poisonous *ressentiment*. Rather than being violently enforced, as is the homelessness of the masses, his unhomeliness is strategically chosen and thus supposedly translated into positive energy. In sum, in Nietzsche's (and Foucault's) radically oppositional thought, we witness a kind of "success story" that claims to be redeeming the repudiated surplus of society without producing any new "social garbage."[11]

To return now finally to the analogy with the Russian Formalists, they almost spontaneously followed Nietzsche in his interiorization of the oppositional thought and directing it against itself. They coerced the national-philological reading of literature to disengage its habitual patterns in the same way Nietzsche forced philosophy, according to Foucault's reading (Foucault 1984d: 90, 93), to deactivate the serious application of its categories and "joyfully" liberate their hidden revolutionary potential. With Russian Formalists, literary theory became a persistently self-defamiliarizing instrument. As one of the prominent inheritors of the Formalist accelerated unworkings of unworkings, Foucault regarded such "eventialization" (or *événementialisation*, i.e. the persistent exemption of the present from the past) (1996: 393, 1990: 47–48)[12] as the distinctive feature of modernity. Instead of being determined by history, each present event contains the potential for disengagement and is summoned to activate it. According to Foucault, this continuous reassessment of one's limits and capabilities (*les pouvoirs*), epitomized in Kant's reflective judgment, is the only Enlightenment legacy worth taking up after two centuries (2001a: 1587).

In accordance with the logic of persistent self-re-description thus appropriated, in a series of works from the 1970s Foucault even reapplied Nietzsche's rhetoric of counter-violence by insistently defying memory with counter-memory, knowledge with counter-knowledge, and history with counter-history. As if echoing the Russian Formalists' *politics of estrangement* as well as the early German Romanticist and Nietzschean "narrative of permanent displacement" in its background, Foucault makes all that is close and familiar the distant and strange (*redoublement*, an echo of Romanticist *Verdopplung*), forcing the theorist to start its

---

[11] Inasmuch as the surplus of people, as the epitome of that which is wrong in democracy, is rendered negotiable rather than irredeemable by Rancière (1999), his vision of democracy, in my opinion, belongs to the same redemption narrative. For more on this, see chapter twelve. However, he remains ambiguous on this question and can also be interpreted in the way as I have done in previous chapters.

[12] As is well known, the "event" is an important concept in Foucault's vocabulary, but as regards "eventialization," he nevertheless asks his audience to pardon *l'horreur du mot*.

history always wholly anew (*recommencement*). There is indeed a remarkable continuity in Foucault's untiring insistence to break free from the delusions of the past. Thus, archeology "deprives us of our continuities [...] dissipates that temporal identity in which we are pleased to look at ourselves [...] bursts open the other, and the outside [...] establishes that we are difference, that our reason is the difference of discourses, our history the difference of times, our selves the difference of masks" (1972: 131). On the way from early German Romanticism, through Nietzsche and the Russian Formalists up to Foucault, the cosmopolitan legacy of Kant's reflective judgment adopted pressing, offensive, and imperative traits.

Via this route, naive confidence in the emancipating power of slavish negation, as Hannah Arendt (1970: 56) has cautioned, reaffirmed and enhanced in its turn the master's violence in place of suspending it. Unleashing "destructive creativity," revolutions degenerate into the tyrannies they have dethroned. The weapon of abstraction employed by "adversarial thinkers" (Nehamas 1989: 183) ultimately displays more extensive violence than the particular instance negated by it was capable of. Precisely by the act of opposing, the abstraction restages its opponent's operations in the same way as, according to Bakhtin and Medvedev, the artistic negation reintroduces the exclusion performed by the particular form disempowered by it. Nietzsche's method of switching perspectives, therefore, neither does break out of the vicious circle of the metaphysical thinking it defies (Hanssen 2000: 282) nor does it absolve the plebeian revolutionary tradition it believes to have translated into the positive. Despite his conviction to have disengaged the violent legacy of popular *ressentiment* in his allegedly life-affirming genealogy, he inadvertently reengaged its perilously discriminating operations. The same equivocal heritage burdens the oppositional thought of modern literary theory.

9 The All-Devouring Modern Mind: Bakhtin's Cosmopolitan Self

9.1 Confronting mind with self-displacing life

Bakhtin's first reading of Kant is usually associated with his time as a student at Petersburg University, during which Neo-Kantianism was a widespread phenomenon among Russian university teachers. Subsequently, he continued to be involved in intense philosophical debates in intellectual circles in Nevel and Vitebsk. At the time, he was strongly influenced by Matvei Isaevich Kagan, who returned to Russia in 1918 after studying in Marburg with the prominent Neo-Kantian philosopher Hermann Cohen. Cohen unilaterally emphasized the transcendental aspects of Kant's complex synthesis between the world and the mind. He concentrated on a priori concepts instead of the thing-in-itself. Focusing on the "logic of pure knowing" (*Logik der reinen Erkenntnis*, 1902), he tried to interpret the operations of the mind in accordance with the systematic mathematical, physical or biological laws, which impose upon the world an all-encompassing oneness (*Allheit*). Despite his respect for Kagan, who transferred these ideas of Cohen's to Russia, Bakhtin was actually closer to another philosopher of the Marburg Neo-Kantian School, Ernst Cassirer, whose *Philosophy of Symbolic Forms* offered a reading of Kant from the world-related perspective of the philosophy of life (Tihanov 2005: 24). In an apt summary of Michael Holquist,

> Bakhtin is perhaps best understood as a figure who is trying to get back to the other side of Kant's synthesis, the world, rather than the mind (and in particular the rational mind), the extreme to which Cohen tended. The original Kantian concept of heterogeneity of ends is much closer to Bakhtin's work than the later Neo-Kantian lust for unity. (Holquist 2002: 6)

Following this thread, between 1918 and 1924 Bakhtin investigated how the ongoing dialogue between the mind and the world influences the constitution of these entities. Not being established unities, both the world and the mind appear as an unfinalizable process. This emphasis on *the process of their correlated becoming* connects Bakhtin's thought at that time, beyond Neo-Kantianism, with the tradition of the philosophy of life (as exemplified in early German Romanticism and thereafter in Nietzsche). The correlated connection to Marxism was brought to expression in the first place in the works of Bakhtin co-authored with Medvedev and Voloshinov, but published under their names. According to Galin Tihanov (2000: 84), Bakhtin participated in all three traditions in an equally passionate and critical way, trying to subject them to "mutually challenging examination."

This permanent challenging of one by another deserves to be re-emphasized, especially in view of the many attempts to reduce Bakhtin's early work to Cohen's and Natorp's Neo-Kantianism (Clark and Holquist 1984; Freise 1993; Poole 1995; Scholz 1998). In order to understand the development of Bakhtin's crucial concept of wholeness (*tseloe*), we need a different rendering of Kant's philosophy from the one we get with Neo-Kantianism, with which Bakhtin never ceased to take issue. A world-related Kant who seriously considered the resistance of the thing-in-itself to its appropriation by the mind needs to be rescued from oblivion.

Even Holquist, whose interpretation of Bakhtin's dealing with Kant's philosophy is otherwise illuminating, is sometimes perplexing in his exegesis. On the one hand, he cautions that Bakhtin is "closer to Kant himself than to Cohen, in so far as he rethinks the problem of wholeness in terms of what is an essentially *aesthetic* operation" (Holquist 2002: 7). This esthetic operation, as Holquist understands it, implies an authoring action of the self in which the other (as a constitutive part of the same wholeness of the world-in-the-making) is "consumed" (*zavershen*) "with care and with the constant awareness" that s/he is "an active consciousness too" (11). Following Kant, who envisioned knowledge (*Erkenntnis*) as a constant dialogue between the conquering mind and the opposing world (4), Bakhtin represents this authoring as an active understanding that offers the other the opportunity to reply in this dialogue. Through such an interpretation of Kant's philosophy, he made its living complexity resilient to the Neo-Kantian unilateral reification in the same way as, a good half-century later, Tihanov and Holquist resisted the Neo-Kantian reductions of Bakhtin's work itself. Subjecting to permanent reflection a priori conditions of knowledge germane to "pure reason," Bakhtin turned upside down the dominant understanding of Kantian philosophy, and interpreted the *Critique of Pure Reason* through the lenses of the *Critique of Judgment*. Intervening thus in the very core of the contemporaneous philosophy of consciousness, he transferred the cognitive relationship between the mind (the subject) and the world (the object) into aesthetic terms. Knowledge became an operation of Kant's reflective judgment.

Yet Holquist on the other hand, turning to the discussion of the chronotope, abandons Bakhtin's "esthetic" Kant to return to Cohen's "scientific" Kant. Making Bakhtin firmly committed to "the historical particularity of any act of perception as it is actually experienced by living persons from their unique place in existence," he strongly contrasts him with Kant, who supposedly "gives exclusive attention" to "the general, repeatable aspects of perception." "Kant's abstraction omits" Bakhtin's "unrepeatable dimension" of perception rooted in "lived experience" (2002: 148) or the most immediate reality (*sammoi real'noi deistvitel'nosti*, in the sense of everyday or common reality too (Bakhtin 1981: 85n)). In this astonishingly simplified interpretation of Kant, his philosophy is reduced to a purely negative foil in order to sharpen the originality of Bakhtin's redescription. Bakhtin supposedly opposes the situated, located consciousness to Kant's "general consciousness" (Holquist 2002: 151). What happened to the world-related Kant who insisted on the thing-in-itself? What happened to his "heterogeneity of ends?" What happened to the Kant of Cassirer, affiliated to the philosophy of life?

Correcting this artificial contrast between Bakhtin and Kant, Tihanov (2000: 84) reminds us that bringing together Neo-Kantianism, *Lebensphilosophie* and Marxism was "a significant element of Russian intellectual life ever since the latter half of the nineteenth century." It instantiated a permanent dialogue between, on the one hand, forms bestowed upon life by the laws of perception, which tend to render themselves as definite (*zakonchennie*) and, on the other hand, life that forces those forms to pass through an interminable process of appropriation wherein they are "consummated" (*zavershennie*) anew. As the German sociologist Georg Simmel put it in 1918: "Life can express itself and realize its freedom only through forms; yet forms must also necessarily suffocate life and obstruct freedom" (Simmel 1971: 375, quoted after Tihanov 2000: 93, 22n). Like Bakhtin, Simmel hails the essential heterogeneity of life (termed by early Romanticists "the exuberant abundance of life"), which triumphs over each particular human act of its homogenization. Whenever human practical, perceptual or artistic form establishes familiarizing borders, life takes care to defamiliarize them. This estrangement strikingly recalls the aesthetic quality defined in § 46 of the *Critique of Judgment* (136–137) as the ability of the work of art to deactivate its familiar perception or mobilize the human mind through the disengagement of its automatic application. The important difference is that it is now ascribed to life in lieu of art. Bakhtin attributes to the wholeness of life the same quality that Kant had attributed to the work of fine art (produced by genius guided by nature). Such aestheticization lends life a supreme authority that in Bakhtin's philosophy "authors" all human achievements including art.

In accordance with the tradition of the philosophy of life, stemming from early German Romanticism and transmitted to him most notably by Dilthey and Simmel, Bakhtin treats the wholeness of life as an *unfathomable performer of self-exemption* from all forms of its appropriation, including the artistic ones. Life manifests itself exclusively through a *permanent self-displacement*. In his polemics against Russian Formalism, Bakhtin accordingly insists that the artistic work is a mere *refraction* of the ideological horizon of a given epoch and social group (Medvedev and Bakhtin 1978: 21–23). Instead of being absolute, art for him is a derivate of something that transcends it. Conceived as a "particular mode of orientation in reality," "the thematic unity of the given work" results from the "chemical combination" of "artistic construction" with the "extraartistic ideologeme," which precedes and surrounds it (23).

> It is true that this ideology of a *raznochinets*, upon entering the novel and becoming a dependent structural element of the artistic whole, in no way ceases to be an ethical, philosophical ideologeme. On the contrary, it brings to the structure of the novel all its extraartistic ideological meaning, all its seriousness, and the fullness of its ideological responsibility. An ideologeme deprived of its direct meaning, of its ideological bite, cannot enter the artistic structure, for it does not provide precisely what is necessary and constituent to the poetic structure – its full ideological acuity. (22)

This disturbing surplus of life also seems to characterize Kant's thing-in-itself, which is enmeshed, in the *Critique of Judgment*, in the process of nature's becoming. Conceived in these mobile terms, it undermines the smooth application of the transcendental principles of the human mind. Confronted with such evasiveness of life, can the subject find any reliable refuge in his or her a priori schemata? Struck by the rapid and violent dissolution of inherited values, patterns and norms of post-October Soviet society, Bakhtin was preoccupied with this question throughout his life. Searching for an appropriate manner in which to relive and mobilize these rigid schemata, he developed the aforementioned conception of the mind's *authoring activity*, conceived as the never-ending dialogic consummation of life's inexhaustible forms. According to Holquist (2002: 149–55), the concept of the chronotope developed in the thirties is to be understood as this dynamic operation rather than the static transcendental structure of the mind. Static structure may have been valid in pre-modern times but, after the modern disintegration of society, the chronotope does not pertain to all minds equally. Because of the accelerated transfiguring interaction between the mind's habitual forms and evasive life, chronotopes are forced to become creative:

> However forcefully the real and the represented world resist fusion, however immutable the presence of that categorical boundary line between them, they are nevertheless indissolubly tied up with each other and find themselves in continual mutual interaction; uninterrupted exchange goes on between them, similar to the uninterrupted exchange of matter between living organisms and the environment that surrounds them. As long as the organism lives, it resists a fusion with the environment, but if it is torn out of its environment, it dies. The work and the world represented in it enter the real world and enrich it, and the real world enters the work and its world as part of the process of its creation, as well as part of its subsequent life, in a continual renewing of the work through the creative perception of listeners and readers. Of course this process of exchange is itself chronotopic: it occurs first and foremost in the historically developing social world, but without ever losing contact with changing historical space. We might even speak of a special *creative* chronotope inside which this exchange between work and life occurs, and which constitutes the distinctive life of the work. (Bakhtin 1981: 254)

Along with the exchange between the chronotope and life, modernity instantiated a continuous exchange between chronotopes themselves, which are "interwoven with, replace or oppose one another, contradict one another or find themselves in ever more complex interrelationships." This dialogue "enters the world of the author, of the performer, and the world of the listeners and readers" (252). Essentially, Bakhtin understands modernity as the age in which people begin to experience their existence as an *open life event without transcendental guarantees*. Bearing in mind that the ordinary Russian word for event, especially when paired with being (*sobytie bytija*, as Bakhtin regularly terms it), etymologically points to the meaning *shared being*, we could define modernity, in Bakhtin's sense, as the age in which the mind becomes aware of the challenge addressed to it by different dispositions of other minds. In making the self aware of the necessity of dialogue, these others call on it to *share in their uniqueness*, i.e. to share its individuality with theirs.

Instead of constraining each other's individual liberty in order to serve the preordained spatial-temporal order of society, as was the case in pre-modern times, from now on *the self and the other are rendered equal only via their absolutely individual claim to life*. There is no other transcendental principle that unites them beforehand, since individuals are authorized by this all-transcending life to exempt themselves from any such principle. It is the key feature of modernity that its unity, at least nominally, remains open to determination by all individuals, regardless of the enormous differences between them. Rather than just representing the examples of a universal rule, individuals now freely *unite their singularities*. To pinpoint this paradox of uniting singularities within the changing order of humankind – always determined anew through the open dialogic interaction of its self-redescribing individuals – the early Bakhtin frequently refers to "the unique and unified event of being" (*edinstvennoe i edinoe sobytie bytija*) (Holquist 2002: 24–25).

9.2 A utopian cosmopolitan community

This utopian modern community of unique individuals, esthetic in nature by virtue of its attachment to life, comes into being through reflective judgment. It is established *on the assumptive basis* in the sense in which Kant speaks of the assumptive establishment of *sensus communis*. At stake is an essentially hypothetical, subjectively projected, *imagined cosmopolitan community* (Robbins 1998: 2). Dealing with the judgment of taste in § 20, Kant (2007: 68) states: "The judgement of taste, therefore, depends on our presupposing the existence of a common sense" and is unimaginable without this presupposition. What he understands by *sensus communis*, as we learn from § 40, is not a logical common sense (*Gemeinsinn*) in the ordinary meaning of sound understanding but an aesthetic common sense in the elevated meaning of public sense (*gemeinschaftlicher Sinn*). Accordingly, an imagined cosmopolitan community can be established exclusively through the esthetic, i.e. reflective and not intellectual, i.e. determining judgment (125).

Yet, however assumptive the establishment of a common sense appears to be, it spawns solid claims. Unlike objective intellectual judgments founded on the concepts of general validity, aesthetic judgments are founded on the subjective feeling of pleasure *demanding the universal consent of everyone* (26; Introduction, §7). Because such pleasure is independent of all interest (§2), the subject assumes s/he is judging completely freely, and therefore expects similar delight to be expressed by everyone.

> Accordingly he will speak of the beautiful as if beauty were a feature of the object and the judgment were logical [...] although it is only aesthetic, and contains merely a reference of the representation of the object to the subject; because it still bears this resemblance to the logical judgement, that it may be presupposed to be valid for everyone. [...] The result is that the judgement of taste, with its attendant consciousness of detachment from all interest, must involve a claim to validity for everyone, and must do so apart from a universality directed to objects, i.e. there must be coupled with it a claim to subjective universality. (43)

Unlike determining logical judgments, aesthetic judgments *require* the agreement of other subjects. From the perspective of the reflective judge, these subjects' joining of the esthetic community is tantamount to *a must*:

> He judges not merely for himself, but for everyone, and then speaks of beauty as if it were a property of things. Thus he says the thing is beautiful; and it is not as if he counted on others agreeing in his judgement of liking owing to his having found them in such agreement on a number of occasions, but he *demands* this agreement of them. (44)

Kant accordingly insists on the *apodictic character* of the judgment of taste, stating that it "*imputes* this agreement to everyone" looking for its confirmation "from the concurrence of others" (§8, 47). He repeatedly returns to this amazing question[1] of why "the pleasure felt by us is expected from everyone as necessary, just as if, when we call something beautiful, beauty was to be regarded as a quality of the object," even if it is obviously just a subjective quality. However, he postpones the answer to it (§9, 49–50). If we accept that reflective aesthetic judgment underlies the whole regulative idea[2] of the purposiveness of nature and, through it, fine artistic work, such hesitation is understandable. Any premature solution

---

[1] In the Introduction he calls it "strange or out of the way" (2007: 26).
[2] Kant does not speak here of the *transcendental principle* because the latter must be taken from an "other quarter" (2007: 15).

would spawn huge consequences. Yet Kant seems nonetheless to provide an answer: "The purposiveness of nature is, therefore, a particular *a priori* concept, which has its origin solely in reflective judgement." (16) If purposiveness is attributed to nature or a work of fine art just for the sake of aesthetic pleasure, then the following cluster of questions, a sort of *Summationsschema* of Kant's hesitations, appears to be of a purely suggestive character:

> But does such a common sense in fact exist as a constitutive principle of the possibility of experience, or is it formed for us as a regulative principle by a still higher principle of reason, that for higher ends first seeks to produce in us a common sense? Is taste, in other words, a natural or original faculty, or is it *only the idea of one that is artificial and to be acquired by us*, so that a *judgement of taste, with its expectation of universal assent, is but a demand of reason for generating such unanimity in this sensing*, and does the "ought," i.e. the objective necessity of coincidence of the feeling of all with the particular feeling of each, only betoken the possibility of arriving at some sort of agreement in these matters, and the judgement of taste only adduce an example of the application of the principle? (§ 22, 70 [emphasis mine])

If Kant's enlightened man projects a higher purpose into the diversity of *nature* to make it conform "to our faculty of cognition" (23) and derive a feeling of pleasure from it, then Bakhtin relegates this assumptive all-uniting property to *life*. Generated in the same way, life mediates between its heterogeneous forms just as "divinely" as Kant's purposive nature. Because the modern individual loses its previously familiar site in the "proximate world" of his/her kin, nation, state, or culture (Bakhtin 1990: 165), life rises as the horizon of universal reconciliation. Bakhtin pushes this individual, confronted with the heteroglot grammar of disjointed norms, toward the dialogic search for identity that leads him/her beyond any particular horizon. He obliges his/her identity construction by his/her constitutive relatedness to life. Pointing out the "necessarily obligating" "uniqueness of present-at-hand being," "*my non-alibi in being*" (Bakhtin 1994: 40), Bakhtin represents this new responsibility toward life as the guarantee of human freedom. Since all warrants of human commonality are put in question, "my unity for myself is a unity perpetually yet-to-be," i.e. to be accomplished in a way "no one else can ever accomplish" (Bakhtin 1990: 126). This cosmopolitan freedom is a tough accomplishment; rather than being a simple given for anyone, it has to be won through persistent effort.

Challenged by other individuals with whom s/he shares the same being, Bakhtin's individual seeks a completely new life form that escapes determination. In order to accomplish it, s/he must persist in disentangling his/her mind from the morass of preordained forms of identification, i.e. freeing himself/herself from any recognizable place that would enable the others to constrain him/her. Early Bakhtin follows this *compensatory cosmopolitan orientation* as an almost *natural determination* of any subject even if the great majority of Soviet subjects at that time were strictly constrained by "local" political and social norms – or precisely because of that. He lends this ethical obligation (*dolzhestvovanie*) of the modern individual an unconstrainedly universal character. No particular community authorizes his/her activity, but rather the super-addressee, the Supreme Judge of all imaginable communities (Bakhtin 1979: 30–36). In Bakhtin's understanding, these superior authorities represent for their part all-encompassing "life." Only inasmuch as the modern individual is resolutely directed toward this life will s/he be able to resist "consummation" by the others.

In complete harmony with Friedrich Schlegel's conception, Bakhtin interprets this self-authoring individual as both the mobilizer and result of the consistent cosmopolitan self-expansion. He was a lifelong adherent of Schlegel's "cosmic irony" or "universal poetry," which break through all the firm identity abodes. As Schlegel clarified in his *Philosophical Apprenticeship* (1796–1806), inasmuch as God demands all earthly incompleteness to be completed by its earthly opposite, and follows this "dialogics of reversals" ad infinitum, He is the ultimate warrant of the freedom of man's formation (*Bildung*). Bakhtin's godlike entities are nothing but replicas of this God as the authorizer of the individual's endless self-revolutionizing. "For a man who has achieved a certain level of the universality of formation, his inner being is an ongoing chain of the most enormous revolutions."[3] (Schlegel 1963: 82–83)

9.3 The authorial operation: expanding the self by consummating the others

At the beginning of the thirties, Bakhtin elaborates on the strategies for a relentless and systematic dialogic extension of the self's horizon. His objective is the gradual relinquishment of the *body*, which occupies a recognizable spatial-temporal site in favor of *consciousness* that "can have neither a beginning nor an end" (Bakhtin 1984: 291). Bakhtin's *Bewusstseinsphilosophie* is therefore clearly opposed to Nietzsche's philosophy of the body but he consents neither with the Formalist interpretation of the esthetic dissolution of mind patterns. Whereas the reader's a priori schemata are in Formalist interpretation *subjected* to permanent literary estrangement, in Bakhtin's theory the reader's reason is engaged in

---

[3] For the overlap of Bakhtin's ideas with those of Friedrich Schlegel (whom Bakhtin mentions in several instances), especially in the *Athenäum-Fragments* and the *Letter on the Novel* in the *Dialogue on Poetry*, see Tihanov 2000: 58–59, 145, and 250.

the authorial operation of an *active understanding*, consistently transgressing its schematic boundaries. The cosmopolitan expansion of its horizon is induced not by literary work but him/her himself/herself. The reader's reaction is a conscious dialogic action rather than a compulsive corporeal response to the challenge of the literary work. Whereas the body observed from without is finite, consciousness is "infinite, revealing itself only from within" (Bakhtin 1984: 290). Yet Bakhtin is at the same time aware that "consciousness comes second" (290), which is why it is constantly reminded of its corporeality, its site in life (*Sitz im Leben*), i.e. its location in the net of other perceptions which never stop challenging it. Holquist points out (2002: 167) that the body "is our 'address' in existence, an address expressed not in numbers, but by our proper name." It is only because of such an identified location that we can speak at all. This explains why Bakhtin introduces the concept of "answerability" (*otvetstvennost'*): our action is nothing but an active answer designed to pull ourselves out of this corporeal address.

To become a self-authoring individual means to consistently and in a strategic manner disembody, i.e. exempt, oneself from this deactivating address. This operation implies a systematic self-expansion through the putting of oneself in the place of others, i.e. enriching one's own point of view through the surplus of perspectives external to it. The analogy with the cosmopolitan duty of the world citizen elaborated by Kant is obvious. Beyond Kant and early German Romanticism, however, Bakhtin's operation of self-authoring seems to be evoking a much older Renaissance colonialist technique dubbed by Stephen Greenblatt (1980: 230) "displacement plus absorption." After all, European modernity set out with Renaissance colonialism. According to Greenblatt, this technique skillfully links empathy with the other with its exploitation for the sake of the strengthening of the self (224). Emphasizing exclusively its positive, empathic side and suppressing the exploiting aspect, Bakhtin called this assimilating technique of the self – in a free Russian translation of the German term *Einfühlung* – *vzhivanie* or live-entering, even though he admitted that it ends with the profitable "returning to my own place" (Bakhtin 1990: 25). The final aim of this *Einfühlung* is the same as Herder, the inventor of the term envisaged it, i.e. the self-aggrandizement. It is through such a profitable *authorial detour* that the other is esthetically "consummated" (*zavershen*), i.e. transferred in the self's terms. Being in the constant making, the authoring self, for its part, escapes the "consummation" by the other. Authorized by the inaccessible life, it is conceptualized as the pure energy of self-exemption. "My unity for myself is perpetually yet-to-be," states Bakhtin in the name of this modern authoring self (126). As Herder is the ultimate author of this exemplary pattern of European modernity, this is the right place to recall his groundbreaking statement: "I am the one in whom creation peaks, who pours into all beings and whose self is full of them all!"

This *operation of the imperial self-empowering through an attentive assimilation of the other* is exemplified in the novel and historiography, two epitomes of European modern literary and scientific genres. Their authors clearly target supreme authority, taking distance from their figures, other specimens of the same genre and other genres. For example, by allocating to "unreasonable" colonized people, peasants and women either a pre-modern place "elsewhere" or outdated time "not yet," historicism "posited historical time as a measure of cultural distance" (Chakrabarty 2000: 7). "[T]he method does not allow the investigating subject to recognize himself or herself as also the figure he or she is investigating. It stops the subject from seeing his or her own present as discontinuous with itself." (239) The same holds for the novel. In fact, within the historicist model, the historian's self treats the other(s) in the same manner as the novelistic author treats his/her figures: they are "consummated" with much care so that the author as their *metteur-en-scène* can escape any such "consumption" and protect his/her unlimited freedom.

While suppressing the aforementioned colonial and imperial overtones inherent in such an authorial attitude – and in the whole "hospitable" or "affirmative" cosmopolitanism carried by it – Bakhtin philosophically constructs an *abstract universal relationship* between the self and the other through a number of oppositions such as openness vs. completeness, immediacy vs. mediacy, center vs. margin, non-referentiality vs. referentiality, etc.

> The other is in the realm of completedness, whereas I experience time as open and always as yet *un*-completed, and I am always at the *center* of space. [...] When I look at you, I see your whole body, and I see it as having a definite place in the total configuration of a whole landscape. I see you as occupying a certain position vis-à-vis other persons and objects [...] Moreover, you not only have definite physical characteristics, specific social standing, and so on, but I see you as having a definite character as well. [...] If we imagine a self and other in painterly terms, the former would be non-figurative and the latter extremely hard-edged. (Holquist 2002: 25–27)

In fact, I desperately need the other to be visible and concrete in order to realize *what I am not*. As Michael Holquist (31) succinctly put it, reminding us of the constitution of Luhmann's modern individual, the "most precise characteristic" of the self is "being what the others are not." As if following this model espoused by Bakhtin, the historicist also tends to wipe out whatever came earlier in order to free the "true present" as an unquestioned "zero point" of history (Chakrabarty 2000: 244). He thereby exemplifies how the modern self permanently authors itself by means of others, i.e. treating them as the mere material for its contrastive self-fashioning. Using the European novel based on this pattern as a self-evident point of departure, Bakhtin represents the whole existence as an *injunction for the self-authoring at the expense of the other.* "Ontologizing" the novel in such an unproblematic way, he disconnects it from particular historical examples of the genre such as Rabelais's or Dostoevsky's novels. For Bakhtin they are just exemplary manifestations of the universal condition of human beings. As one might expect, Bakhtin calls this putatively universal condition, based on the particular examples of the genre, novelness (*romannost'*).

Confronting the modern self with such an eminently novelistic task of self-authoring, in the manner strongly reminiscent of Luhmann, Bakhtin surreptitiously engages the Hegelian legacy of "double negation" as the principle of its "narrative progression." The double negation means that each consecutive instance of progression (of both novelistic and historiographic plots) *negates* the reality introduced by previous instances, because this reality, being established by a restricted perspective, *negates* the "unlimited complexity" of the world. The intention of such a consistent "negation of the negation" is to revive the vast multitude of the world's excluded possibilities. Beyond the restricted *reality*, the modern individual self aims for the *world* as a realm of chaotic contingency. To cite Niklas Luhmann (1970: 34; 1971: 34), another important inheritor of the Early German Romanticist legacy, the world is the final and insurmountable horizon of all particular choices made by its inhabitants (*Woraus-aller-Wahlen*). Bakhtin includes the world perspective in the form of the Supreme Judge who sets the terms of the dialogue between the two adjacent instances of narrative progression. Recourse to this authority enables each subsequent instance to transgress the preceding one and, by redescribing it, emancipate itself from the limits set by it. As argued above, such an extension of the spatially and temporally restricted human possibilities into the substantially elongated space and time-horizon of humanity also constitutes the core of Kant's cosmopolitan argument that establishes his idea of Enlightenment. This remedial grasping toward a stabilizing form of commonality explains why Bakhtin regards the Enlightenment to be the turning point of human history. According to him, it was at that time that the idea of the world as the guarantee of universal human freedom arose on the historical horizon. When, under the extremely sinister Soviet circumstances, he attaches the violently uprooted self to the vague prospect of a large-scale world existence, Bakhtin seems to be developing his peculiar modernist utopia under the spell of this tradition.

9.4 A counterfactual compensatory project

How is world expected to mediate in the earthly human dialogue? Bakhtin interprets this constitutively missing "third person" (*tret'e litso*) in the dialogue as a sort of super-addressee, ensuring an ultimate absolute understanding between interlocutors well beyond the restricted immediate understanding temporarily provided by one of them (Bakhtin 1979: 305–306). Alternatively, he interprets this Third as a "man you'll never know" or, in an explicitly Kantian manner, a "representative of 'all others' for the 'I'," which guarantees that the presently antagonistic perspectives will be reconciled in the distant future (Bakhtin 1984: 264). The authorization of this Third induces in the final analysis such an abstraction of the speaker that it becomes a "pure 'man in man'," "deprived of any social or pragmatic real-life concretization," "independent of all real-life, concrete social forms (the forms of family, social or economic class, life's stories)" (264). As if furtively embodying Bakhtin's carnival utopia, this huge harmonizing horizon of absolute freedom finally obliterates all social, economic, cultural and gender differences between the given interlocutors. It erases all weighty power-related inequalities among earthly human beings, including even the principal rift between the past and the future, which is constitutive of human history. It implies that nothing is lost or dead, no thing that ever happened is irrecoverable.

While Bakhtin projects this utopian world of limitlessly mobile identities, he blithely overlooks the immense "pockets of immobility" both within it and outside it that function as its *invisible condition of possibility*. As Louis Dumont (1980: 12) puts it, "[w]hilst equality is good, it is above all an ideal which man introduces into political life, to compensate for the ineluctable fact of inequality." Since, from the end of the eighteenth century onwards, society as a whole is far from functioning as its political domain is increasingly expected to do, the Western idea of the full autonomy of each person gradually becomes a defensive hypertrophy. The economic dependence of humans on each other is greater than ever before in modern global society (11). Instead of abolishing the harsh national, economic, social and political inequalities of tsarist Russia as it had promised, Bakhtin's post-imperial Soviet Union deepened them to an almost grotesque extent. I interpret this traumatic constellation as the real source of Bakhtin's utopia of an all-equalizing world. This "cruel optimism" (Berlant 2011) explains why in the concluding paragraph of his treatise *Toward the Methodology of Human Sciences* Bakhtin emphatically states:

> There is neither the first nor the last word, there are no limits set to the dialogic context (it extends into the unlimited past as well as into the unlimited future). Even meanings born in the dialogue of the remotest centuries can never be stabilized (once and forever completed, finished). They will always be changed (renewed) in the process of the subsequent, future development of the dialogue. Vast, unlimited, masses of forgotten meanings participate in each particular moment of this dialogic development, but at a given moment in the dialogue's later course they will be recalled, relived, in a renewed context and aspect. There is nothing absolutely dead; every meaning will experience the holiday of its rebirth. (Bakhtin 1979: 373, my translation)

If it is thus impossible to establish definitely the boundaries of meaning, constant transformation determines everything that exists. The *object-world* of given *things* is transformed into the *historical world* of *projects* aiming at an open, uncertain future capable of revising the past. Whereas the spatially-temporally given things are nothing but blind objects of historical temporality, projects are its vivid material embodiment, "*marks of the passage of time*" (Bakhtin 1986: 25). The latter phrase appears in the discussion of Goethe as an author, who was the first to regard the world as being "at the point of transition," involved in the process of incessant becoming (*stanovlenie*) without predestined direction (23).

> Necessity [...] became the organizing centre of the Goethean sense of time. He wished to pull together and connect the present, past and future with the ring of necessity. This Goethean necessity was very distant both from the necessity of fate and from mechanical natural necessity (in the naturalistic sense). It was a visible, concrete, material, but materially creative, historical necessity. (39)

What makes this historical necessity *creative* in Bakhtin's interpretation is the same constitutive moment that made the self and the novel creative: the authority that the world attributes to each particular instance of its progression to author the preceding instances by taking a superior stance to them. This is a retroactive historical necessity that *reflects* upon the inherited *determining* order of causes and effects. In short, Goethe's idea of historical necessity announces the modern age by establishing the *autonomy* of its particles as the measure of its historical development. Modernity deprives the past of the right to rule over the present by letting the latter have the upper hand. Goethe's younger contemporary Alexis de Tocqueville (1945: 17–18) posits that "the woof of time is any instant broken, and the track of generations effaced [...] democracy breaks the chain and severs every link of it." Each segment of historical progression acquires individual, instantaneous quality. "What is still called 'society' is the means, the life of each man is the end." (Dumont 1980: 9) As all humanity is deemed present in each human's unconstrained freedom, humans "are apt to imagine that their whole destiny is in their own hands"; democracy "threatens in the end to confine [every human] entirely within the solitude of his own heart" (Tocqueville 1945: 18–19).

In this sense, Goethe's time can be regarded as the historical point at which the novel, the self and history come together to adopt the *dialogic pattern of narrative progression* through an incessant creative renewal, or continuous individual detachment from the mass of fellow beings. By gradually affecting elected minds, this operation of the self's empowering through the assimilation of others becomes the order of the day. Conceived along the same lines, Goethe's idea of world literature was also envisaged to consolidate, alongside his personal self, the contemporaneous German. According to Bakhtin, his educational novel shifted the focus from the preordained plot to the possibility of the transformation of its hero, whereby the "change in the hero itself acquires *plot significance*" (Bakhtin 1986: 21). Yet placing transition within the hero instead of the plot would hardly be imaginable had not the modern world made possible self-transcendence within the bounds of earthly life, had it not reintegrated the pre-modern and religious "otherworldly future, torn from the horizontal of earthly space and time" back into the worldly and "real flow of time" (43). This is why Goethe's hero "becomes together with the world," why he is put under the pressure of the historical becoming of the world "to become a new, unprecedented type of human being" (23). As Tocqueville noted, through the world's permanent intervention, the bond of human affection gradually extends toward the whole of humankind, but substantially relaxes with regard to any particular human. As the modern world encouraged its inhabitants to draw apart from family and friends in order to achieve unlimited individual freedom, the novelistic hero too acquired the habit of emancipation at the expense of his or her neighbor.

Yet the reverse is also the case, because the novel for its part powerfully influenced the emergence of the new historical world as well as the emergence of the self. Bakhtin wrote to his friend Kozhinov that the novel prepared the way for a "new *being* of the person" (Bakhtin 1992: 147). If the world and, through it, the self were transformed into historical projects saturated with possibilities of further becoming stored in their repudiated past, this also happened because the novel was charged with the role of this world's and this self's author. In a way, the novel was authorized to make the world and the self into unfolding *artifacts*. As Ken Hirschkop (1999: 235) put it:

> For if in Goethe's world 'everything is visible, everything is concrete, everything is bodily, everything is material in this world, and at the same time everything is intensive, meaningful, and creatively necessary', then everything is, in short, part of an aesthetic whole, and beautiful by definition.

As pointed out by Hannah Arendt (1992: 43), Kant was the first philosopher who made the world an inaccessible artifact supervising human reflective judgment. Goethe contributed to this idea with his educational novel, which demonstrated what the human as a *freihandelndes Wesen* can make of itself. Kant teaches the human the same lesson that Goethe teaches his Wilhelm Meister: to recognize the liberating effect of the world introduced into the restrictive terms of one's reality. Ultimately, in his political philosophy he observes the world from the same impartial cosmopolitan perspective and with the same *uneigennütziger Teilnehmung* (unselfish participation) that in the *Critique of Judgment* he required for the judging of fine art (Kant 2007: 73). If this estheticizing of the world toward the close of the eighteenth century was initiated by Kant and Goethe in the "heart" of Europe, it celebrated its heyday more than a century later with Bakhtin at its Eastern "margin."

What Goethe formulated as the interaction between the pressing *narrative forces* of the world-in-becoming and the liberating *dialogic forces* of its inhabitants, Bakhtin translated not just into his conceptions of the self and the novel, but also of *historical poetics*. If Goethe's comparative morphology of life forms was located at the point of the transition of the German people into a nation, then Bakhtin's historical poetics developed in the circumstances of the national consolidation of post-October Russian society. Nation is, for both, a dynamic *Gattung* inserted into the *Menschengattung* or man*kind* in the same way as mankind is only a constituent of life's becoming. Both "genres" are participants in a constant dialogue between the legislating past and the redescribing present, relentlessly resuming the inheritance stored in their memory. They are projects rather than givens, which means that both Goethe and Bakhtin oppose their benighted compatriots' idea of national self-sufficiency. Separated by around a century, Goethe's morphology and Bakhtin's historical poetics share the idea that the present is authorized to choose its past instead of being determined by it. Bakhtin states:

> Always preserved in a genre are undying elements of the *archaic*. True, these archaic elements are preserved in it only thanks to their constant *renewal*, which is to say, their contemporization. A genre is always the same and yet not the same, always old and new simultaneously. (1984: 106)

The genre progresses in the same self-reflective way as the novel, the self or history, i.e. by repeatedly reaching back into the temporarily foreclosed repository of their earlier stages in order to recreate their future course. The agent of this peculiar kind of progression is the author who discloses the delusion of his/her figures while at the same time exposing his/her own delusion to the forthcoming authoring. In Bakhtin's historical poetics the representative of the genre is, because fully oriented toward the redescription of its past, blind to that which is forthcoming. Like Kant's work of (fine) art, genre history is "purposive without (external) purpose," conceived of as a sequence of intermediate stages that surpass each other in the name of an open, unpredictable future which is expected to pass the ultimate judgment. Because of this constitutive exposure to the supposed "absolute understanding," for Bakhtin genre is an essentially open category. It establishes its identity as a reply in the dialogue whose further reply is uncertain and yet-to-come. Genre identity is nothing but a project exposed to contestation by the forthcoming projects.

9.5 The divine and the devalued other – a constitutive interdependency

Holquist (2002: 148) rightly emphasizes Bakhtin's firm commitment to historical particularity as against generic regularity, which implies that Bakhtin treats the historical development of genres in similarly interminable terms as the development of the novel or the self-authoring modern self. In accordance with the operation of the empowerment of the self through the assimilation of others, all three of these affirm themselves only through the *consistent devaluing of proximate human others in the name of the most remote, divine Other*. It might be helpful here to recall Tocqueville, who pointed to the individual's neglect of his or her fellow creature in favor of mankind; or Luhmann (1989: 244), for that matter, who coined the paradoxical slogan "I am not who I am," implying an affirmation of the absolute self through the undoing of its dependence on the others. In terms of Bakhtin's historical poetics, the role of this absolute subject is occupied by the "genre that is *not* one" that affirms itself only in deactivating the "genre that *is* one." Once again, historical time is taken as a measure of cultural distancing: the belated other is relegated to a "waiting room of history" (Chakrabarty 2000: 8), and history on the move cannot afford to wait for him/her to arrive.

Bakhtin leaves no doubt as to how he asymmetrically distributes his sympathies between the "straightforward" genres and the anti-generic non-self-identity. The historically, socially and culturally finished, concrete and particular "proper genres" are merely the necessary basis of the non-genre's transgredient character; they are the visible, objectifiable material needed for the invisible, non-representable spirit of the latter to be established. This is how the individual, the novel, history and historical poetics, four among many allies in the joint venture of European modernity, respond to the challenge of the other: they make calculated use of it in order to draw closer to the supposed super-addressee somewhere in the indeterminate yet-to-come. It is on behalf of this tacitly authorized messianic "third instance" that the "enlightening appropriation" of "inadequate" subordinate subject positions continuously takes place.

The implications of this enlightening operation have been outlined by postcolonial theory in terms of the relationship between European colonizers and the non-European colonized. Dipesh Chakrabarty (2000: 33) illustrated the *retrospective essence* of this "transitional narrative" of modern European individualism, characterized by a decisive reversal of causes and effects in favor of the latter, by using Marx's significant sentence: "Human anatomy contains the key to the anatomy of the ape." This sentence shows the final consequence of the idea of re-evolution posited in Herder's *Reflections on the Philosophy of the History of Humankind* (1784–1791). The re-evolution in question cannot take place without continuously being fueled by descendants' feeling of "sympathetic superiority" over ancestors. However, the crucial point is that the retroactive capitalization on "regressive" others for the "progressive" purpose of human emancipation amounts to a *constitutive dependence on the "backwardness,"* which was ruled out. The "inferior" other does not cease to invade the most intimate interior of the self that steadily strives to neutralize it by allocating it a properly distant site. While it was rendered inadequate, the narrow-minded other actually became indispensable. Therefore, it is impossible that the self, the novel, history and historical poetics can ever accomplish the autonomy which is so desperately desired. Let us pay closer attention to this key point in terms of historical poetics.

As Graham Pechey (2001: 62) noted concerning poetry and drama as the novel's *generic others*, they "are not just a convenience of Bakhtin's thinking but are inwardly constitutive of it, intimations of the absolute that live in the closest intimacy with its far more developed and overt celebration of relativity." That is to say, the novel is in the final reckoning much more exposed to its generic others than Bakhtin seems ready to allow. He insists on making poetry an accomplice in the process of cultural centralization, an agent of the monologic sociopolitical unity posited against the primal heteroglot stratification of language represented by the novel (Bakhtin 1981: 296). Poetry imagines a counterfactual mythical condition in which one person was everybody because s/he spoke the "language of the gods" (331). However, if poetry suspends dialogism in the name of the "utopia" of the Apollonian *principium individuationis*, then it must be recalled that dialogized heteroglossia "needs the moment of individuation." "[W]ithout individuation, that primal state of all discourse would not only not be known, it would be immobile and would mobilise nothing and nobody." (Pechey 2001: 68) In order for languages and ideologies to intersect dialogically, they must be heard as distinctive voices; otherwise, we would have cacophony instead of polyphony. Thus subverting the primacy of dialogue, "[p]oetry and drama [...] survive as the bearers of this counter-truth to that of the novel" (68).

Yet if Bakhtin or his interpreters systematically neglect the deeply dependent character of the novel by making it a self-understandable transcendental category that determines the modern self and history (as well as, consequently, historical poetics), then the novel turns into a repressive tool with an invisible inbuilt power differential. Then one forgets the deeply divided historical, social and cultural conditions of Kant's, Herder's and Goethe's *Schwellenzeit* under which the novel emerged as the determining force of the self and history, with which Bakhtin identifies. As Ken Hirschkop (1999: 238) puts it:

> For if it is essential to a historical world that the people within it labour creatively and not just 'technically', that it embodies the logic of self-transformation and responsibility, and not

just the satisfaction of human needs, then the world of Goethe was not, and could not have been, historical. Bakhtin may not have been politically astute, but he would have known that what Goethe saw was not the evidence of a generalized human creativity, but the products of societies dominated by minority political and cultural power. Only some of the subjects of Goethe's time laboured 'creatively'; most of them worked technically, to satisfy immediate needs and the commands of their superiors.

Hirschkop's claim is in line with the well-known sociological insight that the individualistic view of man "established, generalized and popularized from the eighteenth century to the age of romanticism and beyond," seriously diverges from what happens *in fact* in modern society. The individualistic view of man was "accompanied by the modern development of the social division of labour" (Dumont 1980: 11). To social division one can certainly add the world division of labor and means. From this perspective, not everybody was expected to apply for the prestigious status of world citizen. On the contrary, the majority of the world population was excluded from the forthcoming race in advance. The global economy introduced the rift into the corps of humankind and spawned the unequal development of various world zones. In the underdeveloped zones, rare individuals were able or willing to accept the European standing invitation to transgress all identity borders, fixity and finitude in the name of "unfinished adventure." As a matter of fact, as Zygmunt Bauman (2004: 12) astutely puts it, the majority of people were expected to serve this expanding European history instead of drawing profit from it. The unification of planet-wide humanity desperately needed its handmaidens, fuel stations and repair workshops to service its laborious process of remaking the world. Those necessary resources and laborers were found among the shy and sedentary, ramblers and roamers, those who would rather live their lives in a world ending at the village fence. Instead of consuming European history, not to mention partaking of it on an equal basis, they were transformed into its secret enablers and collateral casualties. Owing to their inertia, historical belatedness and inherent flaws they were declared ineligible for the test of adequacy or completely disqualified in advance, whatever the results they might eventually have achieved. This constitutive bifurcation of the world population, initiated at the very moment the idea of the world was established, is the reason why humankind can never be unified on the basis of individuality. According to the French social anthropologist Louis Dumont (1980: 20):

> In relation to the [power asymmetry as a] more or less necessary requirement of social life, the idea of equality, even if it is thought superior, is artificial. It expresses a human claim, which also entails the choice of certain ends. It represents a deliberate denial of a universal phenomenon [of hierarchy] in a restricted domain. [...] [I]t is well to understand to what extent it runs contrary to the general tendencies of societies, and hence how far our society is exceptional, and how difficult it is to realize this ideal.

9.5 The divine and the devalued other – a constitutive interdependency

Obstacles to realizing the modern European ideal of individualism (which in Europe finally led to grave disillusionment and the birth of a sociology that socially conditions this individual), were particularly visible in the colonized countries forced to implement this ideal despite the huge resistance of their collective mentality as well as their hierarchical social structure. As Bauman (2004: 13–14) puts it, Europe declared a war of attrition against every kind of otherness that failed or refused to try to rise to the standards it set. The latecomers have been "left to stew in their own juice and to seek, desperately yet in vain, local solutions to globally caused problems" (18). The only prolific industry that the so-called developing countries have been able to set in motion is "the mass production of refugees" (19). The paroles of the new world order such as efficiency, flexibility and marketization "acquire sinister meanings of insecurity, loss of livelihood, precariousness of existence, denial of dignity and cancellation of life prospects once they are translated into the native vernaculars away from the metropolis" (24). Yet the way in which the modern self, the novel and history define the background against which they identify their supremacy is precisely the systematic production of the "human waste." The process of the establishment and reassurance of these substantial categories of European modernity is therefore unimaginable without "the colonial adventure." However, the latter seems not just to be their enabling, but also their disabling condition, which is how the devalued other returns through the back door.

One of the great merits of Paul Gilroy's *The Black Atlantic* was its identification of the complicity between the crucial achievements of European modernity and racial terror in colonial regimes (Gilroy 1993: 38). He urges us to think of modernity as having begun in the constitutive relationships with outsiders that both found and temper a self-conscious sense of Western civilization (17). Seen from this angle, the same constitutive dependence on the "bearer of the counter-truth" that Pechey was able to detect in Bakhtin's historical poetics must hold for the novel and history as well. In both these forms so characteristic of European modernity, the native subjects are usually rendered inadequate because they stick to "feudal," i.e. religious or kinship-based forms of identification, and display an inability to develop modern, i.e. interior and on-the-move forms of individual subjectivity. Yet they are interpreted as "backward" only because both genres unreservedly subscribe to the modernist hierarchy between the lower body and the higher mind. Through its chief representatives, modernity gradually liberates its self-conscious hero of any bodily dependence on others. "Yet while it seeks to obliterate the Other, it is only in a dialectical relationship with that Other that it can define its own subject-position. The Other therefore impinges on the subject, creating disturbance and disrupting the stability it seeks." (Azim 1993: 108) So as to tranquilize this disquiet as it spread in various directions, representatives of European modernity deepened the supremacy of consciousness over materiality. One of the remarkable consequences of this tendency was that, from Romanticism onwards, only fiction based on the imagination was regarded as "proper literature," whereas autobiography, biography and historiography were excluded because of the dependence which they had on "material" reality.

These are some of the unintended discriminating consequences of Bakhtin's modernist ethics, which was generated by a historically specific traumatic constellation and therefore completely dedicated to its compensation. Its neglect of the uneven distribution of individual responsibility makes the heteroglossia of Bakhtin's polyphonic novel unwillingly turn into hegemony and the equal rights of its manifold voices eventuate in a pure utopia. One can hardly expect a real dialogue of free voices when the "emptied centre of authorial perspective" (Banfield 1987) authorized by the hypothetical super-addressee surreptitiously has the last word. This constitutively withheld Master – significantly, analogous to the "empty place of power" in the liberal model of Western democracy (Lefort 2000) – does not need to participate in the dialogue because He sets its rules. Thanks to this privileged position, the obliging network of roles, responsibilities and conventions as well as the ensuing necessity of making choices do not condition His existence in any way. In Bakhtin's counterfactual cosmopolitan projection, He remains above the fray, a "genre that is not one." The fact is, however, that the self, the novel and history are *genres on their own*, i.e. saturated with heavy historical, political, ethical and ideological consequences.

Bakhtin builds his cosmopolitan project on the model of Berlant's "cruel optimism" (Berlant 2011). The unavoidable and deeply frustrating "return of the other" to the self accelerates and intensifies the effort to make the complete freedom from the other the prerogative of the self. To establish a completely sovereign self implies to deny its other; this denial makes the project fail; this failure requires it to be pushed further. According to the well-known verdict of the self-proclaimed philosopher of history, those who do not prove capable of continually contributing something new to the developing unity of humankind are to be enlightened, "consummated" or ultimately dispensed with. In 1780 Lessing (1858: 423, trans. mine) described this self-authorized judge as an avatar of the forthcoming crusade of European democracy, a fanatic (*Schwärmer*) "who cannot expect this future to come. He wishes it to be accelerated and accelerated through him [...] For what would be his profit if what he recognizes as being better does not become better during his lifetime?" In his speech *Sur la Constitution* delivered on May 10, 1793 Robespierre declared that the "grand revolution" of humankind set in motion by the French Revolution is now confronted with the task of acceleration "imposed in particular upon you" (Koselleck 1989: 63).

Bakhtin, who grew up intellectually in the atmosphere of another revolution, seems to have found himself the ideal addressee of this testimonial urge. Confronted with the pressing tempo of the disintegration of inherited patterns of Russian society, he saw his own self as being suddenly deprived of all of the traditional alibis of social existence. Like Walter Benjamin's subject (from *Erfahrung und Armut*), this subject was suddenly devoid of all the richness of its acquired experience, thrown into the spiritual poverty of "revolutionary masses." Bakhtin's answer, uttered individually from this traumatic collective destitution, was to compensate for it through the cosmopolitan extension of the disowned self. He pushed this suddenly homeless entity toward "a unity perpetually yet-to-be" (1990: 126) at an accelerated tempo so as to exempt it from being swallowed by the dismembered mass of the "dispossessed."

Yet the question is whether, if the self is capable of rescuing himself/herself from the traumatic experience only by imposing it in an intensified form upon the others, this self is worthy of being saved, maintained and fostered at all. The well-known denouement of European modernity in the Holocaust and Russian *Arbeitslager*, as the devastating return home of the European long-term colonial atrocities, gives this question a pregnancy worth pondering.

10 Countering the Empirical Evidence: From Immigrant Cosmopolitanism to a Cosmopolitanism of the Disregarded

10.1 Abstracting from natural transcendentals

If Eastern and Central European literary theorists of the twenties and thirties applied the "politics of estrangement" (Tihanov 2005) to the national idea of literature prevalent in their post-imperially reconfigured homelands, the immigrant generation of French literary theorists of the sixties reapplied the same politics to the universalist idea of literature commanding their new domicile. Instead of literary nationalism, they targeted literary universalism. Having broken from the Eastern European countries located at the "national" margins of Europe right into its "supranational" heart, immigrants such as the Romanian-Jewish Goldmann, the Lithuanian-born Greimas, and the Bulgarian-born Todorov and Kristeva (Tihanov 2004: 419) raised modern literary theory through their critical questioning to a significantly higher level of abstraction in a very short time. Except for their direct revolutionary inspiration, the generation of Russian Formalists, nothing can stand comparison with the enormous developmental speed of this generation. Up to the sixties French literary theory was practically non-existent (Compagnon 2004: 1–2). The only literary theorist to hold an academic post in the first half of the twentieth century was the French writer Paul Valéry, who held the chair of Poetics at the Collège de France from 1937 to 1945 (Rabaté 2002: 79). But then, owing to the immigration of these Eastern European exiles and dissidents in the sixties, out of the blue a new French Republic of Letters loomed large on the horizon.

Contrary to the first French Republic of Letters, an international assembly of scholars who opposed religious intolerance in the name of universal human principles, this second "French Republic of Letters" attacked the restrictive foundations of this universalism in its very own home. Whereas the free human individual was the foundation of French universalism in the political domain, the author epitomized it in the literary domain. The so-called Parisian avant-garde, questioning this agency in the revolutionary atmosphere of the sixties, established a kind of elective affinity with the Russian avant-garde (Rabaté 2002: 82–83), which subverted the agency of the *Volksgeist* in the analogous October atmosphere. Thus both the October and Parisian revolutions dispossessed the central agencies of their time in the name of those whom these agencies have bereft of the agency status. Turning Paris into an "East Central European cultural center" and an exemplary meeting point of two avant-gardes through their immigration during the first half of the twentieth century (Neubauer 2009: 76), innumerous prominent East Central European émigrés and expatriates testify to the extent of this political depravation. Although their discrimination started in the homeland, the chosen hostland did not eliminate it. Relegated after immigration in the political zones of indeterminacy, émigrés were sentenced to a doubly estranged life. Two socially, linguistically and culturally remote environments, equally strange and all but smoothly translatable into one another, acted in their consciousness in an incessantly contrapuntal fashion (Said 2000: 149). The avant-garde artistic and theoretical movements were induced by a socially and politically traumatic constellation.

To undo the bastion of the literary author, the East Central European/Parisian avant-garde targeted the thesis that the author, behind his/her figures' illusions, provides to his/her reader firm empirical evidence of the delineated reality. The counterthesis read that, precisely by being empirical, such evidence encapsulates the author and his/her reader within the *domestic* horizon falsely taken to be *universal*. To become truly universal, from the point of view of the homeless immigrants divided between two horizons, our horizon must achieve abstract qualities detached from all the restricted empirical terms. In the final account, immigrant cosmopolitans employed *abstract* transcendentalism to dethrone the *empirical* transcendentalism of French universalists who took the "native" horizon to be universal.

The counter-empirical offensive was first set in motion by the "internal émigré" Roland Barthes, who, as early as 1953, discovered the "writing degree zero" apparently stripped of all empirical traits. His concept referred to the strategically impersonalized literary mode that revolutionizes its addressees by catapulting them out of the entrenched techniques of literary understanding. What confuses the "domestic" reader in this mode, exemplified for Barthes in the work of the "French Algerian" Albert Camus, is that its authorial subject, becoming an anonymous assemblage of sensations, escapes the reader's empirical identification techniques. The formerly sovereign author, as if haunted by guilty consciousness, becomes a destination of the myriad of unconscious forces, which invade and structure his/her actions. Such a revolutionary erasure of his/her sovereignty reduces the literary work to an inarticulate assemblage of anonymous writing (*écriture*) with bewildering effects upon the reader.

Composing his pioneering essay, Barthes may have drawn on the idea of "the neuter" (*le neutre*) proposed in Maurice Blanchot's *The Work of Fire* (1949). In the atmosphere of the postwar and postcolonial guilt of French intellectuals, Blanchot introduced the remorseful self-elimination of the author's agency subsequently elaborated upon in his concepts of unworking (*désœuvrement*) and writing (*écriture*). All these concepts point to the self-evacuation of the central agency of the literary work, undertaken as if out of repentance for the exclusions committed.

According to Blanchot's *The Space of Literature* (1952), published a year before Barthes's essay, Mallarmé was the first writer to dethrone the sovereign literary work by setting loose the energy of *écriture* "always going beyond what it seems to contain and affirming nothing but its own outside" (1993: 259). This remorseful orientation of an established agency toward its castrated enabler spawns a conclusion that modern literature, passionately adhering to what it cannot but repeatedly exclude, "contests itself as power" (Blanchot 1997: 67). "Literature denies the substance of what it represents. This is its law and its truth." (Blanchot 1995: 310) In such a way, the author's agency placed at the empirical level of the reader's perception undergoes unworking and rearticulation within a larger and much more abstract field, i.e. writing that makes its transcendental condition. How to conceptualize this new cosmopolitan field of forces?

Blanchot, for his part, interpreted literary *écriture* not as a derivative but rather as a primal structure "that is beyond the reach of the one who says it as much as of the one who hears it" (1993: 212). Both are bereft of their firm identity sites by a prior intervention of this constitutively "neutral," "third person" structure remaining forever beyond the reach of interlocutors. Being all encompassing in its "neutrality," Blanchot's *écriture* is in fact beyond the reach of *any* of its "users"; it simply belongs to the "other scene" in the way as Bakhtin's Supreme Judge does. However, according to the early Barthes's structuralist understanding, the ultimate terms of literary interaction set by this anonymous "writing" remain inaccessible merely to the author and reader, i.e. its immediate "users," but *not the theorist* him/herself. Given the necessary distance and competence, s/he must be able to identify this *contractual frame* analytically.

As the legitimate inheritors of the Russian Formalists' revolutionary doctrine, French structuralists insist on the theoretical reconstruction of the condition of the possibility of literariness. While disengaging the empirical agency of the author they engage the transcendental agency of the theorist, completely in the spirit of their revolutionary inspirers. Dispossessing an empirically restricted institution, they empower an abstract cosmopolitan instance. Following a long tradition, revolutions do not eliminate the rulers but rather replace them. As Agamben has argued in *The Time That Remains* (2005b: 88–112), the messianic tradition inherent in Blanchot's concept of *désœuvrement* makes disempowerment and empowerment strongly reliant on one another. This is why Luther translated St Paul's *katargeín*, referring to both the disempowering and empowering effect of the Sabbath on working days, by an equally double-edged *aufheben*, later enthusiastically adopted by Hegel's dialectics. Inaugurating structuralist revolution, Barthes remains loyal to this ambiguous tradition. Evacuation of the agency at the lower level of the *work* spawns its reestablishment at the higher level of the *writing*. The deactivated empirical restriction returns in the form of a contractual transcendental.

This fundamental equivocation of the structuralist operation of abstraction finds one of its paradigmatic expressions in the reimplementation of the suspended concept of discourse. Benveniste introduced the latter by re-describing Austin's concept of the performative (Benveniste 1966: 266–276). Whereas Austin insisted on the conventional character of the performative, Benveniste derives discourse from the singular situation of its enunciation associated with the specific intention (*vouloir-dire* (Felman 1983: 6–12)). This makes its meaning heavily contextually dependent. This dependency can be suspended only through the elimination of deictic constituents, i.e. the translation of the *discours* into the impersonal *histoire* seemingly universal in its meaning (Benveniste 1966: 241). However, since all revolutionary dethronements turn out to be replacements, *histoire*, rather than being truly universal, again appears to be restricted to an empirical semantic horizon.

To point out this hideously restricted character of *histoire*, Gérard Genette (1969) reintroduced the particularity of the *discours* into the hi/story's seeming universality. He proposed to understand story and discourse as two necessary *aspects* rather than different *modes* of narrative. If the discursive operation remains indiscernible in *histoire*, this is because it is deactivated rather than eliminated. There is no hi/story without the inbuilt structure of meaning instructions, the latter being the more efficient the more unperceivable it is. In such a way, Genette retranslated the concept of discourse (previously translated by Benveniste from Austin's conventional performative into a singular event) from the contingent personal address back into the impersonal structure of manipulation. It lost situational singularity in becoming conventional.

As this abstract structure now operated as the transcendental condition of hi/story's meaning, the task of the theorist was to lay it bare in order to disengage the manipulation effectuated by it in the process of reading. What the reader empirically perceives as being real is from the theoretical point of view but an "effect of the real," which is operated by the discourse. In lieu of the author, structuralists take the discourse to be guiding reader's understanding of the story. It navigates him/her through the process of reading, "hideously" codifying his or her insight into the world represented. The discursively commanded *communication becomes the condition of the possibility of representation*. Following this replacement of one agency by another, narratologists describe the process of narrative communication as a systematic extension of the reader's representation of the world presented. As the elements of the lower levels underlie a continuous semantic re-description by the elements of the higher ones, the process of the reader's integration of narrative units progresses. Instead of simply advancing toward the resolution of the story, the reader is guided to extend his or her understanding of the story from an ever-higher point of view.

What the narratologically redefined discourse finally amounts to, is the systematic disappropriation of the lower by the higher narrative agencies (Rimmon-Kenan 1983: 91). While higher agencies disempower the lower ones, the empowerment works the other way around (Gibson 1996: 214–215). As soon as an "ordinary reader" identifies with any one of the figures, s/he falls into the trap of the discourse and affirms its agency. This is why the narratologist avoids such identifications. If the reading is proper, it results in the deactivation of lower agencies in favor of the more abstract ones. The empirical identifications *with* make way for an abstract identification *of*. Nonetheless, a great majority of "ordinary readers" firmly adhere to "lower" agencies, neglecting "higher" levels of their redescription. Gripped with infantile curiosity, they passionately follow the unfolding of hi/story disregarding the knowledge to be gained from the unveiling of its discursive structure. The narratologists systematically disqualify such a manipulated consumption of narratives, which in its blind sensuous affection inadmissibly confuses the representation of reality with reality itself. If such a blind empirical reading is to be replaced by the true theoretical knowledge, the sensuous entrapment within the story has to be overcome by the rational insight into the discourse as the transcendental condition of hi/story's possibility.

Albeit widely disseminated among "ordinary readers," the mimetic attitude to literary agencies disregards the fact that modern literature strategically dismissed such comfortable habits of its "benighted" consumers. In one of the manifestos of French narratology, published in 1966, Genette explicitly states that narratives orientated toward representation vanish from the horizon of contemporary literature, making way for those focused on their own discourse (1969: 62, 68–69). Just a year thereafter, in the famous essay "The Discourse of History," Barthes declared that the traditional storytelling historiography belonged to the past; the new historiography focused on the structure of its intelligibility instead of reality (1984: 177). In such a "revolutionary fever" typical of French narratology, "mimetic attitude" was dismissed as belonging to the antiquated literary taste. The age of representation was relinquished and whoever was entrapped in its delusions was labeled as a narrow-minded dillettante. Such a disqualification did not merely pertain to the ordinary readers who used to empathically communicate with lower narrative agencies without being capable of recognizing the higher agencies that guide the latter's action and behavior; it was also relevant to the hermeneutic attitudes similarly entrapped in the representational mechanisms. The hermeneutic insight into the story was also accused of being involved in the discourse, which means that interpreters, at the moment they realize the "plot of resolution," are unknowingly commanded by the "plot of revelation."[1]

The narratologists proclaim that an uninvolved *analysis* must substitute for the involved and therefore empirically restricted *interpretation*. By drawing attention to the discursive plotting of the narrative, which surreptitiously manipulates all its interpretations, they not only point to the imperial extension of narrative manipulation via various kinds of its empirical consumption. They simultaneously exempt the impartial "cosmopolitan" perspective of *literary theory* from such inadmissible identifications devalued as the "ideologically projective" *literary critique*. By letting the all-embracing discourse dispossess the agencies of the author, reader and finally critic, they eventually raise the claim to be in the sovereign possession of this all-dispossessing agency. Raising it to the status of the supreme agency, they turn out to be its exclusive proprietor. Nobody else can take the discourse into possession. This is how the empirical restriction reenters the putative transcendental. Let us closer inspect this crucial point.

In his famous essay on the way ideology captures its victims – a sort of death knell to the French structuralism – Althusser (1982: 111–114) proposed an analogy with the scene of the sudden street interpellation "Hey you there!" This *indirect* address, performed by an anonymous voice from the other side of the street (the "other scene" or "shore"), connects ideology with the way fictional narrative addresses its readers. This explains its enthusiastic adoption by so-called performative narrative theory (Currie 1998: 38). Who of the hundreds of accidental passers-by (i.e readers) is actually meant by this anonymous interpellation located outside the field of visibility and therefore addressed to "whomever it might concern?" So as to find this out, those reached by the call turn their eyes toward the source of the voice. Yet why would somebody turn his or her eyes toward the bearer of the voice if they felt uninvolved or found this call of no concern whatsoever? To illustrate this equivocal point, Althusser (1982: 112) draws an analogy with the ringer of our doorbell who, addressed with our question "Who's there?," laconically replies "Me!" Would we ever open the door without having recognized the bearer of this voice? In the same way, before turning ourselves toward the bearer of the street call "Hey you there!" we must have recognized its authorization by a legal institution. Our visualization of the Voice of the Law is just an external check of its previous internal resonance in the "voice of our consciousness" (Butler 1997: 107). We feel the need to identify the bearer of the discourse because of our involvement with him or her in a pre-discursive plot that obliges us toward him

---

[1] For these two types of the plot that refer, via Barthes's narratological résumé (1966), to the relationship between Benveniste's axes of *distribution* and *integration*, see Chatman 1978: 48.

or her. Althusser's point would therefore be that the addressee, at the moment of his or her "recognition" of the caller, is necessarily already "recognized" by the caller's discourse. The "pinning down" follows from this involvement, which is why it must be projective.

To put it differently, the addressee's response does not merely *identify* but *invents* the caller, contributing by this invention to its power and constituting its ultimate authority. This moment is essential in the articulation of Althusser's thesis (Žižek 1999: 260). He insists on the *mutual constitution of the agency and its enabler through the interpellation* because, strictly speaking, neither the caller nor its addressees exist in their distinctive property *before* the call (Althusser 1982: 123). As Borch-Jacobsen (1988: 231) spells out in his analysis of the "Freudian subject," the subject's identity does not precede this interpellation but is an *after-effect* of it. The process of this constitution cannot be preordained in advance, which means that the manner by which the addressee identifies herself/himself depends on the way s/he identifies the caller. One can identify the voice of the street call "Hey you there!" as belonging either to the policeman, police, law, state, homeland, humankind or divine providence, which makes him or her the participant of a completely different plot and raises him or her to a completely different kind of subject. None of these substantially different identifications follows from the deliberate choice of a given addressee but emerges from his/her respective disposition.

Transposed in narrative terms, the same holds for the attribution of the narrative voice to the hero, narrator, implied author, genre, writing or discourse. Each of these agencies is in the final analysis "empowered" by the reader's response who in this way "empowers" himself/herself. However, if every identification of the ultimate narrative agency simultaneously empowers the reader's self, does not the establishment of the principal difference between the *empirical* and *theoretical* (self-) identification amount to the establishment of a *power-difference*? If the theoretical identification is raised to the universal status as opposed to the reader's empirical one, then it is authorized to exert pressure upon the latter to follow its putatively universal law. Once officially instituted by its inventors, the discourse displays more validity than the author does, in the same way the call of Providence does if compared to the call of the police. This is why, in introducing this agency to deactivate the reader's empirical identification with the author, narratologists aimed at a self-empowering superior to the others.

10.2 Dis/empowering the cosmopolitan police

Since the structuralist attempt to interrogate the sovereign agency of the author as the epitome of the French universalist idea of literature resulted in the establishment of an equally sovereign agency of the discourse, the revolutionary politics of the immigrant cosmopolitanism turned into police. One empirical evidence was replaced by another that was equally restricted but more powerfully supported and widely disseminated. Because of such an unexpected empirical perversion of the transcendentalist argument, the idea that the empirical evidence needed to be dismantled in order for universal reality to come through lost its credibility. This "universal reality" turned out to be the result of the imposition of the new transcendental.

The resistance to such *theoretical policing* corresponded with the resistance to the French *political policing*, as the former was experienced to be an echo of the latter. Even if Todorov, Greimas and Kristeva were immigrants, they disseminated their ideas in the French language and through French institutions, which, ironically, colored the reception of their theory. Despite its initial directedness against French universalism, it gradually acquired the latter's traits. As opposed to the culturally and intellectually more homogeneous structuralist generation of Eastern European immigrants, the prominent figures of the poststructuralist generation such as Althusser, Bourdieu, Derrida, Lyotard, Cixous, or Rancière,[2] generated their resistance to the structuralist theoretical evidence out of their various *heterotopias* within French culture.[3] Although their cosmopolitanism was once again induced "from below," the global extension of colonization implied the resistance of its scattered "disregarded" that was more diverse than the Eastern European immigrant cosmopolitans' resistance.

A number of consequences follow from this difference between structuralist immigrant cosmopolitanism and poststructuralist cosmopolitanism of the disregarded. First, rather than deactivating the central universalist truth of the literature of their new domicile in the manner of their structuralist forerunners, the poststructuralists disengaged the truths established by the policing theoretical discourse from their dispersed (ethnic, class-, race-, gender- and/or culture-related) "zones of indeterminacy" in an incomparably larger "radiation field." Second, because the structuralist "cosmopolitan policing" enjoyed such a global

---

[2] All of them, in one way or another, were associated with decolonized Algeria (Young 2001: 413), as was Barthes's "literary hero" Camus after all.

[3] Foucault states of these heterotopias that they "dessicate speech, stop words in their tracks, contest the very possibility of grammar at its source [...] dissolve our myths and sterilize the lyricism of our sentences" (1971: 18).

dissemination, no discourse, including the discourse of literary theory, was spared its infiltration. And third, as the unity of this theoretical policing covered the huge diversity of its subordinate constituencies, the sites of its subversion from below were scattered and heterogeneous in nature. Having been compelled to use, in one way or another, the all-pervading policing discourse, the poststructuralist "complicitous" theorists replaced the structuralist "neutral" analytical discourse with the systematically deferred speech. Rather than authoritatively publicizing, they were clandestinely indicating their cosmopolitanism. Modern theory thus entered the postmodern age of a ventriloquist theoretical discourse, a perpetually masked performance that, as if haunted by the traumatic "repetition compulsion," *distanced any evidence established by the distancing*. This was perceived as the only way to prevent the empirical identification of the theoretical truth.

As the theoretical subject now wore the same actor's mask as did any literary agency as the object of its analysis, the theorist's commanding post was abandoned and the "bondsman's" subversive *miming* of literature substituted the "lord's" sovereign *representation*.[4] As Robert Young put it, Hegel's parable of the lord and the bondsman "mimics at a conceptual level the geographical and economic absorption of the non-European world by the West" (Young 1990: 3). The inference is unavoidable that the European structuralist theorist, pressing the non-European others into his imperial transcendental, "builds an Empire of the Same, and installs at its center a tyrannical dictator" (Fuss 1995: 145). The others are forced to obey this transcendental in order not to be excluded, scorned or punished. Their vast diversity is expected to be ultimately translated into the all-embracing unity and the unabsorbed remainder, the "rest of the West" is to be dropped and discarded as a mere *quantité négligeable*. Once "the part that has no part" is expelled from the field of intelligibility and deprived of any access to identity, the path is wide opened for this identity's huge symbolic capitalization. Relying on previous chapters, we can identify the structuralist approach with the Roman assimilating type of cosmopolitanism.

From the enabler's point of view, as testified by Fanon's postcolonial rewriting of Hegel's "master narrative," instead of *representing* the other in one's own triumphant terms, the theoretical self *enacts* the other *in his/her own terms* in order to undo the effects of his/her violent appropriation in foreign terms. To translate this into the terms of the poststructuralist critique, precisely because structuralist theory assimilates literature into its own terms, it turns out to be its *inventor* rather than neutral *identifier*. Uncovering this obliterated self-empowering of the-

---

4 In rendering *Herr* as lord and *Knecht* as bondsman, I am following A. V. Miller's translation of Hegel's *The Phenomenology of Spirit*. I find these terms more appropriate than master and slave.

ory through the empowerment of literature, the poststructuralist critique dismantles literary agencies established through structuralist theory, searching after literature's own terms. Yet what are literature's *own* terms? As Fanon has spelled out in his rewriting of the agency-enabler relationship from the enabler's point of view, this permanent self-exemption from the agency's delusions amounts to pathogenic consequences, turning my self into an object of constant obsession and self-reproach (Fanon 1986: 210–217). As if repenting the establishment of literature through a theory that sacrifices everything not conforming to it, the poststructuralist critic relentlessly dismantles theoretical projections as devastating empirical delusions about literature. Inasmuch as his/her counter-empirical crusade is now redirected from his/her object toward his/her deluded subject, it proceeds on the model of self-exempting cosmopolitanism that follows the interminable logic "I am what I am not." This crusade, not a bit less determined than its structuralist antagonist, acts in the name of the radical Other disregarded by any imposed identification.

10.3 At the empowering service of a powerless victim: Emmanuel Levinas

Abstract and general as it is, considering the heterogeneity of poststructuralism, this argument needs elaboration and specification. An especially systematic negation of an (empirical) someone other (*l'autrui*) by the (transcendental) universal Other (*l'autre*) was undertaken by the Lithuanian-Jewish French philosopher Emmanuel Levinas. His insistent hypertrophy of the Other calls for an analogy with the aforementioned Fanon's re-description of the lord-bondsman relationship "despite the ostensible dissimilarities that separate the one from the other" (Hanssen 2000: 201). If the repressed European colonialist legacy experienced its boomerang effect in the Nazi genocide (Césaire 2000: 36), then this analogy between the remorseful theorist of the postcolonial and the self-accusing philosopher of the Holocaust trauma loses its initially bewildering character. From different angles, both thinkers subscribe to a cosmopolitanism of the disregarded. Translated into theoretical terms, the poststructuralist discourse places itself at the service of various pariahs of the structuralist transcendental agency.

Starkly opposing the imperial Hegelian self, which subjugates all others to its commanding specular gaze, Levinas undertakes a meticulously elaborated non-reciprocal rewriting of the lord-bondsman relationship. His aim is to counter the politically conquering assimilation of alterity by an ethically responsible "substitution for another" (Levinas 1974: 99–105). Defying Western metaphysical tradition, Levinas re-conceptualizes the idea of the *face* from the safeguard of the Self's identity into an epiphany of the Other's difference, defining it as a "way in which the other presents himself, *exceeding the idea of the other in me*" (1969: 50 [emphasis mine]). He thus makes the face *the* locus of alterity, which resists all attempts at empirical identification. Instead of being a tranquil object of someone's gaze, it becomes its disquieting subject "which prohibits me with the original language of its defenseless eyes" (Levinas 1996: 12). "The eyes break through the mask – the language of the eyes, impossible to dissemble" (Levinas 1969: 66). "*Regarder ce qui [...] vous vise: c'est regarder le visage*" (Levinas 1976: 6). Considering this etiology of the word *visage*, one might interpret it, next to meaning a face, as a noun derived from the verb *viser* (to point to, aim at, target), which would better explain not only its stubborn withdrawal into a targeting position, but also the uprightness (*droiture*), the directness of its interpellation (Eskin 2001: 48). The face pertains to me in an immediate, preconscious way using no linguistic roundabouts but only proximate contact that touches the nudity of my skin (Levinas 1987c: 118). "This is the original language, the foundation of the other one" (116). "This relationship of proximity, this contact inconvertible into a noetico-noematic structure, in which every transmission of messages, whatever be those messages, is already established, is *the original language*, a language without words or propositions, *pure communication*." (119, [emphasis mine]) What is at stake with the face, therefore, is "the ethical event of communication which is presupposed by every transmission of messages" (125).

Following these introductory clarifications we are better equipped to understand what Levinas aims at when claiming that (theoretical) "consciousness is always late for the rendez-vous with the neighbor" (119). It cannot resist "the obsessive proximity of the neighbor" (119) which "breaks up the equality [...] of consciousness, its equality with the object it understands intentionally" (120). This neighbor (*prochain*, as distinct from *voisin*) engraves its trace in my skin besetting my corporeality. Because I cannot take cognizance of an instance haunting and obsessing me in such a traumatizing way, I lose the Other as a comfortable, confirming mirror of my (representational) identity. "The place of the one who speaks to me," clarifies Lyotard (1985: 39), "is never available to me to occupy." That is why "[t]he relationship with the other puts me into question, empties me of myself" (Levinas 1986b: 350). Resisting the implementation of representational practices of my empirical perception, the other disturbs my self-sufficiency, eliminates the very substance of my Ego. This breakthrough of the face "consists in undoing the form in which every entity [...] is already dissimulated." The other appears as a "surplus over the inevitable paralysis of manifestation" (351–352). "His presence consists in coming towards us, *making an entry*." (351) Instead of participating with me in a communion relying on a common footing, he befalls upon me out of a radical exteriority in the form of unexpected events. "[T]he encounter with a face that at once gives and conceals the Other, is the situation in which an event happens to a subject who does not assume it, who is utterly unable in its regard ..." (Levinas 1985: 45)

Levinas renders this disruptive signification of the face alternatively as *expression*, *trace* or *command*. The distinctive feature of all three terms is that they ultimately turn whole signification into self-reference. "We have called face the auto-signifyingness par excellence." (Levinas 1987c: 120) This *signifiance* of the face means that it always signifies more than we are able to attribute to it. The face is a "movement that already carries away the signification it brought [...] It enters in so subtle a way that unless we retain it, it has already withdrawn. It [...] withdraws before entering" (Levinas 1987a: 66), it "has left before having come" (68). These paradoxes mark the constitutively anachronistic structure of interpellation that interrupts my present from an irretrievable, immemorial past impossible to recollect or re-present (65, 1986b: 345). "To *be* qua *leaving a trace* is to pass, to depart, to absolve oneself." (1986b: 357) In a word, the Other inhabits "the other scene," a "beyond" in every possible sense of the word (preconscious, pre-linguistic, pre-present, pre-representative, pre-signifying etc.); it reaches my empirical self out of a *space of radical exteriority*.

However, because of its unfathomable character, Levinas's radically transcendental face appears to be significantly ambiguous, simultaneously degraded and privileged, completely bereft of power and terribly violent. It is on the one hand urging me out of an "eternal exile," which deprives it of any effective power. Levinas frequently describes it in *Totality and Infinity* as a naked, destitute, hungry, and/or helpless stranger, orphan, widow and/or proletarian. But it also has a violent aspect. The way it raises its *powerless* claim is a non-repressive mode of *mauvaise conscience* (Levinas 1989: 81), which *demands* a "responsibility that goes beyond what I may have done to the Other or whatever acts I may or may not have committed" (83). Beyond any particular action, it challenges my very "place in the sun" for having unintentionally usurped someone else's place by way of excluding, stripping or starving him (82). "The other's man death calls me into question, as if, by my possible indifference, I had become the accomplice of the death to which the other, who cannot see it, is exposed..." (83) "It poses the question of my right to be which is already my responsibility for the death of the Other, interrupting the carefree spontaneity of my naive perseverance." (86)

Yet in what way does this claim of *mauvaise conscience* for the defacing of my habitual face occur? It seems to be displaying the same profound equivocation. Levinas renders it as a call of someone who, while naked, destitute and exposed as if about to be shot at point blank range (83), nevertheless resolutely demands: "Thou shalt not kill." He explains the paradox of this unprotected face that does not hesitate to address imperatives as "an absolute resistance in which the temptation of murder is inscribed [...]. This temptation of murder and this impossibility of murder constitute the very vision of the face. To see a face is already to hear: 'Thou shalt not kill'" (Levinas 1990a: 8). What frustrates me to the point of my readiness to kill the Other – in theoretical terms, to immobilize, objectify, mortify or turn him or her into an empirical item – is the stubborn tendency of His spectral face to disown my ego. The Other seems determined to remove my social and political identity marks, raise himself to my master (*maître*) and lord (*seigneur*) who never stops keeping me under his irritating surveillance. Levinas's *visage* is, covertly, also the peculiar French translation of Husserl's German verb *vermeinen* (intending, having in mind, envisaging) (Eskin 2001: 48): it implies the condition of permanent supervision, i.e. the same supervision that was forbidden to the Self. To underline this profoundly disconcerting, haunting, accusing aspect of the face's activity, in *Otherwise than Being* Levinas re-describes another concept of Husserl's, *Ausdruck*, in a similarly original way: he renders it as the continuous drive of the transcendental face to ex-press (tear out) all the empirical identity attributes of the self from their protected residence (*demeure extraterritoriale*).

In sum, there is an *obvious violence exerted in this seemingly powerless interpellation*; a pressure is inherent to its helplessness; a "high above" is manifested in its "far below;" the aggressive overreaction of the self's response would otherwise be unexplainable. Far from being a purely ethical instance, as the philosopher is at pains to present it, Levinas's face is also the agent of domination. The one conditions the other. The same equivocation holds for our response to it: Whereas we are politically disempowering the face's wounding address, defacing it by our *visual representation*, we are simultaneously ethically empowering the *speaking remainder* of the face. It survives our immobilizing gaze, providing an unexpected justification to the claim "Thou shalt not kill." Hence the face is never just *looked at* but also *attended to*. The theorist's profoundly fissured response – defensive reaction and responsible action – reflects its political-ethical undecidability.

Levinas rejects this disturbing undecidability, introducing in its place a clear opposition: he associates the theoretical activity of *seeing* the face with *murdering* it and the theoretical passivity of *hearing* the face with *serving* it. He thus presents the double-edged, uneasy response to the equivocal urge of the face as a completely free choice between the two unequal options. "It is up to us, or, more exactly, it is up to *me* to retain or to repel this God without boldness, exiled for allied with the conquered, hunted down and hence absolute [*ab-solu*, also in the sense of departed, passed away], thus disarticulating the very moment in which he is presented and proclaimed, un-representable." (Levinas 1987a: 66) After all, as Lyotard reads it, the silent command "Thou shalt not kill" has no other purpose but to turn our powerful, violently reacting I into a receptive, responsive You (1988:

110–111). Following this idea, Jill Robbins remarks that "the sense of killing must be enlarged here beyond its literal meaning to a more general sense" (Robbins 1999: 64). It includes all instances of transcendental violence such as representation, knowledge or vision that attempt to master the Other by bringing it in accordance with the self. "Much of the force of Levinasian ethics revolves around the premise that violence first arises *conceptually* [...] Violence arises when the self makes prejudgments about the Other before the Other speaks to the self [...] By extension, violence also arises in the will to comprehend the Absolute as ground, to name the Infinite." (Schroeder 1996: 19) However, is the wish to understand and comprehend the Other always to be explained as a blamable determination for violence? Do we not sometimes visualize the face out of the sheer necessity to defend ourselves from its violence? Levinas seems to seriously underestimate the violence of the face.

He interprets practical physical violence as a sheer extension of the ontological "imperialism of the same" (Levinas 1969: 39). Instead of introducing necessary distinctions between them, he uncritically conflates vision, knowledge and violence, thus displaying the same indifferent and inconsiderate imperialism he is at pains to defy. The result is his diagnosis of a murderous "alliance of logic and politics," knowledge and power, which "plunders the world for the booty of its self-seeking interest" (Rose 1996: 37). The imperial Self (*moi*) or Same (*même*) is blamed for approaching the other obliquely, i.e. via the detour of linguistic representation instead of frontally, i.e. via the direct face-to-face contact. But how to avoid this detour if to encounter the face *as* a face (i.e. ethically rather than politically) necessarily means to listen to its *discourse* (Robbins 1999: 57), to receive it *in actu*, on the move and not as an immobile object? "To see a face," states Levinas himself, "is already to hear it" (1990a: 8). "[T]he manifestation of the face is *already* discourse" (Levinas 1969: 66). However, does not exactly this discursive moment, instead of keeping intact the ethical singularity of the face, imply its transference to the political realm of difference and deferral? Is language not necessarily the reign of substitutions that forces everything entering it to become defaced and replaceable? Levinas's attempt to align seeing with merciless murder and hearing with putting oneself at the disposal of the face seems therefore to be separating the inseparable. If hearing also defaces the face, then ethics is always contaminated by politics.

"What characterizes a violent act," states Levinas, "is the fact that one does *not* face" (i.e. expose oneself to the regard of the face) but catches sight of an angle (i.e. takes the targeting position toward it) (1987b: 19). Yet how to make oneself *directly* vulnerable to an interlocutor who *resonates* in the infinite citational chain of the discourse? After all, the face *cites* its (biblical) command "Thou shalt not kill." In addition, if it reaches us out of an irretrievable past, what is it expected to display if not a divided, double, *grave* voice? If the speaker of this command addresses us from a "beyond," if we are "encountering [his or her] being through an interdiction" (21), are we not in the place of the face ultimately facing a mask, echo or effect instead of an identifiable interlocutor? This might have had Maurice Blanchot in mind, who asserts that "I am not indispensable, in me anyone at all is called by the other [...] the un-unique, always the substituted" (Blanchot 1986a: 13). "I cannot draw any justification from a demand that is not addressed to anyone in particular, that demands nothing of my decision and that in any case exceeds me to the point of disindividualizing me." (21) The singularity I address is only borrowed and temporary, because I just happened to be at the place summoned by the face. I am exposed as anyone else could be in my place, it is not exactly *my* but *anybody's* place.

After all, for Levinas the Good becomes meaningful only through its representation in the concept. "Thus the Good is present [...] only as the *idea* of the Good" (Schroeder 1996: 34). Hence "when Levinas gives the face *as* voice [...] he in a sense de-faces it, gives it as *figure*" (Robbins 1999: 57). This transfer of the face from the observing gaze to the summoning voice is by itself a prosopopeia (Derrida 1997: 101). Trying to unmask its deceitful appearance, Levinas inadvertently masks his face into a trope, depriving it of the straightforwardness and rectitude he otherwise claims for it. While banishing rhetoric from the *inter*subjective relationship, he retrieves it on the *intra*linguistic level by making the deceitful figure inherent in the face. "This means that the face is to some extent a face-mask or a figure-face. It also means that there can be 'face' in figure." (Derrida 1997: 68) However, if there is a figure inscribed into the face, and if the face for its part also permeates the figure, then, despite Levinas's meticulous efforts to strictly separate face and mask, facing and angle, uprightness and obliqueness, self-reference and signification, justice and violence, ethics and politics, their contagious interference is unavoidable. His claim that to become ethical the theorist's self must be "devastated, traumatised, unthroned," stripped of its identity, sacrificed in a sublime "passivity beyond passivity," in an unconditioned obedience to the face of the Other (Rose 1996: 37), in its conspicuous "sacrificial logic," gains relevance less as a philosophical argument than as an inadmissible self-empowering by the victim's trauma. This unconditional trauma signs for the unfathomability and intractability of the self's transcendental. This is how Levinas's politics of trauma, unnoticeably and unwittingly, becomes policing.

10.4 The disabling enablement of the theorist: Maurice Blanchot and Michel Foucault

Although Levinas raises the Other to the summoning agency and degrades the self to the summoned enabler, i.e. reverses the usual distribution of roles, he persists in claiming continuity between them. Exactly this continuity is targeted by Blanchot's critique. For Blanchot the Other (as the agency) and the self (as the enabler) are irreconcilably external one to another, which induces between them a paradoxical relationship of the *disabling enablement*. Accordingly, the principal disagreement between Blanchot and Levinas pertains to the possibility of making language unconditionally serve the Other. Levinas interprets the call of the Other as a direct address on the model of face-to-face, i.e. oral, communication. For him, the face is beyond all attributes and categories, operating exclusively *kath 'auto*, i.e. without any representational mediation. "A face has a meaning not by virtue of the relationships in which it is found, but out of itself [...]" (Levinas 1987b: 21). This ensures the "coincidence of the expressed with him who expresses" (Levinas 1969: 66). To disclose the hidden phonocentrism of this conception of the face, Derrida pointed to the metaphysical presence to oneself as being typical of the "plenitude" (Levinas 1969: 96) of oral discourse (Derrida 1978: 101–102). Only oral discourse permits immediate translation of an utterance into the person authorizing it. Supporting this critique of Levinas's pre-structuralist (i.e. phenomenological) conception of language, Blanchot observes that "this speech once again becomes the tranquil humanist" (1993: 56). It is clearly attributable to an outside speaker who takes responsibility for it in the *first person*, as is regularly the case in the spoken language and "contrary to what happens with what is written." This elucidates Blanchot's resolute introduction of the concept of "writing:" It "does not stand between; it stands outside" (Libertson 1982: 279) the interlocutors. Blanchot's "writing," therefore, acts in the same way as Bakhtin's exotopic "Third in the dialogue."

Surprisingly, in his effort to demonstrate this writerly displaced character of language Blanchot does not find recourse in Jacques Derrida (who also took recourse to the concept of writing) but in Michel Foucault. In discussing Foucault's *The Order of Things* in his *The Infinite Conversation* (257), Blanchot approvingly points out the principal thesis that the classical age breaks free from the domination of the sovereign logos exercised through vocal speech. To escape "this obscure dictation," language introduces anonymous writing that "turns away from the detestable Self" with the aim of ordering, i.e. organizing and systemizing, all human experience. Accordingly, there is nothing left over outside this order, no transcendental (divine or human) instance, no reality and no self, and thus language henceforth self-referentially represents only its transcendental order itself,

10.4 The disabling enablement of the theorist — 273

the perfection of its disposition (*ordonnance*). To draw on Kant, whose philosophy Foucault represents (in this book) as the culmination point of the classical idea of language, man becomes the *invisible principle* instead of the *visible subject* (in both senses of the word subject) of linguistic order. By such a "redoubling of the empirical into the transcendental" (1993: 249) – Foucault's principal discovery in *The Order of Things* – the figure of man disappeared before it was designated (Blanchot 1993: 249; *à peine cette figure est-elle désignée qu'elle disparait* (Blanchot 1969: 371)). Significantly, here Blanchot uses a distinctively Levinasian formulation, "left *before* having come" (Levinas 1987a: 68, "*parti* avant *d'être venu*" (Levinas 2001a: 294)) and "withdraws before entering" (Levinas 1987a: 66, "*se retir avant d'entrer*" (Levinas 2001a: 290)). Is he hinting that he is not just going to correct the "phenomenological" (or pre-modern) Levinas through the "structuralist" (or modern) Foucault but also, in a second step, vice versa? I will return to this characteristically poststructuralist "redoubling" or "folding back" of Blanchot's argument shortly. The crucial point to be maintained is that, for Foucault, the classical age is "the first age of 'structuralism'" (Blanchot 1993: 257): in this era, language that speaks through the human replaces the human who speaks through language. Henceforth all attempts to find recourse in pre- or extralinguistic instances, such as the one Blanchot has criticized in Levinas's work are clearly out of place. This is how, in the first step, Foucault's "structuralism" is engaged to correct Levinas's "phenomenology."

However, by making itself a transcendentally invisible instance of language, the figure of the human has not really disappeared from the world, as Foucault is frequently but mistakenly taken to have claimed in *The Order of Things*. According to Blanchot's distinctively Levinasian formulation, it has only entered into "the new manner of being which disappearance is" (Blanchot 1987: 76), opening the posttraumatic age of its dispersal, discontinuation, redoubling. It has only withdrawn into "the absent" of language out of which it henceforth simultaneously enables and disables everything that is made present in the linguistic order of empirical knowledge. "Enables" because there would be no empirical order without this absent transcendental instance, "disables" because this haunting transcendental enabler of all empirical agencies undergoes for its part also an empirical figuration. Blanchot's argument amounts to the following: As opposed to the divine, unbeatable transcendental status of Levinas's absent face, Foucault limits the sovereignty of the transcendental enabler in an operation entirely atypical of structuralism. Man's "absence is not pure indetermination, it is also always and each time [...] determined" by a given distribution of empirical order (Blanchot 1993: 250). In such a "poststructuralist" reading of Foucault's argument, Blanchot insists that the transcendental principle does not only *determine* the empirical agency of knowledge but also *results* from this agency as its after-effect. From *The*

Order of Things on, the transcendental principle becomes the "future anterior." This parenthesizes its *a priori* character and weakens its determining force, producing "an impure alloy of an historical a priori and a formal a priori" or a "flawed transcendentalism" (Blanchot 1987: 71–72).[5]

Ever since the moment this *aporetic empirical-transcendental circuit* was established, reads Blanchot's Levinasian-Foucauldian thesis, a continuously "shifting ambiguity" (1993: 250) has been inherent to it. Whatever Foucault's "real" argument in *The Order of Things* may be, this is the way Blanchot reads his important concept of *redoubling*: Neither the empirical agency nor the transcendental enabler are original and autonomous as both originate "abroad," which at the same time *founds* and *ruins* them. Several years later Foucault states in *The Archeology of Knowledge* (1972: 128): "The formal a priori and the historical a priori neither belong to the same level nor share the same nature: if they intersect, it is because they occupy two different dimensions." Neither can be completely founded by the other because it itself founds the other too. Yet even though I resist it, my determination comes from the Other who persists as the point of my orientation. Commenting on the permanent tension between the present and the actual in *The Archeology of Knowledge*, Deleuze and Guattari (1994b: 112) warn: "The actual is not what we are but, rather, what we become, what we are in the process of becoming – that is to say, the Other, our becoming-other." Emerging from the perspective of the enabler, poststructuralism substitutes such unremitting *othering of the self* for the agency's smooth *assimilation of the other* characteristic of structuralism.

In the same self-denying spirit, Blanchot asks "how does rebeginning – the non-origin of all that begins – found a beginning? Would it not first of all ruin it" (1993: 249)? Since the interval that separates the self from itself turns into "a new power of determination," the "relation at a distance" characteristic of the modern age becomes "explosive" (251). With modernity, as Blanchot interprets Foucault, *a disabling enablement of the two incompatible terms, the transcendental and the empirical,* arises: The one simultaneously empowers and undermines the other. "Transcendence is brought down, the empirical rises up, the modern era is ushered in." (255) Drawing from this mutual dispossessing a number of important consequences, Blanchot asks: "What speaks when the voice speaks? It situates itself nowhere [...] but manifests itself in the space of redoubling, of echo and resonance where it is not someone, but rather this *unknown* space [...] that speaks without speaking." (258) Does not this multiplied spectral voice, bereft of definite

---

5 It is worth noting here that the French term *vicieux* (Blanchot 1986b: 23) better invokes the *circulus vitiosus*, i.e. desperate circling between the empirical and transcendental forever prevented from completing itself than does the English "flawed."

meaning and representation and addressing us from a resonating "other scene," signal a re-entry of Levinas's exceeding face into Foucault's argument from *The Order of Things*? Therefore, if in the first step of Blanchot's argument Foucault was invoked to "correct" Levinas, then in the second step of the same *entretien infini* Levinas is called upon to "correct" Foucault.

In this second redoubling of the vanishing human figure, a traumatized folding back that disfigures this figure's transcendental face, an equivocal surplus emerges beyond the transcendental linguistic order. It is even more spectral than the Kantian transcendental principle, destined to retreat perpetually like a Levinasian trace that "left before having come" and "withdrew before entering" (Levinas 1987a: 66, 68). Specifying its peculiar profile, Blanchot states that "anterior to beginning, it indicates itself only as anteriority, always in retreat in relation to what is anterior" (1993: 259). In order not to be assimilated into the imperial linguistic order, this simultaneously evasive and invasive leftover retreats into a cry or murmur of "man in passing" (both in the sense of "dying" and "redoubling itself"; Blanchot 1993: 262: "*il crie mourant; il ne crie pas, il est le murmure du cri*" (1969: 392)). Exposed to the repeated linguistic articulation, this simultaneously traumatized and traumatizing Other withdraws in such a way that he "absents himself in dying" (Blanchot 1983: 9). Such a spectral re-entry of the Levinasian grave *voice* into Foucault's *writing* institutes Blanchot's coupling of the transcendental with the reiterative quasi-empirical unworking (*désœuvrement*) of its terms. "Writing ceases to be a mirror. It will constitute itself [...] as always going beyond what it seems to contain and affirming nothing but its own outside [...] affirming itself in relation to its absence, the absence of (a) work, worklessness" ("*l'absence d'œuvre ou le désœuvrement*" (Blanchot 1969: 388)) (1993: 259). In Blanchot's Levinasian re-description of Foucault, the transcendental is exposed to the persistent *désœuvrement* by its quasi-empirical "disregarded." In such a way, the hitherto traumatized "disregarded" henceforth occupies the traumatizing position.

Blanchot adheres to *désœuvrement* not just out of the *intellectual* experience of the "theoretical collaborator" (of structuralism), but also from the *empirical* experience of the practical collaborator of an anti-Semitic regime (he worked throughout the 1930s as a journalist for various right-wing papers; Haase and Large 2001: 85–95). In the sixties, the rise of the Holocaust alongside the postcolonial consciousness exposed both the political and theoretical collaboration with the rule of exclusion to serious critical examination. As the inassimilable otherness henceforth prevented any smooth assimilation, it was raised to the point of departure of a *cosmopolitanism of the disregarded*. The quasi all-embracing theoretical Self was opened toward the non-integrable moment of the guilt toward the Other, which paved the way for grieving self-examination. As more recent readers of Blanchot's legacy, such as Steven Ungar (1995) or Michael Rothberg (2000), have convincingly argued, his disconcerted and disconcerting thought exemplifies an irresolvable guilt, which surmounts all attempts to pin down the sacrificed Other (*autre*) in the empirical terms of "someone other" (*autrui*). His consistent reflection on the limits of any such representation draws its intensity from the traumatic resilience of this disregarded. This also elucidates the "Levinasian" mode of his reading of Foucault.

However, concerning the relationship between Levinas's and Foucault's ethics several caveats are necessary. As opposed to Levinas's absolute transcendental agency that hauntingly *enters* and *engraves* itself upon the self's vulnerable skin, Foucault's quasi-transcendental horizon of the Other is consistently *striven after* by this self. The movement of defacement starts *inside* rather than *outside* the self, requires from the self a transgressing *activity* rather than obeying *passivity*, and implies opening and *enrichment* rather than expiation and *renouncement*. Finally, it departs from the present *self* (toward the evasive Other) rather than the absent *Other* (toward the present self). We can therefore speak of two opposite conceptions of the relationship between the (theoretical) agency and its enabler. If in Levinas's conception the powerless victim is the source of the defacing action, in Foucault's conception it is the remorseful theorist. In the conception of Emmanuel Levinas, in which politics and ethics are clearly separated from and opposed to one another, the agency of the self has the choice between *politically defacing* the Other or *being ethically defaced* by it. As we have seen, Levinas clearly privileges the latter option. In the conception of Michel Foucault, in which politics and ethics are mutually implicated, the ambiguous self has the choice between *politically asserting* its agency by adopting the political face of the Other or *ethically defacing* its agency by surrendering to the ethical face of the Other. Foucault opts for the latter but *it is again up to the self to make the decision*. Opponents agree concerning the freedom of self's choice, but Foucault favors self-revolutionizing action over expiating passion.

Mirroring his "religious" opponent Levinas, the "revolutionary" Foucault advocates the ethical defacing of the theoretical self in a reverse form. Haunted by his experience of collaboration, Blanchot sympathizes with this advocacy. Although he had already developed his conception of *désœuvrement* in the early fifties (Blanchot 1992: 42–48), in extending and elaborating upon it in the sixties, he finds an important ally in Foucault's unworking of the theoretical transcendental. At the time Blanchot introduced his concept, he seems to have taken it from Alexandre Kojève, the crucial intellectual figure of postwar France. Kojève designated the idle man of *posthistoire* as a *voyou désœuvré*, i.e. a man in the condition of the eternal Sabbath (Kojève 1952: 396). However, he refuses to share Kojève's apocalyptic Hegelianism that postpones the Sabbath to the end of history, because it surreptitiously re-introduces theology into philosophy. The theological synthesis that violently captures the totality of history, renouncing the compromising involvement of the philosopher in its course, has to be unworked. To accomplish that, Blanchot uncouples *désœuvrement* from philosophy, aligning it with Mallarmé's modern, self-subverting idea of literature. This literary redescription of Hegelian transcendentalism reminds us of Friedrich Schlegel's former redescription of Kant or Niklas Luhmann's later redescription of Habermas's transcendentalism, as analyzed in previous chapters.

Yet if *désœuvrement* is an eminently literary operation, then it cannot figure as the transcendental condition of the modern linguistic order, as Foucault seems to be claiming in *The Order of Things*. Blanchot remains profoundly ambiguous on this question. "Literature denies the substance of what it represents," reads the definition of its "essence" in the early *The Work of Fire* (1949). "This is its law and its truth" (1995: 310). Yet earlier in the same book, Blanchot states that this inexorable "logic of permanent opposition" holds for the whole language as well. "Inherent in [language], at all its levels, is a connection of struggle and anxiety from which it cannot be freed. As soon as something is said, something else needs to be said. Then something different must again be said to resist the tendency of all that has just been said to become definitive [...] There is no rest..." (22) Is the unworking inherent in the modern linguistic order *per se* or is it a strategy of literary resistance directed *against* this order? If the first is the case, then literature loses its messianic profile as the principle emancipator of the "transcendentally imprisoned" people; if the second, then the ethical literary unworking, setting itself the task of enlightening such people, becomes politically normative. Blanchot's hesitation seems to be redoubling Foucault's line of thought, which oscillates equally between these uneasy alternatives.

To demonstrate this, let us scrutinize his subversion of the theoretical self by subjecting it to the literary outside. In his essay on Blanchot, Foucault supports Blanchot's claim that the modern age is dictated by literature which, sooner and more than any other discourse, leads us "to the outside in which the speaking subject disappears" (Foucault 1987: 13). This insight is crucial because "the being of language only appears for itself with the disappearance of the subject" (15). Even more than de Sade, Nietzsche, Mallarmé, Artaud, Bataille or Klossowski (18), all of them prominent representatives of "the thought from outside," Blanchot consistently testifies to this void in language. He thus treats both discourses he regularly uses, the reflexive and the fictional one, as being outside themselves, i.e. pushes reflexive discourse to the edge of fiction and fictional discourse to the edge of reflection. In the same way that Foucault, according to Blanchot (1987: 71–72), made the formal and historical *a priori* undecidably confront each other, Blanchot, according to Foucault, makes reflection and fiction enter an interminable dialogue.

Foucault points out "[t]his patient reflection, always directed outside itself, and a fiction that cancels itself out in the void where it undoes its forms intersect to form a discourse [...] free of any center [...] a discourse that constitutes its own space as the outside toward which, and outside of which, it speaks" (Foucault 1987: 24–25). So one might infer that Blanchot's peculiar discourse "neither-nor" merely lends expression to the fundamental structure of language in the modern age. Yet such an inference would be misleading if one considers Foucault's characteristically oscillating argument. He claims that Blanchot not only *displays* emptiness genuine to language (12), but *contests* an "entire tradition wider than philosophy," which denies that emptiness by filling it always anew with the particular content (13). In other words, instead of merely representing modern linguistic order, Blanchot offers ethical resistance to the dominant tradition of its conceptualization.

Foucault argues that Blanchot was courageously negligent of this powerful tradition because he was desperately attracted, amidst the dense structure of language, by "an absence that pulls as far away from itself as possible [... and that] has nothing to offer but the infinite void" (28). This attraction to the disregarded "non-linguistic outside" makes Blanchot negligent of the politically established linguistic order. "To be susceptible to attraction a person must be negligent." (28) This negligence is nonetheless extremely dangerous because the inarticulate outside, through its endless withdrawal, gradually removes the human subject from his or her articulation (34), making his or her past, kin and whole life non-existent (28). Levinas would say, the inarticulate outside tears the human subject out of his or her abode. As if hinting at Levinas's always retreating, ab-solving, ambiguous face, Foucault describes this spectral outside as "a gaze condemned to death" (28), averting and returning "to the shadow the instant one looks at it" (41). As soon as its withdrawal from the field of *vision* occurs, however, its underground *voice* begins to become discernible (47). In a curious repetition of the gesture of his interlocutor and intellectual affiliate, Foucault's reading of Blanchot suddenly becomes Levinasian. "Is not this voice – which 'sings blankly' and offers little to be heard – the voice of the Sirens, whose seductiveness resides in the void they open, in the fascinating immobility seizing all who listen?" (45) Alongside his friend Bataille, Blanchot was powerfully seduced by this lethal void, no matter the price of denial and solitude paid for this fascination (Blanchot 1993: 201). This price is yet another reason for Foucault to interpret Blanchot's "thought from outside" as an *ethical resistance to the politically dominant linguistic order*, which was undertaken (out of bad conscience) in the name of its disregarded outside.

Blanchot for his part sees Foucault as equally strongly drawn by the insanity (of Hölderlin, de Sade, Nietzsche and Artaud), which folds back upon the world of sanity with powerful voiding effects. Foucault on different occasions focused upon these figures beset by madness as a paradigmatic *limit-experience*. In the homonymous chapter of *The Infinite Conversation*, which significantly gives the title to the entire section of this book too, Blanchot indicates the manner in which he is going to bespeak *Madness and Civilization*. That madness is an exemplary limit-experience, confirms Foucault himself: "It is for the other world that the madman sets sail in his fool's boat; it is from the other world that he comes when he disembarks. The madman's voyage [...] develops [...] a *liminal* position [...] his exclusion must enclose him [...] He is put in the interior of the exterior, and inversely." (1965: 11) As Blanchot reads Foucault's work, admitting that he is recalling "the marginal idea that came to be expressed in this book" (1993: 196), Foucault actually investigates the inarticulate liminal zone between the madness (*folie*) and the unreason (*déraison*). This zone was forgotten at the moment the unreason was expelled from reason and thus allowed madness to enter it. "The demand to shut up the outside, that is, to constitute it as an *interiority* of anticipation or exception, is the exigency that leads society – or momentary reason – to make madness exist, that is, to make it *possible*." (196)

But the condition of the empirical possibility of madness makes the condition of the empirical impossibility of unreason, turning the latter into the unintended but necessary remainder of the first. Unreason is the inadmissible Other of the admitted other of madness, a disregarded limit-experience. Concentrating on the idea of the redoubling, Blanchot interprets unreason as something that remains in the form of the *neuter*,[6] after the process of empirical differentiation into the *positive* (reason) and the *negative* (madness) has been carried out as far as possible; after "the clear knowledge of science" has finished its job (199). As he clarifies later on in *Michel Foucault as I Imagine Him* (1987: 65), Foucault in *Madness and Civilization* deals not so much with madness as with the question of how and with which consequences unreason conditions reason to produce madness. That which reason ultimately obliterates in its ongoing normative production of differences is "the difference itself," "which (does not) differentiate itself in nothing" (Blanchot 1993: 199, translation modified: *la différence même, ce qui (ne) se différencier en rien* (1969: 297)). Akin to Derrida's *différance*, it "does not differentiate itself in nothing" because it makes the ultimate, transcendental condition of the possibility of all empirical differences.

Following on the one hand Foucault, who highlighted this quasi-transcendental liminal zone that conditions all operations of differentiation while completely escaping them, and on the other Levinas, who pointed to the lawgiving face that operates in similar fashion, Blanchot stresses the irresistible "ap-

---

[6] The French *le neutre* (1969: 297) is misleadingly rendered as "the neutral" in the American translation (1993: 199).

peal of *indifference*" (1993: 199) to being subjected to further differentiation. His *neuter* thus presents itself both as a "differentiated *indifference*," which is continuously *outlawed by* the operations of power and an "indifferent *differentiation*," which continuously *sets the new horizon* for these operations. Its "flawed transcendentalism," such as that of Foucault (Blanchot 1987: 72), is on the permanent quasi-empirical move. "Preventing the sick from dying in the street, the poor from becoming criminals, the debauched from perverting the pious is not at all reprehensible but is a sign of progress, the point of departure for changes that 'responsible authorities' would approve of." (65–66) Blanchot admits that the continuous introduction of oppositions and distinctions is necessary to make the world intelligible. However, the ethical task undertaken by Foucault is to let the disregarded, which is located "outside everything visible and everything invisible" (Blanchot 1993: 256), to re-enter the articulated order created by these operations. Blanchot unreservedly reads his early "book from such a perspective" (196). As this remainder is also located beyond the empirical reach (being precisely for this reason quasi-empirical), Foucault's "redoubling" makes a messianic *promise never to be fulfilled but nonetheless forwarded through the postponement*. He was aware that his search for the truth is irrevocably enmeshed in "the myriad configurations of power" (Blanchot 1987: 68), which pervert his imperatives. This is why he used to "proceed to the very limit" of a given discourse and then, starting the same route again, "turned toward other horizons" (69). (In a sense, he thereby proceeded like Blanchot himself, who untiringly played out fiction against reflection.) A "man always on the move," he toyed "with the thought that he might have been, had fate so decided, a statesman (a political advisor) as well as a writer [...] or a pure philosopher, [unqualified worker, i.e. nothing or nobody in particular]" (68).[7]

At this point, one is well advised to recall that Lacan considered this *je ne sais quoi* ("nothing particular" but at the same time "something unfathomable"), i.e. the "real" as the disregarded moment of the symbolic order, to be *the decisive, most powerful instance in the constitution of the human subject*. In this light, Foucault's readiness to completely dissolve his identity, to let his thought pass "through what is called madness," to "withdraw from itself, turn away from a mediating and patient labor [...] toward a searching that is distracted and astray [...] without result and without works" (Blanchot 1993: 199), presents itself as an unprecedented *self-empowerment*. This insistent self-*désœuvrement*, in its turn, redoubles Blanchot's unworking of his own self. Gradually and imperceptibly, in

---

[7] The parenthesized section ("*travailleur sans qualification, donc un je ne sais quoi ou un je ne sais qui*" (Blanchot 1986b: 17)) is astonishingly dropped from the American translation.

both works, the resistance to the imposed transcendental condition turns into the new transcendental condition imposed upon all modern selves, notwithstanding the huge power differences between them. This is the final consequence of the "ethical" privileging of incessant redoubling.

The delineated ethical shaping of the self forgets that, to be without qualities at the *symbolic* level is substantially different from being bereft of them at the *political* level: the first freely chosen de-identification implies an unlimited mobility while the second enforced condition of "boat people" or *sans-papiers* condemns people to harsh immobility. To render this in Elisabeth Povinelli's terms: "As a result a gap seems to open between those who reflect on and evaluate ethical substance and those who are this ethical substance" (2011: 11). Despite being extremely remote from each other and "never having to meet," these *agencies* and *enablers* appear to be firmly coupled. Is the famous brake-release that facilitates the overall mobility of the First World not somehow connected to putting the brakes on the movement "outside the walls" through a finely balanced combination of economic, administrative and sanctionary policies?

> The first travel at will, get much of their travel [...] are welcomed with smiles and open arms [...] The second travel surreptitiously, often illegally, sometimes paying more for the crowded steerage of the stinking unseaworthy boat than others pay for business-class gilded luxuries – and are frowned upon [...] arrested and promptly deported, when they arrive. (Bauman 1998: 89)

How ethical is it to demand mobility from the selves that are extremely deprived of it? Is this immobility not the disregarded moment of mobility's raising to the transcendental principle, is it not this principle's neglected empirical prerogative and the silenced basis of its legitimacy? Whatever might be the answer to these disquieting questions, Blanchot was not the right person to direct them to his elected affiliate Foucault. Neither was Foucault the right person to address them to Blanchot. Consequently, they remained obliterated by both of them.

10.5 Empowering the literary transcendental: Jacques Derrida

This raising of modern literature to the new and pressing political transcendental characterizes the poststructuralist cosmopolitanism of the disregarded *per se*. Associating the singularity of community members with the "never assured or guaranteed," i.e. heterotopic status of literature, Derrida tacitly supports Foucault's and Blanchot's deduction of the "poetics of rebeginning" from (modern) literature. "[I]t receives its determination from something other than itself." (Derrida 2000a: 28–29) The literary fascinates the Derrida of the late 1990s because it proposes to its audience a realm of possible referents that are *as if* shared among them, though both the author and reader know they cannot be really shared as they belong to an altogether other world (Clark 2005: 150). The same holds for the "singular plural" literary community in which "we know in common that we have nothing in common" (Derrida 2001a: 58) and yet act and behave *as if* we do. This is how the literary subverts the empirical political bond, occupies "the site of its articulation" (Clark 2005: 152), introduces into it "the ordeal of undecidability," and produces a literary community relying on an unknown future yet-to-come. Such community is bound to remain absolutely hospitable (2000b: 83) to this unpredictable alterity that is always on the way to arriving.

Following the logics of the enabler who sacrificially surrenders to the unfathomable Other in order to receive his authorization, Derrida joins the company of Levinas, Foucault and Blanchot. All of them *empower the powerless*. This peculiar *supreme powerless agency*, which Derrida in the late 1990s renders in distinctively literary terms, appears in his early work in the form of *différance*. Via traces, breakthroughs, shifts, delays and folds this "law of laws" ceaselessly disappropriates all identities, but for its part resists any such disappropriation (Derrida 1985: 121). "The law of laws" was probably an allusion to Levinas's ethics labeled by Derrida (1967a: 164) as "the ethics of ethics" because it resists historical recollection (Levinas 1961: 136). Inasmuch as Derrida places the *différance* equally beyond historical "pindownability," in the irretrievable past behind the back of history, it promises an equally discontinuous future: *à-venir*, yet-to-come. In the late 1990s, he replaces the former concepts such as *différance*, trace or undecidability with the rewritten concepts of the gift *(don)* and specter *(Gespenst)*, and, finally, the *messianic promise* of the literary (Beardsworth 1996: 36). He did not even hesitate to call this all-differentiating structure that resists all differentiation *justice*, in order to establish a clear opposition to law *(droit)* that reduces and represses it.

The delineated argumentative steps undertaken by Derrida spawn a *stark binary opposition* between ethics and politics, justice and law, literature and philosophy, which escapes his attention, remaining surprisingly spared deconstruction. When he equates his concept of justice with Levinas's concept of ethics based on their common undeconstructibility,[8] he seems to have forgotten two important caveats. First, Levinas uses the concept of justice primarily in order to empha-

---

8 To be more accurate, Derrida avoids the concept of *ethics* (because he criticized its use by Levinas), choosing instead "sanctity" in order to align with it his concept of justice. However, as Levinas himself explains (Poirié 1987: 95), he replaced the Greek term *ethics* with *sainteté* only in order to avoid the connoted subordination of ethics to ontology and not to change its basic meaning. Accordingly, there is no substantial difference between his use of the terms ethics and sanctity.

size exactly the opposite, i.e. the legal aspect of the original French word *justice* (Levinas 1961: 188, 1992: 132–133, Levinas and Nemo 1982: 94–95). Second, Derrida himself once criticized Levinas's concept of ethics for not having taken into consideration its philosophical and historical "memory" (Derrida and Labarrière 1986: 76), i.e. for freeing its urging face of any representation that would undermine its irresistibility. Although Derrida in this and other ways repeatedly drew attention to the possibility of a violent implementation of such an alleged "command from beyond" (1997: 65),[9] of its perilous proximity to "the bad, even to the worst" (1992b: 28),[10] he simultaneously *unreservedly reiterates the welcome, irrefutable and obligatory character* of this *tout autre*. Accordingly, he states that it underlies no satisfactory translation but just *acceptance, affirmation and obedience*.

From this perspective, one can understand why one of Derrida's most authoritative American interpreters, John Caputo, translated his conception of the Altogether Other into the idea of God of the medieval philosopher Saint Anselm. "God is in-finite by definition. [...] God's measure is to be without measure. God is the sheer excess of never containable or comprehensible excess, Who is always more than anything we can say or think [...]" (Caputo 2000: 180, 183). Derrida himself richly underpins this "hermeneutic" interpretation when he openly equates the Altogether Other with God: "God looks at me and I don't see him and it is on the basis of this gaze that singles me out [*ce regard qui me regard* (1992e: 87, 59, 67)] that my responsibility comes into being" (1995: 91, 51, 67). Since such a hypostasis serves as the hideous instrument of deconstruction's authorization – Derrida unreservedly proclaims, "deconstruction is justice" (1992b: 15) – his enabler's perspective presents itself as a mirror *inversion of the hermeneutic perspective of the agency*. Uncritically used as a categorical imperative, "the trope of the Other [...] must a priori fail to do justice to the complex activity, creativity, and engagement of those whom it figures simply as relegated objects" (Sedgwick 1993: 147). Such an imperial flattening of important historical, political and cultural differences

---

9 As for the "other ways," Derrida explicitly warns that pure face-to-face communication with the Other (i.e. without the mediation of the "small [political] other") might result in perilous consequences, i.e. the impossibility of distinguishing between good and evil, love and hate, giving and taking etc. (1997: 66).

10 Published as a separate book *a posteriori*, the French original contains an addition that is even more explicit in this regard: "Abandonnée à elle seule, l'idée incalculable et donatrice de la justice est toujours au plus près du mal, voire du pire car elle peut toujours être réappropriée par le calcul le plus pervers. C'est toujours possible et cela fait partie de la folie dont nous parlions à l'instant. Une assurance absolue contre ce risque ne peut que saturer ou suturer l'ouverture de l'appel à la justice, un appel toujours blessé." (Derrida 1994c: 61)

among the empirical others might ultimately elucidate why Levinas's face, which lurks behind each "human other" (*autrui*), demands an "unconditional obedience" (Levinas 1961: 23, Levinas 1996: 19).[11] Levinas states that, in welcoming the Other, I welcome the Most High to which my freedom is subordinated (1961: 335). Even though Derrida, Foucault and Blanchot oppose Levinas's philosophical rendering of the Other, the literary in their programs of ethical redemption nonetheless functions in the same way as Levinas's despotic Absolute Other does.

But if Blanchot reminds us that modern literature is tightly co-dependent with modern political identity, if it is always weakened, undermined and ruined by the latter, if it is but a remainder of the latter's techniques of differentiation, then why should we be *absolutely hospitable* and *unconditionally surrender* to it? To prevent this we have to argue *with* Foucault, Blanchot and Derrida *against* them: Absolute hospitality implies a divine sovereignty of Levinas's absent face whereas, according to Blanchot's "Foucauldian" correction, "absence is not pure indetermination, it is also always and each time [...] determined" by the given distribution of an empirical order (Blanchot 1993: 250). Far from being a pure transcendental force, modern literature is just "an impure alloy of an historical a priori and a formal a priori" (Blanchot 1987: 71–72), one of the historical figures of the enduring human redoubling forever prevented from completing itself. Why should we unquestionably other our empirical face, recommence our empirical identity, and renounce our empirical brother for the benefit of this always equally problematic, i.e. empirically refracted exteriority? If this outside cannot but be represented, and its voice broken, then its demand for everybody's unconditional and interminable repentance and expiation is obviously misplaced. "What speaks when the voice speaks? It situates itself nowhere [...] but manifests itself in the space of redoubling, of echo and resonance where it is not someone, but rather this *unknown* space [...] that speaks without speaking." (Blanchot 1993: 258) Even though Blanchot and Derrida explicitly and Foucault implicitly critically reexamined Levinas's transcendental ethics, it seems that this ethics nonetheless reentered Foucault's revolutionary technology of the self, Blanchot's remorseful elaboration of *désœuvrement* and Derrida's messianic concepts of friendship, gift, specter and justice. It did so in the "inimical" guise of literature. Through such a literary reentry, something that was envisioned to be purely and strictly ethical acquired a biased political shape of literary community. *Pace* Levinas, Foucault, Blanchot and Derrida, the ethical and the political on the one hand and the transcendental and the empirical on the other appear to be doomed to an unwanted proximity.

---

11 Derrida blends each other with the Altogether Other in the same way: "*Tout autre est tout autre* (Each other is Altogether Other)" (1992e: 68, 76–77, 1995b: 68, 78).

11 Political and/or Literary Community: From Class to Messianic Cosmopolitanism

11.1 Singularity – a European mission?

Among the concepts that frequently cross the various roads of the humanities at the outset of the twenty-first century, one seems to do so in a particularly insistent way: singularity. From its rich disciplinary background and complex theoretical genealogy, meticulously traced by Derek Attridge in *The Singularity of Literature* (2004) and Timothy Clark in *The Poetics of Singularity* (2005), in what follows I shall single out only the explosive relation between singularity and community. In recent debates, the latter concept was at least seriously reexamined, if not exactly replaced by the former. If the idea of community acquired its prominence in the wake of the transition from Literary to Cultural Studies, then the idea of singularity took center stage, conversely, through the deconstruction of "culturalism." The latter was critically targeted for the reimplementation of the imperial cosmopolitan model that was now to be unworked through literature in favour of an emancipating model. In the conclusion of his book *Europe, or the Infinite Task* (2009), Rodolphe Gasché elucidates this new connection as follows:

> Throughout this book I have insisted on the intrinsic link between the universal and the singular. From Husserl's discussion of a universal rational science having its roots in the life world, to Heidegger's linkage of an originary world to the history of a people, to Patočka's conception of a community of responsibility predicated on the absolute singularity of its members, to Derrida's claim that the concept or idea of universality as an infinite task emerges in a finite space and time, we have seen that singularity can only identify itself by simultaneously appealing to universality. (343)

After this model, the closed communal horizon saturated by particularities is pierced by "hospitality to the foreigner" (342) in order to open its every "here and now" to unforeseeable alterity (Gasché 2007: 308). Gasché claims that such unlimited hospitality characterized European culture from its very nascence. If a European type of universality is unimaginable without singularity, this is because welcoming the radical stranger is inherent to European cultural heritage. Emerging in the culture of ancient Greece as the cradle of Europe, the idea of a universal humanity not only suspended limitations brought upon particular identities by their respective communities, but also broke open "Europe's self-immanence toward transcendence, toward the other, and what is other than Europe" (Gasché 2009: 27). Europe is in Gasché's view an epitome of community "based on mutual help through mutual critique and subsequent correction" (27), even at the risk of thinking that other cultures and traditions are "deemed to be stuck in particularity, incapable of self-transcendence" (343). In Clark's interpretation, these self-enclosed traditions are exemplified by the American self-aggrandizing multicultural "identity politics" based on provincial ignorance and prejudices concerning the others (Clark 2005: 17–19, 23–27).[1] Unlike such oppressive mentalities that permanently reinforce their own norm, Europe is conceived as a *singular event*. "Gasché thinks the irreducible alterity at the heart of this singular event and recalls that the heritage of this event named Europe carries not only a responsibility but a promise." (Birmingham 2009: 108)

Gasché is not the first European thinker to insist on originary heterogeneity as the guarantee of Europe's singularity in comparison with other civilizations. He can count on an abundantly documented tradition of European cosmopolitan self-perception singled out against the background of others' provincialism. The first self-congratulatory statement of Europe's superiority in this regard is Aristotle's famous opposition between the dialogically open and democratic Europeans (Westerners) and the self-enclosed and barbaric Asians (Easterners) (*Politics*: III, 1285a 6–7; VII, 1327b 24–33). As Roberto Dainotto (2007: 52–87) has shown in his investigation of the modern imaginary shape of Europe, Montesquieu was the first to translate this Aristotelian division between the Western and Eastern civilizations into an intra-European opposition between the Northern and Southern Europeans. Thereupon, Voltaire transformed it into the opposition between Western and Eastern Europe. The polemics of Voltaire against Montesquieu notwithstanding, the superiority of French culture benefited from both these reconfigurations. To whomever the superiority was allocated on given political, social, religious and cultural circumstances – and the extra-European and intra-European asymmetries crisscrossed through the history of modern Europe in various ways – the pattern of the enlightened democrats emancipating themselves from the benighted barbarians persisted. Europeans traditionally perceive themselves as latecomers into the world dominated by telluric customs who find themselves obliged to take responsibility for its democratization. This explains why modernism follows Enlightenment in the systematic practice of relinquishing, antiquating, and storing this past in museums. Stating that humankind's hapiness

---

[1] For a similarly Manichean confrontation of American fundamentalism and conservative ideology with European democracy and tolerance, see Said 2002. Inasmuch as the global order of today's world still clearly displays national infrastructure, such anti-Americanism "which divides good and evil by polluting the United States and purifying any collectivity, ideology or region that comes to represent the other side," "elides the systemic processes at play" in it, i.e. the inevitable power asymmetry between the nation-states (Alexander 2012: 162).

cannot be reached through remembrance but only redemption, modernist historicism keeps the Enlightenment's promise of steady progress (Clark 2005: 20).

Since redemption always implies postponement, the European spirit distinguished itself from the outset through a patient detachment from the "non-European" or "not-quite-European." Detachment makes the core of the European modernist idea. It functioned in the same way as Agamben's normative "anthropological machine," producing the non-human both *outside* and *inside* the human, the latter in the form of "the slave, the barbarian, and the foreigner, as figures of an animal in human form" (Agamben 2004: 37). The cosmopolitan axes human/animal and European/non-European operated hand in hand, engendering "a kind of state of exception, a zone of indeterminacy in which the outside is nothing but the exclusion of the inside and the inside is in turn only the inclusion of an outside" (37). Europe was accordingly bringing its spiritual substance to expression by combining the *extermination* of inadmissible others and the *overcoming* of admitted others. As Herder significantly put it: "The barbarian subjects, the educated overcomer cultivates" (*Der Barbar beherrscht, der gebildete Überwinder bildet*) (1989: 706). Being "naturally" prone to cultivation, the European behavior displays human as opposed to animal traits. Herder's distinction from the *Essay on the Origin of Language* (1966: 107, 117–121) neatly completes this self-congratulating conclusion: whereas the animal is self-sufficient, the human is other-related. In contradistinction to other civilizations, it was European civilization which operated as an epitome of the human persistently and attentively related to the non-human and less-than-human.

According to Reinhard Koselleck (1973) and Jürgen Habermas (1962), the cosmopolitan idea of Europe was definitely introduced with Voltaire's Republic of Letters, an open community of heterogeneous citizens established against the nationally isolated and despotic model of the eighteenth century's absolutist monarchies. Since then, *a permanent literary education/cultivation of citizens "organically" belongs to European intellectual formation*. Indeed, Herder's cosmopolis leaves no barbarians outside its gates but, as they are now allowed to enter among the citizens of the world, the pressure of the European *Bildungsimperativ* placed upon them grows considerably. With the Enlightenment and especially modernism as its spiritual heir, literature becomes *the* medium of achieving European singularity. As a model expected to be followed worldwide, Europe figures as the prototype of literary (educated/cultivated/detached) community. As regards these expectations brought upon the others, the European model could be applied only by the not-quite-European humans outside and inside Europe who where "naturally" predestined or prepared to educate/cultivate themselves. Those whom nature "was obliged to deny nobler gifts" she has taken care to compensate for this denial by "an ampler measure of sensual enjoyment" (Herder 1997b: 77):

> That finer intellect, which the creature whose breast swells with boiling passion beneath this burning sun, must necessarily be refused, was countervailed by a structure altogether incompatible with it. Since then a nobler boon could not be conferred on the negro in such a climate, let us pity but not despise him; and honor that parent who knows how to compensate, which she deprives. (77–78)

In a word, Herder's tolerant and democratic vision of the broad human brotherhood could not possibly originate in "brute" Africa but merely in "refined" Europe; its birthplace was Europe's assumptive cosmopolitan care for the rest of the world. Herder states that the "general spirit" of Europe amalgamates the "tribe formation (*Stammesbildung*) of many European nations" (1989: 705). Due to numerous modifications and ameliorations of ethnic narrow-mindedness that took place in the course of many centuries in this climatically privileged part of the world, "everything in Europe tends toward a gradual suspension of national characters" (706). Because of its mild climate,

> [i]n no other part of the world did peoples mix with one another like in Europe: in no other part of the world have they changed their dwelling places and with them their art of living and customs so intensely and frequently as in Europe (705).

In sum, in Herder's finely tuned outline of races, which is astonishingly close in its shape to those of his contemporaries and founders of the forthcoming racist doctrines Blumenbach, Lavater and Camper, we find the following:

> Nature has placed the Negro close to the ape and entrusted the solution of its great problem of humanity to all the peoples of all epochs leading from his (the Negro's) reason up to the brain of the finest human development (*Menschenbildung*). That which is most necessary, produced by drives and needs, is to be found in almost each and every people on earth; but only finer peoples of milder climates were capable of producing a finer development of the state of humankind (*zur feinern Ausbildung des Zustandes der Menschheit*). (633–634)

Like all plants, the environmentally bound non-European races and peoples flourish and wither (571), but in the more mobile and advanced European races culture goes forth (*rückt fort*; 628), taking on the seeds of withered peoples in order to continue with nature's vital creation (*lebendige Schöpfung*; 573). This is why cosmopolitan Europeans are predestined to carry the torch of humankind toward the future freedom.

Yet their singular mission seems to have been incessantly generating obstacles, polarizations and asymmetries in the envisaged smooth flow of humankind's progress. As Herder's representative argument demonstrates, despite the reclaimed spiritual inclusiveness, the European idea of the dialogically oriented, generous and self-educating humans rests on geopolitical devaluations, marginalizations and exclusions. While it establishes proper "human nature," it outlaws and/or derogates improper "natural humans." The inclusion and exclusion inextricable penetrate into each other. For example, Herder states that the parasitic Jews are "hanging onto almost all European nations and drawing more or less profit from their juice" (702), and "Gypsies" are "good for nothing but harsh military discipline" (703). Unlike them, Germans "protected the culture that remained after the storm of the epochs, developed the common spirit of Europe and slowly and conspicuously ripened to effectuate all the world regions on earth" (805).

Not long ago, in the face of such discriminations at the heart of Herder's cosmopolitanism, Julia Kristeva leveled accusations against his *Volksgeist*. She blamed it for the national idea rooted in soil, blood and language, praising in contradistinction Montesquieu's *esprit général* for "a texture of many singularities" with which she "wholeheartedly agrees" (Kristeva 1993: 32–33). Yet by glorifying Montesquieu's Europe for having incorporated foreignness, Kristeva also revivified Montesquieu's geopolitical asymmetries, much more ill-reputed than those of Herder. In line with Gasché's definition of Europe, she stated that unlike non-European civilizations inimical to contamination and overlaps with other traditions, Europe from the outset exemplified an exogamous society stipulating alliances outside the bloodline (Kristeva 1991: 45–46). Montesquieu's *esprit général*, as its chief promoter, must therefore defend "proper European cosmopolitanism" from the revival of the perilous German nationalism (Kristeva 1993: 47). Nevertheless, is this peril to be averted by the same French cosmopolitan "crusade for liberty" that initially provoked German remedial ethnocultural reaction (Brubaker 1992: 8)? Michelet epitomized this imperial crusade by describing France as a "glorious mother who is not ours alone and who must deliver every nation to liberty" (Girardet 1983: 13). To praise Montesquieu is to forget the religious, colonial and imperial difference at the heart of his Europeanism.

The European cosmopolitan spirit took recourse in the model of the self-reflexive modern literature so as to come to terms with this stubborn resurgence of an allegedly overcome provincial brutality amidst the European cultivated self from the Enlightenment onwards. Following this thread, a powerful tradition of seeing Europe as an interminable mission rather than a given fact endorses Gasché's interpretation. Europe enjoys the reputation of an extraterritorial, free-floating essence epitomized in Odysseus as a "compulsive and indefatigable wanderer [...] among those who would rather live their lives in a world ending at the outermost village fence" (Bauman 2004: 3). Mobile as it is, Europe permanently reinvents its singularity against the background of external and internal others' particularities. Yet it is precisely because the *singular* European self needs the *particular* non-European others as its enduring background that it cannot bid farewell to them. European selves cannot assert their singularity without exempting themselves from the non-European particularity. Accordingly, Hans-Georg Gadamer points out in *Das Erbe Europas* (1989), "we are all others, and we are all ourselves" (quoted after Bauman 2004: 7). Bauman develops this idea further stating that "we *know* that culture [...] has no *foundation* except [...] the dialogue that thought conducts with itself [...] we, the Europeans [...] have *no identity* – fixed identity [...] 'we do not know who we are' and even less do we know what we can yet become [...]" (12). Unlike other cultures that are unaware of being distinct because they are unrelated to the others, European culture "feeds on questioning the order of things – and on questioning the fashion of questioning it" (12). This ultimately makes it an "infinite task" of consistent self-singularization.

After Derek Attridge, European event-like singularity is a mobile and open nexus or configuration of attributes into which an unexpected event of reconfiguration breaks forever anew, with the effect of outmaneuvering all pre-existing determinations (Attridge 2004: 63). It is effectuated only through reiteration, within the give-and-take of contingent operations; it is an open form in the permanent remaking (111–119) organically linked to the inventiveness and innovation that are the essential properties of Western art throughout its history (13). Harmonizing with Gasché's thesis of Europe as the "infinite task," Attridge roots this inventiveness in Derrida's absolute hospitality offered to the irreducible singularity of the Other (Derrida 2000b: 83). Yet the advent of this Other can be discerned in no other way but through the estrangement of the familiar produced by everyday cultural operations. It pushes at the limits, revaluates and refashions this familiar (Attridge 2004: 18–19). The arrival of the *literary* Other thus reveals its strong *cultural* dependence: it can be brought to expression only against the background of a given "idiocultural" experience (21) and acquire its distinctive profile merely against this "negative foil."

> There is no "absolute other" (or "Other") if this means a wholly transcendent other, unrelated to any empirical particularity [...]. If the other is always and only other *to me* (and hence to my culture, as embodied in my idioculture), I am already in some kind of relation to it [...]. Otherness, that is, is produced in an *active* or *event-like* relation [...] (29).

This event-like relation organically binds mobile and innovative *literature* to immobile and conservative *culture*, as the former can affirm itself only by outmaneuvering the appropriating operations of cultural particularization in the name of a radically empty freedom (Clark 2005: 3–5, 12). The singularity of modern European literature cosmopolitically disengages the particularity of non-European cultures inside and outside Europe. Gradually extending its global ambitions, the celebrated European singularity finally operates as the *subversive literary foundation of every culture's particularity*. This lends it an overarching and explosive quality of incalculable "eventness" that irrefutably infiltrates worldwide cultures. "We know in common that we have nothing in common," formulates Derrida (2001a: 58). This *nothing* that we Europeans have in common is the universal *vanishing mediator* of literary singularity that undermines everything positive in its typically other-related, ex-static existence (2000a: 28–29). Derrida once termed this literary emptying out of all identified cultural phenomena (2001a: 56) "the natality of the everyday" (1995c: 8), associating its intervention with the "unreadability of the secret" (1992c: 152). Pushing its estrangement to "the limit of not understanding" (2000a: 93), this powerful symbolic "'economy' of literature" (1992d: 43) imperatively demands "faith or confidence" (2002: 111), "learning by heart" and "translating the untranslatable" (1995a: 288–299). In instituting the global "jurisdiction" (1992d: 72) of the "most powerful powerless" (Attridge 2004: 131), it ultimately indiscriminately uproots everything grounded in a particular time, space and culture. It "does not collect itself, it 'consists' in not collecting itself" (Derrida 1995a: 354) because its dissemination exceeds, transgresses and elusively surpasses the other. As in their "plea for a common foreign policy, beginning in the core of Europe," Habermas and Derrida (2003) have concluded that, in proceeding thus, Europe assists in a substitution of a fully inclusive human community for a collection of territorially entrenched entities. The crucial unanswered question is, however, whether a human community set on the singular European pattern can really be "fully inclusive."

11.2 The class cosmopolitanism of Cultural Studies

Even though it has been criticized by "singularists" for its tendency toward cultural particularization of the singular literary, British Cultural Studies, when it emerged for the first time around the middle of the twentieth century, did not aim to abandon the study of universal literature for the benefit of the study of particular cultures. On the contrary, it paradoxically *followed the same European ideal as its singularist critique does today*: to reconfigure in a new cosmopolitan spirit the culturally restricted, i.e. elite idea of literature that ruled the day from the 1930s to the 1950s. Through such an extension of the prevailing elite research horizon, literature's differently structured and neglected conceptualizations stemming in the first place from the "subordinate class" were to be included for consideration. Bearing this primary objective in mind, this widening of the perspective envisioned by Cultural Studies might be termed *class cosmopolitanism*.

Beyond the national-philological concept of literature epitomized in the departments of English, the cosmopolitan project in question envisioned redescribing within its new terms comparative literary programs as well. The argument was that, although the latter had adopted an international idea of literature it remained oblivious to its fundamentally biased politics of representation. Despite generous declarations of its openness to various literatures, Comparative Literature reiterated the traditional inclination of Western culture to domesticate the otherness of non-European and Eastern European cultures as well as the "benighted" domestic populace,[2] assimilating them into a picturesque diversity that feeds its progressing historical unity. From the cosmopolitan perspective of Cultural Studies, the broad internationalism of Comparative Literature was accused of the same surreptitious taming of otherness for which, a half-century later, anti-culturalists or singularists targeted Cultural Studies' particularism. They reproach the "culturalists" for the implementation of the same historicist pattern (Clark 2005: 209) that the culturalists previously objected to in the comparatists. Now, if the *motivating force* of an emancipating critique turns over time into the *privileged target* of the same critique, does not this indicate a slippery, re-signifiable character of cosmopolitan ideals? If these bright ideals are, owing to their tight relatedness to their sinister opponents, necessarily equivocal, can the required division between the singular and the particular, or Europe and non-Europe, be maintained in stable terms capable of reliably guiding humankind toward a final freedom?

Whereas literary singularists attack their cultural particularism, Cultural Studies raised the doubts concerning "cosmopolitics" underlying Comparative Literature predominantly from a class perspective. These studies emerged out of adult education programs between the 1930s and the 1950s dealing with the hard everyday life experience of culturally heterogeneous, mature and politically aware students recruited from the subaltern classes (Steele 1997: 2). Through such teaching praxis, centers for permanent adult education revealed the origin of the ruling idea of literature in the cultural, ideological, social and political values of the elite. "Studying English was to study the growth from barbarism to civilization […]. To become English was to become human." (57) An apparently disinterested and disembodied aesthetics, responsible for the dissemination of this idea of literature,

---

[2] For the association between the non-European colonized and the European working populace see the following comment: "[A] colonial metaphor of missionary appropriation, which was first tested on the Indian subcontinent, was subsequently applied to the English working class […]" (Steele 1997: 4). The English working class was blamed for the same deficits as Moslems or Hindus: immorality, sensuality, self-indulgence, corruption, and depravity (57). In such a way, Cultural Studies unveils the operations of Agamben's "anthropological machine" continuously producing exceptions at the same time outside and inside the political realm. The state of exception becomes the normal state of modern Western culture. However, unlike Agamben, Cultural Studies offers a cosmopolitan solution for this injustice.

was unmasked as a practice of cultural discrimination. After all, neither English nor Comparative Literature departments emerged as self-enclosed and organic but as interrelated and artificially constructed frames of references with shifting and permeable boundaries. As soon as their disciplinary idea of literature was put to "natural" use, ignorance toward that which remained outside their disciplinary field of expertise was set to work.

Once the exclusionist profile of the cosmopolitan idea of Comparative Literature is thus laid bare, one is better equipped to understand why the aesthetics associated with it treated non-European or not-quite-European literary works as invalid or failed embodiments of its ideals, or regarded the everyday life literary production as unworthy of scientific attention. Cultural Studies turned toward these "leftover" elements of the preceding disciplinary expertise in a very similar way as did, a century or so ago, the heterogeneous form of the novel. As Michel de Certeau (1984: 78) put it, this form with its predilection for the marginal and shadowy customs of bourgeois society was gradually made into "the zoo of everyday practices since the establishment of modern science," which expelled them from its disciplinary expertise. It is exactly in this subversive way with regard to the official literary scholarship in the form of English or Comparative Literature departments that Cultural Studies saw its agenda. Yet if de Certeau raised such a representative literary genre to the desired model of Cultural Studies – quite an unexpected move if one considers its aforementioned resistance to the elite idea of literature – this happened because he developed an oppositional concept of literature associated with its emergence.

In established Literary Studies, literature sets the measure of "prominence" of particular cultures, and represents the supreme norm against which comparisons between them are undertaken. From de Certeau's point of view, on the contrary, literature speaks for the anonymous mass of those who are dispossessed of a "proper locus" having to act on "terrain [...] organized by the law of foreign power" (37) irrespective of the culture in question. These deprived "human remnants" of all cultures cannot express themselves except by taking an outsmarting detour through the imposed official discourse of a given culture. Being expropriated of an acknowledged agency for literary production on their own, these enablers express themselves through the subversive consumption, the mimicking re-appropriation of the borrowed discourse, and they turn it through such tactical estrangement against its culturally preordained usage. This is how de Certeau interprets the novel's oppositional narrative techniques.

By analogy, far from officially *representing* literature as do the disciplines of English or Comparative Literature, the non-discipline of Cultural Studies subversively *enacts* it. It does not take literature into cognitive possession from the vantage point of any disciplinary norm, but mimics it in its genuine way. As Michael

Taussig (1992) has suggested in his redescription of the concept of mimesis in accordance with its "primordial" meaning, Cultural Studies understands mimesis in the same sense as "primitive communities" do, i.e. as *mimicry* rather than *representation*. Yet if literature is conceptualized in this "performative" rather than "constative" fashion, then it no longer makes a distinctive *domain of research* represented by prominent authors, but rather a marginalized *disappropriating practice* of deprived human beings without a recognizable profile. It is the practice of the "disregarded" in the same sense I have claimed, in the previous chapter, poststructuralism is; and it opposes Comparative Literature in the same way the latter opposes structuralism – that is, as emancipating cosmopolitanism opposes the assimilating one. Finally, as it is anything but culture-specific, it makes the *emancipating cosmopolitan basis of all cultures*. Put in these terms literature for the first time becomes, to engage Derrida's apt phrase, "the mystical foundation of authority" (1992b: 11). Its all-pervading deactivating effects underlie any culture whatsoever.

Undoing all cultural particularities, the idea of culture is characterized by this cosmopolitan operation of literature in Cultural Studies. The decisive point is that, if in English and Comparative Literature the concept of *literature* was tacitly shaped by the particular ruling *culture* of those in power, in Cultural Studies the concept of *culture* is silently subverted by the cosmopolitan *literature* of the disregarded population. *Cultural Studies acts in the name of the indeterminate residue of determinate cultures and disciplines in the same way as its critics, the "singularists," will do in turn.* To authorize their cosmopolitanism, both take recourse to modern literature's consistent self-disempowerment, a relentless detachment from the political power of cultural identities. Both act as the self-appointed agencies of the destitute enablers, conducting a "politics of trauma." As a result, the transition from English and Comparative Literature to Cultural Studies does not translate simply "from literature to culture," as it is usually rendered, but rather "from the culturally determined self-asserting literature to the literary determined self-questioning culture." The opposition between literature and culture, considered to be fierce antagonists, reenters the identity of each of its constituents, attenuating their conflict. Taking the cosmopolitan perspective of the socially disregarded, Cultural Studies persistently deactivates the monolith concept of a culture of Literary Studies to prevent the elite cultural authorization of literature. Instead of literature being defined from the perspective of elite culture, this culture is now defined from the perspective of the hybrid literary practice of the anonymous and expropriated enablers.

This might explain the literary manner in which Richard Hoggart, one of the forefathers of Cultural Studies, in his *The Uses of Literacy* (1957) misappropriated the disciplinary discourse of English Studies, combining it with personal and public history, autobiography and ethnography. Another literary maneuver was undertaken by Raymond Williams, the second forefather of Cultural Studies, who in *The Long Revolution* (1961) interrogated the established meaning of the key disciplinary concepts of English Literature by delving further back into their forgotten past. The borders of the concept of literature were thus extended to include all kinds of writing such as scientific, historical, autobiographical as well as fictional texts. The intention of Williams's reconstruction was to show that such a broad concept of literature prevailed up until the end of the eighteenth century, and underlied division into fictional and factual literature only in the wake of Romanticism. Instead of connecting the past and present into a smooth historical continuity, Williams thus treats the past as the stockpile of alternative and contestable resources, an unstable and asymmetrical ensemble expected to destabilize the present. Confirming our thesis on Cultural Studies' literary techniques of disappropriation, his undoing of the homogeneous present by way of pluralizing the past thus opposes institutional historiography, taking the liberty germane to literary experimentation. Besides, in disappropriating disciplinary history by means of literary memory, he takes recourse to the ancient but meanwhile apocryphal "plebeian" techniques as analyzed by Nietzsche in *The Joyful Wisdom* (see chapter eight).

Hoggart's and Williams's literary disappropriating operations applied to the mainstream disciplinary legacy paved the way for the discourse of British Cultural Studies, which subsequently incessantly maneuvered between various disciplines and freely combined the past and the present. As one commentator put it, the whole British project of Cultural Studies relies on the "ability to plunder the more established disciplines while remaining separate from them" (Moran 2002: 51), i.e. "stealing away [from them] the more useful elements and rejecting the rest" (Johnson 1996: 75). Opposing the growing institutionalization of the field, Stuart Hall (1992: 285) warned that it threatens the transdisciplinary character of Cultural Studies, which draws strength precisely from its marginality within the academy. If the disciplines were to be denied their exclusive rights, then one was surely not expected to establish a new discipline.

But exactly this firm alignment with the plundering tactical maneuvers of the anonymous populace deprived of any recognizable cultural identity may turn out, as Bill Readings (1996: 122) has argued, to be animated by old Kantian nostalgia for an all-inclusive education guided by the idea of unrestrained human freedom. In his famous treatise *The Conflict of Faculties* (1798), Kant accused the disciplinary fragmentation of knowledge of spawning a regrettable triumph of the disciplined expert over the self-reflective philosopher. He set out by offering an analogy between the idea of the university, promoted at that time under the pressure of the necessity of the mass production of knowledge, and the division of labor in the factory (Kant 1979: 23). In his vision, the form of the university makes only a part of the larger "organism" of an emergent society that replaces the centralized monarchy with the democratic republican constitution. Alongside the necessary differentiation of discrete domains, both society and university are expected to strive for a unifying principle that would ensure the commensurability of divergent particles. Stressing the importance of this principle that completely escapes the empirical evidence, Kant claims that each constituent must obey a "thoroughly interconnected whole of experience" (2007: 19) despite the mere hypothetical character of the latter. On this claim, obviously, the requested authority of philosophy rests.

However, in order to keep steadily in touch with this unfathomable idea of the whole, readiness and ability for self-governing are required from the human self. They usually distinguish academic people from the extramural "incompetent populace" which unconcernedly obeys someone else's governance. Unfortunately, even within the academy not all academics appear to be self-governing subjects, since one can clearly distinguish between the true researchers and mere "technicians of learning" (*Werkkundige der Gelehrsamkeit*) (1979: 25). The latter Kant scornfully labels "the tools of the government" (*Werkzeuge der Regierung*) as opposed to the representatives of philosophy which is "by its nature free and admits of no command" (29). Placed in the position of the critical judge of disciplines by virtue of its being "independent of the government's command" (27), philosophy is expected to relinquish the "secondary disciplines" (45) of their "private property" for the benefit of the forthcoming "common freedom" (59–61).

Kant was the first thinker to raise a "quasi-discipline" to the status of the true representative of human freedom. He envisaged for philosophy not just the task to avert the attention of "minor faculties" from their restricted property toward universal freedom, but also to ensure the "enlightenment of the masses" (161). Yet this was an unreal expectation, as he himself admitted, because "the populace consists of idiots" (*das Volk, "welches aus Idioten besteht,"* 25, trans. modified). No wonder, then, that the humanities established in the next century neglected the "public instruction of the people" in favor of the formation of an exemplary subject capable of moving "among the increasingly differentiated spheres of human society" (Lloyd 1998: 33). This representative subject was expected to embody Kant's conviction of "the disposition and capacity of the human race to be the cause of its own advance toward the better," to be the author of its history (Kant 1979: 151). Owing to the exclusion of the masses, the authorization of humankind's history was relegated exclusively to such representative subjects. At the outset of the specialization of British university life in the second quarter of the nineteenth century, the Anglican priest William Whewell raised the imperative of systematic knowledge closely associated with philosophy. In a kind of a revanchiste aristocratic strategy that countered the advancement of the industrial bourgeoisie, he emphasized the necessity of evaluation and justification of discoveries made in particular disciplinary fields, according to their deducibility from the larger body of common scientific knowledge. This latter knowledge, supposed to channel the torrent of university activities in an edifying direction, was supposed to be preeminently theory-driven (Fuller 2000: 79–85).

In the second half of the nineteenth century, in a countermovement to this aristocratic strategy, a new "quasi-discipline" of English Literature, raised by Matthew Arnold to the status of the central agent of the populace's emancipation, substituted the hermetic philosophy that proved inadequate for such a purpose. Literature was more adaptable to the political formation of citizens in the increasingly disintegrated nation-state of the late nineteenth century. Nevertheless, it took several further decades before the study of literature managed to defy the resistance of the established scientific disciplines. Toward the end of the 1920s, with Arnold's academic follower Frank R. Leavis, it raised the claim to become the pivotal subject and point of liaison for all the other disciplines, one that provides a "strong humane centre" to increasingly "specialist studies" (Leavis 1969: 3). But although he envisaged literary study to be a discipline which is not one, since it is "concerned with training of a non-specialist intelligence" (Leavis 1948: 43), Leavis ferociously fought to establish its preeminence over its mighty rivals, the departments of classics and philosophy. He accordingly opted for its *careful disciplinary profiling* in order to prevent "blunting of edge, blurring of focus and muddled misdirection of attention: consequences of queering one discipline with the habits of another" (Leavis 1972: 213). As soon as it becomes part of a hierarchical distribution of power within the university, no "quasi-discipline" can transcend the corrupting influence of the academy, and wipe its hands clean of any interest (Moran 2002: 34). In the 1980s, Cultural Studies finally replaced Literary Studies, appropriating the techniques of subordinate and anonymous social strata excluded from the horizon of the latter. If in all these cases a "quasi-discipline" superseded the narrow-minded disciplines, this was because the *excommunicated residue of an anonymous and "idiotic" populace was placed at the service of its cosmopolitan authorization*. The same legacy would be taken up by the "singularists" who argue in the name of the suppressed "event-like contingency" of the Other.

Unfortunately, the unprecedented mobility of this residue's appointed representative requires the desperate immobility of the represented amorphous masses. In order for the first to remain permanently mobile, the second are expected to remain always easily mobilizable, i.e. flexible, investible and disposable (Fuller 2000: 104, 110). This suppressed asymmetry between the agencies and enablers in the corpus of allegedly emancipated humankind saw daylight as Cultural Studies started to attribute to each "other" his/her appropriate "subject position." Such a "politically correct" practice instituted the custodial relationship akin to the one between Kantian "free thinkers" and the "idiotic populace": the freedom of "representatives" was reinstated through a ceaseless detachment from the passionate "adherents of self-constraining." In order for the first to demonstrate their sovereign self-governing capacity, the latter were relegated to restricted gender, racial, ethnic or sexual positions. Thus the gap between the agencies and enablers, which was expected to be bridged in the agenda of class cosmopolitanism of Cultural Studies, was by its practice ultimately only deepened. Devoid of awareness of its institutional and disciplinary presuppositions, Cultural Studies regressed to the same agency that it was supposed to replace. Since it raised the same representative claims with regard to the all-encompassing anonymous basis as its fiercest opponent, Leavis's Literary Studies did, the political left and the political right turned out to be pure "mirror images" (Hillis Miller 1998: 63–64).

This might be the reason why Timothy Clark (2005: 19–20) recognized in Cultural Studies just a logical outcome of a principle leading from the Enlightenment through to late modernism: If the progressive narrative of emancipation is to succeed, its constitutive surplus of whatever sort is doomed to be victimized. After all, why did Cultural Studies experience such an easy acceptance by the Western universities if it was not owing to its ability to domesticate the inassimilable otherness of women, racial and ethnic varieties or gays and lesbians into a welcome diversity in the triumphant terms of continuous progress? By explaining literary texts in terms of "subject positions," argues Clark (23), the cultural critic "expresses a drive to position oneself as the embodiment of a supposedly fully enlightened eye to whom all these supposed subject positions and identities are visible and morally mappable." They become transparent in their particularism, unlike him or her who remains resilient to such acts of identification.

It was against this violence of cultural stereotyping, i.e. the pressure of the self-exempting literary norm to pin down everybody to its particular cultural identity, that Clark introduced what he called the "poetics of singularity." As he interprets this central concept, singularities are resilient to any kind of classification of their otherness, displaying an exemplary European capability of *vanishing mediation* (Balibar 2004: 203–235). Europe was often regarded as repeatedly becoming "other than the other," being born ever anew, jumping out of any allocated temporal or spatial category, and continuously operating as an invisible enabler of all agencies. As Hannah Arendt, one of the proponents of Clark's poetics would put it, singularity resides "outside determination" by the others' agencies, resistant to their aggressive appropriation since it is completely unpredictable and contingent. Thanks to such characteristics, its untiring enabling mimics and outsmarts all agencies imposed upon it. In the delineated profile of singularity, the legacy of early German Romanticist "exuberant abundance of life" derived from the modern idea of the literary is unmistakable. All advocates of the poetics of singularity as

Clark represents them, i.e., Heidegger, Gadamer, Blanchot and Derrida, therefore tacitly agree that such singularity is epitomized by modern European literature engendered by Romanticism.

As if suppressing this common source, their idea of literature attempts to detach itself from both the elite European literature promoted by the project of Comparative Literature and the outsmarting maneuvers of the socially disregarded applied in the project of Cultural Studies. Both projects were eventually caught up by the identity pattern of narrative progression they initially starkly opposed – and the key "singularist" concepts like the unworked or confronted (Nancy 1986, 2003), unavowable (Blanchot 1983) or coming community (Agamben 1993) ferociously attack this pattern. Paradoxically, in order to deconstruct it they engage a very similar kind of evasive literary performance to that inaugurated by Cultural Studies as their antagonist. In the name of the socially disregarded, "culturalists" also advocated the idea of literature as an "excluded enabling domain" against the representative idea of literature of English or Comparative Literature departments. Since their envisioned emancipation failed, "singularists" now extend the jurisdiction of the modern European idea of literature to serve as the pre-contractual basis of human community.

11.3 Cruelly attached to unfathomable singularity

What opposes the literary community to political communities is that it establishes a co-belonging, which does not rely on any particular identifying predicates attributed to subjects. As Giorgio Agamben explains in *The Coming Community*, with regard to this focusing on singularity literature is similar to love: it introduces an eventful relation between partners that precedes or withdraws their division into subject on the one hand and predicate on the other. I do not love the other because she as a subject possesses particular qualities due to her belonging to a community of whatever kind. Disabling any such self-assuring judgment on my part, she draws me outside myself exactly by being singular, i.e. belonging only to herself. Being expropriated of all identity attributes, the lovable is "never the intelligence of some thing, of this or that quality or essence, but only the intelligence of an intelligibility" (Agamben 1993: 2), i.e. of *being-thus (tale-quale)*. What characterizes the singular mode of *being-thus* is precisely the evacuation of any protective proper nature (102), i.e. a complete exposure, which enables the related singularities to touch their impossibility instead of enjoying power (32), to experience their vulnerability instead of exhibiting self-assurance (39). If singularities so radically skip the tranquilizing identity attributes of existing political communities, this is because they are completely handed over to the *com-*

ing one (11), i.e. they get their face (or determination) from a disquieting empty space beyond representation (67–68). Because of this complete exposure to an absolute non-totalizable exterior they become a singular "whatever" (*quodlibet, qualunque*) (67). What therefore resolutely distinguishes this coming from the existing community is that the first, being completely devoid of attributes, determines its members without dividing the proper from the improper, the intelligible from the unintelligible, the human from the inhuman; it gives them a face without any distinctiveness. People thus belong to each other without any prior condition of that belonging (86). After Agamben, "if humans could [...] not be-thus in this or that particular biography, but be only *the* thus, their singular exteriority and their face, then they would for the first time enter into a community without presuppositions and without subjects, into a communication without the incommunicable" (65). The coming community produces no human face as opposed to inhuman defacement inasmuch as in the place of human essence it establishes a void. Impossible to turn into the means for any human end, *this void forms the ultimate horizon of the idea of singularity*. It prevents singularities from being coupled to any common property, center or identity.

Sketched thus, Agamben's argument, put forth in 1990, establishes a clear family resemblance with the radical techniques of Blanchot's impersonalization and Foucault's self-defacement as delineated in chapter ten. Such placing of their selves under consistent literary erasure – Derrida's *sous rature*, in its turn a translation of Heidegger's *kreuzweise Durchstreichung* – strategically opened a sort of posttraumatic friendship grown from disaster, *l'amitié-des-astres, Sternenfreundschaft*. With this peculiar rendering reminiscent of Blanchot's *L'Écriture du desastre* Derrida points to a bond without a bond established among the de-identified since deceased humans. The basic prerogative of such a posttraumatic friendship is an absolute detachment of friends from all identity attributes ("what-ness"), which enables them to achieve the condition of a pure, singular and irreducible "who-ness" (Blanchot 1980: 50, 1971: 328), tantamount to Agamben's "being-thus" that resists any political denomination (Derrida 1994b: 331). The politics of such a being-in-common is the politics of consistent estrangement, evacuation and emptying of the identified self. As I have tried to demonstrate in the previous chapter, an irrevocable disappearance of their selves in the labyrinth of writing was Blanchot and Foucault's "joint venture" (Foucault 1972: 17, 1985: 9; Blanchot 1971: 328). This longing for an empty emplacement – withdrawal of friends into an irrevocable absence (Blanchot 1983: 21) – receives its authorization from an absolutely open yet-to-come (*à-venir*), a utopian space of unconstrained freedom to which the friends attach their hopes. If "culturalists" argued in the name of the socially disregarded, homeless masses, then "singularists" argue in the name of singular "whos" (lovers, friends and affiliates) departed, deceased, emptied, de-identified, denuded, absolutely detached, irrevocably absent and brought to a traumatic silence. In the argument of singularists, complete ontological void and emptiness substitute for social anonymity and amorphousness.

Such an essentially *hypothetical*, "imagined cosmopolitan community" (Robbins 1998: 2), which is grouped around an "empty space," sets the horizon of Agamben's ideal of singularity (1993: 10). In evoking it, he spontaneously works in the same early Romanticist tradition inaugurated by Kant's assumptive establishment of *sensus communis* (2007: 68), as do Blanchot and Foucault, or Bakhtin with his carnival utopia for that matter. Bakhtin envisages the socially and culturally liberated individuals responsible exclusively to an "exotopic" (*vnenakhodimoe*) Third Person (*tret'oe litso*), the all-uniting horizon of all communities (Bakhtin 1979: 305–306). This divine authority is, in its turn, a replica of Friedrich Schlegel's God, whose redemptive intervention enabled the Romanticist agency's uncoupling from all inherited political, cultural and/or social bonds with its fellow citizens. From His neutral and indifferent vantage point everything appears to be "exchangeable" and "de-personified" (Bakhtin 1979: 371). As regards this divine supreme detachment and disinterestedness, Bakhtin believed that every human being worthy of the name must strive to become an *imago Dei*, i.e. to evacuate systematically all selfish passions and inclinations from his or her earthly self. According to Friedrich Schlegel: "For a man who has achieved a certain level of the universality of formation, his inner being is an ongoing chain of the most enormous revolutions" (1963: 82–83).

By inventing his self-authoring modern self determined to become a "pure 'man in man'," "deprived of any social or pragmatic real-life concretization," "independent of all real-life, concrete social forms (the forms of family, social or economic class, life's stories)," Bakhtin (1984: 264) spontaneously subscribes to this Schlegelian formula. He thereby anticipates Agamben's, Blanchot's and Foucault's "cruel optimism," defined by Lauren Berlant (2011: 1–2) as a passionate attachment to something that actively impedes the aim of this attachment. The delineated tradition fully corroborates her thesis of "a sustaining inclination to return to the scene of fantasy that enables you to expect that *this* time, nearness to *this* thing will help you or a world to become different in just the right way." The same kind of optimism, though certainly mediated by other relays than in the case of Bakhtin or Agamben, resonates in Blanchot's *free gathering of de-identified humans* from May '68. He describes an atmosphere in which "anyone could speak to anyone else, anonymously, impersonally, welcomed with no other justification than that of being another human" (1987: 63, trans. modified) (*un autre home*, 1986b: 10).

In order to establish his messianic community "without presuppositions and without subjects," i.e. consisting of mere singularities, Agamben along the same lines introduces the supreme authority of *bare life* (*la nuda vita*). In the way he elaborates this concept in the essay "Absolute Immanence" (Agamben 1999a), bare life establishes an identifying relationship between the subject and the object, but itself cannot be rendered in terms of any identity whatsoever. In a sense, it operates like "Europe, vanishing mediator," setting up the identities of all others in such a way as to obfuscate its own identity. As Balibar (2004: 220) has formulated in his path-breaking essay, "*Europe is a borderland* rather than an entity that 'has' *borders*." It enables conjunctions and disjunctions between the agencies by circumventing the status of agency – an absolute enabler as it were. We come to the same conclusion if we inspect the crucial terms of Deleuze and Foucault, Agamben's philosophical "relays" in this essay. According to Deleuze, *lived experience* (*le vécu*) (1995: 4) escapes the terms of whatever Something (such as subject, consciousness, truth, person, or individuality); according to Foucault, *life* (2001a: 1593) roots both the subject and the object in the unexplored terrain of errancy (*mépris*) rather than a firm transcendence. Both "lived experience" engaged by Deleuze and "life" engaged by Foucault refer to *utter contingency* germane to the Romanticist concept of life. Building upon this richly resonating and "cruelly optimistic" European tradition, they pave the way for bare life as Agamben's "absolute enabler."

While differentiating the entire political field, bare life analogously escapes all discriminations. Its *vanishing intrusion* into the area of the political is the "foundational event of modernity" (Agamben 1998: 4). Yet Agamben repeatedly reminds us that this modern "inclusion of bare life in the political realm" (6) implies an exclusion of everything that does not conform to the differences established in this realm. With modernity, between the included determinate life and the excluded indeterminate life emerges a strange complicity of "the most implacable enemies" (10). Whereas politically identified life enjoys legal power, bare life stripped of all identity marks affirms itself only through the unworking of the legislated community. "In Western politics, bare life has the peculiar privilege of being that whose exclusion founds the common being of men" (7, trans. modified) (*la città degli uomini*, 10). Modern human community rests on the void; this traumatic hole fatally infects all communal relations. To point out this crux of his argument, Agamben directs all his philosophical attention to the peculiar "non-relation" between political life (conceived as fullness) and bare life (conceived as emptiness). His discussion of Deleuze in the essay *Absolute Immanence* makes clear that these two "conjoined disjunctive realms" operate not only by way of conditioning but also by subverting and dislocating each other. Because of this "mole of the transcendent within immanence," which the latter cannot but "disgorge [...] everywhere" (Deleuze and Guattari 1994b: 46–47), there is no historical continuity in the process of the world's becoming but only a succession of "between-times (*entre-temps*), between-moments (*entre-moments*)" (Deleuze 2005: 29, 1995: 5).

How does Agamben translate Deleuze's thesis? As no rule can establish itself without the relation of the exception to it (1998: 18), *the rule is engulfed in the whirl of exception*, entailing a series of what Agamben terms the thresholds of indiscernability (*soglia d'indifferenza*) or zones of indistinction (*zona d'indistinzione*) (1998: 4, 9, 18, 27, 28 etc., see esp. 63, 112, 181). Their perfect emptiness is "the place of a ceaselessly updated decision in which the caesurae and their rearticulation are always dislocated and displaced anew" (Agamben 2004: 38); they are the motors of an ongoing change. Since the advent of modernity, we live in a world in which the unlocalizable non-juridical state of exception makes the condition of the im/possibility of the localizable juridical order or political territory (20). Each territory is de-territorialized by this excluded enabling domain; nothing can escape the deactivating force of bare life that is irresistible in its vertiginous undoing. As soon as in the medium of *live beings* a distinction between the subject and object is established, it collapses back into the indiscernible medium of bare life that surpasses them both. The ultimate inseparability of the subject from the object explains Agamben's recourse to Spinoza's "undecidable" usage of the verb-as-noun (1999a: 234–235): at that time the so-called middle voice, that unrecognizably collapses the grammatical subject and object was an important topic of Western theory (Pecora 1991; Pepper 1997; White 1999; LaCapra 2001: 19–42).

On the one hand, Agamben's persistently reemerging concepts of the threshold of indiscernability and the zone of indistinction are clearly related to Blanchot's category of the "relation at a distance" (or "relation without relation" (Large 2006: 4)) as a new and "explosive" "power of determination" of the modern self (Blanchot 1993: 251). Blanchot states that with modernity, a disabling enablement of the two incompatible terms, the transcendental (*autre*) and the empirical (*autrui*), arises: The one simultaneously empowers and expropriates the other (1993: 255; Suglia 2001: 59). On the other hand, Agamben's concepts are equally reminiscent of Foucault's *The Archeology of Knowledge* where it is said that "[t]he formal a priori and the historical a priori neither belong to the same level nor share the same nature: if they intersect, it is because they occupy two different dimesions" (Foucault 1972: 128). In Blanchot's and Foucault's quasi-transcendentalism these two incompatible but conjoined a prioris "encounter each other everywhere, establishing a constellation of the utmost ethical and political importance" (Rothberg 2000: 62). Inasmuch as the transcendental not only *determines* the empirical but also *results* from it, their disjunctive conjuncture establishes a discontinuous temporality of the "future anterior." In lieu of smooth historical continuity, the past disrupts the future and the future subverts the past. Beyond Blanchot and Foucault, two important relays of his redemptive thought, Agamben's messianic temporality refers to Walter Benjamin's equivocal concept of the *Ursprung* (origin but, etymologically, also the primordial leap). In *The Origin of the German Tragic Drama*, Benjamin interpreted this concept as neither fully the cause nor fully the effect, but simultaneously both (Benjamin 1980: 226). His *Ursprung* entitles all constituents of becoming to completely rearrange its flow by arbitrarily leaping out of it at any point. As soon as such a leap into the uncertain exterior of the world's becoming takes place, it engulfs (*reißt hinein*) the whole stream of becoming in its unpredictable whirl.

Agamben's firm adherence to Benjamin's messianic time makes him argue that Deleuze derives his concept of "immanence" not so much from *manere* (to remain [within the same]) as from *manare* (to flow out, to spring forth [into something else]) (Agamben 1999a: 223). The effects of immanence do not naturally *emanate* from the continuous substance of life but discontinuously and unexpectedly *spring forth* from it. "Immanence flows forth; it always, so to speak, carries a colon with it. Yet this springing forth, far from leaving itself, remains incessantly and vertiginously within itself. This is why Deleuze can state [...] that 'immanence is the very vertigo of philosophy'." (226) Everything that it has thrown out, immanence takes care to reintroduce into the intermittent and discontinuous stream of becoming. Like Blanchot and Foucault in their quasi-transcendentalism, Agamben privileges this indeterminate whirl of becoming (the Absolute Enabler) over its determinate constituents (agencies), which are located in the realm of the political. He derives this priority of ethical non-relation over political relations also from Deleuze and Guattari's interpretation of Foucault: "The actual is not what we are but, rather, what we become, what we are in the process of becoming – that is to say, the Other, our becoming-other." (Deleuze and Guattari 1994b: 112) That Foucault privileges the whimsical becoming over the given present, follows from his consistent introduction of the exterminated exterior enabler into the acknowledged interior agency in the paradoxical form of the Outside-interior (*le Dehors-intérieur*) (113). Deleuze and Guattari infer: "Perhaps this is the supreme act of philosophy: not so much to think THE plane of immanence as to show that it is there, unthought in every plane, and to think it in this way as the outside and inside of thought, as the not-external outside and the not-internal inside." (59–60)

In compulsively repeating concepts such as the threshold of indiscernability and the zone of indistinction, and in consistently pushing all empirical evidence toward that which remains indiscernible or indeterminate, Agamben pays the highest possible respect to this "plane of immanence." In an exemplary gesture of "cruel optimism," he attaches all of his hopes to this excluded enabling domain that takes care to subvert and crush them. As a result, in Agamben's philosophical narrative "mourning becomes the law" (Rose 1996) of our being-in-common. It threatens to "disarticulate relations, confuse self and other, and collapse all distinctions" in a kind of "post-traumatic acting out" "caught up in the compulsive repetition of traumatic scenes" (LaCapra 2001: 21). A powerful desire to remain within a traumatically empty emplacement of love or friendship partners engenders an excessive restaging of the traumatic scene. The desire is so powerful that in Agamben's political philosophy, akin to Derrida's "messianism without a Messiah," the holy obligation to the radically transcendent and postponed divinity obliterates secular and immediate commitments to the fellow human beings (LaCapra 2004: 145–151). The "passionate attachment" of these ethics to the all-engulfing "vanishing mediator" uncouples it completely from the political realm of norm and law.

As if testifying to this inclination of his thought to absolutize the sublime, Agamben proffers the "localized unlocalizability" of the concentration camp as the most prominent example of Foucault's Outside-interior in the modern political space. "As the *absolute* space of exception, the camp is topologically different from a simple space of confinement" (Agamben 1998: 22, [italics added]), i.e. Foucault's prison. It paradigmatically demonstrates that sovereign law rests on the *structure of the ban*, which not merely excludes but *abandons* the subaltern, i.e. exposes and threatens it at the threshold of its political order (28). The ban therefore consists of a particular kind of non-relation between the political order and a "mass without qualities" (Deleuze). It is primarily in this sense of being *nonrelated* (29) (*l'irrelato* (1995: 35)) that Agamben raises the concentration camp to the paradigm of European modernity (1998: 166). Like Jean-Luc Nancy, from whom he takes the idea of the ban, he does not restrict extermination to Jewish destiny but refers, for instance, to the camps during the war in the former Yugoslavia (Nancy 2000: 145; Agamben 1998: 176). In the globalized state of exception anybody can become the subaltern on given circumstances, which completely accords with Derrida's ill-reputed declaration "Each other is altogether other" (1992e: 68, 76–77, 1995b: 68, 78) that dangerously equates justice with deconstruction. Like Blanchot's friendship or love, Deleuze's "lines of flight" take up this lead, continually drawing away from determinate sovereign identities toward indeterminate subaltern multiplicities, from the life of human beings to bare life. This subterranean force of exception multiplies neighborhood zones inside the political territory. Deterritorialization of political territories is incessantly on its way, drawing every discernible item into its redemptive whirl of becoming. The battle is ultimately won by the power of the cruelly optimistic attachment to an entirely vague prospect.

11.4 The counter-narrative of singularity

Envisioned in these posttraumatic terms, Agamben's "community to come" founded by death clearly resonates, though it is not explicitly mentioned, in the book of his compatriot Adriana Cavarero, *Relating Narratives*, originally published in 1997. Both treat the Altogether Other that is beyond representation as the point of departure of individual and communal self-representation. This entails a constitutive priority of the *ethical non-relation to alterity*, inassimilable to any horizon of communal being, over the *political relation to other human beings* taking place within this horizon.

Cavarero starts with the conception of subject formation developed by Hannah Arendt, one of the philosophers who feature prominently in Clark's genealogy of the idea of singularity. In *The Human Condition* (1958) and *The Life of Mind* (1971) Arendt considers each human being to be unique yet acquiring its irreplaceable who-ness through the exposure to another human being. As it is only through the other's gaze and voice that I am identified in my singularity, I am unable to master my self-display but must always search for it in You. It is because of such constitutive dependency on You that Cavarero originally titles her book *Tu che mi guardi, tu che mi racconti*: regard me, narrate me who I am! With Blanchot from *L'écriture du desastre* (1980: 37–41) and *La communauté inavouable* (1983: 15–20) as a silent supporter, she insists on what Heidegger called "permanent reopening" (*ständige Unabgeschlossenheit*) or Bataille in his turn "the principle of incompleteness" of the self, although without mentioning any one of these "male" thinkers directly. Nonetheless, Cavarero sides with their opinion that the self is fundamentally and enduringly called into question by the *vanishing Other* by opposing Arendt, who highlights *another human being*. Every narrative of the self provided by such an evasive Other can be only provisional and open (and not finished and closed, as stated by Arendt).

Supported by these tacit philosophical "affiliates," she disagrees with Arendt as to the capability of this You to close up my life-story: the latter has to be constantly re-narrated, as no *determinate* external alterity can resolve definitely and in a satisfactory way the uniqueness immanent to the self, not even its death, as Arendt assumes. For if the self is dead, the storyteller cannot but treat it in the third person, cannot but talk about it to someone else as in the epic narrative. Yet the gist of Cavarero's argument goes against the pre-modern impersonal epic in favor of the modern personal narrative: the protagonist has to be in the second and not the third person, a *you* and not *s/he* of the storytelling (Cavarero 2000: 32, 59, 92, 116). For the singularity of my self to come to the fore, a counter-narrative to the traditional epic narrative is needed. "Storytelling is the living's desire for narration, not the desire for the immortal fame of the dead." (100) In the wake of Agamben's presented argumentation, Cavarero states that, similar to love or friendship, this narrative is based on a nude co-appearance (*comparizione*) of *me* and *you*. Deprived of the intermediacy of any *what*, two *whos* are irretrievably exposed to one another and forced to confront their limits. Her thesis finds support also in Blanchot's claim that friends never speak *about* each other but only *to* each other (1997: 291) or Derrida's claim that a friend exists for me only as *who*, never as *what* (Derrida 1994b: 326–327). As the Italian neologism *comparizione* testifies, Cavarero tacitly appeals not only to Agamben's *The Coming Community* but also to Jean-Luc Nancy's *The Unworked Community*, where the French *comparution* is equally peculiarly used with the meaning of co-appearance (or compearance) of two mutually exposed, tightly co-dependent singularities (Blanchot 1993: 66; Nancy 1986: 165). They share nothing except finitude determined by mutual contact zones, which establish between them a relationship of fatal dis/juncture (Nancy 1986: 70). Nancy's being-in-common is a face-to-face preventing any immanence, autonomy and individuality of its constituencies (Dalton 2000: 34–35). What transpires from these covert references to Agamben, Blanchot, and Nancy is a *literary community* established among the friends, love and narrative partners caught in an interminable search for completion.

Like Agamben and Nancy who in the formation of the self prioritize the non-relation to radical alterity over the relation to the fellow human being, Cavarero states: I am desperately given over (*consegnato*) to the otherness of the other in the unprotected fragility of my inaugural existence (2000: 109). What I thereby desire is an equally inassimilable *you* "that comes before the *we* (*noi*), before the plural *you* (*voi*), and before the *they* (*loro*)," that is "truly an other, in her uniqueness and distinction" (90). In repeatedly emphasizing a nudity of the co-apparent self and other, Cavarero means that they cannot *represent* but only *address* each other, which is a radically performative relation between partners that next to love or friendship only personal (counter-)narrative is capable of. Two performative discourses (Cavarero skips Blanchot's and Derrida's discourse of friendship probably because it is, from her feminist perspective, too "manly" an affair) are thus singled out against the negative foil of all the constative others. However, if narrative *performance* comes into being only through the abandonment of everything that characterizes narrative *representation*, it profiles itself as a self-exemption from its pressure. Like lovers who tear down social distinctions in favor of their basically naked selves (110) – and lovers also in Blanchot's view (1983: 83) abandon their identities through the complete exposure to each other – partners in the narrative performance exhibit their "generic selves" against all narrative identifications brought upon them (Cavarero 2000: 10, 53). They push their singularity to the extreme by parenthesizing the resistance of "communal immanence." If society's identification procedures gradually suppress a "totally nude self-exposure

[…] naked and bared of *what*" characteristic of the "first chapter of our life" (38), then love and narrative are supposed to recuperate this lost singularity of our self by suspending identification procedures. Due to its restoring capacity to make my life begin always anew – an operation Foucault in *The Order of Things* termed *recommencement* – Cavarero takes personal narrative of singularization to be systematically emptying out my commonality established by the epic narrative of identification.

By highlighting cosmopolitan operations such as self-exemption, parenthesizing and suspension, Cavarero not only has recourse to a long-term messianic tradition of the unworking of the working days from the perspective of the Sabbath, as elaborated upon by Agamben (2005b: 95–112). She also inserts her personal narrative into a persistent self-evacuation from external identifications germane to the idea of literature in modern literary theory (since the inauguration of the Russian Formalist "politics of estrangement"; Tihanov 2005). She conceives the denuding operation of the literary narrative as a systematic opposition to the oppression of the political community. Bearing in mind this prominent role of literature in achieving the singular self, it is astonishing that her argument of the naked exposure of literary interlocutors strikingly recalls Levinas's naked exposure of the ethical face of the Other. Levinas's face equally deprives our "imperial I" of its ability to judge, disarms and empties it of its acquired habits (2001: 269–270), forces it to become a singular I instead of the mere embodiment of the Mind (1969: 276). This submerged reference to Levinas is astonishing because of his well-known reservations concerning the "feminine allurement" of literary narratives. Due to its "capacity for interrogation" and permanent "unsaying what it has said" (Levinas and Kearney 1986: 22), he regards *philosophy* as the only proper (male) instrument of establishing the "primordial language" of addressing and touching (Levinas 1987c: 313, 319–320).[3] Yet Cavarero for her part resolutely rejects philosophy as the constative (male) identification of the human *in general* in favor of the personal narrative as the (female) performative of human *singularity*.

According to her, what I really am remains forever hidden from myself, beyond the possibility of my positive, constative knowledge. The only access I have to my singularity is through the memory that keeps telling me my personal story.

---

[3] Levinas acknowledges only maternal femininity as a form of responsible existence, not the feminine caress and voluptuosity. "Eroticism is a loss of perspective. It does not aspire to the infinite transcendence required for desire, which is reserved for the absolute alterity of the divine. As an evasion of significance, the feminine can never take on the aspect of divine for Levinas. The dimension of the intimacy in the midst of existence is opened by the feminine, not the dimension of transcendence." (Vasseleu 1998: 106) For further discussion of this question, see also Irigaray (1993: 185–207) and Chanter (2001: 170–224).

But in as much as my natal self is never accessible to its recollecting reach, the story in question achieves no more than to act out this *constitutive void*: instead of being mastered or represented in the form of a narrative object, my I thus comes to the fore in the form of the denuded narrating subject. Due to such an appearance of the naked self that was supposed to be absolved by the narrative, the story of my uniqueness has to be told over and over (Cavarero 2000: 34). Contrary to the closed-up epic narrative characteristic of the narratological account, Cavarero in such a way insists on an unresolved alterity in the midst of narrative, which seeks to be externalized ever anew (42–43).

> What we have called an altruistic ethics of relation does not support empathy, identification, or confusions. Rather this ethic desires a you that is truly an other, in her uniqueness and distinction [...] The necessary other is indeed here a finitude that remains irremediably an other in all the fragile and unjudgeable insubstitutability of her existing. (92)

Cavarero's personal literary narrative accordingly subverts the classic narrative pattern of political identification against which, despite the differences between their philosophies, Levinas too leveled his ethical accusations. He condemned it for turning the plural and discontinuous "living time" opened to "the salvation of becoming" into the linear and homogeneous "fate" of historical temporality (Levinas 1989: 139–145). Toward the end of *Totality and Infinity*, historical narrative is blamed for taming the unlimited possibility of singular past events through their assimilation into a smooth continuous flow.[4] On closer inspection, Levinas's historical narrative coincides with what Nancy in *The Unworked Community* termed "mythic narrative," ascribing it a foundational, structuring power in the matters of communal life (1991: 49). Political community appeals to myth in order to found, confirm and perpetuate the identity of its subjects (50–51). However, in Nancy's as in Levinas's conception, myth and political community coexist and implicate each other in their common effort to compensate for the fundamental incompleteness and dependence of the self on the other.

Nancy's use of the concept of myth invokes a powerful Western tradition. In the sense Aristotle used the term, mythos refers to the process of recognition, i.e.

---

[4] Levinas's insistence on the irreducible singularity of events and his resistance to their assimilation in the historical narrative is a peculiar reversal of Foucault's demand for the "eventialization" (1996: 393; *événementialisation* (1990: 47–48)) of history, i.e. a persistent disengagement of constituencies from the historical whole as well as incessant separation of the present from the past. In Foucault's idea, instead of being determined by history, each present event assumes a potentially determining, that is to say critical position with regard to the past. In Levinas's idea, the resistance to the closing-up of historical narrative comes from the past rather than present events. The unresolved past, and not the present, "perforates" the historical flow.

the passage of the subject from the state of blindness into the state of insight (Cave 1988: 4). Mythos enables the subject to become a communal being, i.e. to establish a belonging to a superior collective agency. Beware that narratology has followed this pattern, transmitted by Hegelian philosophy in an elaborated form, not only in its early definition of the story but also in its understanding of the reading process. These progressions amount to an overcoming of the state of mental bondage and exemplify the process of a successful subject formation. Through such narrative of coming to oneself, the subject becomes accountable, capable of representing itself as well as others. S/he overcomes the natural state of self-ignorance, self-deceit, or self-indulgence to reach the civilized state of self-knowledge, self-consciousness, or self-mastery. Only inasmuch as subjects are capable of standing for themselves and others do they count as political agencies. Those who for any reason are unable to do this – whether due to infancy or old age, physical or mental illness, character weakness, moral corruption, linguistic or cultural incapacity, abnormal inclinations and habits, irresponsible behavior, or lack of recognizable identity – go unaccounted for. This predicament lasts for as long a period as such enablers do not qualify for political community by relinquishing their unaccountability.

Consider, for instance, the early Freudian conception of how the patient's narrative proceeds in the context of therapeutic dialogue. In the course of storytelling, s/he is expected to overcome his/her self-ignorance by self-enlightenment, by getting rid of his/her deceptive past. This well documented European tradition explains why Nancy places myth at the very heart of political community. Myth is for Aristotle the bearer of the responsible, self-cultivating European agency in contradistinction to the irresponsible and self-enclosed Asian enabler. It not merely discursively engenders a self-conscious community (Nancy 1986: 109); it also produces its representative subject entitled to make promises (Nietzsche 1996: 39), or to join past and present in order to form a smooth and reliable identity. Recall that, for Gasché (2009: 26–27), Europe takes responsibility for the promise of universal humankind, self-authorized to execute this "infinite task."

Cavarero, Levinas and Nancy are however not the first thinkers to challenge this European mainstream pattern of subject-formation. Paving the way for their philosophical critique, Nietzsche was the first to call attention to the oblivion, cleavage and discontinuity inherent to the consciousness-raising carried out by it. "Forgetfulness is no mere *vis inertiae*, as the superficial believe; it is rather an active – in the strictest sense, positive – inhibiting capacity" (1996: 39), moreover "a property of all action" (1957: 12). No definite passage from the irresponsible to the responsible subject, enabler to agency, is possible for the reason that the initial opposition *between* them reemerges at the end of the operation *within* the agency itself. According to Nietzsche, one never gives an account of oneself without being called upon by a social authority, put under a form of institutional pressure, and urged to respond to a demand to normalize oneself. This is why every acquisition of the status of agency implies subjection in lieu of sovereignty. Think, for instance, of confession or its modern descendant psychoanalytic therapy, as well as of giving a statement about an event to a police officer, appearing as a witness in court, or even writing down one's memoirs. Does not this official pattern of subject formation spawn a conclusion that one becomes the master of oneself only on condition of obeying a sanctioned authority, i.e. subjecting oneself to it? In taking up this thread of Nietzsche's, Foucault demonstrates in the first volume of *The History of Sexuality* how "pastoral power," originally born within Christian institutions, has survived into modernity. But the bourgeois disciplinary mastering of oneself is based precisely on the disavowal of this surrendering as its condition of im/possibility. In order to rescue oneself from the permanent capillary surveillance of social authorities, one internalizes it over the course of time, spontaneously conforming to the demand for self-mastering. The sovereign subject is someone who has succeeded in adopting the control of the others over itself.

Nietzsche's polemical argument highlights the "bourgeois" obliteration of this self-disciplining as the condition of the im/possibility of sovereignty. Rather than as a way to achieve proper autonomy, he regards the exemplary narrative of subject formation primarily as a foreclosure of unruly bodily drives by codified consciousness. Rendering self-consciousness as a commanding and censorious instance (2010: §354 and 355) rather than the locus of accomplished social consensus, Nietzsche's argument unmasks power dissymmetry between consciousness (as the herd's site) and the unconscious (as the individual's site). This does not mean that he blames human subjects for such a submissive formation of theirs. They have no choice but to obey the social rules of behavior and adopt forgetfulness as the law of their survival. Nietzsche even treats oblivion as the gate-keeper of human happiness: being unable to be rid of a myriad of memories, to select the necessary from the contingent, one is not just deprived of a proper future but at risk of being regarded as unaccountable. Therefore, obedience to external authority is not a matter of free deliberation. *To be a subject means to accept a subjected position, to become a self means to surrender to the Other.* This is why the agency is always an enabler. Whoever attempts to avoid such auto-subjection is subjected to harsh sanctions.

With Nietzsche's dismantling of the European foundational myth in *The Joyful Wisdom* and *On the Genealogy of Morals*, the European exemplary narrative of subject-making was transferred from an instrument of social cohesion to an instrument of political power. The ultimate effects of the European foundational myth are oppressive. This is the point of connection for Nancy's argument. Precisely in as much as it surreptitiously imposes the terms of *commonality*, myth suppresses existence in its *singularity*; to get rid of this suppression, its foundational fictions have to be constantly unworked (*désœuvré*). Invoking Blanchot's concept of *désœuvrement* in the very title of his book, Nancy makes clear how important a place this permanent interruption of mythic narrative, conceived as the repressive political instrument of subject formation, takes in his conception. Not the narrative itself but merely its relentless unworking can take care of freedom.

> It is the interruption of myth which reveals to us the distinctive or hidden nature of community. In myth, community was proclaimed: in interrupted myth, community affirms itself as what Blanchot has called "the unavowable community" [...] the withdrawal of communion or communitarian ecstasy are revealed in the interruption of myth. (Nancy 1991: 58)

However, as is often the case with Nietzsche's provocative and audacious arguments, this one also appears based on a simple "revolutionary reversal": consensus into dissent, continuity into discontinuity, recognition into misrecognition. If it is equally instrumentalized in both cases, is there a substantial difference between the narrative as the liberating and the oppressive instrument of subject formation? Do we give an account of ourselves exclusively after having been pressed by an institutional authority? And is narrative to be unreservedly identified with the discursive rules of that authority? If we were to grant such an assumption, this would imply that no one has the desire to examine the state of his or her self-knowledge until requested to do so. One's familiar self-representation would be broken only upon someone's external insistence. Yet what if narrative comes into being as an attempt to bridge an *already existing break* in my identity, if its discursive otherness is just a necessary means to repair my fundamentally uncertain self? This would turn narrative *from an oppressive agency into an enabling condition of identity* by rendering it as an equivocal and diversely investible instance.

Such a cautious conception is much closer to the later than the earlier Foucault, who uncritically sided with Nietzsche's unilateral rendering of power as force. Inasmuch as it prepares the way for Nancy's *unworked myth* as well as Cavarero's *personal literary narrative*, this more complex concept of the narrative deserves closer inspection. Whereas Foucault in the first volume of *History of Sexuality* (1975) interprets confession in a Nietzschean vein as a practice infiltrated by the Victorian power regime with the aim of eliciting sexual truths from its subjects, several years later he treats it as a speech act enabling the self to appear to the divine Other (Foucault 1983). If one wants to develop one's own truth through speech, one is required to disappear, sacrifice oneself as a real body and real existence. This means that, toward the end of his life, Foucault abandons the idea of power as a self-sufficient force and introduces in lieu of it a mobile and heterogeneous field of codes, rules and norms opened up toward a constitutively *exterior enabler*. According to this new conception hospitable to the unexpected arrival of the Other, the field of power is demarcated not only by a sovereign discursive authority with whose prescriptions all speech acts are supposed to conform, but by an unpredictable *non-discursive enabler* as well. This excluded non-discursive zone lurks behind the borders of discourse and operates as a displaced addressee of the broadest variety of actions performed within it. This Absolute Enabler sets the ultimate horizon of freedom for all agency-formations, which take place within the restrictive field of discourse. Every subject irrespective of his/her particular position within this field is appointed by this exterior Other for the continuous detachment from his/her discursively given agency and thus invited into an interminable process of self-remaking strategically interrupted by re-beginnings.

It is time to return to Adriana Cavarero's argument about singular narrative formation. She takes Foucault's non-discursive Enabler as her starting point. The other whom I am seeking to tell me who I am is as completely beyond identification as I am myself; we are pushing each other's politics of estrangement to the extreme. Cavarero contends that personal narrative is devoted to exhibiting an elusive "generic self" that originates in the singular event of birth. However, her insistence on the essentially *non-discursive* profile of narrative self-formation is as polemically exaggerated as is Nietzsche's argument about its preeminently *discursive* nature. The singular conception of narrative departs from the assumption of a naked baby as a "first chapter of our life." Yet a "totally nude self-exposure [...] naked and bared of *what*," as Cavarero would have it (2000: 38), barely exists at the origin of human life. Suffice to recall Lacan's warning that the total symbolic net envelops human life long before the human being enters the world (1966: 279) or Althusser's reminder that each individual is always a subject, even before its birth, predestined to become such by its firmly ideologically structured family configuration (1982: 128).

Therefore, ethical nakedness is not so much a *prerogative* as a retroactive *effect* of the evacuation of political masks. It results from their unmasking. Nevertheless, Cavarero raises the imperative, "social qualifications must be torn down by lovers" (2000: 110) in favor of the originally naked selves that would otherwise be forgotten. She thus transforms an arbitrary effect into the logical prerogative of an Absolute Enabler. The same holds for her philosophical antagonist Levinas who promotes the elusive face of the Other into the ethical authority that questions me, disarms me and empties me out of my political attributes (2001b: 269–270). His Absolute Enabler equally resists all attempts to be politically attributed. As soon as such an attribution happens, it withdraws, departing into an irretrievable past (271, 275).

The apparent opponents actually mirror one another: What Levinas renders as the face *mutatis mutandis* amounts to what Cavarero calls the uniqueness of the Other (in each other). In both cases, at stake is an Absolute Enabler that addresses the storyteller by "breaking the careless spontaneity of his naïve perseverance in life" (Levinas 1989: 86) and by demanding to be responded to. In Cavarero's view to respond means to resist all attempts at identification, which is the philosophical or masculine way of dealing with alterity. Levinas states that to be a singular I and not just an embodiment of the Mind means to be able to see the face (1961: 276). Both insist on the priority of an immediate relationship face-to-face with the Other over the mediating intervention of the Third, emphasizing that the latter destroys the *who* of the other, defaces it. But in order to prove the counterfactual possibility of a relationship of uncontaminated proximity, both have to *imagine an instrument of establishing it*. This finally leads them to hypothesize a purely performative language stripped of all constative qualities – and to passionately attach their argument to this wishful projection.

Thus Levinas speaks of a "primordial language" of contact, a "pure communication" bared of all "words and sentences" which enables one, instead of transferring any message, to touch the other, to approach its uniqueness (1987c: 313, 319–320), to engrave one's trace upon it (2001b: 282). As if parting company with him on that point – "as if" because she never mentions Levinas explicitly in her book – Cavarero chooses precisely narrative to be this absolute performative. Taking a position diametrically opposite to her argument, ante rem, Levinas condemns narrative for turning the "living time" opened to "the salvation of becoming" into a linear and homogeneous "fate," i.e. for taming the alterity and exteriority of each inserted *event* into a smooth series of narrative *situations* (1989: 139–142). In an almost perfect inversion of Cavarero's thesis, Levinas interprets philosophy as the epitome of performative language, while narrative appears as the constative opposite:

> The greatest virtue of philosophy is that it can put itself into question, try to deconstruct what it has constructed and unsay what it has said [...] And I wonder if this capacity for interrogation and for unsaying (*dédire*) is not itself derived from the preontological interhuman relationship with the other [...] [T]he best thing about philosophy is that it fails. (Levinas and Kearney 1986: 22)

Even if Cavarero's inversion secretly and understandably polemicizes against an influential philosophy with masculine overtones, one crude dichotomy can hardly be efficiently beaten by another. However understandable this polemic exaggeration may be, the result is an equally unquestioned order of priority between the *who* and the *what*, between performative and constative language, the narrative and the philosophical, the political and the literary, the feminine and the masculine. Yet how is the exclusive merit for the constitution of the singular self to be ascribed either to narrative or to philosophy? Would this not mean attributing a very distinctive feature precisely to something that is proclaimed to resist any attribution whatsoever?

11.5 Vanishing mediation

Unlike Cavarero and Levinas, who resolutely take just one of these sides as the final truth about narrative, Nancy seems to be allowing the narrative to be two-sided, at once constative and performative, pre-modern and modern. If community is founded by pre-modern representational or constative narrative, then it is unworked by modern self-referential or performative narrative. This prevents a sharp opposition between literature and philosophy, which, though differently rendered, takes place in both Cavarero and Levinas. For Nancy, philosophy is always already inherent to narrative just as narrative is to philosophy. As an adherent to deconstruction, he prefers mutual implication to sharp oppositions: no pole, however "basic" or "primordial" it might appear, comes up uncontaminated by the other. In the same way, the mythic community based on communion and the literary community related to singularity function as the condition of im/possibility to each other.

The representational narrative of political community is the condition of the possibility of the self-referential narrative of literary community: its identification operations always leave behind an unresolved residue that serves as the foothold of its literary interrogation. The self-referential narrative for its part revivifies the representational narrative by confronting it with its contingency, mobilizing *the process of historical change conceived as the permanent emancipation of the mythic community*. Therefore, performative unworking does not amount to a termination of the operations of the constative identity. Instead, it implies a persistent and interminable literary intervention in the political forms of a social bond in the name of its excluded residue. "Freedom is not a right," points out Nancy (1988: 108) in recognizably Arendtian fashion, "it is the right of what is 'by right' without right." Such absolute freedom cannot be the goal but only an *infinite task* of human being-in-common.

> Community is given to us – or we are given or abandoned to the community: a gift to be renewed and communicated, it is not a work to be done or produced. But it is a task, which is different – an infinite task at the heart of finitude. (Nancy 1991: 35)

Wittingly or not, Nancy's "infinite task" follows Agamben's messianic argument, making the modern "state of exemption" the point of departure. The so-called weak messianism's redemptive thought tends to save the disregarded remnant of the oppressive historical memory from oblivion. Authorizing modern European literature to stubbornly keep alive this inarticulate surplus of the legislated past, Nancy in fact paved the way for Derrida's "messianism without a Messiah." In his various works from the 1990s, Derrida repeatedly raised the claim for an emergent justice for each particular here and now. In such a way, he reconfirmed Nancy's privileging of modern self-referential literature. Appointed the "vanishing mediator" of human community, it holds the same sway over myth as the literary does over the philosophical narrative in Cavarero's rendering. Being "never at home" in its "ecstatic process," it "receives its determination from something other than itself" (Derrida 2000a: 28), thus repeating the cosmopolitan gesture of Europe as the epitome of the hospitality to the foreigner (Gasché 2009: 27). It unremittingly opens the political community toward an unpredictable empty future of absolute freedom, enabling its messianic emancipation.

"In this context, historical change cannot be conceived in terms of a dialectical or teleological process," i.e. one that ends with a final resolution, "but rather in terms of a constant birth or becoming of singular-plural sense that interrupts established foundational narratives and opens the way for future narratives to emerge" (James 2006: 199). Here Cavarero's continuous rebirth achieved through narrative, or Foucault's *recommencement* mobilized through individual will, are obviously well in place: mythic narratives are incessantly contested to take into consideration the alterity they rule out of possibility. Because modern European cosmopolitan literature as exemplified by the early German Romanticist idea of the novel, leads this process of historical emancipation of oppressed human possibilities, it enjoys a privileged position in all these conceptions. As opposed to the retrograde "mythic forces" of the pre-modern age dominated by non-European civilizations, it performs a favorable, future-oriented, enlightening task. In *Specters of Marx*, Derrida (1994a: 88) consequently regards its operations of committed "transformation, re-evaluation and self-reinterpretation" as the "heir to the spirit of the Enlightenment which must not be renounced." Modern Romanticist literature in such a way enlightens the Enlightenment itself as regards its "infinite task."

However, in relegating messianic authority to modern literature, Nancy's and Derrida's deconstruction reaffirms, if it does not reinvigorate the opposition between the retroactive and proactive narrative that it wanted to overcome. According to Derrida (1994a: 90–91) the mythic narrative serves national or religious appropriation of the humans, whereas the literary narrative serves the deconstruction of such appropriation in the name of undeconstructable justice – "in the name of a new Enlightenment for the century to come" (90). It is thus placed at the service of what Derrida terms the "New International:"

> It is an untimely link, without status, without title and without name, barely public even if it is not clandestine, without contract, "out of joint", without coordination, without party, without country, without national community [...] without co-citizenship, without common belonging to a class. (85)

Such a resolute opposition between the appropriated *communities* and the stubbornly disappropriating *communism* ultimately, even if inadvertently, subscribes to the ill-reputed logics "from the rest to the West." Undertaken in the name of the modern "state of exception," the proposed "new Enlightenment" reminds us of Marx's sentence "Human anatomy contains the key to the anatomy of the ape" (quoted after Chakrabarty 2000: 30). It relies on the dubious "retroactive wisdom." As in Freud's famous analogy of the psychosexual maturation of a human being to the "progress" of humankind, whereby both surpass the awkward "figures of arrested development," historical temporality is used as a strategy of exclusion, or as a figure for the assertion of social and cultural privilege. In these two typically colonial narrative patterns, the Marxist phylogenetic and the psychoanalytic ontogenetic one, things reveal their proper essence only when they reach their ideal goal "naturally" coincident with our present terms. This spawns the degradation of the past. Its retrograde and exotic figures can belong to our "now" too, for example in the form of "petty nationalisms," but they are then relegated to anachronous geopolitical or cultural "ghettoes" of our world.

In the final account, Nancy's argument rests on the same pattern of consciousness-raising, which he condemned as a benighted "mythic" operation or which Levinas, in his turn, blamed for an inadmissible assimilation of the past into the present. Nancy identifies pre-modern Oriental myth with constative work, and modern Western literature with its performative unworking. Consider in this context Attridge's remarkably "Orientalist" claim in *The Singularity of Literature* that innovation marks "the striking continuity [of Western art] across thousands of years" (Attridge 2004: 38), that the tendency to deny instrumentalism in favor of unpredictable originality is a distinctive trait central to its practice "from its beginnings to the present day" (13). Does this unquestioned hypertrophy of European literary and artistic modernity, as opposed to non-European pre-modernity, not also delineate the horizon of Nancy's "literary communism," and does it not accordingly entail a historical and geopolitical contamination of his putatively uncontaminated messianic claim? Does this unexpected return of *particular (European) identity* into (modern) literature, which is supposedly *rendered void of all identity attributes*, not ultimately subvert the opposition between the political community based on restricted identity and the literary community related to unrestricted singularity? Does the geo-historical restrictedness of the idea of literature not seriously infect the nature of the "singular plural" literary community advocated not only by Nancy, but also Blanchot, Agamben, Cavarero and Derrida? Beardsworth (2007: 212) pertinently notes that deconstruction "closes the world down *through* the very set of strategies it puts in place *to* open it." It closes it down by surreptitiously raising Europe to the invisible Supreme Demarcator of all non-European or not-quite-European identities – their "powerfully powerless" Absolute Enabler.

> No European "identity" can be *opposed* to others in the world because there exist no absolute *border lines* between the historical and cultural territory of Europe and the surrounding spaces. There exist no absolute border lines because *Europe as such is border line* [...] More precisely it is a superposition of border lines, hence a superposition of heterogeneous relations to the other histories and cultures of the world (at least many of them), which are reproduced within its own history and culture. (Balibar 2004: 219)

The inference is unavoidable: almost all world cultures have contributed to the ultimately non-identifiable cosmopolitan profile of Europe but the restricting border lines of these cultures' identities are drawn solely by Europe. As Balibar has argued, "without this 'vanishing' mediation no transition from the old to the new fabric of society would have been possible" (233). The final meaning of the idea of Europe as the "vanishing mediator" would therefore be: "Europe as the *interpreter of the world*, translating languages and cultures in all directions" (235). Europe seems to be raised here – as Germany was some two centuries ago in Goethe's idea of *Weltliteratur* – to the sovereign moderator of international intellectual traffic, drawing from this position the same benefit money draws from mediating the traffic of commodities. All other cultures are supposed to participate (or serve) with their particular wares in a global exchange whose course is defined by the European vanishing mediation. Europe uses the broadest variety of *particularities* by exempting itself from all of them with the aim of maintaining and strengthening its cosmopolitan *singularity*. This is how its literary narrative permanently open to the advent of the Altogether Other ultimately comes into being.

12 Literature as Deterritorialization: New Vistas for Democracy?

Deterritorialization does not necessarily invoke associations with literature. According to two recent influential philosophical interpretations, it becomes literary only if it aims for emancipation, which is obviously not always the case. Literary deterritorializations appear to be genuinely democratically oriented. Does this mean that literature is democratic by definition?

12.1 Gilles Deleuze: emancipation through dehumanization

In *A Thousand Plateaus* (1987: 508), Gilles Deleuze and Félix Guattari define deterritorialization as movement by which an element escapes from a given territory, inducing the reconstitution of the latter. Elsewhere, the authors describe it as an operation by which a located agency becomes dislocated, undone or disarticulated (1983: 322; 1986: 86). Yet as deterritorialization inheres in all territorialized agencies as their transformative vector – a sort of "secret agent" of the hidden and all-determining power of becoming (*devenir*) – in fact it merely unleashes the fettered or slumbering creative potential of a given agency. It is a *virtual* operation, taking place at the invisible *molecular* level and is therefore ontologically prior to *actual* deterritorializations (or dislocations) performed at the visible *molar* level such as, for example, movements of population away from rural areas toward urban environments. As opposed to these restricted evacuations entailing reterritorialization, virtual deterritorialization creates a new unrestrained earth and new unrestrained people, and is therefore clearly preferable (1987: 55–56). In the authors' view, literature, art, philosophy and music, aim at a nonlinear system of relations (rather than new territory sought by restricted deterritorializations), and are *absolute* deterritorializations. Only the latter result in democratic emancipation.

How do these absolute deterritorializations come into being? Philosophy worthy of its name is instantiated, for example, by a *problem* rather than a *question*: the question seeks an answer, while the problem is something up to its arising unrecognizable or non-identifiable. Only by trying to solve a problem does philosophy extend the power of becoming inherent to its territory, opening this territory to a reconfiguration by radical alterity. As a matter of fact, Deleuze had already proposed this conception of philosophy as time and place-bound problem solving in his famous 1972 conversation with Foucault, *Intellectuals and Power* (Deleuze and Foucault 1977). Solutions offered by philosophy, he says, are not eternal and universal but emerge from a particular practical problem and bear validity only with reference to it. Philosophical concepts cope with the permanently changing field of practice whose constitutive part they make. Many years later, this idea is resumed in the first chapter of Deleuze and Guattari's *What is Philosophy?* It states that philosophical concepts arise within a determinate practical field in response to the challenge arriving from another, foreign and indeterminate field. The provocation reaches the philosopher from abroad, "the other shore," caused by an unfathomable "someone other" (*autrui*) profoundly uncertain and indeterminate (the French word *autrui* is neither feminine nor masculine, neither singular nor plural). The task of philosophy is to meet this ulterior indeterminate, and respond to its challenge.

The latter appears in the form of the Levinasian face (*visage*), regarding something beyond its field and stating "I am afraid" (*J'ai peur*) in view of such an utter exteriority.[1] Confrontation of the philosopher with this frightened face, continue the authors in the same modified Levinasian mode, disquiets his or her tranquil "there is" (*il y a*) because the face is on the one hand a *visible object* and on the other an *addressing (speaking) subject*. Yet in the final analysis, as it belongs to a *possible world* located beyond the philosopher's "there is," it is neither; it rather precedes such a distinction.[2] By escaping determination in terms of the philosopher's practical field in this indeterminate fashion, the face introduces to it something foreign, exterior and unpredictable, initiating its restructuration that induces a new concept. In responding to this face, the induced concept amounts to an unstable combination (*chiffre*) of determinate relations within the philosopher's practical field and indeterminate chaos beyond its borders. In other words, it contains finite coordinates and infinite possibilities of their combining and ordering. This intertwining blurs the boundaries that separate this concept from others by transforming them into a kind of neighborhood zone (*zone de voisinage*) or threshold of indiscernibility (*seuil d'indiscernabilité*) (1994: 19) (1991: 24–25). The same holds for the boundaries between the concept's internal constituents, which remain permanently open along the lines of flight (*lignes de fuite*), to the exterior realm of the inaccessible. Thus the mutual relationship of these internal constituents underlies an event-like reconfiguration too. Using such unstable and fuzzy concepts, the philosopher subversively reintroduces the chaos of becoming into the stabilized empirical horizons that rely on the engagement of transcen-

---

[1] The authors do not explicitly mention Levinas but, considering their vocabulary, the association is unavoidable.

[2] For a similarly ambiguous character of the Levinasian face whose "eye speaks," see 1961: 38, 66, 1976: 8 and 1991: 123–124 as well as Gürtler 2001: 106. According to Butler 2004b: 135, Levinas introduces a face that announces its suffering in an inhuman voice.

dentals (such as God, man, subject, state, perception or communication) to defend human commonality from this chaos. Philosophy thus places itself at the service of pre-philosophical *immanence*. The authors represent this crucial concept of Deleuze's philosophy, the very horizon of its authorization, in the figure of a sieve (42–43; *crible*, 45) that persistently filters transcendentals, and eliminates them from the primordial chaos of becoming.

In countering philosophical transcendentals by obliging philosophy to immanence, Deleuze and Guattari are at obvious pains to separate philosophy from religion, which is by definition characterized by a transcendental foundation. Nonetheless, as the history of philosophy provides a plethora of examples, they must admit that even the plane of immanence genuine to philosophy produces transcendental concepts, which in the history of philosophy subsequently contest and replace each other. Despite all its efforts to reach the "beyond," philosophy repeatedly substitutes transcendental concepts for immanence, obfuscating the truth of the latter by such illusions (49–50; 50–51). This incapacity (55) (*impouvoir*, 55) of philosophy to think that which perseveres in its very interior, escaping reflection, is the very cause of its turns, folds and roundabouts, its stumbling, stuttering, stammering, screaming and moaning, and its traumatized pre-linguistic manifestations amidst the language. The authors therefore infer that in its stubborn search for immanence, philosophy surrenders its human sovereignty, and behaves like a dog making uncoordinated leaps (55). Such "animalization" of its speech – and this is what absolute deterritorialization of a located human agency amounts to – is the only way for philosophy to retain the memory of escaping immanence. This is obviously considered its essential task.

Interestingly enough, these "uncoordinated leaps" of Deleuze and Guattari's "animalized philosopher" recall Benjamin's concept of the *Ursprung* in the meaning of both origin and primordial leap (Benjamin 1980: 226). In Benjamin's interpretation, if we treat historical origin as a primordial leap, it can by its resurgence unpredictably rearrange the smooth stream of historical becoming by breaking the latter's continuity and engulfing its constituents in its chaotic whirl. In this manner, both Benjamin's messianic time and Deleuze and Guattari's "whimsical" becoming – two absolute deterritorializations of human history in the form of unpredictable and uncoordinated leaps – ultimately *warrant the state of exception* (or the state of emergency), *the upper hand over the historical norm*. The former permanently destabilizes the latter, subverts its order, and obliterates its agencies and distinctions. These are effects that, rather than simply being emancipatory as the authors desire, simultaneously associate the devastating consequences of for example capitalist expansion or totalitarian regimes. We will return to this critical point later.

Beyond this unexpected concordance with Benjamin's an-archic idea of historical time, the French philosophers' consistent dehumanization of the human reminds us of Benjamin's systematic extension of the human, to embrace all earthly creatures including the inhuman ones (Hanssen 1998: 108–163). Along this line, Deleuze and Guattari's "animalized philosopher" is suddenly in accord with Benjamin's contemporaneous interpreter Giorgio Agamben as well, who explicitly obliges the human to bear responsibility for the inhuman:

> Human power borders on the inhuman; the human also endures the non-human. [...] This means that humans bear within themselves the mark of the inhuman, that their spirit contains at its very center the wound of the non-spirit, non-human chaos atrociously consigned to its own being capable of everything. (1999b: 77)

Several years before these lines were written, Deleuze and Guattari call upon the philosopher, by making him or her responsible to the "ultimate exterior," to adhere to the "lines of flight" from the human. Charting a similarly deterritorializing trajectory of dehumanization, they make the human – to deploy Agamben's vocabulary – "pass into populations and populations pass into *Muselmänner*" (85), i.e., thoroughly desubjectified creatures robbed of human language. Deleuze and Guattari's philosopher appears to be acting as a representative of these silent and amorphous masses; s/he becomes an agent summoned to evoke their enforced "animalization" by strategically miming it. Astonishingly, s/he therefore bears witness exactly in Agemben's sense of this concept:

> [I]t means that language, in order to bear witness, must give way to a non-language in order to show the impossibility of bearing witness. The language of testimony is a language that no longer signifies and that, in not signifying, advances into what is without language, to the point of taking on a different insignificance – that of the complete witness, that of he who by definition cannot bear witness. To bear witness, it is therefore not enough to bring language to its own non-sense ... [...] It is necessary that this senseless sound be, in turn, the voice of something or someone that, for entirely other reasons, cannot bear witness. (39)

In both these renderings of philosophy's mission, a substantial gap seems to open between those forced to *live* animalization and those authorized to *bear witness* to it. They occupy very different positions within the same traumatic constellation, which does not seem to concern philosophers. It is because they obliterate this crucial difference, however, they unilaterally celebrate dehumanization as the instrument of emancipation.

Agamben's conception of bearing witness to the trauma of the other, proposed in 1998, is not isolated. It corroborates Cathy Caruth's obliging of theory, two years earlier, to deploy "the very possibility of speaking from within a crisis that cannot simply be known or assimilated" (1996: 117). In theoretical writing, the im-

12.1 Gilles Deleuze: emancipation through dehumanization

pact of reference to trauma "is felt, not in the search for an external referent, but in the necessity, and failure, of theory. [...] What theory does [...] is fall; and in falling, it refers" (90). It is only through such "deterritorializing" disruptions and interruptions of the smooth narrative flow and persistent disfiguring of language that trauma can be adequately expressed not only in theoretical but also autobiographic, historic and literary writing.

In the same vein, Deleuze and Guattari interpret this quasi-traumatized "animally" disfigured discourse as the only authentic philosophical as well as literary writing. In their conception, literature constitutes another prominent form of absolute deterritorialization. Only if it is absolute does deterritorialization aim at the indeterminate Outside, which is presented in more detail above. The authors illustrate the blurring effects of such orientation in their famous book on Kafka and minor literature, in which they point out that Kafka does everything to obliterate the traces of the speaking subject, thus hindering the reader from distinguishing between the speech of the narrator and the figure. His "collective assemblages of enunciation," which indicate the potential of language to become an anonymous machine through the systematic deterritorialization of interlocutors, refuse to be pinned down to any recognizable subject. To achieve such de-identification, speaking subjects subversively mime their antagonist's behavior. "A little bit like the animal that can only accord with the movement that strikes him, push it farther still, in order to make it return to you, against you, and find a way out" (Deleuze and Guattari 1986: 59), Kafka blurs the boundaries between his representing and represented subjects, drawing them into an unrestrained field of immanence. Deleuze and Guattari state that it is through such persistent revivifying of indeterminate polyphony that underlies all established agencies that minor literature and language unleashes the suppressed creativity of its major counterparts. It subverts this language from within its identity, i.e., it deterritorializes its monolingual molecules and pushes its subjects beyond the politically acknowledged threshold of representation (1986: 17–18, 1987: 106).

Searching for a completely other kind of consciousness from that established by major literature, minor literature is, the authors argue, a de-identifying medium of a people yet to come. Deleuze and Guattari conceptualize it as the single possible mode of self-identification for minority populations deprived of the acknowledged political modes such as states enjoyed by majority peoples (1986: 16, 1998: 4). In a word, minority literature operates as an instrument of redemption of the "mutes," or those "without right to bear rights." This legitimizing basis of minor literature is structurally analogous to Agamben's later category of the inhuman or animal. This "eternally minor [...] bastard people, inferior, dominated, always in becoming, always incomplete" (4) cannot accept identity brought upon it by the majority people: "I am a beast, a Negro of an inferior race for all eternity. This is the *becoming* of the writer." (4) In this respect, it is worth noting that Agamben required the author's capacity to speak "in the name of an incapacity to speak" (1999b: 158).

> [W]e may say that to bear witness is to place oneself in one's own language in the position of those who have lost it, to establish oneself in a living language as if it were dead, or in a dead language as if it were living [...] (161)

In this quotation, the distance between the suffering "mutes" and their eloquent representatives is expressed in an exemplary way. It is not only that the first desperately need the latter, but also vice versa.

In Deleuze and Guattari's conception of absolute detteritorialization, the writer's becoming is associated with the "molecular detours" (Deleuze 1998: 2) of "a people who are missing," and must therefore invent themselves by way of literature. It is the "measure of health" of the "oppressed bastard race that ceaselessly stirs beneath dominations" (4). Therefore, "[t]o become is not to attain a form [...] but to find the zone of proximity, indiscernability, or indifferentiation where one can no longer be distinguished from a woman, an animal, a molecule [...]" (1). In this task of deterritorializing determinate identities through multiplying their "neighborhood zones" and "thresholds of indiscernability" (Deleuze and Guattari 1994: 19), or of making indistinguishable all that is distinguished, literature is taken to be meeting philosophy. Conceived as oppositional forces of democratic liberation of established agencies, both are expected to be at the service of becoming, testifying by such representation to that which is missing in the codified form of agencies.

However, as Deleuze admits fifteen years later, there is something that disturbs literature and philosophy as the envisaged forces of emancipating deterritorialization: the *fundamental equivocation* of their undertaking. On the one hand they democratically expropriate dominating agencies, but on the other, in introducing through their devastating "delirium" a worldwide "displacement of races and continents," they simultaneously "erect a race" which is "pure and dominant" (Deleuze 1998: 4). "[T]here is always the risk that a diseased state will interrupt the process of becoming [...] the constant risk that the delirium of domination will be mixed with a bastard delirium, pushing literature toward a larval fascism, the disease against which it fights [...]." (4)

Taking into consideration the hitherto neglected gap between the agencies and enablers constitutive of all "politics of trauma," this important and far-reaching inference from "Literature and Life" echoes the dilemma from Deleuze and Guattari's earlier book on Kafka, concerning the final effect of his deterritorializing assemblages: Are they liberating or enslaving, revolutionary or fascist, socialist or capitalist? How can these two inextricable aspects of Kafka's profound destabilizing of the German language be reliably disentangled? Such are the dangers inherent in the all-equalizing polyphony instituted by minor literature. In it, liberation from the "evil powers" of the past runs parallel to the enslavement by the "diabolic powers" of the future exemplified in capitalism, Stalinism or fascism (Deleuze and Guattari 1986: 57). It is impossible to prevent the overturning of emancipation into mastery, which makes becoming a double-edged process, and its advocacy a risky enterprise.

Perhaps to avoid such undesired malformation of emancipation, Deleuze and Guattari do not restrict their argument to the initially delineated binary oppositions between virtual and actual, indeterminate and determinate, molecular and molar or absolute and restricted deterritorializations (the latter being dislocations rather than proper deterritorializations). In order to prevent the re-emergent equivocation of the concepts dominating these oppositions, they introduce the final overarching opposition between *majoritarian* and *minoritarian* deterritorializations. Its aim is to draw the final distinction between the "good" (ethical/democratic) and "bad" (political/oppressive) agencies of deterritorialization. Whenever a deterritorialization spawns reterritorialization, as in the capitalist mobilization of the labor-power that serves established axioms and agencies, Deleuze and Guattari call it majoritarian, renouncing its democratic and underlining its oppressive potential. Capitalist axioms sort social meaning and individual subjects into binary categories, establishing their asymmetric distinction on the majority model. This is why capitalism makes the white, male, adult, and rational individual into the central point, in reference to which all binary distributions are organized (Deleuze and Guattari 1987: 293). Conversely, minorities open the gaps within these axioms by constituting fuzzy, nonaxiomable sets that are pure "multiplicities of escape and flux" (470). Following various lines of flight, their collective assemblages (*agencements*) produce *creative* or inventive terms, in opposition to mere *expressive* or assertive terms of existing majority agencies.

Yet what is the real benefit of this questioning of the whole set of subordinated oppositions if Deleuze and Guattari merely replace it with an equally problematic all-commanding binary opposition? Have the authors not raised binary opposition to the main instrument of capitalist axiomatic? Does a power asymmetry that favors "exuberant abundance of life" really endorse the democratic character of becoming, as, for example, Hardt and Negri trust with their unreserved advocacy of biopolitical circulation and global nomadism (Hardt and Negri 2000: 361–364)? Will everyone benefit equally from the obliterating whirl of deterritorialization, i.e., curious tourists and travelling intellectuals parallel to the exiles, expatriates and refugees? Does this not reaffirm the dangerous equivocation of becoming, in lieu of overcoming it? If the proper human emerges only when its most intimate property, the agency, is displaced into the inhuman, what about those who, in the same movement of "animalization," undergo territorial dispossession? What about those confronting the imperative to either leave their proper place or become riveted to the land they have been dispossessed of, who are delivered to an utter deprivation of belonging (Butler 2013: 21–24)? The desire they have to belong is by such deterritorializations forced to acknowledge the impossibility of ever truly belonging (Probyn 1996: 8). For better or for worse, becoming is an agent of globalization which has, for its part, "created at least as much trouble as possibility" and "contributed as much to exploitation and poverty as to wealth creation and economic participation" (Alexander 2012: 159). Its inclusiveness rests on exclusion, its tolerance on the long history of imperialism and colonialism accompanied by atrocities (Brown 2006: 37–38). Derrida was very explicit with regard to the "monstrous effective inequality" inherent in today's allegedly all-equalizing mobility:

> [N]ever have violence, inequality, exclusion, famine, and thus economic oppression affected as many human beings in the history of the earth and of humanity. […] [N]o degree of progress allows one to ignore that never before, in absolute figures, never have so many men, women, and children been subjugated, starved, or exterminated on the earth. (1994a: 85)

The unilaterality of Deleuze's praise of philosophical and literary deterritorializations comes especially clear to the fore if we compare it with Foucault's concept of governmentality (Foucault 1991b, 2008b, 2010). In an oppositional gesture analogous to Deleuze's treatment of revolutionary becoming, Foucault equally celebrates governmentality's historical emergence. He argues that it dethrones the oppressive political regime of sovereignty by exposing it as a mobile set of tactics, without recourse to a set of prior principles. With the regime of governmentality, in a political field unmoored from its traditional anchors, a diffuse set of tactics arises which draws its meaning from no single source, no unified sovereign subject, and thus suspends law. Yet in a blind spot remindful of Deleuze's, Foucault disregards that the new regime of governmentality becomes the site for the dangerous reanimation, reconstellation, and recirculation of the supposedly suspended sovereignty. Governmentality does not eliminate but rather reproduce, enlarge, strengthen and expand the state power in its legitimacy (Brown 2006: 82). It is precisely the suspension of law it executes that makes room for the reemergence of sovereignty in an illegitimate, extra-legal form, characterized by violence. In the regime of governmentality, sovereignty acquires the grotesque form of whimsical, unpredictable, and tyrannical operations of "petty sovereigns." Since their actions are no longer subject to review by any higher judicial authority, their managerial power is invigorated (Butler 2004b: 61). In the new form of political legitimacy with no built-in structures of accountability, "petty sovereigns" usurp the right to suspend rights, which makes their relation to law exploitative, instrumental, and arbitrary (83).

As a result, population is managed through a deconstitution or "spectralization" of its humanity, a technique that removes responsibility toward the governed "items" by increasing in such a way both their profitability and disposability, ultimately rendering them "consumable" (Bales 1999: 25). In the final analysis, far from eliminating the weakening nation-state, governmentality's rise protects it from erupting fundamentalisms on the one hand, and globalization on the other. It turns out to be a civic disciplinary technique for consolidating, re-legitimating and rejuvenating the endangered nation-state sovereignty (Brown 2006: 96). This conclusion is corroborated by the implementation of governmentality in the British and French colonies from the mid-nineteenth century on, at a time when the colonial state was exposed to crisis (Mamdani 2012). After the politics of integrating of the native population into the national body failed, regenerative measures were taken to legitimate the distinctive character of this population. The result of this "affirmative action" was an "affirmative exclusion." Two major institutions were "set in place, the French nation on the one hand, composed of those 'of French stock,' [...] and on the other, the different ethnic minorities or communities, which serve as a foil to French identity" (Amselle 2003: 12–13). It appears that racist attitude safely perseveres under this generous paternal cloak, resulting in a peculiar sort of "inclusive exclusion" (Ophir and Givoni and Hanefi 2009).

In sum, sovereignty and governmentality reactivate and regenerate rather than exclude or replace each other, which, if we follow the analogy drawn above, implies the same mutually contaminating kind of relationship between Deleuze and Guattari's majoritarian/oppressive and minoritarian/democratic deterritorializations. We can therefore postulate between them a complex relationship of *mutual implication*, rather than simple *resolute opposition*. Neglecting in the main line of their argument this deeply disquieting equivocation of their central concept of becoming (to which they, admittedly, occasionally take recourse), Deleuze and Guattari interpret "proper" literature as a clearly emancipating operation. By this operation, they say, liberating forces of becoming that are suppressed in language are activated, while established forces of oppression are deactivated. Ronald Bogue helpfully interprets this point:

> Every language imposes power relations through its grammatical and syntactical regularities, its lexical and semantic codes, yet those relations are implicitly unstable, for linguistic constants and invariants are merely enforced restrictions of speech-acts that in fact are in perpetual variation. A major usage of language limits, organizes, controls and regulates linguistic materials in support of a dominant social order, whereas a minor usage of a language induces disequilibrium in its components, taking advantage of the potential for diverse and divergent discursive practices already present within the language. (Bogue 2005: 168)

Minor literature therefore refers to the deactivating *usage* of majoritarian language rather than pointing to any particular *minority* that produces it; minority is a practice of resistance rather than a stable identity, which means that any individual or collective agency can take it up under certain circumstances. By its disengaging operations, it blurs majoritarian oppositions like western/non-western, white/non-white, male/female etc., destabilizes the political agency and introduces collective assemblages of enunciation in place of identifiable speaking subjects (Deleuze 1998: 18). Beneath the official molar (commonly available) constituents of language, such as words or meanings, it brings to the fore the molecular (commonly unavailable) component of *affects*. "What is realized in literary affect is not this or that message, not this or that speaker, but the power that allows for speaking and saying – freed from any subject of enunciation." (Colebrook 2002: 106)

It follows that the agencies of speakers, messages and audiences emerge from the reader's habitual preconscious investments in such singular affects. They are not natural givens but social derivates, molar after-effects of the molecular affective investments already taking place in everyday linguistic practice. Language, at its invisible molecular level, is always already deterritorialized, i.e., detached from the speaker's body. We read in *A Thousand Plateaus* (281) that "[m]ovements, becomings, […] pure relations of speed and slowness, pure affects, are below and above the threshold of perception." In opening the realm of the sensible underneath the threshold of the habitual perception of language, minor literature actualizes its subversive virtual state in the same way that proper philosophy actualizes the immanence of life beyond its transcendentals.

It is argued that solely this operation of the *internal evacuation* of the sovereign collective and/or individual agency (as opposed to the *external dislocation* of populations such as expulsions or migrations) has a truly subversive political character. By introducing impersonal in place of personal discourse, it opens room for maneuver for all those who, according to the majoritarian rules, cannot qualify for the status of a person. As we have seen, minor literature is engaged in the creation of a "missing people still to come," consisting of various misfits of majoritarian peoples (Deleuze and Guattari 1986: 15). Since it is deprived of any acknowledged political territory, language and identity, it achieves political effects through the molecular decomposition and reconfiguration of established personal agencies into impersonal collective assemblages. In the wake of such dissolution taking place at the preconscious level of the sensible (or affects), speaking subjects lose their preeminence in language and literature. They undergo assimilation into becoming. Created by this impersonal force via affective investments in language's molecular movements, minor literature replaces established agencies such as authors, characters and readers with anonymous assemblages. It substitutes multitude for the One. This systematic deterritorialization, according to Deleuze and Guattari, bears out the literature's crucial political effect. Literature deserves its name only if it displays this revolutionary cutting edge.

What renders this interpretation of silent literary revolution paradoxical is that it undoes the habitual association of revolution with public action. The public Subject is instead disempowered, deactivated, and turned into a destination of subterranean affections that invade and reconfigure his or her actions, and revolutionize his or her agency. A usually sovereign revolutionary agency is thus replaced with an impersonal sensory assemblage or indeterminate multitude that cannot freely account for itself; moreover, by befalling and invading the subject's speech, action and behavior, amorphous becoming hinders it from operating in a responsible way. S/he is thus transformed into a vulnerable surface exposed to traumatic engravings. Yet the subject's senses can never become an absolutely passive surface of inscription deprived of all sovereignty, since they are socially structured, categorized, and identified from the outset. This social regulation of identity inscribed into the human subject from the very moment of its birth – the process known as subjectivization – reintroduces the sovereign agency into the allegedly unaccountable impersonal sensory assemblage. Concomitantly, the subject's sensory apparatus operates as the field of a permanent confrontation between the majoritarian forces of regulation and the minoritarian forces of emancipation. This is where revolution, in Deleuze and Guattari's view, finds the prominent field of its micro-political operations, and disappears from the macro-political public scene. The shift of the idea of revolution from the "liberation of whole classes in economic and political terms" to the "liberation on the level of the individual" (Ross 2008: 101) suddenly attributes literature, alongside philosophy, a democratic political role. Politics that had up to then been "proper," i.e. mobilizing collectivities, is allocated to oppressive policies.

12.2 Jacques Rancière: emancipation through deregulation

Jacques Rancière is another contemporary French philosopher who places the emancipating operation of literature amidst the clashing forces of the subject's divided interior. This connects his democratically intended re-description of the concept of literature with the delineated project of Deleuze, despite the clearly different backgrounds of their philosophical conceptions. According to these authors, literature, if it does not reshape the subject's interior, and takes the side of suppressed emancipating forces, is considered unworthy of its name. The political regulation from above, in the form of the so-called identity politics, becomes the main target of the oppositional literary deregulation from below. For both Deleuze and Rancière, literary politics consists in the disarticulation of the politically authorized selection of sensations by an unpredictable revolutionary assemblage that escapes it. Being now orientated inwards toward the subject's perception apparatus, instead of outwards toward the dethroning of other political subjects as before, revolutionary politics deactivates the acting agency, departing from an inarticulate molecular area excluded from the scope of its activity. Despite Deleuze's and Rancière's undeniable divergences, this paradoxical "action through non-action" or *sabbatical of action* – the key operation of the so called messianic thought claiming to be representing the disregarded *sans-part* – associates two autonomous conceptualizations of literature-as-resistance by driving their authors into the spell of messianic politics. Oriented toward the "radical passivity" supposedly caused by trauma, messianic thought systematically denies its own participation in such a representation of the latter. It pretends to merge with the traumatized, obliterating the gap that separates their agency from these enablers. While it thus *creates* that which it claims to be only *speaking for*, it performs what has been called "politics of trauma," conducted by means of trauma narratives (Fassin and Rechtman 2009: 8).

As far as Rancière is concerned, this covert affiliation with messianic thought, according to some recent commentators, ultimately induced his "quixotic founding of the political" (Valentine 2005: 58), performed in the typically melancholic manner of the contemporary Left that is passionately attached to non-action (Gibson 2005). Having allegedly put the politics so unconditionally at the service of the "excluded enabling domain," Rancière doomed public action to operate in the restrictive frame of police, thus unwittingly resuming Althusser's asymmetric oppositions (Žižek 1999: 237–238; Biesta 2008: 8; Hewlett 2007: 105). As far as Deleuze is concerned, the affinity of his self-dispossessing orientation with Eastern philosophy (especially Chinese *wu wei*, in which the human I appears as only one of the myriad interconnected manifestations of natural substance) is hardly accidental, as it belongs to the whole European philosophical tradition that inspires Deleuze's neo-vitalist thought.

> While Leibniz was explicitly interested in Eastern philosophy, the 'fatalism' of Spinoza was frequently denounced as converging with 'Chinese atheism'. [...] Isn't it what Spinoza suggests when he describes human beings along with all other natural 'things', as mere 'modes', determined 'modifications' of a substance which is the only reality endowed with the full privilege of agency? (Citton 2009: 124)

The influence of Spinoza and his legacy on the permanent self-deactivation of the Deleuzian subject is indisputable. However, with regard to "action through non-action" as the delineated paradoxical mode of literary revolution, the messianic tradition of European thought appears to be another, much less discussed background of Deleuze's philosophy. If Chinese philosophy was taken up via Spinoza, then the messianic tradition, as epitomized in the early German Romanticist replacement of the sovereign *philosophical* self by an endlessly deferred *literary* self, was probably imported via Maurice Blanchot.

At this point, a small detour might help us understand the problem. Let us first take a closer look at the early German Romanticist intervention in the idea of literature. They made their subject "literary" in order to draw it into a permanent internal revolution and in such a way distinguish from subjects encapsulated into prejudices. As the latter were at the time spontaneously associated with numerous internal (social and intellectual) as well as external (geographic and cultural) "benighted souls," in the final analysis the early German Romanticists tacitly transferred the messianic operation of self-exemption from the religious to political terms. This operation now implemented in the governmental frame, was taken up by citizens and/or civilizers who thus distinguished themselves from "barbarians," "natives" or "primitives." Within the governmental frame, the narrow-minded subjects, as opposed to the intellectually mobile "literary" subject, obtained their clearly marked place in space, time, and life. The "literary" subject for his part[3] continually producing such "abject" domestic and "barbarous" foreign subjects, operated from a conceit of neutrality through escaping any recognizable identity (Brown 2006: 6). Thanks to such properties, he soon became the chief representative of the rising liberal governance. A consistent negation of anything not himself, thereby marked as inferior, deviant or marginal, turned out to be the key operation of this protean self's assertion and maintenance. This resulted in a proliferation of elementary, primitive, unfinished, or mutilated identities in need of tolerance, shelter, and protection (Mbembe 2001: 1–2).

When Herder cautions the European slaveholder not to mistreat the Negro – "you should not oppress, kill or rob him because he is human like you yourself" (1989: 255) – he is actually pioneering the forthcoming paternal imperial attitude. "The barbarian subjects, the educated overcomer cultivates" (*Der Barbar beherrscht, der gebildete Überwinder bildet*) (1989: 706) therefore means that the superior human is expected to protect the inferior. Behind this "enlightened" expectation, one can discern the long tradition of Roman governance over colonies, which is expressed, for example, in Cicero's letter to his brother (*ad Quintum fratrem* I, i, 27): "If fate had given you authority over Africans or Spaniards or Gauls, wild and barbarous nations, you would still owe it to your *humanitas* to be concerned about their comforts, their needs, and their safety." (Wolf 1998: 68) Ro-

---

[3] The use of *his* is done on purpose to indicate the German Romanticist perspective.

mans trusted that their gods destined them to rule and civilize the world, providing a "human" unity to its ethnic, cultural and linguistic diversity. Yet this colonial uniting into an allegedly common *humanitas* implied the introduction of a complex network of distances, or a carefully elaborated hierarchy by which the natives were recruited "to various roles and positions in the social order" (105). An insidious social apparatus took care to endow each person with a specific weight depending on his or her place in a real or virtual group; those classified as being in need of assistance became distinctly stigmatized.

This Roman colonial kind of protection of the other's distinction, taken up by Herder's fatherly care of remote others and elaborated by the early German Romanticist generous advocacy of human diversity, was politically re-implemented in the nineteenth century, first by British and then French imperial governance. (Mamdani 2012; Amselle 2003) Giving up the failed assimilation of the other into the self, the new focus on the "affirmative action" of the self toward the other – which substituted the shaping for eradicating of differences – turned the German Romanticist *intellectual* "invention of the native" into a compensatory *political* strategy. Pinned down to his or her locality and confined to his or her custom, the native was the creation of the colonial state in crisis (Mamdani 2012: 3). Similarly, the whole regime of governmentality emerged to rescue the nation-state in crisis (Brown 2006: 96). As Amselle (2003: 12) puts it, "[a]t the root of this policy is the idea that universalistic principles have failed. [...] Special opportunities must therefore be given to the disabled of every sort, but without any possibility for society's losers to leave their exclusionary zone. In that way, a ghetto is created by regenerating pockets of poverty and disability."

In terms of the "soft racism of multicultural difference," which came into being as a remedy for the failure of the "hard racism of ethnic purity," minority individuals were permitted integration to humanity, yet only as members of marked or stigmatized groups (7). Such "dissimilar items" constitute the basis of contemporary French society as well. If this society refuses to confront its postcolonial condition, this is due to its reluctance to transform a supposedly "common human past" into an uneasy history, shared with masses of absolutely heteronomous yet radically proximate "creatures." Since "French citizen" was never equal to the "French proper" – not to speak about the *sans-part* deprived of all symbolic profits of the citizen status – the question is whether the past of Empire was ever really common. Its very foundations, the plantation and the colony, radically disclaim the possibility of belonging to a common humanity, even if it reclaims itself as the cornerstone of the French Republican idea (Mbembe 2010: 112). This state of affairs has not really changed with decolonization: after having travelled back into the centers of the former Empire, the overseas "dissimilar items" densely populated their suburban zones, giving rise to a new "regime of confinement" amidst governmentality (151). Since this division still holds power in French society today, the French narcissist self continues to maintain its superiority through the dissemination of various "classified" and "unclassified items" across its political and cultural space (94–96).

To prevent the enthusiastic celebration of the early German Romanticist invention of the *mobile "literary" subject*, the latter has to be understood within the delineated (post)imperial and (post)colonial setting. Far from being unconditionally liberating, in the frame of European modernity messianic politics firmly relies on the invention of the *immobile native*, "animally" riveted to his or her soil. Within the regime of protection turned into a technology of governance, the settler and the native make an indivisible couple. They enable, support and corrupt each other. "Claiming to protect authenticity against the threat of progress, the settler defined and pinned the native" (Mamdani 2012: 30), thus making room for his unconstrained liberty. Accordingly, Novalis's famous postulate that the self is nothing but an after-effect of the retroactive "art of invention" must be viewed in this context. His literary self is a result of free artistic construction – and this is unimaginable without the enabler. "The beginning of the self emerges later than the self; this is why the self cannot have begun. We see therefrom that we are in the realm of *art* here ..." (Novalis 1983b: 253, trans. mine). What causes the self's essentially literary nature is the self-imposed obligation to its perpetual reinvention. "We should not take life to be a novel given to us, but one made by us" (Novalis 1981: 563, trans. mine). By a consistent deactivation of the given past, life is directed toward an open future. Friedrich Hölderlin (1961: 264) states that it is "extraordinarily important" for a poet "to take nothing as given [...] or positive." The early German Romanticists conceptualize literature as *ein immerwährendes Durchbrechen von festen Gehäusen* (Behler 1997: 112), i.e. a consistent tearing apart of firm abodes. In their vision, literature is an eternally repeated self-dissolution for the sake of continuous self-recommencement. It imposes upon the self a strict revolutionary imperative. In following that thread, the self's internal revolution becomes a re-evolution, i.e., a persistent dispossession of the former self.

Returning to Blanchot's advocacy of the endlessly deferred self as the distinctive feature of literature, we must keep in mind this deeply equivocal tradition of European modernity. Blanchot claims that Stéphane Mallarmé was the first writer to launch modern literature's search for an absent Outside "in its very realization always yet to come" (Blanchot 1993: 259, 1992: 42, 2003: 224). However, we can now see that Mallarmé merely continued the search for absolute freedom from the constraining others inaugurated by early German Romanticism at the outset of European imperial and colonial modernity. With modernity, the elite European self has instituted a governmental regime of persistent self-exemption from constraints allocated to social, cultural and geographic others. Turned into the pure negative foil of this self's assertion, innumerable others became exploitable, consumable, and disposable. It was at the peak of this controversial imperial development, which was fully disregarded by Blanchot, that Mallarmé undertook the dissolution of the completed literary *work* for the benefit of perpetual literary *writing*. As opposed to self-enclosed literary work, Mallarmé's writing, states Blanchot, constitutes itself "as always going beyond what it seems to contain and affirming nothing but its own outside" (1993: 259). From this persistent self-decomposing orientation of *écriture* toward the missing outside, Blanchot draws the conclusion that the literature deserving this name "contests itself as power", stubbornly adhering to what it cannot but exclude always anew (1997: 67): "Literature denies the substance of what it represents. This is its law and its truth" (1995: 310). However, by emphasizing literature's consistent self-exemption, Blanchot suppresses its discriminating character, as discussed above. While this literature claims to be acting in the name of absolute freedom, it only frees the exploiting self from any responsibility toward exploited others. That is to say, it usurps freedom exclusively for itself, while delivering others to non-freedom. This is the neglected side of its emancipating undertaking.

Since Blanchot was introduced to this argument only as a relay between early German Romanticist thought and Deleuze's philosophy, we must now return to the latter. What makes Blanchot's elitist idea of writing as an imperial dissolution of all identity abodes relevant to Deleuze's idea of minor literature, is that it regards the consistent evacuation of established literary agencies as the most genuine literary operation. As Deleuze (1998: 13) clarifies, explicitly referring to Blanchot's early concept of *le neutre*, minor literature neutralizes the first and second person of literary agencies in favor of the third person of an impersonal assemblage. In both Blanchot's and Deleuze's unilateral interpretations of literature's mission carried out in the delineated imperial and colonial spirit of European modernity, literature performs its self-revolution by successively deactivating all identity marks in order to reopen the space for multiplicities excluded by them. However, as we have seen, these multiplicities are being affirmed exclusively through a subtle network of marked, restricted, stigmatized or disposable positions; they undergo an internal discrimination in the form of a continuously changing "management of differences." Multiplicities are thus put at the service of majoritarian agency that rules them, by a perpetual redistribution of their roles. This is how sovereignty is reintroduced into their plural assemblage and Deleuze's "emancipating apriorism" is subverted. The unleashing of the multitude of the "disregarded" accompanied by obliteration of distinctions and boundaries does not always result in political emancipation. Various radically populist regimes testify to this. Paolo Virno, also an adherent of Spinoza's multitude, therefore prefers the less revolutionary formulation "that the multitude does not clash with the One; rather, it redefines it" (2004: 25). In accordance with the argument developed above, he sees dispersion and unity as mutually implied rather than opposed regimes.

This insight into the equivocal interconnectedness of multitude and the One also underlies Rancière's critique of Deleuze, and it does so most explicitly when he observes that Deleuze's multitude ultimately draws back "to the need for a political subject that would be real" (A never published interview given for the journal *Dissonance* in 2004, quoted after Citton 2009: 130). It is exactly this representation of "missing people" by literature that, according to Rancière, makes Deleuze's neo-vitalism attractive for Negri and Hardt's pantheist Marxism, with its promise of the final reunion of humankind at the sensory level. Rancière comments that such a utopian project, which uncritically blends the aesthetic with the political into a revolution carried out by masses of global migrants, neglects the inevitable reemergence of fissures within the envisaged future community.

> In *Empire*, they write about nomadic movements which break the borders within Empire. However, the nomadic movements which break Empire's borders are groups of workers who pay astronomical amounts of money to smugglers in order to get to Europe, workers who are then parked in confinement zones, waiting to be turned back. To transform this reality of displacements into anti-imperialist political movements and energies is something totally extravagant. (Quoted after Citton 2009: 125)

For Rancière, Deleuze's non-reflected modernist idea of literature abandons the metaphysics of representation with its hierarchies and divisions, only to introduce in its place the performative metaphysics of impersonal becoming, based on the principle of equality. Such an inversion of the hierarchical paternal community into the egalitarian fraternal community, exemplified in the book on Kafka, makes Deleuze uncritically adhere to minor literature as the new "'hero' of the story" (Rancière 2004a: 154). This mythical figure, charged with the political program of inventing "a people to come," expresses by its "action through non-action" the world of the subversive a-signifying atoms (or affects) that subsists beneath the world of representation (or concepts). Accordingly, instead of being a *creative* term as proclaimed, Deleuze's minor literature is merely an *expressive* term typical of majoritarian agencies. With its writer transformed into the pure medium of the irrefutable power of the senses, it allegedly represents the transcendence of life. Yet by being raised to such an agent of transcendence, it only reduplicates the hermeneutic pattern of an all-determining background force. Therefore, "the principle of indifference that characterizes it deprives the fraternal community of any ontological priority it may have over the community of the Father" (Vallury 2009: 234). Both communities operate on the same principle of reintroducing transcendence into their immanence. "We do not go on, from the multitudinous incantation of Being toward any political justice. Literature opens no passage to a Deleuzian politics." (Rancière 2004a: 163–164)

By countering this conceptualization of literary revolution because it repeats the fallacies of its proclaimed opponent, i.e. political revolution, Rancière refuses equivalence of the artistic and political re-description of equality, trying to keep them apart and maintain the tension between their respective claims. "In order for the resistance of art not to disappear in its opposite, an unresolved tension between the two resistances must be maintained" (2008: 35, trans. mine). Let us start with the political resistance to the aesthetic equality. First, how does Rancière interpret this latter concept? Contrary to its usual rendering as art theory in general, aesthetics is for Rancière a configuration of ways of doing, seeing, thinking and speaking, which operate as habitual forms of exclusion and inclusion within the delimited field of the sensible. In other words, aesthetics defines what is doable, seeable, thinkable and sayable under given social and historical circumstances. Politics (*la politique*), however, disrupts this field through an act of *disagreement* (la mésentente),[4] opening a space for the emergence of new modes of subjectivization. They were previously unheard and unseen, but now, after the political performance of the act of disagreement, they are allowed equal participation in the given sphere of experience (1999: 7–13, 43–60). "Disagreement invents names and utterances, arguments and demonstrations that set up new collectives where anyone can get themselves counted in the count of uncounted." (2011b: 41) Yet since political disagreement necessarily aims to legitimize new identities, it must in turn exclude new, non-legitimized ones.

Unlike politics, which takes the indicated approach to disagreement, literature subverts the aesthetic equality through an act of *misunderstanding* (le malentendu). Underneath the reigning relation between words and bodies, the latter introduces "the staging of mute things that are there for no reason, meaningless […], the world of less than human micro-individualities that impose a different scale of magnitude from the scale of political subjects" (44).[5] Hence the literary act of misunderstanding works on the relationship between words and bodies and on the counting of agents from a side other than the political act of disagreement, which takes the counting of agents for granted:

---

[4] Rancière states in the first of his *Ten Theses on Politics* (2001: 1) that "politics is not the exercise of power" but "the political relationship that allows one to think the possibility of a political subject," a distinctive kind of subject who takes part in "the fact of ruling and the fact of being ruled."

[5] For the whole elaboration of the idea of literary misunderstanding, see the second chapter of *The Politics of Literature* (2011b: 31–45).

> In that regime, meaning is no longer a relationship of will to will. It is a relationship of sign to sign, a relationship written on mute things and on the body of language itself. Literature is the deployment and deciphering of these signs written on things themselves. (15)

Or even more explicitly:

> Misunderstanding works on the relationship and the count from another angle, by suspending the forms of individuality through which consensual logic binds bodies to meanings. Politics works on the whole, literature works on the units. Its specific form of dissensuality consists in creating new forms of individuality that dismantle the correspondences established between states of bodies and meanings [...] (42)

Yet the literary rearrangement of units is much more radical, since it aims at a complete dissolution of acknowledged identities through their persistent and systematic de-identification, de-hierarchization, de-regulation, interrogation, disappropriation and disembodiment. Through such uncompromised egalitarian politics, literature aims for an all-inclusive and indifferent equality, as opposed to the partial and provisional equality underlying the political act of disagreement. As Rancière spells out in *The Night of Labor*, French workers of the 1830s and 1840s tried to reconfigure their country's police order (*l'ordre policier*) so as to be recognized as speaking and thinking subjects, to be included in the official counting. Whereas political disagreement is thus set in motion by the historically excluded, to whom a wrong (*la tort*) has been done – "a supernumerary subject in relation to the calculated number of groups, places, and functions in a society" (Rancière 2005: 51) – literary misunderstanding acts in the name of *universal equality*. Excavating inarticulate, anarchic, unconscious and indeterminate sensations beneath the ruling distribution of the sensible (*la partage du sensible*), it interrogates not only aesthetic, but also political equality. Rancière's point is that, if both political and aesthetical equality operate as agents of exclusive (*either-or*) logic, then literature, along with other arts and philosophy, acts as agent of inclusive (*as-well-as*) logic. In Deleuze's conception, this is ultimately comparable with the way in which literature along with other arts and philosophy, acts as an agent of becoming, engulfing everything in its chaotic whirl. Rancière's conception, which clearly draws on Kant's and Schiller's revolutionary aesthetics of self-exemption (thus returning to the same German Romanticist sources as Deleuze), is that literature represents equality as the transcendental force of negation, bereft of any identity.

> The suspension of power, the *neither ... nor ...* specific to the aesthetic state, [...], announces a wholly new revolution: a revolution in the forms of sensory existence, instead of a simple upheaval of the forms of state; a revolution that is not mere displacement of powers, but a neutralization of the very forms by which power is exercised, overturning other powers and having themselves overturned. (Rancière 2009: 99)

In this way, Rancière separates literature from politics and establishes between their modes of equality not just tension or conflict, as he formulates, but a *binary opposition*. There is a similarity between the manner in which he confronts the hierarchical logic of politics and egalitarian logic of literature, and that in which Foucault confronts the discursive and non-discursive, in his *Archéologie* (1970), or in which Lyotard confronts discursive and figural logic, in *Discours, figure* (1971). In other words, despite Rancière's meticulous efforts to take a distance from both Foucault's (2005: 50) and Lyotard's (2009: 88–107) methodology, he reproduces it. Since oppositions by definition contain power asymmetry, in all these oppositions the first pole is homogenized into a hierarchically organized field guided by the exclusionist *either-or logic*, which permits the second pole to gradually reconfigure it with its all-inclusive *as-well-as logic*. Rancière thereby unwittingly reproduces not merely Deleuze's but Foucault's and Lyotard's binaries as well (as he does with Althusser's oppositional thought, as pointed out above). What results from his one-sided presentation of both politics and literature is a never-ending battle between the exclusivist mastery of the former and the inclusivist emancipation of the latter.

However, Rancière not only inadvertently follows Deleuze's critically targeted re-description of revolution, but also places literature at the service of the transcendental force of negation, deprived of all identity marks. In fact, he redoubles Deleuze's method of effectuating this by favoring a persistent dissolution of the identities of subjects, genres, styles, topics and emotions into affects. Apparently the latter allow for less restrained mutual combinations, "open an aleatory distribution of places and cases" and "heighten the contingency of the being-there-together" (Rancière 1995: 90). Rancière does not hesitate to apply Deleuzian vocabulary when he states that Flaubert's "literary indifference" "asserts a molecular equality of affects that stands in opposition to the molar equality of subjects constructing a democratic political scene" (2005: 56). As opposed to the loud public and political revolutions that result in renewed mastery, both philosophers interpret this covert and mute artistic revolution as democratization true and proper. However, as the envisaged community of equals (*la communauté des égaux*) can never really be attained – occurring without taking place (1995: 82), it is rather an "ever to-be-recommended invention" (90) – it operates as the basic presupposition rather than the final goal of "ongoing democratization." It is a vague prospect, a time-elongating cosmopolitan horizon to which hopes are attached. It is a supposition that has to be "endlessly reposited," "forever in need of reiteration" (84). In the spirit of a weak messianic tradition, it implies an eternal delay.

It follows that Rancière's crucial concept of *universal equality*, analogous to Deleuze's immanence, is hypothesized as an ultimate Outside which finds its differential historical and political expression only in the disguised and displaced form, i.e., within particular distributions of the sensible. Although doomed to be eternally withheld, universal equality remains a persistent regulative principle, stimulating a continuous eliciting of the "hidden truth" of its distorted political and historical manifestations. In that particular regard it strongly reminds us also of Blanchot's absent Outside "in its very realization always yet to come" (Blanchot 1993: 259, 1992: 42, 2003: 224), which, as we have pointed out, recalls the early German Romanticist tradition. By representing universal equality as "the part that has no part" (*le part sans part*) in whatever empirical distribution of the sensible, Rancière authorizes the relentless hermeneutic activity to subvert the latter in the name of the former. "The essence of equality is not so much to unify as to declassify, to undo the supposed naturalness of orders and replace it with the controversial figures of division" (Rancière 1995: 32–33).

> And this equality shapes and defines a community, though it must be remembered that this community has no material substance. It is borne at each and every moment by someone for someone else – for a potential infinity of others. (82)

However, if the democratic politics of literature is a pure activity of declassification that follows the empty and constantly delayed ideal, conceived in the spirit of the weak messianic tradition, then the empirical distributions of the sensible are its necessary prerequisites, and must be undone to liberate the universal equality that lies beneath them. Does this persistent exemption of literature from the empirical distributions of the sensible not ultimately entail an interpretive fever of "penetrating into depth" beneath false appearances, comparable to the one which Rancière, exemplifying with the modern novel, described as "hermeneutic profusion" (2011b: 23)? In highlighting "the suspension of power, the *neither… nor…*" logic as a "wholly new revolution" of literature, (Rancière 2009: 99) Rancière in the first place, of course, draws on Kant's reflective judgment, extended thereupon in Schiller's anthropologic argument. Yet early German Romanticism, by following this extension and applying reflective judgment to literature's consistent tearing apart of firm abodes, raised the novel to the representative literary genre. As an imperial "genre that is not one," the novel is, according to Friedrich Schlegel's *Letter on the Novel* (from the *Dialogue on Poetry*), always in the process of self-dissolution. This cancellation of its specific generic boundaries until it completely merges with the world-in-the-making by becoming its *natural representative*, fully accords with Friedrich Schlegel's contention in the *Athenäum*-Fragment no. 116 that the endless number of modern genres, if properly re-described, amount to the same genre: the novel. Accordingly, in Rancière's interpretation, literature becomes a consistent re-description of its former deluded forms by its latter enlightened self. By regarding such a merciless undoing of appearances as the only true mode of revolution, he inadvertently uncovers the novelistic roots of his idea of literature. Literature as he conceives it persistently refers to the hidden world of contingency beyond the empirical distributions of the sensible, in the same way the novelistic author continuously undoes the illusions of his/her figures and of herself/himself. As exemplary representatives of the "indirect rule" characteristic of the liberal imperial governance – or the colonial regime of governmentality for that matter – both Rancière's and early Romanticist agents demonstrate a feverish hermeneutic activity of self-exemption from given identities. Their method of maintaining and reasserting sovereignty consists in untiringly introducing distances from the others by following the lead germane to the permanent state of exception: "I am what I am not."

In *The Politics of Literature* Rancière blames psychoanalysis and Marxism for uncritically inheriting this "hermeneutic profusion" of their methodology from the narrative techniques of the novel, but the structure of his argument on the true democracy also appears to be unmistakably "novelistic." This is why, despite the universal ambition raised by his idea of literature, he ultimately adheres to that interpretation of literature's mission genuine to equivocal European modernity. In lieu of the proclaimed universal equality, this adherence spawns a restricted equality of the few far-seers against the unequal majority of ignorant others in the background. Supported by the same weak messianic tradition as Blanchot's Outside or Deleuze's immanence, Rancière's universal equality thus turns into a biased agent of globalization which, contrary to the envisioned goal, fosters a continuous bifurcation of humankind into agencies (or "thinkers") and enablers (or "workers"). To put this undesired outcome in his own terms, his regulating ideal in the final analysis introduces an asymmetrical "pedagogic relationship" between masters and pupils (Rancière 2011a: 144) among humankind. As this relationship was the main target of Rancière's critique leveled at Althusser's thought, it seems that Rancière reproduces Althusser's blind spots, along with those of Foucault, Lyotard and Deleuze.

12.3 Reintroducing the agent of universality: politics turned into police

The question that has to be raised is therefore whether such messianic rendering of universal equality does not entail the same substitution of the new for the old "'hero' of the story," i.e. the reintroduction of transcendence into immanence, or the overturning of emancipation into mastery that Rancière objects to in Deleuze's "life" (2008: 29). Do we not testify in Rancière's concept of equality to the same monopolizing of universality as in Deleuze's concept of life's becoming? And is not literature, represented by the (European modernist) novel, raised to the natural agent of this universality in both philosophical conceptions? Accordingly, can

12.3 Reintroducing the agent of universality: politics turned into police

Rancière's polemics against Deleuze be interpreted as a philosophical battle over the monopoly of universality? Bearing in mind that Rancière criticized Lyotard's ethical advocacy of the Lacanian "Thing" for the same reason (Rancière 2009: 88–105), does he not replicate Lyotard's tendency "to extricate artistic modernism from political emancipation, to disconnect it in order to connect it with another historical narrative" (103), a narrative no less magnificent and "grand" than the one Lyotard criticized? This "anti-Lyotardian Lyotardian" (Žižek 1999: 172) thus carefully disconnects the all-inclusive modernist artistic resistance to the distribution of the sensible (called "misunderstanding") from the restricted political emancipation from this distribution (called "disagreement"), in order to uncritically reconnect them by turning modernist artistic resistance into the only true manner of political emancipation.

In conclusion, let us inspect more closely how Rancière performs this peculiar "looping maneuver" in his argument. He claims that the aesthetic regime of art, which promotes complete equality of genres, represented figures, topics, writers and readers, was founded by Kant's and Schiller's aesthetic views. The hierarchy of the previous representative regime was definitely abolished by Kant's insistence on the singularity of art, which systematically exempts itself from all imposed norms, constituting a permanent "state of exception." At constant pains to separate the true artwork from the pleasurable consumption, Kant introduces into its reception the principle of double negation: neither-nor (2009: 96–97). This elimination of both understanding and desire from the reception of the true (genial) artwork "enabled the subject, through the free play of those faculties, to experience a new form of autonomy" (91).

> Aesthetic experience is an experience of the twofold separated sensible. It is separated from the law of understanding, which subjects sensory perception to its categories, and from the law of desire which subjects our affects to the search for a good. The form captured through the aesthetic judgments is neither the form of the cognitive object nor the one of the object of desire. This "neither-nor" determines the experience of the beautiful as the experience of resistance. (2008: 15, trans. mine)

Continuing this resistance, Schiller affirms the undistributed sensible of the "free play" that challenges the order of domination represented in the relationship between the form and the matter (2009: 31–32).

> Thanks to this double bind, aesthetic 'free play' ceases to be a mere intermediary between high culture and simple nature, or a stage of the moral subject's self-discovery. Instead, it becomes the principle of a new freedom, capable of surpassing the antinomies of political liberty. (99)

Both Kant and Schiller, it is said, derive literature from freedom and equality of nature, whose power of immanence, through its ceaseless negating activity, abolishes social hierarchies. Leaning on this persistent "neither-nor" negation, literature's new regulative principle becomes dissensus.

> The core argument of the *Letters on the Aesthetic Education of Man* resides in the same double negation that characterizes Kantian aesthetic negation. It states that the latter is subject neither to the law of understanding, which requires conceptual determination, nor to the law of sensation, which demands an object of desire. [...] In itself, the 'free agreement' between understanding and the imagination is already in itself a disagreement or dissensus. [...] [A]esthetic common sense, for Schiller, is a dissensual common sense. (97–98)

Yet Kant's and Schiller's dissensual logic "neither-nor," epitomized in Kant's reflective judgment, is far from being merely an act of resistance, as Rancière regularly renders it. Rather than being historically unique and unprecedented as he desires, it resumes the operation of self-exemption from the application of socially established rules. In the context of European imperial and colonial modernity delineated above, this operation clearly aims at social, intellectual, cultural, political, and/or economic mastery over those entrapped in experiential judgments. As reflective judgment by definition derogates determining judgment, it is exclusive rather than inclusive: its "affirmative action" amounts to "affirmative exclusion" (Amselle 2003). Accordingly, Kant's and Schiller's modern artwork claims for itself a divine "state of exception," as does the simultaneous claim of the French Revolution in the political realm (Agamben 2005a: 25). In the same way that French revolutionaries usurp the representation of society, Kant's aesthetic genius usurps the representation of nature. Both "monopolists of universality" pretend to be the disinterested mediators of the "supreme will," but they are actually its interested inventors, creators or constructors. This explains why not everybody can qualify for the consistent excessiveness of this will, and some must represent or "embody" it for the others.

Although this exclusion underlies Kant's and Schiller's allocating of privilege to reflective over determining judgment, Rancière completely neglects it. Instead he associates the arrival of the aesthetic regime with the arrival of the all-embracing, as opposed to the restricted kind of democracy achieved by political disagreement. In an interview conducted in 2006 by Frank Ruda and Jan Völker, Rancière explains:

> The art of the aesthetic regime has its own democracy, which tends to establish the equality of sensuous events with a measure that beats the political constitution of communal subjects. Between the democracy of the pre-human, impersonal individuations and the big undertakings of the new communities of the sensible are the "populations" gathered by art that are always deficient or excessive in comparison to those manifested by political communities. (2008: 85; trans. mine)

That is to say, the literature of the aesthetic regime acts in the name of an inarticulate "population" rather than the articulate political community of the "people," as does politics. In spite of his critique of Deleuze and Agamben (2009: 119–120), Rancière seems to act as the same self-elected agent of the dehumanized anonymous masses of enablers. In Agamben's words, he speaks "in the name of an incapacity to speak," places himself in language "in the position of those who have lost it" (1999b: 158, 161). In other words, he implies that the "aesthetic" literature, by following the disarticulating "neither-nor" logic, reproduces the *enforced* dissolution of peoples into populations (Agamben 1999b: 85) by way of *reflective* judgment. It thereby allegedly represents the politics of mélange, hybridity, the "heterogeneous sensible" (Rancière 2002: 146) and the "proleptic union of contraries" (Rancière 2003: 31) or, in a typically Schillerian "playful" manner, a reconciliation of human divisions. Yet far from merely representing it, "aesthetic" literature *invents* this inarticulate mass, which epitomizes equality in order to disqualify the "ethical" and "representative" literature as agents of such equality. In obliterating this exclusion of other kinds of literature from the representation of "population," Rancière associates *exclusive* "aesthetic" literature, which actually monopolizes the universality, with the *inclusive* (virtual) community. Concomitantly, he links politics, which he completely berefts of an emancipating dimension, to the *exclusive* (actual) community. Because he completely frees literature from exclusion, he regards this practice as being constitutive merely of politics.

Rancière's silent relegation of the difference *within both* literature and politics to the difference *between* literature and politics paves the way for his privileging of the literary over the political understanding of equality. Such ungrounded favoring arises from the same blending of art with politics proper (and politics improper with the police) with which he reproached Deleuze's conception, interpreting it as an inadmissible absorption of art in the political. Without first eliminating the internal fissure of both literature and politics, Rancière's emancipation of the literary egalitarian "neither-nor" logic from the political hierarchical "either-or" logic would be impossible. In the final analysis, this entraps his argument in the same substitution of the particular for the universal as in Deleuze's and Lyotard's arguments. Through the erasure of this substitution, Kant's and Schiller's elitist reconciliation of humankind triumphs over the irresolvable division between the political and non-political beings constitutive of Rancière's political thought, by spawning his "quixotic founding of the political" (Valentine 2005: 58), which is characteristic of the recent "melancholy of the Left" (Gibson 2005). From the thinker of anarchic disruptions of the very idea of the human, he becomes the thinker of a messianic human reconciliation. To reintroduce exclusion into the emancipation – one which stubbornly denies its exclusionary character by sentencing itself to the frustrating returns of the denied – one would have to recognize the contaminating workings of determining judgment at the very heart of reflective judgment or, for that matter, sovereignty at the very heart of governmentality. They are mutually implicated and therefore internally unstable, ambiguous and unpredictable constellations rather than consistent self-sufficient entities that exclude each other.

Epilogue
The Practice of Recommencing: Toward a Cosmopolitanism of the Dispossessed Belonging

We are living now in the aftermath of what one might call high theory. Yet this does not suggest that "theory" is over and that we can relievedly return to the age of pre-theoretical innocence (Eagleton 2003: 2). After all, this is not the first time that theory has been reported dead and nothing stimulates it more than the proclamation of its death (McQuillan et al. 1999: 9). This *déjà vu* effect of theory's burial introduces a disturbing equivocation with the "post-" in post-theory. How can something be *after* and therefore *new* with regard to the past if it already happened *before* and is therefore *old*, i.e. a constituent of the same past? The unexpected revival of the surmounted mode of thinking – an operation associated by Freud (1947: 232) with "the uncanny" – redoubles the present in the past by suddenly making strange that which hitherto was familiar (Royle 1999: 13). Something that seemed to have been overcome surprisingly turns out to have determined the overcomer from the outset by forcing him or her to affirm the supposedly discarded beliefs against his or her will.

Whichever post-theorist misapprehends this fundamental equivocation of the relationship between theory and post-theory, taking post-theory to simply mean the irrevocable passing of theory, makes him or herself responsible for the regression into the pre-theoretical condition of common sense. In taking such a common sense attitude, however, s/he polices the others, which in Rancière's terms means: imposes on them a "consensus."[6] What characterizes such a post-theory qua pre-theory, which unfortunately dominates today's theoretical scene, is the establishment of a transcendental platform such as History, Politics, Culture, the Aesthetic or Life as a matter of course. Such a platform is proclaimed to invisibly determine all the visible empirical data in the same way God determines all earthly beings (Bennington 1999: 104–107). In the various forms of today's post-theory qua pre-theory we are witnessing such quasi-universal conditions of possibility raised to the consensual basis of all differentiation, or an a priori agreement on what the difference is. Difference thus becomes an object of observation allowing the observer to safely exempt himself/herself from its disturbing operation. The final objective of that self-exemption is the commanding institutional position of the "Police." Yet the problem such a policing has to confront is that, even though the

---

[6] For Rancière's understanding of the "police" (as against the "political") see 1995: 11–20, 1999: 21–42, 61–65, 2001.

observer, by disengaging his or her empirical restrictions, envisions *sensus communis* in the *emancipating* meaning of *public* sense, him or her nonetheless, in the final account, materializes *sensus communis* in the *restrictive* meaning of *common* sense. In Kantian vocabulary, s/he substitutes the *sensus communis logicus* for the *sensus communis aestheticus* (2007: 124–125). Since common sense is by definition restricted, his or her truth cannot but miss universal validity.

Feverishly and systematically counteracting such undesired failures, theory, seen in retroactive perspective, proved to be passionately attached to its own sovereignty. It hardly strived to maintain the superiority of its subject or, to put it with Rancière, the "pedagogic relationship" between the master and the pupil, the knower and the one who lives in illusion (Rancière 2011a: 144). The pedagogical truth can come into being only against the background of delusions or, more accurately, through the dismantling of previous truths as delusions. The truth of the master who "knows better" can be affirmed only through the derogation of the truth of the pupil who knows less. The development of literary theory in the twentieth century testifies to the perseverance of such "pedagogic relationship" in exemplary ways.

As long as post-theory insists on its definite break with "deluded" theory as it predominantly does today, it appears that it follows this unfortunate tradition of policing the others. Confronted with the rising violence, destruction and extinction of our "age of extremes," post-theorists, in a kind of compensatory maneuver, create for themselves a well-protected, allegedly all-encompassing and all-commanding "observatory." Yet in order to achieve such a remedial quasi-sovereignty, they subject to epistemic violence – in a typically policing manner – not merely their *object*, but also the putative *transcendental condition* they claim to be affirming by their activity. For example History, after being unilaterally reduced to the perspective of the victors, becomes a divine authority entitled to pass judgments on all human lives equally, their unequal chances within its frame notwithstanding. But although historical propulsion raised to the transcendental condition implies expulsion as the condition of its possibility, it obliterates this discrimination inherent to it. Conceived in progressive teleological terms History conceals its innumerous collateral victims.

Not only History suppresses its internal equivocation, but at the other side of the power spectrum also the Subaltern. Turned into the blankness of the Radical Other – for its part an unquestioned transcendental platform –, it enables the establishment of the sovereign agency of the postcolonial theorist. As Gayatri Spivak (1999b: 358) has cautioned, while speaking in the name of the putative muteness of the subaltern, in the final analysis the émigré intelligentsia detaches itself from that "racial underclass." Ironically enough, it thereby spontaneously reintroduces the founding operation of the Enlightenment against which it otherwise persistently argues. That is to say, it makes the subaltern legible only within the field of the political in which the theorist conceives his or her inquiry (Spivak 2008: 24), applying to it the finite responsibility of law instead of the infinite responsibility of justice, which accepts no rules in advance. If the subaltern wants to be recognized, it has to comply with the politically given norms by suppressing its inassimilable difference and heterogeneous axiomatic (Cherniavsky 2011: 157). Hence what might be called the *an-archic and ec-static relationship* between the observer and the observed – as they are both *discontinuous* and *dislocated* with regard to one another – is erased in favor of the observer's spatial-temporal sovereignty.

Claire Colebrook (2011: 70) interprets such a self-exemption of the post-theoretical observer followed by the exposure of the observed object as a kind of "reaction formation" or remedial operation of a theorist befallen and disconcerted by its putative "object." The only alternative way she sees for a theory determined not to pervert its "after" into "before," i.e., not to let its judgments relapse into common sense prejudices, is to subvert such a self-deluding compensatory imaginary or the wish-fulfilling fantasy of the transcendental platform by establishing the obligation of post-theory to protect its antecedent in lieu of triumphantly overcoming it. Theory should be attentively taken care of by post-theory instead of being revolutionarily disposed with or left behind forever. Whenever post-theory introduces such a decisive political interval by simply "burying" theory, it inadvertently falls into pre-theory. Its *après coup* degenerates into a *déjà vu*. Only if it searches for the ethical interaction with and remains loyal to its predecessor can it paradoxically interrupt him/her in favor of something new.

For this reason the prefix "post-" in post-theory, like that in postmodernism or postmemory for that matter, does not merely indicate the temporal sequel or break, but also stresses the ongoing influence of the former on the latter and the profound relationship between the two (Hirsch 2012: 5–6). This *political* (or dissensual) sense of the "after" in "after theory" or the "post-" in "post-theory" that engenders a much more complex relationship than is the *policing* "pedagogical" one, meets an instructive further elaboration in the booklet *Life.after.theory* (Payne and Schad 2003). The significant www-punctuation of the title strategically introduces discontinuity both into its logical *and* temporal continuity, which obviously contradict each other. If we follow the logical continuity, then life appears to be always-already theoretical; if we follow the temporal continuity, then the age of theory is replaced by the age of life. In short, punctuation introduces discontinuity in both of these continuous inferential trajectories. It follows that neither does life fully replace theory nor is it thoroughly theoretical from the outset. Instead of such an easy substitution of the one sovereignty for another, an inassimilable "spectral surplus" interrupts the asymmetric "pedagogical" relationship between *theory* and *life*, as does the one between *post-theory* and *the-*

ory or the *observer* and the *observed* for that matter. Due to the intervention of that surplus, between the *agencies* (placed at the commanding position of the delineated "oppositions") and *enablers* (located at the commanded position) arises a paradoxical *conjunctive disjunction* that breaks the clear-cut policing terms of their relationship, multiplies and disperses both "agencies" and "enablers." In such a way, a complex political relationship between them saturated with a number of ethical stakes comes into being. This peculiar *political-ethical* relationship has been attentively examined in the alternative tradition of thought that we are going to engage in the following.

As one of the prominent philosophers of the so called ethical encounter, Jacques Derrida, in a round-table discussion from 2001 titled "Following theory" pointed out the strange alliance between the theorist's fidelity to the text (the latter figuring as a kind of the *Doppelgänger* of the theorist's constitutively absent interlocutor) and the betrayal of it. As I am trying to indicate by introducing into Derrida's discussion the concept of the *Doppelgänger*,[7] in the final account he claims that the "object" of theoretical observation, due to its "spectrality," is *unavailable in terms of the theorist's spatial-temporal belonging*. Assuming the profile of an unprecedented case, this "object" requires that the observer reconfigure his or her habitual rule of judgment. If the appropriate rule of its following were available in advance, if it were still an unquestioned part of the observer's "place on the earth" and history, there would be no such contradiction and thus no responsibility, no ethics of reading would be necessary; there would only be law inhabited from this place and history and waiting to be applied. But because this is now an uncanny encounter with the *Doppelgänger* relegated to outside the time and space of the observer's belonging, the latter has to invent the rule in order to address the new situation of the former. As he or she who is observed has escaped into an irrevocable exile, this observer's invention of the new rule of cohabitation cannot but be a betrayal of the old rule. "You have to betray in order to be truthful" (Derrida 2003: 11). As political obedience to established law would be irresponsible, Derrida obviously advocates a pre-legal, ethical responsibility which, however, must take its chances:

> There are ethics precisely because there is this contradiction... [...] I have to respond to two injunctions, different and incompatible. That's where responsibility starts. [...] You invent the rule when you read the text in a way which produces another rule responding to the text, or countersigning the text. This is very dangerous and you have no guarantee. [...] Ethics is dangerous. (Derrida 2003: 32–33)

---

7 According to Vardoulakis (2010), Jean Paul coined this term to question the metaphysical autonomy of the Enlightenment self-sufficient subject. In the place of self-sufficiency he introduced an essential relationality located in an agonistic political space, to which decisions and judgment are germane.

After the not-self-inflicted rupture of continuity bore upon the observer and the observed, the former is confronted with an uncannily resonant experience of the past. His or her judgment, addressed from the dispossessed "elsewhere," loses its footing, becomes populated by discordant views and divided up into the antagonistic many. What makes this encounter with the exploded past so uneasy, and this experience so incommensurable, is that the observed, by being now out of joint, resists consistency and semantic identity, drawing the observer into infinite responsibility toward its vibrant plurality and heterogeneity. Even if "no finite being can […] be infinitely responsible," Derrida believes "that […] in ethics responsibility is infinite *or* it is not. That's why I always feel guilty" (Derrida 2003: 48–49).

That significant sense of inexhaustible guilt, it appears, results from the new cohabitation with the non-belonging and precarious many after the departure of the belonging and situated companion (in the position of the observed). Considering Derrida's reiterative coming-to-terms with Levinas, here one is unavoidably reminded of the Levinasian destitute "face" that haunts the self by its unremitting ethical demand to preserve its life from erasure. Out of an extreme precariousness this "face" breaks in, befalls and persecutes the self (Levinas 1986b: 51). This interruption from "elsewhere" blasts open the continuum of the self's history, replacing its smooth transmission with the series of displacing encounters. It liberates the unlimited possibility of the discontinuous and plural "living time" from the linear and homogeneous "fate" of historical temporality (Levinas 1989: 139–45). The insistent claim of the face delivers the self to the same irritating targeting – the French word *visage*, etymologically read, means precisely "targeting" – that the self for its part has previously applied, via its monitoring, to this "face." "*Regarder ce qui […] vous vise: c'est regarder le visage*" (Levinas 1976: 6). Levinas speaks of the "preontological interhuman relationship with the other" (Levinas and Kearney 1986: 22). The targeting position of the face, the uprightness of the interpellation of its "defenseless eyes" (Levinas 1996: 12) escape all attempts of the self to cognize them. Concomitantly, instead of communicating with the familiar companion, theory is confronted with the echoes of a dispossessed exile; instead of enjoying a selfish belonging, it is displaced by their iterative urges. "[I]ts equality with the object it understands intentionally" is broken up (Levinas 1987c: 120). If it wants to protect from erasure these scattered remnants that obsessively beset it, call it into question, empty it of itself, (Levinas 1986b: 350) theory for its part must enter the process of self-disempowerment. Since how could it possibly have turned its attention to the dispossessed if it did not undergo dispossession on its own? Without mobilizing the "alterities within," it could not have corresponded with the "alterities without."

This "unchosen cohabitation," (Butler 2012: 24) an everything but self-elected interdependence and co-articulation with the *defaced enabler* in which the theoretical agency appears to be involved in Derrida's and Levinas's rendering of the ethical encounter, obliges the latter to the care addressed above. Paradoxically, the observer is expected to safeguard the same displaced observed that is unremittingly disquieting him or her. After all, theory appears to be, almost by definition, the activity of survivors induced by the traumatic departure of their life companions. To underpin such thesis, John Schad mentions that even Leavis's famous equation of theory with life implied the activities of those accidentally left alive after the devastating battles of the First World War (Schad 2003: 175–177). Theory also remained firmly associated with the posttraumatic condition thereafter. So when Derrida states that he always "feels guilty" (2003: 48) and that "in a certain way the only thing which interests me is the uncanny" (33–34), he obviously links theory with the uncanny experience of living on with the exilic residues of the past. Theory cannot but arrive too late for the rendezvous with its intimate companion; as the latter is now confronted as the spectral "face" alone, it is by definition a post-theory. It has no other choice but re-beginning; a smooth continuation with the gone is equally impossible as is the definite break with its persecuting memory. Sentenced to the "anacoluthic discontinuity" of "standing alone without companion," theory is called upon to investigate the modes of cohabitation with its disseminated leftovers.

This disquieting companionship that haunts theory's observation comes from the resolute refusal of the departed to remain forgotten (Schad 2003: 188–189) or mortified into a historical object for that matter. Because history, written by those who belong, obliterates the suffering of those who do not belong to its official stream, the exile aims at different kind of remembrance requesting the renouncement of theory's belonging. In order for theory to reinvent the cohabitation by maintaining receptivity for such "diasporic injunctions," Derrida finds Nietzsche's *active forgetting* to be a more appropriate solution than *mournful despair* à la Lyotard or Agamben. Unlike despair passionately attached to the continuity with the lost, active forgetting breaks the obedience to the existing law in the name of recommencing. Instead of compulsively adhering to the memory of the gone companion it matches together *experimental, tentative, and fictional companionships* out of the former's "bits and pieces." In that manner it interrupts the homogeneous stream of common history, rearranges its temporalities to crack its amnesia and prevent it in silencing the alarm sounded from "elsewhere."

"Forgetfulness is no mere vis inertiae, as the superficial believe; it is rather an active – in the strictest sense, positive – inhibiting capacity," states Nietzsche in *On the Genealogy of Morals* (1996: 39). In *The Use and Abuse of History for Life* (1957: 12), to which "active forgetting" refers, Nietzsche introduces the creatively pluralizing commemoration precisely to counteract history's unilateral effacement. Rather than taming the past by the allegedly superior wisdom of the present, memory acts in reverse, i.e., releases the liberating potential of the past to transform that which the present has regrettably come to be. Not for the sake of homogeneous dead eternity, it engages the past for the ongoing, plural and heterogeneous needs of life. If the science of history privileges the unifying *après coup* insight, then the art of memory opens itself to the multitude of *déjà vu* experiences, collecting their dissipated shards like a magnet. By delving into the polyphony of the past and rescuing numerous local and personal histories from erasure, it forges unexpected convergences between its suppressed voices and thus offers a counterweight to the triumphant voice of history. Focused on the transformation of the oppressive present, memory rejects the chronological accuracy of the past's reconstruction. Devoted to those deprived of history, it picks up, combines and fits together their ruins in order to establish a remedial alliance with them.

Nietzsche's subversive rewriting of history, especially with regard to this interlocking inclination of the disregarded, surprisingly accords with the one Benjamin worked out in his famous "Theses on the Philosophy of History."[8] Therein he states that "to articulate the past historically does not mean to recognize it 'the way it really was.' It means to seize hold of a memory as it flashes up at a moment of danger" (Benjamin 1969: 255). In developing a dispossessed cosmopolitanism of scattered *enablers* against the generous one of the superior *agency,* both Nietzsche and Benjamin engage the "tactical" operation of memory, generated out of the endangered, disfigured and disowned present, in order to subvert the tranquil "strategic" use of history. By "flashing up" Benjamin seems to be indicating that memory instantaneously, as it were, takes possession of the historian, explodes into his or her present, distracting his or her attention and rearticulating the latter's habitual priorities. Grabbing hold of the historian, it acts pretty much like Levinas's "face." In such a way, the historian is catapulted out of its privileged abode in the present and forced into what Benjamin calls the now-time (*Jetztzeit*). He defines this now-time as an enormous abridgment of the entire history of humankind, an uncanny fusion of divergent temporalities whose far removed "chips" suddenly reverberate with one another, entering a kind of curious "elective affinities." By compounding distinct temporal sequences and letting them resonate in one another, the memory's amalgamating of the dispossessed breaks apart the amnesia of the linear historic affiliations. Pressed by this divine spark of similarity into an unwilled proximity of the complete strangers to one another, one non-belonging suddenly comes to be shedding light on another.

Transforming the disturbing address of the departed companion into an imagined illuminative cohabitation with the unknown enablers deprived of belong-

---

[8] In the following, I am indebted to the illuminating reading of Benjamin offered by Butler 2012: 69–113.

ing – this might be the new political task of theoretical observation, as opposed to its former policing task. Attuning itself to the "elsewhere" of its exiled other, it cannot unite with him or her on any common basis, as it belongs to him or her only through non-belonging. As no *community* with the excluded is possible, what instead remains is a dispossessing *relationship* that disables the communal type of belonging on both sides. In the way I interpret that which Derrida renders as fidelity-by-betrayal, it amounts to the *agency's pre-legal, ethical commitment to its disabled enablers*. Such a commitment maintains audibility for the multiple voices silenced by the existing law and keeps the observer open for their rival recruitments.

As I have tried to demonstrate, the ethical involvement with the obliterated past was, next to Derrida, proposed and examined also by Nietzsche, Benjamin and Levinas. But there is another important thinker that might be engaged in this new political-ethical connection to widen, articulate and enrich it. By associating the theoretical activity with the recommencing search for the missing rule of cohabitation with its exiled enabler, Derrida, probably inadvertently, brings it close to the concept of political judgment as elaborated in the late work of Hannah Arendt. In her recent *Parting Ways* (2012) Judith Butler has made a strong case for the "diasporic" profile of Arendt's political thought against the "communitarian" readings of her work.[9]

Following her ongoing political concern with statelessness and rightlessness, argues Butler (2012: 126), Arendt consistently defends pluralization against universalization and denies anybody's right to set the universal rule of human commonality. What makes the idea of world history monstrous, says Arendt, is that it compresses the irreducible multitude of people into *one* human individual (2010: 12). However, one can become human only in relation of equality with the manifold others and not alone. As for Arendt being human means being free, no man can become free alone but merely "together with his equals and *only* with his equals" (1979: 301). "Indeed," this is how Butler (2012: 148) reads Arendt, "if there is no equality, no one is human" and equality disappears as soon as a self-nominated "agency of humanity," suspending the constitutive cohabitation with its remote and unknown enablers, unilaterally defines its terms. Being an arbitrary and violent act, such a definition of the human cannot but bereave another part of the irreducible *human many* of the right to bear human rights. And Arendt insists that "the right to have rights, or the right of every individual to belong to humanity, should be guaranteed by humanity itself" (1979: 298).

---

[9] See also Butler 2013: 122–123. To be sure, a number of scholars dealing with Arendt's work recently followed the same "agonistic" reading of her philosophy. See for example Disch 1997; Machart 2005; or Meints-Stender 2007.

In her *Lectures on Kant's Political Philosophy*, she interprets political judgment as Kantian reflective judgment exerted in the plural public space in which, following infinite responsibility toward the destitute that it unavoidably produces by its deliberations, it is obliged to engage ever new perspectives. As the public space is shaped exclusively by the practice of judgment, each and every commonality instituted in its frame is based on discriminatory values and therefore, instead of being sovereign and all-embracing as it used to present itself, exposed to dismantling by other judgments. As Linda Zerilli (2011: 124) puts it, "[j]udging may well call into question my sense of political community with some persons and reveal a new sense of community with others." So what we are dealing here with is not a smoothly progressing assimilation of the excluded performed by political judgment, but a series of the latter's transformative encounters caused by their consecutive appeals. As political judgment, in order to make up for one such appeal, induces another, all those that have been excluded by its reconfigured operations can be impossibly traced back to one and the same common denominator. Being discontinuous and displaced with regard to one another, their non-belonging resists a smooth translation into a new belonging, or indeed community for that matter.

Even if I cannot judge without visiting many scattered standpoints, which are beyond my own in order to overcome my own thinking – and this is the gist of Arendt's idea of human natality and recommencing – it is impossible for me to exhaust them all, and I ultimately must admit that my resulting judgment is not beyond question. It cannot but rely on "betrayal." Even if it revealed something new, it would preclude something else. "This sense of community is contestable because I can never compel anyone to agree with my judgment. […] To judge is not only to assume that others share my view of the world, but also to risk discovering that someone does not" (Zerilli 2011: 130). Since the public space thus appears to be not only plural, but also contradictory in its internal constitution – a multitude of conflicting public spaces rather than the one homogeneous public space – theoretical judgment, invited to a permanent rebirth of its imaginary cohabitations, receives calls of the excluded enablers forever anew. The commemoration undoubtedly breaks history's amnesia in an illuminating manner, but by forcefully merging, abbreviating and mistranslating its residues, it is in itself never uncontested either. On the contrary, its rearticulation of the legal norm, undertaken to safeguard the precarious many, is necessarily conjectural, counterfactual and experimental.

This somewhat unexpected point of concordance between Derrida's and Hannah Arendt's otherwise divergent philosophical perspectives is obviously far removed from the normative discourse of the so-called Critical Theory that dominated the Age of Theory characterized by the policing practice. Having been conceived in the Marxian spirit as ideology critique, Critical Theory championed its own judgments at the expense of others' prejudices. Arendt's and Derrida's envisioning of post-theory as an infinitely responsible thought that, necessarily detaching itself from its "object," does not stop searching for an appropriate cohabitation with the latter's precariousness in ever new terms, aims at the abandonment of such perilous sovereignty of theoretical judgment. It clearly resists today's intensified pressure on the humanities to produce "palpable, visible, measurable, and more or less immediately applicable knowledge after the model of the natural sciences" (Smith 2006: 122). Post-theory in the delineated Arendtian and Derridaean sense is not merely uninterested in that kind of "real knowledge," but also denounces the latter as a completely mistaken idea in the global world of antagonistically co-implicated perspectives. Whatever values are championed, they are in competition with other values, whatever choices we make, we face unintended consequences (Rasch 2011: 57). Instead of being directed toward universal consensus as the putative goal of any responsible intellectual activity, post-theory as it is interpreted here finds itself mired in non-deliberate interdependencies. Doomed to *common* rather than envisioned *public* sense, its judgments are anything but sovereign and all-encompassing.

The fundamental fallacy of Critical Theory was the systematic downplaying, if not utter rejection of that unavoidable common-sense short-circuiting of its enlightening long circuits. While on the one hand awakening and eye-opening, theoretical reason on the other hand entails devastation of those who disobey its *ultima linea* common sense judgments. This is the price of its enlightening activity. Its seemingly sovereign judgments always turn out to have been relying on prejudices. While this does not utterly disqualify its observations, it does restrict them. If we simply rejected them as "misplaced prejudices," we would set up a truth putatively superior to their blinded assertions and thus merely redouble the contested argument. Theory certainly must consistently replace prejudices with judgments, but, as Hannah Arendt has put it, "in the course of that replacement it is necessary to trace back these prejudices to the judgments inherent to them and to affiliate these judgments for their part to the underlying experiences which once gave rise to them" (2010: 79, transl. mine). As nobody can survive without prejudices and as our present judgment, somewhere and someday, becomes such a prejudice too, the analytical objective is not to dispose with prejudices altogether because of their failure to realize the universal truth. Nobody is in the possession of such truth.

Arendt therefore finds the necessary – limited and provisional – authority neither "in an untenable absolute, nor in a law of laws, but in the power of reconstitution itself" (Honig 1991: 102). This peculiar authority acquires the form of the persistent "practice of deauthorization" (111), i.e., the self-rewriting from ever-new perspectives. Such a self-constituting practice clearly resists the pre-given and enclosed notion of belonging. However, it entails not so much a self-congratulating progressive authorization of the theoretical agency but rather its responsive readapting to always-new cohabitations with the enablers. This is how Arendt conceives the constitutive freedom of thinking: an operation of the subversion of the reigning law, but permanently addressed and populated by the many, i.e., performed in their disconcerting company.[10] The slippery and heterogeneous character of this many makes such thinking vulnerable and precarious, but, as Judith Butler has convincingly argued (2012: 173–174), thinking cannot protect the precarious condition of its enablers without simultaneously exposing its agency to it. What drives the theorist's agency to cohabitate, converge with and bear upon the dispossession of its enablers is precisely material interdependency, shared precarity and, ultimately, adjacency of agencies and enablers.

Forever in need of reiteration, the aim of such post-theory is to lay bare the claim of prejudices to the status of universal truths as a pretension unsuitable for the incommensurably heterogeneous circumstances of human life and by doing so to open the space for traumatic experiences disregarded or even inflicted by such truths. Instead of being a practice aiming at the final reconciliation of *humankind*, theory thus becomes a recommencing practice of the *human many* unaccounted for. It takes the form of political judgment that systematically inspects "the line separating one life from the other" (Rancière 2004b: 303), which in the first place means the *borderline between the political agencies and the non-political enablers*. Keeping in mind that the political gesture par excellence is the gesture of excluding the enablers from the political, the discriminating effects of theoretical practice have to be constantly scrutinized by this practice itself. Rather than a final unification of incalculable human plurality, post-theory's permanent task is to raise awareness of the violence inherent in such undertakings as well as to renounce the unitary political identity imposed by them.

It is only through its concern for the permanent rebirth with which "something unique comes into the world" (Arendt 1958: 174), that today's post-theory can display its commitment to a profoundly endangered *life*. Because life is transient, perishable and extinguishable, today's post-theory is urged to shelter and treasure it; because life warrants freedom by its leap outside the determination of temporal continuity (Arendt 1993: 152) and thus interrupts the enclosure by the historical law, it deserves our full devotion and continuous care. It cannot happen

---

10 In opposing law, however, Arendt admittedly vacillates between "liberal" (Kantian) recourse to an extralegal sovereignty, which brings her close to Carl Schmitt, and "radical" recourse to the field of irreducible plurality, which brings her close to Benjamin. See Butler 2012: 173–175.

by itself but only by our assuming responsibility for it, our coming-to-terms with it via the "betrayal" of the reigning law. In terms in which Levinas rendered this responsibility, nobody can replace us in this disposition. As "all persons are the Messiah," "the fact of not evading the burden imposed by the suffering of others defines the self" (Levinas 1990a: 89). Arendt for her part interprets responsibility along similar lines. "I am the legislator," writes she (2003: 69), and my sin can be defined "as the refusal to act my part as legislator of the world." Or to render the same idea finally in Benjamin's terms, we never know whether it is not we ourselves who have been invited to rescue the deprived from the tyranny of law. This profound concern for the (legally) dispossessed is how he translates the guideline (*Richtschnur*) "Thou shalt not kill" (Benjamin 1996: 250). The trauma must not be repeated. As guidelines are neither coercive nor enforceable but variously applicable, it is up to us to interpret, adopt and enact them in given circumstances. Such an enactment, constrained by the animosity that haunts our non-deliberate cohabitation with the irritating dispossessed, is undoubtedly a probing, vexed and ambivalent operation. Nonetheless, the political-ethical encounter that takes the interdiction against destroying precarious life seriously remains the key responsibility of theory in the post-theoretical age, the very task of its survival.

References

Abensour, Miguel (2011) *Democracy against the State: Marx and the Macchiavelian Movement* (Cambridge: Polity).
Agamben, Giorgio (1993) *The Coming Community*, trans. M. Hardt (Minneapolis: University of Minnesota Press).
Agamben, Giorgio (1995) *Homo sacer. Il potere sovrano e la nuda vita* (Torino: Einaudi).
Agamben, Giorgio (1998) *Homo Sacer: Sovereign Power and Bare Life*, trans. Daniel Heller-Roazen (Stanford, CA: Stanford University Press).
Agamben, Giorgio (1999a) "Absolute Immanence," in *Potentialities: Collected Essays in Philosophy*, ed. and trans. Daniel Heller-Roazen (Stanford, CA: Stanford University Press), 220–242.
Agamben, Giorgio (1999b) *Remnants of Auschwitz: The Witness and the Archive*, trans. Daniel Heller-Roazen (New York: Zone).
Agamben, Giorgio (2000) *Means Without Ends: Notes on Politics*, trans. Vincenzo Binetti and Cesare Casarino (Minneapolis: University of Minnesota Press).
Agamben, Giorgio (2004) *The Open: Man and Animal*, trans. Kevin Attell (Stanford: Stanford University Press).
Agamben, Giorgio (2005a) *State of Exception*, trans. Kevin Attell (Chicago: University of Chicago Press).
Agamben, Giorgio (2005b) *The Time that Remains: A Commentary on the Letter to the Romans*, trans. Patricia Dailey (Stanford: Stanford University Press).
Albrecht, Andrea (2005) *Kosmopolitismus. Weltbürgerdiskurse in Literatur, Philosophie und Publizistik um 1800* (Berlin and New York: De Gruyter).
Alexander, Jeffrey (2012) *Trauma: A Social Theory* (Cambridge and Malden, MA: Polity).
Althusser, Louis (1982) "Idéologie et appareils idéologiques d'État (Notes pour une recherche)," in *Positions* (Paris: Les Éditions sociales), 67–125.
Amselle, Jean-Loup (2003) *Affirmative Exclusion: Cultural Pluralism and the Rule of Custom in France*, trans. Jean Marie Todd (Ithaca: Cornell University Press).
Appadurai, Arjun (1996) *Modernity at Large: Cultural Dimensions of Globalization* (Minneapolis and London: University of Minnesota Press).
Appiah, Kwame Anthony (2005) *The Ethics of Identity* (Princeton and Oxford: Princeton University Press).
Appiah, Kwame Anthony (2006) *Cosmopolitanism: Ethics in a World of Strangers* (New York and London: Norton).
Apter, Emily (1995) "Comparative Exile: Competing Margins in the History of Comparative Literature," in *Comparative Literature in the Age of Multiculturalism*, ed. Charles Bernheimer (Baltimore and London: Johns Hopkins University Press), 86–97.
Apter, Emily (2006) *The Translation Zone: A New Comparative Literature* (Princeton and Oxford: Princeton University Press).
Apter, Emily (2009) "Literary World-Systems," in *Teaching World Literature*, ed. David Damrosch (New York: The Modern Language Association of America), 44–60.
Arendt, Hannah (1958) *The Human Condition* (Chicago: University of Chicago Press).
Arendt, Hannah (1970) *On Violence* (San Diego and New York and London: Harcourt, Brace & World).

Arendt, Hannah (1979) *The Origins of Totalitarianism* (San Diego, CA: Harcourt, Brace & Jovanovich).

Arendt, Hannah (1992) *Lectures on Kant's Political Philosophy*, ed. and with an Interpretive Essay by Ronald Beiner (Chicago: University of Chicago Press).

Arendt, Hannah (1993) "What Is Freedom?," in *Between Past and Future: Eight Exercises in Political Thought* (London: Penguin), 143–171.

Arendt, Hannah (2003) *Responsibility and Judgment* (New York: Schocken).

Arendt, Hannah (2010) *Was ist Politik? Fragmente aus dem Nachlass*, ed. Ursula Ludz (Munich: Piper).

Aseguinolaza, Fernando Cabo (2006) "Dead, or a Picture of Good Health? Comparatism, Europe, and World Literature," *Comparative Literature*, Special Edition: *The Idea of Europe*, ed. Susan Rubin Suleiman, 58.4, 418–435.

Assmann, Aleida (1985) "Die Domestikation des Lesers. Drei historische Beispiele," *Zeitschrift für Literaturwissenschaft und Linguistik* 57/58.15, 95–110.

Assmann, Aleida (1993) *Arbeit am nationalen Gedächtnis: Eine kurze Geschichte der deutschen Bildungsidee* (Frankfurt/M.: Campus).

Assmann, Aleida (2004) "Zur Mediengeschichte des kulturellen Gedächtnisses," in *Medien des kollektiven Gedächtnisses: Konstruktivität, Historizität, Kulturspezifizität*, ed. Astrid Erll and Ansgar Nünning (Berlin and New York: De Gruyter), 45–60.

Attridge, Derek (2004) *The Singularity of Literature* (London and New York: Routledge).

Azim, Firdous (1993) *The Colonial Rise of the Novel* (London and New York: Routledge).

Badiou, Alain (2003) *Saint Paul: The Foundation of Universalism*, trans. Ray Brassier (Stanford: Stanford University Press).

Bakhtin, Mikhail (1979) *Estetika slovessnogo tvorchestva*, ed. Sergei Bocharov (Moscow: Iskusstvo).

Bakhtin, Mikhail (1981) *The Dialogic Imagination: Four Essays by M. M. Bakhtin*, ed. Michael Holquist, trans. Michael Holquist and Caryl Emerson (Austin: Texas University Press).

Bakhtin, Mikhail (1984) *Problems of Dostoevsky's Poetics*, ed. and trans. Caryl Emerson (Manchester: Manchester University Press).

Bakhtin, Mikhail (1986) *Speech Genres and Other Late Essays*, ed. Caryl Emerson and Michael Holquist (Austin: Texas University Press).

Bakhtin, Mikhail (1990) *Art and Answerability: Early Philosophical Essays by M. M. Bakhtin*, ed. and trans. Michael Holquist and Vadim Liapunov (Austin: Texas University Press).

Bakhtin, Mikhail (1992) "Pisma M. M. Bakhtina," *Literaturnaia ucheba*, 5–6.

Bakhtin, Mikhail (1994) *Towards a Philosophy of the Act*, ed. Vadim Liapunov and Michael Holquist (Austin: Texas University Press).

Bakhtin, M. M. and Medvedev P. N. (1978) *The Formal Method in Literary Scholarship: A Critical Introduction to Sociological Poetics*, trans. Albert J. Wehrle (Baltimore and London: Johns Hopkins University Press).

Bales, Kevin (1999) *Disposable People: New Slavery in the Global Economy* (Berkeley and Los Angeles and London: University of California Press).

Balibar, Étienne (2002) *Politics and the Other Scene* (London and New York: Routledge).

Balibar, Étienne (2004) *We, the People of Europe? Reflections on the Transnational Citizenship*, trans. James Swenson (Princeton and Oxford: Princeton University Press).

Banfield, Ann (1987) "Describing the Unobserved: Events Grouped around an Empty Center," in *The Linguistics of Writing: Arguments between Language and Literature*, ed. Nigel Fabb and Derrek Attridge and Alan Durant and Colin MacCabe (Manchester: Manchester University Press), 265–85.

Barnard, Frederick M. (1965) *Herder's Social and Political Thought: From Enlightenment to Nationalism* (Oxford: Clarendon).

Barnard, Frederick M. (1979) "Natural Growth and Purposive Development: Vico and Herder," *History and Theory* 18, 16–36.

Barnard, Frederick M. (2003) *Herder, Nationality, Humanity, and History* (Montreal and London and Ithaca: McGill-Queen's University Press).

Barthes, Roland (1966) "Introduction à l'analyse structural des récits," *Communications* 8.8, 1–27.

Barthes, Roland (1984) "Le discours de l'histoire," in *Le Bruissement de la langue: Essais critiques IV* (Paris: Seuil), 163–178.

Bauman, Zygmunt (1998) *Globalization: The Human Consequences* (New York: Columbia University Press).

Bauman, Zygmunt (2004) *Europe: An Unfinished Adventure* (Cambridge: Wiley).

Beardsworth, Richard (1996) *Derrida and the Political* (London and New York: Routledge).

Beardsworth, Richard (2007) "The Irony of Deconstruction and the Example of Marx," in *The Politics of Deconstruction: Jacques Derrida and the Other of Philosophy*, ed. Martin McQuillan (London: Pluto Press).

Beck, Ulrich (2002a) "The Cosmopolitan Society and Its Enemies," *Theory, Culture and Society* 19.1/2, 17–45.

Beck, Ulrich (2002b) "The Terrorist Threat – world risk society revisited," *Theory, Culture and Society* 19.4, 39–55.

Beck, Ulrich and Cronin, Ciaran (2006) *Cosmopolitan Vision* (Cambridge and Malden, MA: Polity).

Beck, Ulrich and Grande, Edgar (2007) *Cosmopolitan Europe* (Cambridge and Malden, MA: Polity).

Beebee, Thomas (2011) "What in the world does Friedrich Nietzsche have against Weltliteratur?," *Neohelicon* 38, 367–379.

Behler, Ernst (1993) *German Romantic Literary Theory* (Cambridge: Cambridge University Press).

Behler, Ernst (1997) *Ironie und literarische Moderne* (Paderborn and Munich: Fink).

Beiser, Frederick C. (1992) *Enlightenment, Revolution, and Romanticism: The Genesis of Modern German Political Thought 1790–1800* (Cambridge, MA and London: Harvard University Press).

Benhabib, Seyla (2006) *Another Cosmopolitanism: Hospitality, Sovereignty and Democratic Iterations* (Oxford and New York: Oxford University Press).

Benjamin, Walter (1969) "Theses on the Philosophy of History," in *Illuminations*, trans. Harry Zohn (New York: Schocken), 253–264.

Benjamin, Walter (1974) "Der Begriff der Kunstkritik in der deutschen Romantik," in *Gesammelte Schriften*, ed. Rolf Tiedemann and Hermann Schweppenhäuser, Vol. 1.1 (Frankfurt/M.: Suhrkamp), 7–122.

Benjamin, Walter (1980) "Der Ursprung des deutschen Trauerspiels," in *Gesammelte Schriften*, ed. Rolf Tiedemann and Hermann Schweppenhäuser, Vol. 1.1 (Frankfurt/M.: Suhrkamp), 203–430.

Benjamin, Walter (1996) "Critique of Violence," in *Selected Writings 1, 1913–1926*, ed. Marcus Bullock and Michael W. Jennings (Cambridge: Harvard University Press), 236–252.

Bennington, Geoffrey (1999) "Inter," in *Post-Theory: New Directions in Criticism*, ed. Martin McQuillan and Graeme MacDonald and Robin Purves and Stephen Thomson (Edinburgh: Edinburgh University Press), 103–119.

Benveniste Émile (1966) *Problèmes de linguistique générale*, Vol. 1 (Paris: Gallimard).

Benveniste, Émile (1967) "La forme et le sense dans le langage," in *Le Langage. Actes du XIIIe congrès. Société de Philosophie de langue française*, Vol. 2 (Neuchâtel: A la Baconnière), 29–47.

Berend, Ivan (1998) *Decades of Crisis: Central and Eastern Europe before World War II* (Berkeley and Los Angeles and London: University of California Press).

Berlant, Lauren (2011) *Cruel Optimism* (Durham and London: Duke University Press).

Berlin, Isaiah (1990) *The Crooked Timber of Humanity: Chapters in the History of Ideas*, ed. H. Hardy (Princeton and London: Princeton University Press).

Bernstein, Michael André (1989) "The Poetics of Ressentiment," in *Rethinking Bakhtin: Extensions and Challenges*, ed. G. S. Morson and C. Emerson (Evanston: Northwestern University Press), 197–225.

Bhabha, Homi (1994) *The Location of Culture* (London and New York: Routledge).

Birmingham, Peg (2009) "A Deceptive God of Dazzling Whiteness," *The New Centennial Review* 8.3, 107–117.

Biesta, Gert (2008) "Sporadic Democracy: Democracy, Education and the Question of Inclusion," in *Education, Democracy, and the Moral Life*, ed. Michael S. Katz and Susane Verducci and Gert Biesta (Dordrecht: Springer), 101–112.

Birus, Hendrik (1995) "Goethes Idee der Weltliteratur: Eine historische Vergegenwärtigung," http://www.goethezeitportal.de/fileadmin/PDF/db/wiss/goethe/birus_weltliteratur.pdf (Würzburg: Königshausen & Neumann) (accessed 5 August 2012).

Biti, Vladimir (2002) "The Conflict of Loyalties: Location and Mobility," in *Other Modernities in an Age of Globalization*, ed. Djelal Kadir and Dorothea Löbermann (Heidelberg: Carl Winter), 211–219.

Biti, Vladimir (2011a) "The Divided Legacy of the Enlightenment: Herder's Cosmopolitanism as Suppressed Eurocentrism," in *Old Margins and New Centers: The European Literary Heritage in the Age of Globalization*, ed. Marc Maufort and Caroline de Wagter (Bruxelles: Peter Lang), 73–83.

Biti, Vladimir (2011b) "The Self, the Novel and History: On the Limits of Bakhtin's Historical Poetics," *Orbis Litterarum* 66.4, 255–279.

Biti Vladimir (2014a) "Anschlussfähigkeit und postkoloniale Welt: Zum Stellenwert des Romans in Luhmanns Systemtheorie," in *Riskante Kontakte. (Wie)können sich Postkoloniale Theorien und Systemtheorie beobachten?*, ed. Mario Grizelj and Daniela Kirschstein (Berlin: Kadmos), 251–278.

Biti, Vladimir (2014b) "Katastrophe – Bruch oder Konstellation?," in *Der Erste Weltkrieg als Katastrophe: Deutungsmuster im literarischen Diskurs*, ed. Claude Conter and Oliver Jahraus and Christian Kirchmeier (Würzburg: Königshausen & Neumann), 21–33.

Blanchot, Maurice (1969) *L'Entretien infini* (Paris: Gallimard).

Blanchot, Maurice (1971) *L'amitié* (Paris: Gallimard).

Blanchot, Maurice (1980) *L'Écriture du desastre* (Paris: Gallimard).

Blanchot, Maurice (1982) *The Step Not Beyond*, trans. Nelson Lycette (Albany: State University of New York Press).

Blanchot, Maurice (1983) *La Communauté inavouable* (Paris: Minuit).

Blanchot, Maurice (1986a) *The Writing of the Disaster*, trans. A. Smock (Lincoln: University of Nebraska Press).
Blanchot, Maurice (1986b) *Michel Foucault tel que je l'imagine* (Saint-Clément: Fata Morgana).
Blanchot, Maurice (1987) "Michel Foucault as I Imagine Him," in *Foucault/Blanchot*, trans. J. Mehlman (New York: Zone).
Blanchot, Maurice (1992) *The Space of Literature*, trans. A. Smock (Lincoln and London: University of Nebraska Press).
Blanchot, Maurice (1993) *The Infinite Conversation*, trans. S. Hanson (Minneapolis: University of Minnesota Press).
Blanchot, Maurice (1995) *Work of Fire*, trans. C. Mandel (Stanford, CA: Stanford University Press).
Blanchot, Maurice (1997) *Friendship*, trans. E. Rottenberg (Stanford, CA: Stanford University Press).
Blanchot, Maurice (2003) *The Book to Come*, trans. C. Mandel (Stanford, CA: Stanford University Press).
Blumenberg, Hans (1984) *Arbeit am Mythos*. Third edition (Frankfurt/M.: Suhrkamp).
Blumenberg, Hans (1987) *Das Lachen der Thrakerin: eine Urgeschichte der Theorie* (Frankfurt/M.: Suhrkamp).
Blumenberg, Hans (1988) *Die Legitimität der Neuzeit* (Frankfurt/M.: Suhrkamp).
Bogue, Ronald (2005) "Minoritarian + Literature," in *The Deleuze Dictionary*, ed. Adrian Parr (Edinburgh: Edinburgh University Press), 167–169.
Bohnenkamp, Anne (2000) "Rezeption der Rezeption: Goethes Entwurf einer Weltliteratur im Kontext seiner Zeitschrift 'Über Kunst und Altertum'," in *Spuren, Signaturen, Spiegelungen: Zur Goethe-Rezeption in Europa*, ed. Bernard Beutler and Anke Bosse (Köln and Weimar and Wien: Böhlau), 187–205.
Borch-Jacobsen, Mikkel (1988) *The Freudian Subject*, trans. C. Porter (Stanford, CA: Stanford University Press).
Boubia, Fawzi (1985) "Goethes Theorie der Alterität und die Idee der Weltliteratur. Ein Beitrag zur neueren Kulturdebatte," in *Gegenwart als kulturelles Erbe: Ein Beitrag zur Kulturwissenschaft deutschsprachiger Länder*, ed. Bernd Thum (Munich: Iudicium), 269–301.
Boubia, Fawzi (1988) "Universal Literature and Otherness," *Diogenes* 36, 76–101.
Bowie, Andrew (1997) *From Romanticism to Critical Theory: The Philosophy of German Literary Theory* (London and New York: Routledge).
Brown, Wendy (2006) *Regulating Aversion: Tolerance in the Age of Identity and Empire* (Princeton and New Jersey: Princeton University Press).
Brubaker, Rogers (1992) *Citizenship and Nationhood in France and Germany* (Cambridge, MA and London: Cambridge University Press).
Brubaker, Rogers (1996) *Nationalism reframed: Nationhood and the national question in the New Europe* (Cambridge and New York: Cambridge University Press).
Brubaker, Rogers (2004) *Ethnicity without Groups* (Cambridge, MA and London: Cambridge University Press).
Brunkhorst, Hauke (2014) *Das doppelte Gesicht Europas: Zwischen Kapitalismus und Demokratie* (Frankfurt/M.: Suhrkamp).
Brunner, José (2014) *Die Politik des Traumas: Gewalterfahrungen und psychisches Leid in den USA, in Deutschland und im Israel/Palästina-Konflikt* (Frankfurt/M.: Suhrkamp).

Butler, Judith (1997) *The Psychic Life of Power: Theories in Subjection* (Stanford: Stanford University Press).
Butler, Judith (2003) *Kritik der ethischen Gewalt* (Frankfurt/M.: Suhrkamp).
Butler, Judith (2004a) *Undoing Gender* (London and New York: Routledge).
Butler, Judith (2004b) *Precarious Life: The Powers of Mourning and Violence* (London and New York: Verso).
Butler, Judith (2012) *Parting Ways: Jewishness and the Question of Zionism* (New York: Columbia University Press).
Butler, Judith (2013) *Dispossession: The Performative in the Political: Conversations with Athena Athanasiou* (Cambridge, MA: Polity).
Calhoun, Craig (2007) "Social solidarity as a problem for cosmopolitan democracy," in *Identities, Affiliations, and Allegiances*, ed. Seyla Benhabib and Ian Shapiro and Danilo Petranović (Cambridge and New York: Cambridge University Press), 285–302.
Caputo, John (2000) *More Radical Hermeneutics: On Not Knowing Who We Are* (Bloomington: Indiana University Press).
Caruth, Cathy (1996) *Unclaimed Experience: Trauma, Narrative, and History* (Baltimore and London: Johns Hopkins University Press).
Casanova, Pascale (2004) *The World Republic of Letters*, trans. M. B. Debevoise (Cambridge, MA and London: Harvard University Press).
Casanova, Pascale (2005) "Literature as a World," *New Left Review* 31, 71–90.
Cassirer, Ernst (1951) *The Philosophy of the Enlightenment*, trans. Fritz C. A. Koelln (Princeton: Princeton University Press).
Cavarero, Adriana (2000) *Relating Narratives: Storytelling and Selfhood* (London and New York: Routledge).
Cave, Terence (1988) *Recognitions: A Study in Poetics* (Oxford: Oxford University Press).
Certeau, Michel de (1975) *L'écriture de l'histoire* (Paris: Seuil).
Certeau, Michel de (1984) *The Practice of Everyday Life*, trans. Steven F. Rendall (Berkeley, CA: University of California Press).
Césaire, Aimé (2000) *Discourse on Colonialism*, trans. Joan Pinkham (New York: Monthly Review Press).
Chakrabarty, Dipesh (2000) *Provincializing Europe: Postcolonial Thought and Historical Difference* (Princeton and Oxford: Princeton University Press).
Chanter, Tina (1995) *Ethics of Eros: Irigaray's Rewriting of the Philosophers* (London and New York: Routledge).
Chanter, Tina (ed.) (2001) *Feminist Interpretations of Emmanuel Levinas* (University Park: University of Pennsylvania Press).
Chatman, Seymour (1978) *Story and Discourse: Narrative Structure in Fiction and Film* (Albany, NY: State University of New York Press).
Cheng, Pheah (1998) "The Cosmopolitical – Today," in *Cosmopolitics: Thinking and Feeling beyond the Nation*, ed. Pheah Cheng and Bruce Robbins (Minneapolis and London: University of Minnesota Press), 20–41.
Cherniavsky, Eva (2011) "The Canny Subaltern," in *Theory after 'Theory,'* ed. Jane Elliott and Derek Attridge (London and New York: Routledge), 149–162.
Chytry, Josef (1989) *The Aesthetic State: A Quest in Modern German Thought* (Berkeley and Los Angeles and London: University of California Press).

Citton, Yves (2009) "Political Agency and the Ambivalence of the Sensible," in *Jacques Rancière: History, Politics, Aesthetics*, ed. Gabriel Rockhill and Philip Watts (Durham and London: Duke University Press), 120–140.

Clark, Katherina and Holquist, Michael (1984) "The Influence of Kant in the Early Work of M.M. Bakhtin," in *Literary Theory and Criticism: Festschrift Presented to René Wellek in Honor of his Eightieth Birthday*, ed. Joseph Strelka, Vol. 1 (Bern and New York: Peter Lang), 299–313.

Clark, Timothy (2005) *The Poetics of Singularity: The Counter-Culturalist Turn in Heidegger, Derrida, Blanchot and the later Gadamer* (Edinburgh: Edinburgh University Press).

Colebrook, Claire (2011) "Extinct theory," in *Theory after 'Theory'*, ed. Jane Elliott and Derek Attridge (London and New York: Routledge), 62–71.

Collingwood, Robin G. (1961) *The Idea of History*, ed. T.M. Knox (Oxford: Oxford University Press).

Compagnon, Antoine (2004) *Literature, Theory, and the Common Sense*, trans. Carol Cosman (Princeton and Oxford: Princeton University Press).

Connolly, William E (2000) "Refashioning the Secular," in *What's Left of Theory? New Work on the Politics of Literary Theory*, ed. Judith Butler and John Guillory and Thomas Kendall (London and New York: Routledge), 157–191.

Connor, Walker (1994) *Ethnonationalism: The Quest for Understanding* (Princeton: Princeton University Press).

Coopan, Vilashini (2009) "The Ethics of World Literature: Reading Others, Reading Otherwise," in *Teaching World Literature* (New York: The Modern Language Association of America), 34–43.

Currie, Mark (1998) *Postmodern Narrative Theory* (New York: Palgrave Macmillan).

Currie, Mark (2004) *Difference* (London and New York: Routledge).

Curtius, Ernst Robert (1954) "Goethe als Kritiker," in *Kritische Essays zur europäischen Literatur* (Bern: Francke), 31–56.

Curtis, James M. (1986) "Mikhail Bakhtin, Nietzsche and Russian Pre-Revolutionary Thought," in *Nietzsche in Russia*, ed. Bernice Glazer Rosenthal (New Jersey: Princeton University Press), 331–354.

Dainat, Holger and Kruckis, Hans-Martin (1995) "Die Ordnungen der Literatur(wissenschaft)," in *Literaturwissenschaft*, ed. Jürgen Fohrmann and Harro Müller (Munich: UTB), 116–155.

Dainotto, Roberto M. (2007) *Europe (in Theory)* (Durham and London: Duke University Press).

Dalton, Stuart (2000) "Nancy and Kant on Inoperative Communities," *Critical Horizons* 1.1, 29–50.

Damrosch, David (2003) *What Is World Literature?* (Princeton and Oxford: Princeton University Press).

Damrosch, David (2006) "World Literature in a Postcanonical, Hypercanonical Age," in *Comparative Literature in an Age of Globalization*, ed. Haun Saussy (Baltimore: Johns Hopkins University), 43–53.

Damrosch, David (2009) *How to Read World Literature* (Malden and Oxford: Blackwell-Wiley).

Das, Veena (2007) *Life and Words: Violence and the Descent into the Ordinary* (Berkeley and Los Angeles and London: University of California Press).

Davis, Oliver (2010) *Jacques Rancière* (Cambridge: Polity).

Deleuze, Gilles and Foucault, Michel (1977) "Intellectuals and Power," in Michel Foucault, *Language, Counter-Memory, Practice: Selected Essays and Interviews*, ed. Donald F. Bouchard (Ithaca and New York: Cornell University Press), 205–217.

Deleuze, Gilles and Guattari, Félix (1983) *Anti-Oedipus: Capitalism and Schizophrenia*, trans. R. Hurley and M. Seem and H. R. Lane, Vol. 1 (Minneapolis: University of Minnesota Press).

Deleuze, Gilles and Guattari, Félix (1986) *Kafka: Toward a Minor Literature*, trans. D. Polan (Minneapolis: University of Minnesota Press).

Deleuze, Gilles and Guattari, Félix (1987) *A Thousand Plateaus: Capitalism and Schizophrenia*, trans. B. Massumi (Minneapolis: University of Minnesota Press).

Deleuze, Gilles and Guattari, Félix (1991) *Que-ce que la philosophie?* (Paris: Minuit).

Deleuze, Gilles and Guattari, Félix (1994) *What Is Philosophy?*, trans. Graham Burchell and Hugh Tomlinson (London and New York: Verso).

Deleuze, Gilles (1994) *Difference and Repetition*, trans. P. Patton (New York and London: Columbia University Press).

Deleuze, Gilles (1995) "Immanence: Une vie...," *Philosophie* 47.

Deleuze, Gilles (1998) *Essays Critical and Clinical*, trans. D. W. Smith and M. A. Greco (London: Verso).

Deleuze, Gilles (2005) *Pure Immanence: Essays on a Life*, trans. Anne Boyman (New York: Zone Books).

De Man, Paul (1986) *Resistance to Theory* (Minneapolis: University of Minnesota Press).

Derrida, Jacques (1967a) "Violence et métaphysique: Essai sur la pensée d'Emmanuel Lévinas," in *Écriture et différence* (Paris: Seuil), 117–228.

Derrida, Jacques (1967b) *De la grammatologie* (Paris: Minuit).

Derrida, Jacques (1976) *Of Grammatology*, trans. Gayatri Spivak (Baltimore: Johns Hopkins University Press).

Derrida, Jacques (1978) "Violence and Metaphysics," in *Writing and Difference*, trans. A. Bass (Chicago: University of Chicago Press), 79–153.

Derrida, Jacques (1979) *Spurs: Nietzsche's Styles/Éperons: Les Styles de Nietzsche*, trans. B. Harlow (Chicago and London: University of Chicago Press).

Derrida, Jacques (1985) "Préjugés – devant la loi," in Jacques Derrida and Vincent Descombes and Garbis Kortian and Philippe Lacoue-Labarthe and Jean-François Lyotard and Jean-Luc Nancy, *La faculté de juger* (Paris: PUF), 87–139.

Derrida, Jacques (1986) "Declarations of Independence," *New Political Science* 15, 7–15.

Derrida, Jacques (1989) "Some Statements and Truisms about Neologisms, Newisms, Postisms, Parasitisms, and other small Seismisms," in *The States of Theory*, ed. David Carroll (New York: Columbia University Press), 63–94.

Derrida, Jacques (1992a) *The Other Heading: Reflections on Today's Europe*, trans. Pascale-Anne Braulut and Michael B. Naas (Bloomington and Indianapolis: University of Indiana Press).

Derrida, Jacques (1992b) "The Force of Law: The 'Mystical Foundation of Authority'," in *Deconstruction and the Possibility of Justice*, ed. David Carlson and Drucilla Cornell and Michael Rosenfeld (New York: Taylor & Francis), 3–67.

Derrida, Jacques (1992c) *Given Time I: Counterfeit Money*, trans. Peggy Kamuf (Chicago: University of Chicago Press).

Derrida, Jacques (1992d) "This Strange Institution Called Literature," in *Acts of Literature*, ed. Derek Attridge (London and New York: Routledge), 33–75.

Derrida, Jacques (1992e) *Donner la mort. L'Éthique du don: Jacques Derrida et la pensée du don*. Actes du colloque de Royaumont, ed. Jean-Michael Rabaté and Michael Wetzel (Paris: Transition).

Derrida, Jacques (1994a) *Specters of Marx: The State of Debt, the Work of Morning & the New International*, trans. Peggy Kamuf (London and New York: Routledge).

Derrida, Jacques (1994b) *Politiques de l'amitié* (Paris: Galilée).
Derrida, Jacques (1994c) *Force de loi: Le "Fondement mystique de l'autorité"* (Paris: Galilée).
Derrida, Jacques (1995a) *Points: Interviews 1974–1994*, ed. Elisabeth Weber (Stanford: Stanford University Press).
Derrida, Jacques (1995b) *The Gift of Death*, trans. David Wills (Chicago: University of Chicago Press).
Derrida, Jacques (1995c) *On the Name*, trans. J. P. Leavey and Jr. D. Wood and I. McLeod. (Stanford, CA: Stanford University Press).
Derrida, Jacques (1997) *Adieu* (Paris: Galilée).
Derrida, Jacques (2000a) *Demeure: Fiction and Testimony*, trans. E. Rottenberg (Stanford, CA: Stanford University Press).
Derrida, Jacques (2000b) *Of Hospitality*, trans. R. Bowby (Stanford, CA: Stanford University Press).
Derrida, Jacques (2001a) *A Taste for the Secret*, ed. G. Donis and D. Webb, trans. G. Donis (Cambridge: Polity).
Derrida, Jacques (2001b) *On Cosmopolitanism and Forgiveness*, trans. Mark Dooley and Michael Hughes (London and New York: Routledge).
Derrida, Jacques (2002) *Without Alibi*, ed. and trans. Peggy Kamuf (Stanford, CA: Stanford University Press).
Derrida, Jacques (2003) "Following theory," in *Life.after.theory*, ed. Michael Payne and John Schad (London and New York: Continuum), 1–52.
Derrida, Jacques (2005) *Rogues: Two Essays on Reason*, trans. Pascale-Anne Brault and Michael Naas (Stanford: Stanford University Press).
Derrida, Jacques and Pierre-Jean Labarrière (1986) *Altérités* (Paris: Osiris).
Deutscher, Isaac (1968) *The Non-Jewish Jew and Other Essays* (Boston: Alyson Publications).
Disch, Lisa (1997) "'Please Sit Down, but Don't Make Yourself at Home': Arendtian 'Visiting' and the Prefigurative Politics of Consciousness-Raising," in *Hannah Arendt and the Meaning of Politics*, ed. Craig Calhoun and John McGowan (Minneapolis and London: University of Minnesota Press), 132–165.
Douzinas, Costas (2007) *Human Rights and Empire: The political philosophy of cosmopolitanism* (Milton Park and New York: Routledge-Cavendish).
Du Bois, William E. B. (1990) *The Souls of Black Folk* (New York: Vintage).
Dumont, Louis (1977) *Essays in Individualism: Modern Ideology in Anthropological Perspective* (Chicago: University of Chicago Press).
Dumont, Louis (1980) *Homo Hierarchicus: The Caste System and Its Implications* (Chicago: University of Chicago Press).
Dumont, Louis (1994) *German Ideology: From France to Germany and Back* (Chicago: University of Chicago Press).
Dussel, Enrique (1993) "Eurocentrism and modernity (Introduction to Frankfurt lectures)," in *Postmodernism Debate in Latin America*, ed. X. Albó and J. Beverley and J. Oviedo (Durham, NC: Duke University Press), 65–76.
Dussel, Enrique (1998) "Beyond Eurocentrism: The World-System and the Limits of Modernity," in *The Cultures of Globalization*, ed. Fredric Jameson and Masao Miyoshi (Durham, NC: Duke University Press), 3–31.
Eagleton, Terry (2003) *After Theory* (London: Allen Lane).
Echternkamp, Jörg (1998) *Der Aufstieg des deutschen Nationalismus (1770–1840)* (Frankfurt/M. and New York: Campus).

Eikhenbaum, Boris (1927) *Literatura (Teoriia, kritika, polemika)* (Leningrad: Priboi).
Elias, Norbert (1978) *The Civilizing Process*, trans. Edmund Jeffcot (New York: Wiley).
Engels, Friedrich (1970) "Der demokratische Panslawismus (1849)," in Karl Marx and Friedrich Engels, *Werke*, Vol. 6 (Berlin: Dietz), 270–86.
Erlich, Victor (1965) *Russian Formalism: History – Doctrine* (The Hague: Mouton).
Eskin, Michael (2001) *Ethics and Dialogue. In the Works of Levinas, Bakhtin, Mandel'shtam, and Celan* (Oxford: Oxford University Press).
Esposito, Roberto (2011) "The Person and Human Life," in *Theory after 'Theory'*, ed. Jane Elliott and Derek Attridge (London and New York: Routledge), 205–220.
Evans, Mari (ed.) (1983) *Black Women Writers: Arguments and Interviews* (London: Pluto Press).
Eze, Emmanuel Chukwudi (1995) "The Color of Reason: The Idea of "Race" in Kant's Anthropology," in *Anthropology and the German Enlightenment: Perspectives on Humanity*, ed. K. M. Faull (Lewisburg and London: Bucknell University Press), 200–241.
Eze, Emmanuel Chukwudi (1997) "Introduction," in *Race and the Enlightenment*, ed. E. C. Eze (Oxford and Cambridge: Wiley), 1–9.
Fanon, Frantz (1986) *Black Skin, White Masks*, trans. Charles Lam Markman (London: Pluto Press).
Fassin, Didier and Rechtman, Richard (2009) *The Empire of Trauma: An Inquiry into the Condition of Victimhood*, trans. Rachel Gomme (Princeton and Oxford: Princeton University Press).
Febvre, Lucien (1973) "Frontière: The Word and the Concept," in Lucien Febvre, *A New Kind of History and Other Essays*, ed. Peter Burke, trans. K. Folca (London and New York: Routledge), 208–218.
Felman, Shoshana (1983) *The Literary Speech Act: Don Juan with J. L. Austin, or seduction in two languages* (Ithaca, NY: Cornell University Press).
Felman, Shoshana and Laub, Dori (1992) *Testimony: Crises of Witnessing in Literature, Psychoanalysis and History* (New York and London: Taylor & Francis).
Ferrara, Alessandro (1999) *Justice and Judgment: the rise and prospect of the judgment model in contemporary political philosophy* (London: Sage).
Fine, Robert (2007) *Cosmopolitanism* (London and New York: Routledge).
Fink, Gonthier-Louis (1993) "Kosmopolitismus – Patriotismus – Xenophobie: Eine französisch-deutsche Debatte im Revolutionsjahrzehnt 1789–1799," in *Gesellige Vernunft: Zur Kultur der literarischen Aufklärung*, ed. Ortrud Gutjahr and Wilhelm Kühlmann and Wolf Wucherpfennig (Würzburg: Königshausen & Neumann), 23–42.
Fohrmann, Jürgen (1989) *Das Projekt der deutschen Literaturgeschichte: Entstehung und Scheitern einer nationalen Poesiegeschichtsschreibung zwischen Humanismus und deutschem Kaiserreich* (Stuttgart: Metzler).
Fohrmann, Jürgen (1994) "Geschichte der deutschen Literaturgeschichtsschreibung zwischen Aufklärung und Kaiserreich," in *Wissenschaftsgeschichte der Germanistik im 19. Jahrhundert*, ed. Jürgen Fohrmann and Wilhelm Voßkamp (Stuttgart and Weimar: Metzler), 576–604.
Foucault, Michel (1965) *Madness and Civilization*, trans. R. Howard (New York: Pantheon).
Foucault, Michel (1971) *The Order of Things: An Archeology of the Human Sciences*, trans. A. Sheridan (New York: Pantheon).
Foucault, Michel (1972) *The Archeology of Knowledge & The Discourse on Language*, trans. A. Sheridan Smith (New York: Pantheon).

Foucault, Michel (1977a) *Discipline and Punish: The Birth of the Prison*, trans. A. Sheridan Smith (New York: Pantheon).

Foucault, Michel (1977b) *Language, Counter-Memory, Practice: Selected Essays and Interviews*, ed. D. F. Bouchard (Ithaca: Cornell University Press).

Foucault, Michel (1980) "The History of Sexuality: An Interview with Lucette Finns," in *Power/Knowledge: Selected Interviews and Other Writings, 1972–77*, ed. C. Gordon (New York: Pantheon), 183–192.

Foucault, Michel (1983) "About the Beginning of the Hermeneutics of the Self," *Political Theory* 21.2, 198–227.

Foucault, Michel (1984a) "Politics and Ethics: An Interview," in *The Foucault Reader*, ed. Paul Rabinow (New York: Pantheon), 373–380.

Foucault, Michel (1984b) "Polemics, Politics and Problemizations: An Interview with Michel Foucault," in *The Foucault Reader*, ed. Paul Rabinow (New York: Pantheon), 381–390.

Foucault, Michel (1984c) "On the Genealogy of Ethics: An Overview of Work in Progress," in *The Foucault Reader*, ed. Paul Rabinow (New York: Pantheon), 340–372.

Foucault, Michel (1984d) "Nietzsche, Genealogy, History," in *The Foucault Reader*, ed. Peter Rabinow (New York: Pantheon), 76–100.

Foucault, Michel (1985) *The Use of Pleasure*, trans. R. Hurley (New York: Pantheon).

Foucault, Michel (1986) "Of Other Spaces," trans. Jan Miskowiec, *Diacritics* 16.1, 22–27.

Foucault, Michel (1987) "Maurice Blanchot: The Thought from Outside," trans. B. Massumi, in *Foucault/Blanchot* (New York: Zone).

Foucault, Michel (1988) "The Concern for Truth," in *Politics, Philosophy, Culture: Interviews and Other Writings 1977–1984*, ed. Lawrence D. Kritzman (London and New York: Routledge), 255–67.

Foucault Michel (1990) "Qu-est ce que la critique? /Critique et Aufklärung/," *Bulletin de la Société française de philosophie 84*, 35–63.

Foucault, Michel (1991a) *Remarks on Marx: Conversations with Duccio Trombadori*, trans. R.J. Goldstein and J. Cascaito (New York: Semiotext(e)).

Foucault, Michel (1991b) "Governmentality," rev. Colin Gordon and trans. Rosi Braidotti, in *The Foucault Effect: Studies in Governmentality*, ed. Graham Burchell and Colin Gordon and Peter Miller (Chicago: University of Chicago Press), 87–104.

Foucault, Michel (1996) "What Is Critique?," in *What Is Enlightenment? Eighteenth-Century Answers and Twentieth-Century Questions*, ed. J. Smith (Berkeley and Los Angeles and London: University of California Press), 382–398.

Foucault, Michel (1997) "What Is Enlightenment?," in *Ethics: Subjectivity and Truth*, ed. P. Rabinow (New York: New Press), 303–319.

Foucault, Michel (2001a) "La vie: l'expérience et la science," in *Dits et écrits II, 1976–88*, ed. Daniel Defert and François Ewald in collaboration with J. Lagrange (Paris: Gallimard), 1582–1595.

Foucault, Michel (2001b) "Pouvoirs et strategies (entretien avec Jacques Rancière)," in *Dits et écrits II, 1976–88*, ed. D. Defert and F. Ewald in collaboration with J. Lagrange (Paris: Gallimard), 418–428.

Foucault, Michel (2001c) "Introduction par Michel Foucault," in *Dits et écrits II, 1976–88*, ed. D. Defert and F. Ewald in collaboration with J. Lagrange (Paris: Gallimard), 429–442.

Foucault, Michel (2001d) "La pensée du dehors," *Dits et écrits I, 1954–69*, ed. D. Defert and F. Ewald (Paris: Gallimard), 546–67.

Foucault, Michel (2001e) "Qu'est-ce que les Lumières?," in *Dits et écrits II, 1976–88*, ed. D. Defert and F. Ewald in collaboration with J. Lagrange (Paris: Gallimard), 1381–1397.

Foucault, Michel (2008a) *Introduction à l'Anthropologie de Kant (Genèse et structure de l'Anthropologie de Kant)*, ed. D. Defert and F. Ewald and F. Gros (Paris: Vrin).

Foucault, Michel (2008b) *The Birth of Biopolitics: Lectures at the Collège de France 1978–1979*, Vol. 5 (London: Palgrave Macmillan).

Foucault, Michel (2010) *The Government of Self and Others: Lectures at the Collège de France 1982–1983*, Vol. 7 (London: Palgrave Macmillan).

Freise, Matthias (1993) *Michail Bachtins philosophische Ästhetik der Literatur* (Frankfurt/M. and New York: Peter Lang).

Freud, Sigmund (1947) "Das Unheimliche (1919)," in *Gesammelte Werke*, Vol. 12 (London: Imago), 229–68.

Fuller, Steve (2000) *Thomas Kuhn: A Philosophical History for Our Times* (Chicago and London: University of Chicago Press).

Fuss, Diana (1995) *Identification Papers* (London and New York: Routledge).

Gasché, Rodolphe (2007) *The Honor of Thinking: Critique, Theory, Philosophy* (Stanford: Stanford University Press).

Gasché, Rodolphe (2009) *Europe or the Infinite Task: A Study of a Philosophical Concept* (Stanford: Stanford University Press).

Genette, Gérard (1969) "Frontières du récit (1966)," in *Figures 2* (Paris: Seuil), 49–69.

Genette, Gérard (1972) *Discours du récit: Figures 3* (Paris: Seuil).

Gibson, Andrew (1996) *Towards a Postmodern Theory of Narrative* (Edinburgh: Edinburgh University Press).

Gibson, Andrew (2005) "The Unfinished Song: Intermittency and Melancholy in Rancière," *Paragraph* 28.1, 61–76.

Gilroy, Paul (1993) *The Black Atlantic: Modernity and Double Consciousness* (Cambridge, MA: Harvard University Press).

Gilroy, Paul (2000) *Against the Race: Imagining Political Culture beyond the Color Line* (Cambridge, MA: Harvard University Press).

Gilroy, Paul (2005) *After Empire: Melancholia or Convivivial Culture?* (London and New York: Rotledge, Chapman & Hall).

Ginzburg, Carlo (1996) "Making Things Strange: The Prehistory of a Literary Device," *Representations* 56, 8–28.

Girardet, Raoul (1983) *Le nationalisme français: Anthologie 1871–1914* (Paris: Seuil).

Goethe, Johann Wolfgang (1887–1912) *Goethes Werke*, 50 vols, edition commissioned by Archduchess Sophie von Sachsen (Weimar: Böhlau).

Goethe, Johann Wolfgang (1965–1978) *Goethes Werke*, 22 vols, ed. Siegried Seidel (Berlin: Aufbau).

Goethe, Johann Wolfgang (1987) *Schriften zur Weltliteratur*, ed. Horst Günther (Frankfurt/M.: Fischer).

Goethe, Johann Wolfgang (1986–1999) *Sämtliche Werke. Briefe, Tagebücher und Gespräche*, 40 vols, ed. Friedmar Apel and Hendrik Birus et al. (Frankfurt/M.: Suhrkamp-Insel).

Goodman, Dena (1994) *The Republic of Letters: A Cultural History of the French Enlightenment* (Ithaca and New York: Cornell University Press).

Greenblatt, Stephen (1980) *Renaissance Self-Fashioning: From More to Shakespeare* (Chicago: University of Chicago Press).

Greenblatt, Stephen (2010) "Cultural mobility: an introduction," in *Cultural Mobility: A Manifesto*, ed. Stephen Greenblatt and Ines Županov and Reinhard Meyer-Kalkus and Paul Heike and Pál Nyíri and Frederike Pannewick (Cambridge and New York: Cambridge University Press), 1–23.

Grosrichard, Alain (1979) *Structure du sérail: La fiction du despotisme asiatique dans l'Occident classique* (Paris: Seuil).

Günther, Hans (1990) "'Weltliteratur' bei der Lektüre des *Globe* konzipiert," in *Versuche, europäisch zu denken: Deutschland und Frankreich* (Frankfurt/M.: Suhrkamp), 104–125.

Gürtler, Sabine (2001) *Elementare Ethik: Alterität, Generativität und Geschlechterverhältnis bei Emmanuel Lévinas* (Munich: Fink).

Guha, Ranajit (2002) *History at the Limit of World-History* (New York: Columbia University Press).

Haase, Ullrich and Large, William (2001) *Maurice Blanchot* (London and New York: Routledge).

Habermas, Jürgen (1962) *Strukturwandel der Öffentlichkeit: Untersuchungen zu einer Kategorie der bürgerlichen Gesellschaft* (Neuwied and Berlin: Luchterhand).

Habermas, Jürgen (1996) "Kants Idee des ewigen Friedens – aus dem historischen Abstand von 200 Jahren," in *Die Einbeziehung des Anderen: Studien zur politischen Theorie* (Frankfurt/M.: Suhrkamp), 192–236.

Habermas, Jürgen (2001) "Why Europe Needs a Constitution?" *New Left Review* 11, 5–26.

Habermas, Jürgen and Derrida, Jacques (2003) "February 15, or What Binds Europeans Together: a plea for a common foreign policy, beginning in the core of Europe," *Constellations* 10.3, 291–297.

Habermas, Jürgen (2004) "Hat die Konstitutionalisierung des Völkerrechts noch eine Chance?," in *Der gespaltene Westen* (Frankfurt/M.: Suhrkamp), 113–193.

Habermas, Jürgen (2005) "Eine politische Verfassung für die pluralistische Weltgesellschaft?," in *Zwischen Naturalismus und Religion* (Frankfurt/M.: Suhrkamp), 324–365.

Habermas, Jürgen (2011) *Zur Verfassung Europas: Ein Essay* (Frankfurt/M.: Suhrkamp).

Hägglund, Martin (2011) "The Arche-Materiality of Time: Deconstruction, Speculative Materialism, and Radical Atheism," in *Theory after 'Theory'*, ed. Jane Elliott and Derek Attridge (London and New York: Routledge), 265–77.

Hall, Stuart (1992) "Cultural Studies and its Theoretical Legacies," in *Cultural Studies*, ed. Lawrence Grossberg and Cary Nelson and Paula Trechler (London and New York: Routledge), 277–294.

Halperin, David (2002) *How to Do the History of Homosexuality* (Chicago: University of Chicago Press).

Hansen-Löve, Aage (1978) *Der russische Formalismus: Methodologische Rekonstruktion seiner Entwicklung aus dem Prinzip der Verfremdung* (Vienna: Österreichische Akademie der Wissenschaften).

Hanson, Stephen E. (2010) *Post-Imperial Democracies: Ideology and Party Formation in Third Republic France, Weimar Germany, and Post-Soviet Russia* (Cambridge and New York: Cambridge University Press).

Hanssen, Beatrice (1998) *Walter Benjamin's Other History: Of Stones, Animals, Human Beings and Angels* (Berkeley and Los Angeles: University of California Press).

Hanssen, Beatrice (2000) *Critique of Violence: Between Poststructuralism and Critical Theory* (London and New York: Routledge).

Hassner, Pierre (1991) "L'Europe et le spectre des nationalismes," *Esprit* 175.

Hegel, Georg Wilhelm Friedrich (1956) *The Philosophy of History*, trans. J. Sibree (New York: Dover).
Hegel, Georg Wilhelm Friedrich (1975) *Aesthetics: Lectures on Fine Art*, trans. T. M. Knox, 2 vols (Oxford: Clarendon).
Hegel, Georg Wilhelm Friedrich (1977) *The Phenomenology of the Spirit*, trans. A. V. Miller (Oxford: Oxford University Press).
Hegel, Georg Wilhelm Friedrich (1991) *Elements of the Philosophy of Right*, trans. Allen W. Wood (Cambridge: Cambridge University Press).
Hegel, Georg Wilhelm Friedrich (1997) "Race, History, and Imperialism: Geographical Basis of World History," in *Race and the Enlightenment*, ed. Emmanuel Chukwudi Eze (Oxford and Cambridge, MA: Wiley), 110–149.
Hempel, Wido (1989) "Zu Voltaires schriftstellerischer Strategie," in *Aufklärung und Gegenaufklärung in der europäischen Literatur, Philosophie und Politik von der Antike bis zur Gegenwart*, ed. Jochen Schmidt (Darmstadt: Wissenschaftliche Buchhandlung), 243–261.
Herder, Johann Gottfried (1891) *Auch eine Philosophie zur Bildung der Menschheit*, ed. Bernhard Suphan, *Sämtliche Werke*, ed. Reinhold Stieg, Vol. 5 (Berlin: Adamant).
Herder, Johann Gottfried (1966) "Essay on the Origin of Language," in Jean-Jacques Rousseau & Johann Gottfried Herder, *Two Essays on the Origin of Language*, trans. John H. Moran and Alexander Gode (Chicago: University of Chicago Press).
Herder, Johann Gottfried (1968) *Reflections on the Philosophy of the History of Mankind*, trans. T. O. Churchill ed. Frank. E. Manuel (Chicago and London: University of Chicago Press).
Herder, Johann Gottfried (1985) *Frühe Schriften 1764–1772*, ed. U. Gaier, *Werke in zehn Bänden*, ed. Martin Bollacher et al., Vol. 1 (Frankfurt/M: Deutscher Klassiker Verlag).
Herder, Johann Gottfried (1989) *Ideen zur Philosophie der Geschichte der Menschheit*, ed. Martin Bollacher, *Werke in zehn Bänden*, ed. Martin Bollacher et al., Vol. 6 (Frankfurt/M.: Deutscher Klassiker Verlag).
Herder, Johann Gottfried (1991) *Briefe zu Beförderung der Humanität*, ed. Hans Dietrich Irmscher, *Werke in zehn Bänden*, ed. Martin Bolacher et al. Vol. 7 (Frankfurt/M.: Deutscher Klassiker Verlag).
Herder, Johann Gottfried (1994) "Auch eine Philosophie der Geschichte zur Bildung der Menschheit," in *Schriften zu Philosophie, Literatur, Kunst und Altertum 1774–1787*, ed. Jürgen Brummack and Martin Bollacher, *Werke in zehn Bänden*, ed. Martin Bollacher et al., Vol. 4 (Frankfurt/M.: Deutscher Klassiker Verlag), 9–109.
Herder, Johann Gottfried (1997a) "Journal meiner Reise im Jahr 1769," in *Pädagogische Schriften*, ed. Rainer Wisbert, *Werke in zehn Bänden*, ed. Martin Bollacher et al., Vol. 9.2 (Frankfurt/M.: Deutscher Klassiker Verlag).
Herder, Johann Gottfried (1997b) "Organization of the Peoples of Africa," in *Race and the Enlightenment*, ed. Emmanuel Chukwudi Eze (Oxford and Cambridge, MA: Wiley), 65–78.
Hewlett, Nick (2007) *Badiou, Balibar, Rancière: Rethinking Emancipation* (London: Continuum).
Hirsch, Marianne (2012) *The Generation of Postmemory: Writing and Visual Culture after the Holocaust* (Chicago: University of Chicago Press).
Hirschkop, Ken (1999) *Mikhail Bakhtin: An Aesthetic for Democracy* (Oxford and New York: Oxford University Press).
Hofmannstahl, Hugo (1979) *Reden und Aufsätze I (1891–1913)*, *Gesammelte Werke in zehn Einzelbänden*, ed. Bernd Schoeller, Vol. 8 (Frankfurt/M.: Fischer).

Hobsbawm, Eric (1983) "Introduction: Inventing Traditions," in *The Invention of Tradition*, Eric Hobsbawm and Terence Ranger (Cambridge and New York: Cambridge University Press), 1–14.
Hobsbawm, Eric John (1990) *Nations and Nationalism: Programme, Myth, Reality* (New York: Cambridge University Press).
Hölderlin, Friedrich (1961) *Sämtliche Werke*, ed. Friedrich Beißner, Vol. 4.1 (Empedokles, Aufsätze) (Stuttgart: Cotta).
Holquist, Michael (2002) *Dialogism: Bakhtin and His World* (London and New York: Routledge).
Honig, Bonnie (1991) "Declarations of Independence: Arendt and Derrida on the Problem of Founding a Republic," in *American Political Science Review* 85.1, 97–113.
Honig, Bonnie (2006) "Another Cosmopolitanism? Law and Politics in the New Europe," in Seyla Benhabib, *Another Cosmopolitanism* (Oxford and New York: Oxford University Press), 102–127.
Hörisch, Jochen (1996) *Kopf oder Zahl: Die Poesie des Geldes* (Frankfurt/M.: Suhrkamp).
Husserl, Edmund von (1954) *Die Krisis des europäischen Menschentums und die Philosophie* (The Hague: Nijhoff).
Huyssen, Andreas (2005) "Geographies of modernism in a globalizing world," in *Geographies of modernism: Literatures, cultures, spaces*, ed. Peter Brooker and Andrew Thacker (London and New York: Routledge), 6–19.
Irigaray, Luce (1993) *An Ethics of Sexual Difference*, trans. Carolyn Burke and Gillian C. Gill (Ithaca and New York: Cornell University Press).
Israel, Jonathan (2010) *A Revolution of the Mind: Radical Enlightenment and the intellectual Origins of Modern Democracy* (Princeton and Oxford: Princeton University Press).
James, Ian (2006) *The Fragmentary Demand: An Introduction to the Philosophy of Jean-Luc Nancy* (Stanford: Stanford University Press).
Jameson, Fredric (1990) "Modernism and Imperialism," in Terry Eagleton and Fredric Jameson and Edward Said, *Nationalism, Colonialism, and Literature*, (Minneapolis: University of Minnesota Press).
Johnson, Richard (1996) "What is Cultural Studies Anyway?," in *What is Cultural Studies? A Reader*, ed. John Storey (London: Arnold), 75–114.
Kadir, Djelal (2004) "To World, to Globalize – Comparative Literature's Crossroads," *Comparative Literature Studies* 41.1, 1–8.
Kadir, Djelal (2006) "Comparative Literature in an Age of Terrorism," in *Comparative Literature in an Age of Globalization*, ed. Haun Saussy (Baltimore: Johns Hopkins University Press), 68–77.
Kadir, Djelal (2012) "Ecce Homo: Somewhat Human, Particularly Global, Conveniently Universal, Relatively Unique, Comparatively Incommensurable," in *The Concept of Humanity in an Age of Globalization*, ed. Zhang Longxi (Göttingen: Vandenhoeck), 55–67.
Kant, Immanuel (1977) *Kants philosophische Anthropologie: Nach handschriftlichen Vorlesungen* (1831), ed. Friedrich Christian Starke (Hildesheim: Weidmann, reprinted in Leipzig).
Kant, Immanuel (1956) *Critique of Practical Reason*, trans. L. W. Beck (Indianapolis: Bobs Merrill Company).
Kant, Immanuel (1960) *Observations on the Feeling of the Beautiful and the Sublime*, trans. J. T. Goldtwaith (Berkeley: University of California Press).
Kant, Immanuel (1969) *Kritik der reinen Vernunft: Gesammelte Schriften*, ed. Königlich Preußischen Akademie der Wissenschaften, Vol. 3 (Berlin: De Gruyter).

Kant, Immanuel (1979) *The Conflict of the Faculties/Der Streit der Fakultäten* (1798), trans. Mary J. Gregor (New York: Abaris).
Kant, Immanuel (1985) *Schriften zur Geschichtsphilosophie*, ed. M. Riedel (Stuttgart: Metzler).
Kant, Immanuel (1991) *Schriften zur Anthropologie, Geschichtsphilosophie, Politik und Pädagogik 1: Werke*, ed. Wilhelm Weischedel, Vol. 11 (Frankfurt/M.: Suhrkamp).
Kant, Immanuel (1997a) "On National Characteristics, so far as They Depend upon the Distinct Feeling of the Beautiful and Sublime," in *Race and the Enlightenment*, ed. Emmanuel Chukwudi Eze (Oxford and Cambridge, MA: Wiley), 49–57.
Kant, Immanuel (1997b) "Physical Geography," in *Race and the Enlightenment*, ed. Emmanuel Chukwudi Eze (Oxford and Cambridge, MA: Wiley), 58–65.
Kant, Immanuel (1997c) *Lectures on Ethics*, ed. Peter Heath and J. B. Schneewind, trans. Peter Heath (Cambridge and New York: Cambridge University Press).
Kant, Immanuel (1998) *Critique of Pure Reason*, ed. A. W. Wood, trans. P. Guyer (Cambridge and New York: Cambridge University Press).
Kant, Immanuel (2006a) *Political Writings*, ed. H. S. Reiss, trans. H. B. Nisbet (Cambridge: Cambridge University Press).
Kant, Immanuel (2006b) *Anthropology from a Pragmatic Point of View*, ed and trans. R. B. Louden (Cambridge: Cambridge University Press).
Kant, Immanuel (2007) *Critique of Judgment*, rev. N. Walker, trans. J. C. Meredith (Oxford and New York: Cambridge University Press).
Kastoryano, Riva (2007) "Transnational nationalism: redefining nation and territory," in *Identities, Affiliations, and Allegiances*, ed. Seyla Benhabib and Ian Shapiro and Danilo Petranović (Cambridge and New York: Cambridge University Press), 159–178.
Kittler, Friedrich (2000) *Eine Kulturgeschichte der Kulturwissenschaft*. Second edition (Munich: Fink).
Koch, Manfred (2002) *Weimarer Weltbewohner: Zur Genese von Goethes Begriff 'Weltliteratur'* (Tübingen: Niemeyer).
Kojève, Alexandre (1952) "Les romans de la sagesse," in of *Critique*, Vol 60.
Koselleck, Reinhart (1985) *Futures Past: On the Semantics Historical Time*, trans. Keith Tribe (Cambridge, MA: MIT Press).
Koselleck, Reinhart (1989) *Vergangene Zukunft: Zur Semantik geschichtlicher Zeiten* (Frankfurt/M.: Suhrkamp).
Kozhinov, Vadim (1972) "Istoriia literatury v rabotakh OPOIAZa," *Voprosy literatury* 7.
Kristeva, Julia (1991) *Strangers to Ourselves*, trans. Leon S. Roudiez (London: Columbia University Press).
Kristeva, Julia (1993) *Nations without Nationalism*, trans. Leon S. Roudiez (New York: Columbia University Press).
Kujundžić, Dragan (1997) *The Returns of History: Russian Nietzscheans after Modernity* (New York: SUNY).
Lacan, Jacques (1966) *Écrits* (Paris: Seuil).
Lacan, Jacques (1977) *The Four Fundamental Concepts of Psycho-Analysis*, trans. A. Sheridan (London: Hogarth Press).
LaCapra, Dominick (1998) *History and Memory after Auschwitz* (Ithaca and London: Cornell University Press).
LaCapra, Dominick (2001) *Writing History, Writing Trauma* (Baltimore and London: Johns Hopkins University Press).

LaCapra, Dominick (2004) *History in Transit: Experience, Identity, Critical Theory* (Ithaca and London: Cornell University Press).
Lacoue-Labarthe, Philippe and Nancy, Jean-Luc (1988) *The Literary Absolute*, trans. P. Barnard and C. Lester (Albany: SUNY Press).
Lang, Berel (1990) *Act and Idea in the Nazi Genocide* (Chicago: University of Chicago Press).
Large, William (2006) "Blanchot, Philosophy, Literature, Politics," *Parallax* 12.2, 1–11.
Leavis, Frank R. (1948) *Education and the University: A Sketch for an "English School."* Second edition (London: Chatto and Windus).
Leavis, Frank R. (1969) *English Literature in Our Time and the University: The Clark Lectures 1967* (London: Chatto and Windus).
Leavis, Frank R. (1972) *The Common Pursuit* (Harmondsworth: Penguin).
Lefort, Claude (1988) *Democracy and Political Theory*, trans. D. Macey (Oxford: Wiley & Sons).
Lefort, Claude (2000) *The Democratic Invention: The Limits of Totalitarian Domination* (Baltimore: Johns Hopkins University Press).
Leonard, Philip (2005) *Nationality between Poststructuralism and Postcolonial Theory: A New Cosmopolitanism* (Houndmills and New York: Macmillan).
Lessing, Gotthold Ephraim (1858) "Die Erziehung des Menschengeschlechts," in *Gesammelte Werke* (Leipzig: Göschen).
Levi, Primo (1988) *The Drowned and the Saved*, trans. R. Rosendahl (London: Abacus).
Lévinas, Emmanuel (1961) *Totalité et infini: Essai sur l'extériorité* (Dordrecht: Nijhoff).
Levinas, Emmanuel (1969) *Totality and Infinity*, trans. A. Lingis (Pittsburgh: Duquesne University Press).
Levinas, Emmanuel (1974) *Otherwise than Being or Beyond Essence*, trans. A. Lingis (Dordrecht: Nijhoff).
Lévinas, Emmanuel (1976) *Difficile liberté* (Paris: Albin Michel).
Levinas, Emmanuel (1981) *Otherwise than Being or Beyond Essence*, trans. A. Lingis (Dordrecht: Nijhoff).
Levinas, Emmanuel (1985) *Time and the Other*, trans. Richard A. Cohen (Pittsburgh: Duquesne University Press).
Levinas, Emmanuel (1986b) "The Trace of the Other," *Deconstruction in Context*, ed. Mark C. Taylor (Chicago: University of Chicago Press), 345–359.
Levinas, Emmanuel (1987a) "Phenomenon and Enigma," in *Collected Philosophical Papers*, trans. A. Lingis (Dordrecht: Nijhoff), 61–75.
Levinas, Emmanuel (1987b) "Freedom and Command," in *Collected Philosophical Papers*, trans. A. Lingis (Dordrecht: Nijhoff), 15–25.
Levinas, Emmanuel (1987c) "Language and Proximity," in *Collected Philosophical Papers*, trans. A. Lingis (Dordrecht: Nijhoff), 109–127.
Levinas, Emmanuel (1988) "The Paradox of Morality: an Interview with Emmanuel Levinas," in *The Provocation of Levinas: Rethinking the Other*, ed. Robert Bernasconi and David Wood (London and New York: Routledge), 168–181.
Levinas, Emmanuel (1989) "Ethics as First Philosophy," in *The Levinas Reader*, ed. and trans. Séan Hand (London: Blackwell), 75–88.
Levinas, Emmanuel (1990a) *Difficult Freedom*, trans. Séan Hand (Baltimore: Johns Hopkins University Press).
Levinas, Emmanuel (1990b) "Reflections on the Philosophy of Hitlerism," trans. Séan Hand, *Critical Inquiry* 17, 62–71.
Lévinas, Emmanuel (1991) *Entre nous: essais sur le penser-à l'autre* (Paris: Grasset).

Lévinas, Emmanuel (1992) *De Dieu qui vient à l'idée* (Paris : Vrin).
Levinas, Emmanuel (1996) "Transcendence and Height," in *Basic Philosophical Writings*, ed. Adrian T. Peperzak and Simon Critchley and Robert Bernasconi, trans. S. Critchley (Bloomington: University of Indiana Press), 11–31.
Lévinas, Emmanuel (2001) "La Trace de l'autre, " in *En découvrant l'existence avec Husserl et Heidegger* (Paris: Vrin), 261–282.
Lévinas, Emmanuel (2001a) "Énigme et phénomène," in *En découvrant l'existence avec Husserl et Heidegger* (Paris: Vrin), 283–302.
Lévinas, Emmanuel and Philippe Nemo (1982) *Éthique et infini* (Paris: Fayard).
Levinas, Emmanuel and Richard Kearney (1986) "Dialogue with Emmanuel Levinas," in *Face to Face with Levinas*, ed. Richard A. Cohen (Albany: State University of New York Press).
Lévi-Strauss, Claude (1983) *Structural Anthropology*, trans. Monique Layton, Vol. 2 (Chicago: University of Chicago Press).
Lévy, Benny (2002) *Le Meurtre du pasteur: Critique de la vision politique du monde* (Paris: Grasset Verdier).
Levy, Daniel and Sznaider, Natan (2007) *Erinnerung im globalen Zeitalter: Der Holocaust. Aktualisierte Neuauflage* (Frankfurt/M.: Suhrkamp).
Libertson, Joseph (1982) *Proximity: Levinas, Blanchot, Bataille and Communication* (The Hague: Nijhoff).
Lloyd, David (1998) "Foundations of Diversity: Thinking the University in a Time of Multiculturalism," in *"Culture" and the Problem of the Disciplines*, ed. John Carlos Rowe (New York: Columbia University Press), 15–44.
Lucy, Niall (1997) *Postmodern Literary Theory: An Introduction* (Oxford and Malden: Blackwell).
Luhmann, Niklas (1970) *Soziologische Aufklärung 1: Aufsätze zur Theorie sozialer Systeme* (Opladen and Köln: Westdeutscher Verlag).
Luhmann, Niklas (1971) "Sinn als Grundbegriff der Soziologie," in Jürgen Habermas and Niklas Luhmann, *Theorie der Gesellschaft oder Sozialtechnologie* (Frankfurt/M.: Suhrkamp).
Luhmann, Niklas (1975) "Generalized Media and the Problem of Contingency," in *Explorations in General Theory in Social Science: Essays in Honor of Talcott Parsons*, ed. J. Loubser, R. Baum, A. Effrat and V. Lidz (New York: Free Press), 507–532.
Luhmann, Niklas (1982) *Liebe als Passion: Zur Codierung von Intimität* (Frankfurt/M.: Suhrkamp).
Luhmann, Niklas (1984) *Soziale Systeme: Grundriss einer allgemeinen Theorie* (Frankfurt/M.: Suhrkamp).
Luhmann, Niklas (1986a) "Die Lebenswelt – nach Rücksprache mit Phänomenologen," *Archiv für Rechts- und Sozialphilosophie* 72, 176–194.
Luhmann, Niklas (1986b) "Intersubjektivität oder Kommunikation: Unterschiedliche Ausgangspunkte soziologischer Theoriebildung," *Archivio di Filosofia* 54, 41–60.
Luhmann, Niklas (1986c) "Das Kunstwerk und die Selbstreproduktion der Kunst," in *Stil: Geschichte und Funktion eines kulturwissenschaftlichen Diskurselements*, ed. H.U. Gumbrecht and K. L. Pfeiffer (Frankfurt/M.: Suhrkamp), 620–672.
Luhmann, Niklas (1989) "Individuum, Individualität, Individualismus," in *Gesellschaftsstruktur und Semantik: Studien zur Wissenssoziologie der modernen Gesellschaft*, Vol. 3 (Frankfurt/M.: Suhrkamp), 149–258.
Luhmann, Niklas (1990a) "Das Erkenntnisprogramm des Konstruktivismus und die unbekannt bleibende Realität," in *Soziologische Aufklärung: Konstruktivistische Perspektiven*, Vol. 5 (Opladen: Westdeutscher Verlag), 31–58.

Luhmann, Niklas (1990b) "Weltkunst," in *Unbeobachtbare Welt: Über Kunst und Architektur*, ed. D. Baecker and F. D. Bunsen and N.Luhmann (Bielefeld: Haux), 7–45.
Luhmann, Niklas (1991) "Am Ende der kritischen Soziologie," *Zeitschrift für Soziologie* 20, 147–152.
Luhmann, Niklas (1995a) *Die Kunst der Gesellschaft* (Frankfurt/M.: Suhrkamp).
Luhmann, Niklas (1995b) "Intersubjektivität oder Kommunikation: Unterschiedliche Ausgangspunkte soziologischer Theoriebildung," in *Soziologische Aufklärung 6: Die Soziologie und der Mensch* (Opladen: Westdeutscher Verlag), 169–188.
Luhmann, Niklas (1996) "Eine Redeskription 'romantischer Kunst'," in *Systemtheorie der Literatur*, ed. Jürgen Fohrmann and Harro Müller (Munich: UTB), 325–344.
Luhmann, Niklas (1997) *Die Gesellschaft der Gesellschaft* (Frankfurt/M.: Suhrkamp).
Lyotard, Jean-François (1984) *The Postmodern Condition: A Report on Knowledge*, trans. Geoffrey Bennington and Brian Massumi (Minneapolis: University of Minnesota Press).
Lyotard, Jean-François (1985) *Just Gaming*, trans. W. Godzich (Minneapolis: University of Minnesota Press).
Lyotard, Jean-François (1988) *The Differend: Phrases in Dispute*, trans. G. Van Den Abbeele (Minneapolis: University of Minnesota Press).
Lyotard, Jean-François (1991) "Sensus communis," in *Who Comes After the Subject?*, ed. Eduardo Cadava and Peter Connor and Jean-Luc Nancy (New York and London: Taylor & Francis).
Lyotard, Jean-François (1998) "Terror on the Run," in *Terror and Consensus: Vicissitudes of French Thought*, ed. Jean-Joseph Goux and Philip R.Wood (Stanford, CA: Stanford University Press), 25–36.
Madou, Jean-Pol (1998) "The Law, the Heart: Blanchot and the Question of Community," *Yale French Studies* (The Place of Maurice Blanchot) 93, 60–65.
Mamdani, Mahmoud (2002) *When Victims Become Killers* (Princeton: Princeton University Press).
Mamdani, Mahmoud (2012) *Define and Rule: Native as Political Identity* (Cambridge, MA and London: Harvard University Press).
Mandelkow, Karl Robert (1980) *Goethe in Deutschland: Rezeptionsgeschichte eines Klassikers*, Vol. 1 (1773–1918) (Munich: Beck).
Marchart, Oliver (2005) *Neu beginnen: Hannah Arendt, die Revolution und die Globalisierung* (Wien: Turia + Kant).
Marini, Marcelle (1992) *Jacques Lacan: The French Context*, trans. Anne Tomiche (New Brunswick, NJ: Rutgers University Press).
Martin, Terry (2001) *The Affirmative Action Empire: Nations and Nationalism in the Soviet Union, 1923–1939* (Ithaca and London: Cornell University Press).
Martínez-Bonati, Félix (1981) *Fictive Discourse and the Structures of Literature* (Ithaca and London: Ithaca University Press).
Marx, Karl and Engels, Friedrich (1952) *Manifesto of the Communist Party*, trans. Samuel Moore in *Marx, Great Books of the Western World*, Vol. 50 (Chicago: University of Chicago Press), 415–434.
Marx, Karl (1971) "On the Jewish Question," in *Early Texts*, trans. D. McLellan (Oxford: Bearns & Noble).
Marx, Karl and Engels, Friedrich (1974) "Manifest der Kommunistischen Partei," in *Werke*, Vol. 4 (Berlin: Dietz), 459–493.
Mayer, Hans (1975) *Außenseiter* (Frankfurt/M.: Suhrkamp).

Mazumdar, Pravu (1998) "Über Foucault," in *Foucault*, ed. P. Mazumdar (Munich: UTB), 15–78.
Mbembe, Achille (2001) *On the Postcolony*, trans. A. M. Berrett and Janet Roitman and Murray Last and Steven Rendall (Berkeley and Los Angeles and London: University of California Press).
Mbembe, Achille (2003) "Necropolitics," trans. Libby Meintjes, *Public Culture* 15.1, 11–40.
Mbembe, Achille (2010) *Sortir de la grande nuit: Essai sur l'Afrique décolonisée* (Paris: La Découverte).
McQuillan, Martin and MacDonald, Graeme and Purves, Robin and Thomson, Stephen (eds) (1999) *Post-Theory: New Directions in Criticism* (Edinburgh: Edinburgh University Press).
Medvedev Pavel and Bakhtin, Mikhail (1978) *The Formal Method in Literary Scholarship: A Critical Introduction to Sociological Poetics*, trans. Albert J. Wehrle (Baltimore and London: Johns Hopkins University Press).
Meints-Stender, Waltraud (2007) "Hannah Arendt und das Problem der Exklusion – eine Aktualisierung," *Deutsche Zeitschrift für Philosophie* 16, 251–258.
Memmi, Albert (1967) *The Colonizer and the Colonized*, trans. Howard Greenfield (Boston: Beacon).
Memmi, Albert (1968) *Dominated Man: Notes towards a Portrait*, trans. Jane Brooks et al. (New York: Orion).
Menninghaus, Winfried (1987) *Unendliche Verdopplung: Die frühromantische Grundlegung der Kunsttheorie im Begriff absoluter Selbstreflexion* (Frankfurt/M.: Suhrkamp).
Menninghaus, Winfried (2002) "Walter Benjamin's Exposition of the Romantic Theory of Reflection," in *Walter Benjamin and Romanticism*, ed. Andrew Benjamin and Beatrice Hanssen (New York and London: Continuum), 19–50.
Meyer-Kalkus, Reinhard (2010) "World literature beyond Goethe," in *Cultural Mobility: A Manifesto*, ed. Stephen Greenblatt and Ines Županov and Reinhard Meyer-Kalkus and Paul Heike and Pál Nyíri and Frederike Pannewick (Cambridge and New York: Cambridge University Press), 96–121.
Mignolo, Walter D. (2000) "The Many Faces of Cosmo-Polis: Border Thinking and Critical Cosmopolitism," *Public Culture* 12.3, 721–748.
Miller, David A. (1988) *The Novel and the Police* (Berkeley: University of California Press).
Miller, John Hillis (1998) "Literary and Cultural Studies in the Transnational University," in *"Culture" and the Problem of the Disciplines*, ed. John Carlos Rowe (New York: Columbia University Press), 45–68.
Moran, Joe (2002) *Interdisciplinarity* (London and New York: Routledge).
Moretti, Franco (2000) "Conjectures on World Literature," *New Left Review* 1, 54–68.
Moretti, Franco (2005) *Graphs, Maps, Trees: Abstract Models for Literary History* (London and New York: Verso).
Morgan, Diane (2000) *Kant Trouble: The obscurities of the enlightened* (London and New York: Routledge).
Mosse, George L. (1985) *A History of European Racism* (Madison: University of Wisconsin Press).
Mostov, Julie (2007) "Soft borders and transnational citizens," in *Identities, Affiliations, and Allegiances*, ed. Seyla Benhabib and Ian Shapiro and Danilo Petranović (Cambridge and New York: Cambridge University Press), 136–58.
Musil, Robert (1978) "Der Anschluss an Deutschland (1919)," in *Gesammelte Werke in neun Bänden*, ed. Adolf Frisé, Vol. 8 (Reinbek bei Hamburg: Rowohlt), 1033–1042.
Nancy, Jean-Luc (1986) *La Communauté désœuvrée* (Paris: Christian Bourgeois).
Nancy, Jean-Luc (1988) *The Experience of Freedom* (Stanford: Stanford University Press).

Nancy, Jean-Luc (1991) *The Inoperative Community*, ed. Peter Connor, trans. Peter Connor and Lisa Garbus and Michael Holland and Simona Sawhney (Minneapolis: University of Minnesota Press).

Nancy, Jean-Luc (2000) *Being Singular Plural*, trans. R. D. Richardson and A. E. O'Byrne (Stanford, CA: Stanford University Press).

Nancy, Jean-Luc (2003) "The Confronted Community," trans. Amanda Macdonald, *Postcolonial Studies* 6.1, 23–36.

Nandy, Ashis (1983) *Intimate Enemy: Loss and Recovery of Self under Colonialism* (Delhi: Oxford University Press).

Nehamas, Alexander (1998) *The Art of Living: Socratic Reflection from Plato to Foucault* (Berkeley and Los Angeles and London: University of California Press).

Neubauer, John (2004) "National operas in East-Central Europe," in *History of the literary cultures of East-Central Europe: Junctures and disjunctures in the 19th and 20th centuries*, ed. Marcel Cornis-Pope and John Neubauer, Vol. 1 (Amsterdam and New York: John Benjamins), 514–524.

Neubauer, John (2007) "Introduction" to "Literary Histories: Itineraries of National Self-Images," in *History of the literary cultures of East-Central Europe: Junctures and disjunctures in the 19th and 20th centuries*, ed. Marcel Cornis-Pope and John Neubauer, Vol. 3 (Amsterdam and New York: John Benjamins), 345–355.

Neugebauer, Christian (1990) "The Racism of Kant and Hegel," in *Sage Philosophy: Indigenous Thinkers and Modern Debate on African Philosophy*, ed. H. Odera Oruka (Leiden: Brill), 259–272.

Nietzsche, Friedrich (1957) *The Use and Abuse of History for Life*, trans. Adrian Collins (New York: The Liberal Arts Press).

Nietzsche, Friedrich (1996) *On the Genealogy of Morals: A Polemic*, trans. Douglas Smith (Oxford and New York: Oxford University Press).

Nietzsche, Friedrich (2010) *The Joyful Wisdom*, trans. Thomas Common (Adelaide: Ebooks).

Ning, Wang (2011) "'Weltliteratur': from a utopian imagination to diversified forms of world literatures," *Neohelicon* 38, 295–306.

Novalis, Friedrich von Hardenberg (1981) *Schriften: Die Werke Friedrich von Hardenbergs*, ed. Paul Kluckhohn and Richard Samuel, *Das philosophische Werk 1*, ed. Hans-Joachim Mähl and Samuel Richard and Gerhard Schulz, Vol. 2 (Stuttgart: Kohlhammer).

Novalis, Friedrich von Hardenberg (1983a) "Die Christenheit oder Europa," in *Schriften: Die Werke Friedrich von Hardenbergs*, ed. Paul Kluckhohn and Richard Samuel, *Das philosophische Werk 2*, ed. Hans-Joachim Mähl and Richard Samuel and Gerhard Schulz, Vol. 3 (Stuttgart: Kohlhammer), 507–526.

Novalis, Friedrich von Hardenberg (1983b) *Schriften: Die Werke Friedrich von Hardenbergs*, ed. Paul Kluckhohn and Richard Samuel, *Das philosophische Werk 2*, ed. Hans-Joachim Mähl and Richard Samuel and Gerhard Schulz, Vol. 3 (Stuttgart: Kohlhammer).

Ophir, Adi and Givoni, Michael and Hanefi, Sari (eds) (2009) *The Power of Inclusive Exclusion* (New York: Zone Books).

Patočka, Jan (1990) *Liberté et sacrifice*, trans. E. Abrams (Grenoble: Millon).

Pechey, Graham (2001) "Not the Novel: Bakhtin, Poetry, Truth, God," in *Bakhtin and Cultural Theory*. Revised and expanded second edition, ed. Ken Hirschkop and Stephen Shepherd (Manchester and New York: Manchester University Press), 62–84.

Pecora, Vincent P. (1991) "Ethics, Politics, and the Middle Voice," *Literature and the Ethical Question, Yale French Studies* 79, ed. Claire Nouvet, 203–230.

Pepper, Thomas Adam (1997) "Anamorphoses of Grammar: Derrida on Heidegger," in *Singularities: Extremes of Theory in the Twentieth Century* (Cambridge: Cambridge University Press), 49–87.

Pizer, John David (2006) *The Idea of World Literature: History and Pedagogical Practice* (Baton Rouge, LA: Louisiana State University Press).

Poirié, François (1987) *Emmanuel Lévinas. Qui êtes-vous?* (Lyon: La Manufacture).

Poole, Brian (1995) "'Nazad k Kaganu': Marburgskaia shkola v Nevele i filosofiia M.M. Bakhtina," *Dialog. Karnaval. Hronotop* 1, 38–48.

Povinelli, Elisabeth (2002) *The Cunning of Recognition: Indigenous Alterities and the Making of Australian Multiculturalism* (Durham and London: Duke University Press).

Povinelli, Elisabeth (2011) *Economies of Abandonment: Social Belonging and Endurance in Late Liberalism* (Durham and London: Duke University Press).

Probyn, Elspeth (1996) *Outside Belongings* (London and New York: Routledge).

Rabaté, Jean-Michel (2002) *The Future of Theory* (Oxford: Wiley & Sons).

Rancière, Jacques (1989) *The Nights of Labor: The Worker's Dream in Nineteenth-Century France*, trans. J.Drury (Philadelphia: Temple University Press).

Rancière, Jacques (1995) *On the Shores of Politics*, trans L. Heron (London: Verso).

Rancière, Jacques (1999) *Disagreement: Politics and Philosophy*, trans. Julie Rose (Minneapolis and London: University of Minnesota Press).

Rancière, Jacques (2001) "Ten Theses on Politics," *Theory and Event* 5.3, 1–16.

Rancière, Jacques (2002) "The Aesthetic Revolution and its Outcomes: Emplotments of Autonomy and Heteronomy," *New Left Review* (March/April), 133–151.

Rancière, Jacques (2003) *Short Voyages to the Land of the People*, trans. J. B. Swenson (Stanford: Stanford University Press).

Rancière, Jacques (2004a) *The Flesh of Words: The Politics of Writing*, trans. C. Mandell (Stanford: Stanford University Press).

Rancière, Jacques (2004b) "Who Is the Subject of the Rights of Man?" *The South Atlantic Quarterly* 103 (2/3), 297–310.

Rancière, Jacques (2005) *The Politics of Aesthetics: The Distribution of the Sensible*, trans. Gabriel Rockhill (New York: Continuum).

Rancière, Jacques (2006) *Hatred of Democracy*, trans. Steve Corcoran (London: Verso).

Rancière, Jacques (2007) *Politique de la littérature* (Paris: Galilée).

Rancière, Jacques (2008) *Ist Kunst widerstandsfähig?* ed. and trans. Frank Ruda and Jan Völker (Berlin: Merve).

Rancière, Jacques (2009) *Aesthetics and Its Discontents*, trans. Steven Corcoran (Cambridge and Malden, MA: Polity).

Rancière, Jacques (2010) *Dissensus: On Politics and Aesthetics*, trans. Steven Corcoran. (London: Bloomsbury Academic).

Rancière, Jacques (2011a) *Althusser's Lesson*, trans. E. Battista (London: Bloomsbury Academic).

Rancière, Jacques (2011b) *The Politics of Literature*, trans. Julie Rose (Cambridge and Malden, MA: Polity).

Rasch, William (2005) *Sovereignty and Its Discontents* (London: Birkbeck Law Press).

Rasch, William (2011) "Theory after Critical Theory," in *Theory after 'Theory'*, ed. Derek Attridge and Jane Elliott (London and New York: Routledge), 49–62.

Räthzel, Nora (1997) *Gegenbilder: Nationale Identitäten durch Konstruktion des Anderen* (Opladen: Westdeutscher Verlag).

Rausch, Hannelore (1982) *Theoria: Von ihrer sakralen zur philosophischen Bedeutung* (Munich: Fink).
Ray, Michael (1992) *Marxism and Deconstruction: A Critical Articulation* (Baltimore: Johns Hopkins University Press).
Readings, Bill (1996) *The University in Ruins* (Cambridge: Harvard University Press).
Renan, Ernest (2006) "What Is a Nation," in *Becoming National: A Reader*, ed. Geoff Eley and Ronald Grigor Suny (Oxford and New York: Oxford University Press), 41–55.
Richardson, Ruth Drucilla (1995) "Staël on the Anthropology of the Enlightenment: 'A Game for Thee, but Death for Me'," in *Anthropology and the German Enlightenment: Perspectives on Humanity*, ed. Katherine M. Faull (Lewisburg and London and Toronto: Bucknell University Press), 125–161.
Riffaterre, Michael (1978) *The Semiotics of Poetry* (Bloomington: Indiana University Press).
Rimmon-Kenan, Shlomith (1983) *Narrative Fiction: Contemporary Poetics* (London and New York: Routledge).
Roberts, David (1992) "The Paradox of form: Literature and self-reference," *Poetics* 21, 75–91.
Robbins, Bruce (1992) "Death and Vocation: Narrativizing Narrative Theory," *PMLA* 107.1, 38–51.
Robbins, Bruce (1998) "Actually Existing Cosmopolitanism," in *Cosmopolitics: Thinking and Feeling beyond the Nation*, ed. Pheng Cheah and Bruce Robbins (Minneapolis and London: University of Minnesota Press), 1–20.
Robbins, Jill (1999) *Altered Reading: Levinas and Literature* (Chicago: University of Chicago Press).
Rose, Gillian (1996) *Morning Becomes the Law: Philosophy and Representation* (New York: Cambridge University Press).
Ross, Kristin (2008) *The Emergence of Social Space: Rimbaud and the Paris Commune* (London and New York: Verso).
Rothberg, Michael (2000) *Traumatic Realism: The Demands of Holocaust Representation* (Minneapolis: University of Minnesota Press).
Rothberg, Michael (2009) *Multidirectional Memory: Remembering the Holocaust in the Age of Decolonization* (Stanford: Stanford University Press).
Rougemont, Denis de (1994) "L'aventure mondiale des Européens," in *Écrits sur l'Europe* (Paris: Editions de la Différence), 55–72.
Rousseau, Jean-Jacques (1964a) "Discours sur les sciences et les arts," in *Œuvres complètes*, ed. Bernard Gagnebin and Marcel Raymond, Vol. 3 (Paris: Pléiade), 1–107.
Rousseau, Jean-Jacques (1964b) "Discours sur l'économie politique," in *Œuvres complètes*, ed. Bernard Gagnebin and Marcel Raymond, Vol. 3 (Paris: Pléiade), 241–278.
Rousseau, Jean-Jacques (1965) *Discourse on the Origin of Inequality*, trans. Barande Ilse (Paris: Payot).
Rousseau, Jean-Jacques (1968a) *The Social Contract*, trans. Maurice Cranston (Harmondsworth: Penguin).
Rousseau, Jean-Jacques (1968b) *Politics and the Arts: Letter to M. d'Alembert on the Theatre*, ed. and trans. Allan Bloom (Ithaca: Cornell University Press).
Rousseau, Jean-Jacques (1977) *Émile*, trans. Barbara Foxley (New York: Dutton).
Rousseau, Jean-Jacques (1978) *On the Social Contract*, ed. Roger D. Masters, trans. Judith. R. Masters (New York: St Martin's).
Rousseau, Jean-Jacques (1986) *Essay on the Origin of Language*, trans. J. H. Moran and A. Gode (Chicago: University of Chicago Press).

Rousseau, Jean-Jacques (1990) "Considerations sur le gouvernement de Pologne," in *Discours sur l'économie politique, Projet de constitution pour la Corse, Considerations sur le gouvernement de Pologne*, ed. Barbara de Negroni (Paris: Seuil).

Royle, Nicolas (1999) "Déjà vu," in *Post-Theory: New Directions in Criticism*, ed. Graeme MacDonald and Martin McQuillan and Robin Purves and Stephen Thomson (Edinburgh: Edinburgh University Press), 3–20.

Safranski, Rüdiger (2009) *Romantik: Eine deutsche Affäre* (Frankfurt/M.:Fischer).

Said, Edward (1993) *Culture and Imperialism* (New York: Vintage).

Said, Edward (2000) "Reflections on Exile," in *Reflections on Exile and Other Essays* (Cambridge and London: Harvard University Press), 137–149.

Said, Edward (2002) "Europe against America," *Al-Ahram Weekly* 612, http://weekly.ahram.org.eg/2002/612/op2.htm (accessed 12 November 2012).

Santner, Eric L. (1992) "History beyond the Pleasure Principle: Some Thoughts on the Representation of Trauma," in *Probing the Limits of Representation: Nazism and the "Final Solution,"* ed. Saul Friedlander (Cambridge, MA and London: Harvard University Press), 143–55.

Saussy, Haun (2006) "Exquisite Cadavers Stitched from Fresh Nightmares: Of Memes, Hives, and Selfish Genes," in *Comparative Literature in an Age of Globalization*, ed. Haun Saussy (Baltimore: Johns Hopkins University Press), 3–42.

Saussy, Haun (2011) "The Dimensionality of World Literature," *Neohelicon* 38, 289–294.

Savigny, Friedrich Carl von (1850) "Über den Zweck der Zeitschrift für geschichtliche Rechtswissenschaft (1815)," in *Vermischte Schriften*, Vol. 1 (Berlin: Veit).

Schaap, Andrew (2011) "Enacting the right to have rights," *European Journal for Political Theory* 1/10, 22–46.

Schad, John (2003) "Coming back to 'life': Leavis spells pianos," in *Life.after.theory*, ed. Michael Payne and John Schad (London and New York: Continuum), 168–189.

Schiller, Friedrich (1991) "'Ankündigung' zu Die Horen (1794)," in *Vermischte Schriften*, ed. Herbert Meyer, *Werke*. Nationalausgabe, ed. Julius Petersen and Hermann Schneider, Vol. 22 (Weimar: Böhlau), 106–109.

Schiller, Friedrich (2000) *Über die ästhetische Erziehung des Menschen* (1795), ed. Klaus L. Berghahn (Stuttgart: Reclam).

Schlegel, August Wilhelm (1964) *Geschichte der klassischen Literatur, Kritische Schriften und Briefe*, ed. Edgar Lohner, Vol. 3 (Stuttgart: Kohlhammer).

Schlegel, August Wilhelm (1965) *Geschichte der romantischen Literatur, Kritische Schriften und Briefe*, ed. Edgar Lohner, Vol. 4 (Stuttgart: Kohlhammer).

Schlegel, August Wilhelm (1966) *Vorlesungen über dramatische Kunst und Literatur, Kritische Schriften und Briefe*, ed. Edgar Lohner, Vol. 1 (Stuttgart: Kohlhammer).

Schlegel, Friedrich (1846) *Über die Sprache und Weisheit der Inder, Sämtliche Werke*, Vol. 7 (Vienna: Klang).

Schlegel, Friedrich (1958) *Wissenschaft der europäischen Literatur (1803–1804), Kritische Ausgabe*, ed. Ernst Behler, Vol. 11 (Munich and Paderborn and Vienna: Schöningh).

Schlegel, Friedrich (1961) *Geschichte der neuen und alten Literatur (1812), Kritische Ausgabe*, ed. Ernst Behler, Vol. 6 (Munich and Paderborn and Vienna: Schöningh).

Schlegel, Friedrich (1963) *Philosophische Lehrjahre 1 (1796–1806), Kritische Ausgabe*, ed. Ernst Behler, Vol. 18 (Munich and Paderborn and Vienna: Schöningh).

Schlegel, Friedrich (1966) "Versuch über den Begriff des Republikanismus" (1795), in *Kritische Ausgabe*, ed. Ernst Behler, Vol. 7 (Munich and Paderborn and Vienna: Schöningh), 11–25.

Schlegel, Friedrich (1971a) "Gedanken 1808/9," in *Kritische Ausgabe*, ed. Ernst Behler, Vol. 19.2 (Munich and Paderborn and Vienna: Schöningh), 263–293.

Schlegel, Friedrich (1971b) *Lucinde and the Fragments*, trans. Peter Firchow (Minneapolis: University of Minnesota Press).

Schlegel, Friedrich (1979a) "Über das Studium der Griechischen Poesie (1795–1797)," in *Kritische Ausgabe*, ed. Ernst Behler, Vol. 1 (Munich and Paderborn and Vienna: Schöningh), 217–367.

Schlegel, Friedrich (1979b) "Vom Wert des Studiums der Griechen und Römer (1796)," in *Kritische Ausgabe*, ed. Ernst Behler, Vol. 1 (Munich and Paderborn and Vienna: Schöningh), 621–642.

Schlegel, Friedrich (1988) *Kritische Schriften und Fragmente (1798–1801), Studienausgabe*, ed. Ernst Behler and H. Eichner, Vol. 2 (Paderborn: Schöningh).

Schlereth, Thomas J. (1977) *The Cosmopolitan Ideal in Enlightenment Thought: Its Form and Function in the Ideas of Franklin, Hume, and Voltaire 1694–1790* (London: University of Notre Dame Press).

Schmitt, Carl (1996) *The Concept of the Political*, trans. G. Schwab (Chicago: University of Chicago Press).

Schmitt, Carl (2003) *The Nomos of the Earth in the International Law of the Jus Publicum Europaeum*, trans. G.L. Ulmen (New York: Telos).

Schön, Erich (1987) *Der Verlust der Sinnlichkeit oder Die Verwandlungen des Lesers: Mentalitätswandel um 1800* (Stuttgart: Klett-Cotta).

Scholz, Bernhard F. (1998) "Bakhtin's Concept of Chronotope: The Kantian Connection," in *The Contexts of Bakhtin: Philosophy, Authorship, Aesthetics*, ed. David Shepherd (London: Taylor & Francis), 141–172.

Schroeder, Brian (1996) *Altared Ground: Levinas, History, and Violence* (London and New York: Routledge).

Schulz, Karlheinz (1989) "Kosmopolitismus und Nationalismus bei den Brüdern Schlegel," *Recherche Germanique* 19, 31–67.

Sebastiani, Silvia (2000) "Race as a Construction of the Other: 'Native Americans' and 'Negroes' in the 18th Century Editions of the Encyclopedia Britannica," in *Europe and the Other and Europe as Other*, ed. Bo Stråth (Brussels: Peter Lang), 195–228.

Sedgwick, Eve Kosofsky (1993) *Tendencies* (Durham: Duke University Press).

Shih, Shu-mei (2004) "Global Literature and the Technologies of Recognition," *PMLA* 119.1, 16–30.

Shklovsky, Victor (1973) "The Resurrection of the Word," in *Russian Formalism*, ed. Stephen Bann and John E. Bowlt (Edinburgh: Edinburgh University Press), 41–47.

Sieyès, Emmanuel Joseph (1963) *What is the Third Estate?*, ed. S. A. Finer, trans. M. Blondel (New York: Praeger).

Simmel, Georg (1971) *On Individuality and Social Forms: Selected Writings*, ed. Donald N. Levine (Chicago and London: University of Chicago Press).

Smith, Barbara Herrnstein (1978) *On the Margins of Discourse: The Relation of Literature to Language* (Chicago: University of Chicago Press).

Smith, Barbara Herrnstein (1988) *Contingencies of Value: Alternative Perspectives for Critical Theory* (Oxford: Harvard University Press).

Smith, Barbara Herrnstein (2006) *Scandalous Knowledge: Science, Truth and the Human* (Durham and London: Duke University Press).

Spivak, Gayatri Chakraworty (1999a) *A Critique of Postcolonial Reason: Toward a History of the Vanishing Present* (Cambridge, MA: Harvard University Press).

Spivak, Gayatri Chakravorty (1999b) "Cultural Talks in the Hot Peace: Revisiting the 'Global Village'," in *Cosmopolitics: Thinking and Feeling beyond the Nation*, ed. Phang Cheah and Bruce Robbins (Minneapolis and London: University of Minnesota Press), 329–408.

Spivak, Chakravorty Gayatri (2003) *Death of a Discipline* (New York: Columbia University Press).

Spivak, Gayatri Chakravorty (2008) *Other Asias* (London and New York: Blackwell).

Staël, Anne Germaine de (1978) *Correspondance générale*, ed. Beatrice W. Jasinski, Vol. 2 (Paris: Klincksieck).

Staël, Anne Germaine de (1985) *Über Deutschland*, ed. Monika Bosse, trans. F. Buchholz and S.H. Catel and J. E. Hitzig (Frankfurt/M.: Insel).

Starr, Peter (2005) *Logics of Failed Revolt: French Theory after May '68* (Stanford, CA: Stanford University Press).

Steele, Tom (1997) *The Emergence of Cultural Studies 1945–65: Cultural Politics, Adult Education, and the 'English' Question* (London: Lawrence & Wishard).

Steiner, Peter (1984) *Russian Formalism: A Metapoetics* (Ithaca and London: Cornell University Press).

Suglia, Joseph (2001) "The Communication of the Impossible," *Diacritics* 31.2, 49–69.

Taminiaux, Jacques (1998) *The Thracian Maid and the Professional Thinker: Arendt and Heidegger*, trans. M. Gendre (New York: SUNY Press).

Taussig, Michael (1992) *Mimesis and Alterity: A Particular History of the Senses* (London and New York: Routledge).

Texte, Joseph (1895) *Jean-Jacques Rousseau et les origins du cosmopolitisme littéraire* (Paris: Hachette).

Thomsen, Mads Rosendahl (2008) *Mapping World Literature: International Canonization and Transnational Literatures* (London and New York: Continuum).

Tihanov, Galin (2000) *The Master and the Slave: Lukács, Bakhtin, and the Ideas of Their Time* (Oxford: Cambridge University Press).

Tihanov, Galin (2004) "The Birth of Modern Literary Theory in East-Central Europe," in *History of the Literary Cultures of East-Central Europe: Junctures and Disjunctures in the 19th and 20th Centuries*, ed. M. Cornis-Pope and J. Neubauer, Vol. 1 (Amsterdam and Philadelphia: John Benjamins), 416–424.

Tihanov, Galin (2005) "The Politics of Estrangement: The Case of Early Shklovsky," *Poetics Today* 26.4, 665–696.

Tihanov, Galin (2011) "Cosmopolitanism in the Discursive Landscape of Modernity: Two Enlightenment Articulations," in *Enlightenment Cosmopolitanism*, ed. David Adams and Galin Tihanov (London: David Brown Book Company), 133–152.

Tocqueville, Alexis de (1945) *Democracy in America* (1840), ed. Phillips Bradley, Vol. 2 (New York: Knopf).

Todorova, Maria (1997) *Imagining the Balkans* (New York and Oxford: Oxford University Press).

Trumpener, Kathie (2006) "World Music, World Literature: A Geopolitical View," in *Comparative Literature in an Age of Globalization*, ed. Haun Saussy (Baltimore: Johns Hopkins University Press), 185–202.

Ungar, Steven (1995) *Scandal and Aftereffect: Blanchot and France since 1930* (Minneapolis: University of Minnesota Press).

Valadez, Jorge M. (2007) "The continuing significance of ethnocultural identity," in *Identities, Affiliations, and Allegiances*, ed. Seyla Benhabib and Ian Shapiro and Danilo Petranović (Cambridge and New York: Cambridge University Press), 303–324.

Valentine, Jeremy (2005) "Rancière and Contemporary Political Problems," *Paragraph* 28.1, 46–60.

Vallury, Raji (2009) "Politicizing Art in Rancière and Deleuze: The Case of Postcolonial Literature," in *Jacques Rancière: History, Politics, Aesthetics*, ed. Gabriel Rockhill and Philip Watts (Durham and London: Duke University Press), 229–49.

Vardoulakis, Dimitris (2010) *The Doppelgänger: Literature's Philosophy* (New York: Fordham University Press).

Vasseleu, Cathryn (1998) *Textures of Light: Vision and Touch in Irigaray, Levinas and Merleau-Ponty* (London and New York: Routledge).

Venuti, Lawrence (2012) "World Literature and Translation Studies," in *The Routledge Companion to World Literature*, ed. Theo D'Haen and David Damrosch and Djelal Kadir (London and New York: Routledge), 180–194.

Verdery, Katherine (1996) *What Was Socialism, and What Comes Next?* (Princeton: Princeton University Press).

Villa, Dana R. (1995) *Arendt and Heidegger: The Fate of the Political* (Princeton: Princeton University Press).

Virno, Paolo (2004) *A Grammar of the Multitude: For an Analysis of Contemporary Forms of Life*, trans. Isabella Bertoletti, James Cascaito and Andrea Casson (Los Angeles: Semiotext(e))

Voltaire, François-Marie Arouet (1753) *Le Siècle de Louis XIV* (1751), second enlarged edition, Vol. 1 and 2 (Paris: Chez George Conrad Walter).

Voltaire, François-Marie Arouet (1765) "Histoire," in *Encyclopédie*, ed. Jean-Baptiste D'Alembert and Denis Diderot, Vol. 8 (Neufchatel: Chez Samuel Faulche & Compagnie), 220–225.

Voltaire, François-Marie Arouet (1770–1772) *Questions sur l'Encyclopédie par des amateurs*, 9 vols (Geneva: s. n.).

Voltaire, François-Marie Arouet (1879) "Mélanges /7/," in *Oeuvres complètes*, ed. Jean Michel Moreau et al. Vol. 28 (Paris: Garnier frères).

Voltaire, François-Marie Arouet (1891) "Correspondance /6/," in *Oeuvres complètes*, ed. Jean Michel Moreau et al. Vol. 37 (Paris: Garnier frères).

Voltaire, François-Marie Arouet (1892) "Mélanges /2/," in *Oeuvres complètes*, ed. Jean Michel Moreau et al. Vol. 24 (Paris: Garnier frères).

Voltaire, François-Marie Arouet (1895) "Mélanges /8/," in *Oeuvres complètes*, ed. Jean Michel Moreau et al. Vol. 30 (Paris: Garnier frères).

Voltaire, François-Marie Arouet (1904) "Essai sur le moeurs et l'esprit des nations (1741)," in *Oeuvres complètes*, ed. Jean Michel Moreau et al. Vol. 11 (Paris: Garnier frères).

Voltaire, François-Marie Arouet (1906) "Histoire de Charles XII. Histoire de l'Empire de Russie sous Pierre le Grand (1731)," in *Oeuvres complètes*, ed. Jean Michel Moreau et al. Vol. 15 (Paris: Garnier frères).

Voltaire, François-Marie Arouet (1961) *Dictionnaire Philosophique* (1764), ed. R. Naves (Paris: Garnier).

Voltaire, François-Marie Arouet (1968–1977) *Correspondence and Related Documents*, 51 vols, ed. Therese Besterman (Toronto and Geneva and Oxford: Voltaire Foundation).

Waldenfels, Bernhard (2002) "Levinas and the face of the other," in *The Cambridge Companion to Levinas*, ed. Robert Bernasconi and Simon Critchley (Cambridge: Cambridge University Press), 63–82.

Waldron, Jeremy (2006) "Cosmopolitan Norms," in Seyla Benhabib, *Another Cosmopolitanism: Hospitality, Sovereignty and Democratic Iterations* (Oxford and New York: Oxford University Press), 83–101.

Watkin, Christopher (2007) "A Different Alterity: Jean-Luc Nancy's 'Singular Plural'," *Paragraph* 30.2, 50–64.

Weir, Alison (1996) *Sacrificial Logics: Feminist Theory and the Critique of Identity* (London and New York: Routledge).

White, Hayden (1999) "Historical Emplotment and the Problem of Truth in Historical Representation," in *Figural Realism: Studies in the Mimesis Effect* (Baltimore and London: Johns Hopkins University Press), 27–42.

White, Hayden (2000) "The Discourse of Europe and the Search for European Identity," *Europe and the Other and Europe as the Other*, ed. Bo Stråth (Brussels: Peter Lang), 67–87.

Wiedemann, Conrad (1993) "Deutsche Klassik und nationale Identität. Eine Revision der Sonderwegs-Frage," in *Klassik im Vergleich*, ed. Wilhelm Voßkamp (Stuttgart: Metzler), 541–569.

Wolf, Greg (1998) *Becoming Roman: The Origins of Provincial Civilization in Gaul* (Cambridge and New York: Cambridge University Press).

Wolff, Larry (1994) *Inventing Eastern Europe: The Map of Civilization on the Mind of the Enlightenment* (Stanford: Stanford University Press).

Wolff, Larry (2001) *Venice and the Slavs: The Discovery of Dalmatia in the Age of Enlightenment* (Stanford: Stanford University Press).

Young, Robert (1990) *White Mythologies* (London and New York: Routledge).

Young, Robert J. C. (2001) *Postcolonialism: An Historical Introduction* (Oxford: Wiley).

Zerilli, Linda M. G. (2011) "The practice of judgment: Hannah Arendt's 'Copernican revolution'," in *Theory after 'Theory'*, ed. Derek Attridge and Jane Elliott (London and New York: Routledge), 120–132.

Žižek, Slavoj (1999) *The Ticklish Subject: The Absent Centre of Political Ontology* (London: Verso).

Index

Abensour, Miguel, 103
Agamben, Giorgio, 29, 102, 109, 117, 128, 221, 223, 224, 228, 259, 287, 292, 299–308, 315, 317, 322–324, 342, 343, 350
Albrecht, Andrea, 62, 67, 71, 73, 148
Alexander, Jeffrey, 2, 4, 5, 8, 13, 15, 60, 64, 154, 326
Althusser, Louis, 28, 262–264, 313, 330, 338, 340
Amselle, Jean-Loup, 15, 63, 84, 86, 327, 332, 342
Appadurai, Arjun, 12, 13, 99
Appiah, Kwame Anthony, 6, 36, 58
Apter, Emily, 14, 36, 105, 134, 179, 180, 188
Arendt, Hannah, 17–19, 47, 57, 101–103, 108, 117, 128, 139, 141, 143, 153, 156, 158, 161–163, 166, 167, 171, 182–186, 190, 216, 220–223, 233, 248, 298, 306, 352–356
Aseguinolaza, Fernando Cabo, 173
Assmann, Aleida, 75, 95, 210
Attridge, Derek, 285, 290, 291, 317
Azim, Firdous, 210, 211, 253

Badiou, Alain, 107
Bakhtin, Mikhail, VI, 3, 27, 28, 153, 166, 167, 187, 225, 226, 228, 229, 233, 235–239, 241–255, 259, 272, 301, 381
Bales, Kevin, 327
Balibar, Étienne, 29, 57, 71, 103, 104, 298, 302, 318
Banfield, Ann, 254
Barnard, Frederick M. 69, 80, 81, 85, 93, 94, 96, 118, 121–123, 129, 132
Barthes, Roland, 258, 259, 261, 262, 264
Bauman, Zygmunt, 206, 208, 252, 253, 281, 289, 290
Beardsworth, Richard, 282, 317
Beck, Ulrich, 207 207, 208
Beebee, Thomas, 144, 175
Behler, Ernst, 97, 188, 195–197, 228, 333
Beiser, Frederick C., 62, 66, 99, 118
Benhabib, Seyla, 6, 67, 74, 78, 371

Benjamin, Walter, 5, 12, 88, 102, 179, 180, 187, 188, 195, 255, 304, 321, 322, 351, 352, 355, 356, 369
Bennington, Geoffrey, 345
Benveniste, Émile, 260, 262
Berend, Ivan, 214–216
Berlant, Lauren, 4, 5, 7, 8, 11, 13, 140, 189, 190, 204, 254, 301
Berlin, Isaiah, 69
Bernstein, Michael André, 230
Bhabha, Homi, 180
Biesta, Gert, 330
Bildung, 15, 22, 83, 84, 89, 94, 96
 – *Bildungswesen*, 15, 118, 124, 126, 127
 – education/cultivation (Enlightenment), 50, 51, 72, 79, 87, 95, 123, 143, 287
 – *Selbstbildung*, 75, 87, 88
 – self-formation (Romanticism), 10, 22, 24, 83, 85–90, 138, 190, 228
Birmingham, Peg, 286
Birus, Hendrik, 150, 154, 158
Biti, Vladimir, V, 5, 105, 172
Blanchot, Maurice, 28, 258, 259, 271–282, 284, 299–301, 303–307, 312, 317, 331, 333, 334, 339, 340, 369, 374
Blumenberg, Hans, 48, 123, 181–185, 190, 193, 218
Bogue, Ronald, 327
Bohnenkamp, Anne, 148, 160, 161, 168
Borch-Jacobsen, Mikkel, 83, 263
Boubia, Fawzi, 157
Boundaries, 14, 15, 19, 22, 30, 49, 52, 60, 75, 114, 166, 203, 204, 215, 230, 243, 247, 293, 320, 323, 334, 339
 – horizon of expectation (*Erwartungshorizont*/*Erfahrungsraum* Koselleck), 44, 75
 – national, 47, 187
 – of inherited horizon, 15
Bowie, Andrew, 196
Brown, Wendy, 11, 84, 326, 327, 331, 332
Brubaker, Rogers, 45–47, 65, 215, 219, 289
Brunkhorst, Hauke, 1
Brunner, José, 4, 5, 7, 60, 190

Butler, Judith, 84, 100, 104, 220, 262, 320, 326, 349, 351, 352, 355

Calhoun, Craig, 58–60
Caputo, John, 283
Caruth, Cathy, 322
Casanova, Pascale, 24, 33–35, 39, 42, 58, 59, 71, 72, 127, 130, 131, 136, 137, 162, 169, 170
Cavarero, Adriana, 313, 29, 306–317
Cave, Terence, 310
Certeau, Michel de, 44, 293
Césaire, Aimé, 266
Chakrabarty, Dipesh, 120, 121, 244, 250, 317
Chanter, Tina, 308
Chatman, Seymour, 227, 262
Cheng, Pheah, 135
Cherniavsky, Eva, 347
Chytry, Joseph, 122, 155
Citton, Yves, 330, 335
Clark, Katherina, 236
Clark, Timothy, 282, 285–287, 290, 292, 298, 299
Collingwood, Robin G., 71
Colonialism, 1, 19, 28, 44, 117, 326
– assimilating/hard, 15, 63, 125, 220, 223
– colonial difference, 34, 35, 105, 107, 127
– necropolitics (Mbembe), 16
– postcolonialism, 10, 66, 71, 104, 130, 179, 211, 230, 266, 275, 332, 346
– regenerating/soft, 15, 63, 65
– religious, 34
Colonization, 28, 87, 136, 157, 186, 264
– structuralist, 28
Community, 3, 16, 21, 23, 35, 38, 52–54, 70, 85, 92, 95, 107, 154, 156, 169, 182, 189, 227, 242, 285, 287, 301, 307, 310, 315, 335, 338, 343, 353
– all-inclusive, 29
– *being-in-common* (Nancy), 307, 315
– city-states, 46, 119, 122, 186
– global, 17, 54, 207
– literary, 29, 158, 215, 282, 284, 299, 315, 317
– nation-state, 7, 46, 47, 65, 80, 136, 172, 207, 214, 217, 297, 327, 332
– natural, 75
– of fate (*Schicksalsgemeinschaft*), 66, 75, 77

– political, 9, 29, 44, 72, 75, 77, 107, 308–310, 315–317, 343, 353
– sensus communis (common/public resp. *Verstand/Vernunft*; Kant), 27, 156, 222, 239, 301, 346
– telluric, 44, 92, 93, 105
– "to come" (Agamben) 163, 306
– traditional, 21, 33, 43, 44, 49
– "unavowable" (Blanchot), 299, 312
– "unworked" (Blanchot/Nancy), 299, 307, 309, 312, 315
– utopian, 27, 239
– *Vergemeinschaftung/Vergesellschaftung*, 68, 76
– world, 42, 79, 82, 168, 222 308
Compagnon, Antoine, 218–220, 257
Connolly, William E., 35
Coopan, Vilashini, 37, 136
Cosmopolitanism, V, 8, 10, 16, 36, 39, 51, 58, 61, 65, 71, 73, 92, 136, 141, 146, 160, 165, 171, 186, 187, 192, 208, 218, 220, 289, 351
– assimilating, 294
– axis between agencies and/or enablers, 1, 8, 16, 18, 20
– class, 291, 298
– cohabitation with the "exilic" enablers, 30, 355
– cosmopolitan nationalism, 21, 22, 57
– French Enlightenment, 17
– German Romanticist, 192, 193, 218
– Greek elitist, 17, 18, 20, 57, 139, 155, 158, 171, 216
– immigrant, 28, 257, 264
– international, 27, 214, 219
– intranational, 27, 213, 215, 219
– literary (French), 22, 55, 59, 72, 73, 76, 213
– messianic, 20, 28, 285
– of the dispossessed belonging, 345
– of the disregarded, 20, 28, 257, 264, 266, 275, 281
– political (German and English), 104, 105
– Roman imperial, 17, 20, 57, 149, 153, 164
– situated operation, 6
– traumatic origin, 2
Cruel optimism (Berlant), 11, 204, 246, 254, 301

Currie, Mark, 83, 262
Curtius, Ernst Robert, 58, 161

Dainat, Holger and Kruckis, Hans-Martin, 94
Dainotto, Roberto M., 39, 42, 77, 78, 286
Dalton, Stuart, 307
Damrosch, David, 24, 133, 136, 146–148, 157, 159–162, 164, 166, 169–174
Das, Veena, 2–4, 6, 7, 10
De Man, Paul, 180, 197
Deleuze, Gilles, VI, 3, 13, 29, 30, 197, 198, 274, 302–305, 319–331, 334, 335, 337, 338, 340, 341, 343
Democracy, 1, 11, 16, 18, 23, 30, 100, 101, 118, 140, 163, 164, 254, 342
– and expulsion, 54, 169
– and inequality, 11, 34, 35, 38, 53, 54, 56, 57, 59, 94, 135, 326
– as consensual platform, 2, 12, 14
– as imparity (Rancière), 2, 100
– as opposed to despotism and tyranny, 21, 40, 74, 77, 103, 109
– as opposed to monarchical absolutism, 42, 47, 50, 296
– dissensual concept of, 101
– global, 2, 11, 13, 16, 17, 19
– liberal, 12, 43, 53, 102
– of division (Rancière), 100, 154, 265, 339
– right to bear rights (Arendt), 60, 100, 154, 162, 265, 323, 339
– state vs. practice, 12, 103, 142
Derrida, Jacques, 6, 26, 28, 74, 78, 135, 136, 156, 195, 196, 226, 229, 231, 264, 271, 272, 279, 281–285, 290, 291, 294, 299, 300, 305, 307, 315–317, 326, 348–350, 352–354, 365, 369
Deterritorialization (Deleuze), VI, 30, 319, 323, 324, 326, 327, 337, 338
– disaggregation of speaking subjects into collective assemblages of enunciation, 6
– transcendental (egalitarian) force of negation, 30, 337, 338
Deutscher, Isaac, 216
Disch, Lisa, 183, 352

Discrimination, 13, 24, 35, 46, 51, 55, 60, 80, 82, 93, 104, 112, 120, 126, 132, 166, 173, 205, 227, 258, 293, 302, 334, 346
– gender, 77
– *see* Femininity/Masculinity
– national, 115
– political, 21
– racial, 115
– religious, 21, 35
Douzinas, Costas, 47, 48, 55, 105, 107, 155, 160
Dumont, Louis, 38, 53, 65, 88, 95, 96, 119, 204, 246, 247, 252
Dussel, Enrique, 45, 103, 108

Eagleton, Terry, 345
Echternkamp, Jörg, 61
Eikhenbaum, Boris, 226
Elias, Norbert, 71
Engels, Friedrich, 130, 133, 134
Enlightenment, 23, 34, 38, 53, 74, 77, 79, 91, 92, 99, 105, 118, 202, 206, 209, 245, 286, 287, 289, 298
– against Renaissance, 36, 39, 104
– against Romanticism, 14, 16, 26, 83, 87, 89, 198, 201, 316
– colonial background of, 34, 35, 65, 71, 95, 107, 346
Equality, 11, 34, 38, 41, 43, 48, 52, 54, 66, 69, 95, 101, 107, 131, 252, 327, 335–340, 343, 352
– all-inclusive/universal, 337–340
– partial/provisional, 336
– political vs. literary (Rancière), 337
Eskin, Michael, 267, 269
Esposito, Roberto, 100, 112, 142
Europe, 1, 10, 19, 22, 25, 26, 39, 40, 42, 51, 57, 78, 80, 90, 103, 114, 125, 127, 129, 133, 135, 152, 182, 193, 206–208, 215, 217, 220, 249, 253, 257, 285, 287–290, 298, 310, 316, 318, 335, 342
– against Africa, 117, 190, 331
– against America, 179, 285
– against Asia, 40, 41, 69
– against colonies, 35, 103, 112, 253
– against Orient, 77, 78, 159

388 — Index

– internal division of, 35, 44, 51, 62, 65, 73, 88, 116, 213, 286
– vanishing mediator (Balibar), 29, 291, 302, 305, 316, 318
Evans, Mari, 210
Exile, 26, 39, 136, 144, 171, 179, 181, 185, 216, 257, 268, 325, 348–350
Eze, Emmanuel Chukwudi, 69, 112–114, 148, 190, 366

Fanon, Frantz, 266
Fassin, Didier and Rechtman, Richard, 4, 8, 9, 15, 330
Febvre, Lucien, 47
Felman, Shoshana, 260
Femininity/masculinity, 3, 76, 77, 105, 113, 308, 314, 320
– "feminine allurement" (Levinas), 308
Ferrara, Alessandro, 223
Fine, Robert, 206, 207
Fink, Gonthier-Louis, V, 47, 58, 59, 65, 192, 379
Foucault, Michel, 13, 17, 28, 52, 83, 106, 107, 109, 110, 113, 136, 163, 164, 230, 232, 233, 264, 272–282, 284, 300–305, 308, 309, 311–313, 316, 319, 326, 338, 340, 367, 376
Freise, Matthias, 236
Freud, Sigmund, 345
Fuller, Steve, 297
Fuss, Diana, 83, 265

Gasché, Rodolphe, 182, 186–188, 190, 192, 193, 195, 203, 218, 219, 285, 286, 289, 290, 310, 316
Genette, Gérard, 227, 260, 261
Gibson, Andrew, 227, 261, 330, 343
Gilroy, Paul, 115, 209, 253
Ginzburg, Carlo, 228
Girardet, Raoul, 289
Globalization, 2, 12, 37, 102, 104, 133, 135–137, 163, 171, 172, 326, 327, 340
Goethe, Johann Wolfgang, 2, 3, 10, 16, 24, 63, 66, 71, 90, 91, 93, 122, 130, 131, 133–135, 137–139, 141–162, 164–175, 184, 187, 189, 191, 247–249, 251, 252, 318, 368
Goodman, Dana, 42, 50, 51, 143

Governmentality, see Sovereignity
Greenblatt, Stephen, 136, 243, 376
Grosrichard, Alain, 69, 72
Guha, Ranajit, 7, 11, 101
Günther, Hans, 91, 133, 146, 149, 150, 154

Haase, Ullrich, 275
Habermas, Jürgen, 42, 183, 202, 206, 207, 277, 287, 291, 369, 374
Hall, Stuart, 295
Hansen-Löve, Aage, 218, 228
Hanson, Stephen E., 66, 189, 217
Hanssen, Beatrice, 195, 233, 266, 322
Hassner, Pierre, 104
Hegel, Georg Wilhelm Friedrich, 35, 41, 87, 93, 101, 114–117, 125, 129, 130, 146, 205, 221, 259, 265
Hempel, Wido, 49
Herder, Johann Gottfried, V, 2, 3, 10, 14, 15, 22–24, 46, 62, 63, 71, 75, 78–81, 83–87, 90–96, 99, 101, 102, 104, 105, 118–131, 148, 152, 157, 191, 200, 201, 213, 214, 243, 250, 251, 287–289, 331, 332, 359
Heterotopias, see Zone
Hewlett, Nick, 330
Hirsch, Marianne, 347
Hirschkop, Ken, 248
History
– authorizing principle, 23
– beyond clear oppositions, 61
– break (revolution), 6, 13, 26, 96, 99, 312, 350
– differential self-propelling of the *Volksgeist*, 65, 85, 87
– driven by natural necessity, 30, 247
– genetic lineage (re-evolution), 22, 85
– human/natural, 1, 23, 39, 41, 42, 44, 64, 99, 115, 120, 228, 245
– intermitted by diasporic injunctions, 30, 55, 350
– literary, V, 62, 64, 67, 68, 76, 78, 81, 82, 91, 94, 214, 215
– organicist pattern, 61
– paternal attitude (evolution), 22
– recommencing as an obstinate leaping outside its determination, 12, 61, 103, 350, 352, 353, 355

- relentless separation from, persistent disengagement of ('eventialization', Foucault), 44, 52, 232, 309
- steady individual overcoming of dependencies, 39
- universal (Kant)/national (Schlegel)/world (Hegel), 62, 67, 101, 104, 106, 107, 115–117, 120, 125, 129, 200

Hobsbawm, Eric John, 86
Hölderlin, Friedrich, 97, 195, 278, 333
Holquist, Michael, 235–239, 243, 244, 250, 358
Honig, Bonnie, 6, 354
Hörisch, Jochen, 43
Hospitality, 1, 28, 78, 284, 285, 290, 316
Hostility, 78, 123
Hu/mankind, 1, 16, 22, 29, 35, 41, 49, 52, 57, 65, 69, 75, 82, 89, 91–94, 99, 101, 102, 105, 108, 109, 114, 115, 138, 188, 193, 200, 239, 250, 252, 288, 292, 317, 340, 355
- divided into Christian/infidel, 36
- divided into citizen/foreigner, 36, 47
- divided into man/inhuman (animal, creature), 37, 51, 300
- divided into person/anonymous mob, 167
- divided into enlightened/benighted (illiterate), 37, 14, 191
- founded in individual freedom as against hereditary principle, 39
- progressing unity in diversity, 59

Husserl, Edmund von, 114, 182, 185, 193, 269, 285
Huyssen, Andreas, 38

Identification, 4, 18, 44, 53, 63, 70, 74, 80, 81, 83, 85, 103, 145, 166, 200, 209, 214, 220, 222, 227, 229, 241, 253, 261–263, 265–267, 281, 298, 307–309, 313–315, 323, 337
- and trauma, 13
- by alienation, 79
- individual/collective, 5, 21, 43, 45, 89, 92, 96, 110, 153
- reader's, 84, 258, 263
Imperialism, 77, 270, 326
- imperial difference, 35, 104, 105, 289

Irigaray, Luce, 308
Israel, Jonathan, 34, 35, 49, 170

James, Ian, 316
Jameson, Frederic, 104
Johnson, Richard, 295
Judgment, 18, 67, 73, 76, 102, 108–110, 115, 128, 131, 141, 148, 162, 182, 184–188, 221, 222, 224–226, 239–241, 249, 299, 348, 349, 352–355, 366
- determining/logical (Kant), 8, 222–224, 240, 342, 344
- reflective/aesthetic (Kant), 27, 222, 224, 226, 231–233, 236, 239, 248, 339, 342–344, 353

Kadir, Djelal, 34, 36, 37, 163
Kafka, Franz, 30, 323, 324, 335, 364
Kant, Immanuel, 14–16, 23, 24, 27, 35, 45, 52, 59, 64, 73, 78, 92, 93, 99, 101, 102, 104–118, 120, 121, 124–126, 128, 129, 131, 152, 155, 156, 167, 184, 187, 188, 190, 191, 193, 196, 199–202, 206, 213, 220–224, 231–233, 235–241, 243, 245, 248, 249, 251, 273, 277, 295, 296, 301, 337, 339, 341–343, 353, 375
Kittler, Friedrich, 121
Koch, Manfred, 43, 44, 46, 86, 87, 90, 93, 95, 144, 148, 149, 153, 155, 164–169, 192
Kojève, Alexandre, 276
Koselleck, Reinhart, 42, 44, 72, 75, 86, 109, 115, 254, 287
Kozhinov, Vadim, 225, 248
Kristeva, Julia, 28, 48, 58, 59, 71, 74, 78, 257, 264, 289
Kujundžić, Dragan, 228

Lacan, Jacques, 280, 313, 341
LaCapra, Dominick, 5, 303, 305
Lacoue-Labarthe, Philippe, 195, 196
Lang, Berel, 115
Large, William, 275, 303
Law, 12, 17, 33, 40, 46, 48, 69, 73, 80, 83, 100, 102, 107, 109, 111, 120, 130, 140, 141, 158, 163, 184, 185, 191, 199, 203, 206, 222, 224, 226, 259, 263, 277, 282,

293, 305, 311, 326, 334, 341, 342, 347, 348, 350, 352, 354–356
– iron law of kinship (Rancière), 128, 157
– natural (Herder), 118, 140
– natural/human, 99
– *On the Spirit of the Laws* (Montesquieu), 40, 51, 72
– universal (Kant), 107, 110, 263
– universality of (Benjamin), 12
Leavis, Frank R., 297
Lefort, Claude, 53
Leonard, Philip, 78
Lessing, Gotthold Ephraim, 254
Lévi-Strauss, Claude, 112
Levinas, Emmanuel, 2, 28, 54, 100, 102, 108, 266–279, 282–284, 308–310, 314, 315, 317, 320, 349–352, 356,
Levy, Daniel and Sznaider, Natan, 11
Libertson, Joseph, 272
Life, 6, 27, 48, 50, 92, 95, 117, 142, 181, 197, 218, 230, 232, 235, 237, 239, 241, 243, 253, 258, 298, 302, 303, 308, 313, 331, 333, 340, 347, 356
– aestheticized performer of self-exemption (Bakhtin), 27, 237, 243
– as becoming (*stanovlenie*; Bakhtin/*devenir*; Deleuze), 235, 249, 274, 302, 321, 324, 325, 327
– dialogic consummation of (Bakhtin), 27, 238
– early German Romanticist concept of, 27, 88, 90, 166, 197, 201, 218, 237, 298, 302
– Foucault's concept of, 278, 302, 312
– Nietzsche's concept of, 197, 230–233, 351
– site in (*Sitz im Leben*), 16, 92, 198, 243
Literature, 1, 2, 16, 21, 25, 30, 33, 42, 54, 67, 83, 88, 96, 133, 136, 146, 147, 152, 154, 157, 159, 162, 164, 170, 173, 174, 187, 200, 206, 215, 217, 220, 223, 264, 265, 277, 282, 284, 285, 290, 293, 295, 299, 315, 319, 324, 329, 338, 342, 343
– act of misunderstanding (*le malentendu*, Rancière), 336
– against culture, 29, 44, 59, 72, 82, 151, 179, 186, 291, 292
– epitome of the national spirit (*Volksgeist*), 85
– free dialogic exchange, 43

– identity-confirming/identity-building, 42
– innate strangeness of, 27, 219
– "literariness", 173, 179, 216, 223, 224, 226, 227, 259
– major/minor (Deleuze/Guattari), 30, 323, 325, 328, 334, 335
– proper/improper, 37, 130, 254
– transcendental force of negation (Rancière), 30, 337, 338
– *Weltliteratur* (Goethe), 10, 16, 24, 133, 135, 146, 150, 154, 158, 160, 166, 170, 175, 318
– world/local, 24, 35, 133
Lloyd, David, 296
Lucy, Niall, 14
Luhmann, Niklas, 25, 26, 48, 161, 162, 166, 167, 174, 197–199, 201–206, 209, 211, 244, 245, 250, 277
Lyotard, Jean-François, 28, 48, 108, 155, 156, 190, 221, 264, 267, 269, 338, 340, 341, 343, 350

Mamdani, Mahmoud, 7, 15, 63, 87, 92, 97, 130, 186, 327, 332, 333
Mandelkow, Karl Robert, 144
Mankind, *see* Hu/mankind
Martínez-Bonati, Félix, 174
Martin, Terry, 216
Marx, Karl, 24, 47, 133–136, 179, 223, 250, 316, 317
Mayer, Hans, 179
Mbembe, Achille, 1, 12, 17, 21, 97, 125, 331, 332
McQuillan, Martin and MacDonald, Graeme and Purves Robin, and Thomson, Stephen, 345
Medvedev, Pavel, 225, 226, 228, 229, 233, 235, 237
Meints-Stender, Waltraud, 352
Memory, 23, 60, 75, 80, 81, 85, 86, 89, 93, 119, 165, 168, 169, 203, 232, 249, 283, 308, 315, 321, 350, 351
– collective, 75, 93, 164
– cultural, 75, 149
– literary, 85, 295
– national, 68, 89
– traumatic, 71
Menninghaus, Winfried, 188, 195–197

Messianism, 29, 305, 315
- action through non-action, 30, 330, 335
- disempowering empowerment, 259
Meyer-Kalkus, Reinhard, 63, 71, 151, 158, 160, 191
Mignolo, Walter D., 35, 39, 59, 104, 105, 107, 193
Miller, David A., 210
Miller, Hillis, 298
Mirroring, 89, 91, 160, 168, 206, 276
- implication, 22, 110, 171, 227, 327
- mutual, 150, 166, 189
- reiterated (Bohnenkamp), 161, 165
Montesquieu, Charles-Louis, 40, 41, 51, 69, 72, 73, 76–78, 110, 200, 286, 289
Moran, Joe, 295, 297, 380
Moretti, Franco, 24, 133, 134, 136, 137, 146, 162, 169, 170
Morgan, Diane, 108
Mosse, George L., 119
Musil, Robert, 57

Nancy, Jean-Luc, 29, 195, 196, 299, 305, 307, 309–312, 315–317
Narrative, 16, 20, 30, 51, 78, 160, 165, 198, 206, 211, 227, 249, 250, 260–263, 265, 298, 305–318, 323, 340, 341
- Enlightenment, 15, 80
- of a progressive humankind, 52
- of permanent displacement, 25, 29, 195, 232
- of persistent overcoming, 52
- progression, 245, 247, 299
- Romanticist, 71
- trauma, 2, 3, 8, 10, 13–15, 20, 22, 24, 55, 60, 61, 64, 70–72, 75, 81, 95, 142, 148, 154, 156, 157, 161, 330, *see also* Trauma
Nation, 23, 57, 64, 79, 80, 95, 127, 130, 147–149, 153, 207, 214, 216
- and humankind, 91
- as a "lay aggregate" (Herder), 78
- French, 42, 58, 59, 70, 73, 289, 327
- German, 62, 70, 88, 95, 129
- suppressed, 7
- *Volksgeist*, 22, 26, 64, 67, 84, 85, 88, 92, 93, 95, 96, 128, 131, 132, 217, 257, 289
  - state, *see* Community

Nationalism, 22, 23, 59–61, 67, 92, 134, 135, 138, 179, 180, 206, 207, 219, 257, 289
- and philology, 19, 24, 130, 135, 213–215, 217, 232, 291
- and xenophobia, 47
- as universalism, 21, 22, 28, 57, 149, 201
- battle of transfers, 71
- conjoining (foreign co-nationals)/disjoining (non-national fellow-citizens), 60
- cosmopolitan, 57, 68, 201
- dominating/dominated (Balibar), 21, 57–59
- exclusive ethnonationalism/inclusive (inter)nationalism, 24, 214
- literary (German), 22
- petty, 57, 66, 317
- self-formation through differentiation, 10, 24
- transnational alliances, 66, 72
Nature, 15, 23, 27, 49, 76, 89, 94, 97, 99, 101, 102, 105, 111, 113, 116–121, 123, 125, 127, 130, 131, 138, 140, 164, 196, 199, 224, 237, 239–241, 265, 274, 287–289, 303, 313, 342
- familiar *Umwelt* (fatherly, caretaking), 23, 118, 119
- inimical wildness (despotic, coersive), 93, 118
- naturalness (German)/artificiality (French), 70, 72, 124
- power of n. (Schlegel), 93
Nehamas, Alexander, 233
Neubauer, John, 62, 81, 258
Nietzsche, Friedrich, 97, 144, 175, 182, 185, 196, 197, 221, 228–233, 235, 242, 277, 278, 295, 310–313, 350–352
Novalis, Friedrich von Hardenberg, 15, 64–66, 78, 88, 152, 160, 191, 192, 195, 333

Observation, 26, 28, 112, 142, 193, 203, 204, 209, 221, 345, 350
- first order (Luhmann), 26, 48, 199, 202, 203
- of latency (Luhmann), 48, 202, 204
- of observation (Luhmann), 197, 198
Ophir, Adi and Givoni, Michael and Hanefi, Sari, 327

Part that has no part, *see* Democracy
Patočka, Jan, 193, 285, 377

Pechey, Graham, 251, 253
Pecora, Vincent P., 303
Pepper, Thomas Adam, 303
Pizer, John David, 135, 151–154, 157
Poirié, François, 282
Politics, 7, 9, 12, 21, 40, 54, 103, 135, 172, 329, 330, 333, 336
– act of disagreement (*la mésentente*, Rancière), 336, 337
– and ethics, 270, 271, 276, 282
– and literature, 343
– cosmopolitics, 292
– dissensual, 12, 20, 101, 347
– egalitarian, 94, 337, 338
– identity, 47, 286, 329
– of estrangement (Tihanov), 218, 232, 257, 308, 313
– of literature, 30, 339, 340
– of representation, 292
– trauma, 5, 15, 60, 271, 294, 324, 330
– turned into police, 7, 8, 97, 340
Poole, Brian, 236
Povinelli, Elisabeth, 3, 5, 8, 10–12, 54, 87, 281
Power, 1, 7, 13, 17, 29, 33–35, 38, 45, 46, 49, 60, 62, 79–81, 90, 92–94, 96, 102, 109–111, 128, 129, 131, 134, 136, 149, 150, 172, 184, 197, 199, 200, 209, 228, 230, 233, 246, 251, 252, 254, 259, 263, 268, 270, 274, 280, 281, 286, 293, 294, 297, 299, 302, 303, 305, 309, 311, 312, 319, 322, 325–328, 333–339, 342, 346, 354
– political, 311
– state, 83, 84, 326
Prejudices, 20, 59, 79, 138, 141, 182, 331, 347, 354, 355
– consensual (Arendt), 141
– misplaced, 141, 354
Probyn, Elspeth, 326

Rabaté, Jean-Michael, 181, 218–220, 257
Rancière, Jacques, VI, 1, 2, 7, 12, 13, 16, 20, 29, 30, 48, 51, 54, 100, 102, 103, 128, 139–142, 230, 232, 264, 329, 330, 335–343, 345, 346, 355, 368, 383
Rasch, William, 121, 127, 354
Rausch, Hannelore, 218
Readings, Bill, 295

Renan, Ernest, 201, 214
Richardson, Ruth Drucilla, 76
Riffaterre, Michael, 174
Right to bear rights, *see* Democracy
Rimmon-Kenan, Shlomith, 261
Robbins, Bruce, 6, 38, 239, 301
Robbins, Jill, 270, 271
Roberts, David, 202
Romanticism, 13, 22, 95, 192, 202, 204, 205, 254, 295, 299
– deconstruction's re-description of, 225–230
– early German, 25, 188, 190, 233, 235, 237, 243, 333, 339
– Luhmann's re-description of, 235–239
– modern literary theory's re-description of, 223, 335–340
– Nietzsche's re-description of, 225–229
– Russian Formalists' re-description of, 223, 237, 243, 245, 251, 253–257, 264
Rose, Gillian, 270, 271, 305
Ross, Kristin, 329
Rothberg, Michael, 5, 7, 15, 60, 61, 72, 117, 144, 276, 303
Rousseau, Jean-Jacques, 9, 14, 22, 46, 68–81, 92, 112, 113, 118, 119, 123, 132, 156, 382
Royle, Nicolas, 345

Safranski, Rüdiger, 14
Said, Edward, 179, 211, 258, 286
Santner, Eric L., 52
Saussy, Haun, 83, 135, 172, 380
Savigny, Friedrich Carl von, 120
Schaap, Andrew, 103
Schad, John, 347, 350
Schiller, Friedrich, 62, 106, 131, 145, 147, 155, 156, 192, 200–202, 337, 339, 341–343
Schlegel, August Wilhelm, 61–66, 148, 157, 160, 187, 192
Schlegel, Friedrich, 15, 22, 24, 60–62, 64–68, 74, 76, 77, 79–81, 83, 85–88, 90, 91, 93, 94, 96, 195–197, 200, 202, 204, 228, 242, 277, 301, 339
Schlereth, Thomas J., 71
Schmitt, Carl, 47, 51, 355
Scholz, Bernhard F., 236
Schön, Erich, 209
Schroeder, Brian, 270, 271
Sebastiani, Silvia, 112, 114–116, 125

Self-exemption, 13, 19, 109, 111, 140, 148, 149, 151, 168, 184, 215, 220–223, 228, 237, 243, 296, 307, 308, 331, 333, 334, 340, 342, 345, 347
Shih, Shu-mei, 37, 163
Shklovsky, Victor, 216
Sieyès, Emmanuel Joseph, 46
Simmel, Georg, 237
Singularity, 28, 29, 87, 260, 270, 271, 281, 285–287, 289, 290, 298–301, 306–309, 312, 315, 317, 318, 341
– against particularity, 28, 61, 135, 157, 168, 226, 236, 250, 260, 286, 290
– as a messianic poetics, 29
– as European mission, 285
– of vanishing meditation (Balibar), 29, 298, 315, 318
Smith, Barbara Herrnstein, 161, 174, 354, 364
Sovereignty, 8, 9, 13, 16, 19, 20, 23, 24, 30, 39, 45, 48, 74, 83, 85, 97, 100, 110, 149, 160, 165, 166, 187, 190, 197, 211, 213, 214, 221, 224, 258, 273, 284, 311, 321, 326, 327, 329, 334, 340, 344, 346, 347, 354, 355
– against governmentality, 17, 83, 84, 109, 110, 326, 327, 332, 333, 340, 344
– centralized power of absolutist monarchies, 46, 296
– dispossessed, 2
– pre-political (Asian)/political (European), 40
Spivak, Gayatri Chakraworty, 130, 134, 346
Staël, Anne Germaine de, 22, 64, 75–79, 90, 144, 160
Steele, Tom, 292, 382
Steiner, Peter, 228
Subject, 2, 4, 10, 11, 18, 21, 27, 37, 44, 49, 50, 58, 75, 77, 80, 87, 102, 111, 116, 120, 123, 128, 140, 160, 163, 168, 182, 183, 185, 189, 196, 208, 210, 211, 221, 238, 240, 244, 253, 258, 263, 266–268, 273, 278, 280, 296–300, 302, 303, 309, 310, 313, 320, 325, 328–330, 337, 338, 341, 342
– autological/genealogical (Povinelli), 93
– as the (literary) author, 28
– formation, 306, 310–312
– in a permanent self-revolution, 231, 242, 276, 334

– literary/indigenous (subaltern, barbarian), 10, 13, 15, 121, 224, 287, 331, 346
– lord/bondsman, 150, 265, 269
– mobile/immobile, 45, 127, 270, 331, 333
– modes of subjectivization 329, 336
– political, 30, 330, 335, 336
– political regulation/literary deregulation (Rancière), 30, 329
– representing/represented, 30
– self-authoring, 242, 243, 245, 250, 301
– sovereign/dispossessed, 311, 326
– speaking, 277, 323, 328
Suglia, Joseph, 303

Taminiaux, Jacques, 182, 183
Taussig, Michael, 294
Texte, Joseph, 72, 73, 76
Theory, 12, 20, 26, 71, 169, 172, 179–182, 185, 186, 188, 193, 195, 201–203, 205, 207, 217, 219, 220, 224–228, 233, 242, 257, 262, 264–266, 297, 303, 308, 323, 345, 348–350, 354, 356
– autopoetic system theory (Luhmann), 197, 202
– committed to the truth, 25
– exclusionary logics of modern literary, 96, 218
– exilic consciousness (Apter), 25, 179, 180
– exposed to critical observation, 142
– genealogy of modern literary, 25, 179, 180, 193, 219, 285
– opposite to post-theory, 345–347, 350, 354, 355
– theōría, 25, 181, 190
Thomsen, Mads Rosendahl, 150
Tihanov, Galin, 65, 133, 145, 181, 213, 215–220, 228, 235–237, 242, 257, 308
Tocqueville, Alexis de, 53, 247, 248, 250
Todorova, Maria, 214
Trauma, 2–10, 13–16, 20, 22, 24, 36, 52, 55, 60, 61, 64, 70–72, 75, 80, 81, 95, 123, 142, 148, 154, 156, 157, 161, 163, 172, 179, 180, 266, 271, 294, 322–324, 330, 356
– agencies (witnesses)/enablers (victims), 1, 4, 8, 16–19, 70, 100, 103, 105, 114, 140, 143, 201, 281, 298, 324
– 'anarchic traumatism' (Levinas), 2, 54, 100

– 'carrier group' (Alexander), 4, 6, 8, 10, 11, 13, 59, 61, 72, 74, 156, 192
– collective (public, reclaimed, overt), 2, 60
– community, 7–9
– constellation, 2, 3, 5, 6, 12, 19, 21, 36, 39, 55, 60, 61, 70–72, 78, 86, 91, 100, 104, 120, 122, 141, 189, 190, 246, 254, 258, 322
– constitutive t. of modernity, 35
– denial/abnegation, 2, 10, 35, 36, 97, 120, 123
– experience (*Erlebnis/Erfahrung*), 1, 3–5, 7, 8, 36, 39, 50, 54, 60, 73, 81, 95, 97, 100, 123, 141, 142, 144, 148, 154, 163, 172, 189, 215, 255
– 'free-floating anxiety' (Berlant), 5, 14
– historical/structural (LaCapra), 4
– 'inchoate experience' (Alexander), 5, 14
– individual (secret, denied, covert), 2, 3, 8, 10, 15, 20, 55
– injury/pain/frustration/denigration/ suffering, 3, 4, 6, 7, 9, 10, 12–14, 16, 36, 55, 60, 81, 154, 350
– multidirectional memory platform (Rothberg), 72, 144
– performative concept of, 9, 15
– 'poisonous knowledge' (Das), 2, 3, 10, 12, 36, 55, 139
– politics of, 5, 15, 60, 271, 294, 324, 330
– psychoanalytic concept of, 3, 6
– social concept of, 5, 9
Trumpener, Katie, 172

Ungar, Steven, 276
Universalism, 22, 28, 57, 59, 66, 119, 155
– French, 22, 28, 76, 257, 264
– literary, 70, 257
– national, 57, 149, 201
– religious, 69, 104, 105

Valadez, Jorge M., 60
Valentine, Jeremy, 343
Vallury, Raji, 335
Vardoulakis, Dimitris, 348

Vasseleu, Cathryn, 308
Venuti, Lawrence, 172
Verdery, Katherine, 60
Villa, Dana R., 183
Virno, Paolo, 334
Voltaire, François-Marie Arouet, 2, 3, 21, 22, 33, 34, 36–42, 44–46, 48–50, 53, 54, 58, 69, 72, 73, 77, 79, 80, 84, 99, 110, 142–144, 149, 155, 184, 198, 201, 217, 121, 286, 287

White, Hayden, 75, 303
Wiedemann, Conrad, 146, 148
Wolff, Larry, 79, 84, 159
World Republic of Letters (*La République mondiale des lettres*; Voltaire/Casanova), 2, 16, 21, 33, 40, 42, 45, 50, 52, 54, 217, 287
– and French Revolution, 21, 46, 149
– and Western liberal democracy, 21, 43, 46
– broad dialogue of equals, 42
– divided legacy, 21, 36
– free commerce/circulation of ideas, 34, 37
– limited to social elite, 44
– prerequisites of, 35, 50, 143
– transnational Enlightenment torch, 34, 124

Young, Robert, 264, 265

Zerilli, Linda, 353
Zone, 9, 12, 48, 54, 114, 139, 142, 164, 199, 201, 210, 252, 258, 264, 279, 287, 303–305, 307, 313, 320, 324, 332, 335
– heterotopias (Foucault), 14, 163, 181, 264
– and French poststructuralism, 264
– and world literature, 163, 281
– disaggregating potentiality of, 12, 14
– of sovereignty, 180
– of indeterminacy (Agamben), 12, 53, 54, 139, 142, 258, 264, 287
– of indistinction (Agamben/Povinelli), 303, 304
– of suppressed possibilities (Povinelli), 9, 54
Žižek, Slavoj, 263, 330, 341

www.ingramcontent.com/pod-product-compliance
Lightning Source LLC
Chambersburg PA
CBHW070748230426
43665CB00017B/2287